"In this remarkably lucid and learned monograph, Curtis Freeman suggests a way beyond 'liberalism' and 'fundamentalism' for the Baptist tradition, one that could renew ecumenical vision whilst defending the distinctive history and prophetic role of Baptist spiritual life. This is a masterful piece of ecclesiology, unfettered by false polemics."

—*Sarah Coakley, Norris-Hulse Professor of Divinity,*
University of Cambridge

"*Contesting Catholicity* courageously addresses Baptists who feel pushed to the margins in the present prevailing climate of Baptist life, and succeeds magnificently in its aim of offering Baptists a vision which transcends the modern split between 'conservative' and 'liberal.' Curtis Freeman is thoroughly convincing in urging that Baptists are best understood as a dissenting movement within the 'one holy catholic and apostolic church' rather than outside it. This is an essential theology for Baptists 'recovering' from recent crises, retrieving the spiritual and doctrinal tradition of the church universal. It can and should engage emotions and change minds."

—*Paul S. Fiddes, Professor of Systematic Theology,*
University of Oxford and Director of Research,
Regent's Park College, Oxford

"In this first truly twenty-first-century ecclesiology, Curtis Freeman offers a brilliant argument, not only for revisioning Baptist notions of church life, but for a readjusted notion of Christian catholicity itself. Challenging, rich, and persuasive, Freeman's 'Other Baptist' vision is an important ecumenical event."

—*Ephraim Radner, Professor of Historical Theology,*
Wycliffe College at the University of Toronto

"This learned and well-argued work offers an evangelical and catholic alternative to fundamentalism and lukewarm liberalism. Written for Baptists, it embodies important lessons for other Christian theologians and leaders."

—*Gerald O'Collins, Emeritus Professor, Gregorian University*

"Freeman examines the Baptist tradition with fresh eyes, imagining how Baptists, by retrieving their own heritage, can embody in new ways that catholicity which is authentically Christian."

—*Robert Louis Wilken, William R. Kenan Jr.,*
Professor of the History of Christianity Emeritus,
University of Virginia

"Curtis Freeman is doing for Baptists what other Protestant theologians are doing for their own ailing denominations—retrieving the catholic substance of the Christian tradition to undergird their passion for the evangelical principle. *Contesting Catholicity* contends that a church claiming to be evangelical while ceasing to be catholic is no Christian church at all.

Freeman's evangelical catholic vision is ecumenically promising by virtue of its faithfulness to the essentials of the Baptist tradition."

—*Carl E. Braaten, Professor Emeritus of Systematic Theology,*
Lutheran School of Theology at Chicago

"This is an important contribution to the ongoing study of Baptist and Catholic theological relationships—a Christian relationship that becomes more urgent by the day."

—*David Tracy, University of Chicago*

CONTESTING CATHOLICITY
Theology for Other Baptists

Curtis W. Freeman

BAYLOR UNIVERSITY PRESS

Cover Design by Jeff Miller, Faceout Studio
Cover Image: Ms 481 fol.8v Baptism of Christ, from a Gospel, 1330 (vellum), Guirages, (fl. 1330) / Armenian Cathedral and Museum, Julfa, Isfahan, Iran / Giraudon / The Bridgeman Art Library

Earlier versions of some material that appears in this book were previously published and have been used with permission from the publications: "Alterity and Its Cure," *CrossCurrents* 59, no. 4 (2009): 404–41; "Can Baptist Theology Be Revisioned?" *Perspectives in Religious Studies* 24, no. 3 (1997): 273–310; "Toward a Generous Orthodoxy," chapter in *Evangelicals and Nicene Faith: Reclaiming Apostolic Witness*, ed. Timothy George (Grand Rapids: Baker, 2011), 116–29; "God in Three Persons: Baptist Unitarianism and the Trinity," *Perspectives in Religious Studies* 33, no. 3 (2007): 323–44; "'To Feed Upon by Faith': Nourishment from the Lord's Table," in *Baptist Sacramentalism*, ed. Anthony R. Cross and Philip E. Thompson, in *Studies in Baptist History and Thought*, vol. 5 (Carlisle, U.K.: Paternoster, 2003), 194–210.

Library of Congress Cataloging-in-Publication Data

Freeman, Curtis W.
  Contesting Catholicity : theology for Other Baptists / Curtis W. Freeman.
    478 pages cm
    Includes bibliographical references and index.
    ISBN 978-1-4813-0027-8 (hardback : alk. paper)
    1. Baptists—Doctrines. 2. Theology, Doctrinal. I. Title.
    BX6331.3.F74 2014
    230'.6—dc23

                                    2013049574

For my students—past, present, and future

Contents

Preface

I am an "Other Baptist." My epiphany came one day when reading a statistical report on theological education. Clearly laid out were numbers for the various Baptist subdenominations. At the end of the list was a reference I did not quite understand. It read: "Other Baptist." After studying the report, it finally dawned on me that I was an Other Baptist. Of course I was not alone. From the look of things, there were a growing number of them. The confusing terminology reflected the increasing number of Baptist students who were enrolling in theological schools not connected with any Baptist denomination.[1] "Other Baptist" is a moniker to be worn, but it is not the name to be chosen.[2]

This book offers a theology for other Other Baptists. It is part diagnostic and part therapeutic. The diagnosis is that many Baptists and other Free Church Christians are suffering from a condition that if left untreated results in death. This sickness did not happen all at once. It was gradual. Nor are the signs of its pathology obvious. They are silent and often unnoticed. Yet the result is deadly. The remedy for this sickness

---

[1] *Fact Book on Theological Education for the Academic Year 1997–1998*, ed. Matthew Zyniewicz and Daniel Aleshire (Dayton, Ohio: Association of Theological Schools, 1997–1998), 62, table 2.16, accessed January 31, 2013, http://www.ats.edu/uploads/resources/institutional-data/fact-books/1997-1998-fact-book.pdf; and *Fact Book on Theological Education for the Academic Year 1999–2000*, ed. Louis Charles Willard (Dayton, Ohio: Association of Theological Schools, 1999–2000), 64, table 2.16, accessed January 31, 2013, http://www.ats.edu/uploads/resources/institutional-data/fact-books/1999-2000-fact-book.pdf.

[2] I began using the "Other Baptist" self-description in a series of op-ed pieces that I wrote for newspapers and denominational publications: " 'Other Baptists,' Too, Are Keeping the Faith," *News and Observer*, August 6, 2003, reprinted in *Baptists Today*, September 2003; "Patterson Galvanized the Other Baptists," *Herald Sun*, July 24, 2003, reprinted under the title "Other Baptists and Bossy Preachers," in *Biblical Recorder*, August 22, 2003, and *Baptist Standard*, August 5, 2003; and "What Kind of Baptist Are You?" *Religious Herald*, September 25, 2003.

unto death (John 11:4) is the life that really is life (1 Tim 6:19). This life is not the product of human creativity. It is God's own life, and its curative power is realized by participating in the fellowship of the Father, through the Son, in the Spirit, with the saints. This is the life of the world. In a word the cure lies in the rediscovery of catholicity. Baptist Christians are more familiar with dissent than catholicity, but, as I show, the way of recovery comes by embracing a mode of being in which contestation and catholicity are not opposites but are instead complementary and necessary for the church to be the church.

I once asked a group of exiles from the southern denominational diaspora what kind of Baptists they were. One of them answered back: "A recovering Baptist!" The description echoed William Faulkner's characterization of Baptist religion as an "emotional condition that has nothing to do with God or politics or anything else." This religious situation, Faulkner explained, came from a spiritual starvation that was particularly prominent in the American South, "where there was little or no food for the human spirit, where there were no books, no theater, no music, and life was pretty hard." As a result, Faulkner opined, southern religion "got warped and twisted in the process."[3] This grim diagnosis surely names a condition that deeply affected Baptists in the South, due not simply to a kind of cultural deprivation but also to the peculiar privilege of cultural establishment. Over time things changed, and as they changed so did Baptists. Even in "the Solid South," the homogenous culture that once embodied evangelical religion has dissipated.[4] But the epidemiological analysis of this condition suggests that it is not restricted to the American South. And its effects have been exacerbated by trying to adapt to the rapid changes of modernity.

Dealing with these changes has not been easy. Conservatives have tended to favor continuity over change, while liberals have more readily embraced change over continuity. But, as I have attempted to show, the problem goes deeper and requires a thicker account that attends to the social and historical conditions in the development of religious thought. I have provided a theological vision for Other Baptists that gestures beyond the liberal–conservative alternatives of modernity. Although I once described myself as "a postconservative, postliberal, evangelical

[3] William Faulkner, Press Conference, 202 Rouss Hall, University of Virginia, May 20, 1957, tape T-134, accessed September 10, 2012, http://faulkner.lib.virginia.edu/display/wfaudio17.

[4] Samuel S. Hill, *Religion and the Solid South* (Nashville: Abingdon, 1972). Hill uses the term "Solid South" to denote the homogeneity of white southern culture, in particular its political and economic structures and to some extent its religious ethos, from 1870 to 1960.

catholic,"[5] my account here has followed the postliberal trajectory. Others may imagine what it might look like to hew a postconservative course.[6]

Thinking about my own journey, I have wondered whether perhaps it may be more helpful to think about the discovery of alterity not so much as a journey from liberalism to postliberalism but as an ongoing story of recovering from liberalism. Just as alcoholics, drug addicts, and bulimics or anorectics can never say they *had* a drinking problem, a drug addiction, or an eating disorder, neither should it be expected that liberalism and its seductions are something from which one has *recovered*. Just as in other twelve-step programs, I must admit that I too am powerless and that my life is determined by forces beyond my control, but that I am committed to moving toward a spiritual awakening and to carrying the message to others. Being Baptist, however, has made this recovery story more complicated than I first imagined.

I want to thank the many conversation partners who have helped me to think through these matters, especially Stanley Hauerwas, David Aers, George Mason, Fisher Humphreys, Elizabeth Newman, Steve Harmon, Barry Harvey, Paul Fiddes, Will Willimon, Sujin Pak, Warren Smith, Lester Ruth, and of course Jim McClendon (of blessed memory). I owe special thanks to Aaron Griffith for preparing the bibliography and author index, to Michael Swenson and Laura Levens for proofing drafts along the way, to Callie Davis for providing technical support and assistance, and to Carey Newman, whose encouragement and guidance enabled me to conceive and complete this project.

Several years ago my colleague Geoffrey Wainwright stated that his goal as a teacher of theology was to keep or restore as many Methodist seminarians as possible within recognizable classic Christianity.[7] It seems fitting, then, to confess that this book has grown out of a personal struggle to do the same with my students so that they might lead Baptists to find their place within the one, holy, catholic, and apostolic church. And in that hope these reflections are dedicated to my students past, present, and future.

---

[5] Curtis W. Freeman, "Toward a *Sensus Fidelium* for an Evangelical Church," in *The Nature of Confession: Evangelicals and Postliberals in Conversation*, ed. Timothy R. Phillips and Dennis L. Okholm (Downers Grove, Ill.: InterVarsity, 1996), 162.

[6] Kevin J. Vanhoozer, *The Drama of Doctrine: A Canonical Linguistic Approach to Christian Theology* (Louisville, Ky.: Westminster John Knox, 2005); and Roger E. Olson, *Reformed and Always Reforming: The Postconservative Approach to Evangelical Theology* (Grand Rapids: Baker Academic, 2007).

[7] Geoffrey Wainwright, panel discussion at Duke Divinity School on bilateral Methodist-Catholic and Baptist-Catholic dialogues (March 18, 2008). See also Wainwright, *Methodists in Dialogue* (Nashville: Kingswood Books, 1995), 277–85; and *Embracing Purpose: Essays on God, the World, and the Church* (Peterborough, U.K.: Epworth, 2007), 291–302.

Introduction

Church, Sect, or Self?

William Hordern tells about a talk he once gave in which he claimed that the Apostles' and Nicene Creeds were part of the Protestant faith. When he finished a listener approached him. "You are a graduate of Union Theological Seminary?" the person asked incredulously. "But you believe in the Trinity and the divinity of Christ!" Doctrinal orthodoxy was not what people had come to expect from graduates of the leading liberal seminary in North America. "What," she ironically inquired, "is happening to Union?"[1]

In the mid-twentieth century there were really only two theological options—orthodoxy and liberalism. Each had its own institutions, organizations, publications, and churches. There were variations in this two-party system. However, when it finally came down to the matter of how Christians could live faithfully in the modern world, there were two basic strategies: to reaffirm the faith once delivered to the saints or to reinterpret the faith anew and adapt it to the demands of modernity. Union was a place well known more for interpretation than for affirmation.

The quest for a liberal Christianity had been under way for well over a century by the time of Hordern's talk. There had been a sustained conversation in Europe from Schleiermacher's *Speeches on Religion* (1799) to Harnack's *What Is Christianity?* (1901) and in America from William Ellery Channing's *Unitarian Christianity* (1819) to Walter Rauschenbusch's *Christianity and the Social Crisis* (1907) about ways to reinterpret the symbols of Christianity to provide a progressive religious alternative to atheism and orthodoxy.[2] Liberal theology was never really a static set of beliefs. It

---

[1] William Hordern, "Young Theologians Rebel," *Christian Century* 69, no. 11, March 12, 1952, 306.
[2] Friedrich Schleiermacher, *On Religion: Speeches to Its Cultured Despisers*, trans. John

1

was more a tradition that included a commitment to a mixture of social justice, biblical criticism, historical consciousness, and scientific discovery. Liberal Christians engaged in a lively argument over time about how these commitments are best commended, defended, and extended.[3] Books were surely instrumental in creating the religious culture of liberal Christianity, but theological schools transmitted its religious vision and cultural ethos to the next generation of leaders for the churches.[4]

Liberal theology met significant resistance in staunch defenders of Protestant orthodoxy like the Princeton theologians Charles Hodge and Benjamin B. Warfield, but it was fundamentalism that launched a full-scale assault on liberalism.[5] Concerned about the advance of liberalism in seminaries and churches, Curtis Lee Laws, the editor of the Baptist periodical the *Watchman Examiner*, issued a call in 1920 for those "who

---

Oman (Louisville, Ky.: Westminster John Knox, 1994). The German *Über die Religion: Reden an die Gebildeten unter ihren Verächtern Reden* went through three editions from 1799 to 1831. Adolf von Harnack, *What Is Christianity?* trans. Thomas Bailey Saunders (New York: Putnam, 1901). The German *Das Wesen des Christentums* appeared in 1901. William Ellery Channing, *Unitarian Christianity: Five Points of Positive Belief from a Discourse Delivered at Baltimore, U.S., 1819* (London: C. Green & Son, n.d.); and Walter Rauschenbusch, *Christianity and the Social Crisis* (New York: Macmillan, 1907).

[3] James J. Buckley describes liberalism as a tradition of theologians devoted to shaping Christian teaching in dialogue with or on the basis of philosophy, culture, and social practice. Buckley, "Revisionists and Liberals," in *The Modern Theologians*, 2nd ed., ed. David F. Ford (Cambridge, Mass.: Blackwell, 1996), 327. Alasdair MacIntyre described a tradition as a lively argument extended over time about how the goods and values of that tradition are best understood and defended. MacIntyre, *After Virtue* (Notre Dame, Ind.: University of Notre Dame Press, 1981), 175. Liberalism conceived as a tradition is an example of what W. B. Gallie calls an "essentially contested concept" in that its definition and use are determined by ongoing disputes and continuing disagreement. Gallie, "Essentially Contested Concept," in *The Importance of Language*, ed. Max Black (Englewood Cliffs, N.J.: Prentice-Hall, 1962), 121–46.

[4] Matthew Hedstrom shows that the basic ideas of liberal Protestantism were communicated and popularized in the mid-twentieth century through middlebrow books. Hedstrom, *The Rise of Liberal Religion: Book Culture and American Spirituality in the Twentieth Century* (New York: Oxford University Press, 2013). The making of liberal theology is in large measure the story of three distinct schools: an ecumenical school associated with Union Theological Seminary, a personalist school connected to Boston University, and an empirical school developed at the University of Chicago. Though liberalism was by nature an ecumenical endeavor, it is not unimportant that these three schools were connected with the Presbyterians, the Methodists, and the Baptists, which covered the denominational landscape of the Protestant mainline. The complex story about how the development and spread of these three schools of liberal theology is intertwined with the history of these three institutions is wonderfully told by Gary Dorrien, *The Making of American Liberal Theology*, vol. 1, *Imagining Progressive Religion, 1805–1900* (Louisville, Ky.: Westminster John Knox, 2001), 335–92; and Dorrien, *The Making of American Liberal Theology*, vol. 2, *Idealism, Realism, and Modernity, 1900–1950* (Louisville, Ky.: Westminster John Knox, 2003), 151–215.

[5] Charles Hodge, *Systematic Theology* (New York: Scribner, Armstrong, 1872–1873); and Benjamin Breckinridge Warfield, *Revelation and Inspiration* (New York: Oxford, 1927).

still cling to the great fundamentals . . . to do battle royal" for the faith.[6] Fundamentalists rallied to resist modernist reinterpretations of the faith by urging Christians to reaffirm what they asserted were the historic truths of an inerrant Bible, a virgin-born Savior, a substitutionary atonement, a bodily resurrection, and a miraculous providence.[7] Yet fundamentalism lacked appeal for many traditional Christians. Though it claimed to be simply a reaffirmation of old orthodoxy, it was in fact an orthodoxy grown cultic, seeing "heresy in untruth but not in unloveliness," and while it was uncertain whether fundamentalism had the most truth, it surely had the least grace.[8] For neo-evangelicals like E. J. Carnell, the proper response to modernity was not in asserting the five points of fundamentalism, which was simply a reverse image of the basic commitments of liberalism, but rather in retrieving and defending the historic faith of orthodoxy, which, he claimed, "limits the ground of religious authority to the Bible."[9]

But just at the point that liberalism had established itself in American Christianity, mainline Protestant churches began a steady decline in membership, budgets, and influence. Liberalism seemed in retreat. Yet it might be argued that liberal Christianity was not defeated so much as it became the victim of its own success, as it won a "decisive, larger cultural victory."[10] Indeed, this declension narrative overlooks the important fact that liberalism succeeded not because more people joined liberal churches but because liberal religious beliefs and commitments gradually became shared by the wider culture. And as a result, much of what liberal Christianity once offered "now lies beyond the churches."[11] Hordern was part

[6] Curtis Lee Laws, "Convention Side Lights," *Watchman Examiner*, July 1, 1920, 834.

[7] George M. Marsden, *Fundamentalism and American Culture* (New York: Oxford University Press, 1980), 117 and 262n30. As Marsden points out, the five fundamentals were not fixed, as the deity of Christ was often substituted for the virgin birth and the premillennial return of Christ was sometimes inserted in the place of miracles. The theological outlook of fundamentalism became characterized by a series of books: R. A. Torrey and A. C. Dixon, eds., *The Fundamentals: A Testimony to the Truth*, 4 vols. (1917; repr., Grand Rapids: Baker Books, 1980).

[8] Edward John Carnell, "Fundamentalism," in *A Handbook of Christian Theology*, ed. Marvin Halverson and Arthur A. Cohen (New York: Meridian Books, 1958), 143; and Carnell, "Orthodoxy: Cultic vs. Classical," *Christian Century*, March 30, 1960, 378.

[9] Edward John Carnell, *The Case for Orthodox Theology* (Philadelphia: Westminster, 1959), 6. Other prominent early neo-evangelical voices included Carl F. H. Henry, *The Uneasy Conscience of Modern Fundamentalism* (Grand Rapids: Eerdmans, 1947); and Bernard Ramm, *Protestant Biblical Interpretation* (Boston: Wilde, 1950).

[10] Christian Smith with Patricia Snell, *Souls in Transition: The Religious and Spiritual Lives of Emerging Adults* (New York: Oxford University Press, 2009), 287.

[11] David A. Hollinger, *After Cloven Tongues of Fire: Protestant Liberalism in Modern American History* (Princeton, N.J.: Princeton University Press, 2013), 48–49. Elesha J. Coffman narrates the story of mainline Protestantism by tracing the history of the *Christian Century* magazine in *"The Christian Century" and the Rise of the Protestant Mainline* (New York: Oxford University

of a small but influential number of younger theologians who saw that the way forward was in moving beyond liberalism. Yet whatever was "after liberalism" would have to be more than "a spoon-fed authoritarianism." Pilgrims on this theological journey must acknowledge their "debts to liberalism" while also seeking to "catch the full breadth of orthodoxy."[12] This third way followed the lines of neither the reaffirmation strategy of orthodoxy nor the reinterpretation approach of liberalism. What theology needed was *retrieval* and *revision*.[13]

Press, 2013); and Jill K. Gill tracks the history of liberalism by recounting the involvement of the National Council of Churches in the anti–Vietnam War movement, in *Embattled Ecumenism: The National Council of Churches, the Vietnam War, and the Trials of the Protestant Left* (DeKalb: Northern Illinois University Press, 2011). Jennifer Schuessler provides a rich and sympathetic review of these recent historical reappraisals of American religious liberalism in "A Religious Legacy, with Its Leftward Tilt, Is Reconsidered," *New York Times,* July 23, 2013. Other recent assessments of religious liberalism include Leigh Schmidt and Sally Promey, eds., *American Religious Liberalism* (Bloomington: Indiana University Press, 2012); and N. Jay Demerath III, "Cultural Victory and Organizational Defeat in the Paradoxical Decline of Liberal Protestantism," *Journal for the Scientific Study of Religion* 34 (1995): 458–69. Will Campbell is somewhat less confident about the cultural victory. He describes an encounter with his friend and lapsed Methodist skeptic, P. D. East, who told about how his daughter's purple Easter chick grew into a Rhode Island Red, and, after all the dyed purple feathers wore off, it acted like all the other chickens in the chicken yard. East explained, "The Easter chicken is just one more chicken. There ain't a damn thing different about it." When Campbell reminded him that it still laid eggs, East replied, "Yeah, preacher Will, it lays eggs. But they all lay eggs. Who needs an Easter chicken for that? And the Rotary Club serves coffee. And the 4-H club says prayers. The Red Cross takes offerings for hurricane victims. Mental health does counseling, and the Boy Scouts have youth programs." Campbell, *Brother to a Dragonfly* (New York: Seabury, 1977), 219–20.

   [12] Hordern, "Young Theologians Rebel," 307.

   [13] William Hordern's book *The Case for a New Reformation Theology* (Philadelphia: Westminster, 1959) was published along with one by L. Harold DeWolf, *The Case for Liberal Theology* (Philadelphia: Westminster, 1959) and Carnell, *Case for Orthodox Theology.* Revisionists reject the approach of postliberalism and propose that what is needed is a revised account of the Christian faith "between the two extremes of political-religious fundamentalism and radical postmodernism" that is more in line with aims of liberalism than orthodoxy. Peter C. Hodgson, *Liberal Theology: A Radical Vision* (Minneapolis: Fortress, 2007), 4. Hodgson argues that these challenges are best addressed not by postliberalism or radical orthodoxy but by a radical liberalism. James Buckley names five major revisionist accounts of theology: Edward Farley, *Ecclesial Reflection: An Anatomy of Theological Method* (Philadelphia: Fortress, 1982); Gordon Kaufman, *In the Face of Mystery* (Cambridge, Mass.: Harvard University Press, 1993); Schubert Ogden, *The Reality of God* (New York: Harper, 1966); David Tracy, *The Analogical Imagination* (New York: Crossroad, 1981); and John Cobb, *Christ in a Pluralistic Age* (Philadelphia: Westminster, 1975). Buckley, "Revisionists and Liberals," in Ford, *Modern Theologians,* 327–42. Others make similar recommendations on the future of the liberal project, including Kenneth Cauthen, *The Impact of American Religious Liberalism,* 2nd ed. (Washington, D.C.: University Press of America, 1983); Christopher H. Evans, *Liberalism without Illusions: Renewing an American Christian Tradition* (Waco, Tex.: Baylor University Press, 2010); Michael J. Langford, *A Liberal Theology for the Twenty-First Century* (Aldershot, U.K.: Ashgate, 2001); and Donald E. Miller, *The Case for Liberal Christianity* (San Francisco: Harper, 1981).

Robert Calhoun described such a third way as a "new and chastened liberalism."[14] This vision was not simply a return to Protestant orthodoxy but an ecumenical *ressourcement* (i.e., back-to-the-sources) of the Christian tradition. This theological outlook has been characterized as a "generous liberal orthodoxy"—*generous* in its respectful and charitable openness toward an understanding of others, *liberal* inasmuch as it did not make a sharp break with modern modes of critical reflection, and *orthodox* because of its conviction that the center of Christian theology is the revelation of the triune God in Jesus Christ. Calhoun was joined in this research project by his younger Yale colleagues Hans Frei and George Lindbeck and later David Kelsey in the constructive proposal that became known as postliberal theology.[15] For Calhoun, the transition was "not to neo-orthodoxy, but to a view closer to traditional orthodoxy without abandoning his liberal convictions." A postliberal theology sought to center the plot of the Christian story on a broad consensus within inclusive parameters that found expression in the ancient ecumenical creeds and focused on the christological and trinitarian center of the Christian faith.[16] It imagined an outlook that might be a mixture of the best of *Christian Century* and *Christianity Today*, but what actually emerged was a diverse set of voices that were evangelical and catholic, finding expression in such publications as *First Things*, *Modern Theology*, and *Pro Ecclesia*.[17]

[14] Robert L. Calhoun, "A Liberal Bandaged but Unbowed," in the series "How My Mind Has Changed in This Decade," *Christian Century*, May 31, 1939, 701–4.

[15] Hans W. Frei, *The Eclipse of Biblical Narrative: A Study in Eighteenth and Nineteenth Century Hermeneutics* (New Haven, Conn.: Yale University Press, 1974); Frei, *The Identity of Jesus Christ: The Hermeneutical Bases of Dogmatic Theology* (Eugene, Ore.: Wipf & Stock, 1997); George A. Lindbeck, *The Nature of Doctrine* (Philadelphia: Westminster, 1984); and David H. Kelsey, *Proving Doctrine: The Uses of Scripture in Modern Theology* (Harrisburg, Pa.: Trinity Press, 1999). Frei's own view might be characterized as type four (Barth) with an openness to type three (Schleiermacher), in Frei, *Types of Christian Theology* (New Haven, Conn.: Yale University Press, 1992). On postliberalism, see Paul J. DeHart, *The Trial of the Witnesses: The Rise and Decline of Postliberal Theology* (Oxford: Blackwell, 2006); Mike Higton, "Frei's Christology and Lindbeck's Cultural-Linguistic Theory," *Scottish Journal of Theology* 50, no. 1 (1997): 83–95; George Hunsinger, "Postliberalism," in *The Cambridge Companion to Postmodern Theology*, ed. Kevin J. Vanhoozer (Cambridge: Cambridge University Press, 2003), 42–57; and William C. Placher, "Postliberal Theology," in Ford, *Modern Theologians*, 343–56.

[16] Robert L. Calhoun, *Lectures on the History of Christian Doctrine* (New Haven, Conn.: Yale Divinity School, 1948), 1:14; Hans Frei, "In Memory of Robert L. Calhoun 1896–1983," *Reflection* 82 (1984): 8–9; George A. Lindbeck, *Robert Lowry Calhoun as Historian of Doctrine*, Yale Divinity School Library Occasional Publication no. 12 (New Haven, Conn.: Yale Divinity School Library, 1998).

[17] *First Things* is a periodical published ten times a year by the Institute on Religion and Public Life in New York City, an interreligious, nonpartisan research and education institute whose purpose is to advance a religiously informed public philosophy for the ordering of society. *Modern Theology* is an ecumenical journal that publishes articles addressing issues specific to the discipline of theology and wider issues from a theological perspective. *Pro Ecclesia* is a journal

Anyone undertaking the task of retrieval and revision dare not strike off on the journey without looking to theologians whose projects provide clues and signposts for other pilgrims. When Yves Congar and Henri de Lubac set out to address the questions of modernity from the standpoint of the historic faith, they discovered that the theological renewal of Christianity begins by "returning to its sources." For the aim of the *ressourcement* movement was to "recover Christianity in its fullness and purity."[18] The call to return to the biblical and patristic sources not only enabled them to break with the prevailing anti-Protestant and antimodern animus in Catholic theology; it also prepared the way for the revisioning of the Second Vatican Council.[19] Those seeking theological renewal can learn much from this "new theology" as a model of retrieval and revision.[20]

---

of theology published by the Center for Catholic and Evangelical Theology. It seeks to give contemporary expression to the one apostolic faith and its classic traditions, working for and manifesting the church's unity by research, theological construction, and free exchange of opinion.

[18] Henri de Lubac, *Paradoxes* (Paris: Livre français, 1946), 67–69. Quoted by Susan K. Wood, *Spiritual Exegesis and the Church in the Theology of Henri de Lubac* (Grand Rapids: Eerdmans, 1998), 5.

[19] The story is told that Pope John XXIII said he convened the Second Vatican Council because the time had come for the Catholic Church to open the windows and let in some fresh air. Though the story may be apocryphal, it reinforces the impression that Vatican II was primarily about bringing the church and its teachings up to date (*aggiornamento*). Modernization was one purpose of the council, but the other equally important feature of Vatican II was a return to the sources (*ressourcement*) of the biblical and patristic tradition. Some interpreters have emphasized the continuity (*ressourcement*) of the Second Vatican Council with the historic tradition of the church, as does the recent collection by Matthew Lamb and Matthew Levering, eds., *Vatican II: Renewal within Tradition* (New York: Oxford University Press, 2008), just as others have focused on the discontinuity of the council with past tradition (*aggiornamento*), as is recently done by John W. O'Malley, *What Happened at Vatican II?* (Cambridge, Mass.: Belknap/Harvard University Press, 2008). But still others contend that a more sophisticated hermeneutic of reform was taking place at the council, involving a dynamic process that included both development (*ressourcement*) and reformulation (*aggiornamento*); see Jared Wicks, "Questions and Answers on the New Responses of the Congregation for the Doctrine of the Faith," *Ecumenical Trends* 36, no. 7 (2007): 97–112; and Marcellino D'Ambrosio, "*Ressourcement* Theology, *Aggiornamento* and the Hermeneutics of Tradition," *Communio* 18, no. 4 (1991): 530–55.

[20] The *ressourcement* employed by Congar and Lubac sought to renew Christian theology by returning to the explosive vitality of the apostolic and patristic sources. This "new theology" overcame the rationalism of neo-Thomism and led to a recovery of the hermeneutical richness of premodern biblical exegesis. See Yves Congar, *Divided Christendom* (London: G. Bles, 1939); Henri de Lubac, *The Mystery of the Supernatural* (London: G. Chapman, 1967); Lubac, *Medieval Exegesis: The Four Senses of Scripture*, 3 vols. (Grand Rapids: Eerdmans, 1998–2009). Other exemplars of retrieval include the Mercersburg theology of John Williamson Nevin, *Catholic and Reformed: Selected Theological Writings of John Williamson Nevin*, ed. Charles Yrigoyen Jr. and George H. Bricker (Pittsburgh, Pa.: Pickwick, 1978); and Philip Schaff, *The Creeds of Christendom* (New York: Harper, 1877); and the paleo-orthodoxy of Thomas Oden's three-volume *Systematic Theology* (*The Living God*, *The Word of Life*, and *Life in the Spirit*; San Francisco: Harper & Row, 1987–1992); and Robert E. Webber, *Ancient-Future Faith* (Grand Rapids: Baker, 1999).

Cornell West and Sarah Coakley are two contemporary theologians that have carefully and creatively explored this pattern of retrieval and revision with a special attention to matters of race and gender. Yet, as they remind other theologians seeking a third way, this reflective process is dynamic and requires ongoing interrogation of the sources through the lens of race and gender with an eye toward new theological vision.[21] Theological renewal thus demands a sophisticated hermeneutic of reflection, one that accounts for a process of development and reformulation and includes both retrieval and revision.

It might be asked whether Baptists have anything to contribute to this conversation of theological renewal. This question is especially pressing since, as Baptist theologian James William McClendon Jr. has pointed out, Baptists have not made significant theological contributions thus far. The lack of engagement is largely due to the fact that Baptists have not taken their own tradition seriously, let alone the ancient and ecumenical traditions of the historic church.[22] But perhaps Baptists should pay more attention given that, as Martin Marty has argued, the ecclesial landscape has been thoroughly baptistified.[23] Of course, Marty was not suggesting that the wider church was seriously attending to theological sources in the baptistic tradition or that they were becoming Baptists and adopting immersion, although there is a growing trend toward believer's baptism in other churches.[24] What he meant was that individuals and groups were

---

[21] Cornell West, *Prophesy Deliverance! An Afro-American Revolutionary Christianity* (Philadelphia: Westminster, 1982); and Sarah Coakley, *Powers and Submissions: Spirituality, Philosophy, and Gender* (Oxford: Blackwell, 2002). As Jonathan Tran points out, Willie James Jennings, J. Kameron Carter, and Brian Bantum have recently demonstrated this retrieval-revision of theology through the lens of race by turning "the Enlightenment's claim of liberation on its head, locating in that movement a basis of oppression and looking instead to ancient and medieval Christian theology to free us from contemporary racism." Tran, "The New Black Theology: Retrieving Ancient Sources to Challenge Racism," *Christian Century*, February 8, 2012, 24–27; Jennings, *The Christian Imagination: Theology and the Origins of Race* (New Haven, Conn.: Yale University Press, 2010); J. Kameron Carter, *Race: A Theological Account* (New York: Oxford University Press, 2008); and Brian Bantum, *Redeeming Mulatto: Theology of Race and Christian Hybridity* (Waco, Tex.: Baylor University Press, 2010). Coakley has written *God, Sexuality and the Self: An Essay "On the Trinity"* (Cambridge: Cambridge University Press, 2013), the first volume of a four-volume systematic theology that similarly subverts modern notions of gender by inviting readers to reconceive the relation of human sexuality and the desire for God through the bodily practice of contemplative prayer. Stanley J. Grenz similarly argues for a fresh reinterpretation of evangelicalism in *Revisioning Evangelical Theology* (Downers Grove, Ill.: InterVarsity, 1993).

[22] James Wm. McClendon Jr., *Ethics: Systematic Theology, Volume I* (Waco, Tex.: Baylor University Press, 2012), 20–26.

[23] Martin E. Marty, "Baptistification Takes Over," *Christianity Today*, September 2, 1983, 32–36.

[24] There is a growing ecumenical consensus that recognizes that "baptism upon personal

becoming like Baptists by increasingly adopting "a *baptist style* of Christian life."[25] But for Marty this baptistic style is just one side of a polarity. Its complementary principle is a *catholic style*. These two, he argued, are opposite but complementary forces, and he commended not the embodiment of one or the other but both.

While it is true that the ongoing task of theological renewal for Baptists depends on attention to baptistic sources, if Baptists are in any sense to be a voice of renewal for the whole church, they will also need to look closely at catholic sources.[26] The task of retrieval will require that Baptists draw from a historical consciousness within their own heritage.[27] But the work of revision will also demand considerable theological wisdom to discern how these particular convictions and practices fit within a larger ecclesial narrative.[28] If performed well, such retrieval and revision will result in a theological outlook that is both baptist and catholic.

---

profession of faith is the most clearly attested pattern in the New Testament documents." *Baptism, Eucharist and Ministry* IV.A.11, Faith and Order Paper no. 111 (Geneva: World Council of Churches, 1982), 4.

[25] Emphasis in original.

[26] Roger E. Olson demonstrates how Baptists (and other evangelicals) should think about retrieving the whole Christian tradition in *The Story of Christian Theology: Twenty Centuries of Tradition & Reform* (Downers Grove, Ill.: InterVarsity, 1999).

[27] Baptists have produced remarkably gifted historians of the Baptist tradition, including William G. McLoughlin, *New England Dissent, 1630–1833: The Baptists and the Separation of Church and State* (Cambridge, Mass.: Harvard University Press, 1971); Edwin S. Gaustad, *Liberty of Conscience: Roger Williams in America* (Grand Rapids: Eerdmans, 1991); Robert G. Torbet, *A History of the Baptists*, 3rd ed. (Valley Forge, Pa.: Judson, 1973); Clarence C. Goen, *Revivalism and Separatism in New England, 1740–1800* (New Haven, Conn.: Yale University Press, 1962); Robert E. Johnson, *A Global Introduction to Baptist Churches* (Cambridge: Cambridge University Press, 2010); Walter B. Shurden, *Associationalism among Baptists in America, 1707–1814* (New York: Arno Press, 1980); Bill J. Leonard, *Baptist Ways: A History* (Valley Forge, Pa.: Judson Press, 2003); William H. Brackney, *The Baptists* (Westport, Conn.: Praeger, 1994); C. Douglas Weaver, *In Search of the New Testament Church: The Baptist Story* (Macon, Ga.: Mercer University Press, 2008); H. Leon McBeth, *The Baptist Heritage* (Nashville: Broadman, 1986); James Melvin Washington, *Frustrated Fellowship: The Black Baptist Quest for Social Power* (Macon, Ga.: Mercer University Press, 1986); Mechal Sobel, *Trabelin' On: The Slave Journey to an Afro-Baptist Faith* (Westport, Conn.: Greenwood Press, 1979); A. C. Underwood, *A History of the English Baptists* (London: Carey Kingsgate Press, 1956); B. R. White, *The English Separatist Tradition: From the Marian Martyrs to the Pilgrim Fathers* (London: Oxford University Press, 1971); Murray Tolmie, *The Triumph of the Saints: The Separatist Churches in London, 1616–1649* (Cambridge: Cambridge University Press, 1977); David W. Bebbington, *Baptists through the Centuries: A History of a Global People* (Waco, Tex.: Baylor University Press, 2010); John H. Y. Briggs, *The English Baptists of the Nineteenth Century* (Didcot, U.K.: Baptist Historical Society, 1994); Ian M. Randall, *The English Baptists of the Twentieth Century* (Didcot, U.K.: Baptist Historical Society, 2005); Stephen Wright, *The Early English Baptists, 1603–1649* (Woodbridge, U.K.: Boydell, 2006).

[28] The Baptist theological resources have been treated by William Brackney, *A Genetic History of Baptist Thought* (Macon, Ga.: Mercer University Press, 2004); Curtis W. Freeman, James W. McClendon Jr., and C. Rosalee Velloso da Silva Ewell, eds., *Baptist Roots: A Reader*

The Baptist vision emerged within a movement of radical protest intent on reforming the one, holy, catholic, and apostolic church. It resulted in the founding of a sect committed to maintaining its place at the top of the hierarchy of denominations. It is in danger of becoming, if it has not already become, a set of principles maintained by an affinity group of mystic individuals, determined by personal choice. How did this happen? Roger Williams, who founded the First Baptist Church in America, seems to have passed through all three stages in his pilgrimage from Puritan to Separatist to Seeker.[29] But for the most part the libertarian transformation of the Baptist movement has been more gradual. When Bunyan's Christian warned three sleeping men "out of the way" that danger awaited, the one called Presumption replied, "Every tub must stand upon its own bottom."[30] What Bunyan quoted as the fool's proverb has ironically become the new folk wisdom. The modern myth, appropriating language from the Enlightenment and popular culture, celebrates autonomous agency and rugged individualism, but the story is as old as the primal parents who declared themselves to be "free."[31]

The source of the Baptist vision is not autonomy, because "interdependence is the mark of the converted" and "the search for independence was Adam's sin."[32] Individual freedom is not the core value of the Free Church tradition, for "Christian liberty is acceptance of the yoke of Christ, not autonomy." Indeed, it is a mistake "to suppose that personal responsibility points relentlessly toward the autonomy of the individual conscience and the privatization of religion."[33] Perhaps it is worth asking

---

in the Theology of a Christian People (Valley Forge, Pa.: Judson Press, 1999); James Leo Garrett Jr., *Baptist Theology: A Four Century Study* (Macon, Ga.: Mercer University Press, 2009); Fisher Humphreys, *The Way We Were: How Southern Baptist Theology Has Changed and What It Means to Us All*, rev. ed. (Macon, Ga.: Smyth & Helwys, 1984); and Stephen R. Holmes, *Baptist Theology* (London: T&T Clark, 2012). None of these summaries sufficiently display the African American Baptist theological heritage, in large measure because they have tended to include "classical" rather than "mass" sources. See Benjamin E. Mays, *The Negro's God as Reflected in His Literature* (Boston: Chapman and Grimes, 1938; repr., New York: Negro Universities Press, 1969), 14–18, 245–55.

[29] See my article "Roger Williams, American Democracy, and the Baptists," *Perspectives in Religious Studies* 34, no. 3 (2007): 267–86.

[30] John Bunyan, *The Pilgrim's Progress*, ed. N. H. Keeble (Oxford: Oxford University Press, 1984), 32. Bunyan's original word was "fatt" (i.e., vat; viz., a tub).

[31] Barry Alan Shain displays how a romantic rendering of individual liberty as the animating principle of American culture in time hardened into a libertarian myth. Shain, *The Myth of American Individualism: The Protestant Origins of American Political Thought* (Princeton, N.J.: Princeton University Press, 1994), 10–11.

[32] B. R. White, "The Practice of Association," in *A Perspective on Baptist Identity*, ed. David Slater (Kingsbridge, U.K.: Mainstream, 1987), 29.

[33] Franklin H. Littell, "The Historical Free Church Defined," *Brethren Life and Thought* 9, no. 4 (1964): 78–79; reprinted in *Brethren Life and Thought* 50, nos. 3–4 (2005): 51–52.

whether the Baptist movement might be understood more as a gesture to the horizon of the new creation than a yearning to remain in the land east of Eden inhabited by all sons and daughters of earth. This book represents an alternative account that renarrates the Baptist story as a community of contested convictions within the church catholic. It builds on the suggestion by Carl Braaten that it might be more useful in an ecumenical age for Baptists to understand themselves as "representatives of a spiritual movement *within* the one holy catholic and apostolic Church, rather than, as the radical reformers claimed, a rebirth of the church of the New Testament." "Such a move," it could be argued, "might parallel the reassessment of Luther's magisterial reformation as a confessing movement within the one Church of the West, rather than as the intentional creation of a new and independent church."[34] The suggestion of a baptist catholicity may strike more than a few as odd. Indeed, the conventional wisdom would seem to indicate that the spiritual freedom of the Baptists embodies the very antithesis of churchliness. The pages that follow explore a churchly theology that challenges the assumption that Baptists historically and normatively epitomize the teleology of progressive fissiparation from catholicity to sectarianism.

It was Ernst Troeltsch who famously distinguished church, sect, and mystic as three distinct types of Christianity. Baptists, in this typological description, originated as a sect that existed as "a voluntary society, composed of strict and definite Christian believers bound to each other by the fact that all have experienced 'the new birth.'" Early Baptists, according to this view, fit the sectarian pattern of voluntary societies living apart from the world in small groups, claiming to represent the pure church, and awaiting the apocalyptic in-breaking of the kingdom of God.[35] But over

---

[34] Carl E. Braaten, "A Harvest of Evangelical Theology," *First Things* 61 (1996): 48. Braaten's comments are posed in a review of James Wm. McClendon Jr.'s *Doctrine: Systematic Theology, Volume II* (Nashville: Abingdon, 1994). *Doctrine* was recently reprinted by Baylor University Press (with a new introduction by Curtis W. Freeman; Waco, Tex.: Baylor University Press, 2012).

[35] Ernst Troeltsch, *The Social Teaching of the Christian Churches*, trans. Olive Wyon (New York: Harper Torchbooks, 1960), 2:993; 2:695. Troeltsch draws from Max Weber's description of an ideal type that "is formed by the one-sided accentuation of one or more points of view and by the synthesis of a great many diffuse, discrete, more or less present and occasionally absent concrete individual phenomena, which are arranged according to those one-sidedly emphasized viewpoints into a unified analytical construct." The ideal type, Weber explains, is a "mental construct" and "cannot be found empirically anywhere in reality." Weber, *The Methodology of the Social Sciences*, ed. Edward Shils and Henry Finch (New York: Free Press, 1949), 90. The point of utilizing a type is not as a description of discrete concrete phenomena but rather as a theory to explain the big picture. Typologies then are not true or false but only helpful or unhelpful for further investigation. Although the distorting effect of

time as the Baptists made peace with the world, their radical stance was transformed through patience and hope from "Baptist sects" into "Baptist Free Churches."[36] Yet because the Baptists were a "non-theological" movement needing "nothing beyond the Bible," they were tendentiously inclined to embrace the standpoint of mystic individualism.[37] Troeltsch adapted this social typology from his Heidelberg colleague, Max Weber, who distinguished between sects conceived as voluntary associations and churches defined as compulsory societies.

For Weber, Baptists epitomized the voluntarism and individualism of the sect type. When on a trip to the United States in 1904, Weber attended a Baptist river baptism (curiously described as a "christening") while visiting relatives in Mount Airy, North Carolina. Pointing out one of the candidates, his American cousin indicated that the man was baptized "because he wants to open a bank" in Mt. Airy. Weber inferred from the comment that the man's motive for membership was to ensure success in business, thus illustrating his thesis on the link between ethics and economics. He suggested that baptism for the Baptists was no otherworldly ritual, but rather was part of an inner-worldly asceticism that admitted into membership only those who have been examined and proven themselves to be morally righteous. Furthermore, at each subsequent gathering of the Lord's Supper, members were subject to expulsion for moral offenses resulting in the prospect of diminished economic prosperity through the loss of credibility and social declassification, thus ensuring that each individual's moral character would remain under scrutiny. Membership in a Baptist congregation, Weber theorized, "meant a certificate of moral qualification and especially of business morals for the individual." Thus the inner asceticism of the Baptists and other Puritan sects, he concluded, "formed one of the most important historical foundations of modern individualism," and, he added, "the modern capitalist ethos."[38]

Ernst Troeltsch's church-sect-mystic typology is contested, there can be no dispute about its enormous power in displaying the social teachings of Christian churches.

[36] Troeltsch, *Social Teaching of the Christian Churches*, 2:708.

[37] Troeltsch, *Social Teaching of the Christian Churches*, 2:767.

[38] Max Weber, *The Protestant Ethic and the Spirit of Capitalism*, trans. Talcott Parsons (New York: Charles Scribner's Sons, 1958), 145 and 254–55n173; Weber, "The Protestant Sects and the Spirit of Capitalism," in *From Max Weber: Essays in Sociology*, trans. and ed. H. H. Gerth and C. Wright Mills (New York: Oxford University Press, 1946), 302–22. Weber's *Protestant Ethic* began in two articles published in 1904–1905, which overlap with his visit to North Carolina. See also Marianne Weber, *Max Weber: A Biography*, trans. and ed. Harry Zohn (New York: John Wiley & Sons, 1975), 298–300. William H. Swatos Jr. has attempted to piece together a coherent narrative account of Weber's visit to Mt. Airy based on the incomplete record, in "Sects and Success: *Missverstehen* in Mt. Airy," *Social Analysis* 43, no. 4 (1982): 375–79. Beth Barton Schweiger corrects Weber's account, showing it to ignore the unique

Some Baptist commentators seem content to own the moniker of sectarianism, approving the description of Troeltsch that identifies Baptists with the sect type of Christianity.[39] Others qualify such a portrayal in favor of a more nuanced view, suggesting that the early Baptists in the American South were not massively sectarian, though their fundamental instinct was predominately sectarian. However, as Troeltsch theorized, over time Baptists became more church-like.[40] This more nuanced account follows the same basic line as that of H. Richard Niebuhr, who argued that the centrifugal tendencies of sects give way over time to centripetal forces that transform them into denominations that reflect the majority values.[41] Yet unlike Troeltsch's typology, in which the dialectic is resolved by the transformation of "Baptist sects" into "Baptist Free Churches," Niebuhr posited an ongoing tension between the church and sect types. Though these writers insist that the classification of Baptists as sect-like is a purely sociological description, the deployment of these typological designations is hardly neutral. Indeed, it carries theological assumptions that are biased against "sectarian" Christianity, missing Troeltsch's observation about Baptists and other Free Churches.[42]

John Howard Yoder offered a different sort of typology that envisioned a believers church as standing between and over against theocrats seeking to reform society at large with one blow and spiritualists emphasizing the importance of inward and individual change as key to social reform. The believers church, which includes the Baptists and other baptistic groups, seeks to embody a way of life that conforms to Scripture and exhibits the life of a covenanted fellowship.[43] Although Yoder shifted the

---

relation between culture and religion in "southern evangelicalism." Schweiger, "Max Weber in Mount Airy; or, Revivals and Social Theory in the Early South," in *Religion in the American South: Protestants and Others in History and Culture*, ed. Beth Barton Schweiger and Donald G. Mathews (Chapel Hill: University of North Carolina Press, 2004), 31–66.

[39] A. C. Underwood begins his *History of the English Baptists* with an approving exposition of Troeltsch that identifies Baptists as a sect (15–21).

[40] Samuel S. Hill, *Southern Churches in Crisis Revisited* (Tuscaloosa: University of Alabama Press, 1999), 143, 150.

[41] H. Richard Niebuhr, *The Social Sources of Denominationalism* (New York: H. Holt, 1929).

[42] For an analysis of the sociological types as a normative rather than a purely descriptive account, see Duane Friesen, "Normative Factors in Troeltsch's Typology of Religious Association," *Journal of Religious Ethics* 3, no. 2 (1975): 271–83.

[43] John Howard Yoder, "A People in the World," in John Howard Yoder, *The Royal Priesthood: Essays Ecclesiological and Ecumenical*, ed. Michael G. Cartwright (Grand Rapids: Eerdmans, 1994), 68–73. Baptist theologian Nigel Goring Wright, following Yoder, offers a qualified endorsement of the sect type, in *Free Church, Free State: The Positive Baptist Vision* (Milton Keynes, U.K.: Paternoster, 2005), 26–28, 213–14.

typology from the descending ecclesiality in the church, sect, and mystic types to a one of divergent social strategies in which churches engage the surrounding culture, he retained—as did H. Richard Niebuhr, whom he criticized—the notion of an ongoing tension in his types. To suggest, as Troeltsch did, that Baptists overcame their sectarian origins is surely better than the Niebuhrian pigeonhole of permanent sectarianism. But it might be questioned whether the developmental model accurately represents the ecclesial pattern of the early Baptists.

It has recently been suggested that the earliest Baptists were actually closer to the church type than Troeltsch proposed. The Smyth-Helwys congregation and other early Baptists understood the church as constituted by a two-dimensional covenant—a horizontal aspect between fellow members, and a vertical relation with God. Consequently, early Baptists regarded their churches as gathered communities that were constituted as Free Churches established by God's eternal covenant of grace, not merely as voluntary societies or sectarian assemblies brought together by mutual agreement. The early Baptists understood the church as both the people gathered by Christ and the people who gathered in response to his call. In this explanation of the church, "believers gather because they are *gathered*." But, like the bells that ring on Sunday morning calling the church to the meeting, the initiative lies with God, not humanity. Thus the early Baptists conceived of their gathered communities as local and visible expressions of the church universal, not merely as independent congregations or voluntary associations. Smyth and Helwys made the further and more decisive move of describing this two-dimensional covenant as sacramentally enacted in baptism.[44]

Such divergent accounts reflect fundamental hermeneutical differences. The constitutive nature of Baptist life is a contested question between those with a "churchly" understanding and others with a "nonchurchly" understanding. The churchly perspective "is rooted in the conviction that God's fundamental purpose in Christ was to create for himself a *people*." The nonchurchly outlook "is rooted in the conviction that God's primary interest—indeed, exclusive interest—is in *individual* Christians." One acknowledges the frailty of the individual and the need for interdependency. The other affirms the competency of the individual and exhibits confidence in the capacity of each Christian to know and do

---

[44] Paul S. Fiddes, "Church and Sect: Cross-Currents in Early Baptist Life," in *Exploring Baptist Origins*, ed. Anthony R. Cross and Nicholas J. Wood (Oxford: Regent's Park College, 2010), 33–57. See also Fiddes, *Tracks and Traces: Baptist Identity in Church and Theology* (Carlisle, U.K.: Paternoster, 2003), 21–47.

God's will.[45] The individualistic interpretation of Baptist origins is, as one historian observed, "derived from the general cultural and religious climate of the nineteenth century rather than from any serious study of the Bible."[46] According to this view, the mainstream of early Baptist development in England and America was representative of the churchly understanding and that the nonchurchly interpretations were reflective of later developments including Enlightenment liberalism, Romantic expressivism, and frontier revivalism.[47]

In his book *Baptists through the Centuries*, historian David W. Bebbington also describes the early Baptists as representatives of a churchly theology. He suggests that this churchly theology went into decline in the eighteenth and nineteenth centuries and that a diminished ecclesiology became widespread by the twentieth century. He provides five reasons for the declension of the churchly view: controversialism (defending against denominational detractors), the intellectual climate (Enlightenment rationalism), the Evangelical awakening (conversion experience superseding the ordinances), anti-Catholicism, and respectability (upward mobility). Those seeking a revisioned churchly understanding seek to retrieve "the early Baptists' exalted doctrine of the church," as one of seven dominant strands in contemporary Baptist life.[48]

---

[45] Winthrop S. Hudson, *Baptists in Transition: Individualism and Christian Responsibility* (Valley Forge, Pa.: Judson Press, 1979), 19–20.

[46] Winthrop S. Hudson, "Shifting Patterns of Church Order in the Twentieth Century," in *Baptist Concepts of the Church*, ed. Winthrop S. Hudson (Philadelphia: Judson Press, 1959), 215.

[47] Robert T. Handy, in his foreword to Hudson's book, provides a historical genealogy of the nonchurchly individualism that became established in Baptist life, in Hudson, *Baptists in Transition*, 9–13. See also Mikael Broadway, "The Roots of Baptists in Community, and Therefore Voluntary Membership Not Individualism; or, The High Flying Modernist, Stripped of His Ontological Assumptions, Appears to Hold the Ecclesiology of a Yahoo," in *Recycling the Past or Researching History?* ed. Philip E. Thompson and Anthony R. Cross (Milton Keynes, U.K.: Paternoster, 2005), 67–83.

[48] Bebbington, *Baptists through the Centuries*, 177–95 and 271. Bebbington identifies E. Y. Mullins, William McNutt, and A. H. Strong as reinforcing the decline of the churchly view, and Ernest Payne, H. Wheeler Robinson, George Beasley-Murray, and the Baptist Manifesto as leading voices in the revival of the ecclesiology of the early Baptists. All of the churchly and nonchurchly personalities mentioned by Bebbington appear in the pages that follow. Readers may wish to know that I was one of the drafters of the document known as "Re-envisioning Baptist Identity," also referred to as the Baptist Manifesto, or simply the Manifesto. It first appeared in print in *Baptists Today*, June 26, 1997, 8–10, but was subsequently published in *Perspectives in Religious Studies* 24, no. 3 (1997): 303–10, and as an appendix in Steven R. Harmon, *Towards Baptist Catholicity: Essays on Tradition and the Baptist Vision* (Milton Keynes, U.K.: Paternoster, 2006), 215–23. It is accessible online at http://divinity.duke.edu/sites/default/files/documents/faculty-freeman/reenvisioning-baptist-identity.pdf.

By the churchly account, early Baptists were not fanatical sectarians who rejected the wider Christian community and withdrew from the world. They were rather churchly minded Christians seeking radical reform of the church catholic by reinstating apostolic practices that serve as identifying marks of the new creation on its way. In his important book *The Gathered Community*, Robert Walton characterized the ecclesial standpoint of the early Baptists as "a company of redeemed men and women having discipline and properly appointed leadership, faithfully preaching the Word and regularly observing the sacraments."[49] Living into such an ecclesial vision, however, is not without challenges. It is fair to note that "catholic" is not a term with which Baptists readily identify.[50] Yet to deny the catholicity of the church is to revert to a sectarian stance that turns back from the ecumenical vision of the early Baptists. John Smyth's *Confession of Faith* breathed a startling spirit of catholicity into the Baptist vision by declaring that "all penitent and faithfull Christians are brethren in the communion of the outward church, wheresoever they live, by what name soever they are knowen, [be they Roman Catholics, Lutherans, Zwinglians, Calvinists, Brownists, Anabaptists, or other pious Christians], which in truth and zeale, follow repentance and faith." He continued, "we salute them all with a holie kisse, being hartilie grieved that wee which follow after one faith, and one spirit, one lord, and one God, one bodie, and one baptisme, should be rent into so many sects, and schismes: and that only for matters of lesse moment."[51]

These early Baptists followed in the footsteps of radical "forward" Christians who, though calling for a new reformation without tarrying any further, imagined a new catholic spirit.[52] In his autobiographical ecclesial treatise, *A True and Short Declaration* (1583), Separatist pioneer Robert Browne conceived of gathered churches as those that "joine them selves to the Lord, in one covenant & felloweshipp together, & to keep

---

[49] Robert C. Walton, *The Gathered Community* (London: Carey Press, 1946), 80.

[50] Edward Roberts-Thomson, *With Hands Outstretched: Baptists and the Ecumenical Movement* (London: Marshall, Morgan & Scott, 1962), 35–36.

[51] Smyth, *A Confession of Faith* §69, in *The Works of John Smyth*, ed. W. T. Whitley (Cambridge: Cambridge University Press, 1915), 2:745. The bracketed reference to "Roman Catholics, Lutherans, Zwinglians, Calvinists, Brownists, Anabaptists, or other pious Christians" is included in the version of Smyth's Confession LXXI that appears as an appendix in Benjamin Evans, *The Early English Baptists* (London: J. Heaton & Son, 1862), 1:267.

[52] Robert Browne described himself during his years of study at Cambridge University as one who was "knowne & counted forward in religion." Browne, *A True and Short Declaration*, in *The Writings of Robert Harrison and Robert Browne*, ed. Albert Peel and Leland H. Carlson, vol. 2 of *Elizabethan Nonconformist Texts* (London: George Allen & Unwin, 1953), 297.

& seek agrement under his lawes and government."[53] Yet, even though Browne's covenanting congregation's search of further reform left them ecclesially separated from the Church of England, he maintained that they must be open "for seeking to other churches to have their help, being better reformed, or to bring them the reformation."[54] And in seeking the wisdom of the whole church, Browne hoped an emerging catholicity would serve as a check against the congregational proclivity toward individualism and sectarianism, for, he contended, "the joining & partaking of manie churches together, & of the authoritie which manie have, must needs be greater & more waightie then the authoritie of anie single person."[55]

Of course, the catholicity of the Baptists stopped at the point of infant baptism, which John Smyth identified as the mark of the beast.[56] Smyth's old Cambridge mentor, Francis Johnson, argued that it was a "great error . . . to think that the baptisme in the Church of Rome . . . is not to be regarded, but to be renounced." He continued that it cannot be denied that the Roman Church "was espoused to Christ and in the covenant of grace by the Gospel of salvation" and that this covenant remained "notwithstanding all her adulteries and apostasie." Johnson further argued that the Roman Church maintained an orthodox view of Christ, professed the apostolic faith contained in the ancient creeds, and baptized with water in the name of the Trinity.[57] Though Johnson insisted that he had not retracted his earlier views on the need for separation from the Church of England and Rome, he nevertheless did not regard the Church of Rome to be a false church, as did Smyth and his congregation. Henry Ainsworth, who split off from Johnson's congregation in 1610, replied that by maintaining "a colourable Plea for the Roman church" Johnson had retracted his separatism and fallen into heresy.[58] Ainsworth thus represents

---

[53] Browne, *True and Short Declaration*, in *Writings of Robert Harrison and Robert Browne* (ed. Peel and Carlson), 422.

[54] Browne, *True and Short Declaration*, in *Writings of Robert Harrison and Robert Browne* (ed. Peel and Carlson), 423.

[55] Browne, *True and Short Declaration*, in *Writings of Robert Harrison and Robert Browne* (ed. Peel and Carlson), 399.

[56] Smyth, *The Character of the Beast*, in *Works of John Smyth*, 2:565.

[57] Francis Johnson, *A Christian Plea Conteyning three Treatises* (Leiden: William Brewster, 1617), 27–29.

[58] Henry Ainsworth, preface to *A Reply to a Pretended Christian Plea for the AntiChristian Church of Rome* (1620). Johnson's view of Rome as a church in a qualified sense was shared by contemporary Puritans within the Church of England who also regarded the Roman Church as a church of Christ but always *secundum quid*. Anthony Milton, *Catholic and Reformed: The Roman and Protestant Churches in English Protestant Thought: 1600–1640* (Cambridge: Cambridge University Press, 1995), 134–41.

the strict separatist and congregational view that denied not only the validity of baptisms performed in the Churches of Rome and England (i.e., catabaptism), but also denied their ecclesial status. Many Baptists have chosen to live out this sectarian option, but Other Baptists seek a more excellent way.

The roots of a Baptist sense of contesting catholicity can be traced to William Perkins, the moderate Puritan theologian and fellow of Christ's College at Cambridge University from 1584 to 1593, during the years Smyth was a student, who has been described as "the prince of puritan theologians and the most eagerly read."[59] Perkins was no Anglo-Catholic. He celebrated the Protestant reform of the Church of England, exclaiming, "Therefore we have good cause to blesse the name of God, that hath freed us from the yoke of this Romane bondage, & hath brought us to the true light & liberty of the gospel."[60] Yet he argued that the proper theological description of a Protestant is a "Reformed Catholic," who "holds the same and necessarie heades of religion with the Romane Church" yet "pares off and rejects all errours in doctrine whereby the said religion is corrupted." Perkins thus attempted "to shew how neer we may come to the present Church of Rome in sundrie points of religion: and wherein we must for ever dissent."[61]

It is within this historical stream that the framers of the 1780 church covenant of the New Road Baptist Church in Oxford, England—which was gathered as an ecumenical fellowship of Baptists, Presbyterians, and some Methodists—declared, "We denominate ourselves a *Protestant Catholic Church of Christ*."[62] It is within this historical stream that the Baptist

[59] Patrick Collinson, *The Elizabethan Puritan Movement* (Oxford: Clarendon, 1967), 125.

[60] William Perkins, *A Reformed Catholike; or, A Declaration Shewing How Neere We May Come to the Present Church of Rome in Sundrie Points of Religion* (Cambridge: John Legat, 1598); Perkins, *The Epistle Dedicatory*, in *The Work of William Perkins*, ed. Ian Breward (Abingdon, U.K.: Sutton Courtenay, 1970), 520.

[61] Perkins, *Reformed Catholike*; William Perkins, "Author to the Christian Reader," in *Work of William Perkins*, 521. Perkins' use of the phrase "Reformed Catholicke" was partly rhetorical, to present a more positive view of Protestantism to Roman Catholics. As the quintessential "moderate puritan," Perkins called for separation from Rome and maintained that the Roman Catholic Church was not a true church of Christ. For the complicated ways in which puritans like Perkins understood the Church of England to be "Catholic and Reformed," see Milton, *Catholic and Reformed*, 177.

[62] New Road Baptist Church, Oxford, England, The Church Covenant of 1780, accessed March 26, 2012, http://www.newroadbaptistchurchoxford.co.uk/content/pages/documents/1312454439.pdf. The church covenant was first printed in Daniel Turner, *Charity the Bond of Perfection. A Sermon, the Substance of which was Preached at Oxford, November 16, 1780. On Occasion of the Re-establishment of a Christian Church of Protestant Dissenters in that City City; with a Brief Account of the State of the Society, and the Plan and Manner of their Settlement.* (Oxford: J. Buckland, 1780), 20–22.

Union of Great Britain issued a remarkable statement of Baptist catholicity in March of 1948, which historian Walter Shurden praised as "an extraordinary lucid document" that "deserves serious consideration by Baptists around the world,"[63] declaring,

> Although Baptists have for so long held a position separate from that of other communions, they have always claimed to be part of the one holy catholic Church of our Lord Jesus Christ. They believe in the catholic Church as the holy society of believers in our Lord Jesus Christ, which He founded, of which He is the only Head, and in which He dwells by His Spirit, so that though manifested in many communions, organized in various modes, and scattered throughout the world, it is yet one in Him.[64]

And it is within this stream that two decades ago I offered "A Confession for Catholic Baptists," which affirmed the place of Baptists within the one, holy, catholic, and apostolic church.[65]

The contention of this project is not to assert a monogenetic source of origin for Baptists in this catholic stream of history, nor is there any intention of setting forth a theological account that equates the essence of the Baptist vision with any particular statement of catholicity. Rather, the aim is to provide a theologically constructive narrative of a contesting catholicity based on a retrieval of sources from the Baptist heritage and in conversation with the wider church. In short, at stake is not a quest to determine who the real Baptists are or were, but rather an attempt to imagine how Baptists might understand themselves in continuity with historic Christianity.

The Baptist vision is surely in need of such renewal given the enduring legacy of polarizing divisions. It raises the question of whether a dynamic center can exist as an alternative to the polarization in the culture and the churches without simply splitting the difference between the extremes. Such a way of putting the question resonates with the conviction of Puritan cleric Richard Baxter, who wrote, "I never thought that when ever men differ, it is my duty to go in the middle between both

---

[63] Walter B. Shurden, ed., *Proclaiming the Baptist Vision: The Church* (Macon, Ga.: Smyth & Helwys, 1996), 143.

[64] The Baptist Doctrine of the Church 2, statement approved by the Council of the Baptist Union of Great Britain and Ireland, March 1948, in *Baptist Union Documents 1948–1977*, ed. Roger Hayden (London: Baptist Historical Society, 1980), 5–6.

[65] Freeman, "A Confession for Catholic Baptists," in *Ties That Bind: Life Together in the Baptist Vision*, ed. Gary A. Furr and Curtis W. Freeman (Macon, Ga.: Smyth & Helwys, 1994), 83–97.

(for so that middle will be next taken for an extream, and men must seek out another middle to avoyd that)."[66] Though Baxter considered himself a catholic Christian adhering to mere Christianity, his theological stance was frequently misconstrued as extremist or some variation thereof. So has the notion of Baptist catholicity been described as postmodern and premodern, liberal and fundamentalist, Catholic and Calvinist, Anabaptist and anti-Baptist. It is amazing that a singular standpoint could be misunderstood in such divergent and, indeed, contradictory ways. Perhaps misunderstanding is the risk of those who desire a more excellent way, as its difficulty to fit neatly into existing categories is evidence of a fresh restatement.

Communities guided by this vision of contesting catholicity believe that the church is signified by the proclamation of the Word and the observance of the sacraments, but they maintain that the ecclesial markers extend to a range of shared habits such as holy living, brotherly and sisterly love, binding and loosing, communal discernment, breaking bread, welcoming strangers, faithful witness, gospel suffering, charismatic ministry, and open meetings.[67] For reasons that will become clear in chapter 1, this particular project of retrieval begins among liberal southerners in Baptist life, but it was the Baptist theologian James William McClendon Jr. who explored this revisioned account of contesting catholicity most persuasively and comprehensively.[68] He envisioned a particular ecclesial standpoint that exists in a triadic relation with the more clearly defined Catholic and Protestant approaches, while at the same time seeking to manifest the unity of the one church.[69] Other Baptist theologians have extended this vision in various ways by calling for a renewal of the church

---

[66] Preface to *Richard Baxter's Confession of His Faith* (London: R. W. for Tho. Underhil, and Fra. Tyton, 1655), objection 6, answer 5. Baxter articulated his account of the "truth" as an alternative to "antinomianism" and "papism" but as no mere via media between them.

[67] This list is a compilation of gospel practices from John Howard Yoder. See his "A People in the World," in *Royal Priesthood*, 73–89; "Sacrament as Social Process: Christ the Transformer of Culture," in *Royal Priesthood*, 359–73; *Body Politics: Five Practices of the Christian Community before the Watching World* (Scottdale, Pa.: Herald Press, 1992); "The New Humanity as Pulpit and Paradigm," in *For the Nations* (Grand Rapids: Eerdmans, 1997), 43–46; and "Firstfruits: The Paradigmatic Public Role of God's People," in *For the Nations*, 29–33. Because Yoder gives various names to the practices and lists them in different orders, I have not attempted to resolve the overlapping nomenclature or prescribed sequence.

[68] McClendon, *Ethics*; along with *Doctrine: Systematic Theology, Volume II* (Waco, Tex.: Baylor University Press, 2012); and *Witness: Systematic Theology, Volume III* (Waco, Tex.: Baylor University Press, 2012).

[69] Jeffrey W. Cary critically engages McClendon on the shortcomings of his ecumenical theology in *Free Churches and the Body of Christ* (Eugene, Ore.: Cascade Books, 2012), 21–24 and 156–92.

through sacramental reform rather than pietistic experience or social engagement.[70] This account is offered in the hope that it might be useful for imagining how to live faithfully in an increasingly confusing time. For, as T. S. Eliot described modern existence in his poem *The Waste Land*, the way ahead is unclear. He asked:

> What are the roots that clutch, what branches grow
> Out of this stony rubbish? Son of man,
> You cannot say, or guess, for you know only
> A heap of broken images, where the sun beats,
> And the dead tree gives no shelter, the cricket no relief,
> And the dry stone no sound of water. Only
> There is shadow under this red rock,
> (Come in under the shadow of this red rock).[71]

In this weary land, with these broken images, and in the shadow of that rock, what might it mean to believe the promise that where two or three are gathered Christ is and that where Christ is there is the church?

---

[70] Harmon, *Towards Baptist Catholicity*; Fiddes, *Tracks and Traces*; Nigel Goring Wright, *Disavowing Constantine: Mission, Church and the Social Order in the Theologies of John Howard Yoder and Jürgen Moltmann* (Carlisle, U.K.: Paternoster, 2000); Wright, *Free Church, Free State*; Barry Harvey, *Another City: An Ecclesiological Primer for a Post-Christian World* (Harrisburg, Pa.: Trinity Press, 1999); and Harvey, *Can These Bones Live? A Catholic Baptist Engagement With Ecclesiology, Hermeneutics, and Social Theory* (Grand Rapids: Brazos Press, 2008).

[71] T. S. Eliot, "The Waste Land," ll. 19–26, in *T. S. Eliot: Collected Poems 1909–1962* (New York: Harcourt Brace, 1963), 53.

PART I

SICKNESS UNTO DEATH

1

Alterity and Its Cure

Other Baptists are sick, and they know it. This sickness is terminal, and it is shared by others. But there is good news; there is a cure. Other Baptists find the cure for their alterity by participating in the life of the triune God with the communion of the saints in the one, holy, catholic, and apostolic church.[1] At one time the social location of Baptists on the theological landscape was unambiguous. Now there are Other Baptists—marginalized and no longer at home, even among their own people and sometimes in the churches of which they have been members all their lives. The empire under whose aegis these Baptists once comfortably lived was conquered, and the culture they once inhabited has been replaced.

Finding a way to account for this Baptist otherness without simply becoming the negative image of "the powers that be" proves more problematic than one might suspect. The rhetoric employed by Baptists engaged in the struggle to be Baptists required an Other and indeed is

---

[1] alterity (äl târ i tē), n. from the Latin *alter* 1. the state of being other or different. 2. the character of that which is other in the other. 3. the circumstance of "others" who are nominalized and distanced by hierarchical and stereotypical thinking. 4. technical term in postcolonial studies denoting the condition of otherness resulting from imposition of Western culture. 5. a category such that the markers of difference indicate the alterity of the Other is irreducible and infinite.

Mark C. Taylor prefers the *a* (alt*a*rity) to the more common *e* (alt*e*rity), suggesting that the difference between them is nothing more or less than the spelling. Taylor contends that " 'altarity' is a slippery word whose meaning can be neither stated clearly nor fixed firmly." Taylor, *Altarity* (Chicago: University of Chicago Press, 1987), xxviii–xxix. Rather than attempting to give an encyclopedic definition of "altarity," Taylor offers a genealogical account of difference from Hegel through Kierkegaard. Taylor conceives of altarity as a condition that is neither outside nor enclosed within the structures of self-relation. Because altarity is a state of creative juxtaposition, he believes it contains the potential to subvert the structures of representation and domination. See also Emmanuel Levinas, *Alterity and Transcendence*, trans. Michael B. Smith (New York: Columbia University Press, 2000).

unintelligible apart from it.[2] The residual discourse of controversy illustrates why the protest of exiled Baptists continues to reflect the dominant
order that displaced the old one, and it indicates why it is so difficult to
find a way to speak in a language that does not assume the terms of the
opposition. Such politics are based not in an account of radical otherness,
which is a matter of absolute difference, but rather on a notion of proximate otherness, which involves differentiation from one's near neighbors
who share an anthropological similitude. While exotic otherness can be
tolerated, the real challenge proves to be the near Other.[3] It is tempting to
follow this social and political version of otherness, but what is needed is
an account of alterity in which otherness is not simply the mirror image
of the regnant ideology but something radically other—oriented toward
a new end, toward God. Only from such a standpoint of radical otherness
can there be the leverage to subvert the structures of representation and
domination.[4]

A sustaining alterity neither collapses into an integralism in which
an infinite oneness coercively overcomes otherness nor dissolves into the
pluralistic fetishization of difference in which otherness is relentlessly celebrated.[5] Edward Said described this kind of otherness in his groundbreaking work, *Orientalism*, in which he explained why the alterity of
the Orient was such that its moral landscape could not be interpreted by
offering a panoramic vision of global geography. He suggested instead
that the Other can be understood only by a narrative display that permits

---

[2] A recent collection of first-person accounts by "exiled" moderate Baptist leaders illustrates the difficulty of speaking about their convictions without the shadow of the conservatives who displaced them from power. Carl L. Kell, ed., *Exiled: Voices of the Southern Baptist
Convention Holy War* (Knoxville: University of Tennessee Press, 2006). The volume on the
moderate leaders was preceded by an earlier book that displays how the rhetoric of the conservatives also presupposed and required the moderate opposition. Carl L. Kell and Raymond
Camp, eds., *In the Name of the Father: The Rhetoric of the New Southern Baptist Convention* (Carbondale: Southern Illinois University Press, 1999). Kell's books clearly show that conservative
and moderate Baptists in the South defined themselves as mirror images of one another.

[3] Jonathan Z. Smith, "What a Difference a Difference Makes," in *"To See Ourselves as
Others See Us": Christians, Jews, and "Others" in Late Antiquity*, ed. Jacob Neusner and Ernest
S. Frerichs (Chico, Calif.: Scholars Press, 1985), 47. So, Smith contends, the other is "most
problematic when he is TOO-MUCH-LIKE-US, or when he claims to BE-US." Thus he
continues, "The problem is not alterity, but similarity—at times, even identity."

[4] Gayatri Chakravorty Spivak, "Can the Subaltern Speak?," in *The Post-Colonial Studies
Reader*, ed. Bill Ashcroft, Gareth Griffiths, and Helen Tiffin (New York: Routledge, 1995),
24. To suggest that postcolonial studies may shed some light on our situation is not to imply
that our condition approaches either the scope of hegemony or the scale of alterity produced
by the history of Western colonialism.

[5] The rhetoric of otherness need not devolve into cookie-cutter imperialism or boutique
multiculturalism.

space for the diversity of human experience.⁶ This work offered the vision of a nourishing otherness without collapsing into integralism or dissolving into pluralism.

To move forward Other Baptists must similarly navigate beyond conservatism and liberalism with the hope that the markers of otherness will become visible. The journey must also be situated within the ongoing story of dissenting voices in the tradition of the whole church so that it becomes clear that this story is one of contesting catholicity.⁷ Retrieving these voices of alterity within the tradition of the church catholic is crucial for providing an alternative story to the conquest narrative that has become synonymous with Christendom.⁸

Perhaps an awareness of radical otherness might become an occasion for a kairotic moment like that of Michael Harrington, whose discovery of a hidden poverty that lay beneath the dark underside of an affluent society enabled him to tell the untold story of the invisible poor. His vision captured the imagination of a new generation who began to see beyond the "Other America" to the Great Society.⁹ The reception of Harrington's book was a happy surprise as it became the manifesto for the War on

⁶ Edward W. Said, *Orientalism* (New York: Vintage Books, 1979). Ugandan Catholic theologian Emmanuel Katongole makes a similar move so as to give voice to the otherness of Africa by exploring stories of individual and collective memory as a mode of theological reflection. By reinserting Africa within a reimagined version of catholic Christianity, his account is generating a fresh conversation about the grammar of social discourse on issues from AIDS to xenophobia. Emmanuel M. Katongole, *A Future for Africa: Critical Essays in Christian Social Imagination* (Scranton, Pa.: University of Scranton Press, 2005). Katongole sketched out this narratological approach in his earlier study, *Beyond Universal Reason: The Relation between Religion and Ethics in the Work of Stanley Hauerwas* (Notre Dame, Ind.: University of Notre Dame Press, 2000). His book *The Sacrifice of Africa: A Political Theology for Africa* (Grand Rapids: Eerdmans, 2011) reflects on the stories, visions, and assumptions that sustain nation-state politics in Africa.

⁷ The story of this dissenting tradition is told by Michael Watts in *The Dissenters*, 2 vols. (Oxford: Clarendon, 1978–1995); and Champlin Burrage, *The Early English Dissenters in Light of Recent Research*, 2 vols. (Cambridge: Cambridge University Press, 1912).

⁸ My account of contesting catholicity as a tradition borrows from Alastair MacIntyre the notion of tradition as participation in a community where arguments are extended synchronically in space and diachronically over time in which fundamental dissent is excluded but where lively debate is welcome and even dissonant voices are heard. Alastair MacIntyre, *After Virtue* (Notre Dame, Ind.: University of Notre Dame Press, 1981), 207; and MacIntyre, *Three Rival Versions of Moral Enquiry: Encyclopaedia, Genealogy, and Tradition* (Notre Dame, Ind.: University of Notre Dame Press, 1990), 59–60. Steven R. Harmon provides a brief account of how Baptists might be understood as a community of dissent within the catholic tradition in *Towards Baptist Catholicity: Essays on Tradition and the Baptist Vision* (Milton Keynes, U.K.: Paternoster, 2006), 63–69.

⁹ Michael Harrington, "The Invisible Land," in *The Other America* (New York: Macmillan, 1962), 1–18. For an excellent account of "The Man Who Discovered Poverty," see Maurice Isserman, *The Other American: The Life of Michael Harrington* (New York: Public Affairs, 2000), 175–220.

Poverty. But unlike Harrington, who left the church in search of "the real world" of politics, Other Baptists are looking for radical transformation of the world through the church and the gospel it proclaims.

Other Baptists no doubt are looking for ways to recognize other Other Baptists on this same journey. The surprising signs of Baptist alterity may include frustration with both lukewarm liberalism and hyperfundamentalism; a desire to confess the faith once delivered to the saints, not as a matter of coercion, but as a simple acknowledgment of where they stand and what they believe; a recognition of the Trinity as the center of the life to which they are drawn; a longing to be priests to others in a culture of self-reliance; a hope of sharing a life together that is not merely based on a common culture or determined by shared interests; a commitment to follow the teachings of the Bible that they understand and being open to receive more light and truth that they do not yet understand; trusting God's promise of presence in water and table; a yearning for the fulfillment of the Lord's Prayer that the church may be one. Other Baptists desire to claim the promise given by the Apostle Paul that "all things are yours, and you are Christ's, and Christ is God's" (1 Cor 3:21-23). This is how Other Baptists recognize one another on the journey.

Memoir of a Dixieland Postliberal

Other Baptists are not unaware of their otherness. Many of them discovered it through controversy and contestation. In 1988, at an annual gathering of Baptists in San Antonio, Texas, longtime gadfly W. A. Criswell decried the way liberals attempted to co-opt the language of conservatism. To a cheering audience of pastors, Criswell began his address: "Because of the opprobrious epithet 'liberal,' today they call themselves 'moderates.'" But, he continued, "a skunk by any other name still stinks!"[10] The jeremiad went on to lament:

> To my great sorrow, and yours, we have lost our nation to the liberal, and the secularist, and the humanist, which finally means the atheist

---

[10] W. A. Criswell, "The Curse of Liberalism," speech to the Southern Baptist Convention, June 13, 1988, *The Criswell Sermon Library*, accessed March 30, 2012, http://www.wacriswell.org/Search/videotrans.cfm/sermon/1222.cfm. Criswell's convention speech resurrected the argument he made four decades earlier in a sermon entitled "The Curse of Modernism," which he preached to the First Baptist Church of Dallas, Texas, on June 12, 1949. In that message he described liberalism as a virus that works from within and "ruins the churches, the denominations, the mission fields, the evangelistic work and appeal of the preachers of Christ." James E. Towns, *The Social Conscience of W. A. Criswell* (Dallas, Tex.: Crescendo, 1977), 254.

and the infidel. America used to be known as a Christian nation. It is no longer. America is a secular nation.[11]

America was suffering from "the curse of liberalism," which, he contended, led to the loss of its status as Christian nation that Baptists had founded and that Baptists deserved to reclaim.[12] Liberalism was to blame for leading American public schools, church-related universities, and denominational seminaries down the slippery slope of secularization. The solution was simple: the curse must be broken by taking the Baptists and America back to their conservative Christian roots. To rid the Baptists of liberalism once and for all, it was imperative to have a real conservative as the convention president and continue to purge all denominational institutions of so-called moderates. He succeeded.[13]

Criswell's sermon wove a slender thread of history into the fabric of a myth. John Smyth, the first Baptist, did indeed emerge out of the same congregation of English Christians "who came on the Mayflower," but the Pilgrim Church was not Baptist, nor can the establishing of the Plymouth colony be mistaken as the founding of America.[14] Even if this revisionist history about America's "Baptist" origins were true, it is unclear how the influence of a liberal ideology held by so few could have such enormous consequences on education, society, and the church.[15] Though

[11] Criswell, "Curse of Modernism," 254. The description of Criswell's message as a jeremiad associates it with a long-standing tradition of political sermons in American Protestantism that identify troublesome current events as visitations of divine retribution for betrayal of covenant promises. By the 1660s these political sermons were preached on the annual ceremonial fast day as the whole community gathered around the sermon that "arraigned sins that had caused the judgments, and pointed out what other terrors would descend unless repentance were forthcoming." Perry Miller, *The New England Mind: From Colony to Province* (Cambridge, Mass.: Belknap Press, 1953), 28; also Sacvan Bercovitch, *The American Jeremiad* (Madison: University of Wisconsin Press, 1978).

[12] Criswell, "Curse of Liberalism."

[13] Messengers responded to the challenge by narrowly electing Jerry Vines over moderate challenger Richard Jackson, thus completing the ten-year cycle of conservative presidents and solidifying the conservative control of the Southern Baptist Convention for the foreseeable future. The presidential election was determined by a bare 600-vote margin out of 31,000 ballots cast. Jerry Vines, pastor of First Baptist Church, Jacksonville, Florida, received a majority of 50.43 percent to 49.57 percent for Richard Jackson, pastor of North Phoenix Baptist Church of Phoenix, Arizona. The election of Vines broke the back of the moderate opposition and ensured conservative control of the SBC. For a brief discussion of "the controversy," see Bill J. Leonard, *God's Last and Only Hope: The Fragmentation of the Southern Baptist Convention* (Grand Rapids: Eerdmans, 1990), 134–42.

[14] Burrage, *Early English Dissenters*, 1:357–68.

[15] James Tunstead Burtchaell offers a more sophisticated version of the declension thesis of the secularization of the academy invoked by Criswell in *The Dying of the Light: The Disengagement of Colleges and Universities from Their Christian Churches* (Grand Rapids: Eerdmans, 1998), 819–51. As the thesis goes, because only rarely was the Christian character of American

it was an effective political speech—and this particular preacher was a master of the craft—the message was not resonant, nor was his argument persuasive. Liberalism, rather than a curse, was a blessing to many. Progressive views on the Bible, science, race, gender, and peace were much more attractive than the retrogressive alternatives held by conservatives. And, as it turned out, these so-called liberals were not the scary figures that they were made out to be. They were models of Christian character and theological sophistication. Yet, for many, a liberal education took place largely outside the curriculum.[16]

Many struggling young Baptists found that the story of Clayton Sullivan mirrored their own intellectual journey.[17] They identified with the author's struggle to come to terms with being a liberal among conservatives when he said:

> I was bewildered. I felt I didn't have a friend anywhere. I found myself questioning whether I should have studied to be a preacher. My dream was becoming a question mark. Was it all a mistake? Maybe God had not spoken to me in the kitchen of the Heidelberg Hotel. Maybe I'd been fooled or maybe I'd played a trick on myself. Yet these feelings I suppressed. Instead, I reasoned, "It's too late to turn back now. I've invested eight years beyond college studying to be a preacher. Turning around wouldn't make sense."[18]

---

church-related colleges vitally resident in academics, it consequently became attached to notions of piety and morality that in time were degraded by the intellectual embrace of liberalism and rationalism. The story within the stories of Christian higher education is one of the dying of the light of faith. For a variation on the secularization thesis that seeks to understand the historical processes that lead to the disestablishment of religion from the academy, see George M. Marsden and Bradley J. Longfield, *The Secularization of the Academy* (New York: Oxford University Press, 1992), 5. For a broader discussion, see my chapter "Can the Secular Be Sanctified?," in *The Future of Baptist Higher Education*, ed. Donald D. Schmeltekopf and Dianna M. Vitanza (Waco, Tex.: Baylor University Press, 2006), 219–31.

[16] This was certainly true in my case. Although my professors at the seminary seemed sympathetic with progressive views, most of them felt constrained by the theological conservatism that was sweeping over the Baptists. As I moved on to graduate school, I continued to find the liberal alternative attractive. One of my fellow students became so concerned about me that he persuaded a small church he once served to call me as their pastor in hopes that it would cause me to moderate my views. It did not. The Sunday sermon became an opportunity to think out loud about the questions that were troubling me at the time: evil and suffering, the nuclear arms race, prayer and providence, egalitarian views on race and gender. I expressed doubts about the Trinity, the resurrection, the inspiration of the Scriptures, and miracles. It goes without saying that my take on the issues was at odds with most of the membership. How that congregation of farmers in central Texas endured my preaching and, even more puzzling, how I avoided being fired I do not know.

[17] Clayton Sullivan, *Called to Preach, Condemned to Survive: The Education of Clayton Sullivan* (Macon, Ga.: Mercer University Press, 1985).

[18] Sullivan, *Called to Preach*, 97–98.

They learned to make an uneasy peace with muddling through long after the certainties of faith disappeared, but, unlike Clayton Sullivan, none of their professors likely ever declared, "I've read your dissertation, and I have to tell you that I don't think you have a moral right to be a Southern Baptist preacher."[19]

But abandoning the faith was not the only option. There were Dixieland liberals who struggled to adapt the faith to the modern world. They were a rare species of Baptists, and they were hard to identify because many of them had become adept at blending into the landscape of the surrounding culture. To survive in the ministry, they learned the artful dodge of knowing the balance between lifting a prophetic voice for social justice and lending a priestly ear to struggling souls.[20] "Paying the rent," they sometimes called it. Although conservatives like Criswell continued to raise the specter of growing liberalism, the subversive subculture of progressives remained fairly small, although their influence often exceeded their numbers.[21]

The vanguard of dissenters was led by Carlyle Marney, whose iconoclastic style and indomitable spirit epitomized Dixieland liberalism.[22] For Marney, fundamentalism was "the heresy of the South." He was sharply critical of conservatives like Criswell who retreated into a retrograde religion underwritten by the repressive powers of race, wealth, and militarism. While serving as pastor of prominent churches in Texas and North Carolina, Marney frequently lectured in the university divinity schools at Chicago and Harvard. He served on the editorial boards of the *Christian Century* and *Theology Today*, and he was an ecumenical leader in the National and World Council of Churches (WCC). In the last decade of

[19] Sullivan, *Called to Preach*, 94. Sullivan identifies the professor as Dr. Ray Summers, who came to Southern Baptist Theological Seminary, where Sullivan was a doctoral student, after "the Battle of Lexington Road," which led to the exodus of thirteen professors.

[20] Sullivan describes how southerners hide their doubts behind the mask of piety except in those occasional moments of transparency when the tragic dimensions of life overwhelm their religious masquerade. He tells about one man who poignantly confessed, "Preacher, the greatest fear I have is when I die and pass over to the other side I'll discover God is the bastard I've sometimes feared him to be." Sullivan, *Called to Preach*, 119.

[21] David Stricklin, *A Genealogy of Dissent: Southern Baptist Protest in the Twentieth Century* (Lexington: University Press of Kentucky, 1999), 6. The resistance of Baptists in the South to progressive or social Christianity is told well by John Lee Eighmy, *Churches in Cultural Captivity: A History of the Social Attitudes of Southern Baptists* (Knoxville: University of Tennessee Press, 1987); and Keith Harper, *The Quality of Mercy: Southern Baptists and Social Christianity, 1890–1920* (Tuscaloosa: University of Alabama Press, 1996).

[22] See John J. Carey, *Carlyle Marney: A Pilgrim's Progress* (Macon, Ga.: Mercer University Press, 1980); Carlyle Marney, "Preaching the Gospel, South of God: An Interview with Carlyle Marney," by Bill Finger, *Christian Century*, October 4, 1978, 914–20; and Mary Kratt, *Marney* (Charlotte, N.C.: Myers Park Baptist Church, 1979).

his life, Marney held a teaching appointment at Duke Divinity School, which at the time was identified as a hub for progressive Christianity in the South.[23]

Marney liked to think of himself as a pilgrim on a journey, and his writings were like theological travel narratives mapping the way for fellow strugglers. He embraced a conviction retrieved from his seventeenth-century forebears, declaring his commitment to "follow new light into any place as soon as I knew it to be new light."[24] Following further light glimmering on the horizon of the new creation required gumption, of which Marney had plenty. Yet even his liberal supporters expressed puzzlement over the theological direction to which he gestured in the preface to his 1970 book, *The Coming Faith*:

> I plead also for a renunciation of that fundamental heresy that Jesus is God. This keeps millions from loyalty to our banners. To call Jesus God is an impertinence against Christ and God. For the Son is not the Father. He is Son, and man-son at that. And I long for the Jewish hope to be rediscovered. That hope that knew about a Father. How new this would be! If not spoiled by a frightened, clinging, hearthsick fundamentalism.[25]

But fundamentalism was not the only darkness that threatened to engulf the faith. There was also the growing force of secularity. Marney attempted to envision a way beyond both alternatives.

Understanding that his critics (and even some friends) would regard this account of the faith to be heresy, he responded, "The New in Faith is always a heresy. But look again."[26] His second and more deliberate

---

[23] In 1925, when Duke University president William Preston Few was trying to persuade Edmund Soper to accept the position as dean of the School of Religion, he appealed, "Where else is there another institution that has at once the resources, the purpose to give the Christian program a central place in education, that has a wide open field and the human material, and all this in a liberal atmosphere of Christian freedom and truth and in a section of the country that is growing rapidly, that is full of hope, and that has its face steadily toward the future?" It was under Soper's leadership that Duke became an intellectual center of theological liberalism in the South. Robert F. Durden, *The Launching of Duke University, 1924–1949* (Durham, N.C.: Duke University Press, 1993), 308.

[24] Carlyle Marney, *The Coming Faith* (Nashville: Abingdon, 1970), 141. Marney's embrace of the further light doctrine dates back to John Robinson and other English separatists of the seventeenth century.

[25] Marney, *Coming Faith*, 8. Marney's vision of the coming faith was based on what he took to be glimmers of the new creation that illumined the darkness of secularization and fundamentalism. It followed an earlier path blazed by John A. T. Robinson in his book *Honest to God* (London: SCM Press, 1963).

[26] Marney, *Coming Faith*, 36.

examination revealed signs of continuity with the old. In his last glances at the arc of history, Marney envisioned the new creation as moving beyond humanity to divinity, from incarnation to resurrection, and from individuality to community.[27] Marney clearly saw the limits of liberalism, and although he barely missed "the postliberal transformation of Duke," in some important ways he anticipated it.[28] This vision did not escape the notice of the young James William McClendon Jr., who was mentored during his undergraduate years at the University of Texas by Blake Smith, the longtime pastor of University Baptist Church in Austin, Texas, and one of Marney's closest friends and fellow dissenters.

Marney's theological struggle charted a different kind of path. The truth was that, at the time of Criswell's "skunk" sermon in 1988, there were many in Baptist life as uncomfortable with liberalism as with fundamentalism. They were not satisfied merely to moderate it. They were looking for ways beyond it. It seemed that both conservatives and liberals were stuck on the same problem: conservatives thought everything they believed was true, and liberals held that unless it was true they would not believe. But neither alternative offered a compelling account of the truth that made belief necessary and possible. Neither understood the true possibilities of alterity Marney hinted at.

Then came *The Nature of Doctrine* by Yale theologian George Lindbeck. That parsimonious volume of 142 pages put these persistent questions and problems into theological perspective in a way that made sense. Lindbeck explained that theology was not the propositional statement of objective realities (e.g., fundamentalism) or the religious expression of subjective experiences (e.g., liberalism) but rather the discipline of making regulative claims about religious practice (i.e., postliberalism). Lindbeck called this third way cultural linguistic or intratextual theology.[29] Alterity was being given a name.

---

[27] Marney, *Priests to Each Other* (Valley Forge, Pa.: Judson Press, 1974).

[28] Will Willimon began his eulogy for Marney by lamenting, "No longer would he thunder forth to us from his mountaintop Shiloh." Willimon, "A Prophet Leaves Us: Carlyle Marney," *Christian Century*, July 19, 1978, 695. It was only six years until another "prophet with a southern drawl" came to Duke who, like Marney, was schooled in liberal Protestantism but envisioned a way fully beyond it. Stanley Hauerwas admits that as an undergraduate student at Southwestern University he would sneak away from the Methodists and listen to Marney preach at the First Baptist Church of Austin, Texas. Hauerwas opined (in a personal conversation), "Marney epitomized what deep down we all wanted to be."

[29] George A. Lindbeck, *The Nature of Doctrine* (Philadelphia: Westminster, 1984), 16–19. Lindbeck actually described Augustine as an example of intratextual theology in which "the whole of his theological production can be understood as a progressive, even if not always successful, struggle to insert everything from Platonism and the Pelagian problem to the fall of Rome into the world of the Bible" (117).

Many Other Baptists were drawn to the work of Stanley Hauerwas, which forced those seeking to understand their alterity to explore how the liberal tradition of social ethics that they had embraced began with a commitment to "Christianize the social order," and they ended up puzzling over the question "Can ethics be Christian?"[30] But it was not until the first volume of James McClendon's *Systematic Theology* appeared in 1986 that it became clearer how an alternative postliberalism might fit within a baptist vision.[31]

Yet in a twist of irony, it was not in listening to these contemporary voices of dissent but rather by turning to the ancient texts and traditions of the church that the pathway of otherness became visible. Though theological alterity was practiced by many in the church, Augustine was particularly helpful for those seeking a way forward. He emphasized the distinction between faith (*credo*) and understanding (*intellegere*):

> If thou hast not understood, said I, believe. For understanding is the reward of faith. Therefore do not seek to understand in order to believe, but believe that thou mayest understand; since, "except ye believe, ye shall not understand" (*Nisi credideritis, non intelligetis*).[32]

---

[30] Hauerwas notes that the trajectory of liberalism's commitment to "Christianize the social order" exemplified in Walter Rauschenbusch's *Christianity and the Social Crisis* (New York: Macmillan, 1912) reached its apex in James Gustafson's book *Can Ethics Be Christian?* (Chicago: University of Chicago Press, 1975). Hauerwas, "On Keeping Theological Ethics Theological," in *Against The Nations* (New York: Harper & Row, 1985), 26–39. I began by reading the books of Stanley Hauerwas, who befriended me and took me on as a part of his "Baptist project." The books I first read by Hauerwas were *Character and the Christian Life* (San Antonio, Tex.: Trinity University Press, 1975); *Vision and Virtue* (Notre Dame, Ind.: University of Notre Dame Press, 1981); *A Community of Character* (Notre Dame, Ind.: University of Notre Dame Press, 1981); and *The Peaceable Kingdom* (Notre Dame, Ind.: University of Notre Dame Press, 1983). He encouraged me to write a dissertation on Augustine of Hippo to explore Lindbeck's thesis: Curtis W. Freeman, "Reading St. Augustine's *City of God* as a Narrative Theology" (Ph.D. diss., Baylor University, 1990).

[31] James Wm. McClendon Jr., *Ethics: Systematic Theology, Volume I* (Nashville: Abingdon, 1986). My new introduction to the Baylor University Press 2012 edition of McClendon's *Systematic Theology* is included in all three volumes as pages vii–xxxviii.

[32] Augustine, *Lectures or Tractates on the Gospel According to St. John* 19.6, trans. John Gibb and James Innes, in *The Nicene and Post-Nicene Fathers* (Grand Rapids: Eerdmans, 1971), 7:184. See also Augustine, *On the Trinity* 15.2.2, trans. Arthur West Haddan and Rev. William G. T. Shedd, in *The Nicene and Post-Nicene Fathers* (Grand Rapids: Eerdmans, 1971), 3:200. Augustine's two-step confessionalism was patterned on the Old Latin translations of Isaiah 7:9. Later in life Augustine read Jerome's translation, which rendered the text in Isaiah "unless you believe you shall not stand." Augustine thought the Vulgate provided an even better and less intellectualized statement of confessional faith.

Faith simply opens the door of possibility for understanding. As Augustine affirmed, "Faith seeks, understanding finds."[33] When he was converted and baptized, Augustine was a convinced Neoplatonist. He did not understand the resurrection of the body, yet it was part of the church's confession of the creed and the teaching of Scripture. So he believed. Gradually, Augustine began to understand more about the apostolic faith he confessed with the church.

At conference in Toronto in 1987, Rowan Williams, then a Lady Margaret Professor of Theology at Oxford and later the archbishop of Canterbury, delivered an address in which he said that this relationship between faith and reason in Augustine was like looking for the sun on a cloudy day. The wise person might point to a spot in the clouds and say something like, "Keep looking right there, and the sun will come out." Sure enough it does peek out, and you say, "Oh, I understand." Some, however, laugh at such sky gazing or lack patience to keep looking. Others are willing to give such alterity a try. It becomes a journey of willingness to live with the mystery of God and God's ways that are not understood at the time. By confessing the faith even (and perhaps especially) when not understood, believers join in the ecclesial performance with Christians who have been confessing the same faith since the days of the apostles.[34]

To be an Other Baptist is not simply to adopt a postliberalism framed as a critique of mainline Protestantism (i.e., Lindbeck and Yale).[35] Rather,

---

[33] Augustine, *On the Trinity* 15.2.2 (trans. Haddan and Shedd).

[34] As Lindbeck stated in the final paragraph of *The Nature of Doctrine*, what is needed to make postliberalism intelligible is more attention by theologians to "performance" (135). In 1995 I attended the theology conference at Wheaton College that took up the conversation between postliberals and evangelicals. At the end of the meeting, Lindbeck concluded with this remark: "I will also say that if the sort of research program represented by postliberalism has a real future as a communal enterprise of the church, it's more likely to be carried on by evangelicals than anyone else." Timothy R. Phillips and Dennis L. Okholm, eds., *The Nature of Confession: Evangelicals and Postliberals in Conversation* (Downers Grove, Ill.: InterVarsity, 1996), 252–53.

[35] Robert Jones and Melissa Stewart worry that certain unintended consequences of "Dixieland postliberalism," of which I am identified as one of the arch-exponents, are being unwittingly cathected in unsuspecting divinity students. They contend that the most undesirable effect is the erosion of the already tenuous bonds among southern evangelicals between a church-against-the-world hermeneutics and antinationalistic pacifism. Jones and Stewart argue that in this weakened condition white southern evangelicals are forced to retreat into a viciously self-justifying insularity that reinforces their identity as a persecuted minority and ultimately transforms itself into an ideology of power to be wielded against their enemies. Robert P. Jones and Melissa C. Stewart, "The Unintended Consequences of Dixieland Postliberalism," *Cross Currents* 55, no. 4 (2006): 506–21. It is important to note that about 20 percent of the Baptist students at Duke Divinity School are African American, which suggests that the identification of Dixieland postliberalism as a phenomenon among white evangelicals is off the mark. But if their argument that Dixieland postliberalism fosters violence were true, it would indeed be an undesirable consequence. As I show in this chapter, in fact, the exact

being an Other Baptist involves confessing the ancient apostolic faith, not in a premodern and uncritical way, but in a postmodern and postcritical way. The path to a cure for alterity tracks through liberalism and beyond, back to the doorstep of orthodoxy, yet with a second naïveté.[36] One might be tempted to embark on this journey alone, but true alterity demands others. To be intelligible, this second level of otherness begs to be situated within the church catholic, so it becomes clear that this is a story about the alterity of contesting catholicity.

The Radical Otherness of the Church

"Let the church be the church."[37] It is not apparent though exactly what and where the church is that it might be itself. Some have said that the church is where the bishop is. Others have suggested that the church is where the Word is preached and the sacraments are administered. Still others contend that the church is where true disciples are gathered.[38] Yet,

---

opposite is the case: Dixieland postliberalism understood as a dissenting tradition within the church catholic offers a peaceful alternative to the violent evangelism of constantinianism. Because the argument of Jones and Stewart depends on a caricature of the viewpoint they criticize, I have not attempted to directly repel their attack. Instead I address the central questions Jones and Stewart raise with the hope of revealing that the perceived tendencies they name are in fact misperceptions. Jones and Stewart follow the familiar lines of argument made by James M. Gustafson against Stanley Hauerwas in "The Sectarian Temptation: Reflections on Theology, the Church and the University," *Proceedings of the Catholic Theological Society* 40 (1985): 83–94; and the response by Hauerwas to Gustafson's critique in Hauerwas' *Christian Existence Today: Essays on Church, World, and Living in Between* (Durham, N.C.: Labyrinth Press, 1988), 3–18. My purpose is to narrate my own theological pilgrimage from liberal to postliberal and show why it might rightly be called, after Jones and Stewart, "Dixieland postliberalism." The next chapter, "Beyond Fundamentalism and Liberalism," shows how northeastern liberalism and southern evangelicalism are siblings under the skin and share a common dependence on modern notions of rationality and individualism.

[36] The phrase "second naïveté" is associated with Paul Ricœur, *The Symbolism of Evil* (Boston: Beacon, 1967), 349. What I denote, however, is more akin to G. K. Chesterton, who described his conversion to orthodox Christianity like "an English yachtsman who slightly miscalculated his course and discovered England under the impression that it was a new island in the South Seas." Chesterton, *Orthodoxy: The Romance of Faith* (New York: Image Books, 1959), 9.

[37] John Howard Yoder, "Let the Church Be the Church," in Yoder *The Royal Priesthood: Essays Ecclesiological and Ecumenical*, ed. Michael G. Cartwright (Grand Rapids: Eerdmans, 1994), 168–80. Hauerwas has repeatedly argued similarly that "the first social ethical task of the church is to be the church." What this means, he explains, is that "the church does not have a social ethic" but rather "the church is a social ethic." Hauerwas, *Peaceable Kingdom*, 99.

[38] On the church as the community gathered around the bishop, see Ignatius, *To the Smyrnaeans* 8, in *The Ante-Nicene Fathers* (Grand Rapids: Eerdmans, 1979), 1:89–90. Martin Luther lists the seven identifying marks of the church, which are Word, baptism, sacrament of the altar, keys, ordained ministry, prayer/praise/thanksgiving, and the cross. Luther, *On the Councils and the Church*, in *Luther's Works* (Philadelphia: Fortress, 1966), 41:148–66. Dirk

even with the help of these identifying marks, the struggle to find the church in the world is difficult, and nowhere is it harder than in regions where the church and the world have become deeply interconnected. In such a context, the question of ecclesial identity may come into greater clarity by understanding what the church is not. For this reason, McClendon proposed that Christian theology begins "with the humble fact that the church is not the world."[39] In other words, the church is most distinctively recognized by its otherness.

It is important to note that the world in this formula ("the church is not the world") does not signify creation or nature or even the cosmos so that the relation between the church and the world is entirely negative, or worse, dualistic. Rather, it denotes the fallen and thus sinful form of creation, nature, and the cosmos that resists the creative intents and redemptive lures of providence.[40] This ecclesial stance is not, then, a justification for a retreat into antagonism or insularity. Indeed, no such escape is possible, McClendon explains, "inasmuch as the line between church and world pass right through each Christian heart."[41] Not to be mistaken for pietistic otherworldliness, McClendon's ecclesial starting point is something closer to Augustine's understanding of the church as a

---

Philips states seven ordinances that roughly parallel Luther's list, which include the Word and ministers, baptism and Lord's Supper, foot washing, evangelical separation, love, commandment keeping, and suffering and persecution, in his "The Congregation of God," in *The Writings of Dirk Philips, 1504–1568*, trans. and ed. Cornelius J. Dyck, William E. Keeney, and Alvin J. Beachy (Scottdale, Pa.: Herald Press, 1992), 363–76.

[39] James Wm. McClendon Jr., *Ethics: Systematic Theology, Volume I* (Waco, Tex.: Baylor University Press, 2012), 17 (references to *Ethics* that follow in this chapter refer to the Baylor edition). Finding the church, to be sure, is a struggle, but the opening line of *Ethics* reminds us "theology means struggle." As McClendon confesses, because the line between the church and the world "passes right through each Christian heart," the struggle begins within. For an account of McClendon's personal church-world "struggle" with the gospel of peace, see his article, "The Radical Road One Baptist Took," *Mennonite Quarterly Review* 74, no. 4 (2000): 503–10. For additional perspectives on McClendon's struggle, see Mikael Broadway, introduction to "Festschrift for James Wm. McClendon Jr.," special issue, *Perspectives in Religious Studies* 27, no. 1 (2000): 5–9; Mark Thiessen Nation, "Jim McClendon, Jr.: A Particular Baptist Theologian," *Journal of European Baptist Studies* 1, no. 2 (2001): 51–55; and Terrence Tilley, "The Baptist Theology of J. W. McClendon, Jr., and Practical Faith in a Pluralistic Context," in *Postmodern Theologies: The Challenge of Religious Diversity*, ed. Terrence Tilley (Maryknoll, N.Y.: Orbis Books, 1995), 142–52. McClendon, *Ethics*, 17. The fact that the church is not the world is a recurrent theme in Hauerwas' writings, and this is nowhere more clearly stated than in his Gifford lectures, where in reference to natural theology he reiterated the importance of accounting for "the differences between the church and the world." Stanley Hauerwas, *With the Grain of the Universe: The Church's Witness and Natural Theology* (Grand Rapids: Brazos, 2001), 234.

[40] Yoder, "The Otherness of the Church," in *Royal Priesthood*, 55.

[41] McClendon, *Ethics*, 17.

corpus permixtum (a mixed body) in which the church is in the world, and the world is in the church.[42]

This observation that the convictions of the church are not the standpoint of the world has long been held by Free Churches, which McClendon identifies as his community of reference. He innovatively refers to them as "baptists," using the lowercase "b" (alluding to the German designation *Täufer* simply translated "baptists") to include such diverse groups as Brethren and Baptists to Pietists and Pentecostals. Given the theological importance of the voices of radical dissent, McClendon asks why baptists have produced so little theology.[43] The default answer is that they have largely been marginalized from the social and religious mainstream. Yet this explanation fails to account for why baptists, even when they have flourished economically and socially, have produced no theological tradition and literature proportionate to their Catholic, Reformed, Lutheran, or Methodist counterparts.

The more basic reason is, McClendon contends, that baptists have not often seen their own convictions and practices as a resource for theology. He explains:

> The underlying failure was baptists' distrust of their own vision, their common life, their very gospel; whereas that vision might have been the resource for their theology, and theology in turn the means of exploring that gospel, revitalizing that life, focusing that vision. Failing in this way, baptists became the victim of ideologies left and right—and thereby became less themselves, spiritually impoverishing both themselves and their neighbors in other Christian churches.[44]

Doing theology from this distinctive standpoint of the baptist vision requires recovering a new approach to theological reflection. This vision has a dual focus. *This is that*: the church is the apostolic community, and the commands of Jesus are addressed to us. *Then is now*: we are the end-time people, a new humanity anticipating the consummation of the blessed hope.[45] Thus the church in the formula ("the church is not the world") does not serve as a mere metonym for a particular community, sect, or denomination committed to the recovery of some naïve primitivism. Nor

---

[42] Augustine, *On Christian Doctrine* 3.32, trans. Marcus Dods, in *The Nicene and Post Nicene Fathers* (Grand Rapids: Eerdmans, 1979), 2:569.

[43] McClendon, *Ethics*, 20–26.

[44] McClendon, *Ethics*, 26.

[45] McClendon, *Ethics*, 30; and *Doctrine: Systematic Theology, Volume II* (Waco, Tex.: Baylor University Press, 2012), 45–46.

is it a kind of sociology of ideas that simply describes what baptists believe and practice. Instead it refers to the way of life that belongs to all churches, and therefore may be rightly described as universal, ecumenical, and cath-olic. This is the standpoint of contesting catholicity.[46]

It is not surprising, though, that some critics continue to miss the ecumenical import of contesting catholicity and dismiss this emphasis on the otherness of the church as merely a "sophisticated version of 'testify-ing.' "[47] Such critics contend that "a truly systematic theology attempts to speak in universalistic terms" because the language and life of religion are shared by "both the church and the culture."[48] This position leaves no doubt that the only voices worth hearing are those that are committed to the establishment agenda of "Christianizing the social order." The heirs of the Radical Reformation, however, rarely acquired a majority conscious-ness that presumed to speak for everyone, due in no small measure to the fact that their heritage is rooted in soil watered by the blood of those who dared to differ.

For those who grew up where religion and culture were closely inter-twined, discerning the otherness of the church was differently difficult.[49]

---

[46] McClendon delineates three senses of catholicity. The first (and earliest) sense of cath-olic (*katholikos*) is a generic usage (usually designated with a lowercase "c" = catholicity₁) and is roughly equivalent to the term "universal." It denotes the way of life comprised of "belief, worship, and morals" that is well rounded or typical as opposed to one sided or partial. The second sense of catholic is an inclusive usage that has come to carry basically the same meaning as "ecumenical" (*oikoumene*)—that is, a way of speaking about all churches summed up as one. This second sense of catholicity initially conveyed a more restricted sense of the inhabited earth and corresponds to the etymological meaning of catholic as "whole" (*Kath hollou* = catholicity₂). In modernity this sense of catholicity₂ designates ecumenism as pursued by interchurch cooperation. The third sense of catholic is as a proper name for the Catho-lic Church (Roman or otherwise), which usually appears written with an uppercase "C" (catholicity₃). McClendon (and Yoder) argue for a radical catholicity in which "the believers church or baptist style of life typically displays such wholeness or catholicity₁ as to make for catholicity₂." James Wm. McClendon Jr. and John Howard Yoder, "Christian Identity in Ecumenical Perspective: A Response to Davis Wayne Layman," *Journal of Ecumenical Studies* 27, no. 3(1990): 561–80.

[47] Max L. Stackhouse, review of *Ethics: Systematic Theology, Volume I,* in the *Journal of the American Academy of Religion* 55, no. 3 (1987): 615–17.

[48] Max L. Stackhouse, rejoinder to McClendon, *Journal of the American Academy of Religion* 56, no. 3 (1988): 555–56.

[49] Those who lived in the Christian civilization known as the South frequently heard injunctions to "be not conformed to the world." Though debate raged on about what con-stituted "worldliness," nonconformity was generally confined to the "finger sins": "Don't drink, dance, smoke, chew, cuss, play cards, gamble, shop on Sabbath, go to the picture show, or engage in mixed bathing" (a.k.a. swimming). To be sure, the lists differed according to regions: smoking was not allowed in Texas, frowned on in Tennessee, and practically required in North Carolina. Similarly, you were considered to be a vicious sinner if you played cards but a virtual saint if you were good at dominoes. The biggest indication of worldliness was

As John Howard Yoder clarifies, church and world, which were distinct in early Christianity before the third century, became fused by the fourth century after the christianizing of the Roman Empire by Emperor Constantine.[50] Since then this Constantinian church-world fusion in its myriad of permutations makes the identification of the church's otherness problematic as in the de facto culturally established Christendom of the South.[51] Yoder named a way for the church's otherness to be visible through its embodiment of gospel practices and in so doing to challenge the prevailing culture Christianity. Yoder identified five practices that he suggested were constitutive of apostolic Christianity that could become instantiated in any gathered community that seeks to live them out.[52] These practices include fraternal admonition, breaking bread, believer's baptism, charismatic ministry, and communal discernment.[53] When two or three are gathered in Christ's name—that is, when they are practicing these practices—the gathered community shares communion not only with one another and with strangers but with the risen Lord.

---

alcohol. Drunkards were "churched," and social drinkers were "shamed." But other factors might have been in play. Very few Baptists in the South owned a distillery or a brewery, but quite a few of them farmed tobacco or worked in the cigarette industry. However superficial the finger sins litany might have been, it at least attempted to make them conscious of what was otherwise not clear—namely, that the church is not the world. Yet precisely because Baptists in the South shared in the cultural establishment, and in many ways exemplified it, they could not so easily extract themselves from the resulting habits and ideologies of white supremacy, male domination, economic subjugation, and militaristic nationalism. Samuel S. Hill, *Southern Churches in Crisis Revisited* (Tuscaloosa: University of Alabama Press, 1999), 103–15. Constantinian critics seem unable to grasp that this church-world distinction is not some kind of geographic retreat. The challenge for the church to be culturally disestablished is not a mandate to "drop out" and "turn off." As McClendon's delineation makes clear, precisely because the world is in the church, the church struggles. Consequently, more appropriately descriptive phrases might be to "stand firm" or "engage hopefully."

[50] Yoder, "Otherness of the Church," in *Royal Priesthood*, 54–64.

[51] Yoder, "The Constantinian Sources of Western Social Ethics," in *The Priestly Kingdom: Social Ethics as Gospel* (Notre Dame, Ind.: University of Notre Dame Press, 1984), 135–47. Yoder is careful not to default to a simplistic account of constantinianism that identifies "the fall of the church" with a specific historical event or period. Thus, constantinianism is a trope that denotes Christendom in its various political, ideological, and existential expressions.

[52] Yoder, "Sacrament as Social Process: Christ the Transformer of Culture," *Theology Today* 48, no. 1 (1991): 33–44, reprinted in *Royal Priesthood*, 359–73.

[53] Because Yoder gives various names to the practices and lists them in different orders, I have simplified the nomenclature and followed the sequence that appears in his *Body Politics: Five Practices of the Christian Community before the Watching World* (Scottdale, Pa.: Herald Press, 1992). See also Yoder, "The New Humanity as Pulpit and Paradigm," in *For the Nations* (Grand Rapids: Eerdmans, 1997), 43–46. For another order of the five practices, see "Firstfruits: The Paradigmatic Public Role of God's People," in *For the Nations*, 29–33, in which baptism and the new humanity appear first. McClendon proposed five persistent marks of the shared life in Christ that baptists have lived out: biblicism, liberty, discipleship, community, and mission. McClendon, *Ethics*, 26–30.

Such an account of Christian body politics provides a compelling witness for those looking from the standpoint of radical democracy.[54] Rather than seeing the otherness of the church as a sectarian withdrawal from the world, radical democrats are attracted to the nonviolent model of ecclesial alterity as a strategy of "engaging the world generously and with receptive vulnerability." They see "the binding centrality of the lordship of Christ" as opening up the "dialogical relations between the church and the world in which giving and receiving is possible."[55] What these radical democrats find interesting is how these practices proceed in an open and dialogic way without foreclosing future conflict or holding out the threat of violence. They are particularly drawn to the practice of communal discernment in which the aim of consensus arises out of open conversation and there is no voting in which the majority overruns a minority and no monarchical decision of a leader by virtue of an office.[56] Here Yoder articulates something like the contesting catholicity memorably declaimed by Cardinal John Henry Newman that the consensus of the faithful is the voice of the infallible church.[57] The consensus envisioned by contesting catholicity is, to be sure, harder to attain in practice than it is to affirm in principle, but even in principle it is encouraging.[58]

Contesting catholicity offers an alternative account of the polity and practice of Free Churches that have become democratized by the

---

[54] Romand Coles describes radical democracy (over against liberal democracy) as the politics exemplified by local communities that maximize the practices of listening, receptivity, tabling, and generosity. Coles, *Beyond Gated Politics: Reflections for the Possibility of Democracy* (Minneapolis: University of Minnesota Press, 2005), 216. See also his essay "The Wild Patience of Radical Democracy," in *Radical Democracy: Politics between Abundance and Lack*, ed. Lars Tønder and Lasse Thomassen (New York : Manchester University Press, 2005), 68–85.

[55] Coles, "Wild Patience of John Howard Yoder," in Tønder and Lasse Thomassen, *Radical Democracy*, 112.

[56] Yoder, *Body Politics*, 67.

[57] John Henry Newman, *On Consulting the Faithful in Matters of Doctrine* (New York: Sheed & Ward, 1961), 57–73.

[58] The "openness" that attracts Coles to contesting catholicity and his worries about prematurely foreclosing a communal consensus seems closer to the practice of the Quakers than the Mennonites. Rufus Jones describes the practice of voteless decisions among the Friends:
> The central idea was the complete elimination of majorities and minorities; it became the Quaker custom to reach all decisions in unity. The clerk of the meeting merely performed the function of reporting the corporate sense, i.e., the judgment of the assembled group, and of recording it. If there were differences of view, as there were likely to be in such a body, the consideration of the question at issue would proceed, with long periods of solemn hush and meditation, until slowly the lines of thought drew together towards a point of unity. Then the clerk would frame a minute of conclusion, expressing the "sense of the meeting."
Jones, *Mysticism and Democracy in the English Commonwealth* (Cambridge, Mass.: Harvard University Press, 1932), 56.

pragmatic politics of American culture.[59] Yet rather than following populism in which a majority vote is too often interpreted as a mandate, contesting catholicity follows an alternative ecclesial rule that sees such democratization of gospel practices not as faithful following of the Christian story but as a tragic failure of the church to be the church.[60] In view of the ways in which the deliberative polity of Baptists in North America has been overcome by liberal democratic principles, including majority rule, the Baptist Manifesto called for the revisioning of a more open practice of discernment. It declared:

> We affirm an open and orderly process whereby faithful communities deliberate together over the Scriptures with sisters and brothers of the faith, excluding no light from any source. When all exercise their gifts and callings, when every voice is heard and weighed, when no one is silenced or privileged, the Spirit leads communities to read wisely and to practice faithfully the direction of the gospel.[61]

Fellow Baptists who have grown comfortable with the accommodation of gospel practices with liberal democratic politics pronounced this call to be "dangerous and un-Baptistic," by which they implied it was "illiberal and undemocratic."[62] Sensitive to the modern mistake of

[59] A forgotten historical detail is that during the early days of Baptist life in the South, many congregations were governed by unanimous consensus rather than majority rule. E.g., the Rules of Conference of the North Creek Baptist Church of Christ in Beaufort County North Carolina, formed in 1790, state that at the church meetings "a door [is] to be opened for the admission of members into the Church, but none shall be admitted but by unanimous consent." North Creek Baptist Church, Decorum or Rules of Conference, Article 5. Unanimity, however, proved to be difficult to sustain in practice, and the polity of the Baptist church meetings shifted to majority rule. At the August 1824 conference, the North Creek Church amended their Rules of Conference by united voice "that a majority shall rule in this church in every case except in the election of a minister." Minute book, North Creek Primitive Baptist Church Minutes, 1790–1890, David M. Rubenstein Rare Book & Manuscript Library, Duke University, Durham, N.C., box 1, folder 1.

[60] Henry M. Robert, *Robert's Rules of Order* (Chicago: Scott, Foresman, 1915), originally published as *Pocket Manual of Rules and Order for Deliberative Assemblies* (Chicago: S. C. Griggs, 1876). Robert was a Baptist layman who initially wrote his manual as a guide for the deliberative process of the church meeting. On Robert's Baptist connection, see William Cathcart, *The Baptist Encyclopaedia* (Philadelphia: Louis H. Everts, 1881), s.v. "Robert, Maj. Henry Martyn," 991–92.

[61] Mikael Broadway, Curtis W. Freeman, Barry Harvey, James Wm. McClendon Jr., Elizabeth Newman, and Philip Thompson, "Re-envisioning Baptist Identity: A Manifesto for Baptist Communities in North America," *Baptists Today*, June 26, 1997, 8–10.

[62] Bill Underwood, "Address for Baptist Summit," *Associated Baptist Press*, February 1, 2006, accessed March 30, 2012, http://www.abpnews.com/archives/item/920-address-for-baptist-summit#.UvAwLKW5Mts. Underwood's critique of the Manifesto parallels the criticism of Jones and Stewart, and it shares the standpoint of establishment critics from Gustafson to Stackhouse.

confusing a gospel-formed conscience with the individualistic notion of self-reliance, the Manifesto authors answered their critics:

> We believe with early Baptists and the mainstream Christian tradition that an individual's conscience is inviolable, but not infallible, and therefore we are always under the obligation to see to it that our consciences have been formed by the faithful practices of the church. It is in this context that dissent becomes an expression of the church's commitment to truth and divine justice.[63]

If liberal democrats worry about contesting catholicity, it might be asked what its appeal is to the voices of radical democracy. The attraction is not merely the procedural openness of egalitarian polity. At a deeper level, the attraction seems to be tied to the sense in which the gospel "is in constant need of clarification through—and in some sense more importantly as—encounter with otherness."[64] Radical democrats recognize they have a stake in alterity even more strongly, arguing that "vulnerable relations with outsiders are integral to the otherness of the church and that when this understanding of *caritas* is forgotten and unpracticed, the church loses its otherness and is assimilated to the violence of the world."[65] And if, as they seem to assume, the markers of alterity signify the very essence of the Other's being, then violence is indeed an ever-present danger. One prominent voice of radical democracy asks:

[63] Mikael Broadway, Curtis Freeman, Steven Harmon, Barry Harvey, Elizabeth Newman, Mark Medley, and Philip Thompson, "'Dangerous and Un-baptistic'? A Response from Supporters of the 'Baptist Manifesto,'" *Associated Baptist Press*, February 1, 2006, accessed March 30, 2012, http://www.abpnews.com/archives/item/919-%E2%80%9Cdangerous-and-un-baptistic%E2%80%9D?-a-response-from-supporters-of-the-%E2%80%9Cbaptist-manifesto%E2%80%9D.

[64] Peter Dula and Alex Sider, "Radical Democracy, Radical Ecclesiology," *Cross Currents* 55, no. 4 (2006): 497.

[65] Coles, *Beyond Gated Politics*, 112, see also 147–48. Coles does not elaborate on the nature of alterity, which he regards as essential to the church's ecclesiality, but clearly at the root it is not *psychological*, such that the field of the Other stands over against the subjective self. See, e.g., Jacques Lacan, *The Seminar of Jacques Lacan*, ed. Jacques-Alain Miller (New York: W. W. Norton, 1988), 203–15. Nor is it primarily *social*, such that the Other is historically constituted in the interplay "We are this" and "They are that." See, e.g., Edward Said, "Representing the Colonized: Anthropology's Interlocutors," *Critical Inquiry* 15, no. 2 (1989): 225; and Said, *Orientalism*, 237. Rather, the otherness that Coles argues is constitutive of the church as the church is *ontological*, such that the alterity of the Other is irreducible and infinite. See, e.g., Jacques Derrida, "Violence and Metaphysics," in *Writing and Difference*, trans. Alan Bass (Chicago: University of Chicago Press, 1978), 114.

Might not "Jesus is Lord" constitute a radical deafness to non-believers, and a confinement of prophecy to those within the church, so that the dialogic conditions of *agape* within give way to monological practices toward others outside in a manner likely to proliferate blindness and violence—certainly *not* the careful discernment that might make vital giving and receiving possible? And would not these degraded relations at the borders migrate inward as "members" are suspected of this or that type of "forgiveness" and treated accordingly?[66]

The worry is that the jealous confession of Jesus as Lord situates the church in a posture that slouches toward forms of constantinianism that wears thin its patience, eclipses alterity, and succumbs to a violent integrity.[67]

Although it seems excessive to suggest that radical ecclesiology is inherently militant, there can be little doubt that some examples suggest it is so.[68] Yet to acknowledge these extreme cases of impatience toward difference does not justify violence against the Other in the name of Christ. As George Lindbeck argues, such a claim may be linguistically correct but performatively untrue. For example, "the crusader's battle cry '*Christus est Dominus*' . . . is false when used to authorize cleaving the skull of the infidel."[69] As the crusader's confession "contradicts the Christian understanding of Lordship as embodying . . . suffering servanthood,"[70] so is the confession "Jesus is Lord" falsified when it is employed in ways to violently compel others into silence. Such coercion contradicts the whole form of life called into being by the one who came preaching peace and calling for a disciple community that imitates his example. This contradiction is visible when Constantine spoke of the "life-giving sign" as a reference to "his own imperial symbol, the Labrum, not the cross of Calvary."[71] Anytime the cross is assimilated as a symbol for political ends, it is falsely used. Similarly, when the image of Christ Pantocrator is employed to sanction the rule of political, ecclesiastical, or patriarchal authorities, it is unfaithfully and, indeed, idolatrously

---

[66] Coles, *Beyond Gated Politics*, 119.
[67] Coles, *Beyond Gated Politics*, 135.
[68] Jones and Stewart, "Unintended Consequences of Dixieland Postliberalism," 516.
[69] Lindbeck, *Nature of Doctrine*, 64.
[70] Lindbeck, *Nature of Doctrine*, 64.
[71] Paul S. Fiddes, *Participating in God: A Pastoral Doctrine of the Trinity* (Louisville, Ky.: Westminster John Knox, 2000), 65. Fiddes approvingly cites as an example of a radical catholic trinitarian ecclesiology Miroslav Volf, *After Our Likeness: The Church as the Image of the Trinity* (Grand Rapids: Eerdmans, 1998). However, Fiddes notes that Volf does not sufficiently attend to the catholicity of the English Baptist tradition that provides the germ of his ecclesiology. I have argued similarly in "Where Two or Three Are Gathered: Communion Ecclesiology in the Free Church," *Perspectives in Religious Studies* 31, no. 3 (2004): 259–72.

represented. These examples are only a few of the oppressive forms of dominion theology about which radical democrats rightly worry. One way of addressing these concerns with the christological approach is to frame it within a trinitarian ecclesiology that invites perichoretic participation in the life of the triune God who desires interdependence for the completeness of fellowship.[72] Such a trinitarian eschatology seems able to patiently preserve alterity and community without a propensity toward jealous dominations of integrity.

But the deeper issue is in the pathological fear of the Other that lies at the root of human existence and comprises the essence of sin. This sickness is the substance of modern culture.[73] Death exists because communion and otherness cannot coincide in creation, but the antidote for the fear and alienation from ontological alterity is communion made possible through new birth. The Father, Son, and Spirit are Other, not only from creation, but from one another. Yet within the Holy Trinity of Persons there is communion. By being reconciled to that Being who is radically Other, the redeemed share in a communion of Persons—the new creation. And so, in the church, human beings who are pathologically driven by their otherness to fear the Other and live as strangers find friendship and are destined toward that eschatological reconciliation of all things in the kingdom. Reconciliation with God, the One who is radically Other, then, is the precondition for reconciliation with any Other. Thus, ecclesial communion makes it possible for sinners to share in the full cosmic dimension of sin, which is death, and yet exist in communion with God and one another in God. The cure for alterity is communion in the life of the Trinity, and the community that participates in the divine life of radical otherness is the church.

Receptive Generosity toward the Other

Thus far, two senses of otherness have been delineated in describing the alterity that Other Baptists have come to own. The first is a critical consciousness that arises from the stigma of being represented as Other. The second is grounded in the ontological otherness of the church, which in its earthly pilgrimage instantiates the eternal relations of the triune God by participating in the divine life. But there is a third sense of otherness that exists at the limits of the self and the community. Like Lazarus, this Other lies ever at the doorstep, but never inside the house. Yet, as Karl Barth observed, the light of true witness may shine brighter and

---

[72] Fiddes, *Participating in God*, 108.
[73] John D. Zizioulas, *Communion and Otherness* (London: T&T Clark, 2006), 1–12.

the Word may be more living and active in and through the Other than among those to whom the knowledge of the witness and Word has been committed.[74] By risking the encounter with the Other, the church stands in a place to receive the gift of its own otherness. If the otherness of the church is maintained as it enters into vulnerable relations with outsiders, it must be asked how the church can show receptive generosity toward the Other and in so doing display what it means to be the church. By refusing to engage and welcome the alterity at its borders, the church risks losing sight of the risen Lord who appears unexpectedly as "the stranger" and in its blindness ceasing to be the vanguard of the new humanity gathered from all nations. Any movement toward such patient hospitality begs for concrete examples to display its practice for imitation and innovation.

One case is the ministry of Bartolomé de Las Casas, who in 1512 became the first priest ordained in the New World. By all appearances he had settled into becoming a typical *encomendero* (i.e., a priest entrusted with the care and conversion of the natives), but two years later Las Casas shocked his parishioners by preaching a sermon at Pentecost that strongly criticized the treatment of the aboriginal Amer-Indian people. Las Casas rejected the Spanish *Ostiense* theory, which denied the validity of political authority for non-Christian indigenous people and justified the wars Christians waged against them as infidels. Instead Las Casas affirmed the self-determination of the Indian chiefs and lords. The appeals of Las Casas went unheeded. Under the sign of the cross and with the power of the sword, the Spanish conquerors expropriated Indian lands and justified their colonialism as a necessary consequence of the christianization of the New World. The publication of Las Casas' *Devastation of the Indies* in 1552 did much to undermine the moral authority of Spanish colonialism and became a basis for the so-called Black Legend that sought to discredit the involvement of Spain in America.[75]

It is tempting to claim Las Casas as the progenitor of liberation theology because he linked salvation with justice and lived in prophetic solidarity with the poor. Nevertheless, because his conceptual tools and theological language were not derived from modern theory but were grounded in biblical practice,[76] Las Casas instead exemplifies what has been described as the radically catholic vision of "this is that" and "then

---

[74] Karl Barth, *Church Dogmatics* IV/3/1, trans. G. W. Bromiley and T. F. Torrance (Edinburgh: T&T Clark, 1961), 365.

[75] Bartolomé de Las Casas, *The Devastation of the Indies*, trans. Herma Briffault (Baltimore: Johns Hopkins University Press, 1992).

[76] Gustavo Gutiérrez, *Las Casas: In Search of the Poor of Jesus Christ*, trans. Robert R. Barr (Maryknoll, N.Y.: Orbis Books, 1993), 8–12.

is now." Even though Las Casas rightly recognized the full humanity of indigenous people and repudiated the violent evangelism of Spanish colonialism, he lacked the theological and ecclesiological resources to successfully resist the constantinianism of his day. This unity of faith and nation was proclaimed by Pope Clement VIII on March 21, 1592, when he exhorted the conquered subjects to be fully loyal "to our very dear son in Christ, Felipe the Catholic King of Spain and the Indies."[77] The underlying assumption was that, unless the Indians became "true Christians," they could not be loyal subjects of Spain. The sign of "true conversion" was the sacrament of baptism, which was often administered en masse and without proper catechization. Though Las Casas protested that such conversions, achieved through compulsion or in ignorance, were "a great offense against God," in the end "baptism as an ecclesiastical fact . . . became a political act, an affirmation of Spanish imperial sovereignty."[78] The resulting politicization of baptism vitiated the Constantinian determination that belied the church as the church.

While in many ways Las Casas serves as a striking example of hospitality toward the indigenous people of America, perhaps an even more fruitful case is the life of Baptist Roger Williams. His friendship with Narragansett Indians not only set him apart from Puritan contemporaries but passed on through spiritual descendants habits of receptive generosity that have become embodied in the dissenting tradition of American society. Sometime after he settled in Plymouth in 1631, Williams sent a letter to Governor John Winthrop in which he disputed the right of the English colonists to the land. Williams claimed that the grant issued to the Massachusetts Bay Colony by the king was invalid and that they had no right to the land unless they compensated the Indian people. Apparently the governor and the magistrates ignored Williams, hoping that the issue would eventually pass. Two years later, however, the letter was brought to public attention in Boston. The court examined it and condemned Williams. His offense, according to the account given by Winthrop, included charging King James with lying for claiming in the patent granting them the land that "he was the first Christian prince that had discovered the land" as well as "with blasphemy for calling Europe Christendom, or the Christian world."[79] Williams wrote a letter of explanation to the court

---

[77] Luis N. Rivera, *A Violent Evangelism: The Political and Religious Conquest of the Americas* (Louisville, Ky.: Westminster John Knox, 1992), 216.

[78] Rivera, *Violent Evangelism*, 231.

[79] *The Journal of John Winthrop, 1630–1649*, ed. Richard S. Dunn, James Savage, and Laetitia Yaendle (Cambridge, Mass.: Belknap Press, 1996), 107. See also *Winthrop Papers, 1631–1637*, ed. Allyn Bailey Forbes (Boston: Massachusetts Historical Society, 1943), 3:148–49.

on January 24, 1634, that temporarily mollified their concerns, but by November of the same year they discovered that Williams was continuing to challenge the validity of both the colony's patent and the status of its church. On October 9, 1635, the General Court banished Williams for having "broached and divulged diverse new and dangerous opinions."[80]

After being expelled from Massachusetts, Williams set out to establish a colony at Providence as "a shelter for persons distressed of conscience."[81] As he began to acquire land, Williams followed local Indian customs in agreeing to a fair purchase price with the tribal sachems (leaders). In future transactions Williams continued to respect the rightful ownership of the Narragansett people and in so doing to recognize their legitimate political authority—that is, to respect and honor their otherness. In 1643 a letter written by Boston minister John Cotton to the Salem Church appeared in print. The following year Roger Williams published his reply, in which he vigorously maintained "that the natives are the true owners of [the land], and that we ought to repent of such as receiving it by Pattent."[82] To Williams, depriving the American Indians of their property without compensation was a sin of unjustly usurping the property of the Other and was based upon the blasphemous doctrine of "Christendom" in which Christian kings falsely assert that they "are invested with Right by virtue of their Christianitie, to take and give away the Lands and Countries of other men."[83] Cotton approvingly noted in his rejoinder that the "violent and tumultuous" protest against their patent right was one of the reasons the court banished Williams.[84] Yet, instead of softening his convictions as the court had hoped, the subsequent decade only served to strengthen his resolve that to hold the patent was a national sin and to renounce their charter was a national duty. It was clear that neither magistrates nor ministers had any intention of recognizing the legitimacy of American Indian provenance.

The position of Williams regarding the claim to the land by indigenous people stood in stark contrast to the views of Winthrop, who refused

---

[80] Nathaniel E. Shurtleff, ed., *Records of the Governor and Company of Massachusetts Bay in New England* (Boston: William White, 1853), 1:160–61. No mention was made of his question about the patent, nor is it referred to in the final sentence of banishment.

[81] "Confirmatory Deed of Roger Williams and his wife, of the lands transferred by him to his associates in the year 1638," in *Records of Rhode Island*, also known as *Records of the Colony of Rhode Island and Providence Plantations* (Providence: A. Crawford Greene & Brother, 1856–1865), 1:22–25.

[82] Roger Williams, *Mr. Cotton's Letter Lately Printed, Examined and Answered*, in *The Complete Writings of Roger Williams* (New York: Russell & Russell, 1963), 1:324–25.

[83] Williams, *The Bloody Tenent Yet More Bloody*, in *Complete Writings*, 4:461.

[84] John Cotton, *A Reply to Mr. Williams*, in Williams, *Complete Writings*, 2:324–25.

to acknowledge the otherness of American Indians as economic and political beings. In a letter to John Endecott, Winthrop pressed the point of the patent:

> But if our title be not good, neither by Patent nor possession of these parts as *vacuum domicilum*, nor by good likinge of the natives: I mervayle by what title Mr. Williams himself holds. and if God were not pleased with our inheriting these parts, why did he drive out the natives before us? . . . If we had no right to this lande, yet our God hathe right to it, and if he be pleased to give it to us (takinge it from a people who had so long usurped upon him, and abused his Creatures) who shall control him or his termes?[85]

In the view of Winthrop (and probably most other colonists), the English were warranted by natural right in taking the land that had long been the possession of "the sons of Adam." He stated:

> That which is common to all is proper to none. This savage people ruleth over many lands without title or property; for they inclose no ground, neither have they cattell to maintayne it, but remove their dwellings as they have occasion, or as they can prevail against their neighbours. And why may not christians have liberty to go and dwell amongst them in their waste lands and woods . . . as lawfully as Abraham did among the Sodomites?[86]

Over time, Winthrop continued, as the colonists cultivated and improved the land, this natural right became a civil right. Moreover, there seemed to be divine sanction for their appropriation of native land, in that the great numbers of native people stricken by disease and plague suggested God might soon remove them entirely, leaving the colonists free to inhabit the New World alone.[87] When divine retribution against the Indians seemed to be withheld, the English colonists took matters into their own hands, waging an all-out war in 1675 that sealed the fate of American Indians. Not everyone shared Winthrop's view of the Indians based on the linking of political aims with economic gains. For example, John Eliot, the celebrated apostle to the Indians, advanced the view in his controversial

---

[85] *Winthrop Papers*, 3:149. John Cotton echoes Winthrop's language in justifying the English occupation of the land by *vacuum domicilim cedit occupanti*. See *Reply to Mr. Williams*, in Williams, *Complete Writings*, 2:46–47.

[86] Winthrop, *General Considerations for the Plantations in New England, with an Answer to Several Objections*, in *Winthrop Papers*, 2:120.

[87] Winthrop, *General Considerations for the Plantations*, in *Winthrop Papers*, 2:120.

work *The Christian Commonwealth* (1659) that the American Indians were the lost tribes of Israel. For millenarians like Eliot, the conversion of the Indians held the key to the fulfillment of the blessed hope and the establishment of a new civil government, both drawn straight from the Scriptures.[88]

In contrast to Winthrop, who denied the full humanity of American Indians, and Eliot, who regarded their difference only for its potential utility, Williams recognized the otherness of the indigenous people, yet respecting their alterity did not prevent him from entering into vulnerable relations with them. He established a trading post in 1637 where Indians came often to barter for English goods. Out of his personal experience, Williams published his first book in 1643, entitled *A Key into the Language of America*, which was widely read and well received in England. Part dictionary and part cultural anthropology, the *Key* presented his observations of Narragansett "Customes, Manners and Worship." Contrary to English stereotypes, the Indians "are remarkably free and courteous, to invite all Strangers in; and if any come to them upon any occasion they request them to come in, if they come not in themselves."[89] Given that these others, whose otherness earned them the name "savages," exhibit such civilized manners, Williams asks:

> If nature's sons, both wild and tame,
> Humane and courteous be,
> How ill becomes it sons of God
> To want humanity. [90]

He expresses surprise at the "strange truth that a man shall generally finde more free entertainment and refreshing amongst these Barbarians, then amongst thousands that call themselves Christians."[91] Williams reports the irony that these American Indians often showed greater hospitality than the so-called Christian Europeans:

> I have knowne them leave their House and Mat
> to lodge a Friend or stranger,
> When Jewes and Christians oft have sent
> Christ Jesus to the Manger.[92]

---

[88] Philip F. Gura, *A Glimpse of Sion's Glory: Puritan Radicalism in New England, 1620–1660.* (Middletown, Conn.: Wesleyan University Press, 1984), 134–36.

[89] Williams, *A Key into the Language of America,* in *Complete Writings,* 1:96.

[90] Williams, *Key into the Language of America,* in *Complete Writings,* 1:99.

[91] Williams, *Key into the Language of America,* in *Complete Writings,* 1:106.

[92] Williams, *Key into the Language of America,* in *Complete Writings,* 1:110.

He even confesses that native hospitality had often been the instrument of divine providence, admitting that "it hath pleased God to make them many times the instruments of my preservation." Indeed, had it not been for their generosity during that "sorrowful Winters flight" after his banishment, Williams might well have perished.[93] The sense of moral irony seemed not to be lost among the Indians, as Williams voiced their perceptions:

> We weare no Cloaths, have many Gods,
> and yet our sinnes are lesse:
> You are Barbarians, Pagans wild,
> our Land's the Wildernesse.[94]

In the introductory remarks to the reader in his *Key*, Williams admits that he does not address the question "What Indians have been converted?" But he adds, "I shall further present you with a briefe Additionall discourse concerning this Great Point."[95] His answer came by way of a small pamphlet entitled *Christenings Make Not Christians*, which takes up the question of the "heathen" and their conversion. But rather than answering the question, Williams changed the subject. His English readers no doubt regarded the term as an appropriate designation for all uncivilized people, including American Indians, who had not yet embraced the influence of Christian culture. To their chagrin, Williams announced that "the followers of Jesus, are now the onely People of God," and the "heathen" include all others—"civilized or uncivilized."[96] Europe was regarded as the heart of Christendom (or the Christian world). Yet, he explained, its "Popish Kingdomes" and "Protestant Nations" were peopled not by followers of Jesus but by "AntiChristian" worshipers of the beast. These so-called Christian nations embraced the blasphemous unity of church and state, maintaining their power through national churches that remained "in an unrepentant, unregenerate, naturall estate, and so consequently farre from hearing the admonitions of the Lord Jesus."[97]

Williams further scandalized his readers concerning "the hopes of conversion, and turning the People of America to God" by condemning the colonizing extension of Christendom through the "monstrous

---

[93] Williams, *Mr. Cotton's Letter Lately Printed*, in *Complete Writings*, 1:194, 315.
[94] Williams, *Key into the Language of America*, in *Complete Writings*, 1:227.
[95] Williams, *Key into the Language of America*, in *Complete Writings*, 1:86.
[96] Williams, *Christenings Make Not Christians*, in *Complete Writings*, 7:32.
[97] Williams, *Christenings Make Not Christians*, in *Complete Writings*, 7:34.

and most inhumane" practices of forced conversions and mass baptisms.[98] True conversion can never be achieved through coercion, as Williams argued: "Jesus Christ compells by the persuasions of his Messengers to come in, but otherwise with earthly weapons he never did compell nor can be compelled."[99] Indeed, Williams contended in *The Bloody Tenent of Persecution*—written about the same time as *A Key into the Language* and *Christenings Make Not Christians*—that the use of coercion coincided with the fall of the church into Christendom, stating that "when Christianity began to be choaked, it was not when Christians lodged in cold Prisons, but Downe beds of ease, and persecuted others."[100] To the consternation of most all his contemporaries, Williams revealed both Catholic and Protestant projects to convert the Indians for what they were—theocratic colonizing efforts that merely extended Christendom and produced false conversions. All that true believers could do in the meantime was to wait patiently and peaceably until "the Lamb may please to open unto us that Wonderful Book and the seven Sealed Mysteries thereof."[101]

Such a description of receptive generosity should not be interpreted as a suggestion that Williams' relations with the Narragansett people and other American Indians were free from stereotypical and colonial thinking. His observations reflect the perspective of a latent colonist—even if a sympathetic one—describing the world of the colonized.[102] Yet among his

---

[98] Williams, *Christenings Make Not Christians*, in *Complete Writings*, 7:36.

[99] Williams, *Christenings Make Not Christians*, in *Complete Writings*, 7:38.

[100] Williams, *The Bloudy Tenent of Persecution*, in *Complete Writings*, 3:187.

[101] Williams, *Christenings Make Not Christians*, in *Complete Writings*, 7:41. James Calvin Davis proposes that the "public discourse" of Williams provides a mediating alternative to radical particularists like Stanley Hauerwas that relegate Christians to "standing on the sideline of public moral discourse" and moral universalists like James Gustafson who imperil the distinctiveness of the Christian witness. Davis, *The Moral Theology of Roger Williams* (Louisville, Ky.: Westminster John Knox, 2004), 116–39. Davis unfortunately reads Williams as far too much of a centrist in the Reformed tradition. His anti-Christendom view of the church along with his millenarianism make him much closer to the sort of radical catholicity of Yoder and McClendon than Davis imagines.

[102] According to Edward Said, Williams' *A Key into the Language of America* assumes the terms of a latent colonist perspective: "'We' are this, 'they' are that." Said cautions that "modern thought and experience have taught us to be sensitive to what is involved in representation, in studying the Other, in racial thinking, in unthinking and uncritical acceptance of authority and authoritative ideas, in the sociopolitical role of intellectuals, in the great value of a skeptical critical consciousness." Said, *Orientalism*, 327. In her fascinating archaeological study of the Narragansett Indians, Patricia Ruberstone compares her findings with Williams' *Key into the Language of America*. What she discovers is a different world than the one described by Williams, "when ancestral lands, not wampum and furs had been exchanged by some of their shachems in deals made with the English for instant gratification and unfulfilled promises; and when other Indians prayed to the Christian god." Ruberstone, *Grave Undertakings: An Archaeology of Roger Williams and the Narragansett Indians* (Washington, D.C.: Smithsonian Institution, 2001), xvi.

contemporaries Williams was a dissenting voice from whom there is still much to learn. He did not regard that which is other in the Other to be ultimate so as to prohibit genuine conversation and cooperation despite the difficulties. Rather, Williams conceived of these differences as constitutive of a penultimate state that points toward the coming of Christ. He thus points to an example of "the natural," which, "after the Fall, is directed towards the coming of Christ."[103] And yet, unlike the militant millenarians who would seek to hasten the coming of the kingdom by force (Matt 11:12), Williams awaited the approaching eschaton with patience and hope. In sum, his sense of the otherness of the true followers of Jesus caused him to find affinity with the otherness of those who were othered by the powers that be.

How did Roger Williams arrive at a standpoint that was at such odds with his Puritan-Separatist heritage? It is certainly the case that his rigorous biblicist hermeneutic, and in particular his eschatological reading of the parable of the weeds and the wheat, opened Williams to a more radical understanding of the intersections of the church and the world. But there can be little doubt that his friendship with the Narragansett people also contributed to changing his mind by causing him to read the Bible from their perspective over against his own, thus interjecting new possibilities into the hermeneutical circle.[104] Through the hospitality of his Indian hosts, Williams received the witness of the living Christ. Receiving the gospel from the stranger was a "conversion" of sorts for Williams himself, and thus became paradigmatic for the kind of conversion that was needed for so-called Christendom to become truly Christian. Because mere christening did not make Christians, neither could it distinguish the church from the world. Therefore, in temporal existence, the garden of the church and the wilderness of the world could not be conceived as two discrete spheres. Like the weeds and the wheat they remain mixed together "until the time of harvest" (Matt 13:24-30). Williams thus came to understand that in this penultimate state of existence the vector of a pilgrim people in their wilderness wanderings is indeterminate and unstable. So, when the light of Christ shines from the face of the Other and it is received as light, it signifies the momentary presence of the coming

[103] Dietrich Bonhoeffer, *Ethics*, ed. Eberhard Bethge, trans. Neville Horton Smith (New York: Macmillan, 1955), 144.

[104] I am here suggesting that the millenarian thesis of Gilpin and biblicist interpretation of Byrd are strengthened by the contextual hermeneutic I have described. See Clark Gilpin, *The Millenarian Piety of Roger Williams* (Chicago: University of Chicago Press, 1979); and James P. Byrd Jr., *The Challenges of Roger Williams: Religious Liberty, Violent Persecution, and the Bible* (Macon, Ga.: Mercer University Press, 2002).

kingdom. And so it was that Roger Williams gained through receptive generosity toward the Other at the boundary, as from Christ himself, this remarkable insight of resisting the temptation to zealous coercion.

Perhaps Other Baptists can find in the life and work of Roger Williams an example of one seeking a cure for alterity in an age in which lively debate and even vigorous dissent lead not to violence but to the ways of peace. Nowhere is there greater need for such retrieval than in post-Christendom societies in which both liberal and conservative Christians seek to instantiate a lost world of Christendom thinking that protects difference in the thin tradition of liberal democracy but has all but forgotten how to embody receptive generosity as a Christian practice. Williams anticipated that the Christendom ecclesiology that could only be established and maintained by coercion would ultimately prove as unsuccessful as it was unfaithful. The church catholic stands ever in need of such a tradition of radical contestation to call into question the Christendom assumptions that inhibit the church from being the church. Through practices of vulnerable relations with the Other, it may be possible to imagine an alternative story to the conquest narrative that has become synonymous with Christendom. This is the gift of contesting catholicity to the faithfulness and wholeness of the church. And, by engaging the otherness at its borders, the church may come to terms with its own alterity and in so doing come to understand its true identity.

2

Beyond Fundamentalism
and Liberalism

In his 1965 memoir, entitled "Dayton's Long Hot Summer," Carlyle Marney recounted his remembrance of growing up in Harriman, Tennessee, a mere forty miles over the hills from where the infamous *Scopes* trial was held. The *Knoxville News Sentinel*, which his family read, was on the side of God and good. "Everything is going to turn out all right for Jesus," his parents assured him. "A great dragon-killer named Bryan has been sent by God Almighty to rescue your Bible, home, church, and sanity." But the *Cincinnati Post*, to which his grandfather subscribed, leaned toward Darwin and Darrow. In its pages, the hero Bryan was shown to be made a fool by Darwin-Darrow, the dragon. Reading both newspapers, young Marney found himself pressed to choose between the Devil and Don Quixote. As a God-fearing Christian, Marney knew he was expected to pray for the dragon slayer to prevail, but somehow he found himself secretly pulling for the dragon. Looking back, he wondered whether the crisis of confusion into which he was thrown as an eight-year-old boy might have been one of the few good things to come out of Dayton that summer. The trial featured plenty of drama and spectacle and was reported by scores of journalists, including the acerbic culture critic H. L. Mencken, spitefully known by locals as that "writing fellow," who came to Dayton expecting to witness a *Götterdämmerung* of Appalachia's gods. But, as Marney observed, "fundamentalism wasn't dying; it never did die, it never would die, and if it did die it wouldn't do it in Dayton, Tennessee. It couldn't get killed from there." And, as Marney also perceptively recalled, Mencken "saw what he came to see." What he saw was there, but much more was there than what he saw. So it was that at a young age Marney began to wonder if there was an alternative to the overbelief of the fundamentalists and the unbelief of the infidels.[1]

Not until he enrolled as a student at the Southern Baptist Theological Seminary in 1940 did Marney discover a way beyond fundamentalism that enabled him to welcome the modern world and remain a genuine Christian. When Marney matriculated, Southern Seminary was just emerging from the economic effects of the Great Depression. The new president, Ellis A. Fuller, was eager to lead the seminary with a bold and aggressive vision that he hoped would help bring Southern Baptists into the modern world. A major piece of the seminary's new posture was educating students with an awareness of the most recent scholarship, which required the acquisition of energetic new faculty that included Yale-educated ethics professor Olin T. Binkley and Marney's major professor, church historian Sydnor L. Stealey.[2] At commencement in 1941, graduating student Das Kelley Barnett delivered a controversial address, "The New Theological Frontier for Southern Baptists," which was subsequently published by the seminary journal *Review & Expositor*. Characterizing the prevailing theology among Southern Baptists as "provincial, dogmatic, apocalyptic, and institutional," Barnett pled for embracing a new theology that was "liberal in its attitude, dynamic in its appeal, social in its application, and dedicated in its purpose to the achievement of the intention of God in history." Barnett's address and article set off a firestorm of controversy at the seminary and throughout the Southern Baptist Convention. Outgoing seminary president John R. Sampey and journal editor W. O. Carver both issued apologies distancing themselves from Barnett's views, but the new theology appealed to the younger Marney.[3]

---

[1] Carlyle Marney, "Dayton's Long Hot Summer," in *D-Days at Dayton: Reflections on the Scopes Trial*, ed. Jerry R. Tompkins (Baton Rouge: Louisiana State University Press, 1965), 125–29; Marney, "Preaching the Gospel, South of God: An Interview with Carlyle Marney," by Bill Finger, *Christian Century*, October 4, 1978, 914–15; and Marney, *Structures of Prejudice* (Nashville: Abingdon, 1961), 125.

[2] William A. Mueller, *A History of Southern Baptist Theological Seminary* (Nashville: Broadman, 1959), 216–25; and Gregory A. Wills, *Southern Baptist Theological Seminary, 1859–2009* (New York: Oxford University Press, 2009), 325–50.

[3] Das Kelly Barnett, "The New Theological Frontier for Southern Baptists," *Review & Expositor* 38, no. 3 (1941): 264–76; reprinted in the *Western Recorder*, September 18, 1941, 10–11, 19–20. The *Western Recorder* ran numerous responses, including Victor I. Masters, "Statement of the Seminary Faculty," *Western Recorder*, October 9, 1941, 9; William O. Carver, "Concerning an Article in the Review and Expositor," *Western Recorder*, October 9, 1941, 10–11; John R. Sampey, "A Word from President Sampey," *Western Recorder*, October 9, 1941, 12; William B. Riley, "Professor Carver's Defense of Barnett," *Western Recorder*, October 30, 1941, 4–5; John R. Sampey, "Safeguarding Doctrinal Soundness of Southern Seminary," *Western Recorder*, November 13, 1941, 1; L. E. Barton, "The Barnett Case and Baptist Freedom," *Western Recorder*, December 4, 1941, 1; William W. Stout, "Concerning

Under the guidance of his seminary professors and driven by a voracious hunger to read, Marney enthusiastically embraced the vision of theological liberalism that the Christian faith could be adapted to modern culture.[4] The research reports he submitted to the faculty during his graduate study indicate that he read extensively in the history of Christianity, and especially in the writings of the early church, but he also consulted critical scholarship outside the required reading.[5] He was especially attracted to the developmental thesis of the German church historian Adolf von Harnack, which held that "dogma in its conception and development is a work of the Greek spirit on the soil of the Gospel."[6] Not surprisingly, Harnack's distinction between external expressions and religious essence lies at the core of Marney's doctoral dissertation on the rise of "ecclesiological externalism" in the early church.[7] Recognizing his scholarly promise, his teachers encouraged him to consider an academic career, but Marney decided he was better suited to be a pastoral theologian. It proved a good fit, and he soon became the foremost voice of a small but influential group of Dixieland liberals. By the time he wrote

---

an Adventure in Misunderstanding," *Western Recorder*, February 12, 1942, 4–5; T. E. Smith, "Observations in Connection with the Barnett Issue," *Western Recorder*, February 26, 1942, 1–2; John D. Freeman, "Who Misunderstood What," *Western Recorder*, February 26, 1942, 4–5, 12; William W. Stout, "Wait a Minute," *Western Recorder*, March 12, 1942, 4–5; T. E. Smith, "An Issue Which Must Not Die," *Western Recorder*, April 2, 1942, 4–5; Gordon Hurlbutt, "Prime Issue in the Barnett Case," *Western Recorder*, April 2, 1942, 6, 23.

[4] In his magisterial three-volume history of American theological liberalism, Gary Dorrien describes liberal theology as "mainly about adjustment and accommodation to the modern world," in *The Making of American Liberal Theology*, vol. 2, *Idealism, Realism, and Modernity, 1900–1950* (Louisville, Ky.: Westminster John Knox, 2003), 389. William R. Hutchison suggests that the first and most visible characteristic of "modernism," which functions in his narrative to name the liberal tradition in American Protestantism, is the "adaptation of religious ideas to modern culture." *The Modernist Impulse in American Protestantism* (Cambridge, Mass.: Harvard University Press, 1976), 2. Dorrien defines the essence of liberal theology as "the idea that Christian theology can be genuinely Christian without being based upon external authority." *The Making of American Liberal Theology*, vol. 1, *Imagining Progressive Religion, 1805–1900* (Louisville, Ky.: Westminster John Knox, 2001), xiii. He more specifically defines twentieth-century American theological liberalism as the conviction "that all claims to truth, in theology as in other disciplines, must be made on the basis of reason and experience, not by appeal to external authority" (*Making of American Liberal Theology*, 2:1).

[5] Carlyle Marney, "Report on Graduate Work: Year, 1941–42"; and "Report on Graduate Work: Year, 1943–44," box 121, Carlyle Marney papers, David M. Rubenstein Rare Book & Manuscript Library, Duke University.

[6] Adolf von Harnack, *History of Dogma*, trans. Neil Buchanan (New York: Dover, 1961), 1:17.

[7] Carlyle Marney, "The Rise of Ecclesiological Externalism to 337 A.D." (Th.D. diss., Southern Baptist Theological Seminary, 1946), xiv. Marney's thesis followed the lines of Harnack's famous distinction between the kernel of primitive Christianity and the husk of dogmatic development. Adolf von Harnack, *What Is Christianity?* trans. Thomas Bailey Saunders (New York: Harper & Row, 1957), 12–15.

his 1965 memoir, he had come to see both fundamentalism and liberalism as deficient, describing one as having its window stuck shut and the other as having its window stuck open. And, as he sardonically surmised, "In either event of extreme one loses the use of the window."[8] Marney imagined the possibility that a "new and chastened liberalism" pointed the way to the future.[9] He continued to search for—but never found—not so much a middle ground between fundamentalism and liberalism as an approach beyond them whereby he might regain use of his theological window.[10] He wondered whether there was such a way forward.

Reestablishing Christian Culture

In the popular imagination, the *Scopes* trial was a clash between rural southern fundamentalism and urban northern intellectualism. The tension between rural and urban cultures was real, but the fighting fundamentalism that stood ready to do battle royal for the faith that long hot summer of 1925 originated not in the South but in the North. Fundamentalism as a movement was born in big northern cities and migrated southward only after it was well established.[11] The World's Christian Fundamentals Association (WCFA), led by Minneapolis Baptist pastor William Bell Riley, held its inaugural conference in 1919 at Philadelphia. Not until six years later did the WCFA launch its southern strategy by holding a meeting in May of 1925 in Memphis, where Bryan was a featured speaker. Riding the wave of the Memphis gathering, fundamentalist leaders lobbied for Bryan to join the prosecution of the upcoming *Scopes* trial, to which he agreed.

---

[8] Marney, "Dayton's Long Hot Summer," 135.

[9] Carlyle Marney, "Liberalism: A Continuation—DeWolf on Continuity," *Religion and Life* 32, no. 3 (1963): 359; Robert L. Calhoun, "A Liberal Bandaged but Unbowed," in the series "How My Mind Has Changed in This Decade," *Christian Century*, May 31, 1939, 701–4.

[10] Carlyle Marney, *The Coming Faith* (Nashville: Abingdon, 1970).

[11] George M. Marsden, *Fundamentalism and American Culture* (New York: Oxford University Press, 1980), 184–95; Michael Lienesch, *In the Beginning* (Chapel Hill: University of North Carolina Press, 2007), 34–58; 139–70. Marsden's generalization of the *Scopes* trial as "the clash of two worlds, the rural and the urban," depends on an understanding of fundamentalism as primarily ideological, whereas Lienesch's account, drawing from social movement theory, shows how fundamentalism was transformed from an ideology into a movement. Lienesch's narrative of the *Scopes* trial, however, draws from the classic work by Edward J. Larson, *Summer for the Gods: The Scopes Trial and America's Continuing Debate over Science and Religion* (New York: Basic Books, 1997). Barry Hankins makes a compelling argument for the rejection of northern fundamentalism by southerners in his "Southern Baptists and Northern Evangelicals: Cultural Factors and the Nature of Religious Alliances," *Religion and American Culture* 7, no. 2 (1997): 271–98, esp. 279.

Yet the struggle was not simply one of rural South versus urban North, which became evident in the meeting of the SBC that also convened in Memphis in May of 1925. There, moderates led by Southern Baptist Theological Seminary president E. Y. Mullins turned back attempts by antievolutionist forces to amend the Memphis Articles on the Baptist Faith and Message. The reluctance to endorse the fundamentalist agenda was understandable given that the popular opinion of Baptists in the South was substantially in agreement with the theologically conservative viewpoint of northern fundamentalists. They consequently felt less urgency about defending the faith or the faithful from the onslaughts of evolution. In an attempt to clarify any lingering uncertainty on the matter, SBC president George W. McDaniel concluded his 1926 presidential address by stating that "this convention accepts Genesis as teaching that man was the special creation of God, and rejects every theory, evolution or other, which teaches that man originated in, or came by way of, a lower animal ancestry." Wanting to leave no room for doubt, messengers unanimously approved a motion to adopt McDaniel's statement on evolution as "the sentiment of this convention."[12]

But the theological outlook was even more complex than it appeared. Southern churches, as social historian Wayne Flynt observed, reflected the deep class divisions of southern culture. Denominational leaders, like E. Y. Mullins and G. W. McDaniel, came from "the First Church elite" of "larger, better-educated, and more affluent" congregations located in small towns and big cities. Beneath this upper tier was a significant subclass of churches made up largely of poor whites, whose under- and uneducated preachers worked bivocationally in the same sort of occupations as their members and shared their more conservative theological views. Moderate and progressive leaders like Mullins attempted to steer the populist energy of their denominational constituencies.[13] They capitalized on the aversion for Yankee culture and the belligerence of northern fundamentalists, which was especially unattractive to southern evangelicals who seemed to

[12] *Annual of the Southern Baptist Convention* (Nashville: Marshall & Bruce, 1925), 71–76; and *Annual of the Southern Baptist Convention* (Nashville: Southern Baptist Convention, 1926), 18. See also Walter B. Shurden, *Not a Silent People: Controversies That Have Shaped Southern Baptists* (Nashville: Broadman, 1972), 53–67.

[13] J. Wayne Flynt, *Dixie's Forgotten People: The South's Poor Whites* (Bloomington: Indiana University Press, 1979), 53. See also Bill J. Leonard, *God's Last and Only Hope: The Fragmentation of the Southern Baptist Convention* (Grand Rapids: Eerdmans, 1990), 113–16. Liston Pope made the politics of southern class division poignantly plain in *Millhands and Preachers: A Study of Gastonia* (New Haven, Conn.: Yale University Press, 1942), 162–86. He shows that no ministers "of recognized standing" supported striking mill workers (328–30).

value civility almost as much as truth.[14] Not surprisingly, though he was a competent scholar on matters of faith and science, Mullins refused to enter into the national controversy by being a witness for either the prosecution or the defense and so declined an invitation from William Jennings Bryan and an appeal by Shailer Mathews, the Northern Baptist dean of the University of Chicago Divinity School.[15] And even in the Solid South, the political balance between progressive elites and populist voices varied from state to state. The political dynamics were more complex in other southern states, like North Carolina, where the passage of popular anti-evolution legislation failed by twenty-one votes while Tennessee comfortably approved a bill outlawing the teaching of evolution.[16]

This more complex and granular understanding of the social and religious texture of the South did not escape Marney's notice. Nor did Mencken miss it entirely either, though his use of sarcasm and caricature was flatly one-sided.[17] But it partly explains the conflict that Marney felt. His father, John Leonard Marney, who was raised on a farm outside Harriman and had only a fourth-grade education, worked his entire adult life in a foundry making agricultural tools. His mother, Sarah Mays Marney, was orphaned as a child and came to Harriman to live with a mill-owner family from the North. The Marneys were active members of the Trenton Street Baptist Church. Mr. Leonard, as his father was affectionately known, identified with the downtrodden and developed a ministry to the indigent. Mrs. Marney was more ecumenical, often attending the Methodist church on Sunday morning and worshiping with the Baptists on Sunday night. She pushed the children toward music, literature, and culture.[18] Large numbers of southern Christians like the Marneys resonated

[14] Hankins, "Southern Baptists and Northern Evangelicals," 279. In his local history of civil rights in Greensboro, North Carolina, historian William H. Chafe shows how progressives favored good manners (civilities) over substantial action (civil rights). Politically, this meant pursuing the course of moderation and gradualism, which from the white perspective was making Greensboro a model city of the New South. Chafe, *Civilities and Civil Rights* (New York: Oxford University Press, 1980), 98–141. Progressive and moderate church leaders in the South had similar commitments.

[15] William E. Ellis, *A Man of Books and a Man of the People: E. Y. Mullins and the Crisis of Moderate Southern Baptist Leadership* (Macon, Ga.: Mercer University Press, 1985), 195.

[16] Lienesch, *In the Beginning*, 134–38.

[17] Mencken confessed that he was pleasantly surprised when he came to Dayton and found not "a squalid Southern village" but "a country town full of charm and even beauty." But his reports consistently played to the gallery, invoking caricatures and stereotypes of southern Christians as fundamentalists, morons, hillbillies, etc. See H. L. Mencken, "The Monkey Trial: A Reporter's Account," in Tompkins, *D-Days at Dayton*, 35–51.

[18] John J. Carey, *Carlyle Marney: A Pilgrim's Progress* (Macon, Ga.: Mercer University Press, 1980), 19–20; Marney, "Preaching the Gospel, South of God," 915; and Marney, "Dayton's Long Hot Summer," 128–29.

theologically with the fundamentalist interpretation of Dayton as a struggle between good and evil, iconically dramatized by William Jennings Bryan and Clarence Darrow. They shared concerns about modernistic preachers that were sensationally described by John Roach Straton, pastor of the Calvary Baptist Church in New York City, in his sermon "Shall the Funny Monkeyists Win?"[19] The fundamentalistic jeremiads of Straton and company envisioned a "Christian America" that bore more resemblance to John Winthrop's "city on a hill" than to Roger Williams' "shelter for persons distressed of conscience."[20] Southerners listened sympathetically

[19] John Roach Straton, "Shall the Funny Monkeyists Win?" sermon delivered September 24, 1922, at Calvary Baptist Church, New York City, in *Religious Searchlight* 1, no. 7 (October 1, 1922): 1–8 (published occasionally by the Religious Literature Department of Calvary Baptist Church, New York, Alfred Stokes, manager). Straton's sermon was a response to the sensational 1922 message, "Shall the Fundamentalists Win?" by Harry Emerson Fosdick, published in *Christian Work* 102 (June 10, 1922): 716–22. Straton challenged Fosdick to a series of debates on the inspiration and authority of the Bible, the virgin birth of Christ, the substitutionary atonement, and the second coming of Christ. He stated that Fosdick "declined and excused himself, under circumstances that made me feel that he was really running to cover." John Roach Straton, *The Famous New York Fundamentalist-Modernist Debates: The Orthodox Side* (New York: George H. Doran, 1924/1925), vii. As Fosdick remembered, Straton denounced him as "a Baptist bootlegger," "a Presbyterian outlaw," and as "the Jesse James of the theological world." Harry Emerson Fosdick, *The Living of These Days: An Autobiography* (New York: Harper & Brothers, 1956), 153.

[20] The jeremiad denotes a form of American Puritan sermon that was preached annually in Connecticut and Massachusetts at the election of the General Court each spring. The jeremiads, as Perry Miller noted, followed the Deuteronomic formula: God warns the people, who humble themselves, and they regain God's favor. A classic example was Samuel Danforth's "Brief Recognition of New England's Errand into the Wilderness," delivered in May of 1670, in *The Wall and the Garden: Selected Massachusetts Election Sermons*, ed. A. William Plumstead (Minneapolis: University of Minnesota Press, 1968), 53–80. On the jeremiad, see Perry Miller, *The New England Mind: From Colony to Province* (Cambridge, Mass.: Belknap Press, 1953), 27–39; and Sacvan Bercovitch, *The American Jeremiad* (Madison: University of Wisconsin Press, 1978), 3–30. In the final chapter of *Fighting the Devil in Modern Babylon*, entitled "The Battle over Atheism and Anarchy," Straton argued that America was founded to perpetuate the morals of Christianity and the principles of the Bible. In classic jeremiad style, he typologically identified America with ancient Israel, quoting from the book of Deuteronomy, "And thou shalt remember all the way which the Lord thy God led thee these forty years in the wilderness, to humble thee, and to prove thee, to know what was in thine heart, whether thou wouldest keep his commandments, or no." Straton rehearsed a litany of departures from the Christian vision of founders, singling out the teaching of evolution in the public schools as one of the chief offenses. Warning that "only God and his Word can lead us safely out of our difficulties," Straton forcefully appealed, "so surely as God led forth ancient Israel for a unique and glorious mission, so does He seem to have raised up Christian America for such an hour as this." Straton, *Fighting the Devil in Modern Babylon* (Boston: Stratford, 1929), 245–71, esp. 268–69. John Winthrop, *A Model of Christian Charity* (1630), in *The Puritans*, ed. Perry Miller and Thomas H. Johnson (New York: Harper & Row, 1963), 1:198–99; "Confirmatory Deed of Roger Williams and his wife, of the lands transferred by him to his associates in the year 1638," in *Records of Rhode Island*, also known as *Records of the Colony of Rhode Island and Providence Plantations* (Providence: A. Crawford Greene & Brother, 1856–1865), 1:22–25.

to laments about the impending devastation of Christian civilization, though they were reluctant to join the moral crusade of Straton and cobelligerents William Bell Riley and J. Frank Norris.[21] These northern Free Church fundamentalists seemed to covet the establishment of Christianity they identified with a lost vision. Why would Southern Baptists not readily desire to retrieve a regnant Christian culture in America?

The answer is simple. Dayton, Tennessee, was a long way from the "modern Babylon" of New York City. But more importantly, they felt no pressing need. Southern Baptists were, after all, the first Free Church movement to create a civilization: It is called the South.[22] Baptists flourished in other geographical regions, and their evangelical influence in the South was shared by Methodists and Presbyterians, but the dominant Baptist presence in the South earned them the status of a de facto established church. Unlike their codenominationalists who lamented the declension of Christianity in the North, the residual Christian culture of the South remained more or less intact. To be sure, Baptists adamantly opposed the government establishment of religion in any form, yet even prior to political disestablishment, southern evangelical churches—especially white evangelical churches—were the beneficiaries of powerful popular support. Baptists and other Southern evangelicals were formally committed to the de jure disestablishment of the church, because the power of their de facto establishment rested not on law but on their social function for their communicants.[23] The cultural establishment of evangelical Christianity was unintended in Dixie, where "the Baptists and Methodists, who had only moved into the region in the late colonial period and who had effectively participated in the challenge to the idea of an established church, emerged as the dominant denominations by 1800."[24] The social

---

[21] Marsden, *Fundamentalism and American Culture*, 153–64. Straton's moral agenda is captured in the titles of his two most sensational books, *The Menace of Immorality in Church and State: Messages of Wrath and Judgment* (New York: George H. Doran, 1920); and *Fighting the Devil in Modern Babylon*.

[22] I owe this description of the privileged place of Baptists in southern culture to my colleague Stanley Hauerwas, who is never shy of reminding Southern Baptists of the irony and indeed the scandal of their own constantinianism.

[23] Donald G. Mathews, *Religion in the Old South* (Chicago: University of Chicago Press, 1977), xvii and 57. This thesis has been widely demonstrated in standard texts of the field of southern religion like Samuel S. Hill, *Southern Churches in Crisis* (New York: Holt, Rinehart, and Winston, 1967); Hill, *Southern Churches in Crisis Revisited* (Tuscaloosa: University of Alabama Press, 1999); and more recently by Christine Leigh Heyerman in *Southern Cross: The Beginnings of the Bible Belt* (Chapel Hill: University of North Carolina Press, 1997).

[24] Charles Reagan Wilson, *Baptized in Blood* (Athens: University of Georgia Press, 1980), 2.

and religious ethos of southern evangelical Christianity was sustained in large measure by the myth of the South as the Baptist Zion and Baptists as God's last and only hope for world evangelization.[25] Even after the Civil War, southern Christians clung to the belief that what the Confederacy failed to establish with its armies would ultimately triumph through the superior principles of christianized southern culture. By the time of the *Scopes* trial, southerners still enjoyed the establishment of evangelical Christianity, although they too soon began to lament its decline.

Christendom as Free Church people came to conceive it was inaugurated with the conversion of Constantine in 312, when church and empire became one. The politically privileged faith of Constantine's *corpus christianum* evolved into the legally established religion of Theodosius' *tempora christiana*. Believing that the era of Christian emperors inaugurated a new age, Theodosius proclaimed in his edict of Thessalonica issued on February 28, 380,

> It is Our will that all peoples who are ruled by the administration of Our clemency shall practice that religion which the divine Peter the Apostle transmitted to the Romans, as the religion which he introduced makes clear even unto this day. . . . That is, according to the apostolic discipline and evangelical doctrine, we shall believe in the single Deity of the Father, the Son, and the Holy Spirit, under the concept of equal majesty and of the Holy Trinity. We command that those persons who follow this rule shall embrace the name of Catholic Christians. The rest, however, whom We adjudge demented and insane, shall sustain the infamy of heretical dogmas their meeting places shall not receive the name of churches, and they shall be smitten first by divine vengeance and secondly by the retribution of Our own initiative, which We shall assume in accordance with divine judgment.[26]

Theodosius attempted to systematically eliminate all rivals to Catholic Christianity through political means. Despite his efforts to christianize civilization, things took a very different direction.[27]

---

[25] Bill J. Leonard, *God's Last and Only Hope*, 11–15; Rufus B. Spain, *At Ease in Zion* (Nashville: Vanderbilt University Press, 1967), 12–43; and Wilson, *Baptized in Blood*, 1–17.

[26] Clyde Pharr, trans. and ed., *The Theodosian Code* (Princeton, N.J.: Princeton University Press, 1952), 16.1.2.

[27] Peter Leithart has rightly pointed out the historical inaccuracy of the theological uses of "constantinianism" as a trope for "Christendom," in his *Defending Constantine: The Twilight of an Empire and the Dawn of Christendom* (Downers Grove, Ill.: InterVarsity, 2010). The so-called fall of the church with Constantine is as much myth as history.

The union of the divine and the human to form a "Christian empire" was viewed by Byzantium as evidence for the reign of Christ now manifest. Constantinianism continued in the Caesaropapism of the East until the fall of Constantinople in 1453. The ancient empire religion faded from the history of the West with the fall of Rome and its fragmentation into the barbarian kingdoms of Europe, but the end of the Western empire did not mean the end of Christendom. Through the centuries it took on new shapes and sometimes more subtle forms as the alignments of power were identified with newly emerging social arrangements.[28] The Catholic understanding of the relationship between church and empire was laid out by Pope Gelasius (492–496). He argued that, of the two powers by which the world is sovereignly governed, the authority (*auctoritas*) of the church exercised by the bishops is weightier than the imperial power (*potestas*) wielded by the emperor.[29] With the coronation of Charlemagne in the ninth century, however, this balance was reversed, and a series of marriages between throne and altar endured eight more centuries in the West as the Holy Roman Empire.

Even as the medieval hegemony of church over society began to fragment in the sixteenth century with the Protestant Reformation, the compromise formula *cuius regio eius religio* (in a prince's country the prince's religion) allowed Protestants and Catholics to retain some measure of their establishment as territorial churches. Christendom was shattered, but the remaining shards reproduced smaller versions of the old model. Free Church people generally, and Baptists in particular, do well to remember that the Peace of Westphalia (1648) that ended the Thirty Years War and defined future political and ecclesial arrangements in Europe was an agreement between only Catholics, Lutherans, and Calvinists.[30] The established authorities resolved no longer to resort to violence as a method of settling their theological differences or to hold the threat of the death penalty over their religious enemies. Nevertheless, they often found it

[28] Robert Markus, *The End of Ancient Christianity* (Cambridge: Cambridge University Press, 1990).

[29] Gelasius, letter of Pope Gelasius to Emperor Anastasius (494), in *Readings in European History*, ed. James Harvey Robinson (Boston: Ginn, 1906), 72–73.

[30] The terms of the Peace of Westphalia (1648) adopted the principle of *cuius regio eius religio* delineated in the Peace of Augsburg (1555), which permitted the prince of a given territory to determine the established church there. It delimited the doctrine by setting 1624 as the "normal year" of religious affairs. Whatever religion was practiced then was permitted to continue, which included Catholic, Lutheran, and Reformed churches. Though the ruler might change the state church, he could not interfere with the public worship of subjects or restrict freedom of worship in private homes. Derek Croxton and Anuschka Tischer, *The Peace of Westphalia: A Historical Dictionary* (Westport, Conn.: Greenwood Press, 2002), s.v. "*cuius regio eius religio*," 69.

propitious to keep the peace by throwing the baptists into prison, confiscating their property, or deporting them and their families.[31]

The ecclesiastical domination by the Christian religion, however, did not go unchallenged. It began to come under attack in seventeenth-century Europe and Great Britain with outset of the Enlightenment. A sustained assault against the church was eventually mounted by intellectual, political, and economic powers driven by the forces of rationalism and secularism. The common goal was to banish the Christian religion to the backwaters of modern culture and to create secular nation-states as alternatives to the fragmented kingdoms of Christendom.[32] This sequestering of Christianity might well have proven fatal had not both liberal and conservative theologians adopted a strategy of accommodation rather than opposition to modernity. No feature was more central to the Enlightenment than the foundationalist theory of knowledge that requires all beliefs to be justified by a special class of beliefs that cannot be questioned. René Descartes (1596–1650), the father of the Enlightenment project, realized that what he could not doubt was his own existence as a rational self. His self-awareness was as "clear and distinct" an idea as the axioms of Euclidean geometry. The self, guided by the autonomous powers of reason, became the sole arbiter of all knowledge claims.[33] The foundationalist tradition that stemmed from Descartes and continued through John Locke (1632–1704) branched off in two directions after David Hume (1711–1776). One fork led from the commonsense realism of Thomas Reid (1710–1796) to the Princeton Theology of Charles Hodge (1797–1878) and Benjamin B. Warfield (1851–1921) and finally to modern fundamentalism. The other grew from Immanuel Kant (1724–1804) to Friedrich Schleiermacher (1768–1834) and Albrecht Ritschl (1822–1889) and to modern theological liberalism.[34]

B. B. Warfield exemplified the conservative Protestant version of modern constantinianism when he argued that

> apologetics has its part to play in the Christianizing of the world: and that is not a small part: nor is it merely a subsidiary or defensive part.

---

[31] See Thieleman J. van Braght, *The Bloody Theater; or, Martyrs Mirror*, 3rd ed. (1886; repr., Scottdale, Pa.: Herald Press, 1990), 1122–41.

[32] For a fuller account of the hidden social and political agenda of modernity, see Stephen Toulmin, *Cosmopolis* (Chicago: University of Chicago Press, 1990).

[33] See especially the First, Second, and Third Meditations. René Descartes, *Meditations on First Philosophy*, trans. Michael Moriarty (Oxford: Oxford University Press, 2008), 17–37. See also Charles Taylor, *Sources of the Self* (Cambridge, Mass.: Harvard University Press, 1989), 143–58.

[34] Nancey Murphy, *Beyond Liberalism and Fundamentalism* (Valley Forge, Pa.: Trinity Press, 1996), 4–6.

... [Christianity] has been placed in the world to *reason* its way to the
dominion of the world. And it is by reasoning its way that it has come
to its kingship. By reasoning it will gather to itself all its own. And by
reasoning it will put its enemies under its feet.[35]

Warfield's account of Christian domination would no doubt come as a
surprise to those who have suffered under the sword of Christians. Yet
the conservative endorsement of ideological constantinianism is no more
ironic than that of liberalism. In his groundbreaking work, *Christianity
and the Social Crisis*, Walter Rauschenbusch argued that "the essential purpose of Christianity was to transform human society into the kingdom
of God by regenerating all human relations and reconstituting them with
the will of God."[36] Social gospelers like Rauschenbusch saw this moral
vision being progressively realized in the modern democratic ideas and
policies of "Christian nations." Mainstream Protestant theology after
Rauschenbusch rejected the liberal optimism of "Christianizing the social
order" but continued to underwrite the same basic democratic assumptions.[37] Thus, both modern liberals and conservatives shared a confidence
in the ultimate triumph of Christian culture. In short, the Constantinian
dominion continued as Christianity was transformed into a set of ideas
that could be made credible and defended and, so it was thought, that
would conquer the ideas of the Enlightenment.[38]

In his doctoral dissertation on the development of ecclesiological
externalism, Marney identified the Constantinian union of church and

---

[35] Benjamin Breckinridge Warfield, review of *Der zekerheid des geloofs*, by Herman
Bavinck, *Princeton Theological Review* 1 (1903): 138–43; cited by Mark A. Noll, "Common
Sense Traditions and American Evangelical Thought," *American Quarterly* 37, no. 2 (1985): 228.

[36] Walter Rauschenbusch, *Christianity and the Social Crisis* (New York: Macmillan, 1907;
repr., Louisville, Ky.: Westminster John Knox, 1991), xxxvii.

[37] Gary Dorrien notes that Rauschenbusch used the terms "Christianize," "moralize,"
"humanize," and "democratize" interchangeably, although "Christianize" was his trump
term (*Making of American Liberal Theology*, 2:111). Christianizing, Rauschenbusch asserted,
meant "humanizing in the highest sense." *Christianizing the Social Order* (New York: Macmillan, 1912), 125. On the continuation of the liberal constantinianism in Niebuhr, Ramsey, and
Gustafson, see Stanley Hauerwas, "On Keeping Theological Ethics Theological," in *Revisions: Changing Perspectives in Moral Philosophy*, ed. Stanley Hauerwas and Alasdair MacIntyre
(Notre Dame, Ind.: University of Notre Dame Press, 1983), 16–42. For a close reading of
Ramsey's Constantinian assumptions, see Hauerwas, "How Christian Ethics Became Medical
Ethics," *Christian Bioethics* 1 (1995): 11–28, esp. 17. Interestingly, Dorrien essentially agrees
with the neoliberal assessment of Niebuhr and subsequent Christian realists, in *Making of
American Liberal Theology*, 2:435–531.

[38] See Stanley Hauerwas, *Dispatches from the Front* (Durham, N.C.: Duke University Press,
1994), 91–94. Barry Harvey displays the way constantinianism forms the backdrop for the process of social transformation that occurs in the Cartesian shift of the Enlightenment in *Another
City: An Ecclesiological Primer for a Post-Christian World* (Harrisburg, Pa.: Trinity Press, 1999).

state as one indication of externalism that is a contradiction of the very essence of Christianity.[39] He was particularly critical of his own Free Church tradition for often forsaking its noble heritage of liberty and succumbing to the shameful practices of authoritarianism and establishmentarianism, especially in the South, where "like-minded persons flock together and create for themselves the group's stamp of uniformity."[40] Marney's worry about fundamentalist and liberal versions of Christendom anticipated the more radical calls to renounce establishment thinking that were to come. [41] National surveys confirm Marney's critique of the ongoing disestablishment of Christianity in American culture.[42] With

[39] Marney, "Rise of Ecclesiological Externalism," 341–60. Page numbers denote Marney's revised manuscript.

[40] Marney, *Structures of Prejudice*, 11–21 and 155–56. Marney's sermon "All the Sons of Earth," July 27, 1947, is evidence of objection to the ways Baptist majoritarian thinking led them to forsake their historic convictions about liberty and dissent in favor of prejudice underwritten by their power as the de facto established church. Box 52, Carlyle Marney papers, David M. Rubenstein Rare Book & Manuscript Library, Duke University. The sermon was published in September 1951 after he preached it for the First Baptist Church of Austin, Texas.

[41] In his book *The End of Christendom*, Douglas John Hall begins with an angular thesis: Briefly put, it is my belief that the Christian movement can have a very significant future—a responsible future that will be both faithful to the original vision of this movement and of immense service to our beleaguered world. But to have *that* future, we Christians must stop trying to have the kind of future that nearly sixteen centuries of official Christianity in the Western world have conditioned us to covet. That coveted future is what I mean when I use the term "Christendom"—which means literally the dominion or sovereignty of the Christian religion. Today Christendom, so understood, is in its death throes, and the question we all have to ask ourselves is whether we can get over regarding this as a catastrophe and begin to experience it as a doorway—albeit a narrow one—into a future that is more in keeping with what our Lord first had in mind when he called disciples to accompany him on his mission to redeem the world through love, not power.

Hall's analysis of the crisis of Christendom and future of Christianity may be helpful for understanding the contemporary crisis and identifying a possible future for Baptists who ought to know better than to covet establishment. Hall, *The End of Christendom and the Future of Christianity* (Valley Forge, Pa.: Trinity Press, 1997), ix. Similar prophecies foretelling the collapse of Christendom are not uncommon, though they have become more frequent. For decades John Howard Yoder, Jim McClendon, Stanley Hauerwas, and other fellow travelers have been warning against the perils of constantinianism in its various permutations and calling the church to affirm its radical otherness. See "The Radical Otherness of the Church" in ch. 1 above. Also see John Howard Yoder, "Christ the Hope of the World," in *The Royal Priesthood: Essays Ecclesiological and Ecumenical*, ed. Michael G. Cartwright (Grand Rapids: Eerdmans, 1994), 194–218; and Stanley Hauerwas, *After Christendom? How the Church Is to Behave if Freedom, Justice, and a Christian Nation Are Bad Ideas* (Nashville: Abingdon, 1991); James Wm. McClendon Jr., *Ethics: Systematic Theology, Volume I* (Waco, Tex.: Baylor University Press, 2012), 17.

[42] See Mark Chaves and Shawna Anderson, "Continuity and Change in American Religion, 1972–2006," in *Social Trends in American Life: Findings from the General Social Survey since 1972*, ed. Peter V. Marsden (Princeton, N.J.: Princeton University Press, 2012); and Claude S. Fisher and Michael Hout, "How Americans Prayed: Religious Diversity and Change," in

the future of a post-Christendom era now all but certain, Christians must learn anew to practice the faith without privilege.[43] This is especially true for Other Baptists.

Revising Christian Theology

The Baptist movement grew out of a conviction that the true church is a believers church. Baptists attempted to display this conviction in their practice. As John Smyth, the first Baptist, asserted, "The Church of the Apostolique constitution consisted of Saints only."[44] Membership in the body of Christ was to be first evidenced by the profession of faith followed by the pledge of baptism. Only baptized believers were received into the membership of the church. Thus delivered from the powers of sin and guilt, believers were freed to participate in the church as the free people of God, whose only Lord is Jesus Christ.[45] The Anabaptists of sixteenth-century Europe and the Baptists of seventeenth-century England resisted

---

Century of Difference: How America Changed in the Last One Hundred Years (New York: Russell Sage Foundation, 2006), 186–211.

[43] Bryan Stone, *Evangelism after Christendom: The Theology and Practice of Christian Witness* (Grand Rapids: Brazos, 2007).

[44] Smyth, "A Lettre to the brethren in S." [1606?], in *The Works of John Smyth*, ed. W. T. Whitley (Cambridge: Cambridge University Press, 1915), 2:558. Smyth argued against the apostolic constitution of the Church of England and for the apostolicity of the independent churches of the separation on the basis that apostolicity is evidenced in the sign of a believers church.

[45] On believer's baptism as a necessary practice of the true church, see Balthasar Hubmaier, "On Infant Baptism against Oecolampad," in *Balthasar Hubmaier: Theologian of Anabaptism*, ed. H. Wayne Pipkin and John Howard Yoder (Scottdale, Pa.: Herald Press, 1989), 275–93; Felix Manz, "Protest and Defense," in *The Racial Reformation*, ed. Michael G. Baylor (New York: Cambridge University Press, 1991), 95–100; Pilgram Marpeck, "The Admonition of 1542," in *The Writings of Pilgram Marpeck*, ed. and trans. William Klassen and Walter Klaasen (Scottdale, Pa.: Herald Press, 1978) 292–302; Dietrich Philips, "The Church of God," in *Enchiridion*, trans. A. B. Kolb (Elkhart, Ind.: Mennonite, 1910), 386–88; the testimony of a woman named Claesken, in Braght, *Martyrs Mirror*, 612–16. The years 1640–1645 were the decisive period for Baptists in defining their theology of baptism (or dipping, as they often preferred) as essential to ensuring a believers church. Among the most widely read accounts include Edward Barber, *A Small Treatise of Baptisme or Dipping Wherein Is Cleerly shewed that the Lord Christ Ordained Dipping for those only that professe Repetance and Faith* ([London?], 1641); Andrew Ritor, *A Treatise of The Vanity of Childish-Baptisme* (London, 1642); Thomas Lambe, *A Confutation of Infants Baptisme* ([London?], 1643); John Spilsbury, *A Treatise Concerning The Lawfull Subject of Baptisme* (London: John Spilsbury, 1643); Christopher Blackwood, *The Storming of Antichrist* (London, 1644); William Kiffin, *To Sions Virgins* (London, 1644); John Thombes, *Two Treatises And An Appendix To Them Concerning Infant-Baptisme* (London: George Whittington, 1645); Henry Denne, *Antichrist Unmasked* (n.p., 1645); Hanserd Knollys, *The Shining of a Flaming-fire in Zion* (London: Jane Cob, 1645); Paul Hobson, *The Fallacy of Infants Baptisme Discovered* (London, 1645); Robert Garner, *A Treatise of Baptisme* (n.p., 1645).

infant baptism and state establishment of the church because these prac-tices virtually ensured the identification of state citizenship with church membership. Moreover, by refusing to recognize the authority of the state to establish the church, the baptismal pledge of absolute loyalty to Jesus Christ as Lord was safeguarded from becoming subordinated to the sov-ereignty of the state.[46]

Early Anabaptist and Baptist communities held firm to the conviction that, for the church to be a believers church, liberty must be preserved. Thomas Helwys (1550–1616), who in 1612 founded the first Baptist church on English soil in Spitalfields just outside the city walls of London, wrote *A Short Declaration of the Mystery of Iniquity*, in which he famously declaimed:

> For we do freely profess that our lord the king has no more power over their consciences than over ours, and that is none at all. For our lord the king is but an earthly king, and he has no authority as a king but in earthly causes. And if the king's people be obedient and true subjects, obeying all human laws made by the king, our lord the king can require no more. For men's religion to God is between God and themselves. The king shall not answer for it. Neither may the king be judge between God and man. Let them be heretics, Turks, Jews, or whatsoever, it appertains not to the earthly power to punish them in the least measure.[47]

Helwys was the first Englishman to argue for complete religious liberty that applies to heretics, Turks, Jews, "or whatsoever," as well as to his own community of dissenters.[48] This claim of universal religious liberty con-stituted a radical break from the traditional notion of established religion expressed in the tagline *cuius regio eius religio* that ascribed to Protestant and Catholic sovereigns to the authority to govern over spiritual matters in their territorial churches. The uniqueness of this remarkable plea raises the question of how it is to be understood.

One stream of interpretation takes Helwys' statement as a lodestone for the protoliberal modernity of Baptist theology.[49] As such it contains

---

[46] See Smyth, *The Character of the Beast*, in *Works of John Smyth*, 2:564–73; and Thomas Helwys, *A Short Declaration of the Mistery of Iniquity* (repr., London: Kingsgate, 1935), 179–82.

[47] Thomas Helwys, *A Short Declaration of the Mystery of Iniquity* (1611/1612), ed. Richard Groves (Macon, Ga.: Mercer University Press, 1998), 53.

[48] Ernest A. Payne, *Thomas Helwys and the First Baptist Church in England*, 2nd ed. (Lon-don: Baptist Union, 1966), 18.

[49] A case for the protoliberal identity of the early Baptists is made by Scott E. Bryant, "An Early English Baptist Response to the Baptist Manifesto," *Perspectives in Religious Studies*

the germ of individualistic autonomy and religious pluralism. To be sure, this language may be construed in such a way as to anticipate modern and even romantic notions of the self. Yet the protoliberal reading fails to account for the main question of *The Mystery of Iniquity*: What must the church teach and practice in order to be the true and faithful church? Helwys and the early Baptists were seeking to maintain an ecclesial claim to the catholicity of the church. To read Helwys simply as a Tractarian advocate of the liberty of conscience misses the deeper currents of his thought.[50] He identified the first beast of Revelation 13 with the Roman Catholic Church and the second beast, which imitated the first, with the Church of England. Neither, he argued, were true and faithful churches. He even believed that the other Separatist congregations were false and unfaithful churches because they simply mimicked the bishops and presbyters, and thus the covenants that constituted their congregations were made with the children of the flesh. Helwys argued that God only enters into covenant with those who believe and are baptized.[51] The protoliberal interpretive paradigm of Helwys fails to account for the centrality of this covenantal ecclesiology. If *The Mystery of Iniquity* is read under the

---

37, no. 3 (2010): 237–48. Bryant follows the view of H. Leon McBeth, who claimed that the central theme of *The Mystery of Iniquity* is a "plea for religious liberty for all." McBeth, *A Sourcebook for Baptist Heritage* (Nashville: Broadman, 1990), 70. Robert N. Bellah argues similarly that the Baptists are the genetic source of liberal individualism in "Is There a Common American Culture?" *Journal of the American Academy of Religion* 66, no. 3 (1998): 613–25. Bryant challenges the thesis that the individualistic and voluntaristic emphasis of modern Baptists was an adaptation to modernity. In particular he argues against the view set forth in "Re-envisioning Baptist Identity: A Manifesto for Baptist Communities in North America," coauthored by Mikael Broadway, Curtis W. Freeman, Barry Harvey, James Wm. McClendon Jr., Elizabeth Newman, and Philip Thompson, *Baptists Today*, June 26, 1997, 8–10; also published in *Perspectives in Religious Studies* 24, no. 3 (1997): 303–10; and further defined and defended by my article "Can Baptist Theology Be Revisioned?" *Perspectives in Religious Studies* 24, no. 3 (1997): 273–310; as well as Philip E. Thompson, "Re-envisioning Baptist Identity: Historical, Theological, and Liturgical Analysis," *Perspectives in Religious Studies* 27, no. 3 (2000): 287–302. The Baptist Manifesto received critical reflections from Walter B. Shurden, "The Baptist Identity and the Baptist Manifesto," *Perspectives in Religious Studies* 25, no. 4 (1998): 321–40; Robert P. Jones, "Re-envisioning Baptist Identity from a Theocentric Perspective," *Perspectives in Religious Studies* 26, no. 1 (1999): 35–57; A. J. Conyers, "The Changing Face of Baptist Theology," *Review & Expositor* 95, no. 1 (1998): 21–38.

[50] Three-fourths of Helwys' *Mystery of Iniquity* pertains specifically to ecclesiological matters. Book 1 identifies the Catholic Church and the Church of England respectively with the first and second beasts in Revelation 13. Book 3 attacks Puritanism as being insufficiently separated from the second beast. Book 4 is a critique of Brownism in which Helwys contrasts the Independent ecclesiology of constituting a congregation by voluntary covenant with the Baptist practice of constituting the church through spiritual covenant in believer's baptism. Book 2 makes the case for religious liberty.

[51] Helwys, *Mystery of Iniquity*, 117–25.

assumption that it is an antecedent of modern individualism and liberty, then it will remain, at least for some, a libertarian tract.

But there are deeper questions with the protoliberal paradigm. It transforms Baptists like Helwys into champions of the anthropocentric philosophy of natural rights and heroes of modern individualism, positions subsequently adopted by later Baptists and other Free Church Protestants. Though the early Baptists were radical Puritans who embraced various versions of Reformed theology, this romantic interpretation strips them of their theological concerns and disclaims the theocentric structure of their thought, imposing in its place notions of enlightened, secular liberalism that would hardly have been recognizable to them. While in Amsterdam, Helwys adopted the view that God's offer of grace may be received or rejected. Because he was not an academically trained theologian, it is unlikely that Helwys came to this position by the logic of Arminian theology. It seems more plausible that his theological shift was a reaction to the use coercive force to compel the conscience of Puritans and other dissenters. It is highly improbable that this theological shift was independent of Mennonite influence.[52] Helwys embraced the radical stance, succinctly described by Heinrich Bullinger, that "one cannot and should not use force to compel anyone to accept faith, for faith is a free gift of God."[53] The protoliberal approach seeks to find continuity between early Baptists and later expressivist theories.

A more historicist reading recognizes that for Helwys the liberty of conscience was dependent on the conviction of Jesus Christ as king in his own kingdom, which challenges and limits civil authority. Religious liberty, then, for Helwys was not a right grounded in an autonomous self. Rather, it was a tactical doctrine that made room for a measure of human free will in response to the sovereignty of God and as a limit to the scope of civil authority.[54] On this point Helwys declared that Christ

[52] Pointing to the timing of Smyth's conversion after he had made contact with the Waterlanders, Michael Watts contends that "it was Mennonite influence which was the decisive factor in [Smyth's] break with Calvinism." Watts, *The Dissenters*, vol. 1, *From the Reformation to the French Revolution* (Oxford: Clarendon, 1978), 46.

[53] Heinrich Bullinger, *Der Wiedertäufferen Ursprung, etc.* (Zurich, 1560); cited by Harold S. Bender, *The Anabaptist Vision* (Scottdale, Pa.: Herald Press, 1944), 4.

[54] Helwys argued that "yet GOD giveing grace, man may receave grace, or my [*sic*] reject grace" in "A Declaration of Faith of English People Remaining at Amsterdam in Holland," 4, in William L. Lumpkin, ed., *Baptist Confessions of Faith*, rev. ed. (Valley Forge, Pa.: Judson Press, 1969), 118. For a discussion of the shift by Helwys toward Arminian theology, see Stephen Wright, *The Early English Baptists, 1603–1649* (Woodbridge, U.K.: Boydell, 2006), 38–39. Robert G. Torbet argued that the principle of liberty "has been distorted by many Baptists today so that it no longer signifies a responsible freedom within the recognized limits of the sovereignty of God over the conscience. Instead, it has come to mean that each

alone is king and the only high priest and chief bishop and that "there is no king, no primate metropolitan, archbishop, lord spiritual, but Christ only, nor may be, either in name or power to exercise authority one over another."[55] Summarizing his discussion of the earthly and spiritual kings and kingdoms, Helwys concluded that "the king must needs grant that as he is an earthly king he can have no power to rule in this spiritual kingdom of Christ, nor can compel any to be subjects thereof, as a king, while the king is but a subject himself."[56]

To construe the liberty of conscience as an anthropological notion grounded in the sanctity of human nature is a mistake. It was a theological doctrine, and more particularly a christological one. Since Christ, and not the king, is Lord over the conscience, Helwys was asserting that the king may not judge between God and humanity. Helwys apparently intended to present a copy of his book to King James I with a note inscribed on the flyleaf stating, "The king is a mortal man and not God, therefore has no power over the immortal souls of his subjects, to make laws and ordinances for them, and to set spiritual lords over them."[57] The core of Helwys' argument is the theological conviction that God is sovereign and has chosen to rule the world by giving authority to an earthly ruler. But Helwys was firm in his assertion that the earthly ruler has no authority in the spiritual kingdom, where God in Christ reigns and the conscience is free, for Christ alone rules the church, whose vocation is to seek and do his will.[58] The ground of liberty for Helwys and the early Baptists, then, was not the free conscience by itself but rather Christ the king to whom alone all are accountable in regard to their faith and religious practice.

Moreover, this protoliberal reading imputes into the word "religion" understandings that were later to come into parlance as the modern world came of age. The sense of "religion" that Helwys invoked was not the sort of private religious experience implied in an eighteenth-century notion of moral agency rooted in natural rights or a nineteenth-century sense of religious experience connected with a theology and practice of revivalist conversionism or a description of the inner data based on twentieth-century psychological theories. Rather, Helwys may have been glossing

---

individual is free to believe what he will without any restraints at all." Torbet, "Baptists and Protestantism in America," *Southwestern Journal of Theology* 6, no. 2 (1964): 106–7.

[55] Helwys, *Mystery of Iniquity*, 34.

[56] Helwys, *Mystery of Iniquity*, 39.

[57] Helwys, *Mystery of Iniquity*, vi. There is no evidence that Helwys' text with its personal message ever reached the king.

[58] Brian Haymes, "On Religious Liberty: Re-reading *A Short Declaration of the Mystery of Iniquity* in London in 2005," *Baptist Quarterly* 42, no. 3(2007): 204.

an older and established meaning of "religion" as *religio*, which denoted the condition of persons bound by vows to God—specifically members of monastic orders who were bound by their religious vows. Might it be inferred from this older sense of "religion" implied in the phrase "men's religion to God" that Helwys was appealing to the obligations that bind all Christians to God, not just "the religious" (i.e., the clergy)? Construed this way, he may have been arguing for a radical understanding of the priesthood of all believers as opposed to a priestly class of religious that obliterated the hard line drawn between laity and clergy, as the Lollards advocated. Perhaps this stretches too far. It seems likely that Helwys at least used the term "religion" in the sense of its binding force to denote an action or conduct indicating a particular belief, thus referring to the expression of beliefs and practices beyond the authorized rites and cer- emonies of the established church backed by the power of civil law and ecclesiastical doctrine. In this sense he would be understood as claiming that a person's religion—that is, the beliefs one confesses and practices (including the beliefs of non-Christians) are not subject to the purview of monarch or magistrate. This secondary meaning seems plausible. The protoliberal paradigm, however, draws from an anachronistic understand- ing of "religion" as experience, with an anthropological valence that is more a product of modern revisionism than historical reality.[59]

---

[59] *Oxford English Dictionary Online*, s.v. "religion," accessed July 21, 2009. The first two definitions of "religion" listed in the *OED* pertain to "a state of life bound by monastic vows; the condition of one who is a member of a religious order; or a particular monastic or religious order or rule." For Wyclif, the term "religion" denoted an "order." He wrote, "First, friars say that their religion, founded by sinful men, is more perfect than that religion or order which Christ himself made. . . . Christian men say that the religion and order that Christ made for his disciples and priests is most perfect, most easy and most sure." *Select English Works of John Wyclif*, ed. Thomas Arnold (Oxford: Clarendon, 1869–1871), 3:367 (language modernized). Though Arnold attributed this text to Wyclif, it is now considered more likely to be the work of an anonymous Wyclifite (or Lollard) writer. Thanks to David Aers for calling this quote to my attention. It does then seem plausible that Helwys might have also employed "religion" with this sense of a new "order—i.e., a new priesthood for all believers. Aers offers a fascinat- ing reflection on the development of the Lollard doctrine of the priesthood of all believers out of the English notion of domestic episcopacy in which lay people were authorized as Christian teachers (bishops) in the home. *Sanctifying Signs: Making Christian Tradition in Late Medieval England* (Notre Dame, Ind.: University of Notre Dame Press, 2004), 67–82 and 157–78, esp. 161–63. A secondary set of definitions of "religion" pertain to "an action or conduct indicating a belief in, reverence for, and desire to please, a divine ruling power; the exercise or practice of rites or observances implying this." This secondary understanding of religion permeated Anglican Christianity, as evidenced by the 1549 collect for the seventh Sunday after Trinity by Thomas Cranmer, which reads in part, "graft in our hearts the love of thy name, increase in us true religion." *The Collects of Thomas Cranmer*, comp. C. Frederick Barbee and Paul F. M. Zahl (Grand Rapids: Eerdmans, 1999), 82. Patrick Collinson observes that in the seventeenth century, "religion" denoted "the authorised rites and ceremonies of the established Church"

The location of Christian freedom under the rule of Christ was even more prominent for the large group of early English Baptists who were more inclined toward Reformed theology. The esteemed Baptist leader and London pastor William Kiffin asserted that the gathered churches affirmed "this great truth, [that] Christ is the king of his Church; and that Christ hath given this power to his church, not to a hierarchy, neither to a national presbytery, but to a company of saints in a congregational way."[60] For Kiffin, Christ is king in the gathered community that lives together under his rule. The church is not merely a constellation of autonomous individuals who practice self-rule and voluntarily cooperate for mutual edification and mission. Communion with Christ and with Christ's body is not simply the aggregate of personal choices. The church as a free people realizes its freedom by standing together under the rule of Christ the king. Another classic seventeenth-century English Baptist statement on the freedom of God's people is found in the Second London Confession. Under the theme "Of Christian Liberty and Liberty of Conscience" it affirms that "the Liberty which Christ hath purchased for Believers under the Gospel" consists in *freedom from* the guilt of sin, condemnation of wrath, the rigor of the law, the powers that be, the evil of afflictions, the fear and sting of death, and everlasting damnation. But it also declares that Christian liberty entails *freedom for* free access and loving obedience to God.[61] Christian freedom and the liberty of conscience are thus rooted in the freedom conferred on believers by the gospel and through their participation in the new creation. The freedom of the church is established only by the gospel of Jesus Christ, not by powers and authorities (including the state) from which believers are freed.

Liberty of conscience for Roger Williams (1603–1683), the ur-Baptist of America, was similarly derived from the gospel and not from Enlightenment theories of natural rights. John Locke's *A Letter Concerning*

---

in contrast to the "irregular practice [in conventicles] of what was not properly religion at all." True religion as defined by the Book of Common Prayer was authorized by the Act of Uniformity. Collinson, *From Cranmer to Sancroft* (New York: Hambledon Continuum, 2006), 152. Thomas Grantham, the most important English General Baptist theologian of the seventeenth century, defined the "religion" of Christianity in terms of the bond of religion (*religio*). Grantham held that the Apostle Paul laid "the Foundation of a Religious Life, and the Glory consequent to it, upon the Free Grace of God manifest to all Men, and makes Religion it self to consist." *Christianismus Primitivus; or, The Ancient Christian Religion* II.1.I (London: Francis Smith, 1678), 35–36.

[60] William Kiffin, preface to "A Glimpse of Syons Glory," sermon by Thomas Goodwin in *The Works of Thomas Goodwin* (Edinburgh: James Nichol, 1866), 12:63; cited in Murray Tolmie, *The Triumph of the Saints: The Separatist Churches in London, 1616–1649* (Cambridge: Cambridge University Press, 1977), 85.

[61] The Second London Confession XXI, in Lumpkin, *Baptist Confessions of Faith*, 279.

Toleration, which deeply influenced moral discourse and public policy in America, was not published until 1689, six years after Williams' death.[62] In *The Bloody Tenent*, Williams specifically argued that the soul is free because Jesus Christ is king. He explained:

> God's people since the coming of the King of Israel, the Lord Jesus, have openly and constantly professed, that no civil magistrate, no King nor Caesar have any power over the souls or consciences of their subjects, in the matters of God and the crown of Jesus, but the civil magistrates themselves; yea Kings and Caesars are bound to subject their own souls to the ministry and church, the power and government of this Lord Jesus, the King of Kings.[63]

Williams argued that soul liberty was forever established by the divine kingship of Jesus Christ, whose "kingly power . . . troubles all the kings and rulers of the world" and whose followers are not permitted to constrain others except by gospel preaching and gentle love.[64]

Although early Baptists seemed to find it unnecessary to provide any warrant other than the gospel for Christian liberty and liberty of conscience, subsequent generations increasingly turned to philosophical and political theories to justify these convictions. Isaac Backus (1724–1806), who like Williams advocated for full liberty of conscience, was influenced by John Locke through Jonathan Edwards (1703–1758). Yet a robust theology of human depravity made Backus suspicious of fully integrating

---

[62] For a description of how the distorted perception of Roger Williams as a civil libertarian became established by progressive historians, see my "Roger Williams, American Democracy, and the Baptists," *Perspectives in Religious Studies*, 34, no. 3 (2007): 267–86. This revisionist account of Williams owes much to Vernon Louis Parrington, whose 1927 portrait of Williams remained widely read for decades, in *Main Currents in American Thought* (New York: Harcourt, Brace, 1927), 1:62–75. Parrington presented Williams as a seminal thinker, describing him as an individualistic mystic and forebear of transcendentalism, as a speculative seeker and precursor of unitarianism, but most of all as a political philosopher and forerunner of democratic liberalism. Parrington also portrayed Williams as a proto-Jeffersonian who anticipated Locke and the natural rights school, thus becoming one of the great heroes in the progressive vision of American intellectual life. For a critique of Williams as a civil libertarian, see LeRoy Moore, "Roger Williams and the Historians," *Church History* 32, no. 4 (1963): 432–51; Moore, "Roger Williams as an Enduring Symbol for Baptists," *Journal of Church and State* 7, no. 2 (1965): 181–89; Mauro Calamandrei, "Neglected Aspects of Roger Williams' Thought," *Church History* 21, no. 3 (1952): 239–58; Alan Simpson, "How Democratic Was Roger Williams?" *William and Mary Quarterly* 13, no. 1 (1956): 53–67; and James Wm. McClendon Jr., *Doctrine: Systematic Theology, Volume II* (Waco, Tex.: Baylor University Press, 2012), 482–87.

[63] Roger Williams, *The Bloudy Tenent of Persecution* (1644), in *The Complete Writings of Roger Williams* (New York: Russell & Russell, 1963), 3:76.

[64] Williams, *Bloudy Tenent*, in *Complete Writings*, 3:346.

Locke's philosophy of natural rights into his account of religious liberty. According to Backus, the true liberty of humankind is "to know, obey, and enjoy [the] Creator and to do all the good unto, and enjoy all the happiness with and in, [their] fellow creatures that [they] are capable of."[65] But because the creature rebelled against the Creator, Backus argued that the powers of sin have enslaved humanity and the natural liberty of creation has been lost. He further asserted that it is

> only the power of the Gospel that can set them *free from sin* so as to become the servants of *righteousness*, [and] can *deliver* them from these *enemies* so as to *serve God in holiness* all their days. And those who do not thus *know the truth* and have not been *made free* thereby, yet have never been able in any country to subsist long without some sort of government.[66]

Both the account and the justification of the liberty of conscience were for Backus, as for Williams, biblical and theological; however, the habit of offering warrants that were acceptable to all people of reason became firmly established among Baptists a generation later.

John Leland (1754–1841), a pivotal figure among colonial Baptists, staunchly defended the historic Baptist convictions of the liberty of conscience and the disestablishment of the church from the state. Yet, to justify and display these convictions, he adopted Lockean and Madisonian language, with its theories of natural rights and voluntary associations. Leland defined the liberty of conscience as "the inalienable right that each individual has, of worshiping his God according to the dictates of his conscience, without being prohibited, directed, or controlled therein by human law, either in time, place, or manner."[67] Leland's deep dependence on the philosophical and political theories of Locke, Jefferson, and Madison can scarcely be missed.[68] In the sermon entitled "A Blow at the Root," delivered in 1801 after his return to New England, Leland began with a jeremiad on human depravity and the moral need of government to restrain evil and concluded with a tribute to American democracy and its founders in a tone that can only be described as panegyric rhetoric. He pled:

---

[65] Issac Backus, *An Appeal to the Public for Religious Liberty* (Boston: John Boyle, 1773), reprinted in *Isaac Backus on Church, State, and Calvinism*, ed. William G. McLoughlin (Cambridge, Mass.: Belknap Press, 1968), 309.

[66] Backus, *Appeal to the Public*, 311–312 (emphasis in original).

[67] John Leland, *A Blow at the Root*, in *The Writings of the Late Elder John Leland*, ed. L. F. Greene (New York: G. W. Wood, 1845; repr., New York: Arno Press, 1969), 239. See also Leland, "The Rights of Conscience Inalienable," in *Writings of the Late Elder John Leland* (ed. Greene), 179–92.

Pardon me, my hearers, if I am over-warm. I lived in Virginia fourteen years. The beneficent influence of my hero was too generally felt to leave me a stoic. What may we not expect, under the auspices of heaven, while Jefferson presides, with Madison in state by his side. Now the greatest orbit in America is occupied by the brightest orb: but, sirs, expect to see religious bigots, like cashiered officers, and displaced statesmen, growl and gnaw their galling bands, and, like a yelping mastiff, bark at the moon, whose rising they cannot prevent.[69]

Leland "turned a quest for self-reliance into a godly crusade." His populist version of liberal individualism "combined ideological leverage of evangelical urgency and Jeffersonian promise" and held out a vision of personal autonomy that the grass roots could embrace, and indeed did baptize by full immersion.[70] Leland upheld to the end "an unvarnished, undiluted individualism."[71] The historic Baptist convictions and practices persisted with Leland, but they were given new modern meanings and warrants in terms of liberal individualism. In time the democratic language of rights became so identified with the religious convictions and practices that subsequent generations of Baptists found it difficult to distinguish between the two. The old warrants were then incorporated into the new descriptions.[72]

---

[68] Thomas Jefferson, A Bill for Establishing Religious Freedom, published in 1777 but not approved by the Virginia legislature until 1786, in *The Papers of Thomas Jefferson*, vol. 2, *1777 to June 18, 1779*, ed. Julian P. Boyd (Princeton, N.J.: Princeton University Press, 1950), 545–47; James Madison, "Memorial and Remonstrance against Religious Assessment," in *The Papers of James Madison*, vol. 8, *March 10, 1784 to March 28, 1786*, ed. Robert E. Rutland and William M. E. Rachal (Chicago: University of Chicago Press, 1984), 295–306; and John Locke, *A Letter Concerning Toleration* (New York: Liberal Arts, 1950). On the use of Jeffersonian and Madisonian theories to provide warrant for the Baptist convictions of the liberty of conscience and the disestablishment of the church, see Mikael N. Broadway, in "The Ways of Zion Mourned: A Historicist Critique of the Discourses of Church-State Relations" (Ph.D. diss., Duke University, 1993), ch. 5, "Historicizing American Ecclesiology," esp. 190–201, 217–20.

[69] Leland, *Blow at the Root*, in *Writings of the Late Elder John Leland* (ed. Greene), 255.

[70] Nathan Hatch, *The Democratization of American Christianity* (New Haven, Conn.: Yale University Press, 1989), 101. Hatch provides a broad account of the growing democratization of Christianity in America during the transitional period between 1780 and 1830.

[71] J. Bradley Creed, "John Leland, American Prophet of Religious Individualism" (Ph.D. diss., Southwestern Baptist Theological Seminary, 1986), 239.

[72] Joseph Martin Dawson was one of the leading revisionist voices who identified the Baptists with Leland's liberal individualism. Dawson, *Baptists and the American Republic* (Nashville: Broadman, 1956). The most enduring influence of Dawson, however, was his contention that this pattern of government was transmitted from Roger Williams through Isaac Backus and John Leland to Thomas Jefferson and James Madison. The Backus-Leland tradition exercised widespread influence among Baptists, but it was a view shaped more by looking forward to the politics of American democracy than looking backward at Roger Williams and

This voluntaristic notion of the self and the language of natural rights continued to become more thoroughly individualistic in subsequent generations of Baptists through such influences as populism and revivalism. The growing democratization of religious convictions and practices during the Jacksonian era is reflected in the writings of William Bullein Johnson (1782–1862), the last southern president of the General Baptist Missionary Convention and the first president of the SBC, who defended "the right of each individual to judge for himself in his views of truth as taught in the scriptures," and Francis Wayland (1796–1865), president of Brown University, who championed "the absolute right of private judgment in all matters of religion."[73] Wayland informed his readers that the principle of private judgment is not unique to Baptists but "has been so generally advocated by Protestants, that it does not require any special notice."[74] It is surely the case that Wayland was convinced private judgment was so widely held that it needed no warrant or explanation, but he seemed aware neither of the Reformers' repudiation of private judgment nor of the contemporary social and intellectual currents that informed his own description of the principle and that made it appear self-evident to him.[75] Wayland was swept along in the cultural and intellectual currents of the early nineteenth century in which "the autonomous individual became for some the preeminent value to be preserved and served."[76] The process whereby evangelical Christians began to adjust the Christian message to the themes of democratic ideology is complex, but it is undeniable that they came uncritically to identify their

---

the early Baptists. On the revisionism of Dawson and others, see my article "Roger Williams, American Democracy, and the Baptists"; Edwin S. Gaustad, "The Backus-Leland Tradition," in *Baptist Concepts of the Church*, ed. Winthrop Still Hudson (Chicago: Judson Press, 1959), 106–34; and Moore, "Roger Williams as an Enduring Symbol for Baptists," 186.

[73] W. B. Johnson, *The Gospel Developed through the Government and Order of the Churches of Jesus Christ* (Richmond, Va.: H. K. Ellyson, 1846), 200; and Francis Wayland, *Notes on the Principles and Practices of Baptist Churches* (New York: Sheldon, Blackmon, 1857), 132.

[74] Wayland, *Notes on the Principles and Practices of Baptist Churches*, 146.

[75] On Luther's rejection of the priesthood of all believers as a "private" matter between the individual and God, see Paul Althaus, *The Theology of Martin Luther*, trans. Robert C. Schultz (Philadelphia: Fortress, 1966), 313–18; and Timothy George, *Theology of the Reformers* (Nashville: Broadman, 1988), 95–98. For one of the earliest Baptist accounts of the priesthood of all believers as a practice of *shared discipleship* rather than private judgment, see Hubmaier, "On Fraternal Admonition," in *Balthasar Hubmaier*, 372–85. Although private judgment is not a Reformed doctrine, it is well established in the political philosophy of John Locke. See, e.g., Locke, *Letter concerning Toleration*, 48. Other Lockean language confused with Baptist convictions includes the freedom to follow the dictates of conscience and the church as a voluntary society (19–20).

[76] Barry Alan Shain, *The Myth of American Individualism: The Protestant Origins of American Political Thought* (Princeton, N.J.: Princeton University Press, 1994), 115.

Christian convictions with American democratic ideals. The democratization of Baptist convictions and practices simply reflects this broader Christian-culture synthesis.[77]

The further accommodation to the rightward branch of modern theology is exemplified in Baptist theologians John Leadley Dagg (1794–1884), professor and president of Mercer University, Alvah Hovey (1820–1903), professor and president of Newton Theological Institute, and James Petigru Boyce (1827–1888), professor of the Southern Baptist Theological Seminary, whose works were patterned after Protestant orthodoxy and the Princeton Theology.[78] As a student at Brown University, Boyce was influenced by Francis Wayland, but it was the Princeton theologians, especially Charles Hodge, who left the most lasting impression on the shape of Boyce's theology. The Princeton theologians adopted a view of science that was close to the one set forth by Francis Bacon (1561–1626). According to the Baconian view, science is the strict induction of verified facts. This understanding of science was wedded to the commonsense philosophy of Thomas Reid (1710–1796).[79] In this ordering of faith, science, and reason, the two absolutely fundamental premises were "that God's truth was a single unified order and that all persons of common sense were capable of knowing that truth."[80] Nowhere was the Baconian and commonsense theology more clearly stated than in the *Systematic Theology* of Charles Hodge, who wrote,

> The Bible is to the theologian what nature is to the man of science. It is his store-house of facts; and his method of ascertaining what the Bible teaches, is the same as that which the natural philosopher adopts to ascertain what nature teaches. . . . The duty of the Christian theologian

---

[77] Mark A. Noll, *The Scandal of the Evangelical Mind* (Grand Rapids: Eerdmans, 1994), 67–81.

[78] Alvah Hovey, *Manual of Systematic Theology and Christian Ethics* (Philadelphia: American Baptist Publication Society, 1877); and James Petigru Boyce, *Abstract of Systematic Theology* (Philadelphia: American Baptist Publication Society, 1887). William Brackney describes Hovey as "critically orthodox" (i.e., as a mediating theologian) because of his accommodations to science and his appeal to a more "dynamic" theory of inspiration. These points confirm, as Brackney indicates, that Hovey adapted to modernity. William H. Brackney, *A Genetic History of Baptist Thought* (Macon, Ga.: Mercer University Press, 2004), 285. However, as James Leo Garrett Jr. shows, Hovey's theology was still primarily a restatement of the received Protestant orthodoxy. Garrett, *Baptist Theology: A Four Century Study* (Macon, Ga.: Mercer University Press, 2009), 279–83.

[79] Sydney E. Ahlstrom, "The Scottish Philosophy and American Theology," *Church History* 24, no. 3(1955): 257–72; and Mark A. Noll, "Common Sense Traditions and American Evangelical Thought."

[80] Marsden, *Fundamentalism and American Culture*, 14.

is to ascertain, collect and combine all the facts which God has revealed concerning himself and our relation to Him.[81]

Boyce reflected the view of his mentor by defining theology "as a science" that "is concerned in the investigation of facts." Theology for Boyce "inquires into [the] existence of [these facts], their relations to each other, their systematic arrangement, the laws which govern them, and the great principles which are the basis of this existence, and these relations."[82] Like Hodge and the Princeton theologians, Boyce assumed that the facts about God were propositionally set forth in the Scriptures and immediately available to the individual mind by means of commonsense reason.

It is important to note one omission in the *Abstract* that indicates the growing rationalism and individualism of Baptist theology. Although Boyce has several chapters on practices of the Christian life, there is no chapter of the *Abstract* given to the church or ecclesial practices.[83] In part 4 of his *Systematic Theology* ("Soteriology"), Hodge treats the ecclesial practices of the Word of God, the sacraments, baptism, the Lord's Supper, and prayer.[84] Such an oversight by Boyce is curious indeed. The same question has been raised about the absence of a chapter on ecclesiology in E. Y. Mullins' *The Christian Religion*. The stated reason seems to be that it simply reflects the division between theological and practical studies in the curriculum of Southern Seminary—a curriculum that Boyce helped to design. Matters of ecclesiology were treated in a separate course.[85] Yet even if Boyce had included a chapter on the church, theology would have remained for him, as it was for Wayland, a matter of private judgment. It became less a way of giving warrants for communally held convictions and historically preserved practices as it became more a discourse of classifying and arranging the facts of the Bible. The recession of ecclesiology in the nineteenth century among Baptists also happened alongside the reduction of pneumatology from a corporate to an individual focus. For example, Elias H. Johnson (1841–1906), longtime professor of theology and proponent of "critical orthodoxy" at Crozer Theological Seminary,

---

[81] Charles Hodge, *Systematic Theology* (New York: Scribner, Armstrong, 1872–1873), 1:10–11.

[82] Boyce, *Abstract of Systematic Theology*, 3.

[83] Boyce has a very brief treatment of the Lord's Supper and baptism as regards "the means of sanctification" in which he argues against Catholic and Reformed theologies of sacrament, seal, and sign so as to leave no doubt that in his judgment the ordinances convey no sanctifying grace to the individual believer in his *Abstract of Systematic Theology*, 421–25.

[84] Hodge, *Systematic Theology*, 3:466–707.

[85] Mueller, *History of Southern Baptist Theological Seminary*, 113; and Timothy George and David S. Dockery, eds., *Baptist Theologians* (Nashville: Broadman, 1990), 334.

argued that, "beyond the mystery of the Spirit's relation to the individual (John 3:8), it is not necessary to believe that he holds a relation to the church as an organic whole."[86] Baptists in nineteenth-century America increasingly came to see the church as merely a gathering of like-minded individuals joined to observe the duties of religion rather than as a vital part of the saving process.[87]

The theology of John Leadley Dagg was also deeply influenced by the habits of mind associated with commonsense rationality.[88] Dagg's *Manual of Theology*, a formative book among Southern Baptists, appears to be dependent upon a simple biblicism in that he proposed to derive doctrine by going straight to Scripture.[89] Yet "religious conservatism in the Old South was always as much a matter of philosophical as of biblical considerations."[90] Dagg's *Theology* begins with the declaration that the "obligation that moves us to seek the knowledge of the truth . . . belongs to the constitution of human nature."[91] Implicit in this appeal to human nature were the commonsense notions of morality and rationality. In effect, common sense provided a criterion for theological truth, and biblical revelation was congruous with human rationality. Thus, for Dagg no less than for Wayland, faith and reason were a seamless garment. Although his book follows an order traditional of Protestant orthodoxy (i.e., God, creation and providence, sin, Christ, the Holy Spirit, etc.), each doctrine is introduced by identifying a corresponding "duty" (i.e., to love God, to delight in the will and works of God, to repent, to believe in Christ, to live and

---

[86] Elias H. Johnson, *An Outline of Systematic Theology* (Philadelphia: American Baptist Publication Society, 1895), 187. Thanks to Philip Thompson for calling my attention to the pneumatological shift in Johnson. Thompson traces the movement away from the dominant Baptist ecclesiology of the seventeenth century, which emphasized "the community of believers, the catholic church and a soteriology characterized by individual and corporate sanctification and formation" to the prevailing twentieth-century Baptist ecclesiology and emphasized "the individual believer, the local church as a voluntary association of individuals, and a soteriology weighted toward individual conversion." Philip Edward Thompson, "Toward Baptist Ecclesiology in Pneumatological Perspective" (Ph.D. diss., Emory University, 1995), esp. ch. 2, "Shifting Patterns in Baptist Thought: The Eighteenth and Early Nineteenth Centuries," 120–72, and ch. 3, "Baptist Thought in America From About 1830 to the Present," 173–301.

[87] Cf. Wayland, *Notes on the Principles and Practices of Baptist Churches*, 179–80.

[88] S. A. Grave distinguishes between the theoretical aspects of commonsense philosophy and the more general habits of mind associated with it in "Thomas Reid," *The Encyclopedia of Philosophy*, ed. Paul Edwards (New York: Macmillan, 1967), 7:121.

[89] J. L. Dagg, *Manual of Theology* (Charleston, S.C.: Southern Baptist Publication Society, 1857–1858), 39–42.

[90] E. Brooks Holifield, *The Gentlemen Theologians* (Durham, N.C.: Duke University Press, 1978), 125.

[91] Dagg, *Manual of Theology*, 14.

walk in the Spirit, etc.). In effect, Dagg was suggesting that the truth of Christian doctrine was self-evident if measured by its commensurability with Christian morality and piety.

A. H. Strong (1836–1921) was for four decades professor of theology and president of Rochester Theological Seminary during the years that Baptist theology was coming of age in the modern world. In many respects Strong, like Boyce, transmitted traditional Reformed theology from a Baptist perspective. Reminiscent of the Princeton theologians, Strong defined theology as "the science of God [not of human experience or the Christian religion] . . . and of the relation between God and the universe."[92] For Strong, the science of Christian theology was built upon the "objective facts" of Biblical revelation, which constitute "the ground" of theology.[93] He thus shared the basic foundationalist assumptions of conservative, propositional theology. In 1906, when the winds of theological liberalism were blowing many schools in the new direction, Strong declared to the Rochester trustees, "Let others teach as they will. We will walk in the old paths and hand down to our successors the old gospel."[94] Yet, throughout his career, Strong moved away from a Baconian understanding of science to embrace the emerging science of the nineteenth century by means of what he termed "ethical monism." Strong defined ethical monism as "that method of thought which holds to a single substance, ground, or principle of being, namely, God, but which also holds to the ethical facts of God's transcendence as well as his immanence, and of God's personality as distinct from, and as guaranteeing, the personality of man."[95] Thus, for Strong, "natural causation is the expression of a supernatural Mind in nature."[96] He thereby affirmed the creative activity of God within and through the process of evolution. Strong, furthermore, incorporated an immanent (rather than an interventionist) account of God's providential activity in miracles so as not to violate the laws of nature.[97] It is not surprising, then, that Strong has been described as a mediating theologian whose goal was "to express evangelical orthodoxy in modern thought forms."[98]

---

[92] Augustus Hopkins Strong, *Systematic Theology*, 8th ed. (Philadelphia: Judson Press, 1907), 1:1.

[93] Strong, *Systematic Theology*, 1:13.

[94] Strong, *Annual Report*, New York Baptist Union for Ministerial Education, 1906, 42. Quoted in Paul M. Minus, *Walter Rauschenbusch: American Reformer* (New York: Macmillan, 1988), 139.

[95] Strong, *Systematic Theology*, 1:105.

[96] Strong, *Systematic Theology*, 1:391.

[97] Strong, *Systematic Theology*, 1:118–19.

[98] D. W. Bebbington, "Baptist Thought," in *The Blackwell Encyclopedia of Modern Christian*

Strong's mediating theology, however, does not constitute a rejection of the conservative paradigm (Scripture) for a liberal one (experience) or a hybrid that combines elements of both. To the contrary, he represents an evangelical modification of conservative theology.[99] Yet, even in his evangelical modification of conservative theology, Strong remains within the basic paradigm of conservative theology, which builds on the foundation of the objective facts of Scripture. Fundamentalism, however, continued on the trajectory of the Princeton Theology, but fundamentalists further reduced the facts of the inerrant Scriptures to five essential ideas that they thought would conquer the ideas of liberalism and convince unbelievers of the truth. E. J. Carnell insightfully observed that fundamentalists failed to grasp the irony of the Catholic agreement with the five fundamentals thus revealing their theologically un-Reformed content and neglecting, as George Lindbeck would later argue, the interrelatedness of doctrines and the communal life that they render intelligible.[100] Amzi C. Dixon (1854–1925), John Roach Straton (1875–1929), William Bell Riley (1861–1947), J. Frank Norris (1877–1952), and T. T. Shields (1873–1955) were influential preachers who popularized the theology of *The Fundamentals* among Baptists.[101]

Some Baptists like William Newton Clarke (1841–1911) of Colgate Seminary, George Burman Foster (1858–1919) and Shailer Mathews (1836–1941) of the University of Chicago, Walter Rauschenbusch (1861–1918) of Rochester Theological Seminary, and Harry Emerson Fosdick (1878–1969) of Union Theological Seminary and popular preacher of Riverside Church in New York City enthusiastically embraced the progressive vision of theological liberalism.[102] At a time when Baptists and

---

Thought, ed. Alister E. McGrath (Cambridge: Blackwell, 1993), 29. Grant Wacker describes how Strong came to his settled standpoint by gradually moving from the "consistent ahistoricism" of old Reformed orthodoxy to an "accommodating historicism" of the new liberalism before finally settling more or less with the mediating theology of "accommodating ahistoricism." Wacker, *Augustus H. Strong and the Dilemma of Historical Consciousness* (Macon, Ga.: Mercer University Press, 1985), 162; and Wacker, review of *Autobiography of Augustus Hopkins Strong*, *Christian Century*, May 18, 1983, 502–3.

[99] Nancey Murphy puzzles over how to fit Strong into her two-paradigm account of modern theology. She concludes that he is "an exception that proves the rule" in her *Beyond Liberalism and Fundamentalism*, 75.

[100] Edward J. Carnell, "Fundamentalism," in *A Handbook of Christian Theology*, 2nd ed., ed. Arthur A. Cohen and Marvin Halverson (Nashville: Abingdon, 1984), 142–43; and George Lindbeck, *The Nature of Doctrine* (Philadelphia: Westminster, 1984).

[101] R. A. Torrey and A. C. Dixon, eds., *The Fundamentals: A Testimony to the Truth*, 4 vols. (1917; repr., Grand Rapids: Baker Books, 1980).

[102] Shailer Mathews, *The Faith of Modernism* (New York: Macmillan, 1924); Rauschenbusch, *Christianity and the Social Crisis*; William Newton Clarke, *An Outline of Christian*

most other Protestants in America were still following the paradigm of commonsense realism in the tradition of Protestant orthodoxy, William Newton Clarke began looking to the new theology of Europe for an alternative. Clarke's *Outline of Christian Theology* (1894) was America's (and Baptists') first systematic theology written from a liberal perspective. With acknowledged echoes of Schleiermacher and the Ritschlian theologians, Clarke took religious experience as the starting point for theology. Yet Clarke was not well versed in German theology and rarely made direct use of it. He maintained that his late-career liberalism was a development of his growing understanding of the Bible, and "he insisted that he had worked out his theological position independently of modern theologians, and even his later works did not cite them."[103] Religion was understood by Clarke, as by Schleiermacher, to be a universal, affective faculty of human nature.[104] For Clarke, the intuitive sense of dependence and obligation corresponded to a higher power, and the reality of God is unknowable apart from experience.[105] Moreover, as Schleiermacher derived the second part of his doctrinal system from the consciousness of sin and grace, so Clarke defined theology as the expression of Christian experience—that is, "the saving of men and the renewing of their life."[106] Although Clarke's *Outline* had much in common with Schleiermacher's *Glaubenslehre*, the account of religious experience in one was individualistic, whereas in the other it was communal. For Clarke the experience of God was "private, personal, [and] esoteric," but for Schleiermacher creature-consciousness was felt with all creation and the consciousness of sin and grace shared with the church.[107]

As an undergraduate student at Colgate University, Harry Emerson Fosdick encountered Clarke. To the young Fosdick, Clarke's theology was proof that Christianity could accommodate modern knowledge. Fosdick matriculated one year at Colgate Seminary, where he became Clarke's student and protégé, before enrolling at Union Theological Seminary in New York to study with many of the leading liberal theologians in America.[108] Through his books and sermons, Fosdick became the most

---

Theology (1899; repr., New York: Scribner, 1912); and Harry Emerson Fosdick, *Christianity and Progress* (New York: Fleming H. Revell, 1922).

[103] Dorrien, *Making of American Liberal Theology*, 2:31, 41.

[104] Clarke, *Outline of Christian Theology*, 2.

[105] Clarke, *Outline of Christian Theology*, 118–26.

[106] Clarke, *Outline of Christian Theology*, 18–19; Friedrich Schleiermacher, *The Christian Faith*, ed. and trans. H. R. Macintosh and J. S. Stewart (Edinburgh: T&T Clark, 1928), §§62–169.

[107] Clarke, *Outline of Christian Theology*, 125.

[108] Fosdick, *Living of These Days*, 55–56, 61–62.

well-known voice of liberal theology. For Fosdick, "the one vital thing about religion is first-hand, personal experience . . . of God in Christ."[109] Though the Divinity School at the University of Chicago tacked in a more empirical direction than the evangelical liberalism of Union Seminary or the personalism of Fosdick, Shailer Mathews began from a remarkably similar standpoint. Like Fosdick, Mathews suggested that "the permanent element of our evolving religion resides in attitudes and convictions (i.e., experience) rather than doctrines." Mathews continued, "Theology changes as banner-words change, but Christian experience . . . will continue."[110] Liberal Baptists like Mathews and Fosdick upheld a theology of abiding experience and changing categories.[111] They maintained that theology must turn aside from the secondary and derived features of Christianity to examine the primary element: religious experience. General religious experience and distinctly Christian experience were viewed as discreet sources of theological reflection. Because the givenness of experience was thought to be universal and perennial, it was immediately available to be known and could be correlated to God. Thus the intimate and incommunicable experience of individuals known and interpreted by individuals became for liberalism the foundation of theology. Mathews' Chicago colleague and Strong's former student George Burman Foster also posited experience as the foundation of religious truth, but his historicist approach led him to more radical conclusions. The last chapter of Foster's sensational book, *The Finality of the Christian Religion*, attempted to connect the religious experience of Jesus with the religious experience of humankind. He explained, "Love, or the will directed to the fellowship of autonomous beings, is the disposition, of which Jesus is archetype, and which alone is good." Based on the "experience-religion" of Jesus, Foster reasoned, the meaning of the incarnation was not that Jesus was like God, but rather that "God is like Jesus." He revealed "the humanness of God." This, Foster exclaimed, is the good news: "God is as good as Jesus is."[112] It was a path that led Foster from liberalism to humanism, the Divinity School to the Department of Comparative Religion, and almost but not quite out of the Baptist ministry.

The liberal tradition was mediated to generations of African American Baptist ministers by Benjamin Elijah Mays (1894–1984), as dean of

[109] Fosdick, *Christianity and Progress*, 160, 163.

[110] Mathews, *Faith of Modernism*, 76.

[111] Harry Emerson Fosdick, *The Modern Use of the Bible* (New York: Macmillan, 1924), 97–130.

[112] George Burman Foster, *The Finality of the Christian Religion* (Chicago: University of Chicago Press, 1906), 475–518.

the School of Religion at Howard University and as professor and president of Morehouse College. Mays studied at the University of Chicago, where he learned an empirical approach to theology. His major academic work, *The Negro's God*, examined "mass sources" (e.g., spirituals, sermons, prayers, etc.) and "classical sources" (e.g., poems, speeches, letters, essays, books, etc.) of African American literature. Mays found that the patterns of God in mass literature were primarily compensatory (i.e., magical, spectacular, revengeful, and anthropomorphic), whereas classical sources indicated a constructive and developmental view of God that addressed the social, economic, and psychological needs of African Americans.[113] Mays also adopted the social gospel of his Chicago teachers. However, because he considered racial discrimination to be the original sin of America, he extended the christianizing effects of the gospel to include the racial desegregation of American society.[114] His Morehouse students, Howard Thurman (1899–1981) and Martin Luther King Jr. (1929–1968), embraced Mays' vision of social Christianity and combined it with personalist theology in their graduate studies at Boston University.

E. Y. Mullins (1860–1928), professor and president of the Southern Baptist Theological Seminary, and D. C. Macintosh (1877–1948), professor of theology at Yale Divinity School, also followed the leftward branch of modernity at a moderate pace by adapting the categories of evangelical piety to experiential religion. Like Descartes, Mullins borrowed the image of axioms in Euclidean geometry to discover the axioms of the Christian religion. With these "self-evident" ideas as a foundation, Christian theology was thought to be "grounded" and "justified." Once again the historic Baptist convictions and practices were given new modern warrants. For Mullins the "axiom" of "soul competency" became the interpretive key to Christian experience, whereas for Macintosh evangelical conversion was thought to be empirically describable as a "right religious adjustment."[115] One is left to puzzle, for example, how E. Y. Mullins, like Strong, seemed to stand between fundamentalism and liberalism. During his presidency of the SBC, Mullins skillfully steered the denomination

---

[113] Benjamin E. Mays, *The Negro's God as Reflected in His Literature* (Boston: Chapman and Grimes, 1938; repr., New York: Negro Universities Press, 1969), 14–18, 245–55.

[114] Benjamin E. Mays, "Democratizing and Christianizing America in This Generation," *Journal of Negro Education* 14, no. 4 (1945): 527–34; Mays, "The Moral Aspects of Segregation," in *The Segregation Decisions: Papers Read at a Session of the Twenty-First Annual Meeting of the Southern Historical Association, Memphis, Tennessee, November 10, 1955*, ed. William Faulkner (Atlanta: Southern Regional Council, 1956), 13–18; and Mays, *Seeking to Be a Christian in Race Relations* (New York: Friendship Press, 1957).

[115] E. Y. Mullins, *The Axioms of Religion* (Philadelphia: Judson Press, 1908) 53–56; D. C. Macintosh, *Theology as Empirical Science* (New York: Macmillan, 1919), 142.

on a middle course through the evolution-creation controversy of the 1920s. As chair of the committee that drafted the Baptist Faith and Message (1925), he led the debate against efforts at the convention to add an antievolution amendment.[116] There is no question that Mullins embodied a moderate political strategy between fundamentalism and modernism. He criticized both extremes. It is important, however, not to confuse the political strategy of Mullins with his theological paradigm. In theological matters Mullins seemed to steer a middle course. He was a contributor to *The Fundamentals* associated with the conservative version of modernity as well as a disseminator of moderated liberal theology. Yet his article "The Testimony of Christian Experience," written for *The Fundamentals*, operated not with a dual or blended paradigm but on a single foundation. Mullins left no doubt that the individual experience of regeneration (the liberal vector), not a biblical source book of information (the fundamentalist vector), was the proper foundation of Christian theology.[117]

Theology for Mullins was a correlative activity "wherein [hu]man-[ity]'s upward soaring thought is met by God's descending revelation and love."[118] But for Mullins the vector of theological correlation was from experience to God, not from God to experience. His theological treatise *The Christian Religion in Its Doctrinal Expression* confirms the prominence of religious experience as the source from which all theological interpretation is derived. To be sure, Mullins declared that Jesus Christ is the supreme authority for theology and that the Scriptures were the only source of authoritative information about him, but he noted that, unless the message of Christ and Scripture are "vitalized by experience," they are of no value for theological reflection.[119] Mullins attempted to make "explicit in reason that which is implicit in experience."[120] But he did not

---

[116] For an account of the moderating effect of Mullins' role in the evolution-creation controversy, see Ellis, *Man of Books*, 147–68 and 185–208. During the *Scopes* trial, when the evolution-creation controversy was at its height, Mullins sought the vanishing middle ground by refusing direct appeals to support the cases both of anti- and proevolution forces (195).

[117] E. Y. Mullins, "The Testimony of Christian Experience,"in Torrey and Dixon, *Fundamentals*, 4:314–23. In an earlier article, Mullins developed an account of religious experience drawing from William James. Mullins, "Is Jesus Christ the Author of Religious Experience?" *Baptist Review and Expositor* 1, no. 2 (1904): 55–70.

[118] Mullins, "Testimony of Christian Experience," in Torrey and Dixon, *Fundamentals*, 4:317.

[119] E. Y. Mullins, *The Christian Religion in Its Doctrinal Expression* (Nashville: Sunday School Board of the Southern Baptist Convention, 1917), 3. On the norm of religious experience, see also Mullins, "The Contribution of Baptists to the Interpretation of Christianity," *Review & Expositor* 20, no. 4 (1923): 383–95; and Mullins, *Talks on Soul Winning* (Nashville: Sunday School Board of the Southern Baptist Convention, 1920), 77–84.

[120] Cited by W. Morgan Patterson, "The Southern Baptist Theologian as Controversialist," *Baptist History and Heritage* 15 (1980): 12.

integrate the experiential source into every doctrine.[121] Still, experience remained the operative paradigm in his theology. Yet the "experience" on which Mullins reflected was neither the romantic pietism of Schleiermacher nor the gentle mysticism of Clarke but rather the evangelical revivalism familiar to Baptists South and North. Interestingly, when Mullins declared, "That which we know most indubitably are the facts of inner experience,"[122] he used language nearly identical with the account of private experience described by William James.[123] But the philosophy of Borden Parker Bowne offered personalist categories that Mullins found more congenial to his experiential theology.[124]

As odd as it may seem, the liberal and conservative trajectories of modern Baptist theology share a common ancestry in foundationalism. Whether convictions and practices are viewed to be warranted by natural rights, commonsense reason, axiomatic truths, or empirically verifiable facts, both streams of modern Baptist theology remain committed to foundational principles, thus liberals (and moderates) and fundamentalists (and evangelicals) are siblings under the skin. This is not a new insight. In his posthumously published book, *Types of Christian Theology*, Hans Frei noted the ironic similarity of liberalism and fundamentalism. Both exemplify Frei's second type because they insist that "theology must have a foundation that is articulated in terms of basic philosophical principles."[125] For fundamentalists the foundation is an inerrant Bible. For liberals it is religious experience.[126] Thus, liberals and conservatives inhabit the same type of theology (i.e., modern) even if they operate within different paradigms (i.e., Scripture vs. experience). However, there is an invisible wall between liberalism and fundamentalism. It is possible to moderate liberal

---

[121] Humphreys makes this point in "E. Y. Mullins," in George and Dockery, *Baptist Theologians*, 339.

[122] Mullins, *Christian Religion*, 73.

[123] William James, *Varieties of Religious Experience* (New York: Collins, 1960). James defined religion as "the feelings, acts, and experiences of individual men in their solitude, so far as they apprehend themselves to stand in relation to whatever they may consider divine" (50). He further explained that "the essence of religious experiences . . . must be that element or quality in them which we can meet nowhere else" (62). For a more detailed examination of the appropriation of James by Mullins, see my "E. Y. Mullins and the Siren Songs of Modernity," *Review and Expositor* 96, no. 1 (1999): 23–42, esp. 31–32.

[124] Stewart A. Newman, *W. T. Conner: Theologian of the Southwest* (Nashville: Broadman, 1964), 98, 111. On the personalist philosophy of Borden Parker Bowne, see Dorrien, *Making of American Liberal Theology*, 1:371–92; and on the Boston school of theological personalism, see Dorrien, *Making of American Liberal Theology*, 2:286–355.

[125] Hans W. Frei, *Types of Christian Theology* (New Haven, Conn.: Yale University Press, 1992), 24.

[126] Murphy, *Beyond Liberalism and Fundamentalism*, 6–7, 11–35; see also Lindbeck, *Nature of Doctrine*, 16–19.

theology, and fundamentalists can slide down the slippery slope to evangelicalism. But liberals cannot become fundamentalists, nor fundamentalists liberals, without a paradigm shift.[127] Moderates and evangelicals, then, are not hybrids. Moderate theology still operates in the paradigm of experience, and evangelical theology is grounded on the foundation of Scripture.

Fundamentalism and liberalism are twin trajectories of modern theology—both of which revised Christian theology to accommodate to modernity.[128] The story of the often antagonistic relationship between liberals and conservatives is an inevitable consequence of the interaction between these two rival visions of theology whose divergent paths were guided by incommensurable paradigms. The intensity of the Baptist battles in this century is symptomatic of a deeper underlying crisis of modernity and of the attempt by Baptists to articulate their identity as a free people of God. Theologies that depend on modern notions of rationality for their intelligibility will find them unhelpful for negotiating the transition beyond modernity. Neither fundamentalism nor liberalism possesses sufficient resources for the constructive theological work that lies ahead. Marney's metaphor proved prophetic: neither the stuck window of fundamentalism or liberalism will do for Baptists. Other Baptists must seek another way.

Revisioning the Christian Future

The most conspicuous indicators of the disestablishment of mainline Protestantism are the decline of church membership, the loss of financial prosperity, and the lack of influence in high places. The waning of Christendom may be even more pervasive than religious pundits have been ready to admit. Protestant affiliation has dropped to about half of the U.S. population, while the number of Americans claiming no religious affiliation has risen to just under one-fifth of the public.[129] Although some

---

[127] Murphy, *Beyond Liberalism and Fundamentalism*, ix; cf. Thomas Kuhn, *The Structures of Scientific Revolution*, 2nd ed. (Chicago: University of Chicago Press, 1970) 77–91, esp. 85.

[128] I am grateful for and indebted to William Brackney, *Genetic History of Baptist Thought*; and James Leo Garrett, *Baptist Theology*, for their extensive and insightful accounts of the history of Baptist theology. Garrett, though primarily descriptive and expositional in approach, gestures toward what he calls "Calminian" (i.e., moderately Calvinistic) evangelicalism as a way forward. *Baptist Theology*, 724–25. Brackney commends drawing from a sevenfold genetic heritage and concludes by gesturing toward the importance of individual liberty by the Baptists as a "stream of Christian spirituality that stresses the individual." *Genetic History of Baptist Thought*, 536–38.

[129] Chaves and Anderson, "Continuity and Change in American Religion, 1972–2006"; Fisher and Hout, "How Americans Prayed," 186–211; "'Nones' on the Rise: One-in-Five

establishmentarian vestiges still survive, the gradual disestablishment of Christendom in America is now in full swing. But the current declension is not limited to the mainline denominations. Baptists, and even Southern Baptists, are in decline.[130] Explaining the causes of the cultural disestablishment of Christianity in America presents a puzzle.[131] But the more fundamental crisis is the one created by the Christendom consciousness of the old dominant order. The challenge that lies ahead is whether it is possible to purge the old habits of mind and imagine a way of being in the world without the privileges of Christendom. A theology for Other Baptists must find an alternative to the coveted future that includes a thoroughgoing restatement of the understanding of Jesus, Christian discipleship, and the mission of the church.

Harvey Cox is one Baptist theologian who envisioned a future beyond the culture of Christendom. His book *The Secular City* imagined a positive role for Christianity in a modern secular world after the end of religion. When he revisited his secularity thesis twenty years later, in light of the continuance of religion, Cox observed that although secularization disestablished Christianity from cultural dominance, it is modernity, not religion, that is now coming to an end. He concluded that "with the passing of the modern age, the epoch of 'modern theology' which tried to interpret Christianity in the face of secularization is also over."[132] Cox suggested that secularization did not drive religion from modern society but instead fostered a type of private religion in which the link between religion and politics is lost.[133] If the effect of modernity on theology was the loss of political content, Cox proposed that the way beyond modernity for theology is to recover a political dimension. He examined the resurgence of political theology in two contemporary religious movements, Protestant fundamentalism and Christian base communities, although he concluded that only the latter holds any promise for postmodern theology.

Adults Have No Religious Affiliation," *Pew Forum on Religion & Public Life*, October 9, 2012, accessed January 12, 2013, http://www.pewforum.org/uploadedFiles/Topics/Religious_Affiliation/Unaffiliated/NonesOnTheRise-full.pdf. For an alternative account, see D. Michael Lindsay, *Faith in the Halls of Power* (New York: Oxford University Press, 2007).

[130] Fisher and Hout, "How Americans Prayed," 197; and the "2008 Southern Baptist Convention Statistical Summary," *2008 Southern Baptist Convention's Annual Church Profile*, Nashville: Lifeway Christian Resources, April 20, 2009, accessed July 21, 2009, http://www.lifeway.com/lwc/files/lwcF_corp_news_ACP2008_pdf.pdf.

[131] Robert Wuthnow provides one of the most complete accounts of just how much has changed in the social arrangements between church and state in his *The Restructuring of American Religion* (Princeton, N.J.: Princeton University Press, 1988).

[132] Harvey Cox, *Religion in the Secular City: Toward a Postmodern Theology* (New York: Simon & Schuster, 1984), 21. See Harvey Cox, *The Secular City* (New York: Macmillan, 1965).

[133] Cox, *Religion in the Secular City*, 12.

Cox argued that whereas modern theology became the ally of the bourgeoisie, liberation theology is postbourgeois in its emphasis on solidarity with those at the bottom and edges of society.[134] Ordinary people are encouraged to read the Bible in conversation with one another without scientific exegetes or priestly interpreters closing off the discussion.[135]

If the task of modern theology was to make the Christian message credible to the modern mind (that is, to the white, male), Western, bourgeois mind, theological reflection that arises from reading communities is postmodern insofar as the concerns of people of color, women, the poor, and non-Westerners are given voice. In attempting to get beyond a theology that is determined by the interests of sovereign nation-states, science-based technology, bureaucratic rationalism, profit maximization, and the secularization of religion, Cox contended for a paradigm of the radical demodernization of theology.[136] Unlike the modern congregations that are simply "collections of discrete persons . . . who created a church through a kind of social contract," postmodern Christianity is embodied in a church where the ties that bind make them "members of one another."[137] Such revolutionary changes would require a new reformation, and Cox saw sixteenth-century baptists as anticipating this future.[138] Yet such a reformation of the church in North America that recovers the politics of the theological, Cox argued, would require input from Baptist "folk piety" in moving beyond the secular city by passing through it.[139]

The modern theologian who is most readily identified as having pushed beyond the liberal-conservative continuum is Karl Barth. He not only anticipated the end of modernity; he also recovered the intratextual performance of theology that "redescribes reality within the scriptural framework rather than translating Scripture into extrascriptural categories."[140] For Barth, the revelation of God in Jesus Christ challenged the enlightened knowledge of modernity and called for the creation not of a new and better world but of a renewed and more faithful church. In contrast to his liberal contemporaries, Barth understood that "the theologian's job is not to make the gospel credible to the modern world, but to make the world credible to the gospel."[141] Barth's own thinking about the

---

[134] Cox, *Religion in the Secular City*, 163–67.

[135] Cox, *Religion in the Secular City*, 23, 168–71.

[136] Cox, *Religion in the Secular City*, 183.

[137] Cox, *Religion in the Secular City*, 214.

[138] Cox, *Religion in the Secular City*, 263–64.

[139] Cox, *Religion in the Secular City*, 267–68.

[140] Lindbeck, *Nature of Doctrine*, 118, 135, and 138n35.

[141] Stanley Hauerwas and William H. Willimon, *Resident Aliens* (Nashville: Abingdon, 1989), 24. See Sheila Greeve Davaney and Delwin Brown, "Postliberalism," in McGrath,

church's social stance changed during his years of writing of the *Church Dogmatics*. As John Howard Yoder argued, Barth finally came to embrace a Free Church (or baptistic) ecclesiology that consists in "the exemplarity of the church as foretaste/model/herald of the kingdom."[142] For Barth, the fundamental difference between the Christian community and civil society is that the church confesses that Jesus Christ is Lord whereas the world does not. This confessional identity is doxologically displayed and politically embodied in the worship and witness of the church. Thus the social strategy of the church is to represent to the world what it means for humanity to be sanctified in Christ, not to control the social and political agenda of the wider society.

This journey beyond the liberal-conservative paradigm was antic-ipated for Baptists in the theology of W. T. Conner, who, although a student of Rauschenbusch and Mullins, turned aside from the modern commitments of his teachers in an attempt to rediscover, as did Barth, "the strange new world of the Bible." Like Mullins, Conner assumed that the scientific method, which begins with "facts of experience," is the proper theological method. Yet, for Conner, the locus of Christian theology was not experiential religion or scriptural propositions but "the [biblical] revelation from God centering in the Person of Jesus Christ."[143] Conner went so far as to describe the notion of the "science of religion" as a "vain idea," and he contended that "it is now time that theology

---

Blackwell Encyclopedia of Modern Christian Thought, 453–56. For a promising arrangement between evangelicals—many of whom are Baptists—and postliberals, see Timothy R. Phillips and Dennis L. Okholm, eds., *The Nature of Confession* (Downers Grove, Ill.: InterVarsity, 1996). One Baptist theologian who has explored Lindbeck's postliberal proposal is Douglas Karel Harink, *Paul among the Postliberals: Pauline Theology beyond Christendom and Modernity* (Grand Rapids: Brazos, 2006).

[142] John Howard Yoder, "Why Ecclesiology Is Social Ethics," in *Royal Priesthood*, 106; and Yoder, "Karl Barth: How His Mind Kept Changing," in *How Karl Barth Changed My Mind*, ed. Donald McKim (Grand Rapids: Eerdmans, 1986), 166–71. See Karl Barth, *Church Dogmatics* IV/2 (Edinburgh: T&T Clark, 1958), 719–26. Ernest Payne earlier recognized the congeniality of Barth to Baptist theology. See Payne's preface to Karl Barth, *The Teaching of the Church regarding Baptism* (London: SCM Press, 1948). Another Baptist theologian who finds the *early* writings of Barth to move in a Baptist direction is Elizabeth B. Barnes, *An Affront to the Gospel? The Radical Barth and the Southern Baptist Convention* (Atlanta: Scholars Press, 1987).

[143] W. T. Conner, *Revelation and God* (Nashville: Broadman, 1936), 43, 99. As James Leo Garrett rightly indicates, "Conner drew upon personalism rather than biblical theology to provide the characteristics of human being as spiritual persons." Consequently, his view of general revelation in *Revelation and God* was closer to Brunner than to Barth. Garrett, "Walter Thomas Conner," in George and Dockery, *Baptist Theologians*, 425–28. Yet as Stewart New-man indicated, "Conner was never quite comfortable with the thought of the 'new orthodoxy' of men like Karl Barth and Emil Brunner," even though he came to emphasize the centrality of revelation for theology. Newman suggested that Conner was particularly concerned about the "deliberate irrationalism" of neo-orthodoxy. *W. T. Conner*, 117–21.

declared its independence of science and stood on its own feet."[144] Unlike Mullins, Mathews, and Macintosh, for whom the theological trajectory runs from human experience to God (i.e., religion), for Conner the trajectory is from God to humanity (i.e., revelation).

This vector of Conner's theology is most fully developed by his student, James William McClendon Jr., whose theological project reflects the influence of his teacher. As Frei and Lindbeck extended the postliberal trajectory of Barth, so McClendon pursued a course charted by Conner, although this path clearly ran from Rauschenbusch through Mullins to Conner and beyond.[145] McClendon's multivolume *Systematic Theology* was rooted in the soil of the common life in Christ that he called the baptist vision, which is grounded in the conviction that "the church now is the primitive church," that "we are Jesus' followers," and that "the commands are addressed directly to us."[146] The underlying hermeneutic of this theological viewpoint is postcritical, as the vision is "a trope of mystical identity binding the story now to the story then, and the story then and now to God's future yet to come."[147] Doctrinal theology as a second-order practice is thus inextricably linked to the first-order practices of the church. Such a theological model allows for a great diversity of readings, yet it presupposes a unity that is sufficient to define an authentic style of communal life in which members can know "what the church must teach to be the church."[148] McClendon moved beyond the foundationalism of modern theology that grounds theological discourse in transcendent experience or an inerrant Bible. For McClendon there is no foundation for theology other than Jesus Christ and no warrant except the gospel.

Following the path laid out by McClendon, Other Baptists are committed to continuing the reform and retrieving the tradition of the church. Other Baptists have said farewell to the establishment of Christendom in search of a contesting catholicity. Other Baptists long to see their churches take a new direction that is neither conservative nor liberal nor something in between. Other Baptists affirm the beliefs and practices that have shaped the identity and mission of baptistic communities through the centuries,

---

[144] W. T. Conner, *The Gospel of Redemption* (Nashville: Broadman, 1945), ix.

[145] McClendon, *Doctrine*, 56–60.

[146] McClendon, *Ethics*, 33. For my assessment of McClendon's theological project, see my article "The 'Coming of Age' of Baptist Theology in Generation Twenty-Something," in "Festschrift for James Wm. McClendon Jr.," special issue, *Perspectives in Religious Studies* 27, no. 1 (2000): 21–38; and my introduction in all three volumes of McClendon's *Systematic Theology* (Waco, Tex.: Baylor University Press, 2012), vii–xxxviii.

[147] McClendon, *Doctrine*, 45.

[148] McClendon, *Doctrine*, 46.

but they also desire to be in continuity with the historic Christian tradition. Other Baptists seek to move beyond modernity, yet they are deliberate about retrieving a connection to the faith and practice of the one, holy, catholic, and apostolic church. Other Baptists do not claim to have the final word but rather invite the wider community of Baptists to enter a conversation about the way forward. Other Baptists pursue the direction of a theology that is deliberately baptistic and intentionally catholic.

To be sure, this vision is not the coveted future of Christendom that some Baptists have grown accustomed to expect. Yet, having traced the narrative arc of fundamentalist overbelief and liberal underbelief, Other Baptists choose an alternative way forward. And if, as Marney suggested, liberals have their windows stuck open and fundamentalists have their windows stuck shut, pilgrims sturdy enough to follow this new vector might actually regain the use of their windows by moving beyond fundamentalism and liberalism toward a generous liberal orthodoxy.

3

Toward a Generous Orthodoxy

Oscar Blake Smith preached his first sermon as pastor of the University Baptist Church of Austin, Texas, on February 4, 1943. The church was located adjacent to the University of Texas campus and hosted a vibrant student ministry. After a decade of ministry in his home state of Arkansas, Smith was attracted by the promise of a free pulpit where he could cast a more progressive theological vision drawn from his studies at Yale Divinity School. Smith found Austin to be an intellectually and spiritually open environment. His sermons drew increasingly large crowds. Membership rolls swelled. Soon he was recognized as one of the outstanding preachers in America. Smith's practical approach to the faith was not surprising. At Yale he had come under the influence of the ecumenically minded and socially engaged dean, Charles R. Brown, who stressed the need for a "thorough application of the principles of the Gospel of Jesus Christ to the conditions of every-day life." The theological formation Smith received at Yale instilled in him a prophetic imagination that impelled him to challenge the powers. He led the University Baptist Church to desegregate its membership in 1946—eight years before the U.S. Supreme Court ruling in *Brown v. Board of Education*, and he urged others to follow suit. In his December 12, 1950, radio address, he advocated to his listeners that "they could strike a blow that would shatter this system completely if they would do one thing: announce to the world that on Jan[uary] 1 there would be no segregated churches," demonstrating that "all men are welcome regardless of race." "That," he declared, "would shatter the system because the last stronghold of segregation is the churches." Smith represented the vanguard of Dixieland liberals that included Carlyle Marney and other Other Baptists known as the "Young Turks" who likewise found their way to Austin.[1]

The Yale faculty during Smith's student days included renowned church historian Williston Walker, New Testament critic Benjamin Bacon, and homiletics professor Halford Luccock, and though Yale was nonsectarian, Kenneth Scott Latourette and Douglas Clyde Macintosh, both Baptists, were prominent members of the faculty during Smith's studies. Baptists comprised the third-largest denominational group among the student body. Also, in the 1920s, a theologian little known outside of New Haven named Robert Calhoun joined the faculty. Along with H. Richard Niebuhr, who came a decade later, Calhoun helped usher in a new theological era at Yale that transitioned from liberalism to postliberalism. His vision has been characterized as a "generous liberal orthodoxy." Yet his transition was "not to neo-orthodoxy, but to a view closer to traditional orthodoxy without abandoning his liberal convictions." In his legendary lectures on the history of Christian doctrine, Calhoun traced the plot of the story of Christianity focused on a broad consensus within inclusive parameters that found expression in the ancient ecumenical creeds. His narrative identified three convictions that guided the development of doctrine: Jesus Christ as genuinely human, salvation through Christ, and God alone as able to save humanity from sin and death.[2]

---

[1] *Austin American-Statesman*, February 1, 1948, June 24, 1973, and July 8, 1973; *Oral Memoirs of Oscar Blake Smith*, interviewed by Thomas L. Charlton (Waco, Tex.: Baylor University Institute for Oral History, 1974); Charles Reynolds Brown, *The Social Message of the Modern Pulpit* (New York: Scribner, 1906), 4–5; and Roland H. Bainton, *Yale and the Ministry: A History of Education for the Christian Ministry at Yale from the Founding in 1701* (San Francisco: Harper & Row, 1957 and 1985), 198–259. Oscar Blake Smith, "Race Relations," radio talk, December 12, 1950, box 1, Blake Smith papers, David M. Rubenstein Rare Book & Manuscript Library, Duke University, Durham, N.C. Smith anticipated the often-quoted statement of Liston Pope, who came later to Yale, first as professor and then as dean. Pope intoned, "The church is the most segregated major institution in American society. It has lagged behind the Supreme Court as the conscience of the nation on questions of race, and it has fallen far behind trade unions, factories, schools, department stores, athletic gatherings, and most other areas of human association as far as the achievement of integration in its own life is concerned." Liston Pope, *The Kingdom beyond Caste* (New York: Friendship, 1957), 105. The Young Turks included John Lee Smith (Blake Smith's son and pastor of Highland Park Baptist Church), Ed Bratcher (pastor of Tarrytown Baptist Church), and Riley Eubank (pastor of Woodlawn Baptist Church). They were later joined by Lonnie Kliever (Baptist Student Union director at the University of Texas), Jess Fletcher (Baptist Bible chair at the University of Texas), and Hardy Clemmons (Baptist Student Union director at the University of Texas).

[2] Robert L. Calhoun, "A Liberal Bandaged but Unbowed," in the series "How My Mind Has Changed in This Decade," *Christian Century*, May 31, 1939, 701–4; Calhoun, *Lectures on the History of Christian Doctrine* (New Haven, Conn.: Yale Divinity School, 1948), 1:14; Hans Frei, "In Memory of Robert L. Calhoun 1896–1983," *Reflection* 82 (1984): 8–9; George A. Lindbeck, *Robert Lowry Calhoun as Historian of Doctrine*, Yale Divinity School Library Occasional Publication no. 12 (New Haven, Conn.: Yale Divinity School Library, 1998).

When Blake Smith began preaching in Austin, he could not draw from the theological revisioning that was only then coming to be at Yale. Yet he understood well enough, as did Marney, that the conservative-liberal binary offered an insufficient basis to account for the revelation in Christ. In a 1944 sermon, Smith addressed a subject about which many members of the University Baptist Church were undoubtedly wondering: Was he a liberal or a conservative? Acknowledging that churches across the country were divided along these lines, Smith asked whether Jesus was a conservative or a liberal and, more importantly, "What would He be today?" In good Yale fashion, Smith problematized the question by historicizing it among the socioreligious groups of second-temple Judaism. Then he offered a surprise answer: "Jesus was really a conservative" because "he was bent on conserving the great eternal values that were in the law and the prophets and which had been discovered in the experiences of the people." But, he continued, "Jesus was also a liberal" because "He viewed everything in terms of what He was doing for the people, and the great principle of it all was love and unselfish devotion to God and to the common good." Offering his concluding assessment, Smith announced, "I do not believe that we should be divided between liberals and conservatives, but all of us should strive to preserve the basic values and to move forward to a richer and fuller understanding and experience of them."[3]

One of the students who heard and heeded Smith's appeal that day was James William McClendon Jr. He had enrolled at the University of Texas in the fall of 1941 and shortly thereafter began attending the University Baptist Church. The theological road McClendon traveled led from Austin to Fort Worth with a brief interlude in Princeton. At Southwestern Seminary he studied with W. T. Conner, who taught there for almost forty years (1910–1949). Conner was a student of Strong at Rochester, Foster at Chicago, and Mullins at Southern, but he gradually shifted his attention to voices in the burgeoning biblical theology movement. Known as "the theologian of the southwest," Conner was liberating without being liberal and conserving without being rigidly bound to orthodoxy. Under his guidance McClendon moved beyond the old liberal-conservative paradigm and, more importantly, toward the sort of generous liberal orthodoxy exemplified by Calhoun and his students Hans Frei and George Lindbeck.[4]

[3] Blake Smith, "Jesus, Liberal or Conservative?" sermon (1944), box 1, Blake Smith papers, David M. Rubenstein Rare Book & Manuscript Library, Duke University, Durham, N.C.

[4] James Wm. McClendon Jr., "The Radical Road One Baptist Took," *Mennonite Quarterly Review* 74, no. 4 (2000): 503–10; McClendon, *Doctrine: Systematic Theology, Volume II* (Waco,

The way ahead for those who like McClendon seek to move beyond the stuck windows of fundamentalism and liberalism lies in moving toward a generous liberal orthodoxy as expressed in the ancient ecumenical creeds. Yet to pursue this path demands a deep and sympathetic understanding of the confessional faith that receives regulative guidance from the faith as historically confessed by the church. This decisive move enables Other Baptists to see their gathered communities not as participants in an isolated sect but as churches in historic continuity with ecclesial Christianity. By retrieving a connection in the historic Christian tradition, Other Baptists recover an account that locates their ecclesial movement within the wider ecumenical communion of the one, holy, catholic, and apostolic church. Embracing a generous liberal orthodoxy grounded in the ancient ecumenical creeds of the church offers the gift of a discerning belief that enables them to understand Scripture as the unfolding narrative of the triune God. Confessional faith, regulative guidance, ecclesial Christianity, ecumenical communion, and discerning belief—these are signs of contesting catholicity.

Confessional Faith

John Clifford delivered his presidential address on April 20, 1888, to a distressed assembly of the Baptist Union of Great Britain. Two unsigned pieces had appeared the previous spring in the *Sword and Trowel*, published by Charles Spurgeon. The anonymous author charged that the Union was on a precipitous "Down Grade." Although Spurgeon did not actually write the articles, he gave his unqualified support to the view that the Baptists had begun to slide down the slippery slope toward "a new religion . . . which is no more Christianity than chalk is cheese." He warned that the atoning work of Christ, the inspiration of the Scriptures, the power of the Spirit, the reality of hell, and the resurrection of the dead were under attack by "enemies of the faith" who expect to be counted among the brethren.[5] Spurgeon claimed that even the deity of Christ was

---

Tex.: Baylor University Press, 2012), 59–60; Stewart A. Newman, *W. T. Conner: Theologian of the Southwest* (Nashville: Broadman, 1964), 98–103; James Leo Garrett, Jr., "Walter Thomas Conner," in *Baptist Theologians*, ed. Timothy George and David S. Dockery (Nashville: Broadman, 1990), 424–25; and my article "The 'Coming of Age' of Baptist Theology in Generation Twenty-Something," in "Festschrift for James Wm. McClendon Jr.," special issue, *Perspectives in Religious Studies* 27, no. 1 (2000): 21–38. Conner dedicated his *Christian Doctrine* (Nashville: Broadman, 1937) in memory of Calvin Goodspeed, A. H. Strong, and E. Y. Mullins, whom he called "my three teachers of theology." Marney and Conner were friends, and in fact they were sharing a meal together when Conner suffered the stroke that cut short his teaching career.

[5] C. H. Spurgeon, "Another Word concerning the Down-Grade," *Sword and Trowel*, August 1887.

being called into question, as several ministers had crossed over into unitarianism. He concluded that, where there was no real communion, there should not be a pretense of fellowship, because "fellowship with known and vital error is participation in sin." He asserted that "those who know and love the truth of God" could not "have fellowship with that which is diametrically opposed thereto" and that there was "no reason why they should pretend that they have such fellowship."[6]

Spurgeon was clearly alarmed by the growing acceptance of evolutionary biology and biblical criticism in the wider culture as well as the increasing influence of unitarian and universalist theology among Protestant clergy. His principle concern, however, was the loosening of doctrinal commitments in the Baptist Union. Spurgeon steadfastly refused to identify any unsound ministers, explaining that the Union "has no doctrinal basis whatever" and seems willing to allow "every form of belief and misbelief . . . so long as immersion only is acknowledged as baptism."[7] Their earlier stated agreement with "the sentiments usually denominated evangelical," he argued, no longer held, since the phrase was dropped from the 1873 Declaration of Principle. And even though Spurgeon soon withdrew from the Union, the controversy continued unabated.[8] It is important to note that both Spurgeon and Clifford saw a need for creed, though they conceived of it differently. For Spurgeon the need was to delineate the boundaries, whereas for Clifford the need was more to name the center.

Clifford's address to the assembly came in the morning before the afternoon session that would consider the new and more evangelically inclined declaration drafted by Joseph Angus, the principal of Regent's Park College, with editorial contributions by Spurgeon's own brother, James. Clifford began by reassuring his colleagues that "even strife is a sign of vitality—uncomfortable, irritating vitality, perhaps; . . . but still it is vitality." Yet he wanted the Union to move beyond this uncomfortable and irritating liberal versus conservative vitality toward a deeper

---

[6] C. H. Spurgeon, "A Fragment upon the Down Grade Controversy," *Sword and Trowel*, November 1887. The anonymous articles were written by Robert Shindler, a close associate of Spurgeon. Shindler produced a pamphlet entitled *Creed or No Creed?* that was distributed at the time of the March meeting of the Union. See C. H. Spurgeon, *The Down Grade Controversy*, ed. Bob Ross (Pasadena, Tex.: Pilgrim, 1978).

[7] Spurgeon, "Fragment upon the Down Grade Controversy."

[8] Ernest A. Payne, *The Baptist Union: A Short History* (London: Carey Kingsgate Press, 1959), 127–43. John H. Y. Briggs identifies three liberal Baptist ministers who were most immediately in Spurgeon's thoughts about the Down Grade: W. E. Blomfield, J. G. Greenhough, and James Thew. Briggs, *The English Baptists of the Nineteenth Century* (Didcot, U.K.: Baptist Historical Society, 1994), 181–88.

confessional unity. Knowing that widespread suspicion of creeds and confessions when used as tests of fellowship stood in the way of approving
new principles, Clifford turned their attention to primitive Christian faith
during the apostolic era. He asked, "What was the Christianity of Jesus
Christ, the Christianity of the Great Forty Years?"

The heart of apostolic faith, he answered, lives in the confession of
three primitive creeds. The first and "primordial germ" of all Christian
creeds is the confession of the Apostle Peter, "Thou art the Christ, the Son
of the living God." As the Lord Jesus explained to Peter, this creed is not
of human origin but a gift of divine inspiration. Thus Clifford urged them
to "get that creed as Peter got it," so that they might know the blessing of
God. Beyond the Petrine confession is the Johannine creed, uttered from
the lips of the Apostle Thomas: "My Lord and my God." The confession
of Thomas is more concise than that of Peter. Yet, Clifford continued that
this creed is "not an echo, but a voice; not a recitation, but a conviction;
not an act of memory, but the articulate breath of a living soul." The third
creed comes from the Apostle Paul: "That if thou shalt confess with thy
mouth the Lord Jesus, and shalt believe in thine heart that God hath raised
Him from the dead, thou shalt be saved." In the words of these three
apostolic witnesses—Peter, John, and Paul—the substance of primitive
Christian faith given once and for all was, Clifford argued, "indisputably
established." And these three creeds provide the pattern for all subsequent
confessions of faith.[9]

It was an eloquent and ebullient statement, and by all accounts a passionately and persuasively delivered one. And after such an overwhelmingly
positive reception, it was no surprise that the "Declaratory Statement"
was adopted with only minor opposition. Following the thesis of Clifford's address, the new principles declared the Union to be "an association
of churches and ministers, professing not only to believe the facts and doctrines of the Gospel, but to have undergone the spiritual change expressed
or implied in them." Contemporary scholarship would no doubt be somewhat less sanguine than Clifford about rigorous historicism establishing
the "historical, verifiable, undeniable" facts of the Gospel. Yet his address
gave voice to the historic Baptist conviction that the ties that bind loving
hearts and kindred minds are held together in personal faith. As the new
declaration affirmed, genuine confession of faith presupposes a "spiritual
change . . . and this change is the fundamental principle of our church

[9] John Clifford, "The Great Forty Years," in *A Baptist Treasury*, ed. Sydnor L. Stealey (New York: Thomas Y. Crowell, 1958), 98–113.

life."[10] Early Baptists and other radical Puritans often thought about this change in terms of what they called "the experience of grace," and "experienced Christians" were those who offered confessions to declare their faith after the fashion of Peter, John, and Paul.[11] They were firm that reciting a creed is no substitute for a personal confession of faith.[12] The proto-Baptist John Robinson (1575/76?–1625) expressed this conviction when he argued that, just as the church was built upon the rock of Peter's confession, even so the church continues to be built stone by stone with believers who like Peter confess their faith in Jesus as the Christ.[13] Robinson's onetime colleague and Baptist founder, John Smyth, argued similarly that apostolicity is evidenced in the sign of a believers church.[14]

This historic Baptist insistence on a personal faith may not be as far as some may think from the ancient ecumenical creeds, which begin with

[10] "Declaratory Statement, Adopted by the Baptist Union Assembly, 23rd April 1888," appendix 6, in Payne, *Baptist Union*, 271.

[11] In Puritan theology, "experience" is a technical term that denotes a constellation of convictions and affections between the awakening to sin and the conversion of the sinner through effective grace. See The Westminster Confession of Faith X, in *Creeds of the Churches*, ed. John H. Leith (Garden City, N.Y.: Doubleday, 1963), 206. Christian experience so understood is *theocentric* and *theological* and should not be mistaken for or confused with *anthropocentric* and *psychological* notions of experience associated with evangelical revivalism, Protestant liberalism, or psychological theories. Vavasor Powell, the Welsh Dissenter and Baptist preacher, wrote, in the preface to the immensely popular collection of conversion narratives that presented the experience of the forty-two Christians, that each experience was "a Copy written by the Spirit of God upon the hearts of beleevers." Powell, *Spirituall Experiences, of Sundry Beleevers* (London: Robert Ibbitson, 1653). Two other examples of early Baptist conversion narratives that describe conversion in terms of experience are Jane Turner, *Choice Experiences of the Kind Dealings of God* (1653); and Katherine Sutton, *A Christian Womans Experiences of the Glorious Working of Gods Free Grace* (1663), in *A Company of Women Preachers: Baptist Prophetesses in Seventeenth-Century England*, ed. Curtis W. Freeman (Waco, Tex.: Baylor University Press, 2011), 305–68 and 587–646.

[12] Walter Rauschenbusch appealed to this early Baptist conviction, though recasting it in later evangelical and psychological language, when he wrote:

> The Christian faith as Baptists hold it, sets spiritual experience boldly to the front as the one great thing in religion. It aims at experimental religion. . . . We ask a man: "Have you put your faith in Christ? Have you submitted your will to His will? Have you received the inward assurance that your sins are forgiven and that you are at peace with God? Have you made experience of experience of God?" If anyone desires to enter our churches we ask for evidence of such experience and we ask for nothing else. We do not ask him to recite a creed or catechism. . . . When we insist on experience, and not on ritual or creed, we place religion where it is necessarily free, and then, if it is freely given, it has value in Gods' sight.

Rauschenbusch, "Why I Am a Baptist," *Rochester Baptist Monthly* (November 1905), reprinted in *Colgate Rochester Divinity School Bulletin* (1938): 5.

[13] Robinson, *A Justification of Separation From the Church of England*, in *The Works of John Robinson: Pastor of the Pilgrim Fathers*, ed. Robert Ashton (London: John Snow, 1851), 2:157–58.

[14] Smyth, "A Lettre to the brethren in S." [1606?], in *The Works of John Smyth*, ed. W. T. Whitley (Cambridge: Cambridge University Press, 1915), 2:558.

the Greek or Latin words *pisteuomen* or *credo*, "we believe" or "I believe." Understanding the ancient ecumenical creeds as personal statements of faith is hampered by the fact that there is no English equivalent (viz., "to faith") that translates the Greek verb *pisteuein* in the Nicene Creed. Consequently, the rendering "believe" can be taken, though wrongly, to suggest that this believing is merely a matter of mental assent. But the declaration with the creed "I believe" may be offered as a personal, and indeed a collective, act of faith. Moreover, the act of believing is closely connected with the act of confessing the faith that is believed. Creeds and confessions "have their origin in a two-fold Christian imperative, to believe and to confess what one believes."[15] This double imperative dates back at least as far as the Apostle Paul, who declared, "If you *confess* [*homologēsēs*] with your lips that Jesus is Lord and *believe* [*pisteusēs*] in your heart that God raised him from the dead, you will be saved" (Rom 10:9). To put the matter in slightly more technical language, some Baptists (and other evangelicals) have tended to emphasize the *fides qua creditur* (the "faith by which it is believed"—i.e., personal faith or trusting obedience) more than the *fides quae creditur* ("the faith that is believed"—i.e., faith as knowledge of truth revealed in Christ).[16] Yet both *fides qua* and *fides quae* are necessary, and together they maintain the necessary tension between the essential convictions of liberty of conscience and fidelity to the gospel. Insufficient attention to both dimensions can easily result in an *attenuated liberality* or an *arcane orthodoxy*, but when held together in balance they open the way for a *generous liberal orthodoxy*.

The Baptist Union in its Declaration of Principles gestured in this dual direction. After stressing the necessity of a "spiritual change" (*fides qua creditur*), they enumerated six gospel doctrines (*fides quae creditur*) that included the inspiration and authority of the Scriptures, the sinful state of humanity, the deity of Christ, justification by faith, the work of the Holy Spirit, and the resurrection and final judgment.[17] But they did not appeal to the ancient ecumenical creeds. Indeed, that the Baptist Union held reservations about the confession of creeds became evident at the October 1889 meeting that considered a letter from the archbishop of Canterbury

---

[15] Jaroslav Pelikan, *Credo: Historical and Theological Guide to Creeds and Confessions of Faith in the Christian Tradition* (New Haven, Conn.: Yale University Press, 2003), 35.

[16] Karl Rahner, ed., *Encyclopedia of Theology: The Concise Sacramentum Mundi* (New York: Seabury, 1975), s.v. "Faith," 500.

[17] "Declaratory Statement," in Payne, *Baptist Union*, 271. As Payne notes, the Trinity was curiously omitted from the six doctrines, unlike the initial 1813 constitution of the Union, which began its list with the doctrine of "three equal persons in the Godhead." Payne, *Baptist Union*, 140 and 24.

inviting a Baptist response to the Lambeth Quadrilateral on steps toward reunion.[18] The second condition named acceptance of the Apostles' Creed as a baptismal symbol and the Nicene Creed as a statement of faith.[19] The Baptists resisted, indicating the susceptibility of the creeds to a variety of interpretations. Their objection to confession of the historic creeds was a niggling criticism, especially compared with the fourth, which specified the recognition of the historic episcopate, which the Church of England claimed but the Baptists rejected outright. The Baptists also noted that basic teachings on personal and nonsacerdotal religion, profession of faith, and separation of church and state were missing from the conditions. Nevertheless, the creeds were at least part of what stood in the way of the Baptists moving forward in ecumenical conversations with the Anglicans. Not surprisingly, when the secretary of the Union read the letter in its entirety to the assembly, explaining why they must decline, he "was greeted with uproarious cheers."[20]

Some Baptists have held out even stronger reservations. For example, W. B. Johnson, the first president of the Southern Baptist Convention, when speaking at the inaugural gathering in Augusta, Georgia, declared, "We have constructed for our basis no new creed, acting in this manner upon a Baptist aversion for all creeds but the Bible."[21] Johnson was

---

[18] The text of the Lambreth Quadrilateral reads:
A. The Holy Scriptures of the Old and New Testaments, as 'containing all things necessary for salvation,' and as being the rule and ultimate standard of faith. B. The Apostles' Creed, as the Baptismal Symbol; and the Nicene Creed, as the sufficient statements of the Christian Faith. C. The two Sacraments ordained by Christ Himself—Baptism and the Supper of the Lord—ministered with unfailing use of Christ's Words of Institution, and of the elements ordained by Him. D. The Historic Episcopate, locally adapted in the methods of its administration to the varying needs of the nations and peoples called of God into the Unity of His Church."
E. A. Livingstone, ed., *The Oxford Dictionary of the Christian Church*, 3rd ed. (Oxford: Oxford University Press, 1997), s.v. "Lambeth Quadrilateral," 946.

[19] The liturgical context of the Apostles' Creed as a baptismal confession may be traced to the second century, as is indicated by the baptismal creed of Hippolytus. *The Apostolic Tradition of St. Hippolytus*, 2nd ed., ed. Gregory Dix and Henry Chadwick (London: Alban, 1992), xxi.12–18, 36–37. See also J. N. D. Kelly, *Early Christian Creeds*, 3rd ed. (New York: Longman, 1972), 113–19. Kelly describes how, from the time of the sixth century on, the Nicene Creed came to be almost universally used in both East and West as a eucharistic confession of faith (348–57).

[20] "Letter on Reunion, Accepted at the Autumn Session of the Baptists Union, 1889, as a Reply to a Letter from the Archbishop of Canterbury," appendix 7, in Payne, *Baptist Union*, 272–73 and 145.

[21] *Proceedings of the Southern Baptist Convention* (Richmond, Va.: H. K. Ellyson, 1845), 19. When the SBC in 1925 adopted the Memphis Articles on the Baptist Faith and Message, the committee added caveat "that the sole authority for faith and practice among Baptists is the Scriptures of the Old and New Testaments. Confessions are only guides in interpretation, having no authority over the conscience."

not the first, nor was he the last, to invoke the motto "no creed but the Bible." Walter Rauschenbusch famously argued in a series of 1905–1906 essays that "Baptists are not chained by creeds," because they hold that "the Bible alone is sufficient authority for our faith and practice."[22] During the modernist-fundamentalist controversy, New York pastor Cornelius Woelfkin successfully persuaded the Northern Baptist Convention in 1922 not to adopt a confession of faith but instead to affirm "that the New Testament is the all-sufficient ground of . . . faith and practice."[23] In 1979, when many Southern Baptists were calling for confessional fidelity, John J. Hurt, longtime Baptist state paper editor of the *Christian Index* and the *Baptist Standard*, declared that the "Southern Baptist Convention has no more need for a creed than it has for a pope." He then added, "It won't get the former without the latter and either will destroy it."[24] Jimmy Allen, former president of the SBC, decried a "creeping creedalism" in Baptist life on the basis that "the thing that distinguishes us as Baptists is that the Bible itself is our creed."[25] And Walter Shurden placed at the top of the list of most dangerous threats in contemporary Baptist life a movement "from a Christ-centered to a creed-centered faith."[26]

One of the most notable Baptists to renounce creeds was Harry Emerson Fosdick, who attributed his creedal-averse faith to his upbringing in a Baptist family of solid convictions. Fosdick boasted that he never subscribed to or repeated any creed. Reporting on a 1922 visit to Japan, he said, "I stood up . . . while the whole company shouted the creed and never opened my lips, such being my habit." Though never surrendering his Baptist convictions or ordination, Fosdick served as the pastor of the First Presbyterian Church of New York City. After his controversial sermon "Shall the Fundamentalists Win?" the Presbytery of New York called for him to submit to the doctrinal standards of the Presbyterian

---

[22] Rauschenbusch, "Why I Am a Baptist," 22.

[23] *Annual of the Northern Baptist Convention* (Philadelphia: American Baptist Publication Society, 1922), 133.

[24] John J. Hurt, "Should Southern Baptists Have a Creed/Confession?—No!" *Review and Expositor* 76, no. 1 (1979): 85. Joe T. Odle, in a companion article answered "Yes!" to the same question. Odle, "Should Southern Baptists Have a Creed/Confession?—Yes!" *Review and Expositor* 76, no. 1 (1979): 89–94. In the same issue, Walter Shurden invoked Johnson's "No Creed but the Bible!" against what he argued was the reversal of Johnson's anticreedalism. Shurden, "Southern Baptist Responses to Their Confessional Statements," *Review and Expositor* 76, no. 1 (1979): 69–84.

[25] Jimmy R. Allen, "The Takeover Resurgence Is Creedalism," *Texas Baptists Committed*, August 2004, 14.

[26] Walter B. Shurden, "The Coalition for Baptist Principles," *Baptist Studies Bulletin* 6, no. 6 (2007), accessed August 26, 2009, http://www.centerforbaptiststudies.org/bulletin/2007/june.htm.

Church, which included adherence to the creeds. Fosdick replied that the "creedal subscriptions to ancient confessions of faith is a practice dangerous to the welfare of the church and to the integrity of the individual conscience." He let them know that for him to subscribe to any creed "would be a violation of conscience."[27] In his 1924 Beecher Lectures, Fosdick averred, "This is the nemesis of all creedalism: the creeds are promulgated to protect faith, and then, their forms of thinking being at last overpassed, insistence on them becomes the ruination of faith."[28]

The suspicion of creeds among Baptists and other Free Church Christians is understandable given efforts by established churches to impose uniformity of faith and practice on their sixteenth- and seventeenth-century forebears or, more recently, the coercive and authoritarian practices of modern fundamentalism. To counterbalance attempts at binding their consciences by forced subscription to creeds, they mounted a fierce defense through the doctrine of religious liberty. However, as subsequent generations assumed a posture of protest and dissent, sometimes creeds, not coercion, were mistakenly identified as the object of protest, as credophobia sometimes morphed into credomachia, which opposes all creeds in principle as a threat to the free confession of faith. Edward Wightman (d. 1612), an early Baptist and the last heretic burned in England, defended what he believed to be the true faith against the false doctrine of the Nicolaitans, which he contended was enshrined in the ancient ecumenical creeds of the church.[29] Though he denied the Trinity and the incarnation, Wightman believed he was not simply refuting the doctrines of the Church of England but was setting straight the Christian faith in what he contended had been a sixteen-hundred-year heretical declension from apostolic Christianity.

[27] Harry Emerson Fosdick, *The Modern Uses of the Bible* (New York: Macmillan, 1924), 262; Robert Moats Miller, *Harry Emerson Fosdick: Preacher, Pastor, Prophet* (New York: Oxford University Press, 1985), 107–18; and Fosdick, *The Living of These Days: An Autobiography* (New York: Harper & Brothers, 1956), 172.

[28] Fosdick, *Modern Uses of the Bible*, 262. Fosdick conceded that noncreedal churches unfortunately do not "have a better understanding of what [the creeds] really meant to say." And he added that when he hears "some fresh and flippant modern mind condescending to them, treating the fathers who wrote them as quibblers and fools, I am strongly tempted to bear a hand in their defense." Yet for Fosdick, "what they really meant to say" came down to abiding experience in changing categories (97–130).

[29] James I, "A Narration of the Burning of Edward Wightman," in *A True Relation of the Commissions and Warrants for the Condemnation and Burning of Bartholomew Legatt and Thomas Withman* [*sic*] (London: Michael Spark, 1651), 7–13; Champlin Burrage, *The Early English Dissenters in Light of Recent Research* (Cambridge: Cambridge University Press, 1912), 1:216–20; and Ian Atherton and David Como, "The Burning of Edward Wightman: Puritanism, Prelacy, and the Politics of Heresy in Early Modern England," *English Historical Review* 120, no. 489 (2005): 1215–50.

The aversion for all creeds but the Bible, however, is far from a consensus view among Baptists, for not all have thought so negatively. The nineteenth-century American Baptist pastor and professor Hezekiah Harvey warned prospective ministers in his lectures at Hamilton Theological Seminary against reactionary anticreedalism, suggesting that "the want of a definite creed, in almost all instances, results in an actual departure from the gospel."[30] Andrew Fuller, the guiding voice in the evangelical theological renewal among eighteenth-century English Particular Baptists, noted that the aversion to creeds as an offense against Christian liberty and the rights of conscience is a common theme among some Baptists. Yet, as he pointed out, even those who protest against creeds have a creed of their own, for the person "who has no creed has no belief." The objection to creeds, Fuller continued, "does not lie so much against our having creeds or systems as against our imposing them on others as the condition of Christian fellowship." Moreover, he argued that "if a Christian society have no right to judge what is truth, and to render an agreement with them in certain points a term of communion, then neither have they a right to judge what is righteousness, nor to render an agreement in matters of practical right and wrong a term of communion." Fuller therefore concluded that the objection against subscription to a creed and articles of faith is "trite and frivolous."[31]

Writing to a friend who was more inclined to the view of Spurgeon, John Clifford reflected on the use of creeds:

> I have stated my mind again and again. I do not object to creeds as statements of belief (*credo*). I gave one when I joined the Church; repeated it or something like it when I entered College, restated it when I became a pastor, and have printed one, over and over again, in various books, Church reports, &c. It is not creeds as creeds; it is coercion through and by creeds I object to.[32]

Even embattled Southern Baptist leader E. Y. Mullins, who was understandably cautious about the potential dangers of authoritarianism, maintained that "when used properly" creeds are "the natural and normal

---

[30] Hezekiah Harvey, *The Church: Its Polity and Ordinances* (Philadelphia: American Baptist Publication Society, 1879), 37.

[31] Andrew Fuller, "Creeds and Subscriptions," in *The Complete Works of the Rev. Andrew Fuller* (Harrisonburg, Va.: Sprinkle Publications, 1988 [reprinted from the 3rd London ed. with additions by Joseph Belcher, Philadelphia: American Baptist Publication Society, 1845]), 3:449–50.

[32] Charles T. Bateman, *John Clifford: Free Church Leader and Preacher* (London: National Council of the Evangelical Free Churches, 1904), 148.

expression of the religious life."[33] It seems warranted, then, that concerns about *fidelity to the gospel* are properly guided by regard for *liberty in Christ*. Both are necessary and complementary. Yet each carries potential mistakes and problems. Creeds are misused when they become instruments of coercion, just as religious liberty is abused when it is invoked to legitimate deviation from the living witness of apostolic faith. It might be asked how creeds then can be employed by Baptists and other Free Church Christians so as to balance the convictions of faithfulness and freedom.

One of the most striking examples of the "natural and normal" use of creeds occurred on July 12, 1905, when the Baptist World Alliance met at Exeter Hall in London for its first congress. Its president, Alexander Maclaren, addressed the session and urged that the new body declare before the world where they stand "in the continuity of the historic Church." He exhorted the congress to make its very first act an "audible and unanimous acknowledgment of [the] Faith." Such a step, he said, would clear away misunderstanding and put an end to slander. He then invited his fellow participants to rise to their feet and confess the Apostles' Creed, "not as a piece of coercion or discipline, but as a simple acknowledgment of where we stand and what we believe." The report states that the whole gathering instantly rose and repeated the whole creed slowly and deliberately with Maclaren. Reflecting on the event, editor of the *Baptist Times and Freeman* and secretary of the congress John Howard Shakespeare noted that there had never been an act of such inspiration or a moment so historic among the Baptists.[34] As a simple acknowledgment of where they stood and what they believed, the opening assembly of the centenary meeting of the congress on July 27, 2005, recalled Maclaren's appeal and repeated the creed together. Such expressions of generous orthodoxy are worthy of emulation by other free and faithful Baptists. And perhaps confessing the creed more often than once every century might be a good practice to consider.[35]

---

[33] E. Y. Mullins, *Baptist Beliefs* (Philadelphia: Judson Press, 1925), 6.

[34] *the Baptist World Congress*, London, July 11–19, 1905 (London: Baptist Union, 1905), 19–20 and vii.

[35] Curtis W. Freeman, Steven Harmon, Elizabeth Newman, and Philip Thompson, "Confessing the Faith," *Biblical Recorder*, July 8, 2004. Several news stories were published on the statement, including Steve DeVane, "Educators Support BWA Recitation of Creed," *Biblical Recorder*, July 17, 2004; Russell Moore, "The Moderates Were Right," *Baptist Press News*, July 7, 2004; and Bob Allen, "Proposal Sparks Debate over Baptists and Creeds," *Ethics Daily*, July 16, 2004. The news story written by DeVane went over the Associated Baptist Press wire service and was picked up by the *Baptist Standard* (Texas), the *Religious Herald* (Virginia), the *Western Recorder* (Kentucky), and *Baptists Today* (Independent). Letter to Keith Jones and BWA Resolutions Committee, June 23, 2004. E. Glenn Hinson recommends that Baptists might appropriate the creed as an instrument for carrying out the evangelical commission of the

Regulative Guidance

In 1679 a group of English General Baptists published a confession of faith entitled the Orthodox Creed. It recommended that the Nicene, Athanasian, and Apostles' Creeds "ought [thoroughly] to be received, and believed . . . to prevent heresy in doctrine, and practice."[36] The text of all three creeds was included in the confession. Concern about maintaining a connection to historic orthodoxy was amplified by the spread of a "new Eutychian" theology among the General Baptists that, like the Eutychianism of old, denied the full humanity of Christ in the incarnation.[37] By appealing to the ancient ecumenical creeds of the fourth century, the General Baptists recognized their regulative function in delineating true from false teaching. The regulative function of the creeds has long been recognized as transmitting continuity with the apostolic tradition through creedal-like fragments, baptismal confessions, catechetical formulae, and abbreviated doctrinal summaries (also known as the rule of faith).[38] These varieties of succinct statements were received not as a set of later standards imposed on the Bible but as the preservation of the basic teachings of Scripture of the primitive communities in which the Scriptures were first heard. The regulative aspect of the creeds, to be sure, ruled out heterodox notions that arose, but more importantly they ruled in orthodox ones. Yet how and what the creeds *ruled in* has often been minimized or overlooked, particularly by the Free Church tradition, as attention has more often than not been focused on how and what the creeds *ruled out*.

For example, John Howard Yoder famously suggested that the use of the creeds is mostly negative. He openly wondered whether they do Free Churches much good.[39] Though Yoder affirmed with the creeds the normativity of God's revelation in Jesus, he relativized their theological importance. Summarizing his position, Yoder declaimed that "the Creeds are helpful as fences, but affirming, believing, debating for, fighting for

---

church in his "The Nicene Creed Viewed from the Standpoint of the Evangelization of the Roman Empire," in *Faith to Creed: Ecumenical Perspectives on the Affirmation of the Apostolic Faith in the Fourth Century*, ed. S. Mark Heim (Grand Rapids: Eerdmans, 1991), 117–28.

[36] The Orthodox Creed XXXVIII, in William L. Lumpkin, ed., *Baptist Confessions of Faith*, rev. ed. (Valley Forge, Pa.: Judson Press, 1969), 326.

[37] Thomas Monck, *A Cure for the Cankering Error of the New Eutychians* (London, 1673). Eutyches was the arch-heretic of Constantinople who was condemned at the council of Chalcedon in 451. The new Eutychianism among the seventeenth-century General Baptists will be discussed in detail in the next chapter.

[38] D. H. Williams, *Retrieving the Tradition and Renewing Evangelicalism: A Primer for Suspicious Protestants* (Grand Rapids: Eerdmans, 1999), 71–99.

[39] John Howard Yoder, preface to *Theology: Christology and Theological Method* (Grand Rapids: Brazos, 2002), 204.

the Creeds, is probably something which a radical Anabaptist kind of faith would not concentrate on doing." Yet he found even less reason to join cause with the credomachian liberals. Despite the "dirty politics" behind the creeds, Yoder argued, the creeds tell the story of how "God has chosen to lead his confused people toward perhaps at least a degree of understanding of certain dangers, certain things not to say if we are to remain faithful."[40]

But the exclusive function of the creeds on which Yoder focuses is secondary and misses their more primary inclusive purpose.[41] The exclusive function operates with the assumption that the creeds primarily delineate a *bounded set* with the aim of keeping some people and their ideas out. Understood in terms of their inclusive purpose, the creeds do not offer exhaustive statements of the faith but rather denote a *centered set* that names the nexus of the common life in Christ and seeks to draw those who confess their articles ever toward the communion envisioned therein. To suggest that the first use of the creeds is about orienting faith and practice toward the trinitarian and christological center is different than conceiving them as an *open set* with neither center nor circumference. But a centered approach urges that boundary making need not be the first step. The boundary-making approach of bounded set (or "critical orthodoxy") imagines the line between orthodoxy and heresy as defined by the circumference of a circle.[42] Yet such an approach may not be the most helpful image. A centered-set perspective views the creeds primarily as a rich resource for delineating the vectors that move toward the center rather than a tool for circumscribing the boundaries. This inclusive orientation

[40] Yoder, preface to *Theology*, 223. J. Denny Weaver extends Yoder's argument by further emphasizing the politics of creedal formation that, he argues, served to undergird the stability of the empire. Weaver, "Nicea, Womanist Theology, and Anabaptist Particularity," in *Anabaptists & Postmodernity*, ed. Susan Biesecker-Mast and Gerald Biesecker-Mast (Telford, Pa.: Pandora, 2000), 251–59. A. James Reimer argues against Yoder and Weaver that theological orthodoxy and constantinianism are not intrinsically linked and that in particular the notion of a Constantinian "fall" is historically and theologically problematic in "Theological Orthodoxy, Constantinianism, and Theology from a Radical Protestant Perspective," in *Faith to Creed: Ecumenical Perspectives on the Affirmation of the Apostolic Faith in the Fourth Century*, ed. S. Mark Heim (Grand Rapids: Eerdmans, 1991), 129–61. Alain Epp Weaver problematizes the argument by suggesting that Yoder developed a two-pronged strategy that on the one hand appealed to the creeds in ecumenical conversations but on the other relativized their importance for theology in "Missionary Christology: John Howard Yoder and the Creeds," *Mennonite Quarterly Review* 74, no. 3 (2000): 423–39.

[41] Thomas N. Finger, "The Way to Nicea: Some Reflections from a Mennonite Perspective," *Journal of Ecumenical Studies* 24, no. 2 (1987): 229.

[42] The phrase a "critical orthodoxy" depicted as a circle with a center and a circumference is proposed by Thomas C. Oden, *The Rebirth of Orthodoxy: Signs of New Life in Christianity* (San Francisco: HarperSanFrancisco, 2003), 130–33.

is the basic standpoint of "generous orthodoxy."[43] Such a theology, to borrow a line from Alexander Campbell, operates within a circle of understanding in which Christ is the center and humility is its circumference.[44]

On June 19, 2008, while speaking at a Baptist gathering, John Killinger dismissed traditional Christology as passé and announced, "Now we are reevaluating and we're approaching everything with a humbler perspective and seeing God's hand working in Christ, but not necessarily as the incarnate God in our midst."[45] Killinger's penchant for controversy is well known. His book *The Changing Shape of Our Salvation* tells the story of the development of soteriology in light and breezy prose. Dismissing the outcome of the ecumenical church councils as the result of an unfortunate power struggle that just happened to be won by premodern fundamentalists, he attributes "the final decisions about belief and orthodoxy" in the patristic era to the exercise of sheer "power, politics, and popularity." Against the traditional account of the history of doctrine, he wonders whether perhaps "the Gnostics, the Montanists, the Marcionites, and other heretics" might have been ruled out "merely because they weren't as strong, clever, and numerous as those who voted another

---

[43] Some readers may wonder how the appropriation of Frei's phrase here relates to the project of Brian D. McLaren, *A Generous Orthodoxy* (Grand Rapids: Zondervan, 2004). McLaren's standpoint seems to represent less of a settled position or even a steady pilgrimage and more of a postmodern pastiche that offers fleeting glimpses of a postconservative evangelical "orthodoxy" from a variety of angles. The stance outlined in this chapter is postliberal as it was with Frei, and although there are many similarities between the two, in the end postconservatives and postliberals have divergent points of departure and a different set of assumptions. While I am a sympathetic and appreciative reader of McLaren's work, in the end his project may be more about generosity and less about orthodoxy. The intriguing convergence of postconservative and postliberal theology has been explored by Roger Olson, "Post-conservative Evangelicals Greet the Postmodern Age," *Christian Century*, May 3, 1995, 480–83; and the evangelical and postliberal authors of Timothy R. Phillips and Dennis L. Okholm, eds., *The Nature of Confession: Evangelicals and Postliberals in Conversation* (Downers Grove, Ill.: InterVarsity, 1996).

[44] Alexander Campbell, *The Christian System* (Bethany, Va.: Pittsburg, Forrester & Campbell, 1839; repr., Salem, N.H.: Ayer, 1988), 5. Given Campbell's aversion to creeds, the use of his axiom to illustrate a positive use of creeds may seem ironic. Yet the hermeneutical priority he gives to Christ and humility suggests the direction of the centered theological outlook of a generous orthodoxy.

[45] John Killinger, "The Changing Shape of Our Salvation" (breakout session at the General Assembly of the Cooperative Baptist Fellowship, Memphis, Tennessee, June 19, 2008). Press reports: David Roach, "CBF Presenter Questions Christ's Deity," *Baptist Press*, June 19, 2008, accessed September 10, 2009, http://www.baptistpress.org/bpnews.asp?id=28326; James A. Smith, "Is CBF Baptist? Christian?" *Florida Baptist Witness*, June 23, 2008, accessed September 10, 2009, http://www.gofbw.com/News.asp?id=9034; Jim White, "Dan Vestal Corrects Claim that CBF Is 'Unchristian,'" *Religious Herald*, July 10, 2008, accessed September 10, 2009, http://www.abpnews.com/~abpnews/extras/rh-archive/item/23242-danvestalcorrectsclaimthatfellowshipis%E2%80%98unchristian%E2%80%99#.U2L2exCCUTI.

way." The acceptance of the Nicene doctrine of the deity of Christ, by his account, was simply the whim of a majority vote.[46] Killinger asserts his view with utter confidence, almost as if he were an oracle of the zeitgeist, even though his positions are grounded neither in solid research nor widely representative of the scholarly guilds.[47] That he would question the incarnation without thoughtful reflection, then, should not be surprising. No doubt the ferocious response to Killinger's remarks by some Baptists was due in part to the assertive voice of liberty. There are few things more likely to get under the skin of Free Church Christians than someone claiming to speak for them. If he had simply said, "*I* am reevaluating and *I* am approaching everything with a humbler perspective," many observers would have happily given him the benefit of his viewpoint, even if they disagreed, but his use of the plural "we" left many observers wondering who was being included in the group that shared his revisionist Christology.

The fact that Killinger, like many other liberals, does not acknowledge the creed as naming the trinitarian and christological center indicates one of the most serious challenges that a centered approach faces. Killinger's revisionism seems to have neither center nor circumference. He consequently offers no serious engagement with the historic stream

---

[46] John Killinger, *The Changing Shape of Our Salvation* (New York: Crossroad, 2007), 71–73.

[47] Killinger offers no theoretical framework for his account of doctrinal development. He does not follow the familiar liberal Protestant historicism of Adolf von Harnack, who proposed that "dogma in its conception and development is a work of the Greek spirit on the soil of the Gospel" and who encouraged the retrieval of the gospel kernel from Hellenistic husk. Harnack, *History of Dogma*, trans. Neil Buchanan (New York: Dover, 1961), 1:17; and Harnack, *What Is Christianity?* trans Thomas Bailey Saunders (New York: Harper & Row), 12–18. Nor does he accept the nuanced Catholic thesis of John Henry Cardinal Newman, which conceived of catholic orthodoxy as "the legitimate growth and complement, that is, the natural and necessary development, of the doctrine of the early church." Newman, *An Essay on the Development of Christian Doctrine*, 6th ed. (Notre Dame, Ind.: University of Notre Dame Press, 1989), 169. Instead Killinger assumes a political theory of doctrine in which orthodoxy and heresy are arbitrary conventions based on the result of winners and losers in theological conflict. His thin description could have been strengthened by a more nuanced reading of the history, such as R. P. C. Hanson's revisionist account of Arianism in his massive study, *The Search for the Christian Doctrine of God* (Edinburgh: T&T Clark, 1988); or even the shorter version, Hanson, "The Achievement of Orthodoxy in the Fourth Century AD," in *The Making of Orthodoxy*, ed. Rowan Williams (Cambridge: Cambridge University Press, 1989), 142–56. Through a dazzling treatment of the primary sources, Hanson shows the conventional account of an established orthodoxy challenged by a coherent Arian party to be inaccurate and misleading. His revisionist account displays the development of orthodoxy mixed with the misuse of power. This more complex reading of doctrinal development could have provided Killinger with facts for thoughtful refection instead of stereotypes, caricatures, and unexamined assumptions.

of orthodox Christology, which affirms of our Lord Jesus Christ, in the words of the Nicene Creed, that he was "begotten [*gennethēnta*] from the Father before all the ages" and is "consubstantial [*homooūsion*] with the Father."[48] Baptists, to be sure, have had their fair share of folks with an unbounded and uncentered theological approach who chose against the way of orthodoxy—like Matthew Caffyn, the seventeenth-century English General Baptist messenger who denied the essential divinity of Christ, or Elhanan Winchester, the eighteenth-century American Baptist pastor and evangelist who founded the first Universalist church in Philadelphia, or the unnamed Unitarians against whom Richard Furman in his 1820 "Call" exhorted his readers to unite for missions and education.[49]

George Burman Foster, a Baptist theologian at the University of Chicago Divinity School in the early twentieth century, was so wary about saying "Jesus is God" that he turned the phrase around, asserting instead that "God is like Jesus."[50] According to his pragmatic-functionalist theory of religion, Foster declared that all doctrines, including what he called the "God-idea," were inventions of human creativity that served the needs and purposes of humanity. He argued that because modern experience has no need for the Trinity or the incarnation, these traditional concepts no longer serve a useful purpose and must be laid aside. What was needed, Foster reasoned, was the creation of "a new eternal Messiah" that would be incarnate "in all human souls, born anew in every child."[51] For those who created and adopted it, the notion of a modern Messiah would function as their Ideal. Few Baptists were interested in following the approach of humanistic naturalism. Most of them were simply amazed that liberal theologians like Foster "could have written so much while believing so little."[52]

[48] The Niceno-Constantinopolitan Creed, in Jaroslav Pelikan and Valerie Hotchkiss, eds., *Creeds and Confession of Faith in the Christian Tradition* (New Haven, Conn.: Yale University Press, 2004), 1:162–63.

[49] A. C. Underwood, *A History of the English Baptists* (London: Baptist Union, 1847), 127; Elhanan Winchester, *The Universal Restoration: Exhibited in Four Dialogues Between a Minister and His Friend* (London: T. Gillet, 1792; repr., Bellows Falls, Vt.: Bill Blake, 1819), commonly called *Dialogues on the Universal Restoration*; and Richard Furman, John M. Roberts, and Joseph B. Cook, "Call for a State Convention in South Carolina . . . ," November 8, 1820, in *A Sourcebook for Baptist Heritage*, ed. H. Leon McBeth (Nashville: Broadman, 1990), 246–51.

[50] George Burman Foster, *The Finality of the Christian Religion* (Chicago: University of Chicago Press, 1906), 495.

[51] George Burman Foster, *The Function of Religion in Man's Struggle for Existence* (Chicago: University of Chicago Press, 1909), 57, 86–88, and 142–43.

[52] I have adapted this wonderful phrase, so apt of Foster's modernist theology, from Stephen Webb, review of *Heaven: The Logic of Eternal Joy*, by Jerry L. Walls, *Christian Century*, December 4–17, 2002, 42. Grant Wacker charitably attributes some of the problem to Foster's "richly allusive . . . prose style" in Wacker, *Augustus H. Strong and the Dilemma of Historical Consciousness* (Macon, Ga.: Mercer University Press, 1985), 169. But, as Gary Dorrien

Hopefully these examples are exceptions that prove the rule. For, whenever Baptists have thought deeply together about faith in Christ, they have tended to echo the language of orthodoxy. The Second London Confession (1677/1688) of English Particular Baptists affirmed that Jesus was "the Son of God, the second Person in the Holy Trinity, being very and eternal God."[53] Similarly, the Orthodox Creed (1678) of the English General Baptists declared that "the Son of God, or eternal word, is very and true God, having his personal subsistance of the father alone, and yet for ever of himself as God."[54] The Articles of Religion of the New Connexion (1770), drafted by an evangelical group of English General Baptists that emerged out of the Wesleyan revival, stated, "We believe, that our Lord Jesus Christ is God and man, united in one person . . . in a way which we pretend not to explain, but think ourselves bound by the word of God firmly to believe."[55] Any survey of the historic Baptist confessions of faith yields the conclusion that Baptists have consistently affirmed the mystery proclaimed since the days of the apostles that in Jesus Christ "all the fullness of God was pleased to dwell" (Col 1:19). This conviction is the trinitarian and christological center described in the language of Nicene orthodoxy. Yet reactionary liberals like Killinger and Foster, appealing to "the autonomy of the human soul" as their internal authority, have dismissed all confessional engagements with the trinitarian and christological center as misguided "catholicized" attempts to "out-pope the pope himself in the deification of an external authority."[56] Rather than assuming such a stereotypical caricature of orthodoxy, liberal theology stands ever in need of an ongoing conversation with the theological tradition of the creed that attends to the central conviction of the incarnation—namely, that God was in Christ.

If liberals have too seldom engaged the trinitarian and christological center of the creed, evangelicals have also failed to attend to its affirmations, and in so doing they have often embraced a diminished orthodoxy.

---

documents, Foster's theology was a "humanistic naturalism." Dorrien, *The Making of American Liberal Theology* (Louisville, Ky.: Westminster John Knox, 2003), 2:178. Yet a recent article in a Baptist journal suggests that the problem may be deeper than some care to admit, when it asks, whether the ABC-USA ecclesiology would declare Arius a heretic. The author answers no and then goes on to say that most likely both Athanasius and Arius would be welcomed into the fellowship on the hallowed principle of diversity. George Hancock-Stefan, "Would the ABC-USA Ecclesiology Be Able (Willing) to Declare Arius a Heretic?" *American Baptist Quarterly* 30, nos. 3–4 (2011): 217–23.

[53] The Second London Confession VIII.2, in Lumpkin, *Baptist Confessions of Faith*, 260.

[54] The Orthodox Creed IV, in Lumpkin, *Baptist Confessions of Faith*, 299.

[55] The Articles of Religion of the New Connexion (Article 3), in Lumpkin, *Baptist Confessions of Faith*, 343.

[56] Foster, *Function of Religion in Man's Struggle for Existence*, 73–75.

Few matters among evangelicals are more in need of renewal than their theology of Scripture. Many evangelical Christians are suspicious of the creeds because they think that the Bible alone is sufficient grounds for their faith. They do not seem to understand that they have a stake in the patristic tradition that unmasks the hermeneutical naïveté of readers who think that they can leapfrog from the primitive Christianity of the Bible to the contemporary situation with relative ease. Evangelicals would do well to explore the implications of the fact that the basic core of apostolic doctrine was preserved and passed on in the postapostolic era through the writings of the church fathers and that this apostolic tradition may be retrieved by carefully reading the patristic sources. Of particular importance for evangelicals is the patristic rule of faith that, although like the creed, was a more elastic summary of the basic body of apostolic doctrine. The rule functioned as a hermeneutical guide for reading Scripture, serving as more of an intrinsic précis that disclosed the central teachings of the Bible than an extrinsic standard that was arbitrarily imposed. The orthodox trinitarian and christological doctrines, to which evangelicals are committed, were not derived by the exegesis of Scripture alone but by reading the Scriptures through the lens of the rule and the creeds.[57]

Article 1 of the Baptist Faith and Message (1963) affirms that the Bible "is, and will remain to the end of the world, the true center of Christian union, and the supreme standard by which all human conduct, creeds, and religious opinions should be tried," but it also states that "the criterion by which the Bible is to be interpreted is Jesus Christ."[58] By glossing a christological hermeneutic, the confession recognized the limits of linguistic exegesis and retained a fragment of the ancient rule of faith, albeit as a very slender thread. It nevertheless preserved the conviction that the New Testament is concealed in the Old, and the Old Testament is revealed in the New, with its corresponding prospective and retrospective hermeneutical strategies.[59] It is ironic that the recent revision of the Baptist Faith and

---

[57] Williams, *Retrieving the Tradition and Renewing Evangelicalism*, 95–99.

[58] Baptist Faith and Message (1963), in Lumpkin, *Baptist Confessions of Faith*, 393. It is important to note that the 2000 revision of the Baptist Faith and Message deleted the sentence "The criterion by which the Bible is to be interpreted is Jesus Christ." Accessed September 24, 2013, http://www.sbc.net/bfm/bfm2000.asp. It was replaced by that statement that "all Scripture is a testimony to Christ, who is Himself the focus of divine revelation." The revision significantly altered the hermeneutical force of the christological reference, which functions prospectively (reading forward from the Old Testament to the New Testament) but not retrospectively (reading backward from the New Testament to the Old Testament).

[59] Augustine, *On the Spirit and the Letter* 27.15, in *The Nicene and Post-Nicene Fathers* (Grand Rapids: Eerdmans, 1971), 5:95. See also my "Figure and History: A Contemporary Reassessment of Augustine's Hermeneutic," in *Collectanea Augustiniana. Augustine: Presbyter factus sum*, ed. J. T. Lienhard, E. C. Muller, and R. J. Teske (New York: Peter Lang, 1993), 319–29.

Message by conservative evangelicals replaced the statement about Christ as "the criterion by which the Bible is to be interpreted" with the line that "all Scripture is a testimony to Christ, who is Himself the focus of divine revelation," thus removing the last remaining vestige of rule of faith from the confession. Given the current state of evangelical Bible study, which is still largely determined by the literal sense meaning and the grammatical historical method, the possible hermeneutical benefits of an evangelical *ressourcement* are enormous. Serious Bible readers will find much-needed hermeneutical guidance by returning to the ancient creeds of the church, for the creeds are not a set of doctrinal propositions requiring assent but rather brief summaries of the biblical story. And because the creeds tell the story into which each Christian enters in baptism, confessing them is a renewal of baptismal pledges. Reciting the creeds thus affirms the overarching meaning of the Bible and informs a scriptural imagination.[60]

The need for a creed in retrieving a fuller sense of the Scriptures is more acute than some may suspect or care to admit. For example, among evangelicals the doctrine of the atonement has drawn largely from the Protestant Reformers in terms of satisfaction or substitution. It might be asked how this doctrine could be enriched by a sustained conversation with the affirmation about Christ the Son in the Nicene Creed that "for us humans and for our salvation he came down from the heavens and became incarnate from the Holy Spirit and the Virgin Mary."[61] The theologians of the ancient Church recognized with this article that biblical texts like Romans 8 taught that humanity, and indeed the entire cosmos, was redeemed through the incarnation. They understood that this cosmic reversal of the law of sin and death is the result of the fullness of Christ's life, not only in the sacrifice of his death. In his classic text, *On the Incarnation of the Word*, Athanasius of Alexandria explained that Christ the Word became incarnate to restore the image of God in which humanity was made and from which all have fallen. He asked:

> What, then, was God to do? What else could he possibly do, being God, but renew His Image in [hu]mankind, so that through it [humanity] might once more come to know Him? And how could this be done save by the coming of the very Image Himself, our Saviour Jesus Christ?[62]

---

[60] Steven R. Harmon, "Do Real Baptists Recite Creeds?" *Baptists Today*, September 2004, 27.

[61] Niceno-Constantinopolitan Creed, in Pelikan and Hotchkiss, *Creeds and Confession of Faith*, 1:162–63.

[62] Athanasius, *On the Incarnation of the Word* §13 (Crestwood, N.Y.: St. Vladimir's Seminary Press, 1944), 41. This was a consistent theme for Athanasius, who elsewhere argued,

The Word by whom humanity was created must recreate humanity in one of Adam's heirs. In the incarnation, the immortal Son of God was united with human nature as the Second Adam, and thus all humanity was clothed in incorruption in the promise of the resurrection. To illustrate this divine drama of salvation, Athanasius suggested that, just as in the ancient world, when a king entered a city and lived in one of its houses, the whole city was saved from its enemies, so Christ the Son "has come into our country and dwelt in one body amidst the many, and in consequence the designs of the enemy against [hu]mankind have been foiled, and the corruption of death, which formerly held them into its power, has simply ceased to be."[63]

These patristic interpreters understood the incarnation as having reversed the powers of sin and death. As Athanasius simply stated, in the Word, God "assumed humanity that we might become God."[64] This doctrine, which was called *theosis*, did not imply a crude divinization in which the redeemed literally become gods. Rather, it taught that, just as the Son was united with humanity through the incarnation, so was humanity united with the life of the Son of God through salvation (or divinization).[65] Irenaeus of Lyons made a similar point, stating that "the Word of God, our Lord Jesus Christ, who did, through his transcendent love, become what we are, that he might bring us to be even what he is himself."[66] There are lingering questions about how these patristic understandings of salvation might be appropriated today. The underlying Platonism with its notion of universal humanity in which all were thought to participate no longer carries the persuasive power that it did in the ancient world. Protestants have likewise grown to be suspicious that the Orthodox doctrine of deification does not take seriously enough the continuing sinfulness of Christians. Still, in a sustained engagement with the patristic doctrine of the incarnation, evangelicals might not just find ways of retrieving the theology of ancient Christianity, but they might apprehend

---

"Why did the Word come among us, and become flesh?" To which he answered, "that He might redeem [hu]mankind, the Word did come among us; and that he might hallow and deify them, the Word became flesh." Athanasius, *Four Discourses against the Arians* 3.39, in *The Nicene and Post-Nicene Fathers* (Grand Rapids: Eerdmans, 1978), 4:415.

[63] Athanasius, *On the Incarnation of the Word* §§9, 35.

[64] Athanasius, *On the Incarnation of the Word* §§54, 93.

[65] Christopher A. Beeley argues that Gregory of Nazianzus was the first patristic theologian to advance a developed theory of *theosis* in Beeley, *Gregory of Nazianzus on the Trinity and the Knowledge of God: In Your Light We See Light* (New York: Oxford University Press, 2008).

[66] Irenaeus, *Against Heresies* 5.pref., in *The Ante-Nicene Fathers* (Grand Rapids: Eerdmans, 1979), 1:526.

a fuller sense of apostolic teaching that testifies to the saving significance of the entirety of Christ's life, not only his death.[67]

Evangelicals have historically defended the soteriological theology of satisfaction and penal substitution against moral and exemplary theories put forth by liberals.[68] More recently the evangelical theology of vicarious substitutionary atonement has been under assault by liberation theologians and those who have adapted the scapegoat theory, both of which object to the victimization of Jesus and the notion of divine retribution that seems to underwrite and perpetuate violence.[69] But some of the harshest criticisms of penal substitution have come from within the ranks of evangelicals. Some Baptists have gone so far as to characterize penal substitution as "cosmic child abuse," which they believe stands in contradiction with the statement "God is love."[70] This runaway sound bite ignited a firestorm among evangelicals, with some critics dismissing it as "silly" and some describing it as "blasphemy."[71] Other evangelicals have offered a more constructive and nuanced defense of penal substitution for contemporary Christians that appropriates a wide range of images and metaphors of atonement in the Bible.[72] Such an approach deals responsibly with the

---

[67] It may be of interest to note that in his introduction to the 1953 edition of *On the Incarnation*, C. S. Lewis describes it as "a masterpiece." Athanasius, *On the Incarnation of the Word*, 9. Lewis drew extensively from the dramatic *Christus Victor* theology of Athanasius and the other patristic writers when he wrote his allegory *The Lion, the Witch and the Wardrobe* (New York: Macmillan, 1950).

[68] Augustus Hopkins Strong, *Systematic Theology*, 8th ed. (Philadelphia: Judson Press, 1909), 3:713–75.

[69] Among Baptist (and baptistic) theologians who have offered thoughtful reflections on the atonement from the standpoints of liberation theology, scapegoat theory, and nonviolence are James H. Evans, *We Shall All Be Changed: Social Problems and Theological Renewal* (Minneapolis: Fortress, 1997), 45–66; S. Mark Heim, *Saved from Sacrifice: A Theology of the Cross* (Grand Rapids: Eerdmans, 2006); and J. Denny Weaver, *The Nonviolent Atonement* (Grand Rapids: Eerdmans, 2001).

[70] Steve Chalke and Alan Mann, *The Lost Message of Jesus* (Grand Rapids: Zondervan, 2003), 182.

[71] Among the harshest critics are Steve Jeffery, Michael Ovey, and Andrew Sach, *Pierced for Our Transgressions* (Wheaton, Ill.: Crossway Books, 2007).

[72] Stephen R. Holmes, *The Wondrous Cross: Atonement and Penal Substitution in the Bible and History* (London: Paternoster, 2007). Holmes makes it clear that unlike other critics he does not regard penal substitution to be the *sine qua non* of evangelicalism when he writes, "I will say as clearly as possible now that I do not for a moment suppose that penal substitutionary atonement is the article by which the church stands or falls; nor do I accept that there is any reason to call for those who object to penal substitution to be expelled, on account of that rejection per se, from Evangelical bodies, let alone from the church." Holmes, "Of Babies and Bathwater? Recent Evangelical Critiques of Penal Substitution in the Light of Early Modern Debates concerning Justification," *European Journal of Theology* 16, no. 2 (2007): 93–105. See also Holmes, "Cur Deus Po-mo? What St. Anselm Can Teach Us about Preaching the Atonement Today," *Epworth Review* 36, no. 1 (2009), 6–17; Holmes, "Death in the Afternoon:

issues of guilt transference, law and love, divine retribution, and redemptive violence. What it does not seem to account for, however, is the biblical witness to the conviction that, in John Calvin's lovely phrase, "Christ
has redeemed us . . . by the whole course of his obedience."[73] Yet this
deficiency is shared by many evangelicals for whom exclusive attention
is given to the cross without considering the saving effects of the entire
course of Christ's life, death, and resurrection.[74]

Both liberals and evangelicals are in need of attending more intentionally to the trinitarian and christological center named in the ancient
ecumenical creeds, but in both cases there was only a glimpse of what
a sustained engagement might look like. James William McClendon Jr.
has crafted a christological formulation that indicates what a generous

---

Hebrews, Sacrifice and Soteriology," in *Hebrews and Christian Theology*, ed. Richard Bauckham, Daniel R. Driver, Trevor A. Hart, and Nathan MacDonald (Grand Rapids: Eerdmans,
2009), 229–52.

[73] John Calvin, *Institutes of the Christian Religion* II.16.5, ed. John T. McNeill, trans. Ford
Lewis Battles (Philadelphia: Westminster, 1960), 1:507. William C. Placher, "How Does Jesus
Save?" *Christian Century*, June 2, 2009, 23–27. See also, Placher, "Christ Takes Our Place:
Rethinking Atonement," *Interpretation* 53, no. 1 (1999): 5–20. Placher notes at this point that
both the Apostles' and Nicene Creeds move immediately from Christ's birth to his death
without attesting to the fullness of his life. Calvin observed that the "Apostles' Creed passes
at once in the best order from the birth of Christ to his death and resurrection, wherein the
whole of perfect salvation consists. Yet the remainder of the obedience that he manifested in
his life is not excluded." Calvin, *Institutes* II.16.5 (ed. McNeill), 1:508. It is this great omission that gave John Yoder, Denny Weaver, and other Anabaptists cause for concern about
the creeds. Willard M. Swartley consequently has proposed the following additions to the
Apostles' Creed to address the omission of Christ's life: "Lived obediently to his Abba. Lived
and taught love, peace, and forgiveness. Healed the sick, cast out demons, forgave sins, raised
the dead, confounded the powers." Swartley, *Covenant of Peace: The Missing Peace in New Testament Theology and Ethics* (Grand Rapids: Eerdmans, 2006), 425.

[74] Baptist theologian Fisher Humphreys acknowledges the incarnational dimension of
what he calls "cruciform forgiveness." Though his focus is on Christ's death, Humphreys
states, "Cruciform forgiveness is incarnate forgiveness at its highest pitch. From this it follows that the death and dying of Jesus are one piece with the rest of his historical life."
Humphreys,*The Death of Christ* (Nashville: Broadman, 1978), 124. New Testament scholar
Douglas A. Campbell makes a perceptive and telling observation about evangelical theology at this point when he argues that "the justification by faith perspective on Christ's work,
while placing a satisfactory emphasis on the cross, evacuates his incarnation, much of his life,
his resurrection, and his ascension, of all soteriological value." Campbell, *The Quest for Paul's
Gospel* (London: T&T Clark, 2005), 168. Campbell indicates a variety of texts in which Paul
attributes saving significance to the resurrection (1 Cor 15:17; Rom 4:25) and the incarnation (Rom 8:1-4; 2 Cor 5:21; Phil 2:5–11; etc.). As a result, the full range of the life of Christ
plays no real part in the drama of salvation. Campbell discusses in great detail the divergent
theories of Pauline soteriology and offers a substantive reconstruction, not unlike that of
the patristic theologians, which "understands Christ's atoning work as transformational, and
. . . consequently encompasses his incarnation, life, death, resurrection, and glorification."
Campbell, *The Deliverance of God: An Apocalyptic Rereading of Justification in Paul* (Grand Rapids:
Eerdmans, 2009), 76, see also 210–12.

orthodoxy looks like for Other Baptists. The centerpiece of the second volume of McClendon's *Systematic Theology*, simply entitled *Doctrine*, is his chapter "Jesus the Risen Christ."[75] It takes as its point of reference the christological doctrine as defined first at Nicaea that Jesus Christ "became incarnate from the Holy Spirit and the Virgin Mary [and] became human" and later at Chalcedon, which affirmed the deity and humanity of Christ: two natures existing in one person.[76] The two-natures doctrine, though at the center of orthodoxy, is not without problems. McClendon cites the celestial flesh Christology of Menno Simons and the immaculate conception Mariology of Pope Pius IX as two unfortunate examples of the limitations of the two-natures model.[77] McClendon agreed that modern historiography brought an end to the haunting docetism that explained away Jesus' humanity as simulation rather than reality.[78] Yet he recognized that the historical purge of docetism has not been free of fallout. From the old quest of the historical Jesus to the continuing quest of the Jesus Seminar, historical-critical investigation into the human life of Jesus has stretched the two-natures Christology to its limits and has driven a wedge ever deeper between the Christ of faith and the Jesus of history.[79]

But more pressing still for McClendon was the distillation of the life of Jesus into the philosophical category of nature, which abstracts the humanity of Jesus from the portrait of the humble Savior found in the Gospels. McClendon's concern was grounded in what Hans Frei identified as "the eclipse of biblical narrative" in modern hermeneutics. Both held the deep conviction that doctrine should illuminate stories rather than stories illustrating doctrine. Consequently McClendon maintained, as did Frei, that the identity of Jesus Christ was inextricable from the biblical

---

[75] McClendon, *Doctrine*, 238–79.

[76] As Leo the Great intoned:

We confess one and the same Son, who is . . . coessential with the Father as to his deity and coessential with us—the very same one—as to his humanity, being like us in every respect apart from sin. As to his deity, he was born from the Father before all ages, but as to his humanity, the very same one was born in the last days from the Virgin Mary, the Mother of God, for our sake and the sake of our salvation: one and the same Christ, Son, Lord, Only Begotten, acknowledged to be unconfusedly, unalterably, undividedly, inseparably in two natures, since the difference of the natures is not destroyed because of the union, but on the contrary, the character of each nature is preserved and comes together in one person and one hypostasis, not divided or torn into two persons but one and the same Son and only begotten God, Logos, Lord Jesus Christ.

R. A. Norris, "Chalcedon's Definition of Faith," in *The Christological Controversy*, ed. R. A. Norris Jr. (Philadelphia: Fortress, 1980), 159.

[77] McClendon, *Doctrine*, 256–57.

[78] McClendon, *Doctrine*, 262–63. D. M. Baillie, *God Was in Christ* (New York: Scribner, 1948), 11.

[79] McClendon, *Doctrine*, 257–63.

story.[80] But it is not only the humanity of Christ that the two-natures doctrine struggles to render intelligible. For McClendon some patristic expressions of the doctrine of impersonal personhood (*anhypostasis*) were too weak to account for God's radical gift of salvation in Christ. Following Karl Barth, McClendon contended that in the incarnation, God did not assume pristine, Edenic, human nature but rather "sinful flesh" (Rom 8:3) in the Pauline sense of humanity in opposition to God.[81] In plain style, he explained, "In today's terms, [Jesus] would have had a score on a Stanford-Binet scale, and a personality that could be categorized by a Myers-Briggs test."[82] But the identity of Jesus Christ may prove to be more basic still.

In his book *Jesus and the Disinherited*, Other Baptist Howard Thurman suggested that any attempt to understand the identity of Jesus begins with the remarkably simple historical fact that "Jesus was a Jew."[83] Yet the Jewishness of Jesus has been so occluded by theological reflection that it has become of no value in the history of salvation. The Jewishness of Jesus is more than a mere historical fact. It is crucial to an understanding of his full humanity and to an explanation of how this Jesus became a universal savior. In the narrative of colonialism, the ethnocentric identity of Jesus the Jew became lost in the theocentric translation to the universal Christ. Jesus' Jewishness was universalized, and European whiteness was substituted in its place under the code of universal human experience, thus retaining the cultural particularity of the Jewishness of Jesus while denying its theological necessity. Christian theologians of colonialism created a new christological adoptionism that left Christianity with the legacy of supersessionism and white supremacy. As a result the fact that Jesus was a Jew is simply the first step of the translation project.[84] A Christology more faithful to the apostolic witness may be retrieved by careful attention to patristic texts. For example, Maximus the Confessor, the seventh-century theologian of Orthodoxy, displays how Christ kenotically emptied himself to take the form of "poor enslaved flesh." And by entering into the

---

[80] Hans W. Frei, *The Eclipse of Biblical Narrative: A Study in Eighteenth and Nineteenth Century Hermeneutics* (New Haven, Conn.: Yale University Press, 1974), 1–16; and Frei, *The Identity of Jesus Christ: The Hermeneutical Bases of Dogmatic Theology* (Philadelphia: Fortress, 1975; repr., Eugene: Wipf & Stock, 1997), 59–64.

[81] Karl Barth, *Church Dogmatics* I/2, trans. G. T. Thomson and Harold Knight (Edinburgh: T&T Clark, 1956), 151–55. Barth strongly affirms the *anhypostasia* in *Church Dogmatics* I/2: 163–65 and IV/2: 49–60. Yet Barth maintains that the generic human nature that is anhypostatically inseparable from the eternal Son is *our* humanity and not Edenic humanity.

[82] McClendon, *Doctrine*, 262.

[83] Howard Thurman, *Jesus and the Disinherited* (Boston: Beacon Press, 1976), 15.

[84] Willie James Jennings, *The Christian Imagination: Theology and the Origins of Race* (New Haven, Conn.: Yale University Press, 2010), 132–50.

hurt of the world, he fully identified with humanity to the point of communicating his divinity through them, thereby healing all human flesh.[85] That Jesus was a Jew, and indeed "a poor Jew," is not merely coincidental. It is the material means of salvation.

Bearing in mind the ahistorical inclination of the two-natures doctrine, McClendon proposed a two-narratives Christology that calls attention to two intertwined stories in the Bible: one of Israel's God and the other of God's people, Israel; one the *kenosis* story of God's self-giving, and the other the *plerosis* story of divine fulfillment in human up-reaching. Throughout the Bible these stories point toward one another, yet they remain distinct, until in the life of a faithful son of Israel, Jesus of Nazareth, these two become at last indivisibly one.[86] Of particular importance is McClendon's reading of the primitive Christian hymn in Philippians 2:5-11. Following a line of patristic interpretation, he took the hymn as an example of the earthly *living of Christ*, not the more common understanding of an incarnational story about the heavenly *leaving of Christ*.[87] By so rendering the hymn as a model of Christ's servant Lordship, and correlatively as an example of servant discipleship for those who follow Jesus in the servant way, McClendon avoided the lingering doceticism of the two-natures model that the kenotic Christology addressed by attempting to explain how deity can "empty" itself. It seems accurate, then, to describe McClendon's two-narratives Christology not so much as a corrective but as a reappropriation that renders it valid for contemporary theology.[88]

---

[85] J. Kameron Carter, *Race: A Theological Account* (New York: Oxford University Press, 2008), 368. See also Brian Bantum, *Redeeming Mulatto: Theology of Race and Christian Hybridity* (Waco, Tex.: Baylor University Press, 2010).

[86] McClendon, *Doctrine*, 274–79.

[87] McClendon, *Doctrine*, 266–69. In taking the Christ hymn of Philippians to refer to Christ's earthly life, McClendon follows the minority view of Cyprian in the history of interpretation. The leading contemporary proponent of the nonincarnational reading is James D. G. Dunn, who has argued that "Phil. 2:6-8 is probably intended to affirm that Christ's earthly life was an embodiment of grace from beginning to end, of giving away in contrast to the selfish grasping of Adam's sin." Dunn, *Christology in the Making* (Philadelphia: Westminster, 1980), 121. N. T. Wright is one of the leading proponents of the incarnational reading of the Pauline Christ hymn. Wright, *The Climax of the Covenant: Christ and the Law in Pauline Theology* (Minneapolis: Fortress, 1992), 90–97. McClendon does not take a position in the debate between the "low and slow" developmental Christology of Dunn and the "early high" Christology of Wright. He does, however, find that Cyprian's view of imitating Jesus in his earthly life coalesces nicely with the Christology of John Howard Yoder and its corollary of servant discipleship. One might reasonably argue for a two-narratives Christology based on the sort of incarnational reading supplied by Wright, although McClendon found the appeal to imitate the preexistent Christ to be less compelling than the imitation of Christ in his earthly life.

[88] Robert Barron, *The Priority of Christ: Toward a Postliberal Catholicism* (Grand Rapids:

Anticipating the possible misunderstanding of readers who might take
this two-narratives approach to regard Jesus simply as the "lucky winner"
adopted by God, McClendon affirms "that there was never a time when
God did not intend to raise Jesus from the dead, never a time when the
whole story pointed to anything less than the ultimate exaltation of this
One."[89] And indeed it seems reasonable to extend McClendon's analogy
to suggest that though there are two stories, human and divine, "there
is one storyteller, God, who acknowledges both stories as his own, who
tells himself in both." Thus, "the fully and richly human story of Jesus
is enhypostatically grounded in the intentionality of the divine storyteller."[90] McClendon identifies a possible solution to the problem of the
two-natures Christology (i.e., what it means for two incommensurable
natures to be joined in one *person*) by suggesting that in Jesus, God's ways
are truly human ways and human ways are truly God's.[91] Careful readers
need look no further for McClendon's orthodoxy, but careless readers may
miss the seriousness with which he took the challenge of historicism.[92] As

---

Brazos, 2007), 65; Terrence Tilley, *The Disciples' Jesus: Christology as Reconciling Practice* (Maryknoll, N.Y.: Orbis Books, 2008), 35–36. Tilley suggests that McClendon's two-narratives
model helps to resolve some of the confusion (and conflict) between the epistemological and
ontological questions implicit in the modern and "scientifically inflected" approaches of doing
Christology "from above" and "from below."

[89] McClendon, *Doctrine*, 272.

[90] Barron, *Priority of Christ*, 66. David H. Kelsey suggests that a kind of two-narratives
approach is at work in the Christology of Karl Barth's treatment of "the Royal Man" in *Church
Dogmatics* IV/2, §64.3 (Edinburgh: T&T Clark, 1958), 154–264. For Barth the biblical narrative renders the identity of Jesus Christ as God with us (1) as the revelation of Israel's Messiah
(viz., the disciples' perspective) and (2) by narrating Jesus' death as an act in which he achieved
his intention to live in unbroken response to God's will. Kelsey, *Proving Doctrine: The Uses of
Scripture in Modern Theology* (Harrisburg, Pa.: Trinity Press, 1999), 39–50.

[91] Tilley, *Disciples' Jesus*, 226–27.

[92] Thomas Finger, e.g., maintains that McClendon unwisely critiques the proclivity
of the Chalcedonian definition for minimizing Jesus' humanity. He suggests that, in fact,
McClendon's two-narratives revision of the liberal-historical Christology makes a more
problematic move similar to that of Faustus Socinus. Finger, "James McClendon's Theology
Reaches Completion: A Review Essay," *Mennonite Quarterly Review* 76, no. 1 (2002): 125–26.
See also Finger, *A Contemporary Anabaptist Theology* (Downers Grove, Ill.: InterVarsity, 2004),
398–99. This criticism misses the point of McClendon's qualification and further his postliberal use the historical-critical critique. To answer McClendon, Finger takes refuge in a
metaphysical essentialism that seems to lead back to the sort of Melchiorism invoked by baptists that McClendon was criticizing. (Melchiorism denotes the "celestial flesh" Christology
popularized by Melchior Hoffman, a German Anabaptist preacher of the 1530s who taught
that Jesus did not receive his humanity from Mary but moved through her like water through
a pipe.) Additionally, Finger fails to acknowledge in his exegesis of Phil 2:1-11 that the phrase
"the form of God" is by no means settled in the scholarship as a reference to preexistence. (See
the above discussion of Dunn vs. Wright.) McClendon acknowledged the stream of historical scholarship Finger cites that reads the Pauline hymn as ascribing preexistence to Christ.

the two-natures model provided previous generations of Christians with a useful account of the faith, McClendon hoped that a two-narratives Christology might enable contemporary Christians to faithfully teach what entitles Jesus to be their Lord or why the confession of Christ's Lordship is consistent with the conviction that God is one and finally how Christlike the lives of disciples are to be. Whatever one makes of McClendon's proposal, there is no question that it represents a sustained reflection on the center from the standpoint of a generous postliberal orthodoxy.

Ecclesial Christianity

In 1840 John Williamson Nevin joined the faculty of a small seminary of the German Reformed Church in Mercersburg, Pennsylvania. Over the next two decades, Nevin and his colleague Philip Schaff championed what Sydney Ahlstrom characterized as "the most creative manifestation of the Catholic tendency in American Protestantism."[93] Reflecting on his theological work, Nevin summarized the Mercersburg theology centered on three convictions: Jesus Christ as the object of faith and knowledge, the Apostles' Creed as the rule of faith, and the catholicity of the church as objective and historical.[94] One of Nevin's main concerns was the increasing sectarianism of evangelical Protestantism in America, which had lost touch with and all but forgotten its connection with historic Christianity. His article "The Sect System" in the first issue of the *Mercersburg Review* delineated the fault lines of sectarianism. Nevin identified the Baptist mind-set as paradigmatic of a sect in that they "adhere rigidly to the New Testament as the sole standard of Christianity"[95] and affirm "no creed but the Bible."[96] They also exalt the right of private judgment in interpretation. He admitted that Baptists are not alone in adhering to the Bible and private judgment. Many other sects claimed the same watchword. Yet they disagree with one another. These sectarian divisions, Nevin argued, indicate that these principles are determined by a prior set of beliefs, influenced

---

McClendon, "Philippians 2:5-11," *Review and Expositor* 88, no. 4 (1991): 439–44. However, McClendon followed another line of interpretation that he traced to patristic sources.

[93] Sydney E. Ahlstrom, *A Religious History of the American People*, 2nd ed. (New Haven, Conn.: Yale University Press, 2004), 615.

[94] John Williamson Nevin, "The Theology of the New Liturgy," *Mercersburg Review* 14, no. 1 (1867): 23–45.

[95] John Williamson Nevin, "The Sect System," *Mercersburg Review* 1, no. 5 (1849): 482–507, and *Mercersburg Review* 1, no. 6 (1849): 521–39, republished in *Catholic and Reformed: Selected Theological Writings of John Williamson Nevin*, ed. Charles Yrigoyen Jr. and George H. Bricker (Pittsburgh, Pa.: Pickwick, 1978), 135. Citations of "Sect System" below correspond to the 1978 Pickwick Press edition.

[96] Nevin, "Sect System," 139.

by powerful authorities, and read through a divergent set of hermeneutical lenses, "leading private judgment along by the nose, and forcing the divine text always to speak in its own way."[97] But more problematic for Nevin was fact that the Baptists seemed committed to a belief that the church was "autochthonic, aboriginal, self-springing from the Bible or through the Bible from the skies."[98] The Baptists, he contended, had no sense of continuity with the historic church prior to the Reformation except in occasional flashes of light in the "dark ages." More troublesome still was the power of every congregation "to originate a new Christianity for its own use, and so may well afford to let that of other ages pass for a grand apostasy."[99] Nevin's Mercersburg colleague Philip Schaff argued similarly that sectarianism led to "not the single pope of the city of the seven hills, but the numberless popes . . . who would fain enslave Protestants once more to human authority, not as embodied in the Church indeed, but as holding in the form of mere private judgement and private will."[100]

The Mercersburg assessment may appear overly harsh, but in many ways it parallels the critique of the Baptists by a consummate insider. In 1872 William H. Whitsitt joined the faculty of the Southern Baptist Theological Seminary to teach ecclesiastical history. Having studied at the Universities of Leipzig and Berlin, where he was deeply influenced by the methods of modern historiography, Whitsitt grew increasingly uncomfortable with the ahistorical character of the popular account that traced the Baptists in an unbroken succession back to the time of Christ.[101] In 1893 Whitsitt published thirty-nine signed articles on Baptists in *Johnson's Universal Cyclopedia* in which, among other controversial statements, he suggested that the baptism of Roger Williams in 1639 had been "most likely performed by sprinkling."[102] Three years after the articles appeared

---

[97] Nevin, "Sect System," 141.

[98] Nevin, "Sect System," 145.

[99] Nevin, "Sect System," 146.

[100] Philip Schaff, *The Principle of Protestantism*, trans. John Nevin (Chambersburg: Publication Office of the German Reformed Church, 1845), 121.

[101] The successionist theory was popularized by the Scotch Baptist William Jones, who published his *History of the Christian Church* in 1812 and went through four American editions. Jones claimed that "the Most High has had his churches and people in every age, since the decease of the Apostles," but he made no attempt to trace the actual connection through history. Jones, *The History of the Christian Church, from the Birth of Christ to the XVIII Century: Including the Very Interesting Account of the Waldenses and Albigenses*, 4th ed. (Wetumpka, Ala.: Charles Yancey, 1845), xix. It was G. H. Orchard who actually provided an account that tracked Baptists "from the time of Christ their founder to the 18th century," in his *A Concise History of the Baptists* (New York: Sheldon, Lamport, 1855).

[102] James H. Slatton, *W. H. Whitsitt: The Man and the Controversy* (Macon, Ga.: Mercer University Press, 2009), 163. In 1880 Whitsitt traveled to England, where he had the

in print, Whitsitt prepared a definitive statement of his views. In a monograph entitled *A Question in Baptist History*, Whitsitt posed a pointed question: "Whether the immersion of adult believers was practiced in England by the Anabaptists before the year 1641?" The issue, he assured readers, had nothing to do with theology because Baptist ecclesiology rested on "the Bible" and "the Bible alone." His concern was "purely a question of modern historical research."[103] After a careful examination of the relevant primary source material, Whitsitt concluded that there was no evidence to indicate that Baptists baptized by immersion prior to 1641.[104] Yet his confidence in the historical record did little to persuade many of his fellow Baptists, who were worried about the implications for theology and ecclesiology. Faced by widespread popular opposition from strict denominationalists, Whitsitt, by then president of Southern Seminary, resigned under pressure. Though subsequent historians have vindicated Whitsitt's historical judgment, his appeal to "the Bible" and "the Bible alone" did little to resolve the lingering theological question of how Baptists still might legitimately claim to be part of apostolic Christianity.[105]

Landmarkers and Restorationists resolved the question of an apostolic connection by nullification and restoration. They promulgated the view that at some point in history the true church ceased to be identified with the historic churches and had to be reconstituted according to the New Testament pattern.[106] The belief in the fall of the church became popularly

---

opportunity to look at the Thomason tract collection and other primary source material pertaining to early English Baptists. From June through October 1880, Whitsitt published four unsigned articles in the New York *Independent* in which he challenged the claim that Baptists had baptized by immersion before 1641. Slatton, *W. H. Whitsitt*, 98.

[103] William H. Whitsitt, *A Question in Baptist History: Whether the Anabaptists in England Practiced Immersion before the Year 1641?* (Louisville, Ky.: C. T. Dearing, 1896), 5.

[104] Whitsitt, *Question in Baptist History*, 80–89.

[105] W. Morgan Patterson, *Baptist Successionism: A Critical View* (Valley Forge, Pa.: Judson Press, 1969), 27–29. Other contemporaries, some of them fellow church historians, supported Whitsitt's conclusions. In a review of Whitsitt's *Question*, Henry Vedder of Crozer seminary stated that he found himself "in entire agreement with Dr. Whitsitt on every matter of the least consequence relating to the case of immersion among English Baptists; so far as the facts are known, any other conclusion than his seems impossible." Quoted in Slatton, *W. H. Whitsitt*, 198. Opponents of Whitsitt raised objections to his conclusion, though they offered no new facts. When faced with contemporaneous primary source evidence from the Kiffin manuscript, which suggests that dipping was not practiced by the London Baptists until 1641, Henry Melville King simply dismissed it as "untrustworthy" and of "doubtful character" in his *The Baptism of Roger Williams: A Review of Rev. Dr. W. H. Whitsitt's Inference* (Providence: Preston & Rounds, 1897), 20. Modern historians have upheld Whitsitt's historical conclusion.

[106] Andrew Christopher Smith, "Searching for the Hidden Church: William Jones and the Common Roots of Landmarkist and Restorationist Ecclesiology," *Perspectives in Religious Studies* 36, no. 4 (2009): 421–31.

expressed in the booklet *The Trail of Blood*, where the corruption of the
Catholic Church was exemplified in the union of church and state at
the time of the emperor Constantine and the subsequent establishment
of infant baptism.[107] But successionists were not the first to assert the fall
of the church. John Smyth argued in his book *The Character of the Beast*,
written in 1609, that infant baptism invalidated the churchly status of
those that practiced it. He thus declared that the independent churches
of the separation were of the same false constitution as the churches of
England and Rome.[108] Though Baptists and other dissenters often voiced a
more extensive understanding of the fall of the church, virtually all English Protestants in the seventeenth century regarded the Roman Catholic Church to be apostate. Indeed, the fact that William Laud and the
High Church Anglicans acknowledged the Catholic Church to be a true
though corrupt church aroused suspicions of a crypto-Catholic conspiracy
in the Church of England, which was regarded to be the enemy of both
king and Parliament.[109] Such pervasive anti-Catholic sentiment makes all
the more striking the statement of Francis Johnson that God's covenant of
grace with the Roman Church remained "notwithstanding all her adulteries and apostasie."[110]

In sharing this conviction in common with the Protestant Reformers, Johnson prefigured the sentiments of Other Baptists who, although
they may utilize an anti-Catholic polemic, still assume a narrative of continuity and thus are less antihistorical than Anabaptists and other Free
Churches who have propagated an ecclesiology of discontinuity.[111] A

---

[107] J. M. Carroll, *The Trail of Blood* . . . (Lexington, Ky.: Ashland Avenue Baptist Church,
1931), 16–17. Carroll drew from earlier sources, including Jones, *History of the Christian Church*;
and Orchard, *Concise History of the Baptists*.

[108] Smyth, *The Character of the Beast*, in *Works of John Smyth*, 2:565.

[109] William Laud and John Fisher, *A Relation of the Conference between William Laud, Late
Lord Arch-Bishop of Canterbury, and Mr. Fisher the Jesuit*, ed. C. H. Simpkinson (London: Macmillan, 1901), 144–80. The conference between Laud and Fisher occurred on May 24, 1622.

[110] Francis Johnson, *A Christian Plea Conteyning three Treatises* (Leiden: William Brewster, 1617), 27–29. For the Protestant anti-Catholicism as polemic and policy, see Peter Lake,
"Anti-popery: The Structure of a Prejudice," in *Conflict in Early Stuart England: Studies in Religion and Politics, 1603–1642*, ed. Richard Cust and Ann Hughes (London: Longman, 1989),
72–106; John Coffey, *Persecution and Toleration in Protestant England, 1558–1689* (Essex: Pearson
Education, 2000), 90 and 134–60; and Anthony Milton, *Catholic and Reformed: The Roman and
Protestant Churches in English Protestant Thought: 1600–1640* (Cambridge: Cambridge University Press, 1995), 134–41.

[111] E.g., in contending against the Anabaptists, Martin Luther argued that, despite its
errors, the church under the papacy has resulted in much that is Christian, good, and true,
including the Scriptures, the sacraments, the keys, the ministry, the Lord's Prayer, the Ten
Commandments, and the articles of the creed. *Luther's Works* (St. Louis, Mo.: Concordia;
Philadelphia: Fortress, 1958), 40:231–32.

recurrent theme in these accounts was the invocation of the myth that fall of the church commenced in the fourth century with the reign of Constantine, who exalted Christianity as the state religion. So far had the church fallen from its primitive state that, restitutionists argued, it could not be repaired but instead must be restored in conformity with apostolic faith and practice as described in the New Testament. The restoration-ist vision not only embraced an ahistorical and romanticized view of a pristine primitive Christianity, it also affirmed, sometimes explicitly and sometimes implicitly, an antihistorical narrative that regarded the church from the fourth to the sixteenth century to be degenerate and apostate. Free Churches from the Anabaptists and the Baptists to the Plymouth Brethren and modern Evangelicals have propagated this notion of the church's fall or ruin.[112] Notwithstanding the antisuccessionism that Whit-sitt and subsequent historians have rightly articulated, historically con-scious Baptists still assume an antihistorical sectarianism that rests on "the Bible" and "the Bible alone." This biblicism, however, masks two addi-tional elements necessary for the coherence of the restorationist narrative. It depends on the *ontological* fall of the church as well as a new *historical* point of origin for the church.

Recognizing the problems associated with antihistoricism, John Howard Yoder offered a more nuanced account of the fall of the church. Prior to Constantine, Yoder argued, Christians knew there was a church, but they had to take it on faith that Christ ruled over the world. After Constantine, Yoder explained, Christians could take as fact that Christ was ruling over the world, but they had to believe against the evidence that there was a believing church.[113] Yoder's identification of the church's fall with the Constantinian shift, however, reinforces an existing anti-historical understanding of the church. It is even unclear by this account whether constantinianism also entails the corruption of the trinitarian and christological orthodoxy that followed the reign of Constantine. In short, this view of the church's fall, though nuanced, still underwrites the declension narrative of church history.[114] To be sure, the continued use of

---

[112] Franklin H. Littell, *The Anabaptist View of the Church* (Boston: Starr King, 1958), 48–78; and J. N. Darby, "What the Christian Has amid the Ruin of the Church," in *The Col-lected Writings of J. N. Darby*, ed. William Kelly (Winschoten, Netherlands: H. L. Heijkoop, 1971–1972), 14:272–300, esp. 275. The second edition of Littell's book was published under the title *The Origins of Sectarian Protestantism* (New York: Macmillan, 1964). The change in the title from "church" to "sect" reflects the influence of Niebuhr's reading of American denominationalism as sectarian.

[113] John Howard Yoder, "The Otherness of the Church," in *The Royal Priesthood: Essays Ecclesiological and Ecumenical*, ed. Michael G. Cartwright (Grand Rapids: Eerdmans, 1994), 57.

[114] Williams, *Retrieving the Tradition and Renewing Evangelicalism*, 122–31.

the Constantinian typology is not always transparent so as not to leave those who employ it open to such a critique. But neither does it explicitly identify the fall of the church with a historical event that resulted in an irreversible and ontological descent from ecclesial being to ecclesial non-being. Yoder actually maintained that the church's fallen-ness is reversible, not ontological. When, for example, he suggested that the lack of unity in the church is an indication of its fall, he meant something like: "The gospel is not true here in this place."[115] Or to put the matter in a slightly different way, Yoder's designation of "constantinianism" suggested that the one, holy, catholic, and apostolic church is sometimes and in some places not visible. He did not claim that there is no church catholic, nor did he indicate that in this place the church catholic cannot at some future time be visible. However, he wanted to maintain the possibility of being able to say that the church catholic is not visible here and now.

McClendon and Yoder responded to precisely these objections in a jointly authored essay answering a critique of their nuanced versions of the ecclesial fall. The detractors acknowledged that their accounts of the church's faithfulness are not committed to a "clandestine institutional succession" or "to literal eras of 'fall' and datable periods of 'restitution.'"[116] Indeed, as McClendon put the matter, "the present church, like the New Testament community of disciples, is often errant or fallen, often restored."[117] Yet, as Yoder has written, "There was then a fall, leaving a degenerate state, so intrinsically deteriorated as not to be reparable without discontinuity."[118] Yoder and McClendon do concede that some sixteenth-century Anabaptists believed in a literal fall and restoration of the church. But they ask whether this contradicts their contention that the present church is "often errant or fallen, often restored." They argue instead that the continuity of the church is not broken by a theology of restitutionism if the fall of the church is not historical and irreversible.[119]

Here McClendon and Yoder echo the moderating judgment of A. H. Newman. Appealing to the promise that the gates of Hades will not

---

[115] John Howard Yoder, "The Imperative of Christian Unity," in *Royal Priesthood*, 291.

[116] David Wayne Layman, "The Inner Ground of Christian Theology: Church, Faith, and Sectarianism," *Journal of Ecumenical Studies* 27, no. 3 (1990): 482–83. James Wm. McClendon Jr. and John Howard Yoder, "Christian Identity in Ecumenical Perspective: A Response to David Wayne Layman," *Journal of Ecumenical Studies* 27, no. 3 (1990): 566–67.

[117] James Wm. McClendon Jr., *Ethics: Systematic Theology: Volume I* (Waco, Tex.: Baylor University Press, 2012), 31.

[118] John Howard Yoder, *The Priestly Kingdom: Social Ethics as Gospel* (Notre Dame, Ind.: University of Notre Dame Press, 1984), 124.

[119] McClendon and Yoder, "Christian Identity in Ecumenical Perspective," 566; and Yoder, *Priestly Kingdom*, 133.

prevail against the church, Newman observes "that a church may make grave departures in doctrine and practice from the apostolic standard without ceasing to be a church of Christ must be admitted, or else it must be maintained that during long periods no church is known to have existed."[120] Indeed, Yoder and McClendon contend that a baptistic view need not necessarily be committed to an account of the historical and ontological fall of the church. What is important, they maintain, is that Christians remain open to the possibility of genuine human disobedience and of God's response to such disobedience at any time and place in history. "To display such openness," they argue, "is to be . . . a baptist in one's thinking."[121] Such baptistic thinking lies behind Miroslav Volf's questioning why the ecclesial identity of Catholic and Orthodox communions in Croatia and Serbia are taken for granted when their "members are inclined more to superstition than faith" and they "identify with the church more for nationalistic reasons," while at the same time the churchly character of "a Baptist congregation that has preserved its faith through the crucible of persecution" goes unrecognized.[122]

But the question remains how this Other Baptist historiography can be catholic in a diachronic sense. Restorationists of various sorts, in seeking to supply a connection to apostolic Christianity, leap over the historic church with a single bound to the age of the apostles and ground their claim on "the Bible alone." Yet, by nullifying the history of the church after its literal fall, restorationists are left with a sectarianism that has no historic continuity to apostolic Christianity, and sectarianism has no claim to catholicity. Roger Williams recognized the inherent contradiction of the restorationist strategy that repudiates a fallen church and gathers a pure one. His dream of a restoring the primitive church faded when he faced the reality that even the repristinated churches of the Baptists were irreversibly fallen. The only hope, he believed, lay in awaiting the coming of Christ and his apostolic messengers, who would once again gather

---

[120] Albert Henry Newman, *A History of the Baptist Churches in the United States* (New York: Christian Literature, 1894), 13.

[121] McClendon and Yoder, "Christian Identity in Ecumenical Perspective," 567. One of the key differences between Catholics and Protestants on ecclesiology is whether the church can sin. Catholics regard the church as the spotless bride of Christ and therefore incapable of sin as such. Protestants understand the church as composed of members who are sinners, though justified, and therefore capable of sin. On these distinctions about the church and sin, see *The Nature and Mission of the Church: A Stage on the Way to a Common Statement*, Faith and Order Paper no. 198 (Geneva: World Council of Churches, 2005).

[122] Miroslav Volf, *After Our Likeness: The Church as the Image of the Trinity* (Grand Rapids: Eerdmans, 1998), 133–34.

true churches.[123] Without an apostolic connection, Williams became "a churchless man."[124] But, as McClendon and Yoder recognized, it is not just Trail of Blood Landmarkers and radical Separatists like Williams who are churchless. Restorationism based on a historic fall renders its adherents to be churchless sects with no credible way of claiming historic continuity to apostolic Christianity.

The connection with apostolic Christianity in the Other Baptist vision as McClendon describes it is neither "developmental nor successionist, but mystical and immediate."[125] This mystical aspect of solidarity with the primitive church in one sense maintains the apostolic conviction of living together under the rule of Jesus Christ, who is "the same yesterday and today and forever" (Heb 13:8). But the pressing question is whether Baptists can confess, "We believe in the holy catholic church." Indeed, the voluntary confession of the ancient and ecumenical creeds moves beyond merely a mystical connection so as to avoid the autistic sectarianism of restorationism and brings to voice the conviction that their gathered communities are visible manifestations of the church catholic. Such an approach is both quantitatively catholic, because it participates with the *consensus fidelium* in mystical and historical continuity with the faith of the apostolic church, and qualitatively catholic, in that it joins voices with the apostolic witness to the Bible as the unfolding story of the triune God. Short of such a confessional strategy, it is unlikely that Other Baptists can retain continuity with the one, holy, catholic, and apostolic church.

Ecumenical Communion

The ecumenical movement is arguably the single most significant development for the church in the twentieth century. Yet remarkably the largest Protestant denomination in the United States was not a participant. Why this is the case merits examination. It has been suggested with not a little irony that Baptists in the American South were the first Free Church denomination to create a civilization. Their majority presence earned them the status of being a de facto established church.[126] But

---

[123] Roger Williams, *Mr. Cottons' Letter Lately Printed*, in *The Complete Writings of Roger Williams* (New York: Russell & Russell, 1963), 1:392; and Edmund Sears Morgan, *Roger Williams: The Church and the State* (New York: Harcourt, Brace & World, 1967), 46.

[124] Perry Miller, *Roger Williams: His Contribution to the American Tradition* (Indianapolis, Ind.: Bobbs-Merrill, 1953), 52.

[125] McClendon, *Ethics*, 32.

[126] The percentage of Baptists to the total population in the United States went from 16.9 percent in 1776 to 20.5 percent in 1850. In 1850 Baptists made up 30 percent of the total religious adherents the South, but by 1926 Baptists comprised 43 percent of all religious adherents in the South, whereas in the North, Baptists were 15 percent of the total religious adherents in

cultural establishment is not the same as catholicity. To describe Baptists as the "Catholic Church of the South,"[127] then, is more of a sociological designation than a theological one. But as the early Baptists evolved from sects into churches, so did Baptists in the South grow into their ecclesial sensibilities as they became a dominant expression of church and culture.[128] Yet in their newly acquired ecclesial form they retained some of their old sectarian habits. The Landmark assertion that "unimmersed bodies of Christians are not churches" but "only religious societies" is surely an extreme expression of this sectarian habit.[129] But, truth be told, the wider community of Baptists in the South epitomized something of an antiecumenical spirit. And, as long as their cultural establishment held firm, they were comfortable ignoring other Christian churches with little consequence. Or so they thought.

On May 13, 1914, the SBC adopted the *Pronouncement on Christian Union and Denominational Efficiency*. E. Y. Mullins, who wrote the section of the report on Christian unity, spoke irenically of the "desire and willingness to cooperate in all practical ways in every cause of righteousness." He passionately urged the assembled messengers by God's will to find a way "through the maze of divided Christendom out into the open spaces of Christian union." J. B. Gambrell, who prepared the statement on denominational efficiency, urged the convention to stay the course of denominationalism "by preserving a complete autonomy at home and abroad, unembarrassed by entangling alliances with other bodies holding to different standards of doctrine and different views of church order." When the vote was taken, denominational efficiency won out over Christian unity.[130] Southern Baptists continued down the path of ecumenical isolation in 1938 by approving the *Report on Interdenominational Relations*. The report affirmed interdenominational cooperation but rejected any notion of organic union, which they warned "must inevitably end in a

---

1850 and only 6 percent by 1926. The Southern Baptist Convention had thirty-three members per one thousand Americans in 1890. By 1986 that number had risen to seventy-four members per one thousand Americans. Roger Finke and Rodney Stark, *The Churching of America, 1776–2005: Winners and Losers in Our Religious Economy* (New Brunswick, N.J.: Rutgers University Press, 2005), 56, 158–59, and 183.

[127] Hinson, "Nicene Creed Viewed," 119.

[128] Ernst Troeltsch, *The Social Teaching of the Christian Churches*, trans. Olive Wyon (New York: Harper Torchbooks, 1960), 2:708.

[129] J. R. Graves, "Baptist Corollaries," *Baptist*, July 20, 1867, 2; cited in James A. Patterson, *James Robinson Graves: Staking the Boundaries of Baptist Identity* (Nashville: B&H, 2012), 209.

[130] *Annual of the Southern Baptist Convention* (Nashville: Southern Baptist Convention, 1914), 77–78. See also William R. Estep Jr., *Baptists and Christian Unity* (Nashville: Broadman, 1966), 153; and James Leo Garrett Jr., ed. *Baptist Relations with Other Christians* (Valley Forge, Pa.: Judson Press, 1974), 67–75.

wide apostasy, followed by inertia, indefiniteness, confusion, and waste of spiritual force."[131] The next year the convention received an invitation to join the World Council of Churches, but, upon recommendation of a study committee chaired by George W. Truett, they declined to affiliate.[132] When SBC president Wayne Dehoney addressed the convention in 1965 and indicated a willingness "to seek broader channels of communication and cooperation" with other Christians, he was met by strong resistance.[133] He subsequently explained that he did not mean to imply that Southern Baptists should reject denominationalism in favor of ecumenism, for such a course "would be to reverse the Reformation and turn the clock back to medieval Catholicism."[134] It is surely this general antipathy toward all things ecumenical that "feeds on ignorance and is fomented by misrepresentation" and sometimes seems "to be deliberate and almost malicious."[135] But not all Baptists were antiecumenical. As the only registered Southern Baptist participant at the 1954 WCC Assembly in Evanston, Illinois, Carlyle Marney was exceptional. And he remained enthusiastically engaged in ecumenical work, serving as vice president of National Council of Churches in 1967–1968.[136]

Other Baptists have not been so disinclined toward ecclesial interdependence. Because many early English Baptists emerged out of, and some remained in, congregations where believer- and infant-baptized members shared communion, there was openness toward other Christian churches.[137] Even after the Act of Toleration in 1689, Baptists continued

[131] *Annual of the Southern Baptist Convention* (Nashville: Southern Baptist Convention, 1938), 24.

[132] *Annual of the Southern Baptist Convention* (Nashville: Southern Baptist Convention, 1940), 99. See also Estep, *Baptists and Christian Unity*, 156; and Garrett, *Baptist Relations with Other Christians*, 73–79.

[133] Wayne Dehoney, "Issues and Imperatives," in *Annual of the Southern Baptist Convention* (Nashville: Southern Baptist Convention, 1965), 95.

[134] Dehoney, "Southern Baptists and Ecumenical Concerns," *Christianity Today*, January 29, 1965, 15.

[135] Ernest A. Payne, *Free Churchmen, Unrepentant and Repentant* (London: Carey Kingsgate Press, 1965), 14.

[136] John Carey, *Carlyle Marney: A Pilgrim's Progress* (Macon, Ga.: Mercer University Press, 1980), 85. Carlyle Marney, "World Council of Churches: Christ, Our Hope," sermon delivered at First Baptist Church, Austin, Tex., August 22, 1954, box 57, the Carlyle Marney Papers, David M. Rubenstein Rare Book & Manuscript Library, Duke University, Durham, N.C. Marney says that he was "the only [Southern Baptist] listed in the program, except Billy Graham," who was unable to attend due to illness. But Marney says that he saw several Southern Baptist seminary professors and "more than thirty pastors" at the assembly.

[137] Joel Halcomb, "A Social History of Congregational Religious Practice during the Puritan Revolution" (Ph.D. diss., University of Cambridge, 2009), 144–67; and B. R. White, "Open and Closed Membership among English and Welsh Baptists," *Baptist Quarterly* 24, no. 7 (1972): 330–34.

to see themselves as part of a larger churchly body with Independents, Presbyterians, and other Dissenters. Baptists in early America held a similar attitude toward other Christians. Baptists in Philadelphia participated in open communion, pulpit exchanges, and public worship with Presbyterian churches, and, when the Presbyterians began to have scruples about such open communion, the Baptists wrote a letter on October 30, 1698, extending their offer of mutual fellowship.[138] These examples of positive relations between early Baptists and other Christian churches, though exceptional, indicate both a precedent and a trajectory for future ecumenical communion. So it is understandable that, when the inaugural assembly of the WCC met in 1948, eight Baptists unions joined as founding members and that in 2006 the membership roster of the WCC included twenty-five Baptist unions.[139]

The striking divergence among Baptists on ecumenical matters prompted E. Roberts-Thomson to suggest that "the Baptist world, ecumenically, can be divided into two groups: those who are of the Southern Baptist point of view, or are closely influenced by it, and those who are not."[140] This tension moved McClendon in 1968 to wonder out loud in a Southern Baptist theological journal: "What is a Baptist ecumenism?" He asked, "How can we take the *really* hard forward step of acknowledging that God loves, not just some Methodists, but their church, not just some Catholics, but their church?" Real ecumenism, he argued, begins with simple but concrete acts of love like the passing of the peace at the Lord's Supper. But the goal must be more than "spiritual unity." Instead the aim is "God-given, unshakable unity that expresses itself in words and in works." Such unity, McClendon imagined, would not be some "monolithic, monotonous, monstrous" institution. But, he continued, there can never be real unity where there is "rivalry, enmity, distrust, hatred between Christians." Real unity is based on love for one another in spite of differences. Such love embraces black and white, women and men, fundamentalists and liberals, Protestants and Catholics, and seeks to live into a vision of identity in Christ.[141]

---

[138] Morgan Edwards, *Materials Toward a History of the Baptists in Pennsylvania* (Philadelphia: Joseph Crukshank and Isaac Collins, 1770), 104–9.

[139] Steven R. Harmon, "Baptists and Ecumenism," in *The Oxford Handbook of Ecumenical Studies*, ed. Geoffrey Wainwright and Paul McPartian (New York: Oxford University Press, forthcoming); and Ernest A. Payne, "Baptists and the Ecumenical Movement," in *Free Churchmen, Unrepentant and Repentant*, 120–29.

[140] Edward Roberts-Thomson, *With Hands Outstretched: Baptists and the Ecumenical Movement* (London: Marshall, Morgan & Scott, 1962), 94.

[141] James Wm. McClendon Jr., "What Is a Southern Baptist Ecumenism?" *Southwestern Journal of Theology* 10, no. 2 (1968): 73–78.

As long as southern culture remained intact and Southern Baptists continued to enjoy the privilege of majority presence, there seemed to be no pressing need for wider ecumenical relations. And their cultural homogeneity ensured that the appeal to the Scriptures alone was a sufficient theological basis for cooperation. But as southern culture began to disappear, so did the sense of privilege and a shared social life. As the earlier hermeneutical consensus dissipated, the resulting diversity in biblical interpretation eventually became too much for the Scripture principle. To bolster the belief in biblical authority, former SBC president Jimmy Draper pressed for the convention to adopt a simple "creed" comprised of four fundamentals: the full divinity and humanity of Christ, the substitutionary atonement, justification by faith, and the bodily resurrection.[142] E. Glenn Hinson recommended that, rather than attempting to formulate a new list of fundamentals, it would be better to reaffirm one of the historic creeds on the grounds that it "accords more closely with the traditional Baptist perspective."[143] And if the desire is to be in accord with historic Baptist perceptions of faith and the memory of the apostolic witness from the Scriptures, the ancient ecumenical creeds do both much better than a hastily conceived statement.[144]

Unlike some Baptists who reject any basis for ecumenical conversation, the seventeenth-century General Baptist messenger Thomas Grantham actively embraced the grounds for ecclesial communion. In so doing Grantham presaged Other Baptists who mark the same journey. Though he considered some of the words of the Nicene Creed to be ambiguous, Grantham nevertheless regarded the ancient confessions of the church "to be of most venerable estimation, both for Antiquity, and the solidity of the matter, and for their excellent brevity." He declared that General Baptists were in agreement with the substance of the Apostles' and Nicene Creeds, and he further suggested that affirmation of the creed "might be a good means to bring to a greater degree of unity" in the face of a divided church.[145] In 1687 Grantham published a catechetical exposition of the six principles in Hebrews 6:1-2, which the General Baptists regarded as a kind of apostolic *regula*. The structure of the catechism is a conversation between a father and a son. When their discussion gets to

---

[142] James T. Draper, *Authority: The Critical Issue for Southern Baptists* (Old Tappan, N.J.: Revell, 1984), 105–6.

[143] E. Glenn Hinson, "Creeds and Christian Unity," *Journal of Ecumenical Studies* 23, no. 1 (1986): 25.

[144] Hinson, "Creeds and Christian Unity," 33.

[145] Thomas Grantham, *Christianismus Primitivus; or, The Ancient Christian Religion* II.5.III (London: Francis Smith, 1678), 59–61.

the second principle of faith, the father introduces the Trinity and says, "that thou mayest know how this Great Mystery was understood by the Ancient Church . . . I will shew thee their Confession of Faith."[146] He then quotes the Nicene Creed in full. After hearing the creed, the son replies (echoing Grantham's own description in *Christianismus Primitivus*), "I much reverence this ancient Confession of Faith, for its excellent Brevity, and especially for the solidity of the Matter." Now, he continues, "I desire you to shew me what Scripture-Evidence we have" for what is taught here about the faith.[147]

During the same decade that Southern Baptists were in the throes of a major division over confessing the faith, the Faith and Order Commission of the WCC was embarking on a project that might make it possible for divided churches to make a common confession of the apostolic faith as a visible sign of the unity of the church.[148] They began working on a new study document, *Confessing the One Faith*, as "an ecumenical explication of the apostolic faith as it is confessed in the Nicene-Constantinopolitan Creed." The commission convened a series of international consultations and meetings from 1981 to 1990 for discussion and reflection. As the process was nearing completion, the April 3–11, 1990, meeting of the Apostolic Faith Steering Group reached an impasse, and it appeared that the project might have to be aborted. But then a surprising development occurred. During the deliberation, Horace Russell, a Jamaican Baptist, spoke up forcefully in favor of confessing the creed. His voice was enough to persuade the majority that if common confession of the faith was so important for a Baptist from a historically noncreedal tradition, then it was surely a positive sign of visible unity.[149] The study document was subsequently approved.[150]

There is a place for Other Baptists to develop statements of faith that declare the distinctive way in which they live out their life together, but if Baptists are a part of the one people of God who will ultimately be a

---

[146] Thomas Grantham, *St. Paul's Catechism*, 2nd ed. (London: J. Darby, 1693), 20.

[147] Grantham, *St. Paul's Catechism*, 21.

[148] *Confessing the One Faith: An Ecumenical Explication of the Apostolic Faith as It Is Confessed in the Nicene-Constantinopolitan Creed* (381), Faith and Order Paper no. 153 (Geneva: World Council of Churches, 1991), vii.

[149] *Confessing the One Faith*, 138; and Geoffrey Wainwright, *Embracing Purpose: Essays on God, the World, and the Church* (Peterborough, U.K.: Epworth, 2007), 90, 172–73, and 263.

[150] Steven R. Harmon puts the importance of a common confession succinctly: Reciting the creeds invites us into solidarity with the saints gone before us who for two millennia have confessed this story with these same words. Reciting the creeds declares our solidarity with our sisters and brothers in Christ in other denominations who today embrace the story of the Triune God. Harmon, "Do Real Baptists Recite Creeds?" 27.

reality at the *eschaton*, there is also value in considering how to confess the faith together with all Christians. This is a visible sign of the catholicity of the church.

Discerning Belief

If, as McClendon observed, Catholic and Baptist Christians can agree that Scripture and tradition "are not two separate sources of authority but properly only one, both communities have a key to the role of creeds and confessions of faith as well."[151] Indeed, the Second Vatican Council provided a carefully nuanced definition describing the coinherence of Scripture and tradition as "bound together" in a reciprocal relationship and as "flowing out of the same divine well-spring" that "come together in some fashion to form one thing."[152] With this understanding, McClendon explains, the creeds function "as guides to the reading of Scripture, not as supplements to it."[153] They are, to borrow a phrase from Yves Congar, "monuments of tradition" that indicate how Christians at other times have read the Scriptures, and they are invitations to contemporary believers "to read them that way if we can." But in the end the creeds are, McClendon concluded, "simply hermeneutical aids" that must like any other reading strategy be subordinated to the biblical narrative that they seek to read.[154]

The creeds surely are guides for reading the Scriptures with an eye to seeing how Christians have historically understood them. Yet the invitation "to read them that way if we can" suggests that readers might also proceed without reference to them. Such an approach, however, would be unwise. Because the canon of Scripture and the creeds of the church developed together, neither can be grasped without reference to the other.[155] It is important to remember that the rule of faith enabled the early church to conceive of the two Testaments as one canon, and the creeds summarized

---

[151] McClendon, *Doctrine*, 470.

[152] *Vatican Council II*, vol. 1, *The Conciliar and Postconciliar Documents*, rev. ed. (New York: Costello, 2004); "Dogmatic Constitution on Divine Revelation" [*Dei Verbum*] §9, November 18, 1965, trans. Robert Murray, in *Decrees of the Ecumenical Councils*, vol. 2, *Trent to Vatican II*, ed. Norman P. Tanner (Northport, N.Y.: Costello, 2005), 755. However, because *Dei Verbum* §9 offers several statements differentiating Scripture and tradition, including that they are to be "accepted and venerated with the same sense of loyalty and reverence," Steven R. Harmon argues that while Baptists cannot offer an unqualified endorsement of the doctrine of Scripture and tradition, they can offer qualified approval and find a place within the pattern of theological contestation that produced it. Harmon, "*Dei Verbum* §9 in Baptist Perspective," *Ecclesiology* 5, no. 3 (2009): 299–321.

[153] McClendon, *Doctrine*, 470.

[154] McClendon, *Doctrine*, 471.

[155] Robert W. Jenson, *Canon and Creed* (Louisville, Ky.: Westminster John Knox, 2010), 11–18.

the trinitarian pattern of Christian Scripture.[156] Indeed, without the arc of the Christian story outlined in the creeds (and the rule), it is questionable whether readers will see Scripture as the unfolding narrative of the triune God. Yet to read the whole of Scripture as something other than the gospel story is (from the Christian standpoint) to misread it. Canon and creed are mutually reciprocal. Both canon and creed are needed to protect the church from distortions of the gospel.[157] As the next chapter will show, when Baptist interpreters were left to their own imaginations without the hermeneutical guidance of the historic creeds, they soon began to lose a sense of the trinitarian pattern of Christian Scripture. Reclaiming the mutuality of the canon of Scripture and the creeds of the church strengthens the church's witness to the Christ-centered truth of the gospel.

Yet even sympathetic readers of Scripture may worry that this sort of theological exegesis may not attend sufficiently to historical matters. For example, Robert Jenson suggests that the appearances of the Angel of the LORD in the Old Testament are not merely theophanies, but christophanies where the second person of the Trinity is manifest in human form. When he asks how readers can so easily identify the Angel as Jesus, Jenson points to the creed, in which "the second triune identity is a man, Jesus of Nazareth."[158] The use of the creed as hermeneutical shorthand may well keep readers from wandering beyond orthodoxy, but such a doctrinal rendering that imports the full weight of Christian dogmatic teaching retrospectively into the Old Testament rushes too quickly to a theological conclusion without seeking to listen to Israel's own voice in the plain sense of Scripture.

Brevard Childs offers an alternative strategy of reading the Bible that is both diachronic and theological. In considering how, for example, to understand the relation between the suffering servant of Isaiah 53 and the New Testament's kerygmatic witness to Jesus Christ in the Gospels, Childs points to the morphological fit between the redemptive activity of the servant and the suffering and death of Jesus Christ. The distinction, Childs argues, is between "God's revelation in the continuum of Israel's history" (the economic Trinity) and "the ontological manifestation of the triune deity in its eternity" (the immanent Trinity).[159] Here Childs glosses

---

[156] Jenson, *Canon and Creed*, 27–50.

[157] Jenson, *Canon and Creed*, 32.

[158] Jenson, *Canon and Creed*, 84. In returning to the angelology of patristic exegesis, Jenson parts company with Karl Barth who sharply distinguished between the Angel of the LORD and the Word incarnate in Jesus Christ "who cannot be prefigured by any such being or set alongside it as a fulfillment," in his *Church Dogmatics* III/3 (Edinburgh: T&T Clark, 1960), 487.

[159] Brevard S. Childs, *Isaiah* (Louisville, Ky.: Westminster John Knox, 2001), 423.

Karl Rahner's rule that "the 'economic' Trinity is the 'immanent' Trinity and the 'immanent' Trinity is the 'economic' Trinity," although he takes the relationship to be asymmetrical, thus making room for historical development within the economies of God's revelation.[160] In the final analysis, Childs suggests that there is an ontological relation between the two in the economy of God's redemption so that "in the suffering and death of the servant in Second Isaiah the self-same divine reality of Jesus Christ was made manifest."[161] Such a reading seems to be theologically informed by the arc of the biblical narrative as outlined in the creeds, while also attending to the diachronic development of the story in the canon.

Still some may wonder why the ancient ecumenical creeds should be privileged as guides for discerning belief. Baptists and other Free Church Christians are rightly concerned to emphasize the "I believe" voiced in the creeds. But the historic creeds do more than invite a confession of faith. The verb phrase "I believe" is followed by the preposition "in" as a stark reminder that faith is more than trust. Faith has an object: God—Father, Son, and Holy Spirit. This simple trinitarian structure gestures to the deep mystery of the faith that is the sum and substance of the biblical narrative. Yet it does so with simplicity and clarity. Other confessions and catechisms are also summaries of the Christian faith. But the Apostles' and Nicene Creeds differ in the respect that they attest to the faith in its apostolic form in a way that others do not, and indeed cannot. It is not surprising, then, that by the second century it was widely believed, and with good reason, that the rule of faith as confessed and taught in the church was inherited from the apostles.[162]

These ancient ecumenical creeds provide a basic outline of apostolic preaching and teaching to which the Scriptures attest. They do not possess an authority independent of Scripture but derive their authority from the biblical story that they summarize and ultimately from the triune God whose voice is heard in it. They are not full accounts of "the faith once delivered to the saints," but they do provide a kind of rule of faith that effectively regulates and guides the reading of interpretive communities.[163] That these creeds gained universal acceptance as statements of

---

[160] Karl Rahner, *The Trinity*, trans. Joseph Donceel (New York: Continuum, 1974), 22. E.g., Fred Sanders argues that "Rahner's Rule is inherently unstable, leaning sometimes toward a strict and total identification of economic and immanent Trinity, and sometimes toward a more carefully circumscribed account of the relationship between them," in his *The Image of the Immanent Trinity: Rahner's Rule and the Theological Interpretation of Scripture* (New York: Peter Lang, 2005), 6.

[161] Childs, *Isaiah*, 423.

[162] Kelly, *Early Christian Creeds*, 29.

[163] Freeman et al., "Confessing the Faith."

what the church believes is a testimony to the catholicity of the church as a quantitative expression of a universally inclusive communion of communions spread throughout time and space but also to the catholicity that is a manifestation of the qualitative dimension of existence that names the fullness of Christ and the gifts of Spirit that are determinative of the church's being.

At times in their history, some Baptists have found it necessary to appeal to the Four Fragile Freedoms, the Five Fundamentals, or the Six Principles to safeguard basic beliefs from the neglect or suppression of the majority.[164] Although each of these statements was issued as a corrective and thus was conceived as supplemental rather than elemental, over time there is a tendency for some to regard these qualifying statements as the *sine qua non* of faith, while the trinitarian and christological center described in the historic creeds fades into the background. The proponents of these formulas would undoubtedly look with suspicion on any who might suggest that casting out devils, speaking in tongues, taking up serpents, drinking deadly poisons, and healing the sick should be taken as a normative description, even though these are listed as signs of true faith in Mark 16:17-18. It might be argued that when severed from the larger gospel narrative, these marks name a faith that is more eccentric than catholic. Yet it might also be asked whether Baptist principles without the christological and trinitarian center are any less eccentric or any more catholic.[165]

In 2012 there was a discussion at the Baptist World Alliance annual gathering in Santiago, Chile, on *The Nature and Mission of the Church*, a study document issued in December 2005 by the Faith and Order Commission of the WCC.[166] The conversations were dynamic and lively. The participants readily affirmed the evangelical conviction that the church is the gathering of those who have responded to the gospel in faith and repentance. But they also struggled for language to express an equally

---

[164] Walter B. Shurden, *The Baptist Identity: Four Fragile Freedoms* (Macon, Ga.: Smyth & Helwys, 1993); Baptist Bible Union, Articles of Faith, in Lumpkin, *Baptist Confessions of Faith*, 384–89; John Griffith, *Gods Oracle and Christs Doctrine; or, The Six Principles of Christian Religion as They Were Taught and Delivered by Christ and His Apostles* (London: Richard Moon, 1655).

[165] In his treatment of Baptist theology, Fisher Humphreys thus begins not with Baptist distinctives but with beliefs shared with all Christians, emphasizing the catholicity rather than eccentricity of the Baptists in his *The Way We Were: How Southern Baptist Theology Has Changed and What It Means to Us All*, rev. ed. (Macon, Ga.: Smyth & Helwys, 1984), 15–27; and Humphreys, *Baptist Theology: A Really Short Version* (Brentwood, Tenn.: Baptist History and Heritage Society, 2007), 9.

[166] *Nature and Mission of the Church*.

important truth that, though the gathering community of the converted is wholly the church, it is not the whole church. Everyone expressed a belief in the one, holy, catholic, and apostolic church, but they also struggled to know what language they might use to express this truth. As they wrestled with this question, one of the Latin American participants told a remarkable story. He described being at an ecumenical gathering in which he expressed his disappointment that Roman Catholics have often claimed the term "catholic" as an exclusive reference to themselves. "No one can be a Christian without being catholic," he exclaimed, because "catholic represents a humble way of admitting that God's kingdom is greater than our denomination." Then his conversation partner, a Roman Catholic priest and theologian, shared his regret that Baptists have often claimed the term "evangelical" as an exclusive reference to themselves. He declared, "No one can be a true Christian without being evangelical." The Baptist brother concluded his story, "So here we were, a Baptist pastor proclaiming that one has to be catholic in order to be a true Christian, and a Roman Catholic priest proclaiming that in order to be a true Christian one has to be an evangelical."[167]

Though the way toward this evangelical catholicity is still emerging, Other Baptists have come to believe that it will entail a retrieval of the ancient ecumenical faith with an eye to the future. Baptists share with all Christians the trinitarian import of the historic creeds. Indeed, very few Baptists are inclined to reject the faith of the Apostles' Creed or any other historic creed up to the Chalcedonian formula. However, many Baptists are rightly wary of adopting a creed—even an ancient ecumenical one.[168] That they have consistently stood against the forced subscription to creeds as a matter of coercion or discipline should now be abundantly clear, but Other Baptists have been more open to the use of creeds when not employed to bind the conscience. By voluntarily reciting the ancient ecumenical creeds of the church, Other Baptists move beyond fundamentalism and liberalism and toward the bedrock of catholicity. This is the starting point for a generous orthodoxy. Only by digging through the recent historical layers of soil toward this bedrock can Baptists expect to engage in genuine ecumenical conversation. In so doing they live into the vision of evangelical catholicity exemplified by leaders like Alexander Maclaren and join their voices with a great cloud of witnesses in the unanimous acknowledgment of the faith thus manifesting their continuity

---

[167] Joel Sierra, "Latin American Perspectives on Baptist-Catholic Dialogue" (Baptist World Alliance, Doctrine and Church Unity Commission, Santiago, Chile, July 5, 2012).

[168] Estep, *Baptists and Christian Unity*, 170.

with the historic church. Such acts of confession are surely simple statements of where Other Baptists stand and what they believe, but even more
they move toward the unity for which the Lord Jesus prayed and which
the church must seek.

PART II

LIFE THAT REALLY IS LIFE

4

God in Three Persons

Just after the revised Baptist Faith and Message had been approved by the 1963 Southern Baptist Convention, James William McClendon Jr. offered a penetrating vision of the future of trinitarianism in Baptist life. The Baptist Faith and Message stated the doctrine with clarity and economy: "The eternal God reveals Himself to us as Father, Son, and Holy Spirit, with distinct personal attributes, but without division of nature, essence, or being."[1] McClendon suggested that with a few changes of terms the language might just as well be used to describe "the structure of a denominational agency" or "the floor plan of a new church building."[2] No doubt the key to Baptists becoming the de facto established church of the south often had more to do with organization and buildings than theology. But McClendon maintained that the guidebook tone of the confession, which reads like a quick tour through a theological museum, reflected a growing indifference to trinitarian faith and practice. In many respects, the state of trinitarianism among Baptists today is little different than it was four decades ago. When asked, "What is the doctrine of the Trinity?" most Baptists are probably not far from Dorothy Sayers' catechism of the average churchgoer, which answers, "The Father incomprehensible, the Son incomprehensible, and the whole thing incomprehensible."[3] The Trinity consequently remains for the most part a doctrine to be held despite its seeming lack of theological coherence or practical relevance.

---

[1] The Baptist Faith and Message II, in William L. Lumpkin, ed., *Baptist Confessions of Faith*, rev. ed. (Valley Forge, Pa.: Judson Press, 1969), 393.

[2] James Wm. McClendon Jr., "Some Reflections on the Future of Trinitarianism," *Review and Expositor* 63, no. 2 (1966): 150. McClendon examines the language from the then newly approved Baptist Faith and Message (1963 and 1925) as well as the New Hampshire Confession (1833). I would like to thank Fisher Humphreys for calling my attention to McClendon's article.

[3] Dorothy Sayers, *Creed or Chaos* (New York: Harcourt, Brace, 1949), 22.

Addressing a joint meeting of American and Southern Baptists at the Baptist Jubilee Advance in 1964, Carlyle Marney playfully observed that "we American Baptists are choking on a unitarianism that features a gnostic and superior-feeling smugness associated with the Fatherhood that is virtually childless." But he continued, "We Southern Baptists are victims of a different sort of Unitarianism—we are largely a Jesus-cult dressed like Buster Brown or Little Lord Fauntleroy, with the trappings of a Confederate Narcissus."[4] Though his observation was an obvious caricature, Marney had a point. The piety of many Baptists tilts toward unitarianism of the Second Person, just as for others it leans in the direction of unitarianism of the First Person.[5] Despite their theological confusion, Baptists seem to formally recognize the importance of the Trinity as evidenced in the long-standing tradition of including "Holy, Holy, Holy" as the first hymn in many hymnals. Yet this apparent liturgical priority is not always matched with theological integrity.[6] The rhetoric of "the Bible and the Bible only," while accurately reflecting a deep conviction, nevertheless left Baptists open to the imposition of alternative creed-like statements that have no connection to the historic Christian faith, thus making them ill equipped to discern the deep logic of the Bible as the unfolding story of the triune God. This is what is at stake.

From Mystery to Problem

On April 6, 1693, the General Assembly of General Baptists in England considered the following question:

> Whether Christ as he was the Word of God, John I, I, Albeit that he was God yet he is not of the Uncreeted Substance of his father But God made him a Creature only And secondly that this Creature was made

---

[4] Carlyle Marney, "The Prospect of Baptist Unity," address at Atlantic City, New Jersey, May 22, 1964, box 69, Carlyle Marney papers, David M. Rubenstein Rare Book & Manuscript Library, Duke University, Durham, N.C. To mark the Baptist Jubilee Celebration, the American and Southern Baptist Conventions held separate but simultaneous meetings May 19–22, 1964, at the Convention Center in Atlantic City, New Jersey.

[5] G. Ernest Wright attributed the phrase "Unitarianism of the Second Person" to Elton Trueblood, who applied it to the Christology invoked at the First Assembly of the WCC, which met in 1948 in Amsterdam. Wright, *The Old Testament and Theology* (New York: Harper & Row, 1969), 24. However, two years earlier H. Richard Niebuhr delineated three Unitarianisms in Christianity (i.e., of the Father, the Son, and the Spirit) in his "The Doctrine of the Trinity and the Unity of the Church," *Theology Today* 3, no. 3 (1946): 371–84.

[6] E.g., in *The Baptist Hymnal* (Nashville: Convention, 1991), out of 666 hymns, only 20 are trinitarian (a ratio of 1:33), but 268 of these 666 hymns are christological (a ratio of 1:2.5). Understanding how and why this is so, however, is not as easy as thumbing through the hymn book.

flesh & Blood & Bones in the Virgins Womb Not by takeing flesh of the Virgin Mary But yt ye Matter (viz) the Word was turned into flesh in the Virgins Wombe.[7]

The view in question, which denied both the full deity and humanity of Christ and was widely regarded as heretical, was ascribed to Matthew Caffyn, a messenger of the Assembly from Sussex. The language in question bore a striking resemblance to the charges against the last person burned as a heretic in England, Edward Wightman, who, like Caffyn, was also a Baptist. Among the charges against Wightman were his beliefs "that there is not the Trinity of Persons, the Father, the Son, and the holy Ghost, in the Unity of the Deity," "that Jesus Christ is only Man and a mere Creature and not both God and man in one Person," and "that Christ our Saviour took not human flesh of the substance of the Virgin *Mary* his Mother."[8] The similarity between the two suggested the severity of the question. At the time of the 1693 meeting, Caffyn was one of the most influential and controversial leaders of the General Baptists. His theological troubles began twenty years earlier when Thomas Monck published *A Cure for the Cankering Error of the New Eutychians.*[9] It sounded an alarm among the General Baptists against those who, like the fifth-century presbyter of Constantinople, denied the full humanity of Christ. Although Monck did not name him directly, Caffyn took the book to be a direct attack on his person and theology. The General Assembly rejected Caffyn's appeal to censure Monck but stopped short of condemning Caffyn's heterodoxy. The attempt at a via media did little to calm the growing controversy. A tract war erupted a year later between Caffyn and one of the members of his congregation in Horsham named Richard Haines.

---

[7] W. T. Whitley, ed., *Minutes of the General Assembly of the General Baptist Churches in England* (London: Kingsgate Press, 1909), 1:39–40.

[8] James I, "A Narration of the Burning of Edward Wightman," in *A True Relation of the Commissions and Warrants for the Condemnation and Burning of Bartholomew Legatt and Thomas Withman* [*sic*] (London: Michael Spark, 1651), 7–13. In this chapter, emphasis is original unless noted. Champlin Burrage, *The Early English Dissenters in Light of Recent Research* (Cambridge: Cambridge University Press, 1912), 1:216–20; and Ian Atherton and David Como, "The Burning of Edward Wightman: Puritanism, Prelacy, and the Politics of Heresy in Early Modern England," *English Historical Review* 120, no. 489 (2005): 1215–50. Wightman was put to death in April 1612. That he was a Baptist (Anabaptist) is suggested by two of the charges against him: "That the baptizing of Infants is an abominable custom" and "That the use of Baptism is to be Administred in Water, only to Converts of sufficient age of understanding, converted from Infidelity to Faith." James I, "Narration of the Burning of Edward Wightman," 8. Wightman's case appears in the tract in connection with three other antitrinitarians, Walther, Thomas, and Bartholomew Legate, all of whom were burned at the stake prior to Wightman.

[9] Thomas Monck, *A Cure for the Cankering Error of the New Eutychians* (London, 1673).

Haines characterized Caffyn's doctrine as heretical in language borrowed from Monck's book, claiming, "The errour is his Principle concerning our Blessed Lord and Saviour, of whom Caffin saith, *That he did not take his flesh of the Virgin Mary*, and that he was not *made of the Seed of David*."[10] Caffyn replied immediately, emphatically rejecting the charge of Eutychianism. In an attempt to clarify his view on the humanity of Christ, Caffyn wrote:

> And if by his saying, that *I deny that Jesus Christ took his Flesh of the Virgin Mary*, he means, that the Redemption of Mankind is no more pretious then the Death, and Blood-sheding of a body of Flesh, in the fallen Estate, under Condemnation for Original sin, and that was in the beginning of the Earth, as the first Man *Adam* was, then do I readily declare my dissent thereunto, and so will (in some respect) the Author of that Book, (Mr. M[onck]) and most others.

He continued by offering his view of the incarnation:

> But this I consent unto, and verily believe, that the true Messiah, whom the Father hath sealed to be the Blessed Saviour of the World, was conceived in the Virgin *Mary*, and there took our Nature, and our Form and so was in all points like unto his Brethren, sin excepted; the Son of *Abraham*, the Son of *David*, confessed to be, while the first Man was of the Earth, Earthey, the second Man the Lord from Heaven, I *Cor.* 15.47.[11]

Caffyn did not clearly affirm that flesh of Jesus was truly human, received from his human mother, Mary. The less than unambiguous explanation did little to satisfy his critics. Haines repeated his charges in a second tract to which Caffyn also offered a rejoinder, leading Haines finally to submit an appeal to the General Assembly in 1680.[12]

The theological confusion about Caffyn's Christology is already evident in his 1660 tract *Faith in Gods Promises*, which attacked the Quakers on their denial of the flesh of Christ. There he argued that "the Eternal Spirit which dwelt in the Man, whom the Jews Crucified; which Spirit the Apostles afterwards received in them, is not the Christ, the Saviour of the world, but the visible man, to whom the Spirit was given, *John*

---

[10] Richard Haines, *New Lords, New Laws* (London, 1674), 6.

[11] Matthew Caffyn, *Envy's Bitterness Corrected* (London, 1674), 31–32.

[12] Matthew Caffyn, *A Raging Wave Foming out his own Shame* (London: Francis Smith, 1675); Richard Haines, *His Appeal to The General Assembly of Dependent Baptists Convened in London, from most Parts of the Nation, the Third day of June; 1680* ([London?], 1680).

3.34."[13] Caffyn admonished Quakers for their gnostic-like Christology that denied that Christ was ever physically seen or heard. Yet his own view of the incarnation was heard by some Baptists as falling short of attributing full humanity to Christ. It is possible that Caffyn was drawing on the so-called *extra Calvinisticum*, which extended Chalcedonian Christology to teach that "the eternal Son of God, even after the Incarnation, was united to the human nature to form One Person but was not restricted to the flesh."[14] However, the resistance he encountered suggested otherwise. For Caffyn, the humanity of Jesus did not derive from Mary but was created from nothing and united with the divine Logos, merely passing through the Virgin's womb. He thus seemed to diminish Christ's humanity, calling into question the fullness of the incarnation in ways that were reminiscent of the "celestial flesh" Christology of earlier Anabaptists, Menno Simons and Melchior Hoffman.[15] Caffyn's refusal to appeal to the settled formulations of historic orthodoxy and his deliberate preference for using strict biblical language left him open to criticism. More problematic still was that this denuded account of Christ's humanity seemed to set Caffyn (and those who followed him) on a course toward the antitrinitarian theology of Socinianism that affirmed the humanity of Christ but rejected his deity.

Caffyn was not the first General Baptist to scruple over the Trinity. In 1624 Elias Tookey and a group of seventeen members withdrew from the London congregation founded by Thomas Helwys and John Murton. When the seceding group appealed to be received by the Waterlander Mennonites, it became clear that several of the Tookey fellowship did not believe there were "three different persons in the Deity which manner of speaking is not found in the Scripture."[16] It was a view not unlike that of the notorious Oxford antitrinitarian, John Biddle. When Matthew Caffyn arrived at Oxford in 1643 as a student at All Souls College, Biddle had been gone for two years. Having received his M.A. from Oxford at

[13] Matthew Caffyn, *Faith in Gods Promises The Saints best Weapon* (London: S. Dover, 1660), 38.

[14] David Willis-Watkins, *Calvin's Catholic Christology: The Function of the So-Called Extra Calvinisticum in Calvin's Theology* (Leiden: E. J. Brill, 1966), 2:1.

[15] A. C. Underwood, *A History of the English Baptists* (London: Baptist Union, 1847), 127. Melchiorism denotes the "celestial flesh" Christology popularized by Melchior Hoffman, a German Anabaptist preacher of the 1530s who taught that Jesus did not receive his humanity from Mary. It is possible that Caffyn picked up the Melchiorite Christology through Menno Simons, although there is no clear indication that Caffyn actually read Menno. It seems more likely that his eccentric Christological views were derived from a simple biblicism.

[16] Tookey's correspondence, quoted in H. John McLachlan, *Socinianism in Seventeenth-Century England* (Oxford: Oxford University Press, 1951), 38–39.

Magdalen Hall, Biddle left to become the master of a school in Gloucester. In 1648 he published his own confession of faith, which declared that the Father is the "Most High God, Creator of Heaven and Earth" and that Jesus Christ "hath no other then a Humane Nature" and is "not the Most High God, the same with the Father, but subordinate to Him."[17] There is no indication that Biddle and Caffyn ever met, though they surely imbibed in the same spirit of radical dissent percolating at Oxford in the 1630s and 1640s. For example, Robert Grebby, who died in 1654, was the chaplain of New College during Caffyn's study at Oxford. Grebby escaped wider notice by not publishing his controversial views, although he echoed the Socinian doctrine that the "Trinity of p[er]sons in ye Godhead doe tell us onely of 3 empty names."[18] Caffyn was expelled from All Souls in 1645 for embracing anabaptistical notions, which often was associated with additional expressions of heterodoxy. The Oxford radicalism was part of an emerging theological outlook that soon gained the attention of those in high places. When in February 1652, *The Racovian Catechism* (a compendium of Socinianism) was published in Latin, Biddle translated it into English to ensure the dissemination of its antitrinitarian theology.[19] A protest led by John Owen, Cromwell's chaplain, and other anti-antitrinitarian theologians, resulted in an act of Parliament, ordering all copies of the catechism to be "seized" and "burnt."[20]

Seeking to strike while the iron was hot, Owen and his allies published a set of *Humble Proposals* in March 1652, which urged Parliament to prevent "persons of corrupt judgements, from publishing dangerous Errours, and Blasphemies."[21] Owen and company assumed there would be widespread public support for the suppression of antitrinitarianism. It was a misjudgment. Instead, their action unleashed a torrent of criticism—not to advocate for Arianism but to protect the liberty of conscience that was under threat by Owen and Parliament. Roger Williams, ardent defender of religious liberty and founder of the First Baptist Church in America, offered his own set of "Proposals from the Scriptures" in which he humbly asked "whether it be not the pleasure of God, that the Judgement and Condemnation of such false Teachers and Hereticks be left to [God]

---

[17] John Biddle, *A Confession of Faith Touching the Holy Trinity According to the Scripture*, Articles I, III, and IV (London, 1648), 1, 19, 29.

[18] Manuscript from Queen's College Library, Oxford, cited in Sarah Mortimer, *Reason and Religion in the English Revolution: The Challenge of Socinianism* (Cambridge: Cambridge University Press, 2010), 164. See also Andrew Clark, ed., *The Life and Times of Anthony Wood: Antiquary of Oxford, 1632–1695* (Oxford: Clarendon, 1891), 2:55.

[19] *Catechesis Ecclesiarium Quae in Regno Polonia* (London: William Dugard, 1651).

[20] *Votes of Parliament Touching the Book commonly called The Racovian Catechism* (London: John Field, 1652).

himself?" and "whether for the Civil powers to assume a Judgement in Spirituals, be not against the Liberties given by Christ Jesus to his people?"[22] Other prominent religious and civil leaders spoke out against the *Humble Proposals* and in defense of the freedom of conscience, including Sir Henry Vane junior, a member of Parliament, and John Milton, who as the Commonwealth's secretary for Foreign Languages had likely licensed the publication of *The Racovian Catechism* in the first place.[23] Owen and his ministerial allies surely personified Milton's earlier scornful observation that "New *presbyter* is but old *priest* writ large."[24]

The failure to achieve a politically established antitrinitarian settlement did little to diminish Owen's zeal. In November 1652, just after being named vice chancellor of Oxford, he began lecturing on the Trinity. The result was *Vindiciae Evangelium*, a seven-hundred-page tome attacking Biddle and Socinianism.[25] Biddle's warm reception by members of the Dunning's Alley church, a General Baptist congregation in London led by the physician and elder John Griffith, soon erupted in controversy. The Baptists, who were sticklers for the liberty of conscience, also opposed antitrinitarianism as a dangerous heresy, prompting Griffith to challenge Biddle to a debate, "Whether Jesus Christ be the most High or Almighty God?" The disputation occurred on June 28, 1655, at the Stone Chapel in London where Edmund Chillenden, another General Baptist, was the minister, reportedly drawing an audience of five hundred people. But before a second meeting could be scheduled to continue debate, Biddle was imprisoned and brought before the Council of State on charges that he had publically denied the deity of Christ.[26] His accusers were a group of

---

[21] John Owen et al., *The Humble Proposals* (London: Robert Ibbitson, 1652), title page.

[22] Roger Williams, *A Testimony to the Said Fourth Paper [Presented by Maior Butler] By way of Explanation upon the four Proposals of it* (London: Giles Calvert, 1652), 1–3. Williams makes it clear that *he* is not a heretic in the strict sense of "one *obstinate* in *Fundamentalls*"—namely, the six principles of "Repentance from dead workes, Faith towards God, the doctrine of Baptismes, and of laying on of hands, the Resurrection, and eternall Judgement, *Heb. 6.2.&c.*," in his*The Bloudy Tenent of Persecution*, in *The Complete Writings of Roger Williams* (New York: Russell & Russell, 1963), 3:88–89.

[23] Mortimer, *Reason and Religion in the English Revolution*, 200 and 166. E.g., the anonymous tract, *Several Queries*, published in April 1652, went further to challenge the very substance of the Trinity, arguing that neither Christ nor the apostles seemed to have required trinitarian faith from their converts. *Several Queries* (1652), 1–2.

[24] John Milton, "On the New Forcers of Conscience Under the Long Parliament," [1646?], in *John Milton Complete Poems and Major Prose*, ed. Merritt Y. Hughes (New York: Macmillan, 1957), 144–45.

[25] John Owen, *Vindiciae Evangelicae; or, The Mystery of the Gospell Vindicated, and Socinianisme Examined* (Oxford: Leon Lichfield, 1655).

[26] Firsthand accounts of the Biddle-Griffith debate and Biddle's subsequent imprisonment are conveyed in two anonymous tracts published by Richard Moone: *A True State of the*

overzealous Presbyterian heresy hunters who appealed to the blasphemy law passed (but never repealed) by Parliament in 1648, which carried the death penalty for antitrinitarianism.[27]

Biddle was not without supporters among Independents and Baptists, who made impassioned appeals in his case on grounds of the liberty of conscience. Several anonymous tracts appeared in July arguing for Biddle's release. One of these unnamed supporters, likely a Baptist, admitted that Biddle, though errant in theological judgment, was nevertheless a true believer. The defender wrote:

Case of Liberty of Conscience in the Common-wealth of England (London: Richard Moone, 1655), esp. 2; and *The Spirit of Persecution Again broken loose, By An Attempt to put in Execution against Mr. John Biddle Master of Arts, an abrogated Ordinance of the Lords and Commons for punishing Blasphemies and Heresies. Together with, A full Narrative of The whole Proceedings upon that Ordinance against the said Mr. John Biddle and Mr. William Kiffen Pastor of a baptised Congregation in the City of London* (London: Richard Moone, 1655). Another anonymous tract also supported Biddle, *An Humble Advise To The Right Honorable The Lord Mayor, The Recorder, and the Rest of the Justices of the Honorable Bench. To the good men of the Jury, aud [sic] at the Sessions House in the Old–Bayley, London, in behalf of Mr. John Bidle, prisoner in Newgate* (London, [1655?]). Excellent secondary accounts are provided by McLachlan, *Socinianism in Seventeenth-Century England*, 207–9; and Blair Worden, "Toleration and the Cromwellian Protectorate," in *Persecution and Toleration,* ed. W. J. Sheils (Oxford: Published for the Ecclesiastical Historical Society by B. Blackwell, 1984), 199–233. Griffith's Dunning's Alley congregation and the Stone Chapel congregation led by Edmund Chillenden were both General Baptists in 1655. The Dunning's Alley church, gathered by Griffith about 1640, was the smallest member of the six primary General Baptist congregations of London. The congregation, founded by Edmund Chillenden around 1653, met in the Stone Chapel at St. Paul's and gradually became Particular Baptist. It does not seem to have been part of the General Assembly in 1656, as Chillenden's name does not appear among the signatories of "Ye General Agreement" of the General Assembly of General Baptists. John Griffith, however, is listed as a signatory among the elders, alongside Matthew Caffyn and Thomas Moncke, who are listed as messengers. See W. T. Whitley, *The Baptists of London, 1612–1928* (London: Kingsgate, 1928), 108, 113; and Whitley, *Minutes of the General Assembly*, li–lii, 6–9.

[27] *Spirit of Persecution Again broken loose,* 2. The Presbyterians who laid charges against Biddle became known as Beacon-Firers because of the names of the tracts they published: *A Beacon Set on Fire* (London, 1652); and *A Second Beacon Fired* (London, 1654). They included Luke Fawn, Samuel Gellibrand, Joshua Kirton, John Rothwell, Thomas Underhill, and Nathaniel Webb. They called on Parliament and Cromwell to suppress "blasphemous books" and punish the authors. During the Commonwealth, High Presbyterians were notorious as heresy hunters. Thomas Edwards and Robert Baillie were two of the most (in)famous. Baillie warned that the Baptists were in fact the fount of all heresy in his *Anabaptisme, the True Fountaine of Independency, Brownisme, Antinomy, Familisme, and Most of the Other Errours Which for the Time Doe Trouble the Church of England* (London: M.F. for Samuel Gallibrand, 1647). Edwards was an equal opportunity heresy hunter, providing a "Catalogue and Discovery of many of the Errors, Heresies, Blasphemies and pernicious Practices of the Sectaries of this time, vented and acted in England in these four last years." Edwards, *Gangraena: The First and Second Part,* 3rd ed. (London: Ralph Smith, 1646).

So that these things well weighed in the true balance of Scripture truth, and true Christian charity, we hope it will appear, though he may erre in some part of his Judgement, yet can he not by any means be esteemed a Believer in God through Jesus Christ, and one that exerciseth himself to have alwayes a good Conscience, void of offence toward God and men, having hope of the Resurrection both of the just and unjust; and so not an Heretick, the Characters of such an one not at all appearing in him: and much less a Blasphemer, having never been known to be either a Curser, or Swearer, or Rayler against acknowledged Truths.[28]

The writer concluded by calling for Biddle's release with the caveat that "though he should somewhat mistake the way, yet doubtless, God, who often accepteth the will for the deed, will look upon it as an Error of his zeal and love, and receive him to his mercy."[29] A second anonymous tract offered a strong case against Biddle's arrest on legal grounds, disputing the adequacy of the charges against him, exposing the lack evidence for prosecution, and most importantly arguing that the 1648 blasphemy law was superseded by the Instrument of Government of the Commonwealth, adopted in 1653, which declared that any laws that violate the liberty of "such as profess faith in God by Jesus Christ . . . shall be esteemed as null and void."[30] This second unidentified supporter, also most likely a Baptist, pointed out that, in addition to criminalizing Socinianism, unitarianism, and Arianism, the 1648 blasphemy ordinance also defined Anabaptism as illegal, making it punishable to maintain "that the baptizing of Infants is unlawful." The author explains that the antipaedobaptist clause had already been used in the arrest of William Kiffen, a prominent London merchant and Baptist minister.[31]

---

[28] *True State of the Case of Liberty of Conscience*, 6. The concluding paragraph appeals to the parable of the wheat and tares (Matt 13) in a fashion similar to that of Roger Williams in *Bloudy Tenent*, in *Complete Writings*, 3:97–119. The author also makes the same argument as Roger Williams about heresy as one obstinate in fundamentals (3:88–89).

[29] *True State of the Case of Liberty of Conscience*, 7.

[30] *Spirit of Persecution Again broken loose*, 1–9; The Instrument of Government of the Commonwealth Articles XXXVII–XXXVIII, in Samuel Rawson Gardiner, ed., *The Constitutional Documents of the Puritan Revolution 1625–1660* (Oxford: Clarendon, 1936), 416.

[31] *Spirit of Persecution Again broken loose,* 18–20. That the anonymous author was likely a Baptist is evident by such features as the repeated appeals to the liberty of conscience, reference to Kiffen's Baptist church as "a Baptized Congregation," and rebutting the ascription to Baptists as "falsly so called" Anabaptists. Presbyterian heresy hunters consistently described the Baptists as "Anabaptists." Baptists resisted the moniker because it was intended to conjure up the radical specter of the Münster rebellion, where in 1534 Anabaptist fanatics took control of the north German city as they awaited the return of Christ and the establishment of the millennium. The First London Confession (1644) contains the disclaimer "The Confession of Faith, of those Churches which are commonly (though falsely) called Anabaptists," in Lumpkin, *Baptist Confessions of Faith*, 153.

In September 1655, the Baptists circulated *The Petition of Divers Gathered Churches*, addressed to Oliver Cromwell, asking for the old blasphemy law to be declared "null and void." The petition characterized Biddle as "a man, though differing from most of us in many great matters of faith, yet by reason of his diligent study in the holy Scripture, sober and peaceable conversation, which some of us have intimate good knowledg of, we cannot but judge every way capable of the liberty promised in the Government."[32] Though the Baptists regarded Biddle to be a "most mistaken Christian," they noted that he was "sober and peaceable," and thus his liberty "should have been protected."[33] Indeed, the Baptists did not consider Biddle to be a "blasphemer" but rather looked upon him as a fellow Christian who "did heartily acknowledge Jesus Christ to be his Lord and God, and hoped in Him, and honoured Him, believing, whatsoever he or any other could bring him out of the Holy Scripture concerning Christ."[34] In February 1656, ten gathered congregations issued a seven-page tract addressed to the officers and soldiers of the army. Among names associated with the supporting churches were Thomas Lambe and William Kiffen, two of the leading Baptist ministers in London. They asked of John Biddle, "What's the Blasphemy that this man's guilty of, that he may not be permitted to live among men in a Common-Wealth, but must be buryed in exilement that he must not breath in the sacred air of Liberty?"[35] They continued to press:

> But doth not Mr. *Biddle* profess the Christian Religion, contained in the Holy Scriptures? Hath he not made them his study day and night and fasting and prayer these many yeers? Is he not like *Apollos* mighty in the Scriptures? Doth he assert any thing which is not plainly laid down in the Scriptures? Or is it not his crime that *he believes the Scriptures according to their most obvious and nearest signification, and not according to the mystical and remote Interpretation*? Its confess'd, a man may erre in taking Scriptures to litterally; but is it blaspheymy so to do when a man doth it with a mind ready to be informed?[36]

---

[32] *The Petition of Divers Gathered Churches, and others wel affected, in and about the city of London, for declaring the ordinance of the Lords and Commons, for punishing blasphemies and heresies, null and void* (London, 1655), 2.

[33] *Petition of Divers Gathered Churches*, 4.

[34] *Spirit of Persecution Again broken loose*, 4.

[35] *To the Officers and Souldiers of the Army* (London, 1656), 1–2.

[36] *To the Officers and Souldiers of the Army*, 2–3 (emphasis added). The Baptists seem to recognize that Biddle's errors had their source in a simple biblicism (i.e., attributing to the Scriptures "their most obvious and nearest signification"), while they also seemed to understand that trinitarian theology relied on a "mystical and remote Interpretation."

Biddle was sent into exile until 1658, but in 1662 he was imprisoned again in London where he soon died. Antitrinitarianism, however, continued to thrive.[37]

The Baptist support for Biddle was not a referendum on his antitrinitarianism. They did not commend his theology, but they did defend his liberty to preach and publish his convictions without government interference. They regarded him to be a sincere but misguided Christian. Nevertheless, they shared his suspicion of the ontologically saturated and politically charged language of the Athanasian Creed. They preferred instead to profess their faith in "words that are found in the holy Scriptures" over the "unscriptural words & notions of 'Trinity in Unity, & Unity in Trinity, of three persons in one essence, of the hypostatical Union of two natures in one person, &c.'"[38] The Baptists strenuously objected to such formulas when they were wielded by heresy-hunting Presbyterians to bind the free conscience and restrict religious liberty, the protection of which they celebrated as a "glorious Gem in the Protectorian Crown."[39] Indeed, the Baptists held the strictest conviction on toleration among all dissenters, consistently advocating for religious liberty, not only for themselves, or even for all Christians (as the Instrument of Government made provision), but for *all* people—even those considered to be blasphemers and heretics. The Particular Baptists, led by William Kiffen, maintained a solid trinitarian confession of faith from their inception, but they also held that it was "the magistrates duty to tender the liberty of mens' consciences . . . and to protect all under them from all wrong, injury, oppression and molestation."[40]

The General Baptist statement on the Trinity was decidedly more vague. When they issued the Standard Confession of 1660, Matthew Caffyn was one of the signatories. The statement declared in three separate articles, "We believe . . . that there is but one God the Father (I) . . . that there is one Lord Jesus Christ, by whom are all things (III) . . . [and] that there is one holy Spirit, the pretious gift of God" (VII). However, it provided no hint as to how the three persons are related as one Godhead,

---

[37] Nigel Smith, "And if God Was One of Us: Paul Best, John Biddle, and the Antitrinitarian Heresy in Seventeenth-Century England," in *Heresy, Literature, and Politics in Early Modern English Culture*, ed. David Loewenstein and John Marshall (New York: Cambridge University Press, 2006), 160–84.

[38] *Petition of Divers Gathered Churches*, 4. The quotes are from the Athanasian Creed.

[39] *To the Officers and Souldiers of the Army*, 5.

[40] First London Confession, Article XLVIII, Note, rev. 1646 ed. (Rochester, N.Y.: Backus Book Publishers, 1981), 17–18. The Particular Baptists, though averse to the metaphysically laden language of the so-called Athanasian Creed, nevertheless adopted a statement on the Trinity in Article II with a clear Nicene ring. Lumpkin, *Baptist Confessions of Faith*, 156–57.

and it permitted baptism either "in the name of the Father, Son, and holy Spirit, or in the name of the Lord Jesus Christ" (XI). The statement deliberately avoided using any language from the Athanasian Creed, which Caffyn and others found problematic. Although the Standard Confession commended "the true Church of Christ" to withdraw fellowship from the unorthodox and disorderly (XVII), which many in the Assembly believed Caffyn to be, it also prescribed "that all men should have the free liberty of their own consciences in matters of religion" and declared that any in authority who seek to bind the conscience are acting "expressly contrary to the mind of Christ" (XXIV).[41]

The trinitarian ambiguity of the Standard Confession, which was written in part to appease accusations of radicalism and insurrection after the restoration of the monarchy, proved to be an insufficiently orthodox basis for the unity of faith and practice. Indeed, in his account of the history of Anabaptists in England, Anglican clergyman and historian John Lewis concluded that one is inclined to think that the authors and subscribers of the Standard Confession attempted "to conceal their Opinions of the holy Trinity."[42] In a book published in 1701 and titled *The Vail Turn'd Aside*, Christopher Cooper of Ashford in Kent went so far as to claim that most of the Baptists in Kent and Sussex denied the Trinity because of the influence of Caffynite theology.[43] As Stephen Nye's 1687 book, *A Brief History of the Unitarians*, indicates, antitrinitarianism continued to flourish in England from the Restoration to the Revolution.[44] But because the 1689 Act of Toleration criminalized any denial of "the doctrine of the blessed Trinity" in preaching or writing, proponents of antitrinitarianism practiced their skills of dissimulation when necessary to escape suspicion.[45] Caffyn was a master of theological obfuscation, and the charge of heresy against him, which had been brewing for decades, was not upheld at the 1693 General Assembly. This allowed him to freely disseminate his heterodoxy until his death in 1714 at the age of eighty-six.[46]

---

[41] The Standard Confession or A Brief Confession or Declaration of Faith, in Lumpkin, *Baptist Confessions of Faith*, 225–35; and Whitley, *Minutes of the General Assembly*, 10–22.

[42] John Lewis, *A Brief History of the Rise and Progress of Anabaptism in England* (London, 1738), 111. As a Latitudinarian, or Low Churchman, Lewis criticized High Church theology on the one hand and Anabaptists on the other.

[43] Lewis, *Brief History of Anabaptism*, 91–92; cited in C. E. Whiting, *Studies in English Puritanism from the Restoration to the Revolution, 1660–1668* (New York: Macmillan, 1931), 89–90.

[44] Stephen Nye, *A Brief History of the Unitarians, Called also Socinians in Four Letters, Written to a Friend* (London, 1687). Nye greatly expanded the original 183-page text in his second edition, *The Faith of One God, who is only the Father* (London, 1691).

[45] The Toleration Act of 1689, Article XVII, in E. Neville Williams, ed., *The Eighteenth Century Constitution, 1688–1815* (Cambridge: Cambridge University Press, 1960), 46.

[46] Whitley, *Minutes of the General Assembly*, 40.

Caffyn's theological adversary, Thomas Monck of Buckinghamshire, was also a signatory to the Standard Confession of 1660. Without directly naming Caffyn in *A Cure for the Cankering Error* (1673), Monck attacked the "Erronious and Heretical" opinions associated with him as a revival of Eutychianism. Monck attributed to the Eutychians the view "That our blessed Mediator did not take his Flesh of the *Virgin Mary*, neither was he made of the Seed of David according to the Flesh."[47] Much of Monck's book concerns a defense of the full deity and humanity of Christ without which he could not be the savior, and two of the ten chapters take up questions of the Trinity. Monck's discussion of the Trinity begins with "the proof of it from the Scriptures,"[48] after which he considers "the use" of the doctrine, because many of the old General Baptists held that all articles of faith should be defended "in Scripture Words and terms & no other terms."[49] His Scripture "proofs" are familiar, including the plural divine voice (Gen 1:26), the Lord's baptism (Matt 3:16-17), the great commission (Matt 28:19), the promised Comforter (John 15:26), the great benediction (2 Cor 13:13), and the Johannine Comma (1 John 5:7).[50]

Monck argues by these and other Scriptures that without knowledge of the Trinity living faith and right worship are impossible. As proof Monck quotes Jesus from the Gospel of John, which declares, "This is life eternal, that they might know thee the only true God, and Jesus Christ whom thou hast sent" (John 17:3). For Monck the Trinity is the *esse* of all faith and practice, affirming in language from the Athanasian Creed: "We worship the Trinity in Unity, and the Unity in Trinity."[51] He concludes with a discussion of the uses of the Trinity, which include confirmation of the truth, consolation of believers, and communion with God and one another.[52] Later in the text, Monck quotes the Cappadocian father Gregory of Nazianzus as saying:

---

[47] Monck, *Cure for the Cankering Error*, cover page.

[48] Monck, *Cure for the Cankering Error*, 36.

[49] Whitley, *Minutes of the General Assembly*, 51. In particular many objected to Nicene language as an unbiblical imposition upon the faith.

[50] Monck, *Cure for the Cankering Error*, 36–37. Monck's citations of Scripture conform to the King James Version rather than the Geneva Bible, which was preferred by Puritans.

[51] Monck, *Cure for the Cankering Error*, 42. The phrase is a quote from the so-called Athanasian Creed, 27, in Jaroslav Pelikan and Valerie Hotchkiss, eds., *Creeds and Confession of Faith in the Christian Tradition* (New Haven, Conn.: Yale University Press, 2004), 1:677. Some Baptists were especially averse to Articles 2 and 42, which declared, "Unless one keeps it [the catholic faith] in its entirety inviolate, one will assuredly perish eternally," and "this is the catholic faith. Unless one believes it faithfully and steadfastly, one will not be able to be saved" (1:676–77).

[52] Monck, *Cure for the Cankering Error*, 41–48.

I cannot imagine one, but presently I am compassed about on every side with the brightness of three: neither can I distinguish three, but forthwith I am brought again to one. Further, in the Persons of the Deity there is an order, but there is none inequality: there is a distinction, but no diversity.[53]

Moderates like Thomas Grantham, who found the Trinity in "no way offensive to Christianity" and saw "no inconveniency" in referring to Father, Son, and Holy Spirit as "persons," nevertheless stopped short of promoting the immanent trinitarian language of the Cappadocians, preferring instead to provide a simple biblical account of the Godhead.[54] Yet even though he believed some of the words of the Nicene Creed were "ambiguous," Grantham still reprinted it in his *Christianismus Primitivus*, considering that "the Doctrine therein contained is full of verity."[55] Monck, however, prescribed no cure for the sickness spread by the Eutychian heresy apart from a full affirmation of trinitarian faith.

Six years after the publication of Monck's *Cure*, a group of fifty-five General Baptist messengers, elders, and brethren from the Midlands issued the Orthodox Creed (1679). The confession of faith, which embraced Monck's trinitarian prescription, alluded to Caffyn in the preface: "We are sure that the denying of baptism is a less evil than to deny the Divinity or Humanity of Christ."[56] Article 3 particularly resonates with the language and theology of the Nicene-Constantinopolitan Creed, affirming that in the "unity of the Godhead, there are three persons, or subsistences,

---

[53] Monck, *Cure for the Cankering Error*, 69.

[54] Thomas Grantham, *Christianismus Primitivus; or, The Ancient Christian Religion* II.2.III–IV (London: Francis Smith, 1678), 40, 43. Grantham preferred the Standard Confession, which he edited in 1678. His revised version was approved by the General Assembly in 1691. For a more positive assessment of Grantham's orthodoxy, see Philip E. Thompson, "A New Question in Baptist History: Seeking a Catholic Spirit among Early Baptists," *Pro Ecclesia* 8, no. 1 (1999): 51–72. For a fuller treatment of the moderate position, see Daniel Allen, *Moderate Trinitarian* (London: Mary Fabian at Mercers Chappel in Cheapside, 1699). Allen's "moderate" trinitarianism was addressed to Joseph Taylor, pastor of the White's Alley congregation in London, who is mentioned as one of the leaders of the orthodox anti-Caffyn party. Whitley, *Minutes of the General Assembly*, 56n8. Peter Lake rightly warns against employing the terms "radical" and "moderate" as hypostasized categories. Instead, he suggests that they function as modifiers of substantive terms such as puritan, Calvinist, or whatever. Peter Lake, *The Boxmaker's Revenge: "Orthodoxy," "Heterodoxy" and the Politics of the Parish in Early Stuart London* (Stanford, Calif.: Stanford University Press, 2001), 398–99. For a treatment of how "moderate puritanism" sought this sort of balance between extremes, see Lake, *Moderate Puritans and the Elizabethan Church* (London: Cambridge University Press, 1982), 6 and 77–92. Thus Grantham is described as a moderate General Baptist whose theological moderation sought a balance between enforced orthodoxy on the one hand and unchecked heterodoxy on the other.

[55] Grantham, *Christianismus Primitivus* II.5.III, 60–61.

[56] Lumpkin, *Baptist Confessions of Faith*, 295.

the father, the word, or son, and the holy spirit, of which substance, power, eternity, and will each having the whole divine essence, yet the essence undivided." The Father is described as "neither begotten nor proceeding." The Son is "eternally begotten of the father." The Holy Spirit is "of the father and the son proceeding." The article concludes by quoting the trinitarian formulae in the Johannine Comma (1 John 5:7) and the great commission (Matt 28:19).[57] The articles on the divine nature of Christ (IV), the incarnation (V), the union of the two natures (VI), the communication of properties (VII), and the Holy Spirit (VIII) similarly echo Chalcedonian and Nicene language.[58] Article XXXVIII contains the startling statement that the Nicene, (so-called) Athanasian, and Apostles' Creeds "ought [thoroughly] to be received, and believed . . . to prevent heresy in doctrine, and practice."[59] The rich trinitarian theology of the Orthodox Creed stood in striking contrast to the thin biblicism of the Standard Confession. Yet despite the elegance of its prose and the orthodoxy of its message, it never gained widespread acceptance among General Baptists nor proved to be a basis for unity in the General Assembly.

After their refusal to censure Caffyn in 1693, the General Assembly did not meet for three years. When they gathered again in 1696, a minority of the orthodox party calling itself the General Association organized around a clear trinitarian confession. The association declined to have fellowship with the General Assembly because even moderates like Thomas Grantham tolerated Caffyn and others with his antitrinitarian sentiments. In 1698 a letter from the churches of Northamptonshire was read to the General Assembly. It asked whether the opinion that Christ the Son "was not of the Uncreated Nature & substance of the Father neither of the Created Nature & Substance of his Mother" was "Sound Doctrine or Error." The view, which was identified as belonging to Matthew Caffyn, "was Owned by all Save one" in the General Assembly to be erroneous.[60] It was agreed to hear his case at the next meeting of the Assembly, but, when Caffyn was brought to trial in May 1700, he was again cleared on all charges.[61]

---

[57] The Orthodox Creed III, in Lumpkin, *Baptist Confessions of Faith*, 299.

[58] Orthodox Creed IV–VIII, in Lumpkin, *Baptist Confessions of Faith*, 299–301. On the resonance of Nicene language, see Steven R. Harmon, *Towards Baptist Catholicity: Essays on Tradition and the Baptist Vision* (Milton Keynes, U.K.: Paternoster, 2006), 71–87.

[59] Orthodox Creed, in Lumpkin, *Baptist Confessions of Faith*, 326. All three ancient ecumenical creeds are included in the original.

[60] Whitley, *Minutes of the General Assembly*, 53–54.

[61] Whitley, *Minutes of the General Assembly*, 67. Caffyn was a skilled rhetorician who cleverly eluded his accusers by stating in Scripture terms what he believed, and he apparently escaped conviction by managing in his defenses to avoid plain language about what he did not

Four years later the General Assembly and the General Association attempted to reconcile as one body. The Unity of the Churches (1704) was the basis of that reunion. With regard to the Trinity, it affirmed "in this divine and infinite Being, or Unity of the Godhead, there are Three Persons, the Father, Word, and Holy Ghost, of one substance, power, and eternity." In regard to the matter of Christology, it stated: "We do believe that there is but one Lord Jesus Christ, the second Person in the Trinity, and the only begotten Son of God; and that he did, in the fulness of time, take to himself our nature, in the womb of the blessed Virgin Mary, of whom, in respect of the flesh, he was made; and so is true God and true Man, our Immanuel."[62] The reconciliation was short lived, as Caffyn's followers withdrew and united around the six principles of Hebrews 6:1-2 and the old Standard Confession.[63]

As strong moderate leaders like Thomas Grantham died, the General Assembly grew lax in faith and practice.[64] When both groups finally reconciled again in 1734, the basis of their union was the Standard Confession and the six principles. The decline of the General Baptists was averted somewhat when a young convert of the Wesleyan revival named Dan Taylor affiliated with them, but in 1770 Taylor and other "Free Grace Baptists" separated to form the New Connection of General Baptists. The Articles of Religion of the New Connection contains no trinitarian statement, but Taylor's *Fundamentals of Religion in Faith and Practice* reflects his firm commitment to trinitarian faith "that the human mind is not able to comprehend . . . because it is confessedly incomprehensible." Taylor concluded that it is "folly and absurdity to deny or dispute any part of the account which the infinite Jehovah gives us of himself, because the comprehension of it is above our capacities."[65] Having refused the life-giving

---

believe. It seems clear that he had doubts about the terminology employed in Chalcedonian and Nicene orthodoxy.

[62] Lumpkin, *Baptist Confessions of Faith*, 340; and Whitley, *Minutes of the General Assembly*, 88–89 and 97–98.

[63] John Griffith, *Gods Oracle and Christs Doctrine; or, The Six Principles of Christian Religion as They Were Taught and Delivered by Christ and His Apostles* (London: Richard Moon, 1665).

[64] Clint Bass provides a rich and complicated account of the General Baptists during and after the Caffyn controversy. He makes a strong case that the majority of General Baptists in the latter seventeenth century remained orthodox in theology, though their obsession with the visible church made them increasingly sectarian. Clint C. Bass. *Thomas Grantham (1633-1692) and General Baptist Theology* (Oxford: Regent's Park College, 2013), 179-212.

[65] Dan Taylor, *Fundamentals of Religion in Faith and Practice* (Leeds, 1775), 19. Although the Articles of Religion of the New Connexion does not contain a trinitarian statement, they reaffirmed a high Christology that declared that "our Lord Jesus Christ is God and man, united in one person; or possessed of divine perfection united to human nature" (Article 3). Lumpkin, *Baptist Confessions of Faith*, 343.

grace of the Trinity, the cankering error proved terminal for the old General Baptists just as Thomas Monck had predicted, and the New Connection, which maintained a trinitarian basis of fellowship alone, survived. Yet even for Taylor the Trinity was less a source of vitality for faith and practice and more an incomprehensible mystery to be believed precisely because it is an incomprehensible mystery. By the end of the seventeenth century, the doctrine of the Trinity "ceased being a mystery of faith and became a problem in theology."[66] While Baptists surely witnessed and were even subject to the misuse of creedal formulations and while their natural instinct was to use only the language of the Bible for doctrinal discussion, this history illustrates that the theological reality of the triune God for many ceased to be a mystery to be lived and was reduced to a problem to be solved.

From Problem to Proof

In February of 1719, ministers from the Presbyterian, Congregationalist, and Baptist denominations of London assembled at Salters' Hall. The ostensive reason for the meeting was a request for advice from the Presbyterians of Exeter, who had examined James Pierce, a young candidate who declared, "We cannot be so certain that the Father, Son, and Holy Ghost are one God."[67] When the Presbyterian elders were unable to reach a resolve about his neo-Arian heterodoxy, Pierce appealed to the Nonconformist ministers of London for advice regarding the elements and conditions of Dissenting orthodoxy. The elders in Exeter were reported to have replied, "Salters' Hall! Why, we understand that into that conference Baptists are admitted. We are not going to listen to the advice or decision of any body of ministers including Baptists!"[68] The General

---

[66] Philip Dixon, *"Nice and Hot Disputes": The Doctrine of the Trinity in the Seventeenth Century* (London: T&T Clark, 2003), 1. Paul C. H. Lim has provided a thick and nuanced account of how the Trinity ceased to be understood as an "ineffable mystery" and survived as "a matter of evident truths from the sound reading of Scripture," in his *Mystery Unveiled: The Crisis of the Trinity in Early Modern England* (New York: Oxford University Press, 2012), 327.

[67] James Peirce, *Plain Christianity Defended* (London: J. Noon, 1719), 1:29; cited in Olive M. Griffiths, *Religion and Learning* (Cambridge: Cambridge University Press, 1935), 119. English Presbyterians continued to move in the theological direction of Peirce throughout the eighteenth century. As Matthew Kadane has observed, the concern of "Presbyterian Arminianism" was to elevate human dignity by diminishing Christ's divinity. Kadane, "Anti-Trinitarianism and the Republican Tradition in Enlightenment Britain," *Republics of Letters* 2, no. 1 (2010), accessed October 11, 2011, http://arcade.stanford.edu/sites/default/files/article_pdfs/roflv02 i01_Kadane_121510_1.pdf. By showing Jesus not to be the second person of the Trinity, the atonement would be meaningless, rendering redemption unnecessary and thus freeing humanity from Adamic guilt.

[68] Alexander Gordon, "The Story of Salters' Hall," in *Addresses Biographical and Historical* (London: Lindsey Press, 1922), 134.

Baptist toleration of Matthew Caffyn was widely known, and it greatly diminished the esteem of Baptist principles among Dissenters, but appeal to Salters' Hall including the Baptists they did.

The debate at Salters' Hall divided along the lines of those who thought that fellowship should be determined by a *trinitarian confession* and others who believed the *Scriptures alone* were a sufficient rule of faith. According to one contemporary observer:

> The most controverted Part, in the Course of the Proceedings, was with relation to some *Points of Faith*; and particularly the *Doctrine of the Trinity*. By some it was judged necessary to be express on the main Articles of the *Christian Religion*, as set forth in some Creeds, Catechisms, &c. in order to justify the *Purity, and Orthodoxy of their Faith*; but these were opposed by others, who were for Enlarging the *Conditions of Communion*, so far, as to affect none of the same Faith in Essentials, but only Cases of Imorality, and the like; who were for having only the inspired Writings, in the very Letter thereof, to be made a *Standard of Faith*, and a *Test of Church Membership*; and who were equally against all Forms, Interpretations, or Dictates of fallible Men, in matters of so great Consequence, and what regarded eternal salvation.[69]

When a vote was taken, "it was carried by a Majority that no *humane Compositions, or Interpretations of the* Doctrine of the Trinity, *should be made a Part of those Articles of Advice, they were met to draw up, and agree to.*"[70] The vote was a narrow majority of fifty-seven to fifty-three, leading Sir Joseph Jekyll to remark that "the Bible carried it by four."[71]

The Advices were sent to the Presbyterians, including a letter from the majority that declared that they "utterly disown the Arian doctrine, and sincerely believe the doctrine of the blessed Trinity and the proper divinity of our Lord Jesus Christ."[72] The controversy, however, was far from over. Another meeting was held at Salters' Hall in March of 1719. A group comprised of those who had been in the minority at the February gathering called for subscription to a trinitarian declaration of faith. They subsequently became known as subscribers. Those on the other side, who insisted that "the Bible is the only perfect rule of faith," refused to sign

---

[69] John Shute Barrington, *An Account of the Late Proceedings of the Dissenting Ministers at Salters Hall* (London: J. Roberts, 1719), 6. Shute, later Viscount, Barrington was a Congregationalist and leader of the nonsubscribers.

[70] Barrington, *Account of . . . Dissenting Ministers*, 10.

[71] Alexander Gordon, *Heads of English Unitarian History* (London: Philip Green, 1895), 33–34.

[72] Gordon, *Heads of English Unitarian History*, 34.

the trinitarian declaration and were dubbed nonsubscribers. While both groups apparently opposed the neo-Arianism that had precipitated the controversy, few who sided with the nonsubscriber position in succeeding generations remained trinitarian. The debate at Salters' Hall proved to be a seismic forecast not only of the fault lines of Nonconformist unity but of the future state of trinitarian theology.[73]

James Foster was a young Dissenter from Exeter who began preaching just as the Salters' controversy was heating up. Like James Pierce, he refused to subscribe to a trinitarian creed. In 1720 he published his *Essay on Fundamentals*, in which he denied that the Trinity was an essential doctrine to the Christian faith. Taunting the orthodox, he wrote:

> All the mighty noise which has been made about your explication of the doctrine of the Trinity's being as plain and evident as that the sun is up at noon-day, so that no one can fail of seeing as you do, who is not hinder'd by some vicious prejudice, etc. comes to this; 'tis not deliver'd in express terms in scripture.[74]

Although Foster expressed reservations with some aspects of the unitarian case, he conceded that "the doctrine of the Trinity is an unintelligible, incomprehensible mystery" that "may be true, tho' we can't see how it can be."[75] In the end, he concluded that Trinity was not "a fundamental

---

[73] Michael Watts, *The Dissenters*, vol. 1, *From the Reformation to the French Revolution* (Oxford: Clarendon, 1978), 375–77. See also Roger Thomas, "The Non-subscription Controversy amongst Dissenters in 1719: The Salters' Hall Debate," *Journal of Ecclesiastical History* 4, no. 2 (1953): 162–86. For a list of the publications by the subscribers and nonsubscribers at Salters' Hall, see Hilarius de Synodis, *An Account of the Pamphlets Writ this Last Year each Side by the Dissenters* (London: James Knapton, 1720), 25–36. Of the seventy-eight subscribers, thirty were Presbyterian, twenty-eight Congregationalists, fourteen Particular Baptists, and one General Baptist. Of the seventy-three nonsubscribers, there were forty-seven Presbyterians, nine Congregationalists, fourteen General Baptists, and two Particular Baptists (and one of uncertain affiliation). The Particular Baptist subscribers included Thomas Harrison, John Skepp, William Curtis, David Rees, John Noble, Edward Wallin, Thomas Dewhurst, Mark Key, Edward Ridgway, John Sharpe, Richard Pain, William Benson, John Toms, Richard Glover, and Joseph Matthews. The lone General Baptist subscriber was Abraham Mulliner of the White's Alley Church, which stood firm against Matthew Caffyn and heterodoxy among the Generals. The Particular Baptist nonsubscribers were Nathaniel Hodges and Richard Parkes. The General Baptist nonsubscribers included John Savage, Joseph Jenkins, Joseph Burroughs, Lewis Douglas, Jeremiah Hunt, Isaac Kimber, Nathaniel Foxwell, John Ingram, Thomas Kerby, Thomas Slater, Amos Harrison, James Richardson, Richard Tuddemann, and Matthew Randall. The list with details on each figure is in "Salters' Hall 1719 and the Baptists," *Transactions of the Baptist Historical Society* 5, no. 3 (1917): 181–86.

[74] James Foster, *An Essay on Fundamentals: With Particular Regard to the Ever-Blessed Trinity*, 2nd ed. (London: J. Noon, 1754), 18. The first edition was published in 1720.

[75] Foster, *Essay on Fundamentals*, 30.

of christianity; because 'tis not so clearly reveal'd as to be obvious to every sincere, serious enquirer after truth, of ordinary capacity, or even to men of good sense and learning."[76] In 1724 Foster became pastor of the Barbican Church, a General Baptist congregation on Paul's Alley in London, where he joined Joseph Burroughs, a nonsubscriber at Salters' Hall. Foster soon became one of the most prominent preachers in London, later serving as pastor of the Pinner's Hall congregation (1744–1753), which ironically had been the headquarters of the trinitarian subscribers after the events of 1719.[77]

It is important, but perhaps not surprising, that *all but two* of the sixteen Particular Baptists and *only one of the fifteen* General Baptists at Salters' Hall were subscribers. The Particular Baptists maintained a trinitarian confession from the outset. The First London Confession of 1644 contains a statement of the Trinity in Article 2 that is consistent with Reformed theology and Nicene trinitarianism in the Western *filioque* tradition. It affirmed that each person of the Godhead is the same God but that each member is distinguished from the others, "the Father being from himself, the Sonne of the Father from everlasting, the holy Spirit proceeding from the Father and the Sonne."[78] Although the Presbyterian heresy hunter Robert Baillie attempted to paint the Particular Baptists with an antitrinitarian brush by asserting that the London Confession made no "mention at all of the Trinity," his accusations went largely unheard.[79] The Midland Confession of 1655 omits Nicene language but glosses the Johannine Comma (1 John 5:7) with an explicit trinitarianism, declaring "that this infinite Being is set forth to be the Father, the Word, and the Holy Spirit; and that these three agree in one."[80] The Somerset Confession of 1656, which represents a statement of moderate Particular Baptists in the west of England, invokes no trinitarian formula but instead narrates the economies of salvation history by describing the Son as fully divine and human (Articles 12–18) and the Spirit as leading in all truth (Articles 19–20).[81]

The longest and most explicit statement of trinitarian doctrine occurs in the Second London Confession (1677/1688), which often reiterates almost verbatim the articles of the Westminster Confession (1646). After the pattern of the Westminster Confession, the article on Scripture in the Second London Confession appears first and is followed by the Trinity.

[76] Foster, *Essay on Fundamentals*, 44.
[77] Whitley, *Baptists of London*, 113 and 117.
[78] First London Confession II, in Lumpkin, *Baptist Confessions of Faith*, 156–57.
[79] Baillie, *Anabaptisme*, 98.
[80] Sixteen Articles of Faith and Order, 2nd, in Lumpkin, *Baptist Confessions of Faith*, 198.
[81] The Somerset Confession XII–XX, in Lumpkin, *Baptist Confessions of Faith*, 206–8.

The Baptists, however, expanded on the Westminster language, adding words that resonate with Nicene orthodoxy: "in this divine and infinite Being there are three subsistences, the Father, the word (or Son) and Holy Spirit, of one substance, power, and Eternity, each having the whole Divine Essence, yet the Essence undivided." It continues that "the Father is of none neither begotten nor proceeding, the Son is Eternally begotten by the Father, the holy Spirit proceeding from the Father and the Son."[82] This affinity for the language of Nicene orthodoxy, which was heavily supported with biblical texts in marginal notes, suggests why the Particular Baptists at Salters' Hall subscribed to a trinitarian rule of faith.

Prior to the Act of Toleration in 1689, one of the strongest and most able Particular Baptist defenders of Nicene orthodoxy was John Tombes.[83] His treatise entitled *Emmanuel or God-Man*, written in 1669, is a remarkable scholarly work that reflects the fruits of his Oxford education. Tombes' *Emmanuel* is a general address to insurgent Socinianism without specific opponents, unlike other tracts of the times, which often give lively rebuttals and direct attacks. In the preface to the reader, the author explains that he originally projected the book as part of a larger theological project but was persuaded to publish it when he became aware of an attack on the deity of Christ. Tombes shows how the eternality and consubstantiality of the Son are warranted in Scripture. His careful treatments of John 1 and Philippians 2 display the linguistic and theological skills that earned him wide respect.[84]

---

[82] The Second London Confession II.3, in Lumpkin, *Baptist Confessions of Faith*, 253.

[83] Although Tombes was converted to the view of believer's baptism in 1642, he remained in the established church until his death. Yet his *Apology for the Two Treatises Concerning Infant-Baptisme* (n.p., 1645) and subsequent additions clearly establish his theology of baptism as consistent with the Baptists. Tombes' convictions were like those of Henry Jesse and John Bunyan in terms of the doctrines of both grace and the church. The Leominster congregation he served admitted for membership both those who had been believer baptized and those who had not. They affiliated with the Baptists after the death of Tombes. See Underwood, *History of the English Baptists*, 69–70. Christopher Hill and Claire Cross have persuasively argued that, because sectarian lines were not clearly drawn before the Act of Toleration, consideration should be given to treating those like Tombes and Bunyan as part of the Baptist heritage. See Watts, *Dissenters*, 1:164; Christopher Hill, *A Turbulent, Seditious, and Factious People: John Bunyan and His Church* (Oxford: Clarendon, 1988), 342–43; and Claire Cross, "The Church in England 1646–1660," in *The Interregnum: The Quest for Settlement, 1646–1660*, ed. G. E. Aylmer (Hamden, Conn.: Archon Books, 1972), 99–120. Hill suggested that "when historians speak of 'Baptists' and 'Quakers' as though there were such entities, they are imposing retrospectively an order which did not exist." He continues, " 'Congregationalist' and 'Baptist' groups which can be regarded as ancestors of the later sects had more in common with one another, and perhaps with Ranters, particularly in their radical politics, than they had with the sects which later looked back to them." Hill, *Turbulent, Seditious, and Factious People*, 342–43.

[84] John Tombes, *Emmanuel or God-Man* (London: F. Smith, 1669).

One year after the Act of Toleration, a gifted Particular Baptist layman named Isaac Marlow wrote *A Treatise on the Holy Trinunity*, in which he declared that "the blessed Doctrine of the Holy Trin-unity is the chiefest" treasures of sacred truth. God is revealed, Marlow continued, in the Scriptures, and it is "the duty of every Christian to have a true distinct Knowledg of God, subsisting in the Father, Son, and Holy Ghost."[85] Marlow held to the firm conviction that all doctrine must have biblical warrant. After considering the evidence for the oneness of God, the plurality of divine subsistences, the deity of the Son and the Holy Spirit, and the unity of Holy Trinity, Marlow argued that the Scriptures manifestly declare that the Father, the Son, and the Holy Ghost, each is God, and "that these three are but one God."[86] Marlow's biblical coup de grâce for the Trinity was the "Johannine comma," which in the Authorized Version states that "there are three that bear Record in Heaven, the Father, the Word, and the Holy Ghost, and these three are one" (1 John 5:7). Admittedly, some critics challenged the authenticity of this text by citing manuscripts in which it did not occur, but Marlow explained that these variants were evidence of a grand Arian conspiracy to expunge the Trinity from the Scriptures.[87] Such arguments failed to persuade critical scholars, who exposed the passage as a spurious interpolation.[88] The limitations of this "plain sense" approach to Scripture are apparent, but Marlow's *Treatise* illustrates the persistence of trinitarian orthodoxy among Particular Baptists.

The most influential critic who showed the Johannine Comma to be a spurious interpolation was Richard Bentley, the master of Trinity College Cambridge and the preeminent classicist of the day. In 1716 Bentley announced that he intended to prepare a critical edition of the New Testament and Jerome's Vulgate. Bentley's *Notae in Epistolam Beati Joannis Apostoli Primam* states that the Comma is omitted by Codex Alexandrinus, Wetstenii, as well as ancient Syriac, Coptic, and Ethiopic witnesses. He notes that among the texts he cites, only Cyprian includes the phrase *et hi tres unum sunt*.[89] Word apparently got out that Bentley, who made his

---

[85] Isaac Marlow, *A Treatise of the Holy Trinunity* (London: Richard Baldwin, 1690), "To the Reader."

[86] Marlow, *Treatise of the Holy Trinunity*, 54.

[87] Marlow, *Treatise of the Holy Trinunity*, 151–56.

[88] Erasmus expressed doubts about the authenticity of the *Comma Johanneum*, but he included it in the third edition of the *Textus Receptus* (1522) after a Greek manuscript including it was found (or produced). See Bruce Manning Metzger, *The Text of the New Testament*, 2nd ed. (New York: Oxford University Press, 1968), 101.

[89] Richard Bentley, *Bentleii Critica Sacra*, ed. Arthur Ayers Ellis (Cambridge: Deighton, Bell, 1862), 86.

fame exposing the *Epistles of Phalaris* as fraudulent, planned to exclude the Comma. In a reply to an unnamed writer, dated January 1, 1717, Bentley alluded to his worried recipient's letter "wherein you tell me from common fame, that, in my designed edition of the New Testament I purpose to leave out the verse of John's Epistle I. chap. 5, ver. 7."[90] Although the extant versions of Jerome's Vulgate and the *Textus Receptus* included the Comma, Bentley determined, after careful examination of the oldest and best manuscripts, that it was in neither Jerome's exemplar nor John's autograph. He explained, "But by this you see, that, in my proposed work, the fate of that verse will be a mere *question of fact*. You endeavor to prove, (and that's all you aspire to,) that it *may* have been writ by the Apostle, being consonant to his other doctrine. This I concede to you; and if the fourth century knew that text, let it come in, in God's name; but if that age did not know it, then Arianism in its height was beat down without the help of that verse: and, let the *fact* prove as it will, the *doctrine* is unshaken."[91]

[90] Richard Bentley, *The Correspondence of Richard Bentley, D.D.*, ed. Christopher Wordsworth (London: John Murray, 1842), 2:529.

[91] Bentley, *Correspondence of Richard Bentley*, 2:530. Gregory of Nazianzus quoted 1 John 5:8 without the Comma in his *he Fifth Theological Oration: On the Holy Spirit* XIX, in *The Nicene and Post-Nicene Fathers*, Second Series (Grand Rapids: Eerdmans, 1976), 7:323. If it had been known, he surely would have cited it as proof. Bentley received at least one letter from a supporter urging him to expose the Comma as a fraud. The writer argued, "The blessed Trinity require it at your hands in vindication of their honour, and of the truth of those sacred oracles that have been graciously given as the sole rule of doctrine for men which ought to be freed from a spurious interlineation foisted therein." J. Shaw to R. Bentley, March 29, 1717, in *Correspondence of Richard Bentley*, 2:531. See also *Dr. Bentley's Proposals for Printing a New Edition of the Greek Testament, and St. Hierom's Latin Version* (London: Printed for J. Knapton, 1721). In his first edition of *The Scripture Doctrine of the Trinity*, Samuel Clarke commented on 1 John 5:7 as Scripture text #1248. He argued that the unity affirmed by John is a unity of testimony, not essence or nature. Clarke stated that "this passage since it does not certainly appear to have been found in the Text of any Greek Manuscript, should not have too much stress laid upon it in any controversy." Clarke, *The Scripture Doctrine of the Trinity*, 1st ed. (London: James Knapton, 1712), 238. In the 2nd and 3rd editions (1719 and 1732) Clarke omitted any comment on the Comma. For more on the Comma and the critics, see Joseph M. Levine, *The Autonomy of History* (Chicago: University of Chicago Press, 1999), 192–205; and August Blundau, "The Comma Johanneum in the Writings of English Critics of the Eighteenth Century," *Irish Theological Quarterly* 17, no. 1 (1922): 66–67. Bentley's criticism did not put an end to appeals to the Comma, but its authority within the English trinitarian debates was greatly diminished thereafter. Raymond E. Brown observed that "even if the Comma had won the battle for acceptance in the sixteenth and seventeenth centuries, the war was not over; for in 1764 J. S. Semler challenged it, thus opening a new campaign of rejection." Brown, *The Epistles of John* (New York: Doubleday, 1982), 780. Among the Baptists, John Gill accepted the Johannine Comma as genuine and dismissed criticisms of its textual authenticity in his *An Exposition of the New Testament* (London: George Keith, 1774–1776), 5:387. Even Andrew Fuller, writing at the beginning of the nineteenth century, thought it more likely that 1 John 5:7 was an omission than an interpolation. *The Complete Works of the Rev. Andrew Fuller* (Harrisonburg, Va.: Sprinkle Publications, 1988 [reprinted from the 3rd London ed. with additions by Joseph Belcher, Philadelphia: American Baptist Publication Society, 1845]), 1:709.

In 1719, the same year of the Salters' Hall debate, John Gill became the pastor of the Horselydown Church in London, where he held forth for over fifty years. When Gill began his ministry, Samuel Clarke's 550-page treatise, *The Scripture Doctrine of the Trinity*, was one of the most widely read and discussed books of the day.[92] Clarke's ambiguity led to doubts about his orthodoxy. One reader opined, "Well, it may be Scripture, or it may not; it certainly is not the doctrine of the Trinity."[93] Gill published *The Doctrine of the Trinity Stated and Vindicated* in 1731 in hopes of laying all doubts to rest, and not a few of his contemporaries considered it to be a tour de force of orthodoxy. From the outset he makes clear that the Trinity belongs to a class of truth based on revelation that is above reason but not contrary to it. The oneness and perfections of God, Gill argued, may be known by natural reason, but the Trinity can be known only by revelation.[94] Because the Trinity is a revealed truth, Gill explained, the Scriptures are and "ought to be our guide in all such abstruse and mysterious doctrines." Too much speculation about the Trinity, he believed, turned away from the Bible. He warned that when theological reflections "are led and govern'd by the false reasonings of our carnal minds, no wonder if we run our selves into mazes, and then find it difficult to get clear."[95] With the loss of the Johannine Comma as a knock-down biblical basis for the Trinity, Gill and other orthodox biblicists were forced to develop more complex arguments that built precept upon precept from the unity of God to the plurality of the Godhead to the personality and deity of each person.[96]

[92] Clarke, *The Scripture Doctrine of the Trinity*. One contemporary observer described the many books written on the Trinity from the time of Clarke's treatise and the events of 1719. Hilarius de Synodis, *An Account Of all the Considerable Books and Pamphlets That have been wrote on either Side in the Controversy Concerning the Trinity Since the Year MDCCXII* (London: James Knapton, 1720). Attributed to Thomas Herne.

[93] Citied in Thomas, "Non-subscription Controversy," 182n4.

[94] John Gill, *The Doctrine of the Trinity Stated and Vindicated* (London: Aaron Ward, 1731), 2. By separating those matters that are *according to reason* from those that are *above reason*, Gill is closer to John Locke's view in *An Essay Concerning Human Understanding*, IV.17.23–IV.18.11, in *Great Books of the Western World*, vol. 35, ed. Robert Maynard Hutchins (Chicago: Encyclopaedia Britannica, 1952), 380–84.

[95] Gill, *Doctrine of the Trinity*, 3.

[96] Four decades after the publication of *The Doctrine of the Trinity*, in his magisterial *Body of Doctrinal Divinity*, the basic argument for the "proofs" of the Trinity remained virtually unchanged. See John Gill, *The Body of Doctrinal Divinity* I.27–31 (London: George Keith, 1769; repr., Atlanta: Turner Lassetter, 1950), 130–71. Although Gill accepted the authenticity of the Johannine Comma, he referred to it only twice in *The Doctrine of the Trinity* and once in *A Body of Doctrinal Divinity*. In neither work does it play a significant role in his argument. Yet in his commentary on 1 John 5:7, Gill argued, "This passage holds forth and asserts the unity of God, a trinity of persons in the Godhead, the proper deity of each person, and their distinct personality; the unity of essence in that they are one; a trinity of persons in that they are three, the Father, the Word, and the holy Ghost, and are neither more nor fewer." Gill,

Gill's grand treatise comes to an abrupt end, expressing hope that he had proven that God is three in one.[97] One has the sense that Gill succeeded in making his points, but readers were left to wonder what difference such an "abstruse and mysterious" doctrine might make for faith and practice.

Not everyone was enamored with Gill's argument. Robert Hall Jr. dismissed it as "a continent of mud."[98] His father was less critical though no more impressed. On May 29, 1776, the subject of the senior Hall's circular letter at the meeting of the Northampton Baptist Association was the doctrine of the Trinity. Annual letters provided an occasion "to explain and defend" the doctrines of grace, but Hall commented that their purpose was "principally of a practical nature." This letter was to be different. Alluding to "awful departures from" and "artful oppositions made to" trinitarian faith among other churches, Hall pronounced it his duty to clarify this fundamental doctrine so that the "saints may be built up in their most holy faith, and others be brought *to the acknowledgement of the mystery of God, and of the Father, and of Christ.*"[99]

Hall Sr.'s argument was no mere outburst of rhetorical flourish. Nor were dangers of antitrinitarianism only in other churches. There were plenty of "awful departures" and "artful oppositions" among the Baptists. One artful opponent of the Trinity was Samuel Mansell, a Baptist pastor in London who condemned his interlocutor for holding the "unbiblical" and "popish" doctrine of the triune Godhead, saying:

Exposition of the New Testament, 5:388. The absence of the Comma in his theological writings on the Trinity suggests Gill knew that the strength of this scriptural witness was offset by the weakness of its textual attestation.

[97] Gill, *Doctrine of the Trinity*, 203–4.

[98] Underwood, *History of the English Baptists*, 170.

[99] Robert Hall, *The Doctrine of the Trinity Stated* (Coventry: J. W. Piercy, 1776), 1–2. Hall does not identify the Unitarians he has in mind. Two decades later Edward Sharmon, a Northamptonshire farmer, published a number of letters addressed to the Baptists in which he argued for unitarianism based on a commonsense reading of Scripture. Sharmon, *A Letter on the Doctrine of the Trinity: Addressed to the Baptist Society at Guilsborough, Northamptonshire* (London: J. Johnson, 1795); Sharmon, *A Second Letter on the Doctrine of the Trinity: Addressed to the Baptist Society at Guilsborough, Northamptonshire* (Market-Harborough: W. Harrod, 1796); Sharmon, *A Caution Against trinitarianism* (Market-Harborough: W. Harrod, 1799); Sharmon, *A Second Caution Against trinitarianism . . . In a Letter Addressed to The Rev. Mr. Fuller, Kettering* (Market-Harborough: W. Harrod, 1800). In his letter addressed to Andrew Fuller, Sharmon asked, "The Bible we both allow to be the only proper standard of infallible truth . . . [and] With the Scriptures before our eyes . . . Wherein then can we differ upon a subject so very plain?" Sharmon, *A Second Caution*, 6. It is doubtful that Sharmon is who Hall had in mind as he began this circular letter, but he suggests the sort of local antitrinitarianism that might have been present earlier.

your method is to call all who differ from you, graceless, empty fools; and men fallen into damnable errors—and declare all damned who live and die rejecting your Popish tenet of Three Co-Equal Gods in one Godhead—though you have not one line of truth in all the Bible, as your authority so saying.[100]

And there were "awful departures," especially among the General Baptists, like Joshua Toulmin, a pastor in Taunton in Somersetshire. When pressed about a statement in his *Life of Socinus* that "many societies of Protestant Dissenters have become communities of professed Unitarians," he admitted that it "was not expressed with sufficient accuracy & precision." He qualified his view that, among the General Baptists and other Dissenters, "many have not disdained the denomination of Unitarians, & on account of the known sentiments of the generality of their members have been stigmatized for their disbelief of the Trinitarian scheme."[101] The remark, though toned down, is nevertheless telling.

Hall's letter is an elegantly written defense of the Trinity that emphasizes the biblical basis for the Cappadocian theology of persons. Unlike Gill's much longer treatise, Hall's letter does not end with the Trinity as a mere placeholder for rational faith and orthodox doctrine. He concludes by proposing "an improvement of the subject, by pointing out . . . its importance and use." Hall argues that "every capital truth in the bible is either founded upon it, or in close connection with it." Without a thoroughgoing trinitarian theology, no sense can be made of the eternal covenant, sacrificial atonement, or sufficient grace. Most importantly, without the Trinity as a hermeneutical key, the Scriptures are unintelligible. Only

---

[100] Samuel Mansell, *A Second Address to Mr. Huntington* (London: J. Parsons, 1797), v–vi. See also Mansell, *An Appeal to the Christian Professing World; or the Doctrine of Three Co-Equal Divine Persons in the Godhead* (London: J. Parsons, 1796). Mansell identified himself as pastor of the Baptist Church in Meeting-House Walk, Snow's-Fields, Borough, Southwark. Whitley identifies Mansell as an Arian who served as pastor of the church in the Snowfields chapel, 1796–1800, though he notes that Rippon ceased mention of the church as Baptist by 1794. Whitley, *Baptists of London*, 133. Mansell was responding to a tract by William Huntington that contended for the Trinity as "the greatest and grandest article of 'the faith that was once delivered to the saints,' and the most weighty and most dangerous matter to be trifled with in all the book of God." Huntington, *Forty Stripes Save None For Satan* (London: G. Terry, 1792), viii.

[101] Joshua Toulmin to Joseph Fownes, Shrewsbury, July 7, 1778, in *Baptist Autographs in the John Rylands University Library of Manchester, 1741–1845*, trans. and ed. Timothy D. Whelan (Macon, Ga.: Mercer University Press, 2009), 36–37. Joshua Toulmin, *Memoirs of the Life, Character, Sentiments, and Writings, of Faustus Socinus* (London: J. Brown, Southwark, 1777), 280. Toulmin was a General Baptist minister in Taunton (1774–1814) and Birmingham (1814–1815). In addition to his work on Socinus, Toulmin wrote books on John Biddle, Joseph Priestly, and other antitrinitarian related subjects.

a way of life that participates in the "three divine Persons in one God . . . is free from absurdity, and agreeable to reason."[102] Hall's letter reaches back to an earlier faith and practice enriched with trinitarian vitality and leans forward into a new form of trinitarian biblicism, but it was not to be a signpost for the future.

From Logical to Inscrutable

On November 8, 1820, a committee from the Charleston Baptist Association led by Richard Furman issued a call for South Carolina Baptists to unite in the causes of ministerial education and missions. They argued that theological education would enhance the social standing of Baptist ministers and offset the potential gains of other denominations that were already preparing leadership to propagate "their peculiar sentiments." But an even weightier reason for Baptists to establish their own theological seminary in the South was to ensure theological orthodoxy. The call sounded a warning:

> Unitarianism is exerting itself with ingenuity, vigor and address, to make proselytes and acquire permanence. Many who were considered as orthodox and even pious christians, have by its adherents been won over to their sentiments. In the Northern States they have made considerable progress, and acquired extensive influence; even Baptist Ministers and Churches (though blessed be God not many) have been corrupted.[103]

Just one year earlier, William Ellery Channing had delivered his sermon on Unitarian Christianity, in which he declared the doctrine of the Trinity to be "irrational and unscriptural" and asserted that "the Father alone is God."[104] The unitarianism of the Father of the sort championed by Channing was clearly what Furman and the Charleston Association was concerned about, but records indicate that Baptists in the United States were firmly trinitarian.[105] Indeed, Francis Wayland averred that American

---

[102] Hall, *Doctrine of the Trinity Stated*, 13–16.

[103] Richard Furman, John M. Roberts, and Joseph B. Cook, "Call for a State Convention in South Carolina . . . ," November 8, 1820, in *A Sourcebook for Baptist Heritage*, ed. H. Leon McBeth (Nashville: Broadman, 1990), 246–51.

[104] William Ellery Channing, "Unitarian Christianity," in *A Sermon Delivered at the Ordination of Rev. Jared Sparks to the Pastoral Care of the First Independent Church in Baltimore, May 5, 1819* (repr., Boston: Hew & Goss, 1819).

[105] The Covenant of Citadel Square Baptist Church, Charleston, South Carolina, written by Richard Furman in 1868, begins: "1. That we will take the only living and true God, one God in three persons, Father, Son, and Holy Ghost, to be our God." Charles W. Deweese, *Baptist Church Covenants* (Nashville: Broadman, 1990), 165.

Baptists had always been trinitarians, who believed "without exception that there is one only living God, and that this God is revealed to us as Father, Son, and Holy Spirit." He went on to assert that he had never known or heard of a single Baptist church that had adopted the Unitarian belief, saying that Baptists "with one accord, always and every where have held Unitarianism to be a grave and radical error."[106]

In 1794 John Asplund published his *Universal Register of the Baptist Denomination in North America*, in which he applied a trinitarian criterion to distinguish churches as "Baptist." Asplund explained that he only counted churches that received members who were baptized after conversion by being "dipped or immersed under the water only one time, in the name of the Trinity, as a token, that all the three persons, Father, Son and Holy Ghost are concerned in man's everlasting salvation."[107] The *Register* also contains *An Abstract of the Principles* said to be held by the Baptists in general, which begins, "We believe in one only true and living God; and that there are three persons in the Godhead, the Father, the Son, and the Holy-Ghost."[108] Apparently Particular and General Baptists, including Six Principle and Sabbatarian Baptists, met the trinitarian standard.[109] That Asplund did not count German Baptists in his census because they practiced triune immersion suggests that he also might have excluded churches that refused to practice immersion in the name of the Trinity had he known of any.[110] The *Register* indicates that between 1791 and 1794 four ministers were excommunicated "for Universal Salvation Doctrine" (and others for immorality, disorder, and Arminianism) but none for Unitarian or antitrinitarian doctrine.[111] By Asplund's account

[106] Francis Wayland, *Notes on the Principles and Practices of Baptist Churches* (New York: Sheldon, Blakeman, 1857), 16–17.

[107] John Asplund, *Universal Register of the Baptist Denomination in North America* (Boston: John W. Folsom, 1794; repr., New York: Arno Press, 1980), 5.

[108] Asplund, *Universal Register*, 83.

[109] The trinitarian commitments of some Six Principle and Seventh Day Baptists may well have been marginal. E.g., the Covenant of Piscataway Seventh Day Baptist Church, Piscataway, New Jersey (1705), suggests a unitarianism of the Father of the sort that was held by General Baptists in England at the time. It states, "We believe that unto us there is but one God, the Father and one Lord Jesus Christ, who is the mediator between God and mankind that the Holy Ghost is the Spirit of God." Deweese, *Baptist Church Covenants*, 134.

110 For an account of the German Baptist view, see James Quinter, *A Defence of Trine Immersion* (Columbiana, Ohio: Gospel Visitor, 1862); Quinter, *A Debate on Trine Immersion, the Lord's Supper, and Feet-Washing* (Cincinnati: H. S. Bosworth, 1867); and Quinter, *A Vindication of Trine Immersion as the Apostolic Form of Christian Baptism* (Huntingdon, Pa.: Brethren's Publishing, 1886).

[111] Asplund, *Universal Register*, 55–62. The first Unitarian congregation in America was not established until June 1796, but Unitarians like Joseph Priestley who came to America in 1794 had been actively promoting the message for some time.

Baptists at the beginning of the nineteenth century were committed to trinitarian doctrine.

The Covenant of the Philadelphia Baptist Association affirmed in 1798 ends with a trinitarian benediction, which suggests that the theology of the Second London Confession adopted by the association in 1742 was still firmly in place.[112] The Charleston Baptist Association likewise adopted the Second London Confession as their standard of faith in 1767 and in 1774 published an ancillary Summary of Church Discipline.[113] The first confession of faith actually written by Baptists in America was the Abstract of Principles of the Kehukee Association of United Baptists, which was approved in 1777 by ten congregations, six of whom were Regular Baptists and four Separate Baptists. The first article of the Kehukee confession begins with an affirmation of faith in the almighty God, who is revealed in the characters of the Father, Son, and Holy Ghost.[114] Baptists tended to stress the three economies and downplay the unity of the Godhead, but to speak of the one being of God revealed in three characters has a distinctly modalistic resonance. The Covenant of the Kehukee Association adopted in 1803 concludes, "These things we do covenant and agree to observe and keep sacred, in the name of, and by the assistance of, the Holy Trinity. Amen."[115] The Terms of Union Between the Elkhorn and South Kentucky Associations, which was drawn up in 1801 as a similar basis for the union of Regular and Separate Baptists in Kentucky, affirmed, "That there is one only true God, and in the Godhead or divine essence, there are Father, Son and Holy Ghost.[116] Still, the Separate Baptists of Virginia had their doubts about their Kentucky brethren, suggesting in 1771, "In Virginia, perhaps, we have been more fortunate; but in Kentucky, and in England, the majority of some of the Baptist churches have become Arians or Socinians."[117] Questions about the trinitarian orthodoxy of Kentucky Baptists remained, leading to an enquiry at the 1803 meeting of the Elkhorn Association of Kentucky Baptists: "Does this Body believe the doctrin[e]of the Trinity as contained in the Confession of Faith." The answer was unanimous, "They do."[118]

---

[112] Deweese, *Baptist Church Covenants*, 150–51.

[113] Summary of Church Discipline (Charleston, S.C.: Charleston Baptist Association, 1774).

[114] Joseph Biggs, *A Concise History of the Kehukee Baptist Association* (Tarborough, N.C.: George Howard, 1834), 42.

[115] Deweese, *Baptist Church Covenants*, 153.

[116] Terms of Union between the Elkhorn and South Kentucky Associations, 2, in Lumpkin, *Baptist Confessions of Faith*, 359.

[117] Robert B. Semple, *A History of the Rise and Progress of the Baptists in Virginia*, rev. G. W. Beale (Richmond, Va.: Pitt & Dickinson, 1894), 75.

[118] William Warren Sweet, *Religion on the American Frontier: The Baptists 1783–1830* (New York: H. Holt, 1931), 496.

In his *Materials Towards a History of the Baptists*, Morgan Edwards only mentions two cases in which trinitarian doctrine was a problem for early Baptists in America. One was the Stono Church in Charleston, South Carolina, which was connected with the General Baptists in England. In 1740 they called a new pastor, about whom Edwards commented, "Mr. Henry Heywood also came from Britain and was a good scholar, but advanced arian and Socinian Doctrines in his preaching."[119] The second concerned a division in the Farewell Street Baptist Church of Newport, Rhode Island, in 1753, which Edwards noted was "occasioned by some who embraced the sentiments of Arius with respect to the Trinity," but he added, "soon this came to nothing."[120] A more typical case is Rev. Nathanael Jenkins, a Baptist minister in Capeway, New Jersey, who also served in the colonial Assembly. Like earlier Baptists in England who, though disagreeing with John Biddle's antitrinitarianism, defended him against punishment by the government on charges of heresy, Jenkins stood for religious liberty and against government reprisal for religious convictions. When a 1721 bill was brought before the Assembly to "to punish such as denied the doctrine of the trinity; the divinity of Christ; the inspiration of holy scriptures," Jenkins stood up in opposition. The bill, Edwards wrote, "was quashed, to the great mortification of them who wanted to raise in New-Jersey the spirit which so raged in New-England."[121]

Associational circular letters suggest that, though Baptists were doctrinally committed trinitarians, there were some among them who differed. The Warren Association warned in 1792 and 1795 against those who would "strip Christ of his eternal Deity."[122] The Ketocton Association of Virginia published a letter on the divinity of Jesus Christ, declaring

[119] Morgan Edwards, *Materials Towards a History of the Baptists*, ed. Eve B. Weeks and Mary B. Warren (Danielsville, Ga.: Heritage Papers, 1984), 2:122. The General Baptists withdrew in 1733 from the Charleston church, which was predominately Particular Baptists, to form the Stono congregation. In 1745 the General Baptists were granted legal right to share the meetinghouse in Charleston. Heywood began preaching on alternate Sundays, but apparently, after an initial positive reception, he was regarded poorly. Basil Manley comments that "Mr. Heywood was immediately introduced into the pulpit in town, and his popular talents drew around him, for a time, a large congregation. But his doctrines soon disgusted the people, and but few came." Manley, *Mercy and Judgment, A Discourse Containing Some Fragments of the History of the Baptist Church in Charleston S.C.* (n.p.: Knowles, Vose, 1837), 25; cited by Robert A. Baker and Paul J. Craven Jr., *Adventure in Faith: The First 300 Years of First Baptist Church Charleston, South Carolina* (Nashville: Broadman, 1982), 118.

[120] Edwards, *Materials Towards a History of the Baptists* (ed. Weeks and Warren), 1:183.

[121] Edwards, *Materials Towards a History of the Baptists* (ed. Weeks and Warren), 1:93; originally published, Edwards, *Materials Towards a History of the Baptists in New Jersey* (Philadelphia: Thomas Dobson, 1792), 41.

[122] William G. McLoughlin, *New England Dissent, 1630–1833: The Baptists and the Separation of Church and State* (Cambridge, Mass.: Harvard University Press, 1971), 2:737.

that Arians and Socinians, though accepting the Scriptures as the rule of faith and practice, nevertheless "deny the proper deity of Christ."[123] In his October 1774 circular letter to the Philadelphia Baptist Association on the Trinity, Samuel Jones attested to "the undivided essence of the Godhead, a trinity of persons, each of them possessed of all divine perfections, and every way coequal, and these three are one, the One God." He urged his readers to "set the Triune God before us in all our ways and enjoyments" being "established in the present truth, nor suffer any to remove us from the firm basis of divine revelation."[124] It raises the question of why there was a need to call the churches to hold the line of trinitarian orthodoxy if it was a settled matter. Indeed, the 1743 meeting of the Philadelphia association wrestled with a case of antitrinitarianism when James Eaton was charged with denying the eternal generation of the Son. Eaton "recanted, renounced, and condemned" his departure from the association's confession of faith. A closing letter urged the people to be content in affirming "the unutterable as well as inconceivable, mysteries of Father, Son, and Holy Ghost, three in one, and one in three, the co-essentiality, the co-eternity, the co-equality, of the three glorious Persons in one eternal God; and that you suffer not a vain and over-curious search to be made thereinto by human reason and worldly wisdom." The letter concluded with a declaration to oppose nontrinitarian heterodoxy:

> We are *nemine contra dicente*, fully united to repel, and put a stop to, as far as we may, unto the Arian, Socinian, and Antitrinitarian systems; protesting unto the world our joint belief of, and our resolution to maintain, the eternal and inconceivable generation of the second Person in the ever adorable Trinity.[125]

Some Baptists, particularly in the northeast, were apparently drawn into unitarianism. In his book *Fifty Years among the Baptists*, David Benedict mentions that in the 1820s, when unitarianism was a growing movement, "a small company of our strong men, mostly ministers, began to falter in their course, and eventually went over to the side. Most of them up to that period had stood firmly on the orthodox platform." The center of this Baptist Unitarian movement was Providence, Rhode Island, about which Benedict concludes his reflections with a pessimistic observation:

---

[123] William Fristoe, *A Concise History of the Ketocton Baptist Association* (Stauton, Va.: William Gilman Lyford, 1808; repr., Harrisonburg, Va.: Sprinkle Publications, 2002), 104.

[124] *Minutes of the Philadelphia Baptist Association* (1707–1807), ed. A. D. Gillette (Philadelphia: American Baptist Publication Society, 1851), 144.

[125] *Minutes of the Philadelphia Baptist Association*, 47–48.

> As I understand the thing, there is a constant downward tendency in the
> Unitarian system, so far as its doctrinal creed is concerned, on the part
> of those who follow their speculations to their final end, till little is left
> of the gospel but its name.[126]

On the whole, Baptists in New England rejected unitarianism, sometimes joining forces with trinitarian Congregationalists and other evangelicals in opposition to unitarianism.[127] But beyond the urban centers of
the northeast, unitarianism may not have posed such a pressing threat to
trinitarian orthodoxy among Baptists. The Principles of the Sandy Creek
Association adopted in 1816 contains an abbreviated declaration of faith,
which begins with these words: "We believe that there is only one true
and living God; the Father, Son, and Holy Ghost, equal in essence, power
and glory; yet there are not three Gods but one God."[128] Likewise, the
New Hampshire Confession of Faith, written in 1833, places an emphasis
like the Kehukee Abstract of Principles on the economies of revelation
within the Trinity rather than the immanent reality of the Godhead. The
New Hampshire Confession affirms that the one true God is "revealed
under the personal and relative distinctions of the Father, the Son, and
the Holy Spirit" that are "equal in every divine perfection, and executing
distinct but harmonious offices in the great work of redemption."[129] Yet
the abbreviated and stylized ways the Trinity is described in these confessions reflects not a denial of the trinitarian doctrine but rather a decreasing
interest in it.

In the mid-nineteenth century, Baptists North and South produced
two hymnals that became widely used: *The Psalmist* and *The Baptist
Psalmody*.[130] Each hymnal contained a selection of doxologies (14 and 16
respectively), of which all but two are trinitarian.[131] *The Baptist Psalmody*

---

[126] David Benedict, *Fifty Years among the Baptists* (New York: Sheldon, 1860), 145, 159.
Benedict oddly does not describe the Baptist Unitarians in his treatment of the history of the
Baptists of Rhode Island in his *A General History of the Baptist Denomination in America and
Other Parts of the World* (New York: Lewis Colby, 1848).

[127] McLoughlin, *New England Dissent*, 2:1133–34.

[128] Principles of Faith of the Sandy Creek Association I, in Lumpkin, *Baptist Confessions
of Faith*, 358.

[129] New Hampshire Confession of Faith II, in Lumpkin, *Baptist Confessions of Faith*, 362.
The New Hampshire Confession became widely known and used by many Baptists through
the publication of J. Newton Brown's *The Baptist Church Manual* (Philadelphia: American
Baptist Publication Society, 1853).

[130] Baron Stow and Samuel F. Smith, eds. *The Psalmist: A New Collection of Hymns for the
Use of Baptist Churches* (Boston: Gould and Lincoln, 1854); Basil Manly and B. Manly Jr., eds.,
The Baptist Psalmody: A Selection of Hymns for the Worship of God (Charleston, S.C.: Southern
Baptist Publication Society, 1851).

[131] *The Psalmist* has fourteen doxologies of which twelve are trinitarian, and *The Baptist*

included 8 trinitarian hymns (6 of them by Isaac Watts) out of a total of 1,295 hymns.[132] The same picture emerges in *The Psalmist*, which has only 9 trinitarian hymns out of a total of 1,180. The introduction of the gospel song in collections like *The Southern Harmony* of the same decade, which had only 2 trinitarian hymns out of 437 total, hints of the growing tendency to prioritize a personal experience with Jesus.[133] This trend suggests an incipient unitarianism of the Second Person, which became even more pronounced in subsequent Baptist hymnals. It is important to note that none of these hymns (individually or collectively) are antitrinitarian, but their publication and reception indicates a practical unitarianism in Baptist worship based on devotion to Jesus that rendered the Trinity increasingly irrelevant.

For many Baptists in America, the Trinity was an obscure teaching about an inscrutable mystery that must simply be believed. This doctrinal obscurity is wonderfully stated by John Leland, the post–Revolutionary era Virginia Baptist minister:

> There are three that bear record in heaven, the Father, the Word, and the Holy Ghost, and these three are one. This is a doctrine of revelation, for a confirmation of which, baptism is performed in the name of the Father, Son and Holy Ghost: but, like the ark of the Hebrews, it is too awful to be pryed into by curious eyes. When eternity can be fathomed and immensity measured—when creation can be accounted for, and the resurrection from the dead be philosophized—when the hidden

---

Psalmody has sixteen of which fourteen are trinitarian. I do not know how these doxologies were actually used in worship. It may be the case that in some churches they were sung in every service of worship, and perhaps at several points in the liturgy. If so, these doxological punctuations would have had the effect of making Baptist worship more trinitarian than Unitarian.

[132] Although Watts' hymns contain an entire book of doxologies modeled on the Gloria Patri, the orthodoxy of his personal views on the Trinity was very much in question. Watts was among the nonsubscribers at Salters' Hall who held that requiring a trinitarian Rule of Faith was not necessary for Nonconformist ministers. In The Christian Doctrine of the Trinity (propositions XV–XVI) written in 1722, he suggested that the Son of God was the human soul of Christ, which was created prior to the creation of the world and was united to the Godhead. Watts, *The Works of the Late Reverend and Learned Isaac Watts* (London: T. and T. Longman, 1753), 6:461–65. In a piece written late in life, Watts expressed his anguished doubt about the Trinity: "Hadst thou told me plainly, in any single text, that the Father, Son, and Holy Spirit are three real distinct Persons in thy Divine nature, I had never suffered myself to be bewildered in so many doubts, nor embarrassed with so many strong fears of assenting to the mere inventions of men, instead of Divine doctrine" (4:641).

[133] William Walker, ed., *The Southern Harmony and Musical Companion*, new ed. (Philadelphia: E. W. Miller, 1854). "Come Thou Almighty King" is one of the two trinitarian hymns in *The Southern Harmony*. It continues to appear in Baptist hymnals to the present.

mystery of God manifest in the flesh, and the guilty sinner being pardoned for the sufferings of an innocent Saviour, are clearly understood, then, and not till then, will limited creatures comprehend the incomprehensible doctrine of a three-one God. If the works of God are past finding out, surely the author of those works must be so.[134]

Again alluding to the warrant of 1 John 5:7, John Leland exclaimed, "That there are three that bare record in heaven, and that these three are one, I believe, because God has said it; but I cannot understand it."[135] Leland was not the first Baptist, nor was he the last, to declare the Trinity an arcane but necessary doctrine. British Baptist pastor and theologian Andrew Fuller affirmed of the Trinity that "whether we can comprehend it or not, we are required humbly to believe it."[136]

The functional irrelevance of the Trinity is supported by the fact that it seems only rarely to have been the subject of Baptist preachers. One notable exception is a sermon by William T. Brantly on February 8, 1824, at the First Baptist Church of Augusta, Georgia, entitled "Trinitarians Rational." Brantly directed his sermons against those of a "presumptuous spirit" who "seem to think that they cannot be genuine sons unless they can trace the resplendent orb over which the great Father has left the glory of his ineffable presence too intense for mortal eyes."[137] The message was so well received that Brantly was asked to submit a copy for publication by the local newspaper. On at least one more occasion, Brantly returned to the subject of the Trinity. After expending most of his homiletical energy arguing that the doctrine of the Trinity is according to reason, he concluded that salvation depends on the Trinity and that where "this doctrine is rejected, the great members of the Christian system are broken off; and a naked, mutilated trunk, without life or comeliness, without reasonable parts or purposes, is presented."[138] The rhetorical force of Brantly's eloquent sermon left no doubt to his hearers that the main point was to ensure the rational basis of the Christian faith, and so the Trinity must be affirmed. The practical relevance of the doctrine of the Trinity, however, undoubtedly escaped the grasp of his congregation.

---

[134] John Leland, "Thoughts," in *The Writings of the Late Elder John Leland*, ed. L. F. Greene (New York: G. W. Wood, 1845; repr., New York: Arno Press, 1969), 534.

[135] Leland, "Thoughts," in *Writings of the Late Elder John Leland* (ed. Greene), 534.

[136] Andrew Fuller, *Letters on Systematic Divinity*, letter 9, in *Complete Works of the Rev. Andrew Fuller*, 1:708.

[137] William T. Brantly, "Trinitarians Rational" (Augusta: Chronicle and Advertiser, 1824), 5. In addition to the First Baptist Church of Augusta, Georgia, Brantly served as pastor of the First Baptist Churches of Beaufort, South Carolina; Philadelphia, Pennsylvania; and Charleston, South Carolina.

[138] Leland, "Thoughts," in *Writings of the Late Elder John Leland* (ed. Greene), 534.

The obscurity of the Trinity is even more pronounced in the writings of Baptist theologians in America. In his *Manual of Theology* published in 1858, John Leadley Dagg was able to develop his doctrines of God, the will and works of God, the fall and present state of man, Jesus Christ, and the Holy Spirit without reference to the Trinity. On page 246, in his treatment of the doctrine of grace, he paused for seven pages to discuss the doctrine of the Trinity. He then continued for another 126 pages to treat the covenant, blessings, and sovereignty of grace, and the doctrine of the future world with no further mention of trinitarian significance.[139] Alvah Hovey, the president and professor of theology at Newton Theological Institution, in his *Manual of Theology and Christian Ethics* written in 1877, devoted a mere page and a half to the doctrine of the Trinity.[140] Elias H. Johnson of Crozer Theological Seminary placed his eight-page treatment of the doctrine of the Trinity about two-thirds of the way through his *Outline of Systematic Theology* published in 1891, as a parenthesis between the offices of the Holy Spirit (§41) and the offices of Christ (§43).[141]

Three years after the publication of his *Manual of Theology*, Hovey made a startling admission: "We call the doctrine of the Triune God a mystery, not so much because it is a *revealed* truth as because it is an *obscure* truth."[142] Although Hovey was attempting to make a case for the Trinity as revealed truth, he gave voice to what most Baptists doubtless thought: the Trinity was an obscure teaching about an inscrutable mystery that must simply be believed. For Baptist theologians the importance and relation of the Trinity in the loci of doctrines was uncertain. The net effect of this inscrutable obscurity of the Trinity was ironically not all that different from Schleiermacher's placement of the Trinity in the conclusion of his *Glaubenslehre*. Although Schleiermacher located the doctrine there because he thought the Trinity was "ecclesiastically framed" and "not an immediate utterance concerning Christian self-consciousness," the Baptists seemed to have no idea what to do with the Trinity, and for neither was the Trinity integral to the work of systematic theology.[143]

---

[139] J. L. Dagg, *Manual of Theology* (Charleston, S.C.: Southern Baptist Publication Society, 1857–1858).

[140] Alvah Hovey, *Manual of Systematic Theology and Christian Ethics* (Philadelphia: American Baptist Publication Society, 1877), 91–92. Hovey's second edition expanded his discussion of the Trinity to two and half pages. Hovey, *Manual of Christian Theology*, 2nd ed. (New York: Silver, Burdett, 1900), 110–12.

[141] Elias H. Johnson, *Outline of Systematic Theology* (Philadelphia: American Baptist Publication Society, 1891), 191–98.

[142] Alvah Hovey, "The Biblical Doctrine of the Trinity," in *Baptist Doctrines*, ed. Charles A. Jenkens (St. Louis, Mo.: Chancy R. Barns, 1880), 362.

[143] Friedrich Schleiermacher, *The Christian Faith* §§170–72, ed. and trans. H. R. Macintosh and J. S. Stewart (Philadelphia: Fortress, 1976), 738–51.

James P. Boyce was one Baptist theologian who seemed bent on demystifying the Trinity. In his 1887 *Abstract of Systematic Theology*, Boyce located the Trinity within the doctrine of God as one of the subheadings along with the divine unity, spirituality, immutability, power, knowledge, holiness, justice, will, and decrees. His discussion begins by referencing the Abstract of Principles of the Southern Baptist Theological Seminary, which states that "God is revealed to us as Father, Son, and Holy Spirit each with distinct personal attributes, but without division of nature, essence or being."[144] Yet Boyce simply repeated a scholasticized summary abstracted from his teacher Charles Hodge, believing that the task of theology was simply to make plain that the doctrine of the Trinity is "a mere statement of the Scriptural facts." Boyce confidently asserted that, by considering the subject "in the utmost simplicity and Scripturalness, the whole truth [of the Trinity] may be attained."[145] His forty pages of plodding propositionalism added little light and indeed simply underscored the arcane and obscurantist nature of this truth.

Writing at the turn of the twentieth century, Augustus Hopkins Strong attempted to transmit the best of the evangelical Calvinist tradition that shaped most Baptist theology while also adapting to the challenges of modernity. Strong worried that the tendency of Baptist theologians like Ezekiel Robinson of Rochester and of Brown to stress the economic and historical aspects of the Trinity said too little about the ontological relations of eternal Sonship and eternal Fatherhood within the Godhead.[146] Strong recognized that the trinitarian biblicism of earlier Baptists was vulnerable to the "new theology." In the preface to the eighth and final edition of his *Systematic Theology*, Strong warned that Christianity was moving toward a "second Unitarian defection" and that he hoped his efforts might "do something to stem this fast advancing tide."[147] Like Gill and others, who held the line of Protestant orthodoxy with its biblicism severed from a received tradition, Strong resisted the antitrinitarianism of modern theology. He offered a rational account, rehearsing with clarity and cogency a chain-link argument of biblical propositions that (1) the Father, Son, and Spirit are recognized as God, (2) these three are distinct

---

[144] James Petigru Boyce, *Abstract of Systematic Theology* (Philadelphia: American Baptist Publication Society, 1887), 125.

[145] Boyce, *Abstract of Systematic Theology*, 125. Cf. Charles Hodge, *Systematic Theology* (New York: Scribner, Armstrong, 1872), 1:447–82.

[146] Augustus Hopkins Strong, "Dr. Robinson as a Theologian," in *Ezekiel Gilman Robinson: An Autobiography, with Supplement by H. L. Wayland and Critical Estimates*, ed. E. H. Johnson (New York: Silver, Burdett, 1896), 194–95.

[147] Augustus Hopkins Strong, *Systematic Theology*, 8th ed. (Philadelphia: Judson Press, 1907), 1:viii–ix.

persons, (3) the tripersonality of God is immanent and eternal, (4) there
is but one divine essence, and (5) these three persons are equal. When all
five propositions were taken together, the conclusion was the doctrine of
the Trinity, which Strong professed was inscrutable yet not contradictory.
Still, one is not left with a sense that the Trinity is any less obscure. Unlike
ethical monism, which Strong maintained was integral to every Christian doctrine, the Trinity has merely "important relations" to other doctrines.[148] The significance cannot be missed. By 1918, when he published
A Tour of the Missions, Strong conceded that his efforts had failed and that
nothing short of the second coming of Christ could halt the advance of
the new unitarianism.[149]

The most extensive rethinking of the doctrine of the Trinity by a
Baptist theologian since the eighteenth century was surely William Newton Clarke. In his *Outline of Christian Theology*, Clarke argued that the
economic Trinity and the essential Trinity should be distinguished as two
separate doctrines: one the divine Trinity that described God's threefold
self-manifestation and the other the divine Triunity that accounted for
God's triune mode of existence.[150] He differed with Schleiermacher in that
"neither of them is discovered in the realm of theism, outside Christianity."[151] Unlike Schleiermacher, Clarke found a basis for both the Trinity
and Triunity of God within the consciousness of redemption. The Trinity was the result of God's manifestation in the history of Israel, the life
of Christ, and the coming of the Holy Spirit at Pentecost. "This," Clarke
wrote, "is the living and practical Trinity of the New Testament," which
was "the only Trinity that was known to the early Church."[152] The Triunity was inferred only later in the history of Christian theological reflection. Clarke showed how the notion of the "eternal generation" of the
Son was rooted in the Fourth Gospel, and he argued much as Augustine
did in *De trinitatis* (albeit with a definite Cartesian twist) from the analogue of self-consciousness by unpacking the statement "The I that I think
of is identical with the I that thinks."[153]

---

[148] Strong, *Systematic Theology*, 1:304–52; and Augustus Hopkins Strong, *Christ in Creation and Ethical Monism* (Philadelphia: Roger Williams Press, 1899).

[149] Augustus Hopkins Strong, *A Tour of the Missions: Observations and Conclusions* (Philadelphia: Griffith & Rowland Press, 1918), 197.

[150] William Newton Clarke, *An Outline of Christian Theology* (New York: Charles Scribner's Sons, 1899), 161. Clarke makes the same distinction in *The Christian Doctrine of God*
(New York: Charles Scribner's Sons, 1909), 227–48.

[151] Clarke, *Outline of Christian Theology*, 162. This is what Schleiermacher developed in
the first part of the system of doctrine as arising from general religious self-consciousness.

[152] Clarke, *Outline of Christian Theology*, 164.

[153] Clarke, *Outline of Christian Theology*, 173.

Clarke concluded that "the practical Trinity which cheered the early Church still supports and illumines Christian experience," and the divine Triunity provided a foundation for the work of redemption "in the eternal being and nature of God."[154] Taken together, Clarke argued, these two doctrines offered a "vastly richer, more vivid and more practical" account of Christian experience without which "God would have been far less loved." Moreover, he contended:

> Whatever harm has come from the doctrine has come because of over-definition, unspiritual discussion of a spiritual mystery, and misuse of the doctrine in its abstract and difficult metaphysical forms as a test of faith and orthodoxy.[155]

Clarke maintained a sense of humor about his theological work. When a group of students once took him to task for his labored effort to "save incredible ideas" in his doctrine of the Trinity, Clarke replied, "Well gentlemen, sometimes when I read that passage over I think I have said something—and sometimes I don't."[156] Despite a radical distinction between the economic and immanent Trinity and an ambiguity of the underlying experientialism in his theology, Clarke does much to display the intelligibility of the doctrine and to reaffirm its significance for Christian faith.

E. Y. Mullins, whose *Christian Religion in Its Doctrinal Expression* in many ways mirrors the work of Clarke, unfortunately reverted back to the Trinity as an inscrutable and obscure doctrine that must be defended against the objections of irrationalism.[157] The eight-page discussion of the Trinity by Mullins occurs only after his chapters on religion, the knowledge of God, Christian experience, other forms of knowledge, revelation, Christology, and the Holy Spirit. And Mullins' contrived treatment of the Trinity is not integrated into Christian experience.[158]

Given this history it is not surprising that McClendon's 1966 article described the state of trinitarian theology in such bland terms. For the most part, in Baptist life the Trinity has been a difficult doctrine needing justification rather than a living conviction seeking clarification. Yet the history of Baptist reflections on the Trinity reveals not so much an

---

[154] Clarke, *Outline of Christian Theology*, 179–80.

[155] Clarke, *Outline of Christian Theology*, 180.

[156] Harry Emerson Fosdick, *The Living of These Days: An Autobiography* (New York: Harper & Brothers, 1956), 65–66.

[157] Edgar Young Mullins, *The Christian Religion in Its Doctrinal Expression* (Nashville: Sunday School Board of the Southern Baptist Convention, 1917), 205–13.

[158] Fisher Humphreys, "E. Y. Mullins," in *Baptist Theologians*, ed. Timothy George and David S. Dockery (Nashville: Broadman, 1990), 339.

indifference to trinitarianism as an implicit nontrinitarianism and some-times an explicit unitarianism. Perhaps even more surprising is the fact that when Baptists embraced unitarianism it was less in response to the challenges of rationalism and more out of the convictions of biblicism. But what this account makes clear is that the Trinity went from being a mystery of faith to become a problem in theology. The most fateful junc-ture of the story occurred when, after the publication of Richard Bent-ley's *Notae* in 1716, serious appeal to the Johannine Comma (in 1 John 5:7) was forever lost. Having given up the connection between canon and creed in favor of the Bible only, the Comma was the last fragment of a *regula* for Baptists that identified the economic Trinity of the biblical witness ("three that bear record in heaven, the Father, the Word, and the Holy Ghost") with the immanent Trinity of eternity ("and these three are one"). With the loss of the Comma, Baptists lost a vital link with patristic reflections and creedal formulations.

Severed from this final vestige of an ecclesial tradition, Baptist exe-getes were left to their own imaginations without historic hermeneuti-cal guides to identify the narrative of Scripture as the unfolding story of the triune God. They sometimes turned to philosophical arguments (e.g., John Gill, J. P. Boyce, and A. H. Strong) in tortured efforts to make the Trinity cohere in Scripture, but in the end these rational justifications sim-ply rendered the Trinity an arcane doctrine about an inscrutable mystery. In the last two hundred years, with few exceptions, most notably William Newton Clarke, trinitarian theology among Baptists suffered from both insistent biblicism and incipient rationalism. Liberals seem inclined to find unitarianism of the First Person as more reasonable, while evangelicals appear prone to regard unitarianism of the Second Person as more rel-evant. One might conclude, then, that Baptists are unitarians that simply have not yet gotten around to denying the Trinity.[159]

From Inscrutable Truth to Living Conviction

That the Trinity for Baptists had become simply a doctrinal placeholder did not escape the notice of some Baptist theologians themselves—some

---

[159] James B. Torrance makes the point that there are essentially two types of worship—unitarian and trinitarian. The unitarian view, which he argues is held by a large number of Protestant Christians, understands worship as an action that religious people do. The trini-tarian view, which Torrance contends is the standpoint of the historic Christian church, sees worship as participation "through Christ in the communion of the Spirit, in the communion of saints." Torrance, *Worship, Community, and the Triune God of Grace* (Downers Grove, Ill.: InterVarsity, 1996), 23. As this chapter shows, Baptists tilt toward the unitarian view.

yearning for another way.[160] The return to biblical narrative in recent the-ology has enabled theologians to move beyond propositionalism and his-toricism by construing Scripture as the story of the triune God.[161] This return in particular became helpful to Other Baptists in their search for a more robust trinitarian theology. The most prominent voice among them was James McClendon. The broad outline of his *Systematic Theology* indicates a deep trinitarian structure that begins with the rule of God, proceeds to the identity of Jesus Christ, and concludes with the fellow-ship of the Spirit. McClendon contended that although "the trinitarian doctrine does not appear in Scripture," the doctrine of the Trinity "was invented in order to encode and protect what does appear in Scripture, the one God who is truly Israel's Father, truly eternal Word, truly life-giving Spirit."[162] Whereas the simple biblicism of the past contributed to an eclipse of trinitarian doctrine, the recovery of biblical narrative has facilitated a trinitarian *ressourcement*.[163]

Catholic theologian Karl Rahner once wondered what difference it would make for Christian faith and practice if the doctrine of the Trin-ity were to turn out to be false and all trinitarian language had to be

---

[160] Fisher Humphreys, "Father, Son and Holy Spirit," *Theological Educator* 12, no. 1 (1982): 78–96; and Dale Moody, *The Word of Truth* (Grand Rapids: Eerdmans, 1981), 120.

[161] Hans W. Frei, *The Eclipse of Biblical Narrative: A Study in Eighteenth and Nineteenth Cen-tury Hermeneutics* (New Haven, Conn.: Yale University Press, 1974); and George Lindbeck, *The Nature of Doctrine* (Philadelphia: Westminster, 1984).

[162] James Wm. McClendon Jr., *Doctrine: Systematic Theology, Volume II* (Waco, Tex.: Bay-lor University Press, 2012), 320. McClendon continues, "The trinitarian doctrine, under-stood as an encoding of the biblical narrative of God, identifies God provided it is recognized as just that—an encoding meant to return us to its source" (321).

[163] It would be hard to imagine a Baptist theologian in America who has been more instrumental in promoting a rediscovery of the triune God than Stanley Grenz. In his work, Grenz stressed the need to move from seeing the Trinity as an obscure teaching about an inscrutable mystery to telling the biblical story as the unfolding narrative of the triune God. See Stanley J. Grenz, *Theology for the Community of God* (Grand Rapids: Eerdmans, 2000), 53. His earlier book *Rediscovering the Triune God: The Trinity in Contemporary Theology* (Minneapo-lis: Fortress, 2004) surveys contemporary trinitarian theology. He began but never completed the series entitled *The Matrix of Christian Theology*, of which there are two published volumes: *The Social God and the Relational Self: A Trinitarian Theology of the* Imago Dei (Louisville, Ky.: Westminster John Knox, 2001); and *The Named God and the Question of Being: A Trinitarian Theo-ontology* (Louisville, Ky.: Westminster John Knox, 2005). Not all agree. Millard J. Erick-son has criticized this narrative-based approach, opting instead for the commonsense realism and turgid propositionalism of the old Princeton theology, in which establishing a trinitarian doctrine is assumed to be merely a matter of arranging the facts of Scripture. Erickson, *The Evangelical Left: Encountering Postconservative Evangelical Theology* (Grand Rapids: Baker Books, 1997), 33–59. His account, which he describes as "a contemporary interpretation," would actually be more at home in the earlier era of John Gill or James Pettigru Boyce when the Trinity was thought to be "free from absurdity and agreeable to reason." Erickson, *God in Three Persons: A Contemporary Interpretation of the Trinity* (Grand Rapids: Baker Books, 1995).

dropped.[164] The shocking truth is that for most Baptist worship nothing would have to change.[165] However, this lamentable fact should not alone be construed as evidence for antitrinitarian theology. Yet Baptist worship, like the worship of wider evangelical Protestantism, is merely monotheistic, not clearly trinitarian. Nothing short of the reformation of worship can (re)turn Baptists to a richer understanding of the triune God. A trinitarian reformation in worship could be the source of renewal for Baptist faith and practice more widely. The theological importance of music in worship cannot be underemphasized. Indeed, the liturgical formula *lex orandi, lex credendi* (the rule of praying is the rule of believing) might function most appropriately for Baptists if reenvisioned as *lex cantandi, lex credendi* (the rule of *singing* is the rule of believing).[166] Still, this absence of a trinitarian dimension does not necessarily suggest a latent antitrinitarian orientation in the theology of Baptists. The christological emphasis, though tending in the direction of a unitarianism of the Second Person, may be redirected toward a more fully trinitarian center.[167] A return to a more doxological and trinitarian pattern of worship is cause for celebration no matter what the style.

Notwithstanding the reassurance that the weak trinitarianism in contemporary Baptist life is not the same as antitrinitarianism, the better part of wisdom seems to lie in the reintegrating of trinitarian practice. Such

[164] Karl Rahner, *The Trinity*, trans. Joseph Donceel (New York: Continuum, 1974), 10–11.

[165] The contemporary music used in a large number of churches shares the same lack of robust trinitarian references. E.g., a survey of Vinyard music found that half were ambiguous "You Lord" songs and almost a third were Son songs, while only 1.4 percent were "Three-Person" songs. Robin Parry, *Worshipping Trinity: Coming Back to the Heart of Worship* (Milton Keynes, U.K.: Paternoster, 2005), 143–46. Lester Ruth observes that all of the top seventy-seven songs in contemporary Christian music between 1989 and 2005 lack any trinitarian dimension in his "How Great *Is* Our God: The Trinity in Contemporary Christian Worship Music," in *The Message in the Music: Studying Contemporary Praise and Worship*, ed. Robert Woods and Brian Walrath (Nashville: Abingdon, 2007), 29–42. See also Ruth, "*Lex Amandi, Lex Orandi*: The Trinity in the Most-Used Contemporary Christian Worship Songs," in *The Place of Christ in Liturgical Prayer*, ed. Bryan D. Spinks (Collegeville, Minn.: Liturgical, 2008), 342–59.

[166] Charles Scalise, review of *Towards Baptist Catholicity*, by Steven R. Harmon, *Perspectives in Religious Studies* 35, no. 4 (2008): 433–35. The old Latin tag *lex orandi, lex credendi*, though normally taken as a rule to stress prayer as the norm for faith, may also be reversed so as to emphasize the rule of faith as the norm for prayer. See Geoffrey Wainwright, *Doxology: The Praise of God in Worship, Doctrine, and Life* (New York: Oxford University Press, 1980) 218.

[167] Christopher J. Ellis, *Gathering: A Theology and Spirituality of Worship in Free Church Tradition* (London: SCM Press, 2004) 240; and Myra Blyth, *Celebrating the Trinity: Faith, Worship and Mission* (Cambridge: Grove Books, 2003). Contemporary Baptists might also imitate the example of their forebears, whose hymnals included multiple trinitarian doxologies. Cf. Stow and Smith, *Psalmist*; and Manly and Manly, *Baptist Psalmody*.

an approach recognizes that a lasting trinitarian faith is not established in a once-for-all confession but instead becomes habituated as a living conviction through iteration. The gracious action of the Father toward the Son is conveyed through sacramental practices by the Spirit.[168] Other Baptists might begin by making it their practice to perform the doctrine of the Trinity when they baptize and lay on hands, offer prayers and pronounce blessings, voice invocations and give benedictions, confess sin and proclaim pardon, and make the sign of the cross and exchange the right hand of fellowship—all in the name and the sign of the Father, the Son, and the Holy Spirit.[169] Their example would undoubtedly invite both congregational imitation and theological reflection. Trinitarian narrations in sermons, observance of communion, and even the polity of the church meeting may require more theological preparation so as to be performed in language that is fitting and faithful.[170]

For the most part the mere monotheism of Baptist faith and practice that stands in need of trinitarian renewal is not intentionally antitrinitarianism. Yet liberal and conservative theological agendas now, as in the past, pull in directions away from trinitarian orthodoxy. For example, *The Chalice Hymnal* used by some liberal Baptist congregations contains several alternate versions of "The Old Hundredth," one of which substitutes "Creator, Christ, and Holy Ghost" for "Father, Son, and Holy Ghost."[171] However, without serious theological reflection, the liberal sensitivity to gender neutrality wanders into heterodoxy. For "Creator" is simply not a suitable substitute for "Father" because it does not adequately convey the clear teaching of Scripture that all three persons of the Trinity are active in creation: God creates *through* the Son and *by* the Spirit. As Gregory of Nazianus explained, to substitute the term Creator for Father is unsatisfactory because it reduces the first person in the Godhead to an action in which case the Son ("Christ" in *The Chalice Hymnal*) "is created and not begotten." And it is not clear how "that which is made [can] be identical with That which made it."[172] The language of the revised doxology is thus

[168] John E. Colwell, *Promise and Presence: An Exploration of Sacramental Theology* (Milton Keynes, U.K.: Paternoster, 2005), 41.

[169] Paul S. Fiddes commends the practices of making the sign of the cross and baptism in the name of the Trinity as two important trinitarian practices from the Free Church/Baptist heritage, in his *Participating in God: A Pastoral Doctrine of the Trinity* (Louisville, Ky.: Westminster John Knox, 2000), 43–44.

[170] *The Book of Common Prayer* (New York: Church Publishing, 1979); Christopher J. Ellis and Myra Blyth, eds., *Gathering for Worship: Patterns and Prayers for the Community of Disciples.* (Norwich, U.K.: Canterbury Press, 2005).

[171] *The Chalice Hymnal* (St. Louis, Mo.: Chalice Press, 1996), #47.

[172] Gregory of Nazianzus, *The Third Theological Oration: On the Son* XVI, in *The Nicene and Post-Nicene Fathers*, Second Series (Grand Rapids: Eerdmans, 1976), 7:307.

modalistic at best and Socinian or Arian at worst, for Christ not sharing the same nature as the Creator implies that he is not divine or perhaps is divine but is still a creature. Even if those who sing the revised doxology *intend* to invoke the Trinity, the language does not properly *refer* to the Trinity.

To be sure, there is good reason to foster language about God in worship and theology that does not underwrite patriarchy and male domination, but the concerns are profoundly mistaken if taken to ascribe masculinity to the personal names of God: Father, Son, and Holy Spirit. In working out the language of the Trinity in the fourth century, the Cappadocians rejected the use of functional language to name the Trinity because they recognized that the persons of the Godhead are more than what they do. As Gregory of Nazianzus argued, to refer to God as Father "is not a name either of an essence or of an action," but rather "is the name of the Relation in which the Father stands to the Son, and the Son to the Father."[173] In other words, the personal language of Father gives voice to the relational dimension of God that functional and essentialist language is incapable of expressing. As the Cappadocian theology of relationality shows, the refusal to use the term Father as a personal name for God "concedes that God the Father is male as patriarchy has defined it," and by adopting functional language as an alternative it "duplicates the unitarianism of the Arians."[174] In other words, revisionist language for the Trinity may satisfy liberal concerns about patriarchal and paternalistic language, but it simply reintroduces ancient heresies in new iterations.[175] Moreover, the relational language of Father, Son, and Holy Spirit, rather than being a source of the oppression of women, is indispensable to opening up to ever-new dimensions of relationship.[176]

But liberals are not alone in departing from trinitarian orthodoxy. A group of conservative Baptist theologians has been on the leading edge of a new and controversial theology that maintains the eternal subordination

---

[173] Gregory of Nazianzus, *Third Theological Oration* XVI, in *The Nicene and Post-Nicene Fathers*, Second Series, 7:307.

[174] Catherine Mowry LaCugna, "The Baptismal Formula, Feminist Objections, and Trinitarian Theology," *Journal of Ecumenical Studies* 26, no. 2 (1989): 243.

[175] David C. Steinmetz, "Inclusive Language and the Trinity," in *Memory and Mission: Theological Reflections on the Christian Past* (Nashville: Abingdon, 1988), 126–34; Geoffrey Wainwright, "The Doctrine of the Trinity: Where the Church Stands or Falls," *Interpretation* 45, no. 2 (1991): 118–24. In addition to the traditional version of "The Old Hundredth" that retains the language of "Father, Son, and Holy Ghost," *The Chalice Hymnal* contains a third version (#48) that meets the editorial guidelines of gender neutrality without veering into heterodoxy, which reads: "Praise God from whom all blessings flow / Praise Christ, all creatures here below / Praise Holy Spirit evermore / One God, triune, whom we adore."

[176] Fiddes, *Participating in God*, 89–108.

of the Son (ESS). This teaching grew out of an attempt to ground the permanent subordination of women to men in the eternal subordination of the Son to the Father.[177] It has even been suggested that the trinitarian doctrine of historic orthodoxy holds that the Son is "equal in being" but "eternally subordinate in role," thus naming an "eternal functional hierarchy within the Trinity" that links "God's *position and authority as God* with the concept of *masculinity* over femininity."[178] Complementarian and egalitarian views of gender relations, therefore, are no longer regarded by proponents of ESS merely as a difference of biblical interpretation. The subordination of women is taken to be ontologically grounded in the eternal relations of the Trinity where the Father rules and the Son obeys.

The not-so-subtle political agenda of ESS should raise theological suspicions. Proponents seem to be attracted to trinitarian theology not as an account of the life in which "we live and move and have our being" (Acts 17:28) but as a knock-down argument that underwrites their complementarian views of gender relations. Those who appeal to trinitarian doctrine for support of their complementarian social agenda should be called to account for this apparent utilitarianism just as much as those who engage in social trinitarian speculations to underwrite egalitarian convictions. Caution must be used in such speculative trinitarian theology, which can easily be co-opted by ideologies of the Right and the Left. It must be remembered that in a strict sense, "there can be no correspondence to the interiority of the divine persons at a human level." Unlike the triune persons, "another human self cannot be internal to my own self as [a] subject of action," because "human persons are always external to one another as *subjects*."[179] This cautionary word is wise. ESS seems to be based on the profound mistake that human relations *imitate* divine relations, when in fact human relations *participate* in the divine life.

<hr/>

[177] Wayne Grudem, *Systematic Theology: An Introduction to Biblical Doctrine* (Grand Rapids: Zondervan, 1995), 459–60.

[178] Bruce A. Ware, "How Shall We Think about the Trinity?" in *God under Fire: Modern Theology Reinvents God*, ed. Douglas S. Huffman and Eric L. Johnson (Grand Rapids: Zondervan, 2002), 269–77. Ware has subsequently published a book on the subject, *Father, Son, and Holy Spirit: Relationships, Roles, and Relevance* (Wheaton, Ill.: Crossway Books, 2005), 72–85. Over time more Baptist theologians have weighed in offering support for ESS—e.g., Andreas J. Kostenberger and Thomas R. Schreiner, eds., *Women in the Church: An Analysis and Application of 1 Timothy 2:9-15*, 2nd ed. (Grand Rapids: Baker Academic, 2005); and Stephen D. Kovach and Peter R. Schemm Jr., "A Defense of the Doctrine of the Eternal Subordination of the Son," *Journal of the Evangelical Theological Society* 42, no. 3 (1999): 461–76.

[179] Miroslav Volf, *After Our Likeness: The Church as the Image of the Trinity* (Grand Rapids: Eerdmans, 1998), 210–11. See also Volf, "'The Trinity Is Our Social Program': The Doctrine of the Trinity and the Shape of Social Engagement," *Modern Theology* 14 no. 3 (1998): 403–23.

It is worth noting that ESS is not a historic doctrine but rather a very new one. It is not part of the received wisdom of the Christian tradition. It is an innovative matter of contemporary speculation that has yet to be tested and proved by any but a very small and unrepresentative group of Baptists and evangelicals. One of the major concerns about ESS is the distinction between functional and ontological subordination. While it is true that the incarnate Son in his earthly life was submissive to the Father, the suggestion that this subordination extends to his eternal exalted state is problematic and suggests deep confusion about the immanent and economic relations of the Trinity.[180] Some critics have argued that ESS appears to be a new version of Arianism.[181] If so, it would not be the first time that a new doctrine was simply another form of an old heresy. The problems, however, are much deeper than simply confusing the economic and immanent relations, as one ESS proponent indicated when he dismissed the "eternal begetting of the Son" and "eternal procession of the Spirit," two of the fundamental features of trinitarian orthodoxy, as "highly speculative and not grounded in biblical teaching."[182]

---

[180] Karl Rahner famously observed that "the 'economic' Trinity is the 'immanent' Trinity and the 'immanent' Trinity is the 'economic' Trinity," in his *Trinity*, 22. However, theological language about the immanent Trinity and the economic Trinity functions differently. Human relationships per se cannot imitate the immanent Trinity, although they can participate in the perichoretic dance of the divine persons. To speak of cooperative relations and mutual submission among the persons of the Godhead, as ESS proponents and opponents do, seems to be a confusion of these theological categories.

[181] Kevin Giles, *Jesus and the Father: Modern Evangelicals Reinvent the Doctrine of the Trinity* (Grand Rapids: Zondervan, 2006), 17–54; and Giles, *The Trinity & Subordinationism: The Doctrine of God & the Contemporary Gender Debate* (Downers Grove, Ill.: InterVarsity, 2002), 76–85. Baptist theologian Millard J. Erickson has weighed in opposition to ESS. Erikson unfortunately muddies already cloudy theological waters by inventing the terms "gradationists" to identify "those who hold that the Father eternally has supreme authority over the Son" and "equivalentists" to denote the view that eternally the Father and the Son have equal authority." Erickson, *Who's Tampering with the Trinity? An Assessment of the Subordination Debate* (Grand Rapids: Kregel, 2009), 21. Since these define generic positions in the controversy, it seems helpful only as a critique of the generic positions he created.

[182] Ware, *Father, Son, and Holy Spirit*, 162. Ironically, Baptist theologians on both sides of the ESS issue reject the Son's eternal generation, which is one of the core elements of Nicene orthodoxy. ESS opponent Millard Erickson contends "that there are no references to the Father begetting the Son or the Father (and the Son) sending the Spirit that cannot be understood in terms of the temporal role assumed by the second and third persons of the Trinity respectively." He further states that "to speak of one of the persons as unoriginate and the others as either eternally begotten or proceeding from the Father is to introduce an element of causation or origination that must ultimately involve some type of subordination among them." Erickson, *God in Three Persons*, 309; and *Who's Tampering with the Trinity?* 179–84. For a balanced assessment of this issue of Nicene orthodoxy and ESS, see Keith E. Johnson, "Trinitarian Agency and the Eternal Subordination of the Son: An Augustinian Perspective," *Themelios* 36, no. 1 (2011): 7–25. A group of evangelical theologians, including Aída

This deviation from orthodoxy is yet more extreme when it infers from the supposed notions of the Son's eternal submission and obedience to the Father that the Son has a will separate and distinct from the Father. By ascribing a division of wills into the Godhead, ESS stands in direct contradiction with the most basic conviction of orthodox trinitarian theology—the unity of God. As Gregory of Nazianzus explains:

> There is One God, for the Godhead is One, and all that proceedeth from him is referred to One, though we believe in Three Persons. For one is not more and another less God; nor is One before and another after; nor are They divided in will or parted in power; . . . but the Godhead is, to speak concisely, undivided in separate Persons.[183]

Gregory of Nyssa similarly observed that to affirm that both the Father and the Son are God means there is "no difference either of nature or of operation" in the Godhead. And because the divine nature is apprehended by every conception as undivided, Gregory concludes, "we properly declare the Godhead to be one, and God to be one, and employ in the singular all other names which express Divine attributes."[184] ESS advocates assume that they are simply putting forth an evangelical version of social trinitarianism, but in fact they have unwittingly reintroduced a new version of the old tritheism that historic orthodoxy long ago laid to rest.

Proponents of ESS veer from orthodoxy on the basis of their simple biblicist hermeneutic, but, more importantly—and what makes this hermeneutic intelligible in the first place—is an individualistic understanding of personhood that is mistakenly read into the relations between members of the Godhead. The most significant contribution of the Cappadocian theology might have been the identification of hypostasis, a term that was already understood as conveying the being (*ousia*) of God, with person (*prosopon*). The whole substance of their theology was grounded in the conviction that the being of the one God is present in each person of the Godhead, which exists not as discrete individuals but as persons in communion.[185] It might better be stated that "in Gregory's psychology,

---

Besançon Spencer, Mimi Haddad, Royce Gruenler, Kevin Giles, I. Howard Marshall, Alan Myatt, Millard Erickson, Steven Tracy, Alvera Mickelsen, Stanley Gundry, and Catherine Clark Kroeger have issued a document that warns that ESS ends up in tritheism: "An Evangelical Statement on the Trinity," accessed December 3, 2011, http://www.trinitystatement .com/wp-content/files/Trinity%20Statement%20Spencer.pdf.

[183] Gregory of Nazianzus, *The Fifth Theological Oration: On the Holy Spirit* XIV, in *The Nicene and Post-Nicene Fathers*, Second Series (Grand Rapids: Eerdmans, 1976), 7:322.

[184] Gregory of Nyssa, *On 'Not Three Gods,'* Letter to Ablabius, in *The Nicene and Post-Nicene Fathers*, Second Series (Grand Rapids: Eerdmans, 1976), 5:336.

[185] John Zizioulas, *Being as Communion: Studies in Personhood and the Church* (Crestwood,

the attribution of a capacity to will is not derived from existence as individual(s), or from the existence of individuals in relation," but rather that the cause of the existence of the will "is wholly unrelated to the reality of individual existence."[186] But, when Gregory does apply psychological categories to the Trinity, it is typically with reference to the Godhead as one person. Even when Gregory does apply psychological language to the three divine persons, there is no indication that their interaction is analogous to the interaction among three distinct human agents.[187] By contrast, the underlying understanding of personhood in ESS is individualistic, so that the will of each divine person is taken to mean there are three individual wills and the three divine persons act as three distinct agents. This is not the Trinity. This is tritheism.

Retrieving the historic trinitarian faith lies in a deep and sustained engagement with the first five centuries of Christianity.[188] But calling for a retrieval of the patristic theology is complicated by the fact that though Baptists tend to read the Bible through a hermeneutical lens inherited from orthodoxy, they also reject the normative status of the postapostolic tradition in which these orthodox doctrines were worked out. Other Baptists seek to correct this lack of historical consciousness by underscoring that the resurgence of trinitarian theology in the twentieth century with its emphasis on the social relations of the three divine persons has its roots in both the biblical narrative and patristic reflections.[189] This attention to patristic sources provides a resource for the critique of individualism that shows how the church participates in the perichoretic life of the triune

---

N.Y.: St Vladimir's Orthodox Seminary Press, 1985), 36–41. For a critique of Zizioulas, see Lucian Turcescu, "'Person' Versus 'Individual,' and Other Modern Misreadings of Gregory of Nyssa," *Modern Theology* 18, no. 4 (2002): 527–39, esp. 536–37. Turcescu criticizes Zizioulas for using the Cappadocian trinitarian theology to combat modern individualism. He argues that "the Cappadocian Fathers were not aware of the dangers of individualism and perhaps that is why they did not make many efforts to distinguish between person and individual." However, Turcescu in no way suggests that modern individualism should be read back into the Cappadocian theology of the Trinity.

[186] Michel René Barnes, "Divine Unity and the Divided Self: Gregory of Nyssa's Trinitarian Theology in its Psychological Context," *Modern Theology* 18, no. 4 (2002): 482. The entire issue, edited by Sarah Coakley, is devoted to rethinking Gregory of Nyssa.

[187] Lewis Ayres, "On Not Three People: The Fundamental Themes of Gregory of Nyssa's Theology as Seen in *To Ablabius: On Not Three Gods*," *Modern Theology* 18, no. 4 (2002): 447.

[188] D. H. Williams, *Retrieving the Tradition and Renewing Evangelicalism: A Primer for Suspicious Protestants* (Grand Rapids: Eerdmans, 1999); Williams, *The Free Church and the Early Church: Bridging the Historical and Theological Divide* (Grand Rapids: Eerdmans, 2002); and Williams, *Evangelicals and Tradition: The Formative Influence of the Early Church* (Grand Rapids: Baker Academic, 2005).

[189] Stephen R. Holmes, *The Holy Trinity: Understanding God's Life* (Milton Keynes, U.K.: Paternoster, 2011).

God who "does not need dependence [yet] freely desires to be dependent on us for the completeness of fellowship, for the joy of the dance."[190] The Cappadocian theology of persons in communion shifts from language of observation to participation, which counters the popular modern hetero-doxy that persons are independent and self-sufficient individuals.[191] The question of how Baptists came to acquire this individualistic account of personhood and why the recovery of catholicity will require giving up on individualism remains to be explored.

Looking to the state of trinitarianism in Baptist life four decades after McClendon's prospective vision, it appears that the disinclination of his fellow Baptists to move toward a more fully trinitarian future has in many respects continued.[192] What lies ahead is uncertain, and it is not an exag-geration to suggest that for more than a few, without radical theologi-cal redirection, the Trinity may be at risk of becoming an artifact of a bygone era, either as an incomprehensible doctrine to be blindly affirmed or an inscrutable mystery to be quietly discarded. Will Baptists today be inclined to listen to the voices of *ressourcement* who nourish, invigorate, and rejuvenate trinitarian faith and practice, or as McClendon suggested will it be back to a future in which the Trinity continues to grow increas-ingly irrelevant? Baptists have learned to be content with a mere mono-theism. Yet because the Trinity is simply the view of God universally shared by Christians around the world and throughout history, a more robust trinitarian faith and life for Baptists lies on the road to recovering a sense of catholicity. But for Baptists to rediscover a more fully trini-tarian faith will require getting over a fascination with denominational identity and recovering a deeper commitment to the universal Christian heritage (to that which is catholic) than merely holding onto Baptist dis-tinctives. Other Baptists seek the recovery of catholicity because there is nothing more qualitatively or quantitatively catholic than the Trinity.[193] The choice is clear.

---

[190] Fiddes, *Participating in God*, 108.

[191] Fiddes, *Participating in God*, 46. Paul S. Fiddes develops this trinitarian ecclesiology more fully in *Tracks and Traces: Baptist Identity in Church and Theology* (Milton Keynes, U.K.: Paternoster, 2003) 70–82, in which he stresses the notion of covenant as the means by which the church gathers and is gathered. The Baptist/Free Church ecclesiology of the gathered community finds strong support in the similar account of Volf, *After Our Likeness.*

[192] McClendon, "Some Reflections on the Future of Trinitarianism," 156.

[193] Fisher Humphreys has suggested that such *ressourcement* will require reconnecting with "the universal Christian heritage . . . which is catholic" in his review of *The Catholicity of the Reformation*, ed. Carl E. Braaten and Robert W. Jenson; *The Catholicity of the Church*, by Avery Dulles; and *Soul of the World*, by George Weigel, in *Perspectives in Religious Studies* 26, no. 1 (1999): 95.

5

Priests to Each Other

"This is the last time I wish to be heard as Baptist for 'Baptist' is an adjective."[1] With that jarring declaration, Carlyle Marney began his 1974 Dickson Lectures at the Myers Park Baptist Church of Charlotte, North Carolina, where for a decade he had been senior minister. In the first lecture, entitled "Hail and Farewell," Marney made it clear that he had no intention of leaving his Baptist identity behind. Still, he loved playing with the notion of leaving. He once reportedly told a group of Baptist ministers, "Now, let me tell you why I left us." But he never really left, nor could he, no matter how many times he may have wanted to or how hard some of his fellow Baptists in the land "South of God" might have wished he would. "If you should drive me away," he asked, "where could I go?"[2] Weighing the options, he just decided to stay. Still, people wondered. Being Baptist, Marney used to say, is like trying to crawl out of a deep, dark, slimy hole. After years of struggling, you finally get to the top. But when you look around and see the way things are in other denominations, you just drop back down into your old familiar hole.[3]

Taking his cue from John Bunyan, who never owned the name Baptist but became arguably the most famous and beloved of all Baptists,

---

[1] Carlyle Marney, *Beyond Our Time and Place* (Charlotte, N.C.: Endowment Fund of the Myers Park Baptist Church, 1975), 35.

[2] Carlyle Marney, "Escape from Provincialism," handwritten notes, 1963, box 69, Carlyle Marney papers, M. Rubenstein Rare Book & Manuscript Library, Duke University, Durham, N.C. Marney concludes, "Let me rest my case tonight on an opening and a close: I shall begin with my debt to Southern Baptists. I shall close with why I have stayed. In between I shall talk about prejudice and religious institutions." These seem to be an early version of what eventually became the 1974 Dickson Lectures.

[3] John J. Carey attributes this story to Marney, citing two anonymous sources, in his *Carlyle Marney: A Pilgrim's Progress* (Macon, Ga.: Mercer University Press, 1980), 138.

Marney affirmed "his first avowed intent, to be a pilgrim," and he invited others to embark on a journey with him "beyond the denominations."[4] Yet unlike Bunyan, whose Christian pressed ever onward in progressive pilgrimage, Marney had watched successive generations of fellow Baptists tread the regressive paths of "the swamp way to the moldy disintegration of a sea-level mausoleum." He understood that postdenominational pilgrimage would involve struggle, growth, and change, but it was a higher road to a promised destiny. It entailed setting out by faith like Abraham without knowing the way, in search of the city whose builder and maker is God (Heb 11:8-10). To be a pilgrim meant that Marney would learn to be *homo viator* (a human traveler)—one whose very existence is defined by the journey. Even if few followed, he was up for the adventure.

Pilgrims Regress

Twenty years earlier, when he was pastor of the First Baptist Church of Austin, Marney took up the subject from a slightly different standpoint, preaching his one and only sermon for the Baptist General Convention of Texas. He began by telling a story about coming upon his old friend Shine one hot day as he was digging a grave back in Beaver Dam, Kentucky. When Marney arrived at the graveyard, Shine was four or five feet down in solid clay and had brought along a "little liquid refreshment" to help him on the job. Every time he bent over with the pick handle, the pint bottle in his hip pocket would rise up a little higher until finally, just before it fell out, Marney reached out and grabbed it and laid it up on the bank. Realizing that his bottle was gone, Shine turned around to look where it had fallen out, and, seeing Marney, he spoke up: "How are you, Preacher?" Marney greeted him with a smile and responded with a question: "Shine, what church do you go to?" "I am a Baptist," he replied. "I believe once saved always saved." Pressing for more, Marney asked, "Shine, what does that mean?" Shine came back as if he were an anxious child reciting the memorized answer from a catechism: "Well, it means if you get right with the Lord, you can live just like you want to the rest of the time." Puzzling over the theological implications, Marney mused, "That is the most convenient thing I ever heard."[5] And it was.

---

[4] John Bunyan, "Who Would True Valour See," in *The Pilgrim's Progress*, ed. N. H. Keeble (Oxford: Oxford University Press, 1984), 247. "Beyond the Denominations" was the title of Marney's second Dickson lecture.

[5] Carlyle Marney, "The Eternal Security of the Believer," sermon preached to the Baptist General Convention of Texas in San Antonio, Texas, 1953, box 55, Carlyle Marney papers, David M. Rubenstein Rare Book & Manuscript Library, Duke University, Durham, N.C.

No struggle, just a convenient truth. And what is more, Marney knew that Shine's doctrine was a whole lot closer to what most Baptists really thought than they would dare admit.

As a twenty-three-year-old student at the Southern Baptist Theological Seminary, Marney listened with rapt attention as his professor Sydnor Stealey articulated a set of Baptist principles that he thought would stand forever unchanged. The list included the competency of the individual to deal with God, the autonomy of the local church, the sufficiency of the Scriptures, the separation of church and state, and the baptism of believers only by immersion. These principles were not entirely Stealey's creation. They were part of a recent tradition of summarizing Baptist beliefs in concise lists. But now, at the end of his career, Marney believed these principles had not only outlived their usefulness; they had become a perversion of pilgrimage. *Soul competency* metamorphosed into atomistic individualism expressed in the folk-lie that "every tub should set on its own bottom," destroying the conviction of the church as a creative fellowship. *Local church autonomy* turned into a kind of ecclesial guerrilla warfare that lost a sense of the church universal. *The sufficiency of the Scriptures* mutated into an idolatrous biblical literalism severing the church from the living memory of Jesus Christ in Christian tradition. *Separation of church and state* became so distorted that Baptists developed a schizophrenic vision of sacred and secular, of world and creation. *Believer's baptism* went so far as to virtually ignore the significance of initiation into the fellowship of Christ. Marney still revered his old teacher, but he admitted, "The authorities have wax noses," and "they have been twisted until now they twist us!"[6] It is unclear what postdenominational pilgrims should make of these old landmarks. Should they be left like a shabby old coat at the door, or did Marney have something else in mind? Not wanting to leave too much room for suspense, he explained, "My point is this: Some points, once you have won them, need no further belaboring, they just need living out."[7] Slavishly adhering to a set of principles, Baptists had become tribesmen rather than pilgrims, determined by the self-destructive myths of race, class, and gender, rather than a vision of a common humanity.

Consider the first principle: soul competency. Understood in terms of modern categories, it has gone to seed, producing "self-styled experts, unbridled complainers, unrefined calumniators, and disjointed demagogues, whose undiluted rancor can mess up folks for fifty years."[8] But

---

[6] Marney, *Beyond Our Time and Place*, 38–41.
[7] Marney, *Beyond Our Time and Place*, 41.
[8] Marney, *Beyond Our Time and Place*, 40.

Marney was not merely calling for Baptist Christians to go against the grain of the just-me-and-Jesus piety that remains so prevalent in American Christianity. He was bumping up against an established account of Baptist identity in the South that enshrined the notion of soul competency as its central tenet. The phrase "soul competency" first appeared in the 1908 Baptist classic *The Axioms of Religion* by E. Y. Mullins, who contended that "the competency of the soul in religion excludes at once all human interference," adding that "religion is a personal matter between the soul and God."[9] Soul competency, Mullins claimed, protects the inalienable right of every autonomous soul for direct and unmediated access to God and establishes "the principle of individualism in religion."[10] He found an enthusiastic supporter in the arch-liberal University of Chicago divinity professor George Burman Foster, who praised Mullins as one of the few scholars "seeking to recover the Baptist position of the autonomy of the human soul, for which our Baptist fathers fought, bled, and died." Foster continued that "while no man has any right to be pope for any other man, he must be his own pope." But he thought that moderates like Mullins stopped short of claiming the radical freedom of the Baptist heritage, invoking soul competency "in a context which usually denies what the phrase affirms."[11]

Advocates of soul competency like Mullins and Foster maintained that this "axiom" was simply a restatement of the earlier Baptist conviction of soul liberty (or liberty of conscience). Yet it was in fact a substantially transformed and thoroughly modern invention. The earlier conviction of soul liberty served a negative and delimiting function: "One cannot and should not use force to compel anyone to accept faith, for faith is a free gift of God."[12] Soul competency became a positive and expressivist theory

---

[9] E. Y. Mullins, *The Axioms of Religion* (Philadelphia: Judson Press, 1908), 53–54.

[10] Mullins, *The Axioms of Religion*, 92–94. Mullins is by no means alone in his individualistic interpretation of Baptist principles. His friend and colleague J. B. Gambrell identified the principle of individualism with the right of private interpretation, general human rights, the constitutional guarantee of religious liberty, and the priesthood of all believers in his "Obligations of Baptists to Teach Their Principles," in *Baptist Principles Reset*, ed. Jeremiah B. Jeter (Richmond, Va.: Religious Herald Press, 1901), 250–51. This individualistic stream of Baptist life was asserted with great conviction on June 13, 1984, by Russell H. Dilday, then the president of Southwestern Baptist Theological Seminary, in the convention sermon of the SBC meeting in Kansas City, Missouri. Dilday argued that the direction out of controversy lay in recovering the Baptist heritage by turning "from *forced uniformity* to the higher ground of *autonomous individualism*," in his "On Higher Ground," reprinted in *Texas Baptists Committed*, April 1997, 11–14.

[11] George Burman Foster, *The Function of Religion in Man's Struggle for Existence* (Chicago: University of Chicago Press, 1909), 74–75, 132.

[12] Heinrich Bullinger, *Der Wiedertäufferen Ursprung, etc.* (Zurich, 1560); cited by Harold S. Bender, *The Anabaptist Vision* (Scottdale, Pa.: Herald Press, 1944), 4. This is the view stated

of moral agency, albeit a scaled-down version of the unencumbered self of American democratic liberalism.[13] It eventually attained the status of a myth, not only in the sense that it is a modern fiction but also because soul competency became a comprehensive theory, albeit a unilinear metanarrative, that explained everything else.[14] Noted Baptist historian of American Christianity Winthrop Hudson sweepingly dismissed Mullins' claim, commenting that "this highly individualistic principle . . . was derived from the general cultural and religious climate of the nineteenth century rather than from any serious study of the Bible."[15] Continuing, Hudson

---

for Baptists in classic form by Roger Williams in *The Bloudy Tenent of Persecution,* in *The Complete Writings of Roger Williams* (New York: Russell & Russell, 1963), vol. 3.

[13] This romantic reading of history is what Barry Alan Shain called "the myth of American individualism" in his *The Myth of American Individualism: The Protestant Origins of American Political Thought* (Princeton, N.J.: Princeton University Press, 1994), 10–11. Shain's thesis is that the misperception of individual liberty as the animating principle of American culture in time hardened into a libertarian myth.

[14] For how this liberal myth became connected with the Baptists, see my article "Roger Williams, American Democracy, and the Baptists," *Perspectives in Religious Studies* 34, no. 3 (2007): 267–86.

[15] Winthrop S. Hudson, "Shifting Patterns of Church Order in the Twentieth Century," in *Baptist Concepts of the Church,* ed. Winthrop S. Hudson (Philadelphia: Judson Press, 1959), 215; and Hudson, *Baptists in Transition: Individualism and Christian Responsibility* (Valley Forge, Pa.: Judson Press, 1979), 142. James Wm. McClendon Jr. grew increasingly less appreciative of Mullins. In the first edition of his *Ethics,* published in 1986, McClendon made a glancing critique of soul competency as not sufficient "to do justice to the shared discipleship that earlier baptists had embraced," but, in the revised edition published in 2002, he characterized soul competency as "Mullins's anthropocentric motto" that "was framed too much in terms of the rugged American individualism of Theodore Roosevelt to do justice to the shared discipleship baptist life requires." See McClendon, *Ethics: Systematic Theology, Volume I* (Nashville: Abingdon, 1986), 30; and, based on the Abingdon 2002, 2nd rev. and enlarged ed., McClendon's *Ethics: Systematic Theology: Volume I* (Waco, Tex.: Baylor University Press, 2012), 29. The Baptist Manifesto, of which McClendon was a coauthor, gestured toward followers of E. Y. Mullins as an example of Baptists who have "embraced modernity by defining freedom in terms of the Enlightenment notions of autonomous moral agency and objective rationality." Mikael Broadway, Curtis W. Freeman, Barry Harvey, James Wm. McClendon Jr., Elizabeth Newman, and Philip Thompson, "Re-envisioning Baptist Identity: A Manifesto for Baptist Communities in North America," *Baptists Today,* June 26, 1997, 8–10. I subsequently wrote a piece that was critical of Mullins' theological method but recognized his significance as a denominational leader. Freeman, "E. Y. Mullins and the Siren Songs of Modernity," *Review and Expositor* 96, no. 1 (1999): 23–42. My criticism of Mullins placed me in the odd company of SBC conservatives, who were critical for similar reasons but with a different agenda—i.e., the justification of the conservative resurgence. See Thomas J. Nettles, *By His Grace and for His Glory* (Grand Rapids: Baker, 1986), 246–47; Nettles "The Rise and Demise of Calvinism among Southern Baptists," *Founders Journal* 19, no. 20 (1995): 17–19; and R. Albert Mohler Jr., introduction to *The Axioms of Religion,* by E. Y. Mullins (Nashville: Broadman & Holman, 1997), 1–32. The Winter 1999 issue of the *Southern Baptist Journal of Theology* was dedicated to the theme E. Y. Mullins in retrospect. It featured articles by R. Albert Mohler Jr., Thomas J. Nettles, Russell J. Moore and Gregory A. Thornbury, and Sean Michael Lucas, all of which faulted Mullins for his emphasis on experience that prepared the way for neoliberalism in

observed, "the practical effect of the stress upon 'soul competency' as the cardinal doctrine of Baptists was to make every[one]'s hat [his or her] own church."[16]

Nevertheless, Baptists committed to the old paths of denominational pilgrimage continued to identify individualism as the distinctive feature that separated them from other bodies and marked them as more authentically Christian.[17] Harry Emerson Fosdick suggested that his grandfather became a Baptist because "he was attracted by their independent individualism," adding that "he was certainly a self-reliant character."[18] Nowhere was this more strikingly evident than in the convenient theology that Marney's old friend intoned back in Beaver Dam: "if you get right with the Lord, you can live just like you want to the rest of the time." Nor is Shine's version all that far removed from the more recently invoked creed of Christian self-sufficiency: "Ain't nobody but Jesus gonna

---

the SBC. The entire Winter 1999 issue of *Review and Expositor* was devoted to an appraisal of the Mullins legacy. Phyllis Rodgerson Pleasants for different reasons concluded that Mullins' mediating theology was unsuccessful in her "E. Y. Mullins: Diplomatic Theological Leader," *Review and Expositor* 96, no. 1 (1999): 43–60. James M. Dunn, Russell H. Dilday, Timothy D. Maddox, and E. Glenn Hinson had more positive assessments of Mullins' project. See Dunn, "Church, State, and Soul Competency," *Review and Expositor* 96, no. 1 (1999): 61–73; Dilday, "Mullins the Theologian: Between the Extremes," *Review and Expositor* 96, no. 1 (1999): 75–86; Maddox, "E. Y. Mullins: Mr. Baptist for the 20th and 21st Century," *Review and Expositor* 96, no. 1 (1999): 87–108; and Hinson, "E. Y. Mullins as Interpreter of the Baptist Tradition," *Review and Expositor* 96, no. 1 (1999): 109–22. More recently, *Baptist History and Heritage* devoted an issue to E. Y. Mullins and *The Axioms of Religion*: *Baptist History and Heritage* 43, no. 1 (2008). My account of Mullins was cited by several of the authors. C. Douglas Weaver and Russell Dilday characterized my work as harshly critical of Mullins, while William Carrell described it as exposing genuine weaknesses in Mullins' theology. See Weaver, "The Baptist Ecclesiology of E. Y. Mullins: Individualism and the New Testament Church," *Baptist History and Heritage* 43, no. 1 (2008): 31n4; Dilday, "The Significance of E. Y. Mullins's *The Axioms of Religion*," *Baptist History and Heritage* 43, no. 1 (2008): 93n3 and 93n5; and Carrell, "The Inner Testimony of the Spirit: Locating the Coherent Center of E. Y. Mullins's Theology," *Baptist History and Heritage* 43, no. 1 (2008): 35. These commentators may leave the impression that my view of Mullins is primarily negative. In response to similar characterizations of my work, I wrote, "Mullins retained the conversionist conviction that previous generations of Baptists had lived out, as well as the evangelical doctrines that his predecessors like J. P. Boyce had thought out. By adapting these convictions and doctrines to modern psychology and theology, Mullins believed he was protecting Christianity from the onslaughts of rationalistic philosophy and skeptical science. His aim was to move Baptists faithfully and effectively into the 20th century. In many ways he succeeded." Letter to the editor, *Baptist Standard*, May 15, 2000, 4, available online at http://assets.baptiststandard.com/archived/2000/5_15/pages/letters.html.

[16] Hudson, *Baptist Concepts of the Church*, 216; and Hudson, *Baptists in Transition*, 143.

[17] J. B. Gambrell, like Mullins, identified the principle of individualism as *the* Baptist distinctive in his *Baptist Principles Reset*, 250–51.

[18] Harry Emerson Fosdick, *The Living of These Days: An Autobiography* (New York: Harper & Brothers, 1956), 11.

tell me what to believe."[19] Yet Marney understood that "individualism is a non-relational creed because it teaches I do not need my neighbour to be myself."[20] To be sure, Marney admired the gumption of self-reliance.[21] He praised Ralph Waldo Emerson for leaving "the Christian ministry because he could no longer conscientiously serve the Lord's Supper." Marney reflected, "I respect Emerson for that. If I ever leave it, I think it will be because I can no longer conscientiously take up an offering." And, he added, "you can't stay in the ministry if you don't take up a collection."[22] But what concerned Marney was the underlying anthropology of soul competency (a dichotomous separation between soul and body) and its accompanying soteriology (salvation as a matter of saving souls, not bodies) that he believed rendered it of little use. And he was not shy in pointing out that this "bastard individualism" (his term) was "a gross perversion of the gospel" (his assessment) and a poor resource for postdenominational pilgrims.[23] In his view, those who venture into the future guided by a new and improved theory of soul competency simply do not possess ballast of sufficient weight to stabilize the transcendental ego and prevent a shipwreck of the faith.[24]

---

[19] James M. Dunn, "No Freedom for the South with a Creed," in *Soul Freedom: Baptist Battle Cry*, ed. James M. Dunn and Grady C. Cothen (Macon, Ga.: Smyth & Helwys, 2000), 83. See also Dunn's chapter in Everett C. Goodwin, ed., *Baptists in the Balance* (Valley Forge, Pa.: Judson Press, 1999); and quoted by Kenneth L. Woodward in "Sex, Sin and Salvation," *Newsweek*, November 2, 1998, 37.

[20] Colin Gunton, *The One, the Three and the Many* (Cambridge: Cambridge University Press, 1993), 32.

[21] Ralph Waldo Emerson, "Self-Reliance," in *The Complete Writings of Ralph Waldo Emerson* (New York: Wm. H. Wise, 1929), 1:138–52.

[22] Carlyle Marney, "For This Cause" (part II), sermon preached at First Baptist Church, Austin, Texas, October 16, 1955, box 61, Carlyle Marney papers, David M. Rubenstein Rare Book & Manuscript Library, Duke University, Durham, N.C.

[23] Carlyle Marney, *Priests to Each Other* (Valley Forge, Pa.: Judson Press, 1974), 12. The concern about individualism has been raised about Protestant Christianity as a whole, American Protantism in general, and Free Churches in particular. Baptists and Pentecostals seem particularly inclined toward individualism. See Philip J. Lee, *Against the Protestant Gnostics* (New York: Oxford University Press, 1987); Robert N. Bellah et al., eds., *Habits of the Heart: Individualism and Commitment in American Life*, updated ed. (Berkeley: University of California Press, 1996); Harold Bloom, *The American Religion: The Emergence of the Post-Christian Nation* (New York: Simon & Schuster, 1992); and Bill J. Leonard, *God's Last and Only Hope: The Fragmentation of the Southern Baptist Convention* (Grand Rapids: Eerdmans, 1990).

[24] Some Baptists, committed to the paths of denominationalism, believe that new versions of soul competency will do just fine. Responding to an earlier version of this essay, Patrick Rogers Horn wrote, "Our lives may show that we hold a distorted version of soul competency. . . . But don't ask us to dump a principle because we can imagine distortions of it. That would make every principle a distorted one, leaving us with no principles at all." Letter to the editor, *Baptists Today*, August 2002, 8; and Curtis Freeman, "Carlyle Marney on Pilgrim Priesthood," *Baptists Today*, June 2002, 28–29.

In his book *Structures of Prejudice*, Marney identified "rugged individualism" as one of four social structures that form a cage or a cell imprisoning human beings in racial prejudice. He asserted that individualism "provides the deepest and most vicious channel for the operation of human prejudice." Yet prejudice, Marney explained, is not inherent to the human condition. It arises from sin, which also results in human estrangement and isolation. The fundamental tenets of this sinful individualism are naked egoism, atomistic materialism, racial hegemonism, naturalistic reductionism, and civil libertarianism. Marney summarized his definition:

> Individualism is a bastardized version of ancient hedonism wearing the garb of modern democratic idealism which claims for itself the same goal as that of classical Greek eudaemonism; that is, self-realization as the end of man, but does this in such a way as to eliminate community, subvert the development of personality, distort all social human values, and has as its end the cutting off of the individual from everything which constitutes personality. It is truly sola-ipsis in that it has neither values nor community that permit the individual ever to come outside the self and therefore is a definition of hell which is the ultimate in isolation. It is always isolationistic, atomistic, and seeks the center of the earth as its own which makes it a god-maker in demonic form.[25]

"In the warm, wet mothering womb of this vicious individualism," Marney argued, "we find the most powerful breeding place of human prejudice."[26] Yet the power of individualism is limited by its incapacity for community, which is the basic condition of personality. It is further constrained by its inability to grasp reality or value and by the depersonalizing misuse of political power.

Marney's indictment was, to be sure, aimed at the sort of individualism that allowed militant segregationists to insulate their racial prejudice from the gospel. He was often critical of those who invoked the old Hamitic myth (Gen 9:20-27) in which black skin and moral degradation were construed to those of African descent as signs of divine punishment and a warrant for racial subjugation that destined them to be "drawers of water" and "hewers of wood."[27] The searching scrutiny of his structural account revealed the religious mysticism of the South for what it was and

---

[25] Carlyle Marney, *Structures of Prejudice* (Nashville: Abingdon, 1961), 198.

[26] Marney, *Structures of Prejudice*, 199.

[27] Carlyle Marney, "From These Stones," in *The Pulpit Speaks on Race*, ed. Alfred T. Davis (New York: Abingdon, 1965), 87–95; and Marney, "The Emancipation of a White," *Christian Century*, November 17, 1954, 1397–98.

displayed the differences between militant segregationists and the Baptist mainstream to be a matter of degree, not of substance. For most of Marney's contemporaries, soul competency justified a piety of indifference to the suffering of African Americans and a politics of inaction toward the segregationist powers in the church and community. They conceived of sin as simply the expression of individual disobedience and salvation as only a matter of saving individual competent souls. None of them sufficiently fathomed the social depths of human depravity or the corporate dimensions of creaturely redemption.

Marney had little patience with his fellow Baptists who, on October 11, 1955, opposed the admission of two African American Baptist congregations, Ebenezer and Nineteenth Street, into the Austin Baptist Association.[28] He had even less respect for preachers who hid behind a gospel of individual salvation, pretending that the cross of Jesus Christ had nothing to do with civil rights. Such a theology allowed militant segregationists to remain church members in good standing without ever challenging their white supremacist politics.[29] This Southern-fried mystic individualism created a culture of white indifference on which the militant segregationists depended. Marney saw through the language of pietism that cloaked a deeper individualistic solipsism. For him individualism was no virtue to be celebrated. It was a vice to overcome. Even when it was dressed up in formal theological language, Marney recognized the sound of the convenient theology intoned by his old friend Shine.

Believer Priesthood

On June 14, 1964, Marney preached a sermon to the Myers Park Baptist Church entitled "The Priest at Every Elbow."[30] The theme was to define the remainder of his ministry. Beginning with a declaration of depravity, it declaimed that human beings use every skill and power at their disposal

[28] Minutes of the Austin Baptist Association, October 10–11, 1955, Texas Baptist Historical Collection, Dallas, Tex., 9–10; and "City Baptists Admit Two Negro Units: Issue Decided on 99–25 Vote," *Austin Statesman*, October 12, 1955, 1.

[29] Such a theology allowed Governor Ross Barnett to remain a member in good standing in the First Baptist Church of Jackson, Mississippi, where Douglas Hudgins was pastor. See Charles Marsh, *God's Long Summer: Stories of Faith and Civil Rights* (Princeton, N. J.: Princeton University Press, 1997), 189–90. See also my articles "'Never Had I Been So Blind': W. A. Criswell's 'Change' on Racial Segregation," *Journal of Southern Religion* 10 (2007), http://jsr .fsu.edu/Volume10/Freeman.pdf; and "*All the Sons of Earth*: Carlyle Marney and the Fight against Prejudice," *Baptist History and Heritage* 44, no. 2 (2009): 71–84.

[30] Marney, "The Priest at Every Elbow," sermon preached at Myers Park Baptist Church, Charlotte, North Carolina, June 14, 1964, box 70, Carlyle Marney papers, David M. Rubenstein Rare Book & Manuscript Library, Duke University, Durham, N.C.

to make themselves "the most savage of all God's magnificent beasts." To beat down this evil, Marney continued, Christians have been given a mighty weapon: "the conviction that the Man Christ could make us whole; and that men who are being made whole could create a well society." Yet, he asserted, "the Christian Church has been a failure at both. We have neither kept the worldliness out nor have we brought the world in." "What shall we do?" he asked. To which he answered, "We must recover the priesthood of every believer or we can't do at all." For such retrieval to have a chance would require radical revision beginning with the clergy. It demanded "a new priesthood" that believed in the redemption of the world and not just a redemption of the church. "No professional clergy," Marney thundered, "can do what the Church is called to do." Calling professional ministers modern-day prophets of Baal and Westernized witch doctors, he scoffed, "We have elevated the clergy into a kept harlotry." In his judgment, the professionalization of the clergy had produced "a hireling ministry" against whom Roger Williams before him loudly protested.[31] But dethroning the clergy called for the laity to own a sense of moral responsibility, which would not be easy. They had grown comfortable with their hand-tamed preachers. Marney jibed, "Most of us church folks are not responsibly free—we are just 'sorta loose.'" Churches hire ministers to tell them that they are free and how to keep this "freedom." And they expect the preacher to tell them a lot of things, "but mostly [they] want him to tell [them] what to do in such a nice way that [they] don't have to do this or anything else."[32]

It was the convenient theology of his old friend Shine raising its head once again. Like the Hydra of ancient myth, destroying it once and for all would require nothing less than a Herculean effort. Reading an essay by Graydon McClellan in a book titled *New Frontiers of Christianity*, Marney stumbled over these words: "the individualistic image of a stipendiary chaplain to a private religious club who, by mastering the arts of unction and inspiration can enlarge the club and further his own career must be smashed."[33] Marney detested the thought that he had become a professional minister and a private chaplain, but he admitted that nowhere had he encountered greater pressure to mash him into a perversion of the priesthood of the congregation than in Myers Park. And he warned them,

[31] Roger Williams, *A Hireling Ministry None of His*, in *Complete Writings*, 7:142–91.

[32] Carlyle Marney, column in the Myers Park Baptist *Church News*, February 27, 1962, box 69, Carlyle Marney papers, David M. Rubenstein Rare Book & Manuscript Library, Duke University, Durham, N.C.

[33] Graydon E. McClellan, "The Ministry," in *New Frontiers of Christianity*, ed. Ralph C. Raughley Jr. (New York: Association Press, 1962), 130.

"The only real protection you have got against my becoming some kind of Pope is not your concern, it is my ego limit and the sharp minds of my brethren of the clergy, and that is not much shelter!"[34]

Marney's understanding of the ministry had been most deeply formed by J. G. Hughes, pastor of the First Baptist Church of Kingsport, Tennessee, and three-time president of the Tennessee Baptist Convention, under whom Marney served before enrolling in Southern Seminary. Through the years, Hughes continued to be Marney's mentor in ministry. When Hughes was in failing health, Marney wrote him an uncharacteristically personal note, in which he said, "As I grow a little older here in Austin and so farther than ever from Kingsport days I find you more and more in my mind and in my heart and not less." And, a decade after his death, Marney described Hughes as an "irresistibly winsome and gracious man, . . . who taught me all I know about true pastors." Hughes, Marney said, "always seemed to preach and teach as if he had just heard from the Almighty. I knew of his discouraged times and tasted the loneliness somedays, but when he came out on Sundays he seemed very sure of the Eternal."[35] Marney had learned well from his old mentor, but he was convinced that the ministry must change. Quoting McClellan again, Marney continued, "The Church needs a tough new tough breed of servant-minded pastors who are willing to lose their lives in building up the ministries of their people."[36] Marney was determined to lose his life, but he still had no idea how to go about building up the ministries of the people. He did not know where to go to discover such a radical understanding of the ministry that envisioned a new partnership between pastors and people.

He turned back to the Luther who, in a letter "To the Illustrious Senate and People of Prague," offered this recommendation on the reform of the church and the priesthood:

> I would confidently advise that you have no ministers at all. It would be safer and more wholesome for the father of the house to read the gospel . . . and . . . to baptize those born in his home, and so to govern himself and his according to the doctrine of Christ even if they never did receive the Lord's Supper. . . . If in this way two houses, three, or ten houses, or a whole city or several cities agreed . . . to live in faith and love . . . even if no ordained, shorn or anointed ever came to them

---

[34] Marney, "Priest at Every Elbow."

[35] Letter from Carlyle Marney to J. G. Hughes, September 11, 1953, box 24, Carlyle Marney papers, David M. Rubenstein Rare Book & Manuscript Library, Duke University, Durham, N.C.; and Marney, *The Carpenter's Son* (Nashville: Abingdon, 1967), 7.

[36] Marney, *Carpenter's Son*, 7.

. . . Christ, without a doubt, would be in their midst and would own them as his church.[37]

Repeating the phrase with emphasis "would own them as his church," Marney asked what Luther could have meant, except simply "the priestliness of every household." Quoting Luther in *The Babylonian Captivity of the Church*, Marney asserted, "As many of us as have been baptized are all priests without distinction." And again, "We are all priests, as many of us as are Christians."[38] But in describing Luther as "writing off the professional priesthood," Marney failed to read him closely and in context. Luther, to be sure, declared that "we are all priests, as many of us as are Christians,"[39] but he also maintained that ministers are one of the visible signs of the true church. "Wherever you find these offices or officers," he declared, "you may be assured that the holy Christian people are there; for the church cannot be without these bishops, pastors, preachers, priests; and conversely, they cannot be without the church."[40] Luther was forced to clarify his view of the royal priesthood after being challenged by Jerome Emser:

> In all my writings I never wanted more than that all Christians should be priests; yet not all should be consecrated by bishops, not all should preach, celebrate mass, and exercise the priestly office unless they have been appointed and called to do so. That was my final intention.[41]

When the Reformers appealed to the priesthood of all believers, they were principally thinking about the right of all Christians to hear a confession of sin. Luther was clearly in favor of making confession, but what he opposed was making it a monopoly the clergy. For Luther, "what all Christians may do privately, the ordained ministry has been set apart to do publicly."[42] Had he looked more carefully, the revolutionary theology Marney thought was in Luther would surely have been found among the Reformation radicals (and later the Baptists) for whom ordained ministry

---

[37] Martin Luther, *Church and Ministry*, in *Luther's Works* (Philadelphia: Muhlenberg, 1958), 40:9–10.

[38] Martin Luther, *Word and Sacrament*, in *Luther's Works*, 36:112–13.

[39] Martin Luther, *On the Councils and the Church*, in *Luther's Works* (Philadelphia: Fortress, 1966), 41:164.

[40] Luther, *On the Councils and the Church*, in *Luther's Works*, 41:164.

[41] Martin Luther, "Dr. Luther's Retractions of the Error forced Upon Him By The Most Learned Priest of God Sir Jerome Emser, Vicar in Meissen," *Church and Ministry I*, in *Luther's Works*, 39:233.

[42] David C. Steinmetz, *Memory and Mission: Theological Reflections on the Christian Past* (Nashville: Abingdon, 1988), 69.

served only the *bene esse* (well being), never the *esse* (essence), of the Church.[43]

Yet Marney discovered an important connection in Luther's doctrine of believer priesthood, which all too often has been missed by interpreters who mistakenly find in it the germ of the modern autonomous self.[44] In *The Babylonian Captivity of the Church*, Luther subtly but clearly linked the priesthood of all believers with baptism. It is in baptism that Christians are united with Christ, and it is in baptism that the baptized hear the words, "You are a chosen race, a royal priesthood, a holy nation, God's own people" (1 Pet 2:9). "Therefore," Luther argued, "we are all priests."[45] Yet Jesus Christ alone is the great high priest. It is from him and in him that baptized believers receive the good news that they are righteous by grace alone, and it is from him and by virtue of union with him that the ministry of priesthood is conferred on every believer in baptism. The priestly ministry of Christ and the priesthood of all Christians are linked, as reconciling faith and the communion of saints constitute the church. In the end, the sacrifice of Christian is Christ's own sacrifice, for "all sacrifice through which the community exists is an offering with and in Christ in that one sacrifice which took place once but is yet everywhere present, which cannot be repeated but lives on in the reality of the community."[46] All Christians are priests because in baptism they share in Christ's priestly office.

This connection between Christ and believer priesthood was only implicit in Marney's 1964 "Priest at Every Elbow" sermon. There is a hint of it near the beginning when he described "a new priesthood that believes in the redemption of the world—not the redemption of the church." Here he looks to the incarnation in which the whole world is redeemed by the presence of Christ. But in *The Recovery of the Person*, published in 1963,

---

[43] See, e.g., Balthasar Hubmaier, "On Fraternal Admonition," in *Balthasar Hubmaier: Theologian of Anabaptism*, trans. and ed. H. Wayne Pipkin and John H. Yoder (Scottdale, Pa.: Herald Press, 1989), 372–85.

[44] As Paul Althaus explains, "Luther never understands the priesthood of all believers merely in the 'Protestant' sense of the Christian's freedom to stand in a direct relationship to God without a human mediator. Rather he constantly emphasizes the Christian's evangelical authority to come before God on behalf of the brethren and also of the world. The universal priesthood expresses not religious individualism but its exact opposite, the reality of the congregation as a community." Althaus, *The Theology of Martin Luther*, trans. Robert C. Schultz (Philadelphia: Fortress, 1966), 314.

[45] Luther, *Word and Sacrament*, in *Luther's Works*, 36:113. Various early Christian baptismal liturgies contain ritual anointing of the baptized, sometimes accompanied with the reading from 1 Pet 2:9-10 that proclaims that the baptized are a royal priesthood. Edward Charles Whitaker, *Documents of the Baptismal Liturgy* (London: SPCK, 1997), 2–7, 30–35, 110–23, 194–96.

[46] Althaus, *Theology of Martin Luther*, 315.

Marney makes this christological link more explicit. There he finds a deep theological trope in the second-century Christian theologian, Irenaeus, who in his work *Against Heresies* declared of Christ, "For he did not seem one thing while he was another. . . . What he was, that he also appeared to be . . . not despising or evading any condition of humanity."[47] Taking it all in, Marney reflected, "He came to us; he became like us."[48] This christological conviction was perhaps the most important and least understood aspect of Marney's theology. In the years to follow, the phrase "He became like us" grew to be something of a leitmotif in Marney's theology.[49] God recapitulated humanity in Jesus Christ.

A month prior to giving his "Priest at Every Elbow" sermon, Marney addressed American and Southern Baptists at the Baptist Jubilee Advance meeting in Atlantic City, New Jersey, on the prospect of Baptist unity. He jokingly criticized American Baptists for holding a unitarianism "associated with a Fatherhood that is virtually childless" and Southern Baptists for being a "Jesus-cult . . . with the trappings of a Confederate Narcissus."[50] Marney's intention was to entertain, and his generalizations were overstated, but his theological analysis was no joke. This theological deficiency endemic to the South was especially prominent in Charlotte. As Marney remarked, "The Bible Belt, in Billy Graham's home town, chokes on its own salvation."[51] But Marney well understood that what he was trying to overturn was the culturally established religion of the South. Reflecting near the end of his life, he observed,

> The heresy of the south is that for 200 years Jesus has been kept so god-like, so divine, that he has not been relevant. Technically the heresy is called docetic gnosticism. Religion in the south has kept Jesus in the heavens. Because if he ever gets in our alley we'll have to be like him. And that'll make us clean it up. My whole ministry has been given to the proclamation that Jesus was human. This implies a real incarnation, because if he's really like us, we have the potential of being like him. But if we keep him God, we don't have to be like him. A person who

---

[47] Irenaeus, *Against Heresies* 2.22.4, in *The Ante-Nicene Fathers* (Grand Rapids: Eerdmans, 1979), 1:391.

[48] Carlyle Marney, *The Recovery of the Person* (Nashville: Abingdon, 1963), 95 and 112.

[49] Carlyle Marney, *He Became Like Us* (Nashville: Abingdon, 1964), 20.

[50] Carlyle Marney, "The Prospect of Baptist Unity," address at Atlantic City, New Jersey, May 22, 1964, box 69, Carlyle Marney papers, David M. Rubenstein Rare Book & Manuscript Library, Duke University, Durham, N.C.

[51] Carlyle Marney, introduction to "Tragic Man—Tragic House" (unpublished manuscript, 1958), 3, box 63, Carlyle Marney papers, David M. Rubenstein Rare Book & Manuscript Library, Duke University, Durham, N.C.

keeps Jesus too godlike doesn't have to be responsible as a human being. Any religion that reduces my responsibility for this earth is a copout.[52]

Yet Marney pushed so hard against the modern-day gnostics in affirming with Irenaeus the reality of God in Christ becoming *like us* that he overlooked the trajectory in Irenaeus of the incarnation's effect in humanity becoming *like God*. This doctrine, which is called *theosis* in the Eastern Church, affirmed that "he became what we are that we might become what he is."[53] Still, it is important to note that what drove Marney toward the humanity of God in Christ was not the worries of liberal historical critics about the man Jesus, though he had read Harnack thoroughly. Rather what informed his insight was the orthodox concern that God must be one with humanity in Christ or else salvation is in jeopardy.[54] The Word became flesh—not a gnostic phantasm, not an adopted Son, not a subordinate creature, not a celestial flesh, but a real person. On this conviction, Marney believed, hung the salvation of the world.

Marney unveiled his incarnational anthropology before a nationally televised audience on Christmas Eve in 1965. The sermon, titled "Peace but Not Yet," was not immediately understood, even by his supporters, as a Christmas message. Though Marney never mentioned the war in Vietnam, it provided the occasion and context for his thesis: peace on earth only through the emergence of "a new kind of man." He intoned:

When God talked peace once he did it by, with, and through a man, the only man, the man none of our wants and desires could entrap and

---

[52] Carlyle Marney, "Preaching the Gospel, South of God: An Interview with Carlyle Marney," by Bill Finger, *Christian Century*, October 4, 1978, 918.

[53] The patristic doctrine of *theosis* as classically stated by Athanasius affirms God "assumed humanity that we might become God." Athanasius, *On the Incarnation of the Word* §54 (Crestwood, N.Y.: St Vladimir's Seminary Press, 1944), 93. The meaning of *theosis* for Athanasius and other Orthodox theologians is not a crude divinization in which the redeemed literally become gods, but rather that as the Son is united with humanity through the incarnation, so is humanity united with the life of the Son of God through salvation (or divinization). Irenaeus makes a similar point, stating that "the Word of God, our Lord Jesus Christ, who did, through his transcendent love, become what we are, that he might bring us to be even what he is himself," in his *Against Heresies* 5.pref., in *The Ante-Nicene Fathers*, 1:526.

[54] Marney's concern to beat back a creeping docetism is grounded in the orthodox concern for the reality of the incarnation. He differs from Maurice Wiles, John Hick, et al. who reject the incarnation as myth, as Herbert McCabe argued, "not because the Church long ago threw it out as an option incompatible with her life, a heresy, but because it is found to be incompatible with the European way of life in the second half of the twentieth century." McCabe, *God Matters* (London: Geoffrey Chapman, 1987), 54. See John Hick, *The Myth of God Incarnate* (Philadelphia: Westminster, 1977). D. M. Baillie attempted to show that one of the positive aspects of the new historicism was that it put an end to docetism, in his *God Was in Christ* (New York: Scribner, 1948), 11–20.

enslave. . . . The star of this hope is a man who weighs as much naked as dressed. He transcends the racial, regional, religious buckets of our existence by his ability to move in and out. He has dimensions of selfhood beyond nation, beyond property, beyond regional views of race. . . . He knows a larger race—the human race. . . . And here, words like white, Protestant, American drop off and out. Mere adjectives! He is the prospect of a gorgeous full-orbed manhood.[55]

That Marney's language was esoteric did not fit well with the prime-time audience, nor did it facilitate an understanding of his point. The *Charlotte Observer* in its article about the service got the anthropology part but missed the Christology, reporting that the "new man . . . must be a man as Christ was a man."[56] This was true enough, but for Marney there was more. The "new man" was possible only because in Christ God became like us. The new human race was not something that Christians could create themselves through sheer force of will or by any other means at their disposal. The "one new human race" began with the incarnation, and in the incarnation humanity and divinity were manifested to be united: "the Word (not silence) was made flesh (not idea) and dwelt among us so that everywhere he passed his grace spilled over on us, and faith (not knowledge) and person (in a community of love) became so vital that any man seized by this grace would forthwith begin to act as if he were creating it all over again."[57] Marney concluded:

> One has gone before us into a manhood and a community that lies within our reach. The method is *dialogical* and requires us to *hear* each other. The setting is *cruciform* and demands our lives and fortunes. The characters are *human*. The drama has consequences—we can afford to work at being brothers to the race because we have met here, and there, too, a very great grace.[58]

Marney's theme: the new history inaugurated in the Man-God, Jesus Christ, makes this new humanity, which was indeed *real* humanity, possible.

---

[55] Marney, "Peace but Not Yet," sermon preached at Myers Park Baptist Church, Charlotte, North Carolina, December 24, 1965, box 70, Carlyle Marney papers, David M. Rubenstein Rare Book & Manuscript Library, Duke University, Durham, N.C. There are several versions of the sermon. One is handwritten. A second is a typescript of Marney's handwritten text. A third is a slightly revised version that was prepared for distribution.

[56] "Marney's Sermon to Nation: Peace Requires a New Man," *Charlotte News*, December 25, 1965, 1A.

[57] Marney, "Peace but Not Yet."

[58] Marney, "Peace but Not Yet."

It was a point lost on many a listener. The sermon received more than five hundred letters and telegrams from across the country. Many were positive, but some were less favorable. Dr. John Landrum, pastor of Kirkwood Baptist Church in Missouri and one of Marney's former classmates at Southern Seminary, wrote, "When you had an opportunity over national television to give a strong witness for our Lord and Savior Jesus Christ, you failed—completely." Rev. Dick Meier, pastor of Bethany Baptist Church in Millard, Nebraska, was even stronger in his response: "I blushed with shame as I watched all the pretentious Phariseeism and the put-on show of meaningless religiosity." Meier continued, "I rebuke you for the sake of your people and for your own sake." The Northside Baptist Church of Charlotte bought ads in the *Charlotte Observer*, announcing that their pastor was going to preach a sermon to the five-thousand-member congregation, asking, "Can Carlyle Marney Save You From Sin?" The answer, as might be expected, was "No!"[59] The Charlotte newspapers ran letters to the editor for several weeks. Mrs. J. C. Eaves exclaimed:

> What a disappointment: There was no Christmas message. What was Dr. Marney trying to tell the thousands who were listening? Not once was Christ mentioned as long as I listened. You would never have known it was Christmas Eve and Christ's birthday.[60]

The *Charlotte News* reprinted the entire sermon, but the letters to the editor continued to come in through February.[61] One person described it as "an incoherent piece of quasi-existentialism, a jumble of non-sequiturs, and a seldom equaled example of inept showing off."[62] For most the essence was lost in the eloquence. The only writer who seemed to understand the sermon was fellow North Carolina pastor Frank Thomas, who explained that the whole message came down to an appeal for "men and women to discontinue 'playing at religion' and begin to love."[63] As Marney later remembered, the critics thought that he had "stripped Christmas of its feathers." Marney tried to act as if it did not matter, but the criticism, especially from his friends, hurt. Scrawled at the top of the sermon manuscript, in Marney's hand, was one word—"condemned."

---

[59] Marion Arthur Ellis, *By a Dream Possessed: Myers Park Baptist Church* (Charlotte, N.C.: Myers Park Baptist Church, 1997), 79–80.

[60] Mrs. J. C. Eaves, letter to the editor, *Charlotte News*, January 6, 1966, 14A.

[61] *Charlotte News*, January 13, 1966, 12A.

[62] Letter to the editor, *Charlotte News*, January 24, 1966, 12A.

[63] Frank Thomas, letter to the editor, *Charlotte News*, January 24, 1966, 12A.

But, well received or not, it was, Marney believed, the only hope of salvation. In this christological anthropology, he had finally discovered how to overcome the convenient theology Shine had voiced that day in the graveyard back in Beaver Dam, as well as its many-headed manifestations that Marney had subsequently encountered. No human could conquer it. Only the Man-God, Jesus Christ, could defeat the theology of convenience and vanquish it once and for all. And only by sharing in the transformed humanity that became incarnate in Jesus Christ was there hope of overcoming it. What Marney discovered in Irenaeus, and what he had tried to argue in that 1965 Christmas Eve sermon, was something like what Karl Barth finally admitted in his little book, *The Humanity of God*: that the deity of God eternally included humanity and that this humanity became incarnate in Jesus.[64] Citing Barth's essay in support of his view, Marney exclaimed:

> The real atonement: He is Me! Jesus Christ is the secret truth about my real nature. This is who I am. Our destiny has overtaken us—and this Jesus Christ is who you are. We have to identify with him because he has already identified with us.[65]

For Marney, retrieving the practice of believer priesthood was not merely another way of restating the widely held assumption that all people are competent to deal with God for themselves, reducing faith to an exclusive one-on-one relationship between God and the individual soul. As he warned, this outlook merely underwrites the widely held but false notion of religious self-sufficiency. Marney understood that the priesthood of believers as an extension of the ministry of Christ is the only antidote to the sickness of individualism—one of the symptoms of alterity. The task that lay ahead was to learn anew what it means to be priests to each other. It is precisely this practice of believer priesthood that Marney was trying to retrieve at Myers Park Baptist Church and later at Interpreter's House. He suggested a way for Other Baptists seeking to move beyond sin-sick individualism in the introduction to his last book, *Priests to Each Other*:

> How does it work, the priesthood of the believer? You, you, take your priesthood wherever you are, to be whatever priests must be. There, where you and *they* are—you, all of you, *are the ministry of the Word*. This does not mean that you are competent to deal with God for yourself. It means rather that you are competent to deal with God and *for*

---

[64] Karl Barth, *The Humanity of God* (Atlanta: John Knox, 1960), 45–46.
[65] Carlyle Marney, *The Coming Faith* (Nashville: Abingdon, 1970), 52.

the neighbor. It was a gross perversion of the gospel that inserted a bastard individualism here and then taught us that the believer's priesthood meant that "every tub must set on its own bottom." Instead of each of us looking to some hired hand who can step down when he wishes to, we priest each other. Yet, in tearing loose from your old dependency on your little Protestant Rome, says Luther, "as always you must reckon with a Cross."[66]

This universal priesthood allows all believers to preach the Word, baptize Christians, hear confessions, celebrate communion, admonish fraternally, pray for others, minister to the needy, sacrifice themselves, and discern the spirits.

Marney suggested that the practice of believer priesthood begins with "the nerve to submit all [our] images of the self to Christ and his people for correction."[67] Shattering the self-deceptions and fictions that determine our lives requires submitting them to the correction of the Christ who appears where two or three are gathered. For only gospel truth can break through the myths that shackle the soul, and only gospel truth can set prisoners free to live by grace. But, as Marney observed, confronting and being confronted with the truth is painful. Paraphrasing Jesus, he warned, "You shall know the truth, and the truth shall make you flinch before it makes you free."[68] What was at stake for pilgrim priests, Marney held, is not so much an attempt to revise an old principle as a struggle to retrieve a lost practice. Believer priesthood is a powerful practice that gives rise to a life-giving way of life. Yet Marney would have done well to display more clearly what such a community of priests might look like in flesh and blood and how the practice of discernment works in a real-life setting.[69] He might have shown why without other practices and habits, like friendship and love, believer priesthood can grow cruel or become legalistic. Here Marney leaves room for fellow travelers to follow his trailblazing effort by suggesting other normative practices that enable the church to faithfully carry out its mission. For Other Baptist pilgrims, the journey is about practices, not just principles; convictions, not merely concepts; communion, not individualism.

---

[66] Marney, *Priests to Each Other*, 12.

[67] Marney, *Priests to Each Other*, 74.

[68] This quote is part of the Marney oral tradition reported by several who heard him say it.

[69] One example of such a theological account is John H. Yoder on "the Rule of Christ," variously called "Binding and Loosing," in his *The Royal Priesthood: Essays Ecclesiological and Ecumenical*, ed. Michael G. Cartwright (Grand Rapids: Eerdmans, 1994), 323–58.

Priestly Pilgrims

As the years passed, Marney became ever more convinced that the true personhood that had become incarnate in Jesus Christ could be recovered through the practice of believer priesthood. Yet he grew progressively less confident in the church as the instrument of recovery. Marney's 1946 doctoral dissertation on the ecclesiology of the early Church studied "the development of ecclesiological externalism," which he was convinced "contradicts the essence of Christianity."[70] Its 365 pages are densely footnoted with extensive references to a wide range of Christian literature in its first four centuries. Marney's brilliance and his reputation for mastery of the writings of the early church became legendary at Southern Seminary. His major professor, Sydnor Stealey, considered Marney to be "in a class absolutely by himself" and remembered him as "the most brilliant" person he had ever known. Others shared that assessment. Southern classmate Theron Price described Marney as being like most other students, only a whole lot smarter.[71] It was from Stealey that Marney learned there is more than the New Testament and the now; it was Stealey who taught him to read the history of the whole church as the story of all God's people; and it was through Stealey that his understanding of the Baptist movement was historicized and relativized.

There was no great moment of enlightenment when Marney awakened from his dogmatic slumber. Yet under Stealey's watchful care, Marney gradually broke through the Landmark clay in which he was planted to find root in richer spiritual soil that lay buried deep beneath the surface, and, with his mentor's wise guidance, Marney stretched his mind toward the light that shone above and beyond the fundamentalist canopy that threatened to engulf Baptists who remained under its shadow. Later in life, having preached and lectured in the most distinguished theological schools in the world, Marney defended his academic training: "A man can get a fairly classic education south of God," he quipped. "He doesn't have to go to New England."[72] It is understandable that over the years his scholarship took on a mythic quality, resulting in the story that he was the

---

[70] Carlyle Marney, "The Rise of Ecclesiological Externalism to 337 A.D." (Th.D. dissertation, Southern Baptist Theological Seminary, 1946), xiv.

[71] Carey, *Carlyle Marney*, 25. Stealey's assessment of Marney was related to me by Randall Lolley, who followed Stealey (and Olin T. Binkely) as president of Southeastern Baptist Theological Seminary in Wake Forest, North Carolina.

[72] Marney, "Preaching the Gospel, South of God," 916.

only student in the history of Southern Seminary who had read all the church fathers in the original Greek and Latin.[73]

Following Harnack, Marney's doctoral dissertation presupposed a tension between the spiritual essence of Christianity and the outward form of religion. Marney explained that "symbols and forms, institutions and dogma will be called on to help finite minds bridge time and space."[74] But he argued that it was a mistake to confuse these external expressions with the religious essence. Nevertheless, he conceded that some externalism must remain. The heart of the problem, Marney suggested, was "how to keep the Spirit of Christ vital in the outworking of Christianity through society."[75] He made no attempt to answer the question, though he hoped his study would be a first step toward doing so, and it proved to be foundational for his ecclesiological viewpoint. Some externalism, he contended, is necessary, "for absence of body and form (ecclesiological and theological) in Christianity produces anarchic confusion."[76] But "undue emphasis on body and form to the extent that an externalism is converted to the status of an end in itself," he continued, "has resulted in stultification, encrustation, and, at times absolute vitiation in the task the Spirit of Christ would see accomplished."[77] Marney asserted, "Christianity has yet to find the high ground between antinomian anarchy and institutional, pedantic stultification." He made clear that his critique of externalism was not a rejection of orthodoxy per se, but with the historical processes of objectification, institutionalism, and mysticism that have distorted and distracted from the essence of Christianity.[78] Though he regarded externalism as a general tendency that "preserves and defends that which is empty at the cost of that which is real," he argued that it was a tendency that "can be directed into a higher form of expression."[79] The upshot of his dissertation was that the institutional Church is a means (not the end) of

---

[73] Carey, *Carlyle Marney*, 28. When a graduate student once asked him whether the story was true, according to Marney, "I took him by the arm, led him to an isolated corner where no one could hear us, looked him in the eye and said, 'Son, it's a lie.'" Marney occasionally quoted Greek or Latin phrases, but his footnote references cite the standard English translations from *The Ante-Nicene Fathers* and *The Nicene and Post-Nicene Fathers*. Nevertheless, his dissertation was a remarkable piece of research for a young scholar.

[74] Marney, "Rise of Ecclesiological Externalism," xi. Marney quoted Goethe from Adolf von Harnack's *The Constitution and Law of the Church of the First Two Centuries*, trans. F. L. Pogson (New York: G. P. Putnam, 1910), 258.

[75] Marney, "Rise of Ecclesiological Externalism," xii.

[76] Marney, "Rise of Ecclesiological Externalism," xii.

[77] Marney, "Rise of Ecclesiological Externalism," xii.

[78] Marney, "Rise of Ecclesiological Externalism," xiv–xviii.

[79] Marney, "Rise of Ecclesiological Externalism," xx.

moral and social transformation, provided it is not overcome by the forces of externalism.

Fresh out of his doctoral studies at Southern Seminary and as a new pastor of the Immanuel Baptist Church of Paducah, Kentucky, Marney attempted to put this ecclesiology into practice. On July 27, 1947, he was invited by his old mentor in ministry, J. G. Hughes, to preach at the Union Avenue Baptist Church in Memphis, Tennessee. The sermon, entitled "All the Sons of Earth," addressed the fight against religious and racial prejudice. Marney argued that, on the matter of racial prejudice, the South was in a moral and spiritual desert. Appealing to the conscience of the congregation, he charged, "The great challenge to our civilization . . . is to learn to live together." He expressed confidence in the Church as the agent of social transformation, asserting, "I believe our hope lies in the Church and I believe frankly, that Southern Churches are best equipped to lead out."[80]

Marney carried this hopeful confidence in the church with him when a year later he was called as pastor of the First Baptist Church of Austin, Texas, where he held forth a progressive vision of society. In September 1955, Marney addressed the recurring themes of individualism and community in a local television program he hosted named *These Things Remain*. He explained:

> In our emphasis on rugged individualism, we have come to believe in the assertion of individuality—and every man is ready to stand up for his rights, whether it be because his water bill he thinks isn't right or something really insignificant. But there is a vast difference between the assertion of one's individuality and the realization of personality. It takes neighbors for that. It takes community for that. It takes things of value for that. Thousands of us came to Austin to live because we thought it would be a wonderful place to rear our children, to exercise our calling, and to do our work. None of us, I say, have really a right to this wonderful place to live who will not become involved in the needs of his neighbors. The urge is not to rugged individualism, the urge is to learn to live together.[81]

---

[80] *Commercial Appeal*, July 26, 1947, 3; *Memphis Press-Scimitar*, July 26, 1947, 3; and the worship bulletin for the Union Avenue Baptist Church, July 27, 1947, in the historical archives of the Union Avenue Baptist Church, Memphis, Tennessee; Marney, "All the Sons of Earth," sermon preached July 27, 1947, in the Carlyle Marney papers, box 52, David M. Rubenstein Rare Book & Manuscript Library, Duke University, Durham, N.C. The sermon was published in September 1951 after he preached it for the First Baptist Church of Austin, Texas.

[81] Marney, "Learn to Live Together," from *These Things Remain*, televised message, September 30, 1955, box 61, Carlyle Marney papers, David M. Rubenstein Rare Book & Manuscript Library, Duke University, Durham, N.C.

If individualism was a sign of the sin-sick soul and community was the antidote, the church in Austin was Marney's spiritual and social experiment. But the harsh realities of structural evil had a chastening effect on Marney's optimistic vision. For example, in 1953, he served on a Travis County grand jury that "no billed" a former justice of the peace who wrote a check for $16,810.89 in unpaid fines and court costs just two days earlier. In the same courthouse, another man was sentenced to a year in prison for stealing a lawn mower, even though the owner got the stolen mower back. That the justice of the peace was white, and the yard man was black did not escape Marney's notice.[82] Mugged by reality, he was forced to confront the fact that the powers that be are resistant to living together. It was clear that he would need more than good will and a sense of humor to persuade them. So did he become a recovering optimist with doubts.

But Marney admitted that his real crisis came in Charlotte, when in September of 1958 he accepted the call as pastor of Myers Park Baptist Church. He had faced the challenge of political power in Austin, but in Charlotte he butted up against a combination of social and economic forces for which he was unprepared. Marney characterized the churchgoing folks of Charlotte as "established enough to be unchallenged," "powerful enough to feel no social pressure," "pious enough to know no conviction for their sin," and "complacent enough to feel no real responsibility anywhere."[83] He aimed to change that, knowing he had his work cut out for him. With the help of his ministerial staff, Marney began to implement new programs throughout the church with the goal of equipping a priesting-laity that was the vision of his 1964 "Priest at Every Elbow" sermon. A host of small groups were formed for prayer, study, and social action, but the most strategic change involved a new policy on reception into church membership. The document was approved by the deacons and adopted by the congregation one month later on March 14, 1966.

The policy declared that membership in the Myers Park Baptist Church "is open to all who believe in Christ as Lord; who indicate their dedication of self and substance as witnesses of Christ; and who subscribe to the founding covenant."[84] It established a three-step process, whereby

---

[82] *Austin Statesman*, July 17, 1953, 1; and Pat Ireland Nixon, *A History of the Texas Medical Association 1853–1953* (Austin: University of Texas Press, 1953), 420–21.

[83] Marney, "We Have This Treasure," Lecture 4 at the Summer School on "The Church and Evangelism," July 9, 1959, sponsored by the Council of Southwestern Theological Schools. Marney delivered the same lectures at the School of Religion, Virginia Union University, July 26–August 12, 1965. The description of religion in Charlotte is in the audio tape of the Southwestern lecture but not in either of the written transcripts. Quoted in Carey, *Carlyle Marney*, 43.

[84] "Special Committee Recommendation on Reception of Members"; and "Open—And

any who presented themselves for membership by professing commitment to Christ were first placed under the watchcare of the church. Candidates were then invited to participate in five weeks of training by the ministers and lay leaders of the congregation. Each participant was responsible for reading about 150 pages of printed material, which centered on three questions: What is it to be human? What is it to be Christian? What is it to be the church? Consideration of these questions was followed by sessions on worship, pastoral care, spiritual growth, Christian education, stewardship, and commitment. Upon completion of the training, candidates were presented for reception into membership by the congregation at the observance of the Lord's Supper.

But even as he moved to renew the church through the equipping of the laity, Marney was growing less sanguine about the church as an instrument of transformation. In *The Recovery of the Person*, published in 1963, he confessed:

> As for myself, I have less and less hope that denominational houses can offer any real redemption for us. Indeed, most times, as formerly, the institutional church seems somehow in the way. I look for, long for, some radical reconstitution, knowing all the time it will likely be preceded by an inevitable great turning away.[85]

Marney was working on a manuscript, tentatively titled *The Recovery of the Church*, which was never published. It included chapters based on a sermon series on recovery that he preached during the first year at Myers Park and was organized in three parts: the Gospel of God—*Leitourgia*; the Gospel of Fellowship—*Koinonia*; and the Gospel of Service—*Diakonia*. The book reflects the peak of Marney's ecumenical vision in search of the center and unity of the faith among the churches that he located in Jesus Christ:

> The Center for us Christians is in what God has done and is doing; in his claim on us; and in our response to all this which He gives, too. It rests on "the conviction that God himself came, and comes, into human history in the person of Jesus Christ." It rests on God and what He has done in Jesus the Lord: incarnation-redemption, crucifixion-resurrection, and history's consummation. It rests on God's Sovereign judgment-grace which is His mercy and issues in the worship-work

---

Responsible Membership," *The Myers Park Baptist Church News*, February 15, 1966, 1. Made available from the historical records of the Myers Park Baptist Church.

[85] Marney, *Recovery of the Person*, 100–101.

of the brotherhood that is the Church at the Center. And the Church stands here, where the Cross-arms intersect to speak of paradox, conflict, tension, and of resurrection, new life, grace. You are not at Church on its fringes, with your arm load of fragments for building private fires in isolated camps. Rather these prospects which we nurture in our hearts grow out of [this] Center, they do not lead *to* it. Buildings and budgets, classes and ministries, missions and programs, organizations and committees; these are *tools*, these are *means*; not ends. These are ways in which we respond to what we get at Center—not the content of that Center. For the Center does not rest on us, not even on our brotherhood.[86]

To be sure, Marney regarded the church that puts at its very center the confession of Christ as Lord to be truly the church. Yet he admitted that more often the church is less than church because it has a Lord that is less than Lord. And, he continued, "Where the church is a fifth-rate power; where the church is a part-time do-gooder; where the church is spiritless, defeated, sidetracked, conformist, stupid or blind—it is like its concept of its Lord."[87] He recognized that real redemption must come through the church of a proper Lord, but, in view of the failure of the church to be the church, he rejoiced in what he called "the church at God's left hand."[88] This alternative church was comprised of dedicated case workers, government agents, health-care personnel, enlightened employers, family counselors, and entrepreneurs of social uplift—all of whom were engaged in the work of ministry.

During his years at Interpreter's House (1967–1978), Marney's ecclesiology grew further removed from the institutional church. The final chapter of his 1971 book, *The Coming Faith*, was entitled "The Coming Church." It contained much of the 1964 "Priest at Every Elbow" sermon, and it gestured in the direction of what he would say in his 1974 book, *Priests to Each Other*. Describing the churches as "closed communions, ghettos, refuges of sick and miserable people,"[89] Marney pointed toward

---

[86] Marney, "The Recovery of Center," in Recovery of the Church Series—Pamphlet 1, published for Members and Friends of Myers Park Baptist Church, Charlotte, North Carolina, 1958. Marney delivered this same message to the American Baptist Convention in Rochester, New York, 1960, box 65, Carlyle Marney papers, David M. Rubenstein Rare Book & Manuscript Library, Duke University, Durham, N.C. This quote summarizes the theme of the book.

[87] Carlyle Marney, "Church and Race: A Never-Ending Winter?" sermon preached at Riverside Church, New York City, October 18, 1964, published in the *Pulpit*, February 1967, 4–6.

[88] Marney, "Church and Race," 4–6.

[89] Marney, *Coming Faith*, 158.

the horizon of the new creation. The means of transformation for the emergence of the new humanity, Marney argued as he did in the 1964 sermon, was the priesthood of believers. But what appeared in this chapter that was not in the original sermon was the image of Interpreter's House from John Bunyan's classic tale, *The Pilgrim's Progress*. In the story, Christian sets out from the City of Destruction on his journey to Mount Zion. He is instructed to make for the Wicket Gate by Evangelist, who tells him that after "he was gone some distance from the gate, he would come at the house of the Interpreter, at whose door he should knock, and he would shew him excellent things." At the gate, Christian is met by Good Will, who says, "We make no objections against any, notwithstanding all that they have done before they come hither, they are in no wise cast out." So it is that Christian, with his burden and half-released guilt, finds his way to Interpreter's House, stating as his reason for coming that "you would show me excellent things such as would be an help to me in my journey." And so, Interpreter instructs him to light the candle of the Spirit's illumination and bids him to follow into a private room, where seven emblems are revealed that strengthen him for what lies ahead in the way: the image of his guide, the gospel that cleanses his soul of sin, the wisdom of patience over passion, the unquenchable fire of grace, the stately palace of fellowship with the saints, the iron cage of despair, and the trembling man who must face his future. Only after this instruction is Christian ready to proceed to the Cross where his burden is finally loosed and it tumbles into the grave where he sees it no more.[90]

Bunyan's ecclesiology, like Marney's, was fuzzy. Interpreter's House stands "in the way," but it is *not* the church. That comes later in the narrative, at House Beautiful, which stands "just by the High-way side."[91] It was Bunyan's way of saying that church membership, though desirable, is not necessary for salvation. Yet Interpreter's House is essential for all wayfaring Christians as a place where the Holy Spirit leads them into deeper truth about themselves and others. In Bunyan's own life story, Interpreter's House was the manse of the Independent (Baptist) Church in Bedford, the private room was the great room of the manse with its large stone fireplace, and Bunyan's guide was none other than John Gifford, the pastor, who eventually baptized him in the Great Ouse River.[92] So

---

[90] Marney, *Coming Faith*, 169. Bunyan, *Pilgrim's Progress*, 23–30.

[91] Bunyan, *Pilgrim's Progress*, 37.

[92] John Brown, *John Bunyan: His Life Times and Work*, 3rd ed. (London: Wm. Isbister, 1887), 92; and Richard L. Greaves, *Glimpses of Glory: John Bunyan and English Dissent* (Stanford, Calif.: Stanford University, 2002), 43–47. Bunyan wrote:

I sat under the ministry of holy Mr Gifford, whose doctrine, by God's grace, was much

Marney envisioned his own Interpreter's House, patterned after the one in Bunyan's story, as a place of refuge for weary pilgrims where they would be received unconditionally and shown excellent things for help in their faith journeys. And just as Interpreter guided Christian to look deeply into his own soul before continuing on, so those who stopped to rest with Marney in the mountains of western North Carolina near the Methodist campgrounds were offered help first by learning to explore the journey inward toward self-understanding before venturing outward, where they would discover how to take up their priestly vocation. For only when inwardness controls outwardness, Marney believed, was it possible to live into the vocation of pilgrim priesthood.[93]

In a posthumously published interview in the *Christian Century*, Marney confessed, "Twenty-five years ago, I was more hopeful about the church as an organization than I am now. But I haven't abandoned the church. I never did stick with it as an end to anything. . . . It's a tool, a means to an end."[94] Buckets are tools. And as Marney was fond of saying: "All our buckets leak."[95] He gave up on the leaky buckets of denominationalism and ecumenism. But he never gave up on the people of God. He was a chastened optimist with doubts to be sure, yet he was not without hope. But his was a hope against hope, as he reflected, "I didn't commit myself to saying I had hope for the church. Hope comes and goes. I would still say I am hopeful, but I would redefine where church is at. Church is right here where two or three are."[96] As faltering as his confidence was in ecclesial institutions, he never lost faith in the great universal Church—"the church of all climes and times," as he called it.[97] And in that sense Marney still believed with old Cyprian, that "no one can have God as Father who does not have the Church as Mother,"[98] and the Apostle Paul

---

for my stability. This man made it much his business to deliver the people of God from all those false and unsound rests that by nature we are prone to take and make to our souls; he pressed us to take special heed, that we took not up any truth upon trust, as from this or that or another man or men, but to cry mightily to God, that he would convince us of the reality thereof, and set us down therein by his own Spirit in the holy Word; for, said he, if you do otherwise, when temptations come, if strongly, you not having received them with evidence from heaven, will find you want that help and strength now to resist, as once you had.

Bunyan, *Grace Abounding to the Chief of Sinners*, 117, ed. W. R. Owens (London: Penguin Books, 1987), 32.

[93] Marney, *Coming Faith*, 174–76.

[94] Marney, "Preaching the Gospel, South of God," 919.

[95] Marney, *Beyond Our Time and Place*, 44.

[96] Marney, "Preaching the Gospel, South of God," 919.

[97] Marney, "Church and Race," 4.

[98] Cyprian, *The Unity of the Catholic Church* 6, in *The Ante-Nicene Fathers* (Grand Rapids: Eerdmans, 1979), 5:423. Marney cites this text in "Rise of Ecclesiological Externalism," 244.

before him, who declared that "Jerusalem above, she is free, and she is our mother" (Gal 4:26). Though for Marney, Bunyan, and other priestly pilgrims before and after them, what really counts as church is the gathered community.

In a conversation as his father was nearing the end of life, the elder Marney wistfully remarked, "I sometimes feel that if I could go back to the point of my beginning the faith-life I could keep it solid." Shocked, Marney answered back, "But Dad, hasn't it been solid for *you*?" Marney thought to himself, "I would have staked my life it was solid!" His father offered a surprising answer: "faith for me has been riddled with holes and gaps—and there are days I do not know." Trying to take it all in, Marney asked, "Then when *is* it right?" And his father answered, "At the meeting! It's always right when I can get to the Meeting!"[99] This is Marney's legacy: Neither rugged individualism nor coercive authoritarianism will do. Only a faith formed and sustained in a community of believer priests is good news to a world of moral strangers.

Threefold Ministry

Other Baptists find in Marney what the cure for alterity looks like. In him they see someone who honestly confronted the sickness of individualism that so long had plagued Baptists and other modern Christians. He understood that the only hope of overcoming this weakened condition lies in recovering the catholic center of the faith—sharing in the transformed humanity that became incarnate in Jesus Christ. If independence was the result of Adam's sin, interdependence was the work of Christ's redemption. Marney confronted the modern gnostic myth by returning to patristic sources: divinity became humanity so that humanity might share in divinity. In Jesus Christ the word of God became flesh—a real person. This is what led Marney to a new understanding of the recovery of the person. But this patristic retrieval of the new humanity in Christ is more than an anthropology. It is a soteriology, for participation in Christ's transformation of human existence is the salvation of the world. It exposed the gnostic counterfeit of individual salvation that fooled Baptists and many evangelicals like Shine into thinking of life in Christ as a kind of transaction where "if you get right with the Lord, you can live just like you want to the rest of the time." Whatever salvation is, it is incarnational and means that the whole of human existence has been taken into the christocentric reality. And in this reality Marney also came to see the

[99] Marney, "The Tent of Meeting," September 22, 1963, box 69, Carlyle Marney papers, David M. Rubenstein Rare Book & Manuscript Library, Duke University, Durham, N.C.

social mission of the church not as an effort to persuade people that the church can be a force of social good but as a social embodiment of the new humanity that exists to persuade people that Jesus Christ has reconciled the world to God. Other Baptists find in Marney the germ of a catholic anthropology, a catholic soteriology, and a catholic ecclesiology.

But Other Baptists also come to embrace through Marney a catholic understanding of life in Christ as vocational. Marney learned by way of Luther the catholic teaching that names the common priesthood of all Christians as a vocation of baptism. The priesthood of all believers is a calling that invites the baptized to share in the priestly ministry of Jesus Christ, the great high priest. For in baptism Christians are summoned from the waters by the words "You are a chosen race, a royal priesthood, a holy nation, God's own people" (1 Pet 2:9). This priesthood that begins with the *confession* of Christ as Lord is built on the *foundation* of Christ as the head and cornerstone and leads to a *vocation* that has its identity in Jesus Christ, who makes them into a new race. Marney recognized that the way through the sinful structures of prejudice lay in all Christians claiming their baptismal identity in Christ. Though he does not pick it up, Marney was in sync with the theological trajectory of the *Epistle of Diognetus*, which describes Christians as a "new race" of people.[100] The issue in question is not a matter of ethnicity but rather of *identity*. That identity is the calling in Jesus Christ to be God's people. Other Baptists recognize that in Free Churches the practice of believer's baptism lays stress on the confession of faith as a mark of the faithful and so like Calvin regards the priestly benefits as extending soteriologically to all Christians.[101] But because in Free Churches baptism follows the confession of faith, the soteriological account converges with the ecclesiological approach of the earlier catholic tradition that identifies general Christian priesthood with baptism. Thus both Anabaptists and early Baptists placed an emphasis on the baptismal candidate's readiness to submit to the mutually reciprocal and communally discipling process as set forth in Matthew 18:15-20.[102]

---

[100] *Epistle of Diognetus* I, in *The Apostolic Fathers*, ed. Bart D. Ehrman, Loeb Classical Library (Cambridge, Mass.: Harvard University Press, 2003), 2:131.

[101] John Calvin, *Institutes of the Christian Religion* IV.1.7, ed. John T. McNeill, trans. Ford Lewis Battles (Philadelphia: Westminster, 1960), 2:1021. Even though he considered baptism to be a sign and seal of the covenant, Calvin held that among the baptized there "are mingled many hypocrites who have nothing of Christ but the name and outward appearance."

[102] *Balthasar Hubmaier*, 373–85. See also Yoder, *Royal Priesthood*, 265. The first generation of *Täufer* like Conrad Grebel spoke about following "the rule of Christ" or "binding and loosing." See Grebel's "Letter to Thomas Müntzer," in *The Radical Reformation*, ed. Michael G. Baylor (Cambridge: Cambridge University Press, 1991), 42–43. That early Baptists in New England followed the "rule of Christ" is evident in the Baptist-Puritan debate of April

These theological conversations about the priesthood of believers that began in the midst of controversy about the reform of the church have resulted in the retrieval of a genuinely catholic understanding remarkably shared by the whole church. This theological renewal has been guided by a return to the biblical sources. God's covenant with Israel was mediated through three offices—prophet, priest, and king. No one in the history of Israel fulfilled all three offices, though some exercised more than one office. Yet all three offices were realized in one life—Jesus the Christ. Protestant theologians from Calvin to Barth have employed them as a framework for displaying the reconciling work of Jesus Christ.[103] As Calvin points out, the threefold office has ecclesiological implications because all Christians share in Christ's ongoing work as mediator.[104] Calvin explains that the anointing of Christ's prophetic ministry "was diffused from the Head to the members" in fulfillment of the prophesy that "your sons shall prophesy and your daughters."[105] All Christians also share the benefits of Christ's kingly ministry in that "he arms and equips us with his power, adorns us with his beauty and magnificence, [and] enriches

---

14–15, 1668, in Boston, in which Thomas Goold defends why he refused to have his daughter baptized in the Congregational church. William G. McLoughlin, *Soul Liberty: The Baptists' Struggle in New England, 1630–1833* (Providence: Brown University Press, 1991), 37–92, esp. 63–72. Modern Baptists have tended to understand the practice primarily in a negative and exclusionary sense, preferring the language of "discipline." See James Leo Garrett Jr., *Baptist Church Discipline* (Nashville: Broadman, 1962); and Gregory A. Wills, *Democratic Religion: Freedom, Authority, and Church Discipline in the Baptist South 1785–1900* (New York: Oxford University Press, 1997). More recently those in the believers church tradition have sought to reclaim the practice in the positive sense of discipleship and discernment. See Marlin Jeschke, *Discipling in the Church* (Scottdale, Pa.: Herald Press, 1988); and Leland Harder, *Doors to Lock and Doors to Open: The Discerning People of God* (Scottdale, Pa.: Herald Press, 1993). Gerald W. Schlabach examines the Mennonite practice of fraternal admonition from the standpoint of Augustine's theology of correction and its influence on the Catholic tradition in "The Correction of the Augustinians: A Case Study in the Critical Appropriation of a Suspect Tradition," in *The Free Church and the Early Church: Bridging the Historical and Theological Divide*, ed. D. H. Williams (Grand Rapids: Eerdmans, 2002), 47–74.

[103] Calvin, *Institutes* II.15 (ed. McNeill), 1:494–503; and Karl Barth, *Church Dogmatics* IV.1–3 (Edinburgh: T&T Clark, 1956–1962). Robert Sherman moves significantly beyond the traditional Protestant treatments of the threefold office as exclusively christological doctrines by providing a wonderful account of the atonement that brings together the threefold office with trinitarian theology that displays how Christ as king achieves the Father's victory, Christ as Priest makes the sacrificial offering, and Christ as Prophet bears witness through the Spirit's life-giving word. Robert Sherman, *King, Priest, and Prophet: A Trinitarian Theology of the Atonement* (New York: T&T Clark, 2004).

[104] Rose M. Beal, "Priest, Prophet and King: Jesus Christ," in *John Calvin's Ecclesiology: Ecumenical Perspectives*, ed. Gerard Mannion and Eduardus Van der Borght (London: T&T Clark, 2011), 93–96.

[105] Calvin, *Institutes* II.15.2 (ed. McNeill), 1:496.

us with his wealth."[106] And all Christians are received as companions in Christ's priestly ministry, to "offer ourselves and our all to God, and freely enter the heavenly sanctuary that the sacrifices of prayers and praise that we bring may be acceptable and sweet-smelling before God."[107]

But the radical account of all baptized Christians participating in the ministry of Christ is not a distinctively Protestant doctrine. It was articulated with great clarity and conviction in the work of Yves Congar, who argued that the laity was not merely the object of ministry of the clergy, but that by virtue of baptism every Christian shares in Christ's threefold office as prophet, priest, and king.[108] Congar was a voice of renewal within the Catholic Church, which declared at Vatican II that "the faithful who by baptism are incorporated into Christ, are placed in the People of God, and in their own way share the priestly, prophetic and kingly office of Christ, and to the best of their ability carry on the mission of the whole Christian people in the Church and in the world."[109] The council went on to affirm that all God's people share in Christ's kingly ministry through "their special vocation . . . to seek the kingdom of God by engaging in temporal affairs and directing them according to God's will."[110] And, because the people have been joined to Christ's life and mission, "he also gives a share in his priestly office, to offer spiritual worship for the glory of the Father and the salvation of [hu]man[ity]."[111] And all the people of God share in Christ's prophetic ministry as he "establishes them as witnesses and provides them with the appreciation of the faith (*sensus fidei*) and the grace of the word (cf. Acts 2:17-18; Apoc. 19:10) so that the power of the Gospel may shine out in daily family and social life."[112]

Yet, in both the Protestant and Catholic accounts, the participation of the laity in the ministry of Christ is decidedly asymmetrical compared to the participation of the clergy. *Lumen Gentium* makes it clear that although the threefold office of Christ gives substance to "the common priesthood of the faithful," their ministerial participation differs "essentially and not only in degree" from the hierarchical priesthood.[113] Thus the sacramental ministry of bishops and priests differs in kind from the ministry of the

---

[106] Calvin, *Institutes* II.15.4 (ed. McNeill), 1:499.

[107] Calvin, *Institutes* II.15.6 (ed. McNeill), 1:502.

[108] Congar, *Lay People in the Church*, trans. Donald Attwater (Westminister, Md.: Newman Press, 1957), 112–308.

[109] *Lumen Gentium* §31, *Vatican Council II*, vol. 1, *The Conciliar and Postconciliar Documents*, rev. ed. (New York: Costello, 2004), 388.

[110] *Lumen Gentium* §31, *Vatican Council II*, 1:389.

[111] *Lumen Gentium* §34, *Vatican Council II*, 1:391.

[112] *Lumen Gentium* §35, *Vatican Council II*, 1:391–92.

[113] *Lumen Gentium* §10, *Vatican Council II*, 1:361.

laity. Likewise, for Calvin the continuation of the ministries of word, sacrament, and discipline, which correspond to the prophetic, priestly, and kingly work of Christ, are primarily to be carried out by those who exercise the offices of ministry—namely, the pastor, teacher, and elder.[114] The Free Church tradition offers an even more radical understanding of ministry, which is open to both lay and ordained ministers, as all members of the church are called to share in Christ's prophetic, priestly, and royal ministry—not as a charism or an office, but as a calling.[115]

Free churches have followed in the example of the English dissenter Henry Barrow, who described the church as "a fellowship of the faithful and holie people gathered in the name of Christ Jesus, their only king, priest, and prophet."[116] All members of the church share freely in the ministry of Christ through word and sacrament. For example, after the English Parliament passed an ordinance against lay preaching on April 26, 1645, forbidding anyone to preach who was not ordained by the Church of England "or some other reformed church," Thomas Lambe, the soap boiler and pastor of the Bell Alley Church in London, was arrested for preaching without a license along with a young weaver named Samuel Oates. They were brought before the mayor, who asked Oates how long he had been preaching. The young man answered that he had been preaching "ever since he was baptized."[117] For the early Baptists, baptism was sufficient warrant to prophesy. When the community gathered for worship, they followed the rule of Paul, that "you can all prophesy" (1 Cor 14:31), so it was not unusual for five or more people to prophesy in succession.[118] Such a radical understanding of the prophetic, priestly, and royal ministry of all Christians is not a distinctive doctrine that belongs only among Free Churches. It is a practice that belongs to all the people of God. It deserves to be reexamined and retrieved for the renewal and transformation of the whole church.

But if every Christian participates in the prophetic, priestly, and kingly ministry of Christ so that there is no one ungifted, no one not called, no one not empowered, it might be asked why the church needs

---

[114] Calvin, *Institutes* IV.3.1–10 (ed. McNeill), 2:1053–62.

[115] John Howard Yoder, *Body Politics: Five Practices of the Christian Community before the Watching World* (Scottdale, Pa.: Herald Press, 1992), 47–60.

[116] Henry Barrow, *A True Description Out of the Worde of God, Of the Visible Church* (1589), A2, reprinted in *The Writings of Henry Barrow*, ed. Leland H. Carlson, vol. 3 of *Elizabethan Non-conformist Texts* (New York: Routledge, 2003), 214.

[117] Thomas Edwards, *Gangraena: The First and Second Part*, 3rd ed. (London: Ralph Smith, 1646), 1.37.

[118] Champlin Burrage, *The Early English Dissenters in Light of Recent Research* (Cambridge: Cambridge University Press, 1912), 2:172–73.

ordained pastoral leadership. The historic Baptist answer, as voiced by the eighteenth-century English Baptist minister Daniel Turner, is "that there be some, one or more in every particular church, invested with official power, is necessary, and of divine appointment, for the due administration of the word and sacraments; the maintaining due order in the church, and due execution of the laws of Christ."[119] Although there is no monopoly in the ministry of the new covenant by the ordained clergy, there is a need, as the Apostle Paul stated, that *"some* would be apostles, *some* prophets, *some* evangelists, *some* pastors and teachers, *to equip the saints* for the work of ministry, for building up the body of Christ, until all of us come to the unity of the faith and of the knowledge of the Son of God, to maturity, *to the measure of the full stature of Christ"* (Eph 4:11-13).

Marney once observed that most ministers are so lacking in prophetic competence that they do not have enough character "to damn a church mouse, much less an entire culture." Nor do they often know how to pronounce priestly "words of consolation" or to exercise the royal ministry "of a proper sedition" by being wise as serpents and harmless as doves.[120] Liberals tend to accommodate to psychotherapeutic models that conceive of the minister's identity as a therapist, and evangelicals are inclined to adapt to concepts drawn from business and the corporate world that define the minister as a manager, but in both cases the ministry is considered to be a profession. By recovering the christological center of the faith, Marney's radical vision, like Congar's, can be a source of renewal, not just for Free Churches, but for the church catholic by calling for the retrieval and revisioning of Christian ministry—lay and ordained. Understood christologically, Christian ministry is a *vocation,* not a *profession,* and so, at the Council of Orange in 529, the church rejected all Donatist and Pelagian notions of competence that rest on human abilities or skills, stating that the reception and exercise of the gifts of the gospel depend on God and God alone.[121] Other Baptists understand that they are priests to one another by participating as ministers in the priestly ministry of Jesus of Christ, the mediator of the new covenant. That is not just a Baptist principle. It is the conviction of the one, holy, catholic, and apostolic church.

---

[119] Daniel Turner, *A Compendium of Social Religion* (London: John Ward, 1758), 49–50.

[120] Marney, "Fundaments of Competent Ministry," *Duke Divinity Review* 41, no. 1 (1976): 5–15.

[121] *Canons of the Second Council of Orange, A.D. 529,* trans. F. H. Woods (Oxford: James Thornton, 1882), 18–19, 23–25. See also by Richard John Neuhaus, *Freedom for Ministry,* rev. ed. (Grand Rapids: Eerdmans, 1992); and William H. Willimon, *Pastor: The Theology and Practice of Ordained Ministry* (Nashville: Abingdon, 2002).

6

Where Two or Three Are Gathered

Watts Street Baptist Church in Durham, North Carolina, was a fairly typical Southern Baptist congregation when Warren Carr became pastor in 1946, but under his leadership they came to share a connection with the wider church. In 1957 he drafted a new church covenant that pledged "to regard as of the household of faith all who worship Christ as Savior and Lord." And though they affirmed a commitment to the Baptist heritage, they also affirmed their resolve to "seek with all Christians a unity of spirit and action."[1] Baptists emphasize the evangelical conviction that the church is the gathering of those who have responded to the gospel in faith and repentance. Yet, as Carr recognized, some Baptists so emphasize a personal experience of salvation that church membership seems to be left to each individual as an option. These evangelically minded folk maintain that the Christian decision is for Jesus Christ, not the church. Carr questioned any theology in which Jesus Christ and the church were thought to be mutually exclusive. He declaimed, "It is decidedly problematic for anyone to assume that he [or she] may make a decision for Christ without reference to the church." He continued, "It is decidedly unbiblical for anyone to ignore the scriptural testimony that the church is the body of Christ." He concluded, "It is decidedly illogical for anyone to think that he [or she] may be related to Christ without His body."[2] To be in Christ is to be in the church: for the church is the body of Christ, or it is not the church at all.

Like his friend and fellow pilgrim Carlyle Marney, Carr recognized the danger of the Baptist notion of soul competency in which personal experience with Jesus Christ constituted the highest authority and there

[1] The Covenant of Watts Street Baptist Church, Durham, N.C., 1957.
[2] Warren Carr, *At the Risk of Idolatry* (Valley Forge, Pa.: Judson Press, 1972), 49.

225

was no need for the community of the faithful to be priests to each other. Such rugged individualism was, he argued, incompatible with a doctrine of the church.[3] If membership was conceived simply as a personal decision, he doubted that such voluntarism could lead to anything more than sectarianism. In his book *Baptism: Conscience and Clue for the Church*, Carr explored an ecumenical ecclesiology that also embraced an evangelical faith. He conceived of the church not merely as a voluntary society made up of like-minded individuals but rather as a new creation of Word and Spirit.[4] Still Carr wondered how to give expression to a church that is both evangelical and ecumenical.

For churches to be the church, Baptists and others in the Free Church tradition believe all that is necessary is a gathered community, understanding the ecclesial minimum to be stated simply in the promise "where two or three are gathered in my name, I am there among them" (Matt 18:20). The Baptist emphasis on the church as it is visible and gathered shares with Anabaptists and other evangelicals a sense of the church as *Gemeinde* or community. And here, at least in some measure, they affirm the Ignatian ecclesial formula that "wherever Jesus Christ is, there is the Catholic Church,"[5] because Jesus Christ promised to be present where two or three are gathered. Though Baptists have not always stressed ecclesiology as strongly as they might, it has been suggested that "the most distinctive feature about Baptists is their doctrine of the church."[6] Yet it is important to note that Baptists do not say, "Where two or three are gathered there is *a* church." Instead, they affirm, "Where two or three are gathered there is *the* church." But such a claim begs for a fuller account of how to understand the ecclesiality of the gathered community that addresses the questions "What is the church?" and "Where is it to be found?"

Ubi Ecclesia?

One September Sunday morning in 1781, between five and six hundred souls gathered on the grounds of the Upper Spottsylvania Baptist Church, about twenty-two miles from Fredericksburg, Virginia. The community that became known as the "Traveling Church" met for worship and to hear a farewell sermon delivered by Elder Lewis Craig, pastor of the Upper

---

[3] Carr, *At the Risk of Idolatry*, 51.

[4] Warren Carr, *Baptism: Conscience and Clue for the Church* (New York: Holt, Rinehart & Winston, 1964).

[5] Ignatius, *To the Smyrnaeans* 8, in *The Ante-Nicene Fathers* (Grand Rapids: Eerdmans, 1979), 1:90.

[6] W. T. Whitley, *A History of the British Baptists* (London: C. Griffin, 1923), 4.

Spottsylvania Baptists, who was leaving the next day with the newly constituted congregation. No one knows exactly how or why they determined to set off together. The sturdy pilgrims made their weary way, first in wagons and then by foot, for nearly six hundred miles over the Blue Ridge Mountains, across the Holston River, through the Cumberland Gap, and into the Kentucky bluegrass, taking with them their communion service, their treasured pulpit Bible, and most every feature of churchly practice except the meeting house itself. Along the way they gathered on the Lord's Day for singing, praying, preaching, baptizing, breaking bread, and feet washing, being careful to omit no feature of orderly service. The journey was dangerous, filled with wind and weather, foul fiends, and great discouragement. But Elder Craig often recounted the story of Israel's wilderness wandering and prayed that, as God sustained his ancient suffering people, they too might be strengthened in their afflictions and guided safely to the promised land. When they finally arrived in Kentucky at Gilbert's Creek, on the second Sunday of December in 1781, as was their custom, they gathered for worship around the same old Bible they used back in Virginia to listen to their pastor preach the word.[7]

The story of the Traveling Church offers one of the most memorable accounts of religious life on the American frontier. It is strikingly reminiscent of another Pilgrim church that departed England for Holland and finally New England, where they established Plymouth Colony inspired by their pastor, John Robinson, the seventeenth-century proto-Baptist. On one level these stories stand as simple reminders that the dangerous journeys of life are meant to be undertaken together, not alone. In 1610 Robinson wrote *A Justification of Separation* as a pointed reply to Richard Bernard, an old friend from his student days at Cambridge.[8] For a short

---

[7] George W. Ranck, *The Traveling Church: An Account of the Baptist Exodus from Virginia to Kentucky in 1781 under the Leadership of Rev. Lewis Craig and Capt. William Ellis* (Louisville, Ky.: n.p., 1910). See also Robert B. Semple, *A History of the Rise and Progress of the Baptists in Virginia*, rev. G. W. Beale (Richmond, Va.: Pitt & Dickinson, 1894), 200; James B. Taylor, *Lives of Virginia Baptist Ministers*, 2nd ed. (Richmond, Va.: Yale & Wyatt, 1838), 85; and John Taylor, *A History of Ten Baptist Churches* (Frankfort, Ky.: J. H. Holeman, 1823), 41.

[8] For a thick account of Robinson in the context of Separatism and the early Baptists, see Walter Herbert Burgess, *John Robinson Pastor of the Pilgrim Fathers: A Study of His Life and Times.* (London: Williams and Norgate; New York: Harcourt, Brace & Howe, 1920), 110–203. The English Baptists have long recognized that their connection with Congregationalists and other Nonconformists as Free Churches lies in a common historical ancestry. Illustrative of this Free Church perspective, J. H. Shakespeare narrated the Baptist story from Robert Browne through Francis Johnson and John Robinson to John Smyth and Henry Jacob, in his *Baptist and Congregational Pioneers* (London: Kingsgate Press, 1907). For a theological analysis of Robinson's separatist ecclesiology, see Timothy George, *John Robinson and the English Separatist Tradition* (Macon, Ga.: Mercer University Press, 1982), 57–167.

time, the two walked together in the path of separation from the Church of England, but Bernard soon returned to his former Anglican parish. In 1608 he published *The Separatists Schisme*, dedicated to a moderate nonseparating Puritanism that stood between "the Schismatical Brownists" on the one hand and "the Antichristian Papists" on the other.[9] Just as Robinson was completing his *Justification*, Bernard published a second book, entitled *Plain Evidences: The Church of England Apostolical, the Separation Schismatical*.[10] Robinson identified "the gathering and governing of the church" as the main subject that needed clarification,[11] and he laid out a range of ecclesiological configurations displayed in the divergent interpretations of Matthew 16:18–19 in which Christ gave to Peter the keys of the kingdom.

The Catholics, Robinson argued, affirm that the power of the keys were given to Peter "as the prince of the apostles, and so to the bishops of Rome as Peter's successors." The Anglicans, Robinson continued, contend that the keys were handed to Peter as "an apostle, that is, a chief officer of the church, and so to [the prelates], as chief officers succeeding him," which he added "is also Mr. Bernard's judgment." The Protestants say that the keys belong to Peter "as a minister of the word and sacraments . . . and so consequently to belong to all other ministers of the gospel equally." "But we," Robinson concluded, "do believe and profess that this promise is not made to Peter in any of these forenamed respects, nor to any office, order, estate, dignity, or degree in the church, or world, but to the confession of faith, which Peter made by way of answer to Christ's question . . . 'Thou art the Christ, the Son of the living God.'" "So," said Robinson, "the building of the church is upon the rock of Peter's confession, that is, Christ, whom he confessed: this faith is the foundation of the church:

---

[9] Richard Bernard, *Christian Advertisements And Counsels Of Peace Also Disswasions From The Separatists Schisme* (London: Felix Kyngston, 1608), in the epistle dedicatorie. It is ironic that Bernard's son-in-law was none other than Roger Williams, who established the first Baptist church in colonial America. When his hopes of a radically pure church faded soon after having been believer baptized, Williams renounced ties to all churches and became, as Perry Miller aptly described him, "a churchless man seeking the pure fellowship." Miller, *Roger Williams: His Contribution to the American Tradition* (Indianapolis, Ind.: Bobbs-Merrill, 1953), 52.

[10] Robinson, *A Justification of Separation From the Church of England*, in *The Works of John Robinson: Pastor of the Pilgrim Fathers*, ed. Robert Ashton (London: John Snow, 1851), vol. 2. Robinson states in the preface that his work was an answer to "Mr. Bernard's book," *The Separatists Schisme*, but, because Bernard's "second treatise," *Plain Evidences: The Church England is Apostolicall, the Separation Schismaticall* (London: T. Snodham for Weaver & Welby, 1610), appeared in print before the completion of his reply, Robinson explains that he answered points of the second book that he considered to be "of weight" in his *Works of John Robinson*, 2:1, 507.

[11] Robinson, *Works of John Robinson*, 2:49.

against this faith the gates of hell shall not prevail."[12] This confession of faith, Robinson explained, must be offered freely and visibly.[13]

Robinson's insistence that for churches to be the church they must be a *communio fidelium* echoed a fundamental conviction of earlier separating Puritans who defined a church as "a company or congregation of the faithful called and gathered out of the world by the preaching of the gospel."[14] The church as a gathered community was identified by its confession of faith in Christ, not by geographical boundaries. Thus the gathered church was distinct from the parish or territorial church. This gathered church ecclesiology found expression in A True Confession of 1596, which declared that Christ was calling his church, "separating them from amongst unbelievers," "gathering and uniting them together as members of one body in his faith, love and holy order."[15] Membership in the gathered and separated community meant to exemplify the conviction of visible sainthood by ensuring that none were "to be received into their communion as members, but such as do make confession of their faith, publicly desiring to be received as members, and promising to walk in the obedience of Christ."[16] Children of church members, though they were incapable of making such a confession of faith, were to be received by baptism into the life of the gathered community in hope that they would in due time come to confess Christ. By limiting membership to those who deliberately and personally confessed the faith, separating Puritans maintained that a confession of faith belongs to the ecclesial *esse* (essence), not just the *bene esse* (well-being), as the magisterial Reformers had argued.

[12] Robinson, *Works of John Robinson*, 2:157–58. Robinson cites Bernard's *Separatists Schisme*, 94, as an example of the Anglican interpretation. He undoubtedly has in mind the sort of Catholic claim stated by St. Ambrose of Milan: "Where Peter is, there is the Church" (*Ubi ergo Petrus, ibi Ecclesia*), in *Enarratio in Psalmum* 40.30, Patrologia Latina 14 (Paris: J. P. Migne, 1882), 1134. Calvin maintained that the preaching of the gospel by the ministers of the church is the ordinary means for communicating the gospel, in his *Institutes of the Christian Religion* IV.1.5, ed. John T. McNeill, trans. Ford Lewis Battles (Philadelphia: Westminster, 1960), 2:1016–17. He argued that "nothing is given to Peter which was not also common to his colleagues" for "the preaching of the same gospel has been entrusted to all the apostles, so also the apostles have been furnished with a common power to bind and loose" (IV.6.4, 2:1105).

[13] Robinson, *Works of John Robinson*, 2:332–33.

[14] John Field, "Confession of Faith" (December 4, 1572), in Daniel Neal, *The History of the Puritans* (London: Thomas Tegg & Son, 1837), 1:191.

[15] A True Confession (1596), 17, in William L. Lumpkin, ed., *Baptist Confessions of Faith*, rev. ed. (Valley Forge, Pa.: Judson Press, 1969), 87. This confession is the work of Separatists (falsely called "Brownists") in Amsterdam and reflects a move toward congregational principles. It may have been the work of Henry Ainsworth, who due to the imprisonment of Francis Johnson in London, was serving as pastor of the Ancient Church in Amsterdam.

[16] True Confession, 37, in Lumpkin, *Baptist Confessions of Faith*, 94.

One year before Robinson wrote *A Justification of Separation*, John Smyth published a critique of Bernard entitled *Paralleles, Censures, Obser-vations* in which he identified himself as the pastor of the church at Gains-borough, near Lincoln. Though he had an earlier association with the parish church there, by this time Smyth considered it to be a false church. Making his point in a jocular tone, he explained:

> A true man may have a wooden leg, an eye of glass: So a true church may have a false ministry and worship, or government. A man carved out of wood, cannot possibly have any truth of a man in him, but all his parts and limbs are wooden, even as the image is of wood: So a false church can have nothing true in it, but all is false, idolatrous usurped.[17]

Since 1606, Smyth had served as the minister of a congregation that was in fellowship with a gathering community in nearby Scrooby under the leadership of Robinson and Richard Clifton. Smyth agreed in principle with Robinson and others of the separation against Bernard that where "two or three gathered together by love, and into the name of Christ by faith, Christ is present to dwell and walk."[18] But by the time he wrote *The Character of the Beast* in 1609, Smyth had reached the conclusion that permitting infants into the fellowship of the church by baptism not only contradicted the conviction of a *communio fidelium*, but in his judgment it invalidated the churchly status of all who practiced it. He argued:

> The true constitution of the Church is of a new creature baptized into the Father, the Son, and the Holy Ghost: The false constitution is of infants baptized. We profess therefore that all those Churches that bap-tise infants are of the same false constitution: and all those Churches that baptize the new creature, those that are made disciples by teaching, men confessing their faith and their sins, are of one true constitution: and therefore the Churches of the separation being of the same consti-tution with England and Rome, is a most unnatural daughter to her mother England, and her grandmother Rome.[19]

The ordinance of baptism, Smyth believed, had to be restored *de novo*. The congregation disbanded, and, believing there to be no true church with which to unite, they reconstituted themselves anew upon the basis

---

[17] Smyth, *Paralleles, Censures, Observations*, in *The Works of John Smyth*, ed. W. T. Whitley (Cambridge: Cambridge University Press, 1915), 2:352.

[18] Smyth, *Paralleles, Censures, Observations*, in *Works of John Smyth*, 2:387.

[19] Smyth, *The Character of the Beast*, in *Works of John Smyth*, 2:565.

of believer's baptism.[20] After baptizing himself, Smyth baptized the others (most likely by affusion rather than immersion) and established the first Baptist church.[21] Smyth's self-baptism has remained a matter of theological debate, but it is widely accepted that he exemplifies how a confessional faith enacted in the practice of believer's baptism became the foremost distinguishing mark of Baptist ecclesiology. Subsequent generations would describe this mark in terms of the "experience of grace," "evangelical conversion," or "regenerate church membership." However expressed, it attests to the conviction that a church is a community of disciples gathered in a common confession of faith in Jesus Christ. So, as to the question, "*Who* is gathered?" the Baptists came to answer, "*Believers.*"[22]

This question leads to asking how believers are gathered. Baptists arrived at an answer to this question, as they did the previous one, from

---

[20] Smyth, *Retractions and Confirmations*, in *Works of John Smyth*, 2:757.

[21] The extent to which the early Baptists may have been influenced by Anabaptists is disputed, as the lively exchanges between Winthrop Hudson and Ernest Payne illustrate. Hudson argued that the historical evidence weighs against any Anabaptist influence on the Baptists, while Payne suggested that it is still likely that Baptists were influenced by continental radicals because, as he put it, "ideas had legs in the sixteenth and seventeenth centuries, as they have today." Winthrop S. Hudson, "Baptists Were Not Anabaptists," *Chronicle* 16, no. 4 (1953): 174–79; Hudson, "Who Were the Baptists?" *Baptist Quarterly* 16, no. 7 (1956): 303–12; Hudson, "Who Were the Baptists?" *Baptist Quarterly* 17, no. 2 (1957): 53–55; Ernest A. Payne, "Who Were the Baptists?" *Baptist Quarterly* 16, no. 8 (1956): 339–42; and Payne, "Contacts between Mennonites and Baptists," *Foundations* 4, no. 4 (1961): 39–55. William R. Estep concluded "that English Baptists arose out of English Separatism under the influence of continental Anabaptism," in his "On the Origins of English Baptists," *Baptist History and Heritage*, 22, no. 2 (1987): 24. Kenneth R. Manley provides an excellent summary of the disputed question and answers in "Origins of the Baptists: The Case for Development from Puritanism-Separatism," *Baptist History and Heritage* 22, no. 4 (1987): 34–46. The extent to which Smyth and his congregation were influenced by the Mennonites in Amsterdam has also been a matter of debate. Stephen Wright notes that it is not known when the Smyth congregation first made contact with the Mennonites in Amsterdam. However, because their interaction came principally after rather than before Smyth's self-baptism in 1609, it is difficult to determine whether or how Mennonite baptismal practice might have shaped Smyth's change of mind. Wright, *The Early English Baptists, 1603–1649* (Woodbridge, U.K.: Boydell Press, 2006), 36–44. Kirsten T. Timmer has resolved some of the questions about the extent of the Mennonite influence on Smyth in her "John Smyth's Request for Mennonite Recognition and Admission: Four Newly Translated Letters, 1610–1612," *Baptist History and Heritage* 44, no. 1 (2009): 8–19. Timmer's research principally challenges the hypothesis suggested by James Coggins that the Smyth congregation was officially accepted and recognized as a "true Mennonite congregation" on May 23, 1610. See Coggins, *John Smyth's Congregation: English Separatism, Mennonite Influence, and the Elect Nation* (Scottdale, Pa.: Herald Press, 1991), 84. Timmer shows that Smyth's congregation continued to have close association with the Mennonites after the failed conference in May 1610, but it was not officially Mennonite until January 1615 when it merged with the Amsterdam Waterlanders.

[22] John Smyth, *A Short Confession of Faith* (1610), 24, in Lumpkin, *Baptist Confessions of Faith*, 108.

within the movement of English Separatists.[23] Henry Jacob, the pastor
of a gathered congregation in London that later gave rise to many of the
early Baptists, asked, "How is a visible church constituted and gathered?"
He answered, "By a free mutual consent of believers joining and covenanting to live as members of a holy society together in all religious and
virtuous duties as Christ and his Apostles did institute and practice the
gospel."[24] The practice of constituting a church of the faithful by covenant
is indicated in Article 33 of A True Confession of 1596, which stated
that those who make "true profession of Christ . . . are willingly to join
together in Christian communion and orderly covenant and by confession
of faith and obedience of Christ, to unite themselves into peculiar congregations."[25] So it was that in the year 1606/1607 the Gainsborough congregation, led by Smyth, followed this pattern and "joyned them selves
(by a covenant of the Lord) into a Church estate, in the fellowship of the
gospell, to walke in all his wayes, made known, or to be made known
unto them, according to their best endeavours, whatsoever it should cost
them, the Lord assisting them."[26] The gathering of the church in 1616 by
Henry Jacob followed a similar pattern, echoing the covenant adopted by
the congregation of Smyth and Robinson. Joining hands, the community made a circle and offered a personal confession of faith, then "they
Covenanted togeather to walk in all Gods Ways as he had revealed or
should make known to them."[27] A branch of the Gainsborough church
soon began meeting at the manor house in nearby Scrooby. Though the
two groups were separated geographically and led by different ministers,
they illustrated the ecclesial vision of walking "by one and the same rule"
and understanding themselves "as members of one body in the common
faith, under Christ their head."[28]

Just over a year after their founding by subscribing to a covenant,
the Gainsborough congregation left England for Holland. Sometime in

[23] For a complete account of covenant making from the continental radicals forward
with particular attention to the Baptists, see Champlin Burrage, *The Church Covenant Idea: Its
Origin and Its Development* (Philadelphia: American Baptist Publication Society, 1904).

[24] "Papers of Henry Jacob's Written during the Years 1603–1605," in Champlin Burrage,
The Early English Dissenters in Light of Recent Research (Cambridge: Cambridge University
Press, 1912), 2:157.

[25] True Confession, 33, in Lumpkin, *Baptist Confessions of Faith*, 92.

[26] William Bradford, *History of Plymouth Plantation, 1620–1647*, ed. William Chauncey
Ford (Boston: Houghton Mifflin, 1912), 1:20–22. Following Bradford's account, Champlain
Burrage showed the covenanting at Gainsborough occurred in the beginning of the year
1606/1607, in Burrage, *Early English Dissenters*, 1:231–32.

[27] Burrage, *Early English Dissenters*, 1:314 and 2:294.

[28] True Confession, 38, in Lumpkin, *Baptist Confessions of Faith*, 94.

1607 prior to their departure, Smyth published a book entitled *Principles and Inferences Concerning The Visible Church* in which he defined a church as "a visible communion of saints" that "is of two, three, or more saints joined together by covenant with God and themselves, freely to use all the holy things of God, according to the word, for their mutual edification, and God's glory."[29] Robinson held to a similar definition, stating that "a company, consisting though but of two or three, separated from the world . . . and gathered into the name of Christ by a covenant made to walk in all the ways of God known unto them, is a church, and so hath the whole power of Christ."[30] Yet the two parts of the community that were gathered in mutual covenant back in Gainsborough soon found themselves divided over baptism. As Smyth continued to move into a more radical understanding of covenant ecclesiology, the part of the congregation led by the more moderate Robinson separated and moved to Leyden. The other part that remained in Amsterdam under Smyth's ministry committed themselves to following the conclusion that, because infants were incapable of believing and taking up the responsibility of discipleship professed in baptism, they could not enter into covenant with God or one another and therefore could not be church members. They subsequently renounced the practice of infant baptism, dissolved their congregation, and reconstituted themselves as a visible community of baptized believers.

By the time he published *The Character of the Beast*, presumably shortly after adopting the practice of believer's baptism in 1609, Smyth moved to the view that "the true form of the church is a covenant betwixt God and the faithful made in baptism in which Christ is visibly put on."[31] Baptism was a covenanting act, and therefore no written covenant was required to constitute the church or for members to subscribe to. When a small group of the Smyth congregation returned to England and established a Baptist congregation outside the walls of London in Spitalfields, Thomas Helwys, the layman who led the returning group, followed Smyth's practice of baptism as a covenanting act that constituted the church. Helwys argued in *The Mystery of Iniquity*, published in 1612, that Christ has made a new covenant with those who believe and are baptized. Believers, not infants, are of the faith of Abraham and enter as Abraham did into covenant with God and the people of God. A written covenant was not necessary.[32]

---

[29] Smyth, *Principles and Inferences Concerning The Visible Church*, in *Works of John Smyth*, 1:252.

[30] Robinson, *Works of John Robinson*, 2:132.

[31] Smyth, *Character of the Beast*, in *Works of John Smyth*, 2:645.

[32] Thomas Helwys, *A Short Declaration of the Mystery of Iniquity* (1611/1612), ed. Richard Groves (Macon, Ga.: Mercer University Press, 1998), 132.

London Baptist pastor Hanserd Knollys indicated that a covenantal theology of baptism became widely accepted among the early Baptists, and though he implied that some congregations did hold formal written covenants, they did not insist on subscription to a covenant for membership. Whoever made a profession of faith was admitted into the membership of the church. But many were admitted "without urging or making any particular covenant with Members on admittance."[33] William Kiffin, another London pastor and Baptist leader, appropriated the Reformed language of "seals" for baptism and the Lord's Supper to denote them as covenantal acts that signify and perform the saving act of God in Jesus Christ. "The covenant," he explained, "binds mutually on Gods part and on ours; and so do the Seals which belong to the Covenant." For, he continued, "the Covenant is sealed by us in Baptism; and it is Renewed in the Lord's Supper."[34] The covenantal framework of this gathered church ecclesiology among the early Baptists has admittedly diminished over time and has been gradually replaced with democratic and bureaucratic notions of voluntary association and denominational cooperation. But attending to the covenant tradition that lies at the origins of Baptist ecclesiology is important for more than historical reasons. A retrieval of covenant theology offers the promise of an ecumenical vision by conceiving of an ecclesial openness to and a historical continuity with the whole covenant people of God throughout the world and the ages.[35] Moreover, although the practice of making and renewing written covenants continued after the early Baptists, it has rarely been understood as constitutive to the ecclesiality of a congregation.[36] The practice of congregations adopting

---

[33] Hanserd Knollys, *A Moderate Answer Unto Dr. Bastwicks Book: Called, Independency not Gods Ordinance* (London: Jane Coe, 1645), 20. An exception to Knollys' account is John Spilsbury, a Particular Baptist pastor in London and one of the primary authors of the London Confession of 1644. Spilsbury argued that "matter and forme constitutes a Church, the matter is a company of Saints, or persons professing faith in the righteousness of Jesus Christ; and living accordingly, that is, in holiness of life. The forme is that by which these are united and knit up together in one fellowship, and orderly body, and that is the covenant of grace that lies between God and his people, by which God visibly becomes the God of such persons, and they his people above all other. That this is the forme of a Church, and not Baptisme, I prove. . . . A people are a church by covenant unto which ordinances are annexed, to confirme and establish the same." Spilsbury, *A Treatise Concerning the Lawfull Subject of Baptisme* (London: John Spilsbury, 1643), 41.

[34] William Kiffin, *A Sober Discourse of Right to Church-Communion* (London: George Larkin, 1681), 103.

[35] Paul S. Fiddes, *Tracks and Traces: Baptist Identity in Church and Theology* (Carlisle, U.K.: Paternoster, 2003), 24.

[36] Charles W. Deweese has compiled an extensive collection of congregational covenants in *Baptist Church Covenants* (Nashville: Broadman, 1990). The number of seventeenth-, eighteenth-, and nineteenth-century covenants compared with those from the twentieth

and renewing local covenants, however, has fallen away and in many cases ceased entirely. Retrieving the congregational practice of covenant making and reciting serves as a reminder that the lives of members are not their own, but are held in relationships of trust. This practice reaffirms the historic Baptist understanding of a church as people bound to God and one another in mutual responsibilities and claims.[37] But if the Baptist understanding is that a church is a community of believers joined by baptism in covenant with God and God's people, it raises the question of by *whom* the church is gathered. The answer lies in a brief retracing of the historical development.

In 1589 Henry Barrow wrote *A True Description Out of the Worde of God, Of the Visible Church* from a London prison where he awaited execution for religious dissent. Barrow strenuously objected to the establishment of the English Church by authority of the queen. He envisioned as an alternative a gathered church living under the reign of Christ and maintaining discipline according to Christ's rule. The church, according to Barrow, is "a company and fellowship of the faithful and holie people gathered in the name of Christ Jesus, their only king, priest, and prophet." This community so gathered worships "him aright, being peaceablie and quietlie governed by his officers and lawes, keeping the unitie of faith in the bond of peace and love unfained."[38] A true church, Barrow argued, could not be formed by coercion of earthly powers but only by free consent of a free people. As he famously intoned, "Here is no intrusion or climbing up an other way into the sheepefolde, than by the holy and free election of the Lorde's holie and free people."[39]

This vision of the visible church under Christ's rule is found in A True Confession of 1596 to which separating Puritans moving toward congregational polity looked for doctrinal guidance. Article XVII reads:

> That in the mean time, besides his absolute rule in the world, Christ
> hath here in earth a spiritual kingdom and a canonical regiment in

---

century suggests that the practice of covenant making declined significantly by the end of the nineteenth.

[37] William C. Turner stands as an exception to the historical trend. He invites African American Baptists to join him in a theological journey of reflection in the National Baptist Church covenant, in his *Discipleship for African American Christians: A Journey through the Church Covenant* (Valley Forge, Pa.: Judson Press, 2002).

[38] Henry Barrow, *A True Description Out of the Worde of God, Of the Visible Church* (1589), A2, reprinted in *The Writings of Henry Barrow*, ed. Leland H. Carlson, vol. 3 of *Elizabethan Non-conformist Texts* (New York: Routledge, 2003), 214.

[39] Barrow, *True Description*, A3, in *Writings of Henry Barrow* (ed. Carlson), 216.

his Church over his servants, which Church he hath purchased and redeemed to himself, as a peculiar inheritance.[40]

As a consequence of Christ's rule, it continued, "every Christian congregation hath power and commandment to elect and ordain their own ministry according to the rules prescribed" and "to receive in or to cut off any member . . . or to move members sequestered from the whole."[41] But, it added, "that for the keeping of this Church in holy and orderly communion . . . Christ hath placed special men over the Church, who by their office are to govern, oversee, visit, watch, etc."[42] John Robinson similarly asserted that "the Lord Jesus is king of his church alone," but he too understood the rule of Christ in a moderately congregational way, explaining that "the Lord Jesus hath given to his church a presbytery, or a college of elders or bishops, for the feeding of the same, that is, for the teaching and governing of the whole flock according to his will."[43] These statements indicate that some separated churches, while moving toward congregational polity, still retained elements of presbyterial rule. It remained for John Smyth and his congregation to venture toward a more radical congregational polity under Christ's rule.

Smyth exclaimed in *Paralleles, Censures, Observations* (against Richard Bernard), "Let this therefore be set down for an invincible truth that the true visible church is the kingdom of Christ, where Christ the king only ruleth and reigneth in his own laws and officers and over his own subjects."[44] Therefore, he continued, "the power of binding and loosing is given to the body of the church, even to two or three faithful people joined together in covenant."[45] Holding that the visible church consists of believers only and that the congregation under Christ's rule is authorized to loose and bind, Smyth took the further step in *The Differences of the Churches of the Seperation*, written in 1608, arguing that "we hold that all the Elders of the church are Pastors: and that lay Elders (so called) are Antichristian," indicating that his church was moving toward a radical understanding of congregational polity.[46] Within a year of baptizing himself and his followers, Smyth began to have doubts about his self-baptism and petitioned the Waterlander Mennonites for membership. In late 1609

---

[40] True Confession, 17, in Lumpkin, *Baptist Confessions of Faith*, 87.
[41] True Confession, 23–24, in Lumpkin, *Baptist Confessions of Faith*, 89.
[42] True Confession, 26, in Lumpkin, *Baptist Confessions of Faith*, 90.
[43] Robinson, *Works of John Robinson*, 2:140–42.
[44] Smyth, *Paralleles, Censures, Observations*, in *Works of John Smyth*, 2:353.
[45] Smyth, *Paralleles, Censures, Observations*, in *Works of John Smyth*, 2:388.
[46] Smyth, *The Differences of the Churches of the Seperation*, in *Works of John Smyth*, 1:273.

Smyth sent them a short confession of faith written in Latin that described a church as "a company of the faithful (*coetum fidelium*); baptized after confession of sin and of faith, endowed with the power of Christ (*potestate Christi praeditum*)."[47]

A small group within the Smyth congregation continued to believe their baptism in 1609 was valid. Seeking to clarify their position, Thomas Helwys drew up a brief confession, also in Latin, which he sent to the Mennonites. Article 9 defined a church as "an assembly of believers" (*coetus populi fidelis*) who are baptized in the triune name upon confession of their faith and sins, thus possessing authority from Christ to preach the word, administer baptism and the Lord's Supper, choose their own ministers, and restore and exclude their own members according to the rule of Christ.[48] In 1611 Helwys drafted a more extensive declaration of faith in which he provided an ecclesial statement clarifying a basis for the validity of the baptisms performed by Smyth two years earlier. Article 11 declared that "though they but two or three, have Christ given them, with all the means of their salvation," they "are the body of Christ and a whole Church."[49] The next article succinctly summarized this vision of ecclesial authority:

> That as one congregation hath Christ, so hath all. And that the Word
> off God cometh not out from any one congregation in particular but
> unto every particular church as it doth unto all the world. And therefore
> no church ought to challenge any prerogative over any other.[50]

And here, he might well have quoted Ignatius, that "wherever Jesus Christ is, there is the Catholic Church."[51] It could be argued that Helwys was the architect of Baptist ecclesiology and the author of the first Baptist confession of faith.[52]

The Baptist leader and London pastor William Kiffin described the gathered churches as affirming "this great truth, [that] Christ is the King

---

[47] Smyth, *Short Confession of Faith*, 12, in Lumpkin, *Baptist Confessions of Faith*, 101; *Corde credimus, & ore confitemur*, in Burrage, *Early English Dissenters*, 2:178–80.

[48] Thomas Helwys, *Synopsis fidei, verae Christianae Ecclesiae Anglicane, Amsterdamiae* 9, in Burrage, *Early English Dissenters*, 2:183.

[49] Thomas Helwys, "A Declaration of Faith of English People Remaining at Amsterdam in Holland," 11, in Lumpkin, *Baptist Confessions of Faith*, 120.

[50] Helwys, "Declaration of Faith of English People," 12, in Lumpkin, *Baptist Confessions of Faith*, 120.

[51] Ignatius, *To the Smyrnaeans* 8, in *The Ante-Nicene Fathers*, 1:90.

[52] William R. Estep Jr., "Thomas Helwys: Bold Architect of Baptist Policy on Church-State Relations," *Baptist History and Heritage* 20, no. 3 (1985): 32.

of his Church; and that Christ hath given this power to his church, not to
a hierarchy, neither to a national presbytery, but to a company of saints in
a congregational way."[53] From Thomas Helwys through William Kiffin to
the present day, Baptists have held to this same conviction. Though sometimes it has been mistakenly identified as the "autonomy" or "independence" of the local church, which conceives of authority in democratic
terms, the Baptists, as Kiffin indicated, have held to an ecclesial authority
that is christologically derived: each local congregation stands under the
rule of Christ and so authorized to govern its own affairs. So in answer
to the question *"How* can churches be the church?*"* Baptists answer, "As a
community of *believers* gathered by *baptism* in *covenant* with God and God's
people to walk together under the rule of Christ." Or, to put the matter
differently, the church is both the community gathered by Christ and the
believers who gather in response to his call. For, as Jesus said, "Where two
or three are gathered in my name, I am there among them" (Matt 18:20),
and where Christ is, there is the church.

Ibi Ecclesia?

The Baptist movement began in large measure with the conviction that
God's purpose in history is the creation of a people—the church. Theirs
was a search for a true church that became visible in the gathered community. These congregations, they believed, were gatherings of the church
under the rule of Christ, which, though congregationally governed, did
not conceive of itself as independent but rather as interdependent with
other gathered communities. In 1644 seven congregations in London
came together to draft a confession of faith that declared:

> Though wee be distinct in respect of our particular bodies, for conve-
> nience sake, being as many as can well meet together in one place, yet
> are all one in Communion, holding Jesus Christ to be our head and
> Lord; under whose government wee desire alone to walk, in following
> the Lamb wheresoever he goeth.[54]

They described the visible church as Christ's spiritual kingdom that is
"called and separated from the world, by the word and Spirit of God, to

---

[53] William Kiffin, preface to "A Glimpse of Syons Glory," a 1641 sermon by Thomas
Goodwin, in *The Works of Thomas Goodwin* (Edinburgh: James Nichol, 1866), 12:63; cited in
Murray Tolmie, *The Triumph of the Saints: The Separatist Churches in London, 1616–1649* (Cam-
bridge: Cambridge University Press, 1977), 85.

[54] Preface to First London Confession (1644), in Lumpkin, *Baptist Confessions of Faith*,
155.

the visible profession of the faith of the Gospel, being baptized into that faith, and joined to the Lord, and each other, by mutual agreement, in the practical enjoyment of the Ordinances, commanded by Christ their head and King."[55] By borrowing language from the earlier separatist statement, A True Confession of 1596, the London Baptists explained that the visible church is not divided but walks together under the rule of Christ the king.[56] Although the early Baptists held the conviction that the church is most visible in the local congregation, they recognized its visibility in wider fellowships.

One group of early Particular Baptists in western England described the gathering of congregations in association as a duty in order "to communicate each to other, in spiritual, and things temporal."[57] In 1677 the Particular Baptists issued a statement of faith known as The Second London Confession, which was widely received in England and adopted in America (with two additional articles) by the Philadelphia Baptist Association in 1742. It described the associational principle in which "many churches holding communion together, do by their messengers meet to consider, and give their advice in, or about that matter in difference, to be reported to all the churches concerned." Yet it continued that, in these associational meetings, the messengers "are not entrusted with any church-power properly" nor "with any jurisdiction over the churches themselves, to exercise any censure either over any churches, or Persons: or to impose their determination on the churches, or Officers."[58] In this confession the Particular Baptists made clear their belief that the wider fellowship was needed to seek the mind of Christ together in matters of difficulty and divergence, but it also noted that the association held no binding authority over the local congregations. The early General Baptists attributed more ecclesiological status to their extracongregational bodies. One group of English General Baptists in their confession of faith, The Orthodox

---

[55] First London Confession (1644) XXXIII, in Lumpkin, *Baptist Confessions of Faith*, 165.

[56] First London Confession (1644) XLVII, in Lumpkin, *Baptist Confessions of Faith*, 168–69. Cf. True Confession, 38, in Lumpkin, *Baptist Confessions of Faith*, 94.

[57] The Somerset Confession (1656) XXVIII, in Lumpkin, *Baptist Confessions of Faith*, 211.

[58] The Second London Confession (1677/1688) XXVI.15, in Lumpkin, *Baptist Confessions of Faith*, 289. For an overview of associationalism in early American Baptist life, see Benjamin Griffith, "Of the Communion of Churches" Article 9, in *A Short Treatise of Church Discipline* (Philadelphia: Philadelphia Baptist Association, 1743); Morgan Edwards, "Of An Association," in *The Customs of Primitive Churches* (Philadelphia, 1768), ch. 54; "Of the Association of Churches," in *Summary of Church-Discipline* (Charleston, S.C.: Charleston Baptist Association, 1774), ch. 6; James Manning, "Sentiments Touching An Association," adopted by the Warren Baptist Association in 1769, in Reuben Aldridge Guild, *Early History of Brown University* (Providence: Snow & Farnham, 1897), 76–77. See also the careful study of Walter B. Shurden, *Associationalism among Baptists in America, 1707–1814* (New York: Arno Press, 1980).

Creed (1678), declared that "General councils, or assemblies, consisting of Bishops, Elders, and Brethren, of the several churches of Christ, and being legally convened . . . make but one church, and have lawful right, and suffrage in this general meeting, or assembly, to act in the name of Christ." The article continued that the general assembly is the best means under heaven to preserve unity and to prevent heresy and superintendency among or in any congregation whatsoever within its own limits or jurisdiction.[59] But though early General Baptists regarded their associations and assemblies to be visible expressions of the one church, they did not ascribe authority to any governing body beyond the congregation to impose a decision on a local church. They protected and prized the liberty of each congregation to make loosing and binding judgments under the Lordship of Christ and the leadership of the Holy Spirit. Consequently, as Baptists have sought to give concrete expression to this wider fellowship, they have joined into associations, societies, conventions, unions, federations, fellowships, and alliances, but they have not organized, nor would they seek to organize, a single entity called "the Baptist Church."

For all the emphasis the early Baptists put on the community of visible saints, they also recognized that there is more to the church than what can be seen. Consequently, The Second London Confession declared that the universal church, which "consists of the whole number of the elect," remains invisible.[60] Yet even though the early Particular Baptists held that the church catholic is invisible, they maintained that it becomes visible in the gathering community. One of the strongest early statements of the catholicity of the church is found in The Orthodox Creed, published in 1678 by a group of English General Baptists who sought to locate themselves theologically within the great tradition of catholic orthodoxy. They affirmed their conviction that the church catholic is visible in the local congregation, declaring, "We believe the visible church of Christ on earth is made up of several distinct congregations, which make up that one catholic church, or mystical body of Christ." Thus the early Baptists envisioned the *invisible catholic church* as comprised of the whole people of God, but they also conceived of the *visible catholic church* made up of all confessing Christians and all true churches. The invisible church catholic, as The Orthodox Creed continued, becomes visible where "the word of God is rightly preached, and the sacraments truly administered according to Christ's institution, and the practice of the primitive church," and where

---

[59] The Orthodox Creed (1678) XXXIX, in Lumpkin, *Baptist Confessions of Faith*, 327.
[60] Second London Confession (1677/1688) XXVI.1; and Orthodox Creed (1678) XXIX, in Lumpkin, *Baptist Confessions of Faith*, 285 and 318.

"discipline and government duly [are] executed, by ministers or pastors of God's appointing, and the church's election."[61] For these early Baptists, then, the *notae ecclesiae* included evangelical proclamation of the word, sacramental observance according to the primitive pattern, and discipleship under the rule of Christ as extensions of the threefold office of Christ as prophet, priest, and king. These marks were not merely indicators of a good Baptist congregation but were, they believed, signs of the one, holy, catholic, and apostolic church. It is conceivable, then, to understand the early Baptist vision as a movement of radical renewal within the church catholic rather than purely a faction of dissent and separation.

The contesting catholicity of the early Baptists has often been forgotten or misremembered in subsequent generations. For example, the popular New Hampshire Confession of Faith, published in 1833, described the visible church but made no reference to the invisible, catholic, or universal church, nor did it have anything to say about associational cooperation or union. The Baptist Faith and Message adopted by the Southern Baptist Convention in 1963 borrowed language from the New Hampshire Confession, adding that the local congregation is "an autonomous body, operating through democratic processes under the Lordship of Jesus Christ." It concluded with an oblique reference to "the body of Christ" as including "the redeemed of all ages."[62] The assertion of congregational "autonomy" became greatly exaggerated in the American South and on the western frontier in the movement known as Landmarkism, which asserted that the only true churches were local Baptist ones and that all other so-called churches were mere human societies without valid ministers or sacraments.[63] But it was not only the Landmarkers who lost sight of the catholicity of the early Baptists. A nonchurchly understanding of Baptist denominational life has gradually displaced the earlier churchly understanding. The nonchurchly understanding was rooted in the belief that God's primary interest is in individuals. Congregational autonomy and democratic processes became more a political method of measuring the mind of the membership and less a spiritual practice about discerning the mind of Christ.[64]

Some Baptists thus have adopted a nativist American form of atomistic and sometimes isolated existence. This democratized account

[61] Orthodox Creed (1678) XXX, in Lumpkin, *Baptist Confessions of Faith*, 318–19.

[62] The Baptist Faith and Message (1963) VI, in Lumpkin, *Baptist Confessions of Faith*, 396.

[63] H. Leon McBeth, *The Baptist Heritage* (Nashville: Broadman, 1987), 447–61.

[64] Winthrop S. Hudson, "Prolegomena to a Theology of Church Order," in *Baptists in Transition: Individualism and Christian Responsibility* (Valley Forge, Pa.: Judson Press, 1979), 19–35.

of congregational independence failed to imagine much connection between the local congregation and the wider fellowship in part because it paid insufficient attention to the vision of the early Baptists, which viewed interdependence as the mark of the converted and independence as Adam's sin.[65] It is important to note that "Baptists at the beginning were Congregationalists but not Independents." They believed that the gathered community was competent in Christ to exercise churchly judgments, but "they set their faces against isolationism."[66] The early Baptists exemplified a return to a more catholic vision in which the "local congregation is not truly a church if it lives an entirely separate life."[67] This perspective offered a corrective against a growing sense of "exaggerated independence, self-sufficiency, and atomism" in Baptist life. It was guided by a vision of "high churchmanship in its inner urge towards communion, fellowship and unity with all those other Christians who *together* make up the Church catholic."[68]

In his book *The Gathered Community*, Robert C. Walton offered a fresh examination of the New Testament and the life and thought of the early Baptists. He claimed, "A Baptist church is a local manifestation of the universal Church, and therefore, Baptist ministers are ministers of Christ's Church."[69] In March of 1948, the Baptist Union of Great Britain approved a statement along similar lines entitled the Baptist Doctrine of the Church, which declared that "although Baptists have for so long held a position separate from that of other communions, they have always claimed to be part of the one holy catholic Church of our Lord Jesus Christ." It continued that Baptists "believe in the catholic Church as the holy society of believers in our Lord Jesus Christ, which He founded, of which He is the only Head, and in which He dwells by His Spirit, so that though manifested in many communions, organized in various modes, and scattered throughout the world, it is yet one in Him."

It also upheld the nature of visible churches, the feature of ecclesiology more familiar to Baptists, but it described gathered companies of believers as "the local manifestation of the one Church of God on earth and in heaven."[70] To put it simply, the statement affirmed that the local

---

[65] B. R. White, "The Practice of Association," in *A Perspective on Baptist Identity*, ed. David Slater (Kingsbridge, U.K.: Mainstream, 1987), 29.

[66] Henry Cook, *What Baptists Stand For* (London: Carey Kingsgate Press, 1961), 84.

[67] Ernest Payne, *The Fellowship of Believers: Baptist Thought and Practice Yesterday and Today*, enlarged ed. (London: Carey Kingsgate Press, 1952), 31. The first edition was published in 1944.

[68] Payne, *Fellowship of Believers*, 37.

[69] Robert C. Walton, *The Gathered Community* (London: Carey Press, 1946), 147.

[70] The Baptist Doctrine of the Church, statement approved by the Council of the Baptist

church is wholly church but not the whole church. Or to borrow another image, the local church is "the outcrop" of the church catholic.[71] These descriptions retrieved a vision of a fuller understanding of the church. And although they did not receive universal acceptance, they succeeded in shifting attention toward a sense of catholicity among the early Baptists that had long been neglected.[72]

It is important to return to the *notae ecclesiae* of confession, covenant, and Christ to which the early Baptists drew attention and examine these marks by placing them in a framework of Free Church ecclesiology that begins with the germ of Matthew 18:20 that "where two or three are gathered in Christ's name, not only is Christ present among them, but a Christian church is there as well."[73] Or to put the matter more pointedly, not "there is *a* church," but "there is *the* church."[74] The ecclesial status ascribed to the gathering community in Matthew 18:15-20 is related to the ecclesial language in Matthew 16:13-20 where Peter is portrayed as the prototype of confessing discipleship that is essential for churches to be the church.[75] The church as a *communio fidelium* is manifested through the multiple and mutual public confessions of faith in Christ. This confessional mark is critical for Free Church theologian Miroslav Volf, who wonders why the ecclesial identity of Catholic and Orthodox communities in his homeland, the former Yugoslavia, was taken for granted when, as he perceived, their "members are inclined more to superstition than faith" and they "identify with the church more for nationalistic reasons." At the same time, the churchly character of "a Baptist congregation that has preserved its faith through the crucible of persecution" goes unrecognized.[76]

Union of Great Britain and Ireland, March 1948, in *Baptist Union Documents 1948–1977*, ed. Roger Hayden (London: Baptist Historical Society, 1980), 5–6.

[71] P. T. Forsyth, *The Church and the Sacraments*, 3rd ed. (London: Independent, 1949), 65.

[72] Ernest A. Payne, *The Baptist Union: A Short History* (London: Carey Kingsgate Press, 1959), 223.

[73] Miroslav Volf, *After Our Likeness: The Church as the Image of the Trinity* (Grand Rapids: Eerdmans, 1998), 136.

[74] Forsyth, *Church and the Sacraments*, 66.

[75] Of all the models of the church in the New Testament, Raymond E. Brown commended the Matthean ecclesiology as having a high respect for Law and authority as well as remarkable nuance in dealing with pastoral issues, in his *The Churches the Apostles Left Behind* (New York: Paulist, 1984), 135–36. It is not surprising that Baptists and others in the Free Church tradition have been drawn to Matthew for ecclesial insight. Cf. John Howard Yoder, *The Royal Priesthood: Essays Ecclesiological and Ecumenical*, ed. Michael G. Cartwright (Grand Rapids: Eerdmans, 1994), 323–58; and Nigel Goring Wright, *Free Church, Free State: The Positive Baptist Vision* (Milton Keynes, U.K.: Paternoster, 2005), 9. Wright borrows extensively from Volf's Free Church ecclesiology to display a distinctively "Baptist" doctrine of the church. See also Cook, *What Baptists Stand For*, 48.

[76] Volf, *After Our Likeness*, 133–34.

The primary concern, however, is not how those outside the Free Church tradition regard this ecclesiology, but with the integrity of the Free Church ecclesiology that is threatened from within by an individualistic understanding of faith, for individualism leads to more than just diminished theology.[77] When freedom-as-autonomy is understood as absolute, it assaults community life and ultimately destroys itself, thus rendering ecclesiology not merely problematic but impossible.[78] Jesuit theologian Michael J. Taylor offered the following stereotypical description of Baptist individualism:

> The Baptist is a Christian not because he is a member of a Christian church but because he has accepted the absolute Lordship of Jesus Christ, whose life and redeeming message are unfolded for him in the Bible. If he has a norm for religious action, an authority to govern him, a creed to teach him, it is the Bible, illumined by the light of the Spirit. The Baptist, armed with the Bible and guided by the Spirit, exercises supreme responsibility over his own soul before God and believes that no state, or religion, or group of ecclesiastics should dictate to him the religious principles that are to govern his life. He is a free soul under God and balks at anything or anyone that might compromise this freedom. Among Christians he stands out as the "rugged individualist," the "priest unto himself," the "Spiritual nonconformist."[79]

Taylor's account accurately characterizes the individualism expressed in much of the popular religion to be found in Baptist churches. The trouble is not that Baptists and other evangelical Christians forsake to assemble (Heb 10:25) but rather that often they understand their assembly as just another voluntary association. Schleiermacher famously distinguished between Protestantism, which makes the individual's relation to the church dependent on a relation to Christ, and Catholicism, which makes the individual's relation to Christ dependent on a relation to the church.[80]

---

[77] Volf, *After Our Likeness*, 2–3.

[78] Wendell Berry, *Sex, Economy, Freedom, and Community* (New York: Pantheon Books, 1992), 144–46. Berry cites Jesus' statement "the truth shall make you free" (John 8:32), but his specific concern is with the often-cited "freedom to be wrong" grounded in Jeffersonian politics. Berry exemplifies his claim in his novel *Jayber Crow*, which narrates the destruction of rural community life by the forces of "progress" justified by freedom. Berry, *Jayber Crow* (Washington, D.C.: Counterpoint, 2000).

[79] Michael J. Taylor, *The Protestant Liturgical Renewal: A Catholic Viewpoint* (Westminster, Md.: Newman Press, 1963), 268; cited by Robert T. Handy, "Areas of Theological Agreement from a Baptist Point of View," *Foundations* 10, no. 2 (1967): 172n30.

[80] Friedrich Schleiermacher, *The Christian Faith* §24, ed. and trans. H. R. Macintosh and J. S. Stewart (Philadelphia: Fortress, 1976); cited by Volf in *After Our Likeness*, 159.

The church-as-voluntary-association model is a radical version of Schleiermacher's Protestant type and, as Catholics and Orthodox critics rightly charge, results in a deficient social reductionism because it conceives of the church as merely a human social group. Moreover, this model adopts a contractual language of faith and a transactional understanding of salvation where both parties give and receive: the individual offers faith and in return God provides salvation. In the economy of this individualistic scheme, salvation is severed from membership in the church, since believers enjoy a private relationship with Christ and must subsequently enter into voluntary association with the church. Under the assumptions of this voluntaristic model, Christians who choose not to unite with fellow believers may be in violation of the admonition not to neglect meeting together (Heb 10:25), but their relation to Christ remains unaffected by their isolation from the church.

Communion ecclesiology offers a radically different account of the church, faith, and salvation in which the church is understood as grounded in the *koinonia* between the Father, Son, and Holy Spirit.[81] Rather than an individualistic account of salvation as a contractual relationship that dominates evangelicalism, in communion ecclesiology the life of salvation is conceived of as participation with the triune God and with fellow believers in the church. The benefits of salvation are mediated not by pious feelings or individual faith but in the fellowship of word and sacrament. As Thomas Helwys wrote, "The Church of Jesus Christ is a company of faithful people, separated from the world by the word and Spirit of God being knit unto the Lord, and one unto another, by baptism upon their own confession of the faith and sins."[82] Through the proclamation of the gospel, the performance of baptism, and the observance of the Lord's table, believers are united with Christ, and in Christ they are united with one another. Believers do not receive faith from the church, yet faith comes through the church and not apart from the church.[83] This interconnection between belief, the believer, and other believers is such that relation with Christ is never simply between the individual and Christ but rather between the believer and "the whole Christ" (*totus Christus*), who is head and body.[84]

---

[81] Dennis M. Doyle, *Communion Ecclesiology* (New York: Orbis Books, 2000), 13, 11–22.

[82] Helwys, "Declaration of Faith of English People," 10, in Lumpkin, *Baptist Confessions of Faith*, 119.

[83] Volf, *After Our Likeness*, 166. Volf further contends that "a person does not become a Christian until he or she is baptized and partakes in the Eucharist, both of which acts emphatically are to take place within the worship service and accordingly also in the local church" (167).

[84] Robert Jenson rightly worries about the tendency of Protestants to fall from

The ecclesial mark of covenant also plays a critical role in a Baptist Free Church ecclesiology, in which the church is "a visible communion of saints . . . joined by covenant."[85] Critics charge that, in Free Church ecclesiology, the church emerges from the voluntary assembly of its members as merely a "free association of independent individuals." This criticism of the Free Church alternative might hold if covenant community and voluntary association were equivalent notions. But they are not, as Baptist theologian A. H. Strong pointed out, suggesting that the idea of the church as a voluntary association "is no more true than that hands and feet are voluntarily united in the human body for the purposes of locomotion and work."[86] To be sure, the church as a community gathers in response to the call of Christ, but it is Christ's gathering, not the community's response, that is determinative of the church. Such a covenantal ecclesiology excludes the notion of the church as merely a voluntary society. No one chooses to be a member of the church; one is made a member of the church. The church is not an affinity group that people join; it is the body of Christ into which believers must be joined. The converts on the day of Pentecost did not add themselves to the church; they were added to the church (Acts 2:38).

The church as a covenant community is not a creation of human action. It is constituted in covenant "from above" by "the Spirit of God, acting through the word of God and the sacraments" as well as "from below" by receiving the gifts of God by faith.[87] Baptism and the Supper are thus constitutive of the church, for just as "by one Spirit we were all baptized into one body" (1 Cor 12:13), so "because there is one bread, we who are many are one body" (1 Cor 10:17). Baptism and the Supper are not simply acts of obedience. They are the means whereby Christians are joined into the body of Christ through the Spirit. The sacraments therefore belong to the *esse* of the church, not merely the *bene esse*, as Free Churches sometimes maintain. Without them, the churches cannot be the church. Through them, but not without them, persons are made Christians and are sustained in faith and union with Christ and his body. Baptism and the Lord's Supper enact the covenant between God and the people of God. But in a Baptist Free Church ecclesiology, because all

---

communion ecclesiology back into typical Protestantism by describing individual union with Christ as the basis for corporate communion in the church in his "Catholic and Evangelical?" *First Things* 86 (1998): 42–43.

[85] Volf, *After Our Likeness*, 175.

[86] Augustus Hopkins Strong, *Systematic Theology*, 8th ed. (Philadelphia: Judson Press, 1909), 3:893. Here Strong is approvingly quoting A. J. Gordon.

[87] Volf, *After Our Likeness*, 176.

believers are united with Christ in baptism and charismatically gifted as priests, the ordained office belongs not to the *esse* but to the *bene esse* of the church.[88] Yet, because even in covenant community human beings are not in communion as the Trinity is, so ecclesial participation on this side of the eschaton corresponds to the perfect unity of the Trinity "in a broken fashion."[89]

Such a trinitarian framing of Baptist Free Church ecclesiology has important implications: Christ is directly present through his Spirit in every gathered community that assembles in his name and professes faith in him. Each congregation is simultaneously independent of and interconnected with other churches through the Spirit that makes Christ present. And the profession of Christ as universal Savior and Lord implies that participation in the church must be open to all people.[90] Here Other Baptists see the gathered community of believers not simply as a congregation with a connection to the larger denomination of Baptists, but as the local manifestation of the one church of God. To be sure, the fullness of catholicity awaits the coming eschatological communion of the entire people of God in the new creation. Catholicity is that toward which the church in pilgrimage is always moving, for "the universal church arises *by way of* the local churches, just as the local churches themselves arise through the pneumatic anticipatory connection to the yet outstanding gathering of the whole eschatological people of God."[91] Yet there is reason for concern that catholicity pneumatologically conceived might simply become an empty cipher, so it is essential that local churches remain connected with the ecclesial whole, which is signified in the relation of a local church to other churches, the openness of each church to other churches, and loyalty to the apostolic tradition.[92] But because such an eschatological vision of catholicity lacks the necessity of visible and indeed institutional expression, it risks becoming merely a spiritual unity without concrete manifestation.

Although some Baptists have insisted that the local congregation is the whole of the church, there was a vision of catholicity among the early Baptists that understood the local church as wholly the church but not the whole of the church. In such a view, the universal church of Jesus Christ is present and manifested in each local congregation. Though Baptists are hesitant to ascribe ecclesial authority to connectional bodies such as associations, unions, conventions, or fellowships, they nevertheless recognize

---

[88] Volf, *After Our Likeness*, 152.
[89] Volf, *After Our Likeness*, 207.
[90] Volf, *After Our Likeness*, 154–58.
[91] Volf, *After Our Likeness*, 202.
[92] Volf, *After Our Likeness*, 274–75.

the ecclesial marks in them. Such an understanding of the church finds fuller display within the Trinity. Other Baptists see the church as a gathered community of believers participating in the fellowship and mission of the triune God. Through the Spirit and the Word, "believers are drawn into the communion of God's own being and become partakers of the divine nature."[93] Yet the Trinity as a "communion of co-equal divine persons" is not merely an analogue for democratic church polity because "the church is not an *icon* of the Trinity."[94] This trinitarian vision of communion ecclesiology provides an account of the reign of Christ in the church through the Holy Spirit that differs slightly from the early Baptists, who conceived of the *regula Christi* in more of a christological sense (as an extension of Christ's kingly office) than in pneumatological terms. But because the trinitarian communion ecclesiology conceives of the local church and the universal church as participating in the *koinonia* between the Father, Son, and Holy Spirit, the local and universal are held together in a perichoretic unity.[95]

Baptist Free Church communion ecclesiology as *a communion of churches*, however, differs from Catholic communion ecclesiology as *a communion of representatives of churches*—namely, the bishops. As Pope John Paul II explained, "full and visible communion" requires as a necessary condition for unity "communion of the particular Churches with the Church at Rome, and of their Bishops with the Bishop of Rome."[96] But from the standpoint of the Baptist Free Church tradition, whenever a community of believers is gathered in baptismal covenant around word and table, Christ is directly present with them, and through the Spirit they share communion with the whole people of God. It is important, then, to explore what the implications of such an ecclesiological account has for thinking about how Catholics and Baptists understand local churches as participating in the one true church.

---

[93] Wright, *Free Church, Free State*, 233.

[94] Wright, *Free Church, Free State*, 233.

[95] Robert Sherman argues that the work of Christ as prophet, priest, and king must be placed within a trinitarian narrative so that the atonement is seen as the work of the triune God, in his *King, Priest, and Prophet: A Trinitarian Theology of the Atonement* (New York: T&T Clark, 2004). Christological accounts of the church likewise beg for trinitarian ecclesial narration such as offered by Wright and Volf.

[96] John Paul II, *Ut Unum Sint*, May 25, 1995, §97, accessed January 29, 2013, http://www.vatican.va/holy_father/john_paul_ii/encyclicals/documents/hf_jp-ii_enc_25051995_ut-unum-sint_en.html.

Quis Ecclesia?

In April 2001, the Catholic magazine *America* published an article by Cardinal Walter Kasper entitled "A Friendly Reply to Cardinal Ratzinger on the Church." Ratzinger responded with an article entitled "The Local Church and the Universal Church" in a November 2001 issue of the same magazine. It was an unusually public venue for such a contentious conversation between two of the leading theological voices in the Catholic Church: Cardinal Kasper, then president of the Pontifical Council for Promoting Christian Unity, and Cardinal Ratzinger, then prefect of the Congregation for the Doctrine of the Faith (CDF; later Pope Benedict XVI). To witness these two Catholic theologians respectfully but firmly disagreeing was a refreshing reminder that catholicity is a contested concept, which is especially important for outsiders, who too often are inclined to think about Catholic theology in undifferentiated terms. But whatever else this debate conveyed, it sent a clear signal to observers that the nature and relation of the local and universal churches were contested at the highest levels of the Catholic Church.[97]

The nub of their disagreement was the question of ecclesial priority: Which church is first, universal or local? Ratzinger's stated view was that "the temporal and ontological priority lies with the universal Church."[98] Kasper agreed with Ratzinger's reasoning that the universal church was not simply the end result of the coming together of local churches, but he rejected the further argument "that the local churches exist 'in and from' the universal church."[99] For Kasper, this thesis went too far, destroying the right balance between the universal church and the particular churches. The universal church, as Vatican II defined, "subsists" in the Roman Catholic Church (*Haec Ecclesia . . . subsistit in Ecclesia catholica*), but the one church of Christ also exists "in and from" the local churches. Thus, he argued, "just as local churches are not mere extensions or provinces of the universal church, so the universal church is not the mere sum of the local churches."[100] Kasper contended that the historical case for

---

[97] Walter Kasper, "A Friendly Reply to Cardinal Ratzinger on the Church," *America*, April 23, 2001, 8–14; and Joseph Ratzinger, "The Local Church and the Universal Church," *America*, November 19, 2001, 7–11. Kilian McDonnell provides an excellent summary and analysis not only of the articles in *America* but of the previous statements by Ratzinger that occasioned Kasper's "Friendly Reply," in his "The Ratzinger/Kasper Debate: The Universal Church and Local Churches," *Theologial Studies* 63, no. 2 (2002): 227–50.

[98] Joseph Ratzinger, *Call to Communion* (San Francisco: Ignatius Press, 1991), 44; cited in McDonnell, "Ratzinger/Kasper Debate," 228.

[99] Kasper, "Friendly Reply," 11.

[100] Kasper, "Friendly Reply," 12.

priority cannot be sustained by the documents of the biblical witness, nor do the Scriptures support the thesis of the preexistence of the universal church. Instead, Kasper stated that the Scriptures do support the doctrine of "the simultaneous preexistence of the universal church and the particular churches."[101] Kasper concluded his article by suggesting that Ratzinger's ecclesiology was Platonic, leading to an increasing centralization and a diminished capacity for ecumenism.

Ratzinger responded by downplaying the impression that Kasper's "sharp critique" revealed "a longstanding theological dispute" between the two theologians. He expressed gratitude to Kasper for clarifying that both of them affirmed the perichoretic unity between the local church and the universal church. Yet Ratzinger remained resolute about the priority of ontological unity, which closes the door to sociological notions of the universal church as a federation of local and national churches. Avery Cardinal Dulles weighed in on the side of Ratzinger, declaring that "the ontological priority of the Church universal appears to me to be almost self-evident." He concluded that, in an age of globalism, the Catholic Church must have a vigorous curial office to safeguard "the unity of all the particular churches in the essentials of faith, morality, and worship."[102] Catholic ecumenical theologian Jean-Marie Roger Tillard approached the universal and local question differently. Tillard did not reject the question of priority of the universal church but rather argued that the universal church is a communion of local churches. For Tillard, "each local church exists only in communion with that universal church of churches, and the universal church exists only in, through, and from the local churches." In short, the universal church is the communion. To raise the issue of priority, then, "betrays a misunderstanding of the relationship of the local and the universal, or unity and diversity."[103]

The Kasper-Ratzinger exchange, however, represents only a small range among the contested interpretations of the statement in *Lumen Gentium* that the universal "Church of Christ . . . subsists in the Catholic Church, which is governed by the successor of Peter and the bishops in communion with him."[104] Although the settled view prior to Vatican II was one of "full identity" between the Catholic Church and the church

---

[101] Kasper, "Friendly Reply," 13.

[102] Avery Cardinal Dulles, "Ratzinger and Kasper on the Universal Church," *Inside the Vatican*, June 9, 2001, 12–14.

[103] Christopher Ruddy, *The Local Church: Tillard and the Future of Catholic Ecclesiology* (New York: Herder & Herder, 2006), 100.

[104] *Lumen Gentium* §8.2, *Vatican Council II*, vol. 1, *The Conciliar and Post Conciliar Documents*, rev. ed. (New York: Costello, 2004), 357.

Christ founded, some theologians contend that the participants in the Second Vatican Council did not intend to soften this identity by changing the language of "is" (*est*) in the initial draft of *Lumen Gentium* to "subsists in" (*subsistit in*) in the final text.[105] A number of divergent understandings of "subsists in" challenge the exclusive identity thesis of traditionalists.[106] The most radical is that the church of Christ is an eschatological ideal that cannot subsist in history. It is unclear whether any Catholics have espoused such a view, but among the Baptists Roger Williams (the first Baptist in America) held something like it. Williams envisioned a radical ecclesiology in which the garden of the church must be separated from the desert of the world. Initially he thought this could be achieved by weeding the garden, first according to the Separatists and later the Baptists. When his hopes of a pure church faded, soon after having been believer baptized, he renounced ties to all churches. He lamented that God had broken down the wall and the worldly vines had choked out the garden. The only hope was to await the coming of Christ, the heavenly gardener, who would prune back the weeds so that the roses might again bloom.[107]

Those who hold to a second view suggest that the church of Christ subsists in a federation of local churches taken together.[108] It is conceivable that some Baptists with strong federated connection like the European Baptist Federation might understand their participation in fuller catholicity in a similar way. From this standpoint their practices of believer's baptism, missionary activity, and separation of church and state might be understood as gospel practices that enhance the richness of the discipleship of all gathered communities.[109] Some hold a third interpretation that affirms that the church of Christ subsists in the Catholic Church but also in other non-Catholic churches.[110] The CDF issued a strong statement

---

[105] Karl J. Becker, *L'Osservatore Romano*, December 14, 2005, subsequently published in *Origins* 35, no. 31 (2006): 514–22. See also Christopher J. Malloy, "*Subsistit In*: Nonexclusive Identity or Full Identity?" *Thomist* 72 (2008): 1–44.

[106] The summary of the four nonexclusive identity positions are laid out clearly by Malloy, "*Subsistit In*," 9–14.

[107] Roger Williams, *Mr. Cottons Letter Lately Printed*, in *The Complete Writings of Roger Williams* (New York: Russell & Russell, 1963), 1:392. Thus Perry Miller aptly described Williams as "a churchless man seeking the pure fellowship," in his *Roger Williams*, 52. Clark Gilpin demonstrates that millennialism was not only the basis of Williams' separating ecclesiology but was "the axis of his religious thought," in his *The Millenarian Piety of Roger Williams* (Chicago: University of Chicago Press, 1979), 51, 174.

[108] Malloy, "*Subsistit In*," 9. Hans Küng is a Catholic proponent of nonexclusive identity with sympathy for this position, in his *The Church* (Garden City, N.Y.: Image Books, 1976), 365.

[109] Keith G. Jones, "Rethinking Baptist Ecclesiology," *Journal of European Baptist Studies* 1, no. 1 (2000): 4–18.

[110] Leonardo Boff promulgated the view that the church of Christ can subsist in other

against this view, explaining its position that "there exists only one sub-sistence of the true Church" and that "outside of its visible structure there exist only elements of Church."[111] It is likely the case that Free Church communion ecclesiologies and many of those in the early Baptist *ressource-ment* movement that aspired to a fuller catholicity might be understood, at least by some Catholic interpreters, as examples of something like this third category.

A fourth view understands "subsists in" (*subsistit in*) to mean that the church of Christ exists fully in the Catholic Church but also in lesser and varying degrees in other Christian churches and ecclesial communities.[112] This view inveighs against the traditionalist contention that equates *est* and *subsistit in* so as to understand *Lumen Gentium* as perpetuating full and exclusive identity of the church of Christ and the Catholic Church. Proponents of this fourth view point to the language of the text and from council discussions that indicate the one true church is found in the Cath-olic Church but that it nonetheless extends, though lacking its fullness, beyond the Catholic Church. They cite as evidence the next sentence in *Lumen Gentium* 8.2, which states that "many elements of sanctifica-tion and of truth are found outside" the "visible confines" of the Catho-lic Church, as implying the presence and salvific role of churches and ecclesial communities that are not in full communion with the Catholic Church.[113] They argue that "what motivated the approval of the change from *est* to *subsistit in* was that it would make it possible for the council to acknowledge the fact that outside the Catholic Church there are not only elements of the Church, but that there are churches and ecclesial commu-nities." And they argue, in summary, that "the doctrinal commission that approved this change must have understood it to mean no longer claim-ing an exclusive identity between the Church of Christ and the Catholic Church."[114]

When the CDF issued its "Responses to Some Questions Regarding Certain Aspects of the Doctrine of the Church" in June 2007, some Baptists joined other Protestants in decrying the notion that their congregations

---

Christian churches in his *Church, Charism and Power: Liberation Theology and the Institutional Church*, trans. John Diercksmeier (New York: Crossroad, 1985), 75.

[111] *Acta apostolicae sedis* 77 (Vatican: Typis Polyglottis Vaticanis, 1985), 758–59; cited by Francis A. Sullivan, "The Meaning of *Subsistit in* as Explained by the Congregation for the Doctrine of the Faith," *Theological Studies* 69, no. 1 (2008): 118.

[112] Francis A. Sullivan has forcefully defended this interpretation of *Lumen Gentium* and other documents of Vatican II in his "A Response to Karl Becker, S.J., on the Meaning of *Subsistit in*," *Theological Studies* 67, no. 2 (2006): 395–409.

[113] *Lumen Gentium* §8.2, *Vatican Council II*, 1:357.

[114] Sullivan, "Response to Karl Becker," 402.

were "ecclesial communities" rather than churches in the proper sense. Some pronounced ecumenical conversations with Catholics to be dead in the water. Others portrayed the CDF document as evidence that Benedict XVI was intent on undoing Vatican II. What such reactions failed to take into account was that the "Responses" echoed earlier papal teaching in *Ut Unum Sint* that envisioned the possibility that "the church of Christ is present and operative in the churches and ecclesial communities not yet fully in communion with the Catholic Church, on account of the elements of sanctification and truth that are present in them."[115] "Responses" further reiterated language of Vatican II's *Unitatis Redintegratio*, that while separated churches and communities "suffer from defects" (chiefly the absence of historic apostolic episcope and valid eucharistic worship), they are nevertheless "deprived neither of significance nor importance in the mystery of salvation," and that "the Spirit of Christ has not refrained from using them as instruments of salvation."[116]

By acknowledging that Christ may be genuinely present elsewhere and that the Spirit may be sanctifying work not under Catholic control, the CDF offered language for which Baptists can be grateful. This opens space for future conversations concerning what ecclesial elements make it possible to discern in the common lives of the other signs of the one church of Jesus Christ. For Baptists to receive such admonition from their Catholic brothers and sisters, they must recognize that their tradition of dissent is not self-sufficient and thus rediscover their place within the larger catholic whole. But such reception cannot be asymmetrical. It demands that Catholics likewise be humble enough to embrace the corrective embodied in the communal witness of their Baptist conversation partners. It might be conceivable, for instance, to understand the Rite of Christian Initiation for Adults, which acknowledges adult baptism as the norm, as one possible example of such humble receptivity.

Pope Benedict's hermeneutic of continuity—which insists that new statements must be understood in coherence with existing teaching—has

---

[115] Congregation for the Doctrine of the Faith, "Responses to Some Questions regarding Certain Aspects of the Doctrine of the Church," accessed January 29, 2013, http://www.vatican.va/roman_curia/congregations/cfaith/documents/rc_con_cfaith_doc_20070629_responsa-quaestiones_en.html. The CDF softened Pope John Paul II's stronger statement that "the elements of sanctification and truth" are "present and operative beyond the visible boundaries of the Catholic Church" (*ultra fines visibiles Ecclesiae catholicae inveniuntur et operantur*). John Paul II, *Ut Unum Sint* §§11–12; accessed January 29, 2013, http://www.vatican.va/holy_father/john_paul_ii/encyclicals/documents/hf_jp-ii_enc_25051995_ut-unum-sint_en.html. Though issued by Pope John Paul II, *Ut Unum Sint* was drafted by Jean-Marie Roger Tillard.

[116] *Unitatis Redintegratio* 3.4, *Vatican Council II*, 1:456.

its limitations. Vatican statements are often so subtle as to be inscrutable to most Baptists and other Free Church Christians. When, for example, the way "Responses" considers the doctrine of *Lumen Gentium* that "the Church of Christ subsists in the Catholic Church," it seems to suggest a return to a pre–Vatican II ecclesiology.[117] From the range of contested interpretations, it is clear that there are those who would wish to push toward greater exclusivity. But it may be more likely that the CDF was actually making the reverse move by quietly distancing itself from recent revisionists, who argued that "subsist" entails full, exclusive, robust, undifferentiated, and exhaustive identity between the church of Jesus Christ and the Catholic Church.[118] This bit of welcome news eluded most Baptists. Only a more sophisticated hermeneutic of reform, one that accounts for a process of development and reformulation and includes both *ressourcement* and *aggiornamento*, can enable readers to detect such subtle nuances.

Though Baptists are happy to receive insight from this Catholic way of realizing fuller catholicity, too few possess the theological and historical resources to employ it wisely. Catholics might ask how they can help their Baptist sisters and brothers become better ecumenical conversation partners. Wondering about what Baptists can learn from this Catholic way of expressing catholicity raises the question of whether there is a Baptist style of catholicity. For it is not only Catholics who must seek to embody the unity for which Jesus prayed. Baptists also must ask what it might mean to realize the Lord's petition "that they all may be one . . . so that the world may believe" (John 17:21). If all Christians have a fundamental duty to display this unity, Other Baptists wonder what might be ways of realizing it. James William McClendon Jr. and John Howard Yoder have suggested that there is a Free Church or baptist style of Christian life that leads to greater unity.[119]

McClendon and Yoder describe three ways the word "catholic" has been used from the apostolic era to the present. The first, or catholic$_1$, denotes a quality in congregations of being whole, typical, or ordinary.

---

[117] Sullivan, "Meaning of *Subsistit in*."

[118] Jared Wicks, "Questions and Answers on the New Responses of the Congregation for the Doctrine of the Faith," *Ecumenical Trends* 36, no. 7 (2007): 97–112. See also Wicks, "Not-So-Fully Church: The Pope's Message to Protestants—and Catholics," *Christian Century*, August 21, 2007, 9–11. Wicks mentions Alexandra von Teuffenbach and Karl Becker as two of the revisionists the CDF statement was likely meant to address.

[119] James Wm. McClendon Jr. and John Howard Yoder, "Christian Identity in Ecumenical Perspective: A Response to David Wayne Layman," *Journal of Ecumenical Studies* 27, no. 3 (1990): 562. Yoder uses the terms "believers church" and "Free Church" interchangeably, just as McClendon uses "baptist" in lower case to include the wide range of Christian communities that descend from the Radical Reformation.

It consists not only of beliefs and convictions but practices and refers to a way of living. The second, or catholic$_2$, might be translated ecumenical (*oikoumene*) and signifies the sense of catholicity shared by all Christian churches. The third, or catholic$_3$, describes its ecclesial use in the "Roman" Catholic Church.[120] It is implied in the words of Vatican II's decree on ecumenism, *Unitatis Redintegratio*, which states that a lack of unity among Christians "openly contradicts the will of Christ, scandalizes the world, and damages the holy cause of preaching the Gospel to every creature."[121] Yet McClendon and Yoder suggest that the Catholic way of ecumenism assumes that "the Catholic Church as the Ecumenical Church is the goal that the modern ecumenical movement pursues, that Scripture enjoins, that Christ our Lord petitioned in prayer."[122] This Catholic approach suggests that the path to unity comes through a greater understanding of catholic$_3$, but the Baptist way of seeking greater unity comes through a deeper understanding of the communal practices (catholic$_1$) that from the beginning marked the whole or ordinary Christianity of the church. The Baptist heritage thus lays legitimate (though not uncontested) claim to the legacy called catholic$_1$—that is, to the display of "elements of sanctification and of truth" that mark the "ordinary" Christianity of the church.[123] In the process of describing the Baptist vision of catholicity, the question changes from "Who has the truer deposit of faith?" to "How shall we proceed in the search to locate the church catholic$_2$ that we confess?" The typical Baptist answer is for gathered communities to engage in discerning, reconciling dialogue.[124]

This search for greater catholicity was at work in the first-century churches of Samaria (Acts 9:4-25) and Antioch (Acts 11:19-26). The church of Samaria had its origin in the preaching of Philip (Acts 8:12), who though not an apostle was one of the seven, so chosen because he was "full of the Spirit and of wisdom" (Acts 6:5). The Samaritans enthusiastically received Philip's message. But though they heard an authentic proclamation of the gospel and received Christian baptism from Philip, they did not receive the Holy Spirit (Acts 8:15). When the Jerusalem church heard of the events, they sent Peter and John to Samaria. Only after the apostles prayed and laid their hands on the Samaritans did they receive the Spirit (Acts 8:17). It is a complicated story that defies simple explanations.

---

[120] McClendon and Yoder, "Christian Identity in Ecumenical Perspective," 562–63.

[121] *Unitatis Redintegratio* 1.1, *Vatican Council II*, 1:452.

[122] McClendon and Yoder, "Christian Identity in Ecumenical Perspective," 564.

[123] McClendon and Yoder, "Christian Identity in Ecumenical Perspective," 572; and *Lumen Gentium* 8.2, *Vatican Council II*, 1:357.

[124] McClendon and Yoder, "Christian Identity in Ecumenical Perspective," 578.

The reasons the baptism they received at the hands of Philip was regarded as so defective and the Spirit was withheld under conditions that it would be expected are not immediately apparent. There is no clear presumption in this text or in the rest of Acts that the laying on of hands must accompany every baptism to ensure its validity. Nor is there a stated requirement that an apostle must be the actual administrator of the rite. Yet the Spirit was graciously bestowed when the apostles were reconciled with Philip and the Samaritans were received by the Jerusalem church. The laying on of hands thus signifies fellowship among the churches as well as the gift of the Spirit.[125]

The founding of the church in Antioch was the result of the witness of humble Hellenistic Christians scattered after the persecution of Stephen (Acts 11:19-20). Yet despite its lack of apostolic origins, there is no suggestion that it was defective in its constitution or gifts. Indeed, when Barnabas, as a messenger of the church in Jerusalem, arrived in Antioch, he witnessed "the grace of God" present among them (Acts 11:23) and found the practice of evangelism there advanced beyond the church in Jerusalem (Acts 11:21). Though he was "full of the Holy Spirit and faith" (Acts 11:24), there is not a hint that Barnabas was sent to repair their baptism or lay hands on them so that they might receive the Spirit. The gist of his appeal was that they should "remain faithful to the Lord with steadfast devotion" (Acts 11:23). Here the church in Antioch has a gift for the church in Jerusalem, and by their mutual exchange and conversation the churches realize a greater sense of *oikoumene* (catholic$_2$), as the witness of the risen Lord is extended from Jerusalem to "Judea and Samaria and to the end of the earth" (Acts 1:8). Because the apostles were excluded from this widening catholicity (Acts 8:1), the church of Jerusalem stood in need of receiving instruction on evangelism from the church at Antioch, but the church in Antioch also received the approval and blessing of the church in Jerusalem, resulting in a wider sense of fellowship between the churches.[126]

These stories illustrate what the early Baptists envisioned when they described themselves as committed "to walk by one and the same rule, and by all means convenient to have the counsel and help one of another in all needful affairs of the church, as members of one body in the common faith under Christ their only head."[127] Such a vision holds "the balance

---

[125] G. R. Beasley-Murray, *Baptism in the New Testament* (Grand Rapids: Eerdmans, 1962/1990), 112–17.

[126] Beasley-Murray, *Baptism in the New Testament*, 114–16.

[127] First London Confession XLVII, in Lumpkin, *Baptist Confessions of Faith*, 168–69.

between the privileges of the local church on the one hand, and on the other the necessity to seek the guidance of God from others."[128] This is the Baptist way of "counsel and help," which entails mutual exchange and conversation in order to display the ordinary faith (catholic$_1$) that characterized the wider communion of churches from the beginning (catholic$_2$). Catholicity is a two-way street, with mutual exchange and expressions of gifts and graces. Baptists might ask whether they can better and more fully realize the unity for which the Lord prayed by seeking the path aimed toward catholic$_3$ with their Catholic sisters and brothers. And Catholics might ask whether they are prepared to face the challenges and receive the gifts that may come through discerning, reconciling dialogue with the gathered churches of the Baptists. The answer to these questions and to the renewal of catholicity each path envisions lies not in the recovery of a lost past but in pilgrimage (*ecclesiolae in via*) together, seeking along the way to understand more fully what it means for the churches to be the church.

Subsistit in Ecclesiae Baptisticae?

Other Baptists believe that *embracing a greater sense of catholicity* offers hope of being sustained in the ecclesial pilgrimage through the wilderness of life after Christendom. They draw from the fuller catholicity affirmed by the early Baptists expressed in The Orthodox Creed, which stated that as Israel "had the manna to nourish them in the wilderness to Canaan; so have we the sacraments, to nourish us in the church, and in our wilderness-condition."[129] Such a vision is not a forced either-or choice between the Baptist heritage and the Catholic faith. It is a both-and approach that envisions Baptists as a pilgrim community of contested convictions within the church catholic. Contestation within the tradition is not a good in itself but is "a state of affairs that is necessitated by the current failures of the church to embody the unity that is an eschatological mark of the church." Such difference can even be a step toward unity, but only if it is "pursued as a conversation that requires contestation because of the present participation of the church in the fallen nature of humanity en route to the eschatological realization of the unity of the church."[130]

---

[128] Fiddes, *Tracks and Traces*, 55. I am grateful to Ian Randall for this way of describing local catholicity in his excellent "'Counsel and Help': European Baptists and Wider Baptist Fellowship" (paper presented at a symposium on the local church at the German Baptist Seminary in Elstal, March 21–24, 2007).

[129] Orthodox Creed XIX, in Lumpkin, *Baptist Confessions of Faith*, 311–12.

[130] Steven R. Harmon, *Towards Baptist Catholicity: Essays on Tradition and the Baptist Vision* (Milton Keynes, U.K.: Paternoster, 2006), 66. Harmon commends Catholics for embodying

Baptists who seek to give fuller expression to the catholicity of the faith, while at the same time maintaining a contesting voice, must acknowledge the fundamental ambiguity of such a position. Yet some may still remain suspicious, believing "sectarian orthodoxy" to be "deeply incoherent."[131]

Other Baptists, however, emphatically deny that their ecclesial vision is sectarian, but rather than crossing the Tiber they choose to maintain their catholicity as Baptists.[132] They resonate with the catholicity of many early Baptists and with other Other Baptists like Daniel Turner, an eighteenth-century English Baptist minister who described Baptists as a "small porch" annexed to the "grand temple" of the whole church.[133] With Turner's leadership, the Baptists in Oxford denominated themselves "a Protestant Catholic Church of Christ," understanding their congregation, with all true gospel churches, to belong to the whole church.[134] Toward just such an ecclesial reality, Other Baptists affirm that their congregations are fully church, that the catholic church subsists in them, and their celebrations of the Lord's Supper are indeed valid celebrations of the Eucharist in which Christ is present when they gather in his name, recount the words of institution and the story of his Passion, re-present his sacrificial work, and participate in that which the bread and wine signify. In the meantime, Other Baptists must see to it that there is enough catholicity existing among them to be recognized by Christians within

---

the practice of conciliar contestation, which is complementary with the proposal of Baptists as a community of dissent within the church catholic, in his "*Dei Verbum* §9 in Baptist Perspective," *Ecclesiology* 5, no. 3 (2009): 299–321.

[131] Richard John Neuhaus, "The Unhappy Fate of Optional Orthodoxy," *First Things* 69 (1997): 57–60. Neuhaus declaimed that "where orthodoxy is optional, orthodoxy will sooner or later be proscribed." For a counterexample to the suspicion of Neuhaus, see the forum in which Richard Crane, Nicholas M. Healy, Elizabeth Newman, and Maureen H. O'Connell express appreciation for the ecclesial vision of Harmon's *Towards Baptist Catholicity* while also expressing concerns about the prospects of Baptists becoming more fully catholic, in their "A Book Symposium on Steven R. Harmon, *Towards Baptist Catholicity*," *Pro Ecclesia* 18, no. 4 (2009): 367–92.

[132] Here Other Baptists echo the resolute protest of Lutheran evangelical catholic James Nuechterlein, "In Defense of Sectarian Catholicity," *First Things* 69 (1997): 12–13.

[133] Daniel Turner, *Charity the Bond of Perfection. A Sermon, The Substance of which was Preached at Oxford, November 16, 1780. On Occasion of the Re-establishment of a Christian Church of Protestant Dissenters in that City; with a Brief Account of the State of the Society, and the Plan and Manner of their Settlement* (Oxford: J. Buckland, 1780), quoted in Paul S. Fiddes, "Daniel Turner and a Theology of the Church Universal," in *Pulpit and People: Studies in Eighteenth-Century Baptist Life and Thought*, ed. John H. Y. Briggs (Milton Keynes, U.K.: Paternoster, 2009), 113.

[134] This phrase appears in the church covenant of congregation, now the New Road Baptist Church in Oxford, which was most likely drafted by Turner. A text of the covenant may be found in Turner, *Charity the Bond of Perfection*, 20–22; see also Rosie Chadwick, ed., *A Protestant Catholic Church of Christ: Essays on the History and Life of New Road Baptist Church, Oxford* (Oxford: Alden, 2003), 401–3.

the wider church.[135] Other Baptists want to see to it that there is sufficient catholicity in their ecclesial communities for it to be recognized that the church of Jesus Christ subsists in their congregations. They want to know whether it might be that important elements of the one, holy, catholic, and apostolic church that have been widely neglected or ignored are present and operative in gathered communities of the Baptists. And they want to know how to understand their historical pilgrimage so as to bear witness to "Jerusalem above" as "our mother" (Gal 4:26).[136]

Other Baptists confess *the church is one*. The churches, however, are divided, and their division is a great scandal that hinders the witness of each and all. The divisions are not simply between Lutherans and Catholics or Methodists and Baptists. The denominational families are as deeply divided among themselves as against one another, and ecumenical progress toward the realization of greater unity looks ever less likely. Separation among the churches is a tragic reality resulting in separation from the whole of Christ and the fullness of the Spirit. Yet even though the churches are divided, the church is not. These divisions are historical, not ontological. If the church were truly divided, there would be, indeed there could be, no church. Despite the division of the churches, the church is one because it is gathered by one Spirit, serves one Lord, confesses one faith, and practices one baptism (Eph 4:4-5). As Carlyle Marney thundered in his May 22, 1961, address to the Pastors' Conference of the SBC,

> What if we sectarians are already church? What if "we are not divided"? What if our unity does not hang on some preliminary to *parousia* to occur here and soon? What if our unity is not even a hybrid eschatological hope? What if we have never *been* divided? What if our unity is something not in our power to divide because it does not rise in us? What if the unity of the faith that we are to keep is not in men but somewhere else? What if our oneness is given? What if God *hath* made both one and hath broken down the wall of partition between us? What if that holy feeling of affection we have known for men behind other fences is real and we are truly brothers? What if our oneness is

---

[135] Steven R. Harmon, "Why Baptist Catholicity, and by What Authority?" *Pro Ecclesia* 18, no. 4 (2009): 392.

[136] The Niceno-Constantinopolitan Creed, in Jaroslav Pelikan and Valerie Hotchkiss, eds., *Creeds and Confessions of Faith in the Christian Tradition* (New Haven, Conn.: Yale University Press, 2004), 1:162–63. In an earlier essay, I attempted to answer these questions by turning the same four *notae*. Curtis W. Freeman, "A Confession for Catholic Baptists," in *Ties That Bind: Life Together in the Baptist Vision*, ed. Gary A. Furr and Curtis W. Freeman (Macon, Ga.: Smyth & Helwys, 1994), 87–94. See also Harmon, *Towards Baptist Catholicity*, 3.

something we may sin against and deny, but cannot divide? What if the oneness of faith is the oneness of the body that is Christ?[137]

But as Marney knew, there is no "what if?" when it comes to the unity of the church. Either the church is one, or it is not the church at all. Yet, because the unity of the church is not empirically evident, it must be confessed as a matter of faith. Contestation, then, is not in itself a good, though it can serve the good, albeit in proximate ways, if and only if it is understood as a step toward the realization of the ultimate unity of the church. But, where the Baptist tradition of dissent devolves into the celebration of diversity, multiplicity, or plurality as a foundational principle of alliances and unions, it builds on wood, hay, and stubble and belies the unity and indeed the very existence of the church.[138]

Thus the divided churches may confess the oneness of the church knowing that the unbroken fullness of communion with the Father, through the Son, and in the Spirit is not possible until the church reaches its heavenly rest. Yet, in union with Christ and indwelt by the Spirit, the church is already one. Living into this unity in the already-but-not-yet time requires active waiting. But the churches must resist the temptation of thinking that an eye fixed on the eschatological gathering of the whole people of God inevitably engenders the quietist supposition that all signs of visible unity must be deferred to the end. Indeed it is just as mistaken to conceive of the church's unity as a reality postponed for the eschaton as it is to lay claim to a communion that is overly realized in history.[139] The

---

[137] Carlyle Marney, "The Unity of the Faith," Pastors' Conference, Southern Baptist Convention, May 22, 1961, in *The Recovery of the Church* (unpublished manuscript), ch. 1, Carlyle Marney Papers, David M. Rubenstein Rare Book & Manuscript Library, Duke University, Durham, N.C.

[138] Karl Barth, *Church Dogmatics* IV/1 (Edinburgh: T&T Clark, 1956), 668–85; and Barth, *The Church and the Churches* (Grand Rapids: Eerdmans, 1936/2005), 5–59. As James Wm. McClendon Jr. and James M. Smith argue, the celebration of diversity as a strategy of resisting convictional imperialism often results in the incoherent viewpoint of cultural relativism that regards convictional differences as an "inevitable, ineradicable, and ultimate fact of human existence and denies the existence of any common elements relevant to mutual understanding." McClendon and Smith, *Convictions: Defusing Religious Relativism*, rev. ed. (Valley Forge, Pa.: Trinity International, 1994), 8.

[139] Steven R. Harmon, "Baptists, Praying for Unity, and the Eschatology of Ecumenism," in *A Century of Prayer for Christian Unity*, ed. Catherine E. Clifford (Grand Rapids: Eerdmans, 2009), 119–20. Miroslav Volf charges Orthodox theologian John Zizioulas with a eucharistic communion ecclesiology that results in an overrealized eschatology. Volf, *After Our Likeness*, 101. Volf consequently pushes the unity and catholicity of the church so far toward the horizon of "the eschatological gathering of the whole people of God" that it is difficult to discern how such "broken" unity and "partial" catholicity in gathered communities signifies and participates in the fullness of the church in heavenly communion (268–69). My chapter "A Confession for Catholic Baptists" tilted perhaps a bit too far toward eschatological unity, although in

unity signified by the church in its earthly pilgrimage, while it can never be fully realized, can be anticipated in real ways by the pilgrim people of God in communion with the saints at rest.[140] The critical task, then, is to discern visible signs of the one Lord, one faith, and one baptism not to achieve or create unity but to display it and thus the subsistence of the one church in history. This raises the question of how Baptists might contribute to a fuller display of the church.

Theologians working on Catholic ecclesiology might benefit from reading Baptist theology. Although the constitutional disestablishment of religion requires Catholicism in the United States to be one of many Free Churches, Catholic theology has often presumed a Constantinian polity that portrays themselves as "the One True Church" and "worthy of support by and laden with authority over the state (although other sects and ecclesial bodies might be tolerated)."[141] Catholic life and thought "is riddled with Constantinian presumptions."[142] As a result, Catholic ecclesiology has reached an impasse between "unity" and "uniformity." Catholics have to choose. They "can have uniformity on an authoritarian Catholics United for the Faith model by paying the price of disunity," or "they can have the nominal unity a liberal model provides by paying the price of internal incoherence." But it must be recognized that "the marriage of uniformity and unity possible in a Constantinian polity has dissolved as that polity has died."[143] By attending to the theology of the Baptists and the other marginalized traditions of the Free Churches, Catholics might find a third way beyond this impasse that allows for "diversity in unity." The theology of James McClendon might be helpful to Catholics in understanding what it means to be a true and Free Church in a free society.[144] Such an ecclesiological transformation requires the disavowal of constantinianism, with its presumptions of power that obstruct rather than extend the mission of the

---

that piece I was attempting to provide an account for the appropriation of spiritual practices that might display the unity of the church, in Furr and Freeman, *Ties That Bind*, 88.

[140] *Lumen Gentium* §§48–51, *Vatican Council II*, 1:407–13.

[141] Terrence W. Tilley, "Why American Catholic Theologians Should Read 'Baptist' Theology," *Horizons* 14, no. 1 (1987): 129.

[142] Tilley, "Why American Catholic Theologians Should Read 'Baptist' Theology," 130. Tilley rightly points out that although *Dignitatis Humanae* affirmed religious freedom as a political human right and the freedom of the church in carrying out its mission, it did not (nor did any other documents from Vatican II) oppose state establishment of religion on theological or practical grounds (129).

[143] Tilley, "Why American Catholic Theologians Should Read 'Baptist' Theology," 137.

[144] Tilley, "Why American Catholic Theologians Should Read 'Baptist' Theology," 137. See esp. James Wm. McClendon Jr., *Ethics: Systematic Theology: Volume I* (Nashville: Abingdon Press, 1986), 73–75, 176; and *Ethics: Systematic Theology: Volume I* (Waco, Tex.: Baylor University Press, 2012), 168, 181–82.

church.[145] Disavowing a quest for sacred power and living faithfully under the rule of Christ is a way for Baptists to witness to what it means for the churches to be the one church of Jesus Christ.

Other Baptists confess that *the one church is also holy* because by the one Holy Spirit many members are baptized into the one body of Jesus Christ (1 Cor 12:13). Recognizing the marks of the church "is not merely a question of the continuity of the word—the maintenance of the original doctrine—but also of the continuity of a life; that is life flowing from the Holy Ghost."[146] Here Baptists stand in the stream of a pentecostal ecclesiology that emphasizes the presence and power of the Holy Spirit as a mark of the true church.[147] Yet the holiness of the church is neither a quantitative sum of virtuous character nor moral excellence exemplified by the individual members but is rather a qualitative distinctive made possible by participation in the *koinonia* of the Holy Spirit that indwells the church.[148] When its individual members fall into sin and even when as a community it is unfaithful and in need of reformation and renewal, the church by virtue of its union with Christ and the indwelling presence of the Spirit remains holy. As Karl Barth observed, the church may become a beggar, a shopkeeper, or a harlot, but it is still and always the bride of Christ.[149]

The doctrine of the church's holiness was tested to the limits in the fourth century by the Donatist churches in North Africa who conceived of holiness in terms of moral conduct over against the Catholics who understood holiness as a sacramental effect. The Donatists maintained that Catholic purity was tainted by the toleration of unfaithful bishops who surrendered the Scriptures during the persecution of Diocletian (A.D. 303–305).[150] In response, Augustine of Hippo reconciled the Donatist emphasis of a faithful church with the Catholic ecclesiology of a sacramental communion. Drawing from the African theologian Tyconius, Augustine provided the doctrinal formulation for Catholic ecclesiology

---

[145] Nigel Goring Wright, *Disavowing Constantine: Mission, Church and Social Order in the Theologies of John Howard Yoder and Jürgen Moltmann* (Carlisle, U.K.: Paternoster, 2000), 9; and Wright, *Free Church, Free State*, 270–79.

[146] Emil Brunner, *The Misunderstanding of the Church*, trans. Harold Knight (Philadelphia: Westminster, 1953), 47.

[147] Lesslie Newbigin, *The Household of God* (London: SCM Press, 1953), 87–88. Newbigin characterized Catholic ecclesiology as emphasizing continuity with apostolic faith and practice and Protestant ecclesiology as emphasizing the correct proclamation of the Word and proper administration of the sacraments.

[148] Freeman, "Confession for Catholic Baptists," in Furr and Freeman, *Ties That Bind*, 89.

[149] Barth, *Church Dogmatics* IV/1, 691.

[150] W. H. C. Frend, *The Donatist Church: A Movement of Protest in Roman North Africa* (Oxford: Clarendon, 1952), 10.

by distinguishing between "the true and the mixed body of the Lord."[151] Tyconius was not a typical Donatist because he did not believe the Donatists were the only true church but part of the church catholic, even though they were not in communion with the Catholics. Augustine adapted Tyconius' notion of the Lord's *corpore biparto* to conceive of the church as a *corpore permixto*, which contained both wheat and chaff (Matt 13:24-30).[152] The mixed body is the church as it is (*Ecclesia est qualis nunc est*); the unmixed body is the church as it will be (*Ecclesia est qualis tunc erit*).[153] Only at the winnowing out on judgment day will the holiness of the church be visible.[154] Holiness then, like unity, is an eschatological mark.

Some critics have contended that Baptist ecclesiology is simply Donatism revived. The former separatist Henoch Clapham dismissed all rebaptizers as Donatists who "have synned that fearfull and horible syn" against the Holy Ghost and "do build stubble, strawe, tymber" rather than gold, silver, and precious stones of the one and holy church.[155] Admittedly, the early Baptist emphasis on the visible church has at times tended toward the moralism of Donatism. Yet Other Baptists have attempted to distinguish the visible church from the invisible church rather than collapsing them into one another. They further maintain that though the local congregation is wholly the church, it is not the whole of the church. Thus the Baptist sense of local catholicity mitigates their identification as Donatists.[156]

---

[151] It is accepted that Augustine adapted his two-city analogy from Tyconius, though much of Tyconius' commentary on the Apocalypse has been lost. Writing in his commentary on Revelation in the eighth century, Saint Beatus of Liebana drew from Tyconius: "Behold two cities, the city of God and the city of the Devil" (*Ecce dua ciuitates, unam Dei et unam diaboli*). Beatus, *Sancti beati a liebana commentarius in Apocalypsin* (Rome: Typis Officinae Polygraphicae, 1985), 2:2296. The Turin fragment of Tyconius' Revelation commentary states, "There are two people [*populi*] in the church: there is that part that is of God [*pars Dei*] furnished with light and that part that is of the devil [*pars diaboli*] surrounded by the obscurities of darkness." *Tyconii Afri in Apocalypsis* §172, in *The Turin Fragments of Tyconius' Commentary on Revelation*, ed. Francesco Lo Bue (Cambridge: Cambridge University Press, 1963), 96.

[152] Augustine, *On Christian Doctrine* 3.32, in *A Select Library of the Nicene and Post-Nicene Fathers of the Christian Church*, ed. Philip Schaff, trans. J. F. Shaw (Grand Rapids: Eerdmans, 1977), 2:569; see also *On Christian Doctrine*, Patrologia Latina 34 (Paris: J. P. Migne, 1887), 82.

[153] Augustine, *City of God* 20.9, in *The City of God, Books XVII–XXII*, Fathers of the Church 24, trans. Gerald G. Walsh (Washington, D.C.: Catholic University of America Press, 1954), 276; and see also *City of God*, Patrologia Latina 41 (Paris: J. P. Migne, 1900), 673.

[154] Augustine, *City of God* 20.5, in *The City of God, Books XVII–XXII* (trans. Walsh), 257.

[155] Henoch Clapham, *The Syn, Against the Holy Ghoste* (Amsterdam, 1598), 7. Against the Anabaptist who "baptiseth himselfe . . . and then he baptiseth another," Clapman appealed to Augustine, who confuted "rebaptization." Clapham, *Antidoton; or, A Soveraigne Remedie Against Schisme and Heresie* (London: John Wolfe, 1600), 33.

[156] Timothy George argues similarly that John Robinson and English Separatism was not "Donatism writ English," in his *John Robinson and the English Separatist Tradition*, 100–105.

Baptists, however, could take more concrete steps toward such an account of holiness.

For example, there are no clear fundamental reasons that would prohibit Baptists from affirming the Joint Declaration on the Doctrine of Justification with the Lutherans, Catholics, and Methodists.[157] Indeed, the joint declaration provides an excellent basis for theological conversations between Baptists and Catholics on justification, although the doctrines of *simil justus et peccator* and the criteriological position of justification as the "first and chief article" would be less problematic for Baptists than for Lutherans. The sacramental understanding of the ordinances and the theological justification of infant baptism, both of which are assumed in the consensus affirmations of the joint declaration, are more difficult matters for Baptists.[158] It is nevertheless conceivable that, through the joint declaration's principle of differentiated consensus, Baptists might find a way to affirm believer's baptism by immersion not as a Baptist distinctive but as a catholic practice maintained by Baptists in hope that one day it will be fully received within the one, holy church. In so doing Baptists would take a huge step toward demonstrating that they affirm with their sister churches the conviction that the church is holy "because Christ himself is our righteousness, in which we share through the Holy Spirit in accord with the will of the Father."[159]

Other Baptists affirm that *the church that is one and holy is also catholic* every time they lift their voices to sing "elect from every nation yet one o'er all the earth."[160] This quantitative sense of catholicity as a universally inclusive fellowship spread throughout the world was crucial in Augustine's critique of the Donatists for lacking catholicity, precisely because they were not in communion with churches outside of Africa. Yet there is a deeper qualitative catholicity that names the fullness of Christ and the gifts of Spirit that are determinative of the church's being. From the day of Pentecost, the church was catholic both quantitatively as a transnational fellowship and qualitatively as a community gifted by the Holy Spirit. Catholicity is thus a mark of the church established by Christ and

---

[157] The Lutheran World Federation and the Catholic Church, Joint Declaration on the Doctrine of Justification, accessed February 8, 2010, http://www.vatican.va/roman_curia/pontifical_councils/chrstuni/documents/rc_pc_chrstuni_doc_31101999_cath-luth-joint-declaration_en.html. The World Methodist Council affirmed the joint declaration in 2006.

[158] Tarmo Toom, "Baptists on Justification: Can We Join the Joint Declaration on the Doctrine of Justification?" *Pro Ecclesia* 13, no. 3 (2003): 305.

[159] Joint Declaration on the Doctrine of Justification, 3.15.

[160] Samuel Stone, "The Church's One Foundation" (no. 236), in *The Baptist Hymnal* (Nashville: Convention Press, 1975).

gathered by the Spirit. The confession of catholicity has been maintained among Catholics and Protestants, although too often Free Churches have abandoned it because they mistakenly considered it to be an attribute of the Roman Church. Sometimes they have gone so far as to describe their communities as a-catholic. Yet, by forsaking the conviction of catholicity out of a fear of "catholic tendencies," they risk alienation from the very being of the community in communion with Christ through the Spirit that they wrongly disavow. In this sense it is correct to say that any claim to churchly identity must include the mark of catholicity, for "where it is not 'catholic,' it is not the true church, the church of Jesus Christ," for "a church is catholic or it is not the church."[161]

The contestation of early Baptists caused them to internalize habits of suspicion about catholicity into its tradition. For example, The Second London Confession, signed by thirty-seven Baptist ministers in 1688, declared that the pope is "that Antichrist, that Man of sin, a Son of perdition, that exalteth himself in the Church against Christ, and all that is called God; whom the Lord shall destroy with the brightness of his coming."[162] That all but the last phrase was borrowed almost word for word from The Westminster Confession of 1646 indicates that the Baptists were probably impelled to demonstrate their agreement with fellow Puritans as much as they were interested in expressing their animus against Catholics.[163] Nevertheless, shrill caricatures like this one became entrenched in the doctrinal tradition, even when they are latent in the collective memory. These old anti-Catholic spirits were conjured up anew when R. Albert Mohler, president of the Southern Baptist Theological Seminary, intoned on March 22, 2000, for *Larry King Live* that the pope holds a false office, leads a false church, and teaches a false gospel.[164] His pre–Vatican II predecessor, E. Y. Mullins, identified Catholicism as an example of a deficient proxy religion, declaiming that "Romanism asserts at every point the soul's incompetency."[165] B. H. Carroll, founding president of Southwestern Baptist Theological Seminary, promoted a view held by many of the earliest Baptists from John Smyth to Roger Williams that identified

---

[161] Barth, *Church Dogmatics* IV/1, 702.

[162] Second London Confession XXVI.4, in Lumpkin, *Baptist Confessions of Faith*, 286.

[163] The rejection of Antichrist was not limited to the extreme millenarian minority but was defended by all the Protestant archbishops of Canterbury from Cranmer to Abbot and was regularly defended in the universities. See Anthony Milton, *Catholic and Reformed: The Roman and Protestant Churches in English Protestant Thought, 1600–1640* (Cambridge: Cambridge University Press, 1995), 93–127.

[164] "Mohler Calls Catholicism False Church," *Baptist Standard*, April 3, 2000.

[165] E. Y. Mullins, *The Axioms of Religion* (Philadelphia: Judson Press, 1908), 60.

the Catholic Church with the Whore of Babylon described in the Book of Revelation.[166]

The Baptist proclivity for anti-Catholicism comes out in less obvious ways too. The historic Baptist stance of religious liberty has often been little more than a thin disguise for attack rhetoric. The May 16, 1920, address by George W. Truett, delivered from the east steps of the nation's capitol is widely cited as a classic statement on Baptist identity. One of the most respected voices in Baptist life at the time, Truett defined the Baptist position by invoking oppositional rhetoric. He asserted that while Baptists defend the full liberty of conscience, the Catholic Church thrusts "all its complex and cumbrous machinery between the soul and God, prescribing beliefs, claiming to exercise the power of the keys, and to control the channels of grace," adding that "all such lording it over the consciences of men is to the Baptist mind a ghastly tyranny in the realm of the soul and tends to frustrate the grace of God, to destroy freedom of conscience, and to hinder terribly the coming of the Kingdom of God."[167] So in 1971 when Southern Baptists passed a resolution calling members "to work for legislation that will allow the possibility of abortion under such conditions as rape, incest, clear evidence of severe fetal deformity, and carefully ascertained evidence of the likelihood of damage to the emotional, mental, and physical health of the mother," who could doubt they were guided by the conviction that if the Catholics were against abortion, then Baptists should probably be for it?[168]

Protestants and Catholics have already taken steps in personal conversation and by binding agreement to acknowledge that their mutual condemnations "are no longer applicable."[169] The process began by coming

---

[166] Benajah Harvey Carroll, *The Book of Revelation* (New York: Fleming H. Revell, 1913).

[167] George W. Truett, *Baptists and Religious Liberty* (Nashville: Baptist Sunday School Board, 1920), 3–36, reprinted in *Christian Ethics Today* 7, no. 1 (2001), accessed November 25, 2011, http://christianethicstoday.com/cetart/index.cfm?fuseaction=Articles.main&ArtID=266. It is noteworthy that H. Leon McBeth published Truett's speech, omitting the sections "Exact Opposite of Catholicism," "Papal Infallibility or the New Testament," and "Direct Individual Approach to God," which contain the anti-Catholic references, in his *A Sourcebook for Baptist Heritage* (Nashville: Broadman, 1990), 467–77. Joseph Early Jr., ed., omits the same sections of Truett's speech in *Truett Readings in Baptist History: Four Centuries of Selected Documents* (Nashville: B&H, 2008), 145–52.

[168] "Resolution no. 4—on Abortion," in *Annual of the Southern Baptist Convention*, June 1–3, 1971 (Nashville: Executive Committee, Southern Baptist Convention, 1971), 72. After the *Roe v. Wade* decision, the SBC adopted a resolution at the 1974 meeting that reaffirmed the 1971 resolution, which "reflected a middle ground between the extreme of abortion on demand and the opposite extreme of all abortion as murder." "Resolution No. 5—on Abortion and Sanctity of Human Life," *Annual of the Southern Baptist Convention*, June 11–13, 1974 (Nashville: Executive Committee, Southern Baptist Convention, 1974), 76.

[169] "Official Documents of the Joint Ecumenical Commission with Regard to the

to terms with their history, which enabled them to see the old doctrines in new light. It is surely time for Baptists to reconsider their controverted convictions about all things catholic. Anyone who does so carefully will discover that these historical pronouncements were formulated in reaction to the Council of Trent or Vatican I and do not accurately describe the present-day Catholic Church. Such a reappraisal might liberate Baptists from medieval stereotypes and modern caricatures so that they might be able to recognize and appreciate the subsistence of catholicity in the Catholic Church and foster catholicity in their own fellowship. The challenges of such a proposal became apparent in a seminar of Baptist doctoral students that gathered to discuss the book *Towards Baptist Catholicity*. After expressing appreciation for the tone and the content of the book, one of the participants suggested that the message might be better received if the word "catholic" had been omitted. It is reminiscent of another time when an evangelical press expressed interest in reprinting the book *The Peaceable Kingdom*.[170] After praising the book, the publisher said they would need to "take out the parts on pacifism." The book was never republished. It would seem that there is at least as much difficulty getting Baptists to think about catholicity as getting evangelicals to think about peace. But, if the Baptist claim that the church of Jesus Christ subsists in gathered communities and wider associations outside the Catholic Church is to make any sense at all, they cannot remain anticatholic or even a-catholic. Baptists must learn to embrace catholicity as sign of the one and holy church. For either a church is catholic or it is not the church.

Other Baptists affirm with the ancient ecumenical creed that *the church that is one, holy, and catholic is also apostolic*. The mark of apostolicity means that the church today lives in continuity with the faith and practice of the apostolic community. From the early centuries of Christianity, the apostolic succession of ministry was recognized as a manifestation of faithfulness to the apostolic tradition.[171] The succession of ministers is thus a sign of continuity with the apostolic church. Yet apostolicity cannot

---

Assignment 'The Condemnations in the Protestant Confessions and in the Doctrinal Decisions of the Council of Trent Which No Longer Apply to Our Partner Today,'" May 6–7, 1981, in Karl Lehmann and Wolfhart Pannenberg, eds., *The Condemnations of the Reformation Era: Do They Still Divide?* (Minneapolis: Fortress, 1990), 168–69; Joint Declaration on the Doctrine of Justification, 5.41–42.

[170] Stanley Hauerwas, *The Peaceable Kingdom* (Notre Dame, Ind.: University of Notre Dame Press, 1983).

[171] Irenaeus, *Against Heresies*, 3.3.1, in *The Ante-Nicene Fathers* (Grand Rapids: Eerdmans, 1979), 1:415. Irenaeus does not limit the succession of ministry to the bishops, but includes presbyters as a communal sign of continuity with apostolic faith and practice; *Against Heresies* 3.2.1, 4.26.2, in *Ante-Nicene Fathers*, 1:415, 497.

be reduced to historical continuity. It is a confession of faith, not merely a statement of fact, and so apostolicity may be affirmed but not proven. Some Baptists have countered with their own version of apostolic succession by asserting that the one true church Christ established was Baptist in its membership, ordinances, polity, and discipline. The Landmarkers contended that these apostolic churches have descended in uninterrupted succession from the days of the first Baptist—John.[172] All "paedobaptist" Protestant denominations, they argued, were offspring of the apostate Roman Catholic Church. Landmarkers maintained that though Baptist churches as the manifestation of apostolic faith and practice have persisted since the time of the John the Baptist, they have been persecuted by the apostate church and forced underground throughout most of history. The succession of these apostolic churches, they argue, may be traced by the crimson trail of blood.[173]

Admittedly, few Baptists embrace the trail of blood succession myth, but it is also the case that more than a few remain suspicious of the thought that apostolic Christianity is actively present outside baptistic communities, and fewer still are open to the possibility that there is genuine apostolicity and ecclesiality in the Catholic Church.[174] Many Baptists have followed the Protestant formulation that identifies apostolicity as "wherever we see the Word of God purely preached and heard and the sacraments administered according to Christ's institution."[175] But Other Baptists, in sympathy with McClendon's account of "the baptist vision," have equated the Scripture principle with apostolicity as a hermeneutical standpoint that envisions the church today as the apostolic community to whom the commands of Jesus are addressed directly.[176] These divergent

---

[172] G. H. Orchard, *A Concise History of the Baptists* (Nashville: Graves, Marks, & Rutland, agents of Tennessee Publication Society; New York: Sheldon, Lamport, 1855). The subtitle continues: "From the Time of Christ Their Founder to the 18th Century." Landmark Baptist minister and publisher J. R. Graves republished Orchard's book and wrote an introduction in which he asserted that "all Christian communities during the first three centuries were of the Baptist denomination" and that these Baptist churches never disappeared (introductory essay, xiv).

[173] J. M. Carroll, *The Trail of Blood . . .* (Lexington, Ky.: Ashland Avenue Baptist Church, 1931).

[174] James Leo Garrett Jr. is one notable exception of a Southern Baptist theologian who was an observer at Vatican II and stressed the need to move beyond a polemical and evangelistic approach toward Catholics to dialogue and fraternal conversations between Baptists and Catholics. Garrett, *Baptists and Roman Catholicism* (Nashville: Broadman, 1965), 42–45.

[175] Calvin, *Institutes* IV.1.9 (ed. McNeill), 2:1023. See e.g., The Orthodox Creed (1678) XXX, in Lumpkin, *Baptist Confessions of Faith*, 318–19.

[176] James Wm. McClendon Jr., *Doctrine: Systematic Theology, Volume II* (Waco, Tex.: Baylor University Press, 2012), 45–46.

understandings of apostolicity seem to lead to an impasse, with Catholics on one side standing for the authority of the church and Baptists on the other side holding firm on the authority of the Bible. Other Baptists seek a way beyond this apparent divide between incommensurable accounts in search of a fuller instantiation of apostolicity.

Baptism, Eucharist and Ministry suggests that continuity with the apostolic church includes "witness to the apostolic faith, proclamation and fresh interpretation of the Gospel, celebration of baptism and the eucharist, the transmission of ministerial responsibilities, communion in prayer, love, joy and suffering, service to the sick and the needy, unity among the local churches and sharing the gifts which the Lord has given to each."[177] Catholics, along with Orthodox and Anglicans, have maintained episcopal succession as a necessary condition for continuing in the apostolic tradition. But if episcopal succession is understood as *"a sign,* though *not a guarantee"* of continuity with apostolic faith and practice across space and time, there seems to be a way beyond the impasse.[178] Baptists and other Free Churches, which rely on the Holy Spirit working providentially to keep the churches in the apostolic tradition, can welcome episcopal succession as *a sign of apostolicity* in the life of the whole church, though they do *not* regard it as *a necessary condition for valid apostolic ministry and gifts.* Catholics might conceive of the possibility that there could be expressions of the one, holy, catholic, and apostolic church outside of the Catholic Church, and they might even consider whether some of the better parts of the church and the best elements of truth that they have neglected may be found outside rather than inside that Catholic Church.[179]

Baptists have maintained a witness to another, and often overlooked, sense of apostolicity derived from the literal meaning of the word *apostolos* as "one who is sent out." In 1792 William Carey published *An Enquiry into the Obligations of Christians to Use Means for the Conversion of the Heathens* in which he asked "whether Commission given by our Lord to his Disciples be not still binding on us." The prevailing view among his contemporaries, Carey observed, was that the commission had been fulfilled by the apostles and that "if God intends the salvation of the heathen, he will some way or other bring them to the gospel, or the gospel to them."[180] The fact that the faith was already extended to the four corners of the

---

[177] *Baptism, Eucharist and Ministry* IV.A.34, Faith and Order Paper no. 111 (Geneva: World Council of Churches, 1982). Hereafter *BEM.*

[178] *BEM* IV.B.38.

[179] Barth, *Church Dogmatics* IV/1, 713.

[180] William Carey, *An Enquiry into the Obligations of Christians to Use Means for the Conversion of the Heathens* (Leicester, 1792; repr., London: Carey Kingsgate Press, 1961), 8–9.

earth, it was assumed by many, guaranteed the catholicity of the church. But Carey countered that if the Great Commission was restricted to the first generation of Christians, then so were the commands to baptize and teach as well as the promise of divine presence. He contended that each generation must manifest apostolicity by continuing to go into all the world making disciples. The embrace of this missional conviction led to the formation of the Baptist Missionary Society with Carey as its initial appointment.[181] The apostolic vision inspired Ann and Adoniram Judson to lead American Baptists to venture into international missions, as well as Johann Oncken, whose motto *Jeder Baptist ein Missionar* impelled the spread of missionaries throughout Europe.[182] Baptists have attempted to live out the conviction that missional churches are manifestations of apostolic practice, and to the extent that they have been faithful in upholding the missionary impulse they have maintained a vital sense of apostolicity needed for the churches to be the church.

Because the fullness of Christ (the *plene esse*) to which apostolic faith and practice gave witness is found in the church as a whole, the life of the churches can be enriched, as Pope John Paul II observed, not simply through the exchange of ideas, but by the exchange of gifts.[183] Receptive ecumenism is one approach that seeks to foster the mutual exchange of ecclesial gifts in the hope of a fuller realization of apostolic faith and practice. Participants begin by asking "What do we need to learn from other traditions?" rather than "What do they need to learn from us?"[184] This strategy encourages each tradition to take responsibility for receiving from others and being willing to facilitate the growth of others without conditions or expectations. Just as the church of Jerusalem received a vision of world mission from the church of Antioch and Antioch gained from Jerusalem a closer connection with Apostles and their teaching (Acts 11:19-26; 13:1-3), so it is hoped that contemporary churches by mutual

[181] Brian Stanley, *The History of the Baptist Missionary Society 1792–1992* (Edinburgh: T&T Clark, 1992), 9–15.

[182] Robert G. Torbet, *Ventures of Faith: The Story of the American Baptist Foreign Mission Society* (Philadelphia: Judson Press, 1955), 15–30; Ian M. Randall, *Communities of Conviction* (Schwarzenfeld: Neufeld Verlag, 2009), 49–69; and Randall, "Every Apostolic Church a Mission Society," in *Ecumenism and History*, ed. Anthony R. Cross (Carlisle, U.K.: Paternoster, 2002), 281–301.

[183] John Paul II, *Ut Unum Sint* §28.

[184] *Receptive Ecumenism and the Local Church*, newsletter of the project in Receptive Ecumenism, accessed February 14, 2010, https://www.dur.ac.uk/theology.religion/ccs/projects/receptiveecumenism/phasetwo/. Steven R. Harmon, "A Time for Exchanging Ecclesial Gifts," *Baptists Today*, January 2010, 18; Harmon, *Ecumenism Means You, Too: Ordinary Christians and the Quest for Christian Unity* (Eugene, Ore.: Cascade Books, 2010), 67, 116–17; and Paul D. Murray, ed., *Receptive Ecumenism and the Call to Catholic Learning: Exploring a Way for*

exchange can learn what it means to be the church together. For example, as the Catholic Church seeks to engage in "a new evangelization," perhaps they might benefit by learning from the Baptist practice of evangelism, just as Baptists can surely learn from Catholics to be faithful to the Great Commission by being the contemporary mission of the church with its historic witness to the gospel.[185] Yet, as McClendon observed, at minimum receptive ecumenism requires "an acknowledgment of the grace of God in places other than our place, in persons other than ourselves, in churches other than our churches."[186] Baptists have freely received much from the historic tradition of the church, and they have gifts to share that could enrich the life of the church and bring it into a fuller manifestation of apostolic faith and practice.

That Baptists identify the church in gathered communities is commendable, but their most pressing ecclesiological challenge lies in learning how to show that these gatherings are related to the church as the whole people of God. Some Baptists may think that confessing the church to be one, holy, catholic, or apostolic is contrary to fact because in historical existence the church does not clearly manifest these marks. Yet the church's nature is not empirically recognizable for any and all to see, for the ecclesiality of the church is an ontological reality, not a sociological one. A trinitarian ecclesial vision provides a way of seeing the church as a creature of Word and Spirit. Through this lens it becomes clear that communion among members and between communities is grounded in communion with the triune God. To put it simply, gathered communities are seen to be outcroppings of the whole church. This is a deep conviction of contesting catholicity. It is not contrary to the basic convictions of a gathered church ecclesiology but rather a necessary condition for the church to be the church. For either the church is one, holy, catholic, and apostolic or it is not the church at all. Other Baptists, then, seek to manifest expressions of this reality in their worship, work, and witness. The following chapters will indicate the sort of future that might be possible if gathered communities were to more intentionally engage in reading Scripture, celebrating communion, and baptizing disciples as shared practices in which the life of the whole church is enriched.

Contemporary Ecumenism (New York: Oxford University Press, 2008).

[185] Benedict XVI, "Homily of First Vespers on the Solemnity of the Holy Apostles Peter and Paul," accessed September 1, 2013, http://www.vatican.va/holy_father/benedict_xvi/homilies/2010/documents/hf_ben-xvi_hom_20100628_vespri-pietro-paolo_en.html.

[186] James Wm. McClendon Jr., "What Is a Southern Baptist Ecumenism?" *Southwestern Journal of Theology* 10, no. 2 (1968): 73.

7

More Light from the Word

Trying to imagine "the new breed" of minister that the coming faith would require, Carlyle Marney reflected back on the principles that had guided his own ministry:

> Twenty-five or so years ago I set out to [the] Holy City determined to be one of the new breed. On my blithe way I took three oaths: (1) I would never become economically victimized by a job. (2) I would never want anything a denomination could give me to the point of paying too much to get it. (3) I would follow new light into any place as soon as I knew it to be a new light.[1]

The pledge to follow new light was a recurring theme in Marney's reflections. As he described it in his book *The Recovery of the Person*, the light revealed in the incarnation illumines the pathway to a new humanism. It leads to a journey of "faith seeking understanding." Yet the first, and perhaps most neglected, word that guides pilgrims along the way is the word "obey." But obey what? Answering his own question, Marney replied: "The light we have." Embarking on the journey "may well indeed wait on our obedience," and, as he was quick to add, "I have always had more light than I have been willing to follow, and so have you."[2] The Christian vocation of living into the reality of the new humanity "is the life of obedience to a light, a word we have heard from behind us."[3] The quest for more light begins with "obedience to light I already have."[4] But it does

---

[1] Carlyle Marney, *The Coming Faith* (Nashville: Abingdon, 1970), 141.
[2] Carlyle Marney, *The Recovery of the Person* (Nashville: Abingdon, 1963), 37–38.
[3] Carlyle Marney, "Fundaments of Competent Ministry," *Duke Divinity School Review* 41, no. 1 (1976): 9.
[4] Carlyle Marney, *Priests to Each Other* (Valley Forge, Pa.: Judson Press, 1974), 114.

not end there. As Marney knew all too well, there is more light than that
which lies behind. The light shining from eternity, which broke into time
when God in Christ became human, points to a future yet to be and to a
coming faith. Ahead is new light that promises to illumine the pilgrimage
of the new humanity on its way.

The conviction to follow new light has a long tradition among Baptists, going back to the early English Separatists.[5] It finds classic expression
in the much-celebrated saying of John Robinson that "the Lord has more
truth and light yet to break forth out of his holy word."[6] Life together for
the early Baptists was a quest of unfolding truth. With the Bible in their
hands, they promised to walk in the ways made known as they were led
by the Spirit to ways yet to be known.[7] What distinguishes Baptists is not
so much a doctrine of Scripture, much less a theory of inspiration, but
rather a standpoint and a conviction that the church now is the apostolic
community and the commands of Jesus are addressed to *us*. As James William McClendon Jr. has argued, Baptists are defined primarily by a way of
seeing: "this is that." It correlates with an eschatological outlook that *we*
are also the end-time people, a new humanity anticipating the consummation of the blessed hope. He designates this standpoint as a hermeneutical motto that he calls "the baptist vision."[8] Such a viewpoint leaves room
for liberty of interpretation while also calling for obedience to the truth
and light received. Yet as a hermeneutical stance it faces resistance from
a literalism that diminishes the complexities of interpretation under the
assumption that "the Bible says what it means and means what it says."
McClendon's teacher and Marney's friend W. T. Conner was quick to

---

[5] B. R. White, *The English Separatist Tradition: From the Marian Martyrs to the Pilgrim Fathers*
(London: Oxford University Press, 1971), 123. See also Stephen Brachlow, *The Communion of
Saints: Radical Puritan and Separatist Ecclesiology 1570–1625* (Oxford: Oxford University Press,
1988), 110–11, also 79, 82–83, and 104–6.

[6] Edward Winslow, *Hypocrisie Unmasked: A True Relation of the Proceedings of the Governor
and Company of the Massachusetts Against Samuel Gorton of Rhode Island* (London: Rich. Cotes,
1646; repr., New York: Burt Franklin, 1968), 97; and William Bradford, *Bradford's History
"Of Plimouth Plantation" from the Original Manuscript with a Report of the Proceedings Incident to
the Return of the Manuscript to Massachusetts* (Boston: Wright and Potter, 1899), 71–83. See also
Walter Herbert Burgess, *John Robinson, Pastor of the Pilgrim Fathers: A Study of His Life and Times*
(New York: Harcourt, Brace & Howe, 1920), 239–40; Robinson, *The Works of John Robinson:
Pastor of the Pilgrim Fathers*, ed. Robert Ashton (London: John Snow, 1851), 1:xliv–xlv.

[7] Ernest Payne, *The Fellowship of Believers: Baptist Thought and Practice, Yesterday and Today*,
enlarged ed. (London: Carey Kingsgate Press, 1952), 18.

[8] James Wm. McClendon Jr., *Ethics: Systematic Theology, Volume I* (Waco, Tex.: Bay-
lor University Press, 2012), 30; *Doctrine: Systematic Theology, Volume II* (Waco, Tex.: Baylor
University Press, 2012), 45–46; and Curtis W. Freeman, James Wm. McClendon Jr., and C.
Rosalee Velloso Ewell, eds., *Baptist Roots: A Reader in the Theology of a Christian People* (Valley
Forge, Pa.: Judson Press, 1999), 4–7.

point out that this uncritical approach fails to distinguish between *wording* and *meaning*. He deliberately intoned, "The Bible does not always say exactly what it means, nor does it always mean exactly what it says. It means what it *means*."[9] But the distinction between wording and meaning, as Conner knew, carries its own set of problems, illustrated in the familiar two-step hermeneutic of historical criticism in which the work of biblical scholars is to determine "what it meant" and the task of theologians is to formulate "what it means."[10] Yet exactly how one moves from *meant* to *means* is far from clear. But there is a deeper and more ironic problem here in that, for both uncritical literalism and historical criticism, the ultimate goal of biblical interpretation is the same: the resolution of all questions so that *no new light is necessary*. Other Baptists seek a way beyond this hermeneutical impasse.

Walking in the Light: Reading in Communion

Edward Winslow, one of the members of the pilgrim church that set sail on the *Mayflower* in 1620 from Delft Haven in Holland, recounts that in his farewell speech John Robinson directed their attention to the church covenant, "whereby wee promise and covenant with God and one with another, to receive whatsoever light or truth shall be made known to us from his written Word: but withall exhorted us to take heed what we received for truth, and well to examine and compare, and weigh it with other Scriptures of truth, before we received it."[11] The covenant to which Winslow referred was made some thirteen years earlier, when Robinson with John Smyth gathered a Separatist congregation in England at Gainsborough near Lincoln. There they "joyned them selves (by a covenant of the Lord) into a Church estate, in the fellowship of the gospell, to walke in all his wayes, made known, or to be made known unto them, according to their best endeavours, whatsoever it should cost them, the Lord assisting them."[12] Just prior to adopting believer's baptism, Smyth defined

---

[9] Stewart A. Newman, *W. T. Conner: Theologian of the Southwest* (Nashville: Broadman, 1964), 108.

[10] Krister Stendahl, "Biblical Theology, Contemporary," in *The Interpreter's Dictionary of the Bible*, ed. George A. Buttrick et al. (Nashville: Abingdon, 1962), 1:420.

[11] Edward Winslow, *Hypocrisie Unmasked*, 97–98. Thus Edmund S. Morgan observed that "the only ostensible requirements for admission to the church were a profession of faith, subscription to the covenant, and good behavior." Morgan, *Visible Saints: The History of a Puritan Idea* (New York: New York University Press, 1963), 58.

[12] William Bradford, *History of Plymouth Plantation, 1620–1647*, ed. William Chauncey Ford (Boston: Houghton Mifflin, 1912), 1:20–22. Following Bradford's account, Champlain Burrage showed the covenanting at Gainsborough occurred in the beginning of the year 1606/1607, in *The Early English Dissenters in Light of Recent Research* (Cambridge: Cambridge

"the true form of the church" as "a covenant betwixt God and the faithful made in baptism in which Christ is visibly put on."[13] Theirs was a progressive covenant, as the quest for more light led Smyth and his congregation to dissolve their earlier church covenant and reconstitute themselves anew as a visible community of baptized believers forming the first Baptist church. The Smyth congregation, and the Helwys group that broke away and returned to England, retained this covenant theology as the basis of their churchly estate, as did the Baptists who followed in their steps.[14]

As the early English Baptists began to identify their life together, covenant language figured prominently in their statements about how they envisioned it. The seven congregations of London who drew up a confession in 1644 admitted that they were distinct bodies, yet they declared that all are "one in Communion," holding Jesus Christ as their "head and Lord" and desiring to "walke" together in following the Lamb.[15] The expression "walking together" is ecclesiological shorthand for being in covenant with one another.[16] Such a vision conceives of the church as a community of disciples gathered by Christ in baptismal covenant around the Word. It has as members fellow pilgrims on a journey bound by cords of mutual trust. It requires a commitment to seek the mind of Christ together for ministry and mission. And it generates a distinctive approach of reading the Bible in communion.[17] The practice of the church meeting is a time and place in which members gather to search for the purpose of Christ. Because in Baptist thinking "Christ alone rules in the congregation, and the task of the local church gathered in covenant community together is to *find his mind for their life and mission*," discerning the mind of Christ relies on a corporate interpretation of Scripture, or exegesis by the

---

University Press, 1912), 1:231–32. On the relation between Robinson and Smyth, see Nick Bunker, *Making Haste from Babylon: The* Mayflower *Pilgrims and Their World* (New York: Vintage Books, 2011), 170–77.

[13] Smyth, *The Character of the Beast*, in *The Works of John Smyth*, ed. W. T. Whitley (Cambridge: Cambridge University Press, 1915), 2:645.

[14] Thomas Helwys, *A Short Declaration of the Mystery of Iniquity* (1611/1612), ed. Richard Groves (Macon, Ga.: Mercer University Press, 1998), 117–25. See my explanation of Helwys' covenantal ecclesiology in ch. 2, "Beyond Liberalism and Fundamentalism."

[15] Preface to First London Confession, in William L. Lumpkin, ed., *Baptist Confessions of Faith*, rev. ed. (Valley Forge, Pa.: Judson Press, 1969), 155.

[16] This language of walking together occurs in First London Confession, Article XLVII, where they declare that those in the visible church "walk by one and the same Rule," and Article LI, in which they declare their common commitment together "to walk in obedience to Christ" no matter whether they have support from the Magistrates or not. Lumpkin, *Baptist Confessions of Faith*, 169–70.

[17] Paul S. Fiddes, *Tracks and Traces: Baptist Identity in Church and Theology* (Carlisle, U.K.: Paternoster, 2003), 21–22. See also Richard Kidd, ed., *On the Way of Trust* (Oxford: Whitley, 1997).

community of the church. Baptists, to be sure, value the importance of the personal reading of Scripture, and they look to the Holy Spirit for guidance to understand what they read, but it would be incorrect to suggest that private interpretation of Scripture is the primary approach to reading Scripture in the Baptist tradition. Individual interpretation "is always subject to 'congregational hermeneutics,' to the mind of the whole community, gathered in the presence of Christ."[18]

Reading in communion allows for—indeed it encourages—individual and personal engagement with Scripture. But, as the early Baptists understood, walking together under the rule of Christ means bringing insights into the Word back to the community for conversation and testing, to discern together whether it is more light or not. And if these insights are indeed determined to be light, then they are also life that proceeds from Christ under whose rule the church lives. The congregational hermeneutic is complemented by an associational connection (and even wider by an ecumenical communion), because no local congregation possesses sufficient resources to go it alone and because Christ also rules in other communities gathered in covenant. This hermeneutics of peoplehood has its roots in the Radical Reformation, "where the working of the Spirit in the congregation is validated by the liberty with which the various gifts are exercised, especially by the due process with which every prophetic voice is heard and every witness evaluated."[19]

Something like this congregational hermeneutic was envisioned in a 1997 statement on Baptists identity that declared:

> We affirm Bible Study in reading communities rather than relying on private interpretation or supposed "scientific" objectivity. . . . We thus affirm an open and orderly process whereby faithful communities deliberate together over the Scriptures with sisters and brothers of the faith, excluding no light from any source. When all exercise their gifts and callings, when every voice is heard and weighed, when no one is silenced or privileged, the Spirit leads communities to read wisely and to practice faithfully the direction of the gospel.[20]

---

[18] Paul S. Fiddes, "Dual Citizenship in Athens and Jerusalem: The Place of the Christian Scholar in the Life of the Church" (Founders Day address for a conference on Christian Life and Witness, "From the Academy to the Church," Georgetown College, Georgetown, Ky., January 24, 2012). See Fiddes' chapter by the same title in *Questions of Identity: Essays in Honour of Brian Haymes*, ed. Anthony R. Cross and Ruth Gouldbourne, Centre for Baptist History and Heritage Studies 6 (Oxford: Regent's Park College, 2011), 137.

[19] John Howard Yoder, *The Priestly Kingdom: Social Ethics as Gospel* (Notre Dame, Ind.: University of Notre Dame Press, 1984), 22.

[20] Mikael Broadway, Curtis W. Freeman, Barry Harvey, James Wm. McClendon Jr.,

The affirmation calls for a congregational hermeneutic that rejects "private interpretation" as an end in itself, but it also encourages a lively engagement with Scripture, *"excluding no light from any source."* Some members of a covenant community may be moved to share insights from their "family and secret devotion."[21] Others may be inclined to contribute from their study of biblical commentaries or theological books. Still others engaged in such practices as *lectio divina* or *lectio continua* may offer discoveries from their reading.[22] Even the Sunday sermon may become part of the congregational deliberation and contestation over meaning when it is brought into the loop of conversation. To put it simply, interpretation may start out as an individual matter, but it is not done well if it stops there. For the responsibility of discerning the mind of Christ lies not with any one member but rather with the whole community that enters into covenant with God and one another. Whereas individualism turns the Bible into a private book and limits its scope of insight, reading in communion opens the Scriptures each time afresh with hope of new light and truth from the Word.

While the general church meeting is model for hermeneutical conversations, a more familiar example of reading in communion may be in Sunday school classes. When Baptist churches began establishing Sunday schools, proponents argued that the benefits would include a union of moral and intellectual education, the early conversion of children, biblical literacy among Christians, due observance of the Lord's Day, calling out the called into ministry, and an extension of every benevolent ministry of the church.[23] The Old School (or Primitive) Baptists who rejected the call to establish Sunday schools declined into relative obscurity, while Missionary (or Convention) Baptists who took up the challenge of Christian education multiplied like the children of Israel in the land of Goshen. It does not require too much of a leap in logic to conclude that studying the Bible together in small groups with the guidance of a denominational

---

Elizabeth Newman, Philip Thompson, et al., "Re-envisioning Baptist Identity: A Manifesto for Baptist Communities in North America," *Baptists Today*, June 26, 1997, 8; and also Freeman, "Can Baptist Theology Be Revisioned?" *Perspectives in Religious Studies* 24, no. 3 (1997): 304–5.

[21] This phrase comes from the popular and widely used Baptist church covenant in J. Newton Brown, *The Baptist Church Manual* (Philadelphia: American Baptist Publication Society, 1853), 23–24.

[22] The practice of *lectio divina* is popular but relatively new among many Baptists, but the practice of *lectio continua* is more common, although it is known in daily Scripture reading provided by such sources as *Our Daily Bread, Open Windows, Through the Bible*, etc.

[23] Basil Manly Jr., *A Sunday School in Every Church* (Charleston, S.C.: Southern Baptist Publication Society, 1858).

curriculum was a crucial factor in the transformation of Baptists in the South from a group of scattered and independent congregations to a large, national denomination. There is surely much more that could be said about what is (or at least should be) learned in Sunday school, but there can be little doubt about the importance of biblical literacy beginning at an early age and in particular the practice of studying the Bible together in small groups.[24]

Although Baptists have their origins in an open process of seeking more light and truth through reading in community, it is surely a mistake to think that all of their forebears embraced the further light doctrine with an eye to "the evolution of truth" or "continuous revelation."[25] For seventeenth-century radicals like Gerrard Winstanley, whose journey from Baptist to Digger to Quaker was based on his equation of the "Word of God" with the light that "dwells in a man's heart," experiential religion could indeed lead to new revelation.[26] And Isaac Robinson, John Robinson's son, seemed to believe he was following his father's admonition to be ready to receive more light when he embraced the Quaker faith and established a meeting on Cape Cod.[27] But for moderate Separatists like Robinson and Smyth, new light did not mean new revelation. As biblicists they rejected the spiritualized imaginings of the Quakers. "More light" was a hermeneutical motto expressing a deep conviction that the church is always being reformed (*ecclesia reformata, semper reformanda*).[28] The stated belief of the early Baptists was that the meaning of the Bible as the revealed word of God is sufficiently plain to be understood by each and all, affirming that "in this written Word God hath plainly revealed whatsoever he hath thought needful for us to know, beleeve and acknowledge,

---

[24] Small-group study continues to shape religious life in America, as is indicated in Robert Wuthnow, ed., *"I Come Away Stronger": How Small Groups Are Shaping American Religion* (Grand Rapids: Eerdmans, 1994).

[25] Christopher Hill, *The World Turned Upside Down* (New York: Penguin, 1991), 366. Hill lumps together all sectarians from "Lollards to Levellers" as part of "continuing underground tradition," in his *The Collected Essays of Christopher Hill*, vol. 2, *Religion and Politics in 17th Century England* (Amherst: University of Massachusetts Press, 1986), 107. However, this explanation is reductionistic and too simplistic to account for on-the-ground expressions that, in the words of Peter Lake, were more "acts of creative bricolage, kaleidoscopic combinations and recombinations of ideological materials, drawn from a number of sources." Lake, *The Boxmaker's Revenge: "Orthodoxy," "Heterodoxy" and the Politics of the Parish in Early Stuart London* (Stanford, Calif.: Stanford University Press, 2001), 400.

[26] Gerrard Winstanley, "A Letter to the Lord Fairfax," in *The Works of Gerrard Winstanley*, ed. George H. Sabine (Ithaca, N.Y.: Cornell University Press, 1941), 289.

[27] Philip F. Gura, *A Glimpse of Sion's Glory: Puritan Radicalism in New England, 1620–1660* (Middletown, Conn.: Wesleyan University Press, 1984), 151.

[28] Theodore Dwight Bozeman, *To Live Ancient Lives: The Primitivist Dimension in Puritanism* (Chapel Hill: University of North Carolina Press, 1988), 126–27.

touching the Nature and Office of Christ, in whom all the promises are Yea and Amen to the praise of God."[29] In language borrowed from their Presbyterian contemporaries in the Westminster Confession, the same group of Baptists in 1689 again declared a commitment to the plain-sense understanding of the Scriptures: "that not only the learned, but the unlearned, in a due use of ordinary means, may attain to a sufficient understanding of them."[30] Yet the same article begins with an important qualification that "all things in Scripture are not alike plain in themselves, nor alike clear unto all."[31] This caveat indicates that from their origins Baptists shared with other Protestants the conviction that biblical perspicuity is fraught with hermeneutical complexity. They understood that the Bible is "both clear and obscure, not merely clear or obscure."[32]

The doctrine of the perspicuity (or clarity) of Scripture was affirmed by the Protestants at the Diet of Speyer in 1529, who declaimed, "This holy book is in all things necessary for the Christian; it shines clearly in its own light, and is found to enlighten the darkness."[33] Luther, Zwingli, and other Reformers expressed confidence in the perspicuity of Scripture, but it was primarily from Calvin that the Baptists drew this hermeneutical principle.[34] For Calvin, the light of the Word makes clear the way of salvation like spectacles enable those with weak eyes to read the words on a page.[35] For Calvin the Word is inseparable from the Spirit, as the same Spirit that inspired the Scriptures confirms the Word through an inward illumination.[36] Yet Calvin emphatically denied that the Spirit's ongoing illumination might in any way be construed as new revelation. Rather,

---

[29] First London Confession VIII, in Lumpkin, *Baptist Confessions of Faith*, 158.

[30] The Second London Confession I.7, in Lumpkin, *Baptist Confessions of Faith*, 251; quoting verbatim from the 1646 Westminster Confession.

[31] Second London Confession I.7, in Lumpkin, *Baptist Confessions of Faith*, 251.

[32] James Patrick Callahan, "*Claritas Scripturae*: The Role of Perspicuity in Protestant Hermeneutics," *Journal of the Evangelical Theological Society* 39, no. 3 (1996): 357.

[33] Cited in Robert Newton Flew and Rubert Eric Davies, *The Catholicity of Protestantism* (London: Lutterworth Press, 1951), 14. There is no full English translation of *Die Bescherung und Protestation*, written to protest the majority edict of the Second Diet of Speyer in 1529. The full German text of the *Protestation* may be found in Julius Ney, *Geschichte des Reichstages zu Speyer im Jahre 1529: Mit einem Anhange ungedruckter Akten und Briefe* (Hamburg: Angentur des Rauhen Hauses, 1880).

[34] Martin Luther, "On the Bondage of the Will," in *Luther and Erasmus: Free Will and Salvation*, Library of Christian Classics, trans. and ed. Gordon Rupp and Philip Watson (Philadelphia: Westminster, 1969), 109–112, 158–69; Huldrych Zwingli, "Of the Clarity and Certainty of the Word of God," in *Zwingli and Bullinger*, Library of Christian Classics, ed. G. W. Bromiley (Philadelphia: Westminster, 1953), 49–95.

[35] John Calvin, *Institutes of the Christian Religion* I.6.1., ed. John T. McNeill and trans. Ford Lewis Battles (Philadelphia: Westminster, 1960), 1:70.

[36] Calvin, *Institutes* I.7.4 (ed. McNeill), 1:79.

the Spirit seals the minds of the faithful with the clear teaching that is commended in the gospel.[37] Stated simply, the perspicuous meaning of Scripture is its spiritual teaching. To be sure, the "sublime mysteries" of the kingdom of God are set forth in "rude simplicity" of human language.[38] But though the text of Scripture is clearly stated, it is not always clearly understood. Indeed, Calvin admitted that in the Scriptures "there is sometimes obscurity, which the unlearned take as an occasion to wander off to their own destruction."[39]

Yet as the case of the Ethiopian eunuch illustrates, when readers approach the Scriptures with openness and docility, though some passages may remain obscure without the further light of spiritual guidance, there is much that is clear and immediately useful for edification. Calvin noted that even though "many things were hidden from [the eunuch] . . . the irksomeness of it did not make him throw the book aside." He then drew an important hermeneutical conclusion: "There is no doubt that this is the way we also must read Scripture; we ought to accept eagerly and with a ready mind those things which are clear, and in which God reveals His mind; but it is proper to pass by those things which are still obscure to us until a clearer light shines." To which he added, "But if we shall not be wearied by reading, the final result will be that constant use will make us familiar with Scripture."[40] Right reading of Scripture, then, for Calvin proceeds on the basis of what is clear and awaits further light on those matters that are obscure. And as the Ethiopian eunuch came to understand from Philip that what he was reading pointed to Christ, so by reading in communion is the understanding illumined by a sense of Christ as the goal and soul of Scripture. As Calvin commented, "let us learn, without Christ, the *Sun of righteousness* (Mal. iv.2) there is no light even in the law, or in the whole word of God."[41]

But where for Calvin perspicuity was primarily *a semantic principle* that pertained to the clarity of the words of Scripture, for the Baptists

[37] Calvin, *Institutes* I.9.1 (ed. McNeill), 1:94.

[38] Calvin, *Institutes* I.8.2 (ed. McNeill), 1:82.

[39] John Calvin, *Calvin's Commentaries: The Epistles of Paul the Apostle to the Hebrews and the First and Second Epistles of St. Peter*, ed. David W. Torrance and Thomas F. Torrance, trans. William B. Johnston (Grand Rapids: Eerdmans, 1963), 12:367.

[40] John Calvin, *Calvin's Commentaries: The Acts of the Apostles 1–13*, ed. David W. Torrance and Thomas F. Torrance (Grand Rapids: Eerdmans, 1965), 6:243–48; see Timothy George, *Reading Scripture with the Reformers* (Downers Grove, Ill.: InterVarsity, 2011), 132–33.

[41] John Calvin, *Calvin's Commentary on the Epistles of Paul the Apostle to the Corinthians* (Grand Rapids: Eerdmans, 1948), 2:183. See Wulfert de Greef, "Calvin's Understanding and Interpretation of the Bible," in *John Calvin's Impact on Church and Society, 1509–2009*, ed. Martin Ernst Hirzel and Martin Sallmann (Grand Rapids: Eerdmans, 2009), 87–89.

it was chiefly *a principle of religious accessibility* to the truth of Scripture. And whereas for Presbyterians perspicuity was tied to *the teaching office*, for the Baptists the plain sense freed *all members of the covenant community* to read the Scriptures as together they discerned the light of Christ. The radical danger of a biblically literate laity did not go unnoticed. Royalist army officer William Cavendish, Duke of Newcastle, warned young Prince Charles (later King Charles II) about "Bible mad" Dissenters, saying that "the Bible in Englishe under every wever's and chambermayde's arme hath done us much hurte."[42] Putting the Bible in the hands of every Christian and freeing them to "open the book and read therein" is indeed a radical notion that equalizes and destabilizes, but it is the Baptist way.[43]

Yet to believe that the Word is *plainly revealed* does not mean that all Scripture is *plainly understood*. For example, Jane Turner, a member of the London Baptist congregation led by John Spilsbury, puzzled over why she was unable to see the teaching of believer's baptism for so long, even though it was "so plainly expressed in Scripture." She explains that it was not until, like the Ethiopian eunuch, she was "instructed in the waies of God" that her eyes were opened. She thus observed "that light discovers darkness, and though Truth be never so plainly expressed, yet ignorance cannot apprehend it."[44] The church meeting thus becomes a liminal space where participants in the conversation of discernment are invited to journey from old ways of thinking toward new hermeneutical horizons of understanding.[45] By creating opportunities for transformation that can rightly be described as "the hermeneutics of conversion," liminal experience opens blind eyes to see how the biblical narrative fits into a larger story told by the community.[46] When the vigorous conversations between covenant partners push the hermeneutical limits of the community, awaiting more light can be a means of forestalling further division. In the meantime, community members continue to walk in the light that has already been received. The conviction of further light has been important for Baptists "not because Christ Himself has in any way

---

[42] William Cavendish, "Letter of Instructions to Prince Charles," cited in Arthur Stanley Turberville, *A History of Welbeck Abbey and Its Owners, 1559–1715* (London: Faber & Faber, 1938), 60 and 173–74.

[43] John Bunyan, *The Pilgrim's Progress*, ed. N. H. Keeble (Oxford: Oxford University Press, 1984), 8.

[44] Jane Turner, *Choice Experiences of the Kind Dealings of God (1653)*, 83, 91–92, in Curtis W. Freeman, ed., *A Company of Women Preachers: Baptist Prophetesses in Seventeenth-Century England* (Waco, Tex.: Baylor University Press, 2011), 337, 339.

[45] Victor Turner, *The Ritual Process* (Ithaca, N.Y.: Cornell University Press, 1969), 95–97.

[46] Gary A. Furr and Curtis Freeman, eds., *Ties That Bind: Life Together in the Baptist Vision* (Macon, Ga.: Smyth & Helwys, 1994), 33, 39–43.

changed, but because God by His spirit has taught us to see in Him treasures of wisdom and power that our fathers did not discover."[47] And over the years, Baptists have been committed to walking in the light with the hope of more light to come.

Though walking together in the light of the Word has been a source of strength for Baptists, it has also provided occasions for controversy and division—particularly in the twentieth century when the irresistible force of historical criticism met the immovable object of commonsense realism. The resulting battles for the Bible have left Baptists largely divided into two camps: those who contend that "the Bible says what it means" (inerrantists/fundamentalists) and those who argue that "the Bible means what it means" (historical critics/liberals).[48] George Lindbeck has noted that the disagreement of both parties was over the factual veracity of the text. Inerrantists have tended "to insist that everything which could by any stretch of the imagination be supposed to be a factual assertion must be so interpreted and accepted as accurate." Historical critics look to the text "as a source of data for reconstructing what could . . . be plausibly taken to be the originating events, personalities, or situations (e.g., the historical Jesus)." There are, of course, gradations between these extremes, "but for all the participants in the debate from fundamentalist rigorists to hyperskeptical liberals, the narrative meaning had collapsed into the factual and disappeared."[49]

Lindbeck's observation of the collapse of narrative extends the argument of his Yale colleague and onetime Baptist theologian Hans Frei, whose monumental study of biblical hermeneutics, *The Eclipse of Biblical Narrative*, displayed how earlier realistic readings of the Bible became displaced on two fronts: higher criticism and apologetic theology. Critical

[47] Henry Cook, *What Baptists Stand For* (London: Carey Kingsgate Press, 1961), 28.

[48] The hermeneutical divide in the recent Baptist battles for the Bible can be traced out between inerrantists—Harold Lindsell, *The Battle for the Bible* (Grand Rapids: Zondervan, 1976); and L. Russ Bush and Tom J. Nettles, *Baptists and the Bible: The Baptist Doctrine of Biblical Inspiration and Religious Authority in Historical Perspective* (Chicago: Moody Press, 1980)—and noninerrantists—Clark H. Pinnock, *The Scripture Principle* (San Francisco: Harper & Row, 1984); and Robison B. James, ed., *The Unfettered Word: Southern Baptists Confront the Authority-Inerrancy Question* (Waco, Tex.: Word Books, 1987). The division in Baptist life follows the same basic lines as the inerrancy vs. noninerrancy debate in wider evangelicalism. D. A. Carson and John D. Woodbridge, *Scripture and Truth* (Grand Rapids: Zondervan, 1983); and Jack B. Rogers and Donald K. McKim, *The Authority and Interpretation of the Bible: A Historical Approach* (New York: Harper & Row, 1979).

[49] George A. Lindbeck, "Scripture, Consensus and Community," in *Biblical Interpretation in Crisis: The Ratzinger Conference on Bible and Church*, ed. Richard John Neuhaus (Grand Rapids: Eerdmans, 1989), 93; and Lindbeck, *The Church in a Postliberal Age*, ed. James J. Buckley (Grand Rapids: Eerdmans, 2002), 209.

interpreters mistook the history-likeness of the Bible for ostensive references to historical events, and, when the meaning of ostensive reference was shown to be historically unreliable, they sought meaning in ideal reference.[50] Apologetic readers ascribed the veracity of the Bible to moral or theological notions beyond the text, and so Scripture was read so as to conform to non-narrative dependent accounts of truth.[51] Yet in both instances the truth of the Bible was severed from its meaning as its message was reduced to principles that could be apprehended without future reference to the text.

But Frei's underlying identification of the literal sense with realistic narrative, and in particular with Protestant perspicuity, is deliberately ambiguous. In his essay "The 'Literal Reading' of Biblical Narrative in the Christian Tradition," Frei asked whether the *sensus literalis*, which he suggested is the closest thing to a *sensus fidelium* in the Christian church, may "break" under the strain of disputes about hermeneutical theory or whether it may prove supple enough to "stretch" to accommodate a range of interpretive theories within a unified cultural-linguistic framework. He proposed that "the less entangled in theory and the more firmly rooted not in a narrative (literary) tradition but in its primary and original context, a religious community's 'rule' for faithful reading, the more clearly it is likely to come into view, and the stronger as well as more flexible and supple it is likely to look."[52] Moreover, he questioned whether attempts to warrant "established or 'plain' readings" by any hermeneutical theory beyond conformity to a particular religious community's rules for reading amounts to anything more than a "last-ditch" effort to hold on to the waning of a wider cultural consensus.[53] What is needed, Frei contended, is attention to the beliefs, ritual, practices, and narrative of the entire semiotic system within which Scripture is enacted—or to borrow Lindbeck's compacted phrases, the "cultural linguistic" and "intratextual"

---

[50] Hans Frei, *The Eclipse of Biblical Narrative: A Study in Eighteenth and Nineteenth Century Hermeneutics* (New Haven, Conn.: Yale University Press, 1974), 10, 134, 324. George A. Lindbeck took up Frei's thesis in the context of ecumenical theology, in his "The Bible as Realistic Narrative," *Journal of Ecumenical Studies* 17, no. 1 (1980): 81–85.

[51] Frei, *Eclipse*, 101.

[52] Hans Frei, "The 'Literal Reading' of Biblical Narrative in the Christian Tradition," in *Theology and Narrative: Selected Essays*, ed. George Hunsinger and William Placher (New York: Oxford University Press, 1993), 139. Following Frei, Kathryn Greene-McCreight shows how Augustine, Calvin, and Barth work out the literal or plain sense as the hermeneutical interplay between the verbal sense and ruled reading. Thus for Greene-McCreight, and it would seem for Frei as well, there is a suppleness and elasticity to the "plain sense" that may encompass what is called "figural" as well as "literal." Greene-McCreight, *"Ad Litteram": How Augustine, Calvin, and Barth Read the "Plain Sense" of Genesis 1–3* (New York: Peter Lang, 1999), 21–22.

[53] Frei, "'Literal Reading,'" in Hunsinger and Placher, *Theology and Narrative*, 144.

interpretive frame.[54] In the end, Frei's answer about the literal reading is inconclusive, and the divisiveness of the Baptist battles for the Bible waged over the last century make his question more fraught than ever. Some may wonder, then, whether there is a future for the plain-sense reading of Scripture as generations of Baptist Christians have believed there was and would be.

Those who criticize the approach Frei commended express concern that intratextuality devolves into a crude kind of populism in which the hermeneutical process merely becomes a cipher for what is conventional, or that it leads to subjectivism or, worse still, to a self-refuting relativism in which there are an infinite number of possible meanings, none of which has priority. The end result, they argue, would be a world of hermeneutical chaos in which anything goes. It has been suggested that such criticisms also apply to reader response theory, which contends that the text of Scripture can only be rightly understood in the context of an "interpretive community."[55] Though the larger aim of many who employ such a hermeneutical strategy is to restore the Bible to its rightful place in the church, there is reasonable concern that this approach—which apparently assumes that texts have no inherent meanings, but only ascribed ones—may be "true neither to the actual functions of Scripture in the theological discourse of classic Christianity nor to the general human conviction that texts have determinate ranges of meaning."[56] And, without the assumption that texts have at least a limited range of meaning, these critics contend that ordered social discourse would seem to be impossible.[57]

The notion that texts have no meaning but rather "only emerge as the consequence of interpretive acts" at first blush may indeed seem

---

[54] Frei, "'Literal Reading,'" in Hunsinger and Placher, *Theology and Narrative*, 146–48; and George A. Lindbeck, *The Nature of Doctrine* (Philadelphia: Westminster, 1984), 16–19.

[55] Stanley Hauerwas, *Unleashing the Scripture: Freeing the Bible from Captivity to America* (Nashville: Abingdon, 1993), 21. See Stanley Fish, *Is There a Text in This Class? The Authority of Interpretive Communities* (Cambridge, Mass.: Harvard University Press, 1980), 11–16.

[56] Richard B. Hays, *The Moral Vision of the New Testament: A Contemporary Introduction to New Testament Ethics* (San Francisco: HarperCollins, 1996), 8 and 266.

[57] Hays, *Moral Vision*, 11n24. To illustrate this point, Hays suggests that the word STOP on a traffic sign is not subject to an infinite number of meanings. Anyone who has spent any length of time in North America would concede the point. Yet it is possible to conceive of circumstances where there might be alternate meanings derived from the same sign. Consider someone from the Australian Outback (like Crocodile Dundee) visiting the United States who speaks English but is unfamiliar with American driving laws and customs, or an African bushman (like Xi the Ju'hoansi tribesman in *The Gods Must Be Crazy*) who does not understand English but finds his way to the city from the Kalahari Desert. Both might see the word STOP on a traffic sign and arrive at different conclusions as to its meaning.

dangerously anarchic.[58] But it is precisely this assumption that Stanley Fish set out to undermine in the following story that provided the title to his book *Is There a Text in This Class?*

> On the first day of the new semester a colleague was approached by a student who, as it turned out, had just taken a course from me. She put to him what I think you would agree is a perfectly straightforward question: "Is there a text in this class?" Responding with a confidence so perfect that he was unaware of it (although in telling the story, he refers to this moment as "walking into the trap"), my colleague said, "Yes; it's the *Norton Anthology of Literature*," whereupon the trap (set not by the student but by the infinite capacity for language for being appropriated) was sprung: "No, no," she said, "I mean in this class do we believe in poems and things, or is it just about us?"[59]

The professor exhibits one way to answer the question, taking it literally as an inquiry about whether there is a required book for the course. Anyone who has paid the bill of a college student understands this interpretation. Call it meaning$_1$. The student's response requires a more specialized understanding of literary theory, and in particular the hermeneutical debates between new critics and deconstructionists. Bearing in mind these technical discussions, the student's answer also makes good sense. Call it meaning$_2$. But there are other possible meanings not identified in the story. Imagine, for example, another student returning to the room where her class met earlier that day. She interrupts the conversation of the student and the professor to ask, "Is there a text in this class?" She wonders whether they have seen her lost textbook. In this context, the question takes on yet another literal sense. Call it meaning$_3$. One might infer from this story that there are an infinite number of possible meanings to the question "Is there a text in this class?" But it is a long way from three to infinity. And even if there may be an unlimited number of possible meanings, there are only as many determinate meanings as there are practices to sustain them.[60] What emerges upon reconsideration of Fish's

---

[58] Hauerwas, *Unleashing the Scripture*, 19. Fish argues that "interpretive strategies are not put into execution after reading; they are the shape of reading, and because they are the shape of reading, they give texts their shape, making them rather than, as is usually assumed, arising from them." Fish, *Is There a Text in This Class?* 13.

[59] Fish, *Is There a Text in This Class?* 305

[60] I have borrowed this analysis of Fish's story from James Wm. McClendon Jr., "A New Way to Read the Bible" (the A. O. Collins Lectures, Houston Baptist University, Houston, Tex., April 1995). Umberto Eco makes a similar observation from the story of an Indian slave messenger and a basket of figs, criticizing the semiotic notion that every text, "once it is

thesis, rather than a dangerous relativism of an absolute indeterminacy of texts, is actually a picture of their relative determinacy.[61]

Still less clear is what makes the meaning(s) of a text determinate. Linguistic philosopher John Austin theorized that meaningful "speech acts" are determined at three levels. The first is the *locutionary* force of the words—namely, the actual utterance comprising phonetic, phatic, and rhetic acts. At the next level is the *illocutionary* force of an utterance, which is its intended meaning. And finally the *perlocutionary* force of the words names the actual effect or uptake, intended or not.[62] Whether speech-act theory answers the questions at issue may be debated, but what this sort of analysis seems to display is that the determinacy of a text (and in particular of the biblical text) is not narrowly dependent on an analysis of the grammar, syntax, or semantics of the language in question, but rather (as Hans Frei suggested) it hangs on a complex combination of the beliefs, practices, and narrative of the entire semiotic system within which Scripture is enacted. A group of theologians and biblical scholars has recently contributed to "the Scripture project," which provides some indication of how to imagine the sort of hermeneutical vision suggested by the Yale school of Frei and Lindbeck. The proposals of this project challenge the current division between theology and biblical studies in the curricula of most Christian seminaries, in which biblical exegesis comes first and supplies the raw materials for theological reflection. Among the themes to emerge from their reflections are unifying the narrative of Scripture, reading Scripture with the communion of the saints, and seeking more truth and light through fresh readings of Scripture in bearing witness to the Christ-centered truth of the gospel.[63] In the end what this hermeneutical vision calls for is a "deep, sympathetic, critical, and imaginative" engagement with Scripture and the Christian tradition.[64]

---

separated from its utterer (as well as from the utterer's intentions) and the concrete circumstances of its utterance (and by consequence from its intended referent) floats (so to speak) in the vacuum of a potentially infinite range of possible interpretations." Eco, *The Limits of Interpretation* (Bloomington: Indiana University Press, 1990), 2.

[61] McClendon calls this view of relative determinism "perspectivism," in which convictional conflict is "expected, but not inevitable, fundamental but not ultimate, enduring but not inherently ineradicable," as opposed to imperialistic and relativistic. James Wm. McClendon Jr. and James M. Smith, *Convictions: Defusing Religious Relativism*, rev. ed. (Valley Forge, Pa.: Trinity Press, 1994), 8–10.

[62] John L. Austin, *How to Do Things with Words*, 2nd ed. (Oxford: Oxford University Press, 1975), lecture 8, 94–108; and John R. Searle, *Speech Acts* (London: Cambridge University Press, 1969), 22–26.

[63] Ellen F. Davis and Richard B. Hays, eds., *The Art of Reading Scripture* (Grand Rapids: Eerdmans, 2003), 1–5.

[64] Maggie Spini, "Hays Named New Divinity School Dean," *Chronicle*, February 14,

This hermeneutical excursus provides an opportunity to think again about the baptist vision, which, as McClendon characterized it, arises from a sense of the immediacy of Scripture—*This is that*: the church is the apostolic community, and the commands of Jesus are addressed to us.[65] "Baptists," as one observer notes, "read the Bible in present tense, not as a document written a long time ago that can only be interpreted through a biblical hermeneutic."[66] The plain sense of reading Scripture is the dominant aspect of Baptist hermeneutics.[67] This interpretive stance is rooted in the conviction that the Holy Spirit who inspired the Scriptures continues to constitute the church, so that the Bible and the church comprise a continuous story. Given this sense of continuity, McClendon notes that in the baptist vision, "there is a strong link between the plain sense of Scripture and the church's self-understanding as a continuation of the biblical story."[68] But, as has already been noted, this sense of the plain sense differs from the notion of perspicuity as defined by Calvin, which as a semantic principle is linked more closely to the literal words of Scripture and the interpretive office of the elder and which understands the role of the Holy Spirit more in terms of the inward illumination of the individual reader. The plain sense in the baptist vision also differs from a more generic evangelical account in which the Spirit guides individual readers into an understanding of the biblical text by commonsense reason.[69] Ironically, the plain sense within the baptist vision is somewhat akin to apostolic figural readings (and to subsequent patristic and medieval forms of spiritual exegesis) that see a typological connection between the prophetic "that" and the pentecostal "this" (Acts 2:16) and where illumination is closely connected with the fellowship of the Holy Spirit in the church. This way of conceiving of the spiritual sense of Scripture was largely eclipsed by the grammatical and semantic readings of the Protestant Reformers.

2012, accessed March 3, 2012, http://dukechronicle.com/article/hays-named-new-divinity-school-dean.

[65] McClendon, *Ethics*, 30; McClendon, *Doctrine*, 45–46.

[66] Brad Elliott Stone, "Making Religious Practices Intelligible in the Public Sphere: A Pragmatist Evaluation of Scriptural Reasoning," *Journal of Scriptural Reasoning* 10, no. 2 (2011), accessed March 6, 2012, http://jsr.lib.virginia.edu/volume-10-no-2-december-2011-public-debate-and-scriptural-reasoning/making-religious-practices-intelligible-in-the-public-sphere/.

[67] Helen Dare and Simon Woodman, eds., *The "Plainly Revealed" Word of God? Baptist Hermeneutics in Theory and Practice* (Macon, Ga.: Mercer University Press, 2011), viii.

[68] McClendon, *Doctrine*, 44.

[69] Calvin, *Institutes* I.7.4 (ed. McNeill), 1:79; George M. Marsden, *Fundamentalism and American Culture* (New York: Oxford University Press, 1980), 14. For a more in-depth discussion of fundamentalism, common sense, and hermeneutics, see ch. 2 above, "Beyond Fundamentalism and Liberalism."

The baptist vision, then, represents a parallax view, and walking together in the Word provides a means of retrieving a primitive practice.[70] As in earlier precritical ways of reading, the immediacy of the Spirit in the baptist vision conceives of God's speaking "to us" as more communal than individual. McClendon puts it emphatically:

> I would not be misunderstood here. I am not making the smaller claims that community Bible study is helpful, or even that it is commanded, though both are true. I am saying that without the community of its readers there can be no Bible reading at all. To read the Bible as *Bible*, God's holy book, requires membership in the biblical reading community—the people of God. Either Gideon Bible readers in their solitary motel rooms are members of that community or they are clueless and more likely to get it wrong than right.[71]

The hermeneutical problem laid out in this way is about the sort of interpretive community that is needed to read the Bible. Those committed to the individualistic hermeneutics of modernity may attest that no community is necessary to read effectively. The baptist vision, however, follows a plain-sense approach of reading in communion. Such reading in covenant community demands an "active, diverse and ongoing engagement with the biblical texts" that permits "interpretive diversity and disagreement as a hallmark of the church's life" without insisting on "particular interpretive decisions as the necessary hallmark of being 'biblical.'"[72] And, because reading in covenant is messy, it requires that ongoing conversations within a community be shaped by relationships of friendship and mutual trust.[73] This account of the baptist vision may be helpful in moving beyond the hermeneutical impasse of fundamentalism and liberalism. Its provisional nature of the church creates a dynamic process that "allows not only a view of self-correction of baptist ecclesiology (and interpretation) in the historical process, [but also] the coexistence of other forms of ecclesiology (and interpretation)."[74] Given the current state of Bible study in churches, which is still largely determined by the plain-sense meaning

---

[70] Curtis W. Freeman, "The 'Eclipse' of Spiritual Exegesis: Biblical Interpretation from the Reformation to Modernity," *Southwestern Journal of Theology* 35, no. 3 (1993): 21–28.

[71] McClendon, "New Way to Read the Bible."

[72] Sean Winter, *More Light and Truth? Biblical Interpretation in Covenantal Perspective*, the Whitley Lecture (Oxford: Whitley, 2007), 28, 30.

[73] Sean Winter, "Persuading Friends: Friendship and Testimony in Baptist Interpretative Communities," in Dare and Woodman, *"Plainly Revealed" Word of God?* 253–70.

[74] Edgar V. McKnight, "How to Read and How Not to Read the Bible: Lessons from Münster," *Perspectives in Religious Studies* 24, no. 1 (1997): 87.

and grammatical historical method, the question that arises is whether the baptist vision might be lifted beyond the literal sense and toward the horizon of the catholicity of the church.

Receiving New Light: Reading with Openness

As the Pilgrim Church prepared to depart from Holland, John Robinson challenged them "to begin the great worke of Plantation in *New England.*" And he instructed them to judge his ministry and teaching by the example of Christ and the message of Scripture. If what he taught them was truth and light it would not be cancelled out or contradicted by the revelation of new truth and light from "any other instrument" of God: "for he was very confident the Lord had more truth and light yet to breake forth out of his holy Word."[75] Having faced fractious separatism first in England and later in Holland and anticipating more of the same in the New World, Robinson made a rather remarkable plea not to limit God to the light of the past but to be open to receive more truth and light. And he went so far as to suggest that if Luther and Calvin—"precious shining lights in their times"—were still living, "they would bee as ready and willing to embrace further light, as that they had received."[76] At the heart of this hermeneutical vision was an openness "to receive whatsoever light or truth shall be made known" to them in the journey as they walked together. Yet the new did not simply supersede the old, for, as Robinson emphasized, they must "take heed what [they] received for truth, and well to examine and compare, and weigh it with other Scriptures of truth, before [they] received it." And he urged them to prepare for a long journey, because the revelation of new light and truth would come gradually over time rather than all at once.[77]

Not everyone was inspired to join in the journey. Lapsed Separatist Henoch Clapham accused baptists, like the Donatists before them, of sinning against the light revealed and building on wood, hay, and stubble.[78] When Roger Williams wrote Anne Sadlier, the daughter of his early benefactor Sir Edward Coke, about having learned new light "in the wilderness of America," she replied that she planned to stick with "the glorious lights of the church of England." Referring to the new lights that Williams had urged her to follow, she declared, "I believe, in the conclusion, they will prove but dark lanterns," signing her letter, "your friend in

---

[75] Winslow, *Hypocrisie Unmasked*, 97.
[76] Winslow, *Hypocrisie Unmasked*, 97–98.
[77] Winslow, *Hypocrisie Unmasked*, 97–98.
[78] Henoch Clapham, *The Syn, Against the Holy Ghoste* (Amsterdam, 1598), 7.

the old way."[79] Williams acknowledged her suspicion of the new light and her affection for the old way, but he urged her to consider the Bereans, who "welcomed the message very eagerly and examined the scriptures every day to see whether these things were so" (Acts 17:11). And he then listed a number of Scripture texts she might read for illumination. Her third and final reply expressed chagrin that Williams continued to bother her: "I should never have heard of you any more; but it seems you have a face of brass, so that you cannot blush." She suggested that he and one of the books he recommended "would make a good fire," concluding her letter with the plea to "trouble me no more with your letters, for they are very troublesome to me."[80]

Early Baptist communities were committed to walking together in the light of the Word, but they were also open to more light each time they gathered around an open Bible.[81] In 1643 the English General Baptists Thomas Nutt and Edward Barber published a one-page challenge of debate to the Westminster Divines, which concluded with an appeal that all God's people everywhere might "walk after the light."[82] The General Baptists prefaced their 1654 statement, True Gospel-Faith Declared According to the Scriptures, with the admonition to weigh their confession by Scripture, "and if it be according to the Scriptures, there is light in it." Yet they continued that even though the theological formulations worked out with the illumination of old light may later be recognized as inadequate when examined from the viewpoint of new light, neither is new light discontinuous with old light. This further light they sought was not the "light within" of the Quakers. Remembering the conviction that the Lord has more truth and light to break forth out of the Word, the General Baptists admonished, "Let the Scripture therefore be the rule of thy faith and practice."[83] Benjamin Cox was a former Anglican clergyman, who along with Hanserd Knollys joined the Particular Baptists after the first edition of the London Confession of 1644 that expressed confidence in the "plainly revealed" Word. Cox contributed to the second

---

[79] Roger Williams to Anne Sadlier in Roger Williams, *The Complete Writings of Roger Williams* (New York: Russell & Russell, 1963), 6:241.

[80] Anne Sadlier to Roger Williams, in Williams, *Complete Writings*, 6:251–52.

[81] Anthony Cross argues that the further light doctrine was a "vitally important part of the original Baptist vision, and one that we would do well to make our own again," in his "Through a Glass Darkly: The Further Light Clause in Baptist Thought," in Cross and Gouldbourne, *Questions of Identity*, 105.

[82] Thomas Nutt and Edward Barber, *The Humble Request of Certain Christians Reproachfully Called Anabaptists* (London, 1643).

[83] True Gospel-Faith Declared According to the Scriptures, in Lumpkin, *Baptist Confessions of Faith*, 191.

edition of the London Confession in 1646 and published an appendix that stated, "Although we know that in some things we are yet very dark, and in all things as yet we know but in part, and do therefore wait upon God for further light; yet we believe that we ought in our practice to obey, and serve, and glorify God, in the use of that light which he hath given us; and not neglect the good using of that light which God hath already given us, under pretence of waiting for more."[84]

Baptists in America followed this same hermeneutical principle. When on September 25, 1682, William Screeven and nine others gathered at a Baptist church in Kittery, Maine, they covenanted "to walk with God and one with another . . . according to the grace of God and light at present through his grace." Like Robinson, the Kittery church pledged to follow further light that God might "make known to us through his Holy Spirit according to the same blessed word all the days of our lives."[85] The covenant of the Grassy Creek Baptist Church in Granville County, North Carolina, written in 1757, suggests that Baptists moving on to the frontier also affirmed the further light doctrine, as it stated the belief of being "guided by the word and Spirit of God, and by the help of Divine grace" yet holding out hope of "still looking for more light from God, as contained in the Holy Scriptures, believing that there are greater mysteries to be unfolded and shine in the church, beyond what she has ever enjoyed."[86]

This practice of walking together in the light received while being open to receiving more light was grounded in a sense of the immediacy of the Spirit that flourished in the English market-town prophesying meetings of the late sixteenth and early seventeenth centuries.[87] Divergent understandings of prophesy emerged from these gatherings of the godly. Some participants followed the traditional Puritan pattern of William Perkins, for whom "the whole and onely matter" of prophesying was the preaching of "the word of God."[88] His book *The Arte of Prophecying* was a

---

[84] Benjamin Cox, An Appendix to A Confession of Faith or A More Full Declaration of the Faith and Judgement of Baptized Beleevers XXI (London, 1648), in *Confessions of Faith*, ed. Edward Bean Underhill (London: Haddon, Brothers, 1854), 59.

[85] Covenant of the Kittery Baptist Church, in Charles W. DeWeese, *Baptist Church Covenants* (Nashville: Broadman, 1990), 134. See also Chaplin Burrage, *The Church Covenant Idea: Its Origin and Its Development* (Philadelphia: American Baptist Publication Society, 1904), 181–84.

[86] Robert I. Devin, *A History of Grassy Creek Baptist Church, from Its Foundation to 1880, with Biographical Sketches of Its Pastors and Ministers* (Raleigh, N.C.: Edwards, Broughton, 1880), 45.

[87] Geoffrey F. Nuttall, *The Holy Spirit in Puritan Faith and Experience* (Oxford: Basil Blackwell, 1946), 76; and Patrick Collinson, *The Elizabethan Puritan Movement* (Oxford: Clarendon, 1990), 168–239.

[88] William Perkins, *The Arte of Prophecying; or, A Treatise Concerning the Sacred and Onely*

guide for preachers on the proper exegesis of Scripture and the proclamation of its truth. Others looking to the account of John Robinson went further, describing prophesying as "the practice of all reformed churches" that was to be observed "not only by ministers but also the teachers, and of the elders and deacons, and even of the very common people."[89] Robinson argued that the practice of prophesying by all Christians was a means to the preservation of the purity of doctrine, for "as by the beating together of two stones fire appeareth, so may the light of the truth more clearly shine by disputations, questions, and answers."[90]

Some expressions of prophecy were even more radical than the practice as advocated by Perkins and Robinson. In John Smyth's congregation, because prophesying was regarded as part of spiritual worship, the Scriptures were laid aside so that the word of prophecy might come from the heart. This notion of spiritual worship was closer to the Dutch Collegiant notion of free prophecy, whereas most Baptists tended to follow moderate expressions like Perkins or even Robinson.[91] Worship in the Smyth congregation was an all-day affair. They prayed, sang Psalms, and expounded on the Scripture, but mostly they worshiped by prophesying with five or more people exercising in succession.[92] This pattern of multiple prophesying, following the Rule of Paul (1 Cor 14:29-33), seems to have been common among the early Baptists, although critics like the Presbyterian heresiographier Thomas Edwards portrayed prophesying in Baptist meetings as confusing and disorderly.[93]

At the top of Edwards' list of cankerous offenses was permitting women to prophesy. Based on the injunction that all may prophesy (1 Cor 14:24), Robinson proposed what might be described as the prophethood of all believers. He upheld every member of the church (men and women) as prophets with a responsibility to prophesy publicly, although

---

True Manner and Methode of Preaching (London: Felix Kyngston, 1607), 1 and 4, in *The Work of William Perkins*, ed. Ian Breward (Abingdon, U.K.: Sutton Courtenay, 1970), 333.

[89] Robinson, *The People's Plea for the Exercise of Prophecy*, in *Works of John Robinson*, 3:334.

[90] Robinson, *A Just and Necessary Apology*, in *Works of John Robinson*, 3:58.

[91] Smyth, *The Differences of the Churches of the Seperation* (1608), in *Works of John Smyth*, 1:18. Smyth argued that "because as in prayer the spirit only is our help & ther is no outward help given of God for that kind of worship. So also in prophesying & singing. 1 Cor. 11.4 & 14.6" (Smyth, *The Differences of the Churches of the Seperation*, 10.7, in *Works of John Smyth*, 1:283).

[92] Letter from Hughe and Ann Bromehead to their cousin Sir William Hammerton c. 1609, in Burrage, *Early English Dissenters*, 2:172–73. The Bromeheads seem to distinguish from propounding (from the Scripture) and prophesying (from the heart).

[93] Thomas Edwards, *Gangraena: The First and Second Part*, 3rd ed. (London: Ralph Smith, 1646), 1:36.

he maintained that women were not permitted to prophesy openly in the church meeting, in part because of the injunction for women to be silent in the churches (1 Cor 14:34).[94] Women in the Smyth congregation were likewise not allowed to prophesy in the open meeting, but other Baptists did allow women to prophesy freely in public. For example, when one London congregation considered the objection to the preaching of Anne Harriman, they examined the Scriptures together and determined that "a woman, (maid, wife or widow) being a prophetess (1 Cor. 11) may speak, prophesy, pray, with a veil."[95]

In seeking to characterize the hermeneutical approach that leads to such radical conclusions, McClendon observed that the baptist vision is a way of reading the Bible by those who accept the plain sense as the dominant way of connecting their lives with the biblical story. But, he added, there is something beyond the literal sense going on that enables them to "see past and present and future linked by a 'this is that' and 'then is now' vision." This spiritual hermeneutic arises from "a trope of mystical identity binding the story now to the story then, and the story then and now to God's future yet to come."[96] Robinson's expression of the baptist vision fixes the element of continuity in "Scripture and its Christ, while declaring the biblical word to be an agent of change that must itself change, releasing afresh the mighty, transforming power of God."[97] Just as the pilgrims would open their sails to the winds that would bring them safely to the shores of the New World, those who walk in the way of the baptist vision must ever learn to adjust their sails to the winds of the Spirit as they are guided in the journey to a world of new light and truth.

This journey, McClendon suggests, is nowhere better exemplified than in that of Roger Williams.[98] Like his Puritan contemporaries, Williams held that "the Scripture is full of mystery and the old Testament of types."[99] John Cotton and the Massachusetts Bay Puritans looked to establish historical continuity between them and Old Testament figures. Believing that their commonwealth fulfilled the types of Israel, they justified the use of civil power by church authorities to punish those with whom they disagreed. Williams countered that the relationship between

[94] Robinson, *A Justification of Separation*, in *Works of John Robinson*, 2:215–16.

[95] Claire Cross, "The Church in England, 1646–1660," in *The Interregnum: The Quest for Settlement, 1646–1660*, ed. G. E. Aylmer (Hamden, Conn.: Archon Books, 1972), 116–17; cited in John H. Y. Briggs, "She-Preachers, Widows and Other Women: The Feminine Dimension in Baptist Life since 1600," *Baptist Quarterly* 31, no. 7 (1986): 341.

[96] McClendon, *Doctrine*, 45.

[97] McClendon, *Doctrine*, 451.

[98] McClendon, *Doctrine*, 482–86.

[99] Roger Williams to John Winthrop, July 31, 1637, in *Complete Writings*, 6:54.

Israel and the church was merely figural, "typing out the *Christians Churches* consisting of both *Jews* and *Gentiles,* enjoying the true power of the *Lord Jesus,* establishing, reforming, correcting, defending in all cases concerning his *Kingdome* and *Government.*"[100] By insisting that the link between Israel and the church is spiritual rather than historical, Williams challenged the fundamental premise that warranted their commonwealth. Israel, he argued, was a type of Christ and his church, not a type of the Massachusetts Bay Colony. He thus obliterated the biblical basis for any union of church and state. And, in fulfilling all the offices of ancient Israel (prophet, priest, and king), Jesus as the Christ who proclaimed, served, and ruled though suffering love showed the civil government to be scripturally invalid.[101] For Christ compels only through the persuasion of his messengers, Williams contended, not by the power of earthly weapons.[102] As McClendon concludes, "From Jesus onward, government interference in anyone's faith, be that faith false or true, constituted disobedience to Jesus himself."[103]

This vision could lead to remarkably sophisticated hermeneutical judgments, as John Bunyan illustrates in his agonizing account of the journey made possible by receiving new light. Bunyan's awakening began when he heard a group of women discussing "with such pleasantness of Scripture language" that he was drawn to "look to the Bible with new eyes, and read as [he] never did before."[104] No longer was the Bible "a dead letter, a little ink and paper."[105] It became a living Word. Not long afterward he had a vision of light shining on a mountain. Between him and the light stood a wall, which kept him shivering in the cold away from the light. After some time he found a narrow gap in the wall, and he came into the heat and light of the sun. When the vision faded, Bunyan understood that the mountain signified the church and the sun symbolized the

---

[100] Roger Williams, *The Bloudy Tenent of Persecution,* 109, in *Complete Writings,* 3:16.

[101] Perry Miller, "Roger Williams: An Essay in Interpretation," in Williams, *Complete Writings,* 7:10–21; James P. Byrd Jr., *The Challenges of Roger Williams: Religious Liberty, Violent Persecution, and the Bible* (Macon, Ga.: Mercer University Press, 2002), 31–52; and Lisa M. Gordis, *Opening Scripture: Bible Reading and Interpretive Authority in Puritan New England* (Chicago: University of Chicago Press, 2003), 113–44. The Massachusetts clergy expected that opening the Scripture would supernaturally lead to greater theological consensus. As Gordis shows, Williams' obstinacy undercut the Puritan theory of scriptural clarity and threatened the established consensus.

[102] Roger Williams, *Christenings Make Not Christians,* in *Complete Writings,* 7:38.

[103] McClendon, *Doctrine,* 487.

[104] John Bunyan, *Grace Abounding to the Chief of Sinners,* ed. W. R. Owens (London: Penguin Books, 1987), §38 and §46; 14–15.

[105] Bunyan, *Sighs from Hell,* in *The Complete Works of John Bunyan,* ed. John P. Gulliver (Philadelphia: Bradley, Garretson, 1872), 783.

Word of God. The gap in the wall was Jesus Christ, who is the way. Yet Bunyan's imaginative reading, though helpful, was not fully liberating. He worried that he might not be one of the elect, and he wondered whether the day of grace for him had passed.[106]

Bunyan's doubts persisted, and he became lost in despair, believing he had committed the unforgivable sin of Esau, who despised his birthright and lost his opportunity for repentance (Heb 12:16-17).[107] Again he received relief through further light. First, he came to understand that Esau was unable to repent not because he lost his birthright but because he lost his blessing. Second, Bunyan came to believe that the birthright signified regeneration and the blessing symbolized the eternal inheritance.[108] He was able to discern that although he had at one time despised the regenerative work of the Spirit, in the end he received the blessing of salvation. When the truth finally sank in, Bunyan said, it was as if chains fell from his legs and loosed him to boldly approach the throne of grace.[109] Later he observed, "I believe that the great end why God committed the Scriptures to writing was, that we might be instructed to Christ, taught how to believe, encouraged to patience and hope for the grace that is to be brought unto us at the revelation of Jesus Christ; also that we might understand what is sin and how to avoid the commission thereof."[110]

But even though the openness to receiving new light is part of the baptist vision, it is not a baptist invention. It finds an analogue in the church catholic. Augustine tells how as a young man he found the stories of the Old Testament particularly offensive, with their crude and sometimes immoral language. When he moved from Rome to Milan, he went to listen to Ambrose for the eloquence of his preaching, not its content. As he listened, the passages of the Bible that had previously "killed" him when he took them literally now became intelligible when explained "spiritually" by way of allegory.[111] Yet the longer he studied, the better he understood that the New Testament is concealed in the Old and the Old Testament is revealed in the New.[112] And the more closely he read the whole of Scripture, the more clearly he came to understand that the literal

---

[106] Bunyan, *Grace Abounding*, §§53–57; 18–19.

[107] Bunyan, *Grace Abounding*, §136; 36.

[108] Bunyan, *Grace Abounding*, §226; 58.

[109] Bunyan, *Grace Abounding*, §230 and §239; 59–61.

[110] Bunyan, "Of the Scriptures" §3, *A Confession of My Faith . . .* , in *The Works of John Bunyan*, ed. George Offor (Glasgow: W. G. Blackie & Son, 1854), 2:601.

[111] Augustine, *Confessions* 5.13–14, trans. John K. Ryan (New York: Image Books, 1960), 130–31.

[112] Augustine, *On the Spirit and the Letter* 27.15, in *The Nicene and Post-Nicene Fathers* (Grand Rapids: Eerdmans, 1971), 5:95.

(or "letteral") sense of the text is Christ. His was a literalism that attended to the letter of the entire canon of Scripture in light of Christ.[113] This hermeneutical approach may then be described as christological plain sense in which the literal words of the biblical text refer to Christ, indeed to the whole Christ (*totus Christus*), that includes his members in the church.[114]

To the extent, then, that the baptist vision sees the literal as spiritual with Christ at the center it is actually quite catholic. To be sure, the offer issued to all invites participation in a lively hermeneutical experiment, making room for freedom of interpretation with differing emphases and styles. Yet at the heart of its practice is the christological key, for as the eternal Word of God, Jesus Christ is mediated *through*, discovered and encountered *within*, existent *before*, and authoritative *above* Scripture.[115] It is unlikely that old John Robinson could have imagined the new truth and light that would break out at Plymouth Plantation or among their more radical descendants. Yet his wisdom still reaches out today: for as the Pilgrim Church looked to the winds of the Spirit to fill their sails on their hermeneutical journey, so they trusted in Christ as the ballast that steadied the ship through turbulent interpretive waters. But those who embark on this journey must learn to set their course toward the full light that glimmers from beyond the horizon, and to that heading our reflections must now turn.

Awaiting Full Light: Reading with Patience

One final word of caution—neither old light nor new light is full light. Each is penultimate and awaits the fulfillment that will come at the last day. When the Apostle John envisioned the new Jerusalem, he described it as a place of perpetual light, where "the glory of God is its light, and its lamp is the Lamb" (Rev 21:23). Pilgrims behold the Lamb who calls them to follow him through troubled waters and who illumines the dark path of the journey, but their eyes are also fixed on the eschatological horizon. So they stand on this side of the river and sing:

---

[113] Jason Byassee, *Praise Seeking Understanding: Reading the Psalms with Augustine* (Grand Rapids: Eerdmans, 2007), 205–19. The wonderfully insightful phrase "christological literalism" is Byassee's invention.

[114] Augustine, *On the Epistle of John* 1.2, in *The Nicene and Post-Nicene Fathers* (Grand Rapids: Eerdmans, 1971), 7:461.

[115] James Gordon, "Spirituality and Scripture: The Rule off the Word," in *Under the Rule of Christ: Dimensions of Baptist Spirituality*, ed. Paul S. Fiddes (Macon, Ga.: Smyth & Helwys, 2008), 131.

On Jordan's stormy banks I stand,
And cast a wishful eye
To Canaan's fair and happy land,
Where my possessions lie.[116]

This is that: the church today is the apostolic community, and the commands of Jesus are directly addressed. *Then is now*: the church at this moment is the end-time people of God, and these are the last days. This is the baptist vision.[117]

Yet there is good reason to worry that as a hermeneutical principle this vision can run amuck. Why did it mislead those militant Anabaptists in 1534 to insist that Münster was the new Jerusalem? How could it permit the Fifth Monarchy movement to believe that their revolt in 1661 would hasten the return of king Jesus? And who can explain Nat Turner's visions of the apocalypse that resulted in the 1831 Southampton slave revolt or William Miller's disappointing predictions of the cleansing of the earth in 1843 or J. N. Darby's dispensational scheme and inventive rapture teaching that propagated the great premillennial myth and spawned exuberant apocalyptic speculation? If there is an explanation for these missteps, perhaps it is that none of them sufficiently appreciated the ultimacy of the full light that will only begin to shine on the final day "when the faith shall be sight" and "the clouds be roll'd back as a scroll."[118] But for now, as the Apostle Paul wrote, "We see in a mirror, dimly, but then we will see face to face" (1 Cor 13:12). The further light doctrine thus calls for theological modesty because it stands as a reminder that no one yet has the final word.

Still, if there is the possibility for such huge mistakes, it leads to ask whether and how this vision might serve as a faithful guide in the journey toward more light and truth. The paradigm for discerning the direction of the Spirit is Pentecost. It begins when someone asks, "What does this mean?" (Acts 2:12), and it requires another to explain, "this" is "that" (Acts 2:16). Yet connecting the pentecostal "this" and the prophetic "that" requires remarkable insight. It presupposes that participants are open to seeing the world through this hermeneutical lens, for Pentecost gives a glimpse of a new humanity, redeemed and reconciled to God. The great outpouring of the Spirit is accompanied by a great overturning of the social order, as sons and daughters, young and old, bond and free, break

---

[116] Samuel Stennett, "On Jordan's Stormy Banks I Stand," in *The Baptist Hymnal* (Nashville: Convention Press, 1975), 490.

[117] McClendon, *Doctrine*, 44–46.

[118] Horatio G. Spafford, "It Is Well with My Soul," in *The Baptist Hymnal*, 339.

loose together in prophetic proclamation of God's mighty works. It is a subversive vision in a social world where biblical warrants are often used to reinforce the subjugation of the other. Yet it also imagines a world in which among the baptized there is no longer Jew or Greek, slave or free, male and female, for all are one in Christ Jesus (Gal 3:28). It is both a hermeneutical principle and an ecclesial standpoint. This is that, and then is now. This biblicism that characterizes Other Baptists is not so much a fixed doctrine like plenary verbal inspiration or a proven technique like the historical-critical method. It is more of an ongoing practice of learning to read in communion, with openness and with patience.

The preaching women among the early baptists caught sight of this radical hermeneutic. As Pricilla Cotton and Mary Cole reminded their male interlocutors, disputed texts that seem to silence women must be read closely, for just beneath the surface lie subversive meanings waiting to be discovered.[119] Or, as Anne Hutchinson attested to the Massachusetts General Court, "The Lord knows that I could not open scripture; he must by his prophetical office open it to me."[120] Or, as Sarah Wight suggested, the new light that pours out on God's sons and daughters is but "a taste now of what shall be."[121] Or, as Katherine Sutton exclaimed, "The spirit of truth joynes with the word of truth," meaning that "the more of this light comes into the soul, the more it thirsteth after light."[122] Or, as Anna Trapnel asserted, the "Spirit takes the Scripture all along, and sets the soul a swimming therein."[123] Some Baptists have found it difficult to grasp such a radical vision given by women. "Let your women keep silence in the churches: for it is not permitted unto them to speak" (1 Cor 14:34). "It says what it means, and it means what it says," they confidently intone, but Other Baptists have learned to see a fuller meaning when the

---

[119] Priscilla Cotton and Mary Cole, *To the Priests and People of England We Discharge Our Consciences, and Give Them Warning* (London: Giles Calvert, 1655), 6–8. Cotton and Cole subvert the text to argue that their male interlocutors are in fact the women who are commanded to be silent because they prophesy outside the protective covering of Christ their head. See Freeman, *Company of Women Preachers*, 10–11.

[120] "The Examination of Mrs. Anne Hutchinson at the Court at Newtown," in *The Antinomian Controversy, 1636–1638: A Documentary History*, ed. David D. Hall, 2nd ed. (Durham, N.C.: Duke University Press, 1990), 336. Her appeal to "immediate revelation" was rejected out of hand by the court as an anarchic threat to the Puritan consensus.

[121] Henry Jessey, *The Exceeding Riches of Grace Advanced* (London: Matthew Simmons, 1647), 90, in Freeman, *Company of Women Preachers*, 220.

[122] Katherine Sutton, *A Christian Womans Experience of the Glorious Working of Gods Free Grace* (Rotterdam: Henry Goddaeus, 1663), 34, in Freeman, *Company of Women Preachers*, 632.

[123] Anna Trapnel, *The Cry of a Stone* (London, 1654), in Freeman, *Company of Women Preachers*, 445.

hermeneutical gaze is directed toward the horizon of the new creation instead of backward to the Edenic fall as the following story suggests.

Addie Davis began attending services at the Watts Street Baptist Church of Durham, North Carolina, early in 1963. After graduating from Meredith College, she had served as education director of First Baptist Church of Elkin, North Carolina, and dean of women at Alderson-Broadus College in Phillipi, West Virginia. By the time she arrived at Watts Street, Davis was a student at Southeastern Baptist Theological Seminary in Wake Forest, North Carolina. One Sunday she approached Warren Carr, the pastor of Watts Street. She told him that she had tried other forms of religious service, but that the call to be a "preaching minister" was "firm and definite." As Carr recalled, she explained, "That's what God had called her to do, and that's the only thing she could do." It was not easy for Davis to reach this conclusion. Though the Presbyterians and the Methodists had already begun ordaining women, as had some Baptist groups, no Southern Baptist church had ever ordained a woman to the ministry.[124] She asked Carr straight out whether he would consider ordaining her. A shocked Carr answered, "Addie, I suppose you're asking this question before you join the church?" She replied, "Honestly, yes." Carr responded that he could not promise her anything to get her to join the church. "You have to do that as a matter of faith, as a matter of preference," he told her. He explained that he was open to her ordination, but that the members of Watts Street would have to get to know her first before they were ready to talk about other possibilities. He admitted that he did not think that they should ordain her before she had been called to

---

[124] United Methodists and Presbyterians both approved full clergy rights for women in 1956. Russell E. Richey, Kenneth E. Rowe, and Jean Miller Schmidt, *The Methodist Experience in America: A History*, vol. 1 of *The Methodist Experience in America* (Nashville: Abingdon, 2010), 346–48, 402–3; Lois A. Boyd and R. Douglas Brackenridge, *Presbyterian Women in America: Two Centuries of a Quest for Status*, 2nd ed. (Westport, Conn.: Greenwood Press, 1996), 128–29. Although American Baptists began ordaining women to the ministry before the turn of the twentieth century, there were very few ordained women in the American Baptist Churches until they adopted a resolution in 1965 on the status of women that urged churches to work for the equality of women in society, employment, education, and the law and to "secure full participation of women in the life and work of the church (including the pastorate)." *Year Book of the American Baptist Convention: 1965–66* (Valley Forge, Pa.: Judson Press, 1965), 74. Free Will Baptists in the South began ordaining women to the ministry in 1911, although it was not common. See Michael R. Pelt, *A History of Original Free Will Baptists* (Mt. Olive, N.C.: Mt. Olive College Press, 1996), 265–66. Mark Chaves reports that from 1970 to 1990 the number of female clergy rose from 3 percent to 10 percent of the total U.S. clergy population, in his *Ordaining Women: Culture and Conflict in Religious Organizations* (Cambridge, Mass.: Harvard University Press, 1997), 1.

a church, adding, "I'm not saying that we won't; maybe in the last analysis we will before you leave seminary."[125]

Addie Davis joined Watts Street Baptist Church. On March 13, 1963, she was granted a license to preach and invited to fill the pulpit on Sunday evening May 5.[126] The conviction that God was leading her to a ministry of the Word grew stronger. Remembering what Carr had said about not ordaining her without a congregational call, she continued to seek a church that might be willing to consider her as pastor. But, when she would talk to churches without ministers, they would always say, "We can't find a place for you." Davis realized that "they would rather have nobody than a qualified woman."[127] She contacted several Southern Baptist state executives, but they all told her the same thing—they did not know any churches that were open to considering a woman as pastor. As she later recalled, "The truth is, that they weren't willing to recommend a woman to any church." She decided to press the leadership of Watts Street. In a letter dated May 14, 1963, Davis wrote the chair of the deacons, Vivian Parks. She expressed her appreciation for approving her license to preach, but she inquired whether it might be feasible to consider her ordination in "the immediate future." She reminded him that the rule of requiring a congregational call before ordination was not universally or equally observed, stating that "some of our men are ordained before they have a call to a church." Was it not possible to do the same for her? But, she conceded, "what is best in my case is . . . entirely up to the Watts Street Church."[128] She acknowledged that she did not expect getting started to be easy but that being ordained before she was called to a church might be beneficial. Parks reiterated the judgment of the pastor and deacons "that ordination should await a definite call to a church," and he continued, "in our view, the service of ordination would at that time be more meaningful and more in keeping with its purpose." Parks closed his letter with the request to let them know whenever she received the good news of a call, and they would be pleased to discuss plans for her ordination.[129]

---

[125] Warren Carr, *Oral Memoirs of Warren Tyree Carr: April 18, 1985*, Baylor University Religion and Culture Project (Waco, Tex.: Baylor University Institute for Oral History, 1988), 32–34; Pamela R. Durso and Keith E. Durso, eds., *Courage and Hope* (Macon, Ga.: Mercer University Press, 2005), 18–24.

[126] Watts Street Baptist Church, Minutes of Church Meeting (March 13, 1963), 1.

[127] Addie Davis quoted in the *Herald Sun*, July 30, 1994, B1.

[128] Addie E. Davis to Vivian A. Parks Jr., May 14, 1963, Watts Street Baptist Church Heritage Room, Durham, N.C.

[129] Vivian A. Parks Jr. to Addie E. Davis, May 24, 1963, Watts Street Baptist Church Heritage Room, Durham, N.C.

Then one day Elizabeth Miller, an old friend from Meredith, called Davis to tell her that the First Baptist Church in Readsboro, Vermont, was looking for a pastor. Miller recommended her to the Readsboro church, and in good time they called her to be their pastor. The Readsboro church sent a request to Carr asking Watts Street to proceed with Davis' ordination. Carr took the request to the Deacon Board and announced, "Addie Davis," whom you now know, has told me that God will not let her rest until she has answered and is able to fulfill a call to parish and pulpit ministry." He explained, "Her sex is a secondary consideration to me." Carr continued, "What I hear is a call, and I hear it as a genuine call." He appealed, "I'm here to recommend that we ask her to stand for ordination, and I'm here to say, 'I ain't going to get in God's way.' If you want to, that's up to you." But, he concluded, "I believe God has called Addie Davis, and I do not intend to impair that, to hinder that in any way." The deacons concurred and recommended that she stand for ordination pending approval by the church conference, which was passed "subject to the approval of the Examining Council."[130] And therein lay the dilemma.

According to Baptist polity, the Watts Street church could recommend Addie Davis for ordination, but the practice in those days was for candidates to be examined by a committee from the local Baptist association. Carr went to the associational examining committee and warned, "Now I simply will organize my own examining council out of the church if you're going to have a prejudice beforehand. If you can consider this person on her merits, all right, but I don't want you all on there saying at the same time 'no women.'" When the time for the examination came, the committee considered two candidates. The other prospective ordinand examined by the committee was a young campus minister whose doubtful opinions on the virgin birth gave the committee cause for concern. Indeed, the council had good reason to worry. Reports of growing heterodoxy among young North Carolina ministers had already drawn the attention of denominational leaders. When queried by officials from the General Board of Baptist State Convention of North Carolina, one Baptist campus minister in Durham stated, "I do not deny the virgin birth, and I do not affirm it. My mind is still open." The ambiguous answer did not satisfy his superiors on the General Board, who summarily dismissed him and two other campus ministers. One supporter of the board's action

---

[130] Carr, *Oral Memoirs of Warren Tyree Carr*, 32–33; Watts Street Baptist Church, Minutes of Church Meeting, February 26, 1964, 7; and July 29, 1964, 2; Watts Street Baptist Church, Deacon Board, Minute Book, July 21, 1964, 203; and August 18, 1964, 205.

commented, "A man who doesn't believe in the virgin birth is no more a Baptist than the Pope of Rome."[131]

When it came time to examine Davis, "She was superb," Carr recalled. And "when they asked her about the virgin birth and those kinds of arguments . . . she came through with flying colors." Her theology posed no problems for the council. But, as Carr had suspected, "the old prejudices of the brethren began to rise." Two members of the council confessed that, despite their assurance to remain open, they could not in good conscience approve a woman for ordination. A heated argument ensued, and they were about to vote her down, when a young minister on the council named John Keith spoke out. He said, "Brethren, you leave me confused. In the case of our first candidate you were quite insistent that he believe that a virgin bore the word. How is it that you are now so adamant that a virgin should not preach the word?" Laugher broke out. The committee took a vote, which passed unanimously, and Addie Davis became the first woman ordained by a church in the Southern Baptist Convention on August 9, 1964.[132]

It is important to ask how this complex process of discernment led to the conclusion that Addie Davis should be ordained to the ministry. For some Baptists the Bible seemed clear: women are not permitted "to teach or to have authority over a man" (1 Tim 2:12). This text and others, they argued, categorically excluded women from pastoral leadership and ordination. It was an argument Davis no doubt heard countless times, including from the pastor of her home church in Covington, Virginia, who refused to consider her for ordination, and from Baptist newspaper editors across the South who criticized her, saying that the teaching of

---

[131] "Baptist Dismissals," *Time*, April 12, 1954, 84. The minister quoted in the article was Max Wicker, the Baptist campus minister at Duke University, who soon afterward became a Methodist elder. The other two dismissed by the General Board were J. C. Herrin, the Baptist campus minister at the University of North Carolina, and James W. Ray, the Baptist Student Union state director. Ray came under fire from the Baptist State Convention for inviting Nels Ferré as a speaker for the state Baptist student convention. Nels Ferré's book *The Christian Understanding of God* (New York: Harper, 1951) raised questions about the virgin birth.

[132] Carr, *Oral Memoirs of Warren Tyree Carr*, 33–34; and Carr, *Reflections on the August 9, 1964 Ordination of Addie Davis*, Watts Street Baptist Church, Durham, N.C., August 8, 2004. Rev. John M. Keith Jr. was an associate at Temple Baptist Church in Durham and a divinity student at Duke. Davis and Parks had another exchange of letters after her ordination in which she expressed her appreciation to the deacons and members of Watts Street Baptist Church for their support. She stated, "I know that we are united through the living Word and my prayer is that I shall be a faithful and good steward of God's Word in this high calling of God in Christ Jesus." Letter from Addie E. Davis to Vivian A. Parks Jr., August 13, 1964; and letter from Vivian A. Parks Jr. to Addie E. Davis, August 20, 1964, Watts Street Baptist Church Heritage Room, Durham, N.C.

the New Testament "is plain that only men are to be considered for the gospel ministry."[133] Yet as the early Baptists expressed and as Addie Davis shows, the Scriptures that some wanted to claim as "plainly revealed"[134] "are not alike plain ,in themselves, nor alike clear unto all."[135] As Pricilla Cotton and Mary Cole or Katherine Sutton and Anna Trapnel before them, Other Baptists like Addie Davis looked to different texts, such as "you are all one in Christ Jesus" (Gal 3:28), and sometimes to the same texts in different ways, like the injunction that women may indeed pray and prophesy (i.e., preach) in public worship (1 Cor 11:4-5). These Scriptures, they argued, were *more* plainly revealed and in their view *clearly* warranted the ordination of women.

Although the broad contours of this conversation fit the fundamentalism–liberalism paradigm, the above resolution does not. The Southern Baptist opponents of ordination for women did seem to approach the issue with the assumption that the Bible contains the unchanging, inerrant, and authoritative answer to the question. So Jack Gritz, editor of the *Baptist Messenger* of Oklahoma, publically chastised R. C. Briggs and Luther Copeland, the two Southeastern Baptist Seminary professors who participated in the ordination of Addie Davis, exhorting them to "go back and read the New Testament," adding that "they might just find some interesting things there."[136] And, to be sure, Warren Carr was a major voice of the Dixieland liberals who consistently challenged the growing fundamentalist juggernaut in the SBC, but Carr's theological outlook was shaped less by the autonomous experientialism of neoliberal theology and more by the biblical realism of Karl Barth and Lesslie Newbigin. But, most of all, the hermeneutical conversation was not about one group appealing to Scripture for warrant and the other looking to experience and reason. Both opponents and proponents of women's ordination looked to Scripture for light and truth. They just looked differently.[137]

---

[133] Jack L. Gritz (editor of the *Baptist Messenger* of Oklahoma), quoted by W. G. Stracener (editor of the *Florida Baptist Witness*), "The Ordination of a Woman Pastor," *Alabama Baptist*, December 10, 1964. Southern Baptists eventually codified this interpretation in the 2000 revision of the Baptist Faith and Message, which states that "the office of pastor is limited to men as qualified by Scripture." Baptist Faith and Message VI, accessed February 21, 2013, http://www.sbc.net/bfm/bfm2000.asp#vi.

[134] First London Confession VIII, in Lumpkin, *Baptist Confessions of Faith*, 158.

[135] Second London Confession I.7, in Lumpkin, *Baptist Confessions of Faith*, 251.

[136] Gritz, quoted in Stracener, "Ordination of a Woman Pastor."

[137] Eileen Campbell-Reed shows how liberals and conservatives read the Bible differently in her "Anatomy of a Schism: How Clergywomen's Narratives Reinterpret the Fracturing of the Southern Baptist Convention" (Ph.D. dissertation, Vanderbilt University, 2008), 284–93, accessed February 10, 2014, http://etd.library.vanderbilt.edu/ETD-db/available/etd-07232008-000207/unrestricted/Campbell-Reed+Dissertation7-24-08.pdf. The termi-

Another explanation theorizes that external social forces, not internal theological reasons, are the source of changing policies on women's ordination. According to this sociological account, church policies are only apparently about biblical, theological, and ecclesiological matters, yet they are actually more about cultural achievement than theological necessity.[138] No doubt the clash between the established traditions of the 1950s nuclear family and the rising tide of 1960s women's liberation played out in the theological arguments for and against the ordination of women in general, and Addie Davis in particular. It is surely the case that most scholars who have studied the Baptist Battles, even when they have attended to the social and cultural forces in play, have told the story as a male-oriented contest, thus reducing the matter of the role of women to a mere symbol of the real issues, which were thought to be biblical and theological.[139] Yet if liberals have largely ignored the external social forces, conservatives have all but denied that they were relevant to the question. So, for example, Southern Baptists resolved that the question of women's ordination should not be decided "by modern cultural, sociological, and ecclesiastical trends or by

---

nology of Campbell-Reed's otherwise careful and very helpful analysis of the controversy over women's ordination in the SBC unfortunately leaves the impression that the matter can be simply explained as a conflict between "biblicists" who appealed to an inerrant Bible for warrant and "autonomists" who were guided by the liberty of individual conscience. Mark Chaves sufficiently demonstrates that commitment to inerrancy does not settle the question of the ordination of women. He points out that not all inerrantists oppose women's ordination. Indeed, some inerrantists actually make a case for ordaining women on biblical grounds. Chaves, *Ordaining Women*, 91–101.

[138] Chaves, *Ordaining Women*, 3–9.

[139] Elizabeth H. Flowers, *Into the Pulpit: Southern Baptist Women & Power since World War II* (Chapel Hill: University of North Carolina Press, 2012), 5. Flowers elegantly shows how a proper telling of the story of the Baptist Battles requires taking into account the role of women as determinative rather than peripheral. By narrating the stories of eight Baptist clergywomen, Campbell-Reed's *Anatomy of a Schism* nicely displays the way their perspectives contribute to a greater understanding of the SBC controversy. The exemplary studies by Bill J. Leonard and David T. Morgan pay attention to the social history of the Southern Baptist conflict. Leonard describes the denominational fragmentation as the inevitable result of the breakdown of southern culture, whereas Morgan sees it partly as a bid for power. See Leonard, *God's Last and Only Hope: The Fragmentation of the Southern Baptist Convention* (Grand Rapids: Eerdmans, 1990), 1–24; and Morgan, *The New Crusades, the New Holy Land: Conflict in the Southern Baptist Convention, 1969–1991* (Tuscaloosa: University of Alabama Press, 1996), ix–xi. Yet neither Leonard nor Morgan gives the role of women a prominent place in the controversy. In his social history of the Southern Baptist controversy, Barry Hankins treats "the women's issue" as a key piece of "cultural resistance" for conservatives. In line with his larger thesis, Hankins argues that the theological importance of role of women in the church for conservatives was imported from northern evangelicalism by way of Carl Henry. Hankins, *Uneasy in Babylon: Southern Baptist Conservatives and American Culture* (Tuscaloosa: University of Alabama Press, 2002), 229–32.

emotional factors" but rather on "the final authority of Scripture."[140] But the fact that these external pressures were so strongly registered indicates that the resolution, rather than being formulated strictly from the Scripture, was constructed in direct response to these influences, thus simply creating a mirror image of them. Yet even though this sociological explanation is powerfully explanatory, it risks reducing what is theologically relevant to what is empirically demonstrable. As a consequence it leaves little room for the work of the Spirit in these conversations.

A more promising alternative for Other Baptists is the hermeneutical rule laid out by the Apostle Paul in 1 Corinthians 14:26-40. This open process allows for interplay between the literal sense of the Word and the ruled readings of the community, but it also leaves room for the Spirit to reveal more light and truth. A radically democratic catholicity is not determined by the internal theological logic of established paradigms, nor is it reducible to the external pressures of social and cultural dynamics. It names a hermeneutical process that is receptive to epiphanies of the Spirit.[141] McClendon describes this hermeneutical approach as comprised of two basic steps: someone to ask, "What does this mean?"(Acts 2:12), and another to answer, "This is that" (Acts 2:16). Yet as John Yoder indicates the process is more complex. The Apostle Paul states that "when you come together, each one has a hymn, a lesson, a revelation, a tongue, or an interpretation" (1 Cor 14:26). In other words, when the question "What does this mean?" is asked, the "this is that" may come through several voices. Each participant in the conversation has something important to contribute, not out of respect for their democratic rights to participate, but because everyone is gifted. When fully engaged this process will involve prophets (viz., agents of direction), scribes (viz., agents of memory), teachers (viz., agents of linguistic self-consciousness), and elders or bishops (viz., agents of order and due process).[142] The end result is not purely theological or procedural. Rather, it is more about a process of weighing the truth and discerning the mind of Christ as "God's will is known by the Spirit working in the meeting."[143]

---

[140] *Annual of the Southern Baptist Convention* (Nashville: Southern Baptist Convention, 1984), 65.

[141] Molly T. Marshall argues that "minding the Spirit" in exegesis presupposes participation in the church, attending to the lives of the saints and conversations with others outside the church, in her "Reading Scripture with the Spirit," *Baptistic Theologies* 3, no. 2 (2011): 8–12.

[142] Yoder, *Priestly Kingdom*, 28–34.

[143] John Howard Yoder, *Body Politics: Five Practices of the Christian Community before the Watching World* (Scottdale, Pa.: Herald Press, 1992), 67–69.

There were a few prophets in the conversation who envisioned the possibility of new light illuminating the way for Addie Davis to be ordained. There were also plenty of scribes who challenged the process of seeking new light and argued not to neglect the light God had already given. There was no shortage of teachers who cautioned not to follow new light until they knew it to be light. And there were some elders who ensured that the discernment process was orderly. Still even more important than the process of conversation were two decisive "this is that" moments that led to new light being received and followed. The biblical paradigm for this approach, as Yoder suggested, is the decision to include Gentiles in the church, which in large measure turned on a vision by Peter, who explained his conversion in thinking to the elders in Jerusalem by saying "God has shown me" (Acts 10:28). He later defended his view, suggesting that since God had given the same Holy Spirit to Jews and Gentiles alike, the matter was settled. Who was he to hinder God (Acts 11:17)?

The first epiphany of understanding came as Addie Davis arrived at a firm sense of calling. She was a prophetic voice, standing over against the community of discernment in her home church and the wider Southern Baptist community of readers. She challenged them to walk with her on a journey in following this new light. Their resistance led her to Southeastern Seminary and finally to Watts Street Baptist Church in search of covenant partners who were open to the possibility of more light. The second epiphany occurred in Warren Carr's deliberation with the Watts Street deacons. His recommendation echoed the words of Peter. Convinced that Addie Davis had heard the same call to the ministry that he had heard, he realized he could not stand in God's way. What turned their thinking to ordain a woman was not that they were a progressive church and that this was the next and most obvious step for progressives to take. When it came to the matter of ordination, they kept alive the old practice of calling out the called in the traditional Baptist way. This practice has its roots in the Reformed distinction between the "outer and inner call." The outward call pertains to "the public order of the church," and the inward call attains to the "witness of our heart." The key to this practice is fostering a community that discerns ministerial vocation by discovering whether a candidate is "fit and competent to exercise it."[144] This pattern of calling ministers goes back to the early days of the Baptists, who held that "the church of Jesus Christ with its ministry may from among themselves, make choice of such members, as are fitly gifted and qualified by Christ."[145]

[144] Calvin, *Institutes* IV.3.11 (ed. McNeill), 2:1062–63.
[145] The Somerset Confession XXXI, in Lumpkin, *Baptist Confessions of Faith*, 212.

When Warren Carr met Addie Davis, he recognized there was little question about the inner call: it was "firm and definite." What he wondered about was whether she was gifted and qualified. Over time Carr came to see both the inner and the outer call confirmed in Addie Davis. Gender was not an issue. Ordination was not even the issue. A call and fitness for ministry were issues. The growing consensus eventually led Carr, the deacons, and the members of Watts Street to conclude that they would not impair or hinder her call in any way. And their discernment was confirmed when the Readsboro church extended a call to Addie Davis to become their pastor. Carr later reflected back on the church's action: "You were the first Southern Baptist church ever to ordain a woman, but you didn't ordain her because she was a woman. You ordained her because she was called to preach. And believe you me she preached."[146]

The final decisive hermeneutical moment occurred in the deliberations of the ordaining council. Because according to Baptist ecclesiology ordination into the gospel ministry is recognized by other churches, it is not entirely the prerogative of the congregation that recommends a candidate. For this reason Carr convened an ordination council from the local Yates Baptist Association, seeking the discernment and blessing of the wider church. Far from a spiritual laissez-faire approach, Carr took seriously his moderating role as an agent of order in a conversation that he knew could easily become disorderly. In articulating the rules for the deliberation, he made it clear that he would not allow prejudiced opinions to highjack the examination. Although several members had reservations about ordaining a woman, they pledged to enter into deliberation with openness and receptivity to more light. Yet they found it difficult to remain open. For a time it appeared that the council would refuse to approve Davis for ordination. Then the unexpected happened, as John Keith's comment became the occasion for an epiphany of understanding by the council in which they could say with one accord, "It has seemed good to the Holy Spirit and to us" (Acts 15:28).

This extended reflection displays what it looks like to engage in a robust hermeneutical conversation where every voice is heard and none is silenced or privileged, where no outcome is predetermined and all gather with the hope of discerning together the mind of Christ. It is an open process that allows for freedom of expression, and yet it risks the possibility of conversion to new perspectives. Advocates and adversaries are essential to the search for new light and truth, as all participants must listen and be

---

[146] Warren Carr, "A Prayer for Durham, N.C.," sermon preached at Watts Street Baptist Church, Durham, N.C. December 12, 1993.

heard. Dissenting views cannot be trumped by majority opinion, nor can the conversation be ended merely by the assertions of the loudest voices. It listens carefully to the ruled readings of the community and attends closely to the plain sense of Scripture. It seeks to move toward a greater understanding of the text but hopes even more to find a path to the reconciliation envisioned in the text. It does not default to the presumed answers of fundamentalism or liberalism, nor can it be reduced to the shortcuts of autonomy or authority.

Participating in this process demands conviction to walk in the light already received, openness to receive new light in the journey, and patience to wait for the coming of the full light that shines from the horizon of the future. It means walking by faith in the ways known until Christ leads to those ways yet to be known.[147] Catholicity so conceived cannot be made visible by simply appealing to the settled consensus of the past. It requires openness to the emerging accord of communities that seek to discern the mind of Christ and the direction of the Spirit in the widest and fullest sense. There are no shortcuts to the manifestation of catholicity, and many judgments of contesting communities will no doubt be disputed. Most of all, it needs disciples who continue in the Word that they may prove themselves to be disciples indeed. Other Baptists can with expectant hope offer this prayer:

> O Father, Son, and Spirit, send us increase from above;
> Enlarge, expand all Christian souls to comprehend thy love;
> And make us to go on to know with nobler powers conferred;
> The Lord hath yet more light and truth to break forth from His
> Word.[148]

This is the hermeneutical standpoint of contesting catholicity, which begins with the question of what might happen if each time the Bible were opened it was met with the shared conviction of expecting more light and truth.

---

[147] Cross attributes this way of putting the further light doctrine to Brian Haymes, in Cross and Gouldbourne, *Questions of Identity*, 118.

[148] George Rawson, "We Limit Not the Truth of God," in *The Baptist Church Hymnal* (London: Psalms & Hymns Trust, 1900), 211.

8

Evangelical Sacramentalism

In September of 1957, a study group that included Carlyle Marney, the pastor of the First Baptist Church of Austin, Texas, and James I. McCord, the dean of Austin Presbyterian Seminary, presented a *Report on the Table of the Lord* at the North American Faith and Order Study Conference in Oberlin, Ohio. The Oberlin meeting took up the challenge of the 1952 Faith and Order statement, "The Unity We Have and the Unity We Seek," which acknowledged the differences that stand in the way of the unity of the church but which nevertheless expressed the desire to work toward "a time when all Christians can have unrestricted communion in sacrament and fellowship with one another."[1] The Austin study group stated that it was their unanimous conviction to see the *totus Christus* presented as both subject and object in the celebration at the table. And since, in their view, Christ is actively present in the entire eucharistic celebration, they pronounced the nominalist interpretation of "symbol," in which the sign simply points to another reality, "inadequate to express the biblical meaning of symbol," where "the sign both points to and actually conveys the reality which is both signified and represented." They further declared that "while Christ's presence in the Eucharist is not contingent on faith, it is only through faith as an 'empty vessel' that the believer received the crucified and risen Christ and the fruits of his redemption, including the forgiveness of sins, justification, sanctification, newness of life and communion with the brethren." They concluded that the uniqueness of Christ's presence at the table eliminates "any possibility of human

---

[1] "The Unity We Have and the Unity We Seek," the Third World Conference on Faith and Order at Lund, Sweden (1952), in *Creeds of the Churches*, ed. John H. Leith (Garden City, N.Y.: Doubleday, 1963), 578.

311

control over God's gracious giving of Himself in Christ." In this understanding, "the 'sacrament' is not liable to any 'magical' or '*ex opere operato*'
connotation."[2]

Like Marney and his ecumenical conversation partners, Warren Carr
also shared the desire to recover an evangelical sacramentalism. Carr
and Marney understood that the whole doctrine of the church is contained in the theology of the sacraments. To think little of them was to
think little of the church. And to think much of them was to contend
for their worthy interpretation. Carr wondered why Baptists and other
Free Churches thought so little of them. That the writings of Baptist and
Free Church theologians were characterized by a studied indifference to
things sacramental suggested that they gave little thought to the church.
Carr pointed to the complete neglect of ecclesial matters by the respected
theologian E. Y. Mullins as an indication of the alarming movement of
Southern Baptists toward denominational isolation.[3] Carr stood against
that trend and looked toward some kind of evangelical sacramentalism
that addressed the promise and presence of God. Yet he expressed a desire
to find a language beyond ordinance and sacrament. The word "sacrament," although theologically rich, conjured up popular notions of magic
that seemed impossible to dispel, while the term "ordinance" was "bereft
of mystery," leaving "no place for God" to work. "What language shall
we borrow," he wondered, to describe the mystery of participation in
life of the triune God?[4] Answering Carr's question is not easy, but Other
Baptists might begin by imagining what it might mean to move toward
an evangelical sacramentalism.

From Simple Faith to Sacramental Participation

The efforts of Marney and Carr to recover a sacramental faith and practice
address the basic question of how to speak meaningfully of Jesus Christ as
living and present in the gathered community. The answer, as narrated in
the second chapter of Acts, is that *Jesus Christ is present in the church through
the Holy Spirit*. As the church at Pentecost gathered in the awful reality
of the absence of Christ to wait and to pray, so in that awful absence the
church must still live. Yet, as Carr confessed, "I am not undone because I

---

[2] Austin Study Group, *Report on the Table of the Lord*, North American Conference of Faith
and Order, September 3–10, 1957, box 111, the Carlyle Marney Papers, David M. Rubenstein
Rare Book & Manuscript Library, Duke University, Durham, N.C.

[3] Warren Carr, *Baptism: Conscience and Clue for the Church* (New York: Hold, Rinehart
and Winston, 1964), 12–15. For more on E. Y. Mullins and ecclesiology, see ch. 2 above,
"Beyond Liberalism and Fundamentalism."

[4] Carr, *Baptism*, 169–71.

know that usually at eleven o'clock on Sunday morning, there is a place I can go to a people who understand because they also wait—the Body of Christ waiting, with no more than a prayer and a promise, for the Spirit to come."[5] Such faith leaves still unanswered the questions of how the Spirit comes, and what the modes of Christ's spiritual presence are.

The most obvious sign that points to the presence of the risen Christ through the Spirit is the Word as it is read, studied, and proclaimed. So the community gathers in the shared conviction that "the Lord has more truth and light yet to break forth out of his holy word."[6] The road toward an evangelical sacramentalism naturally begins as the church gathers around the Word to receive the mystery of the gospel in the confidence that, as the Apostle Paul describes it, preaching is a means of grace, for "it pleased God by the foolishness of preaching to save them that believe" (1 Cor 1:21). The sacramentality of the Word is thus grounded in God's promise to take human words and transform them into God's own Word. And in the ministry of the Word, the church is invited to feed upon the bread of life. This mystery of the giving and receiving of the life-giving Word cannot be demystified. It can only be received by faith that comes, as the Apostle Paul declaimed, from hearing (Rom 10:17). As John of Damascus observed, the Word of God was conceived in the ear of Mary as she heard and received it by faith, and so is the Word incorporated by those that hear and receive it still.[7] The ministry of the Word thus re-presents the living Lord, so that, as Christ is made audibly present through the Word, Christ becomes visibly present in his body as the Word creates life anew.[8] Other Baptists can thus affirm with Luther that "wherever you hear or see this word preached, believed, professed, and lived, do not doubt that the true *ecclesia sancta catholica* . . . must be there," because, he adds, "God's word shall not return empty."[9]

---

[5] Warren Carr, "The Community Which Waits," sermon preached at the Watts Street Baptist Church, Durham, N.C., March 4, 1973.

[6] For more on the communal interpretation of Scripture, see ch. 7 above, "More Light from the Word."

[7] John of Damascus, *The Orthodox Faith* 4.14, in *A Select Library of the Nicene and Post-Nicene Fathers of the Christian Church* (Grand Rapids: Eerdmans, 1976), 9:86.

[8] This description of the sacramentality of the Word draws from P. T. Forsyth, *The Church and the Sacraments*, 3rd ed. (London: Independent Press, 1949), 141. It is also stressed by Alexander Maclaren, e.g., in his sermon "In Remembrance of Me," in *Expositions of Holy Scripture: Corinthians* (repr., Grand Rapids: Baker, 1974), 174–75.

[9] Martin Luther, *On the Councils and the Church*, in *Luther's Works* (Philadelphia: Fortress, 1966), 41:150. Calvin similarly names the preaching of the Word as one of the marks of the church. John Calvin, *The Institutes of the Christian Religion* IV.1.9, ed. John T. McNeill and trans. Ford Lewis Battles (Philadelphia: Westminster, 1960), 1023. B. A. Gerrish describes

This mystery of Christ's presence with the community gathering around the Word raises the issue of his presence with the community gathering around the table, for as the church engages in the reading, study, and proclamation of Scripture the question of Christ's eucharistic presence will inevitably arise. The *lectio continua* of the church eventually leads to inquiry into what it means in the bread of heaven discourse when Jesus declares that "those who eat my flesh and drink my blood have eternal life" (John 6:54). The history of interpretation has fallen along predictable lines, with Catholic interpreters pointing to the sacramental nature of these images and Protestant scholars seeing the language of eating and drinking as metaphorical allusions to faith.[10] Baptists and other evangelicals have long been suspicious of sacramental theology that disconnects the operations of grace from personal faith. This suspicion would appear to be justified by a close reading, given Jesus' pronouncement that "whoever believes has eternal life" (John 6:47).[11] So, in reading, the evangelically minded see faith alone as the biblically warranted condition of salvation, and the sacramentally conscious find eucharistic participation as a divinely promised means of grace. The result is that Baptists have too often found themselves caught between the unhappy extremes of *empty formalism* and *mere symbolism*. Indeed, reading with a second naïveté,[12] it

---

Calvin's theology of the Word as sacramental, in his *Grace and Gratitude: The Eucharistic Theology of John Calvin* (Minneapolis: Fortress, 1993), 82–86.

[10] Catholic biblical scholar Raymond E. Brown points to the eucharistic shape of John 6:51-58, which, he contends, is consistent with the rest of the discourse in the chapter and thus represents true Johannine thought. Brown's account makes implausible Bultmann's theory that a later redactor added these verses to correct the chapter and render it more acceptable to the Church. Brown, *The Gospel according to John* (Garden City, N.Y.: Doubleday, 1966), 1:284–94; and Brown, *New Testament Essays* (Garden City, N.Y. : Doubleday, 1968), 108–27; cf. Rudolf Bultmann, *The Gospel of John: A Commentary* (Philadelphia: Westminster, 1971), 218–37. Brown further suggests that it is not implausible to conceive that John 6:51–58 was spoken by Jesus in Capernaum. Martinus C. de Boer, following M. J. J. Menken, argues that John 6:51–58 is christological rather than eucharistic. Therefore, to eat Jesus' flesh and drink his blood means "to believe in him as the one who dies for the life of the world." Boer, *Johannine Perspectives on the Death of Jesus* (Kampen, Netherlands: Kok Pharos, 1996), 226–28. Huldrych Zwingli argued, "His body is eaten when it is believed that it was slain for us. It is faith, therefore, not eating, about which Christ is speaking here" Zwingli, *Letter to Matthew Alber Concerning the Lord's Supper* (November 1524), in *Huldrych Zwingli: Writings*, trans. H. Wayne Pipkin (Allison Park, Pa.: Pickwick, 1984), 2:134. Zwingli equates the words "eat" and "believe" in his writings.

[11] Of course, for those who with Brown read John 6:54 as sacramental, this statement is also understood eucharistically, just as those who with Menken interpret the previous passage as christologial take John 6:47 to be the same. Zwingli, e.g., intones that "the meaning of Christ's words was, 'No one will live except he believes that I have been delivered up to death for his salvation." Zwingli, *Letter to Matthew Alber*, in *Writings*, 2:133.

[12] Paul Ricœur, *The Symbolism of Evil* (Boston: Beacon, 1967), 349.

is hard to miss that the clear and plain sense seems to link salvation and communion in Christ with eucharistic participation. Other Baptists seek an evangelical sacramentalism that comes to the Lord's table for spiritual nourishment and calls for the reception of God's grace in the Eucharist through personal faith.

In his sermon to a group of catechumens preparing to receive the Eucharist on Easter, Augustine explained that what they see with their eyes is the bread and the cup but what they must learn to perceive by faith is that the bread is the body of Christ and the cup is the blood of Christ. Quoting the prophet Isaiah, he alluded to his famous tagline: "unless you believe you will not understand" (*nisi credideritis, non intelligetis*). He then stated, "My friends, these realities are called sacraments because in them one thing is seen, while another is grasped. What is seen is a mere physical likeness; what is grasped bears spiritual fruit."[13] Augustine was referring back to Isaiah 7:9, to which he often turned to delineate between believing and understanding.[14] His point to the catechumens was simply that, unless those who come to the table believe the bread and the cup are the body and blood of Christ, they will not understand the mystery of his presence. Put more simply: *Believing is seeing.* These realities are sacraments because there is more going on here than meets the eye. Augustine offered no theorized account to the catechumens to make the real presence intelligible. He merely reminded them that this mystery will become intelligible only when it is believed. For unless it is believed *that* Christ is present in the Eucharist, it will not be understood, no matter how well the theories explain *how* Christ may be known to be present.[15]

Though the early Baptists resisted highly theorized accounts of sacramental practice, they nevertheless often held a higher view of Christ's presence at the table than is thought to be the case. In the difficult years before the Act of Toleration in 1689, one group of the General Baptists of England confessed that as Israel "had the manna to nourish them in the wilderness to Canaan; so have we the sacraments, to nourish us

---

[13] Augustine of Hippo, sermon 272, *Ad Infantes, de Sacramento*, in Patrologia Cursus Completus, Series Latina 38, ed. J. P. Migne (Paris: Migne, 1844–1865), 1246–48. Augustine's sermon on the sacrament was delivered to catechumens on Easter 405–411. Allan D. Fitzgerald, ed., *Augustine through the Ages: An Encyclopedia* (Grand Rapids: Eerdmans, 1999), 784.

[14] E.g., Augustine, *Lectures or Tractates on the Gospel According to St. John* 19.6, trans. John Gibb and James Innes, in *The Nicene and Post-Nicene Fathers* (Grand Rapids: Eerdmans, 1971), 7:184; and Augustine, *On the Trinity* 15.2.2, trans. Arthur West Haddan and Rev. William G. T. Shedd, in *The Nicene and Post-Nicene Fathers* (Grand Rapids: Eerdmans, 1971), 3:200.

[15] Augustine does have a semiotic understanding of the sacraments that are mysteries precisely because they are signs of sacred things. Augustine, *On Christian Doctrine* 3.9.13, in *The Nicene and Post-Nicene Fathers*, trans. marcus Dods (Grand Rapids: Eerdmans, 1979), 2:560.

in the church, and in our wilderness-condition."[16] They understood that their survival in the spiritual desert depended on more than a formal ritual that overlooked the necessity of personal faith and an informal spirituality that emphasized the importance of piety but neglected the practice of the Supper. For these General Baptists, the living Christ was true spiritual food to be received by faith, and this heavenly manna was to be gathered at God's table. Thomas Grantham (1633/1634–1692), one of their most important theological voices, maintained that at the Lord's Supper there is a real offer of the flesh and blood of Christ "to feed upon by faith."[17] "This bread and this Cup," Grantham wrote in his catechism for children, "is the Real Body and Blood of Christ, but not carnally and corporally."[18] By emphasizing that the presence of Christ is *real*, Grantham was searching for language to speak of the mystery of Christ's presence. He could have borrowed from Augustine that what they see with their eyes is the bread and the cup, but what they must learn to perceive by faith is that the bread is the body of Christ and the cup is the blood of Christ, though he would be quick to add that this presence is *spiritual* not *carnal*.

While Grantham did not draw from Augustine, he did borrow from the Book of Common Prayer. The language of feeding by faith would have been immediately recognizable to his contemporaries as an allusion to Thomas Cranmer's famous revision of the words of administration in the 1552 prayer book that were repeated at the distribution of the bread: "Take and eate this, in remembraunce that Christ died for the[e], and *fede on him in thy heart by faith*, with thankes gevyng."[19] In this phrase, Cranmer attempted to find a middle way between Reformed and Catholic theology of the Eucharist, for he insisted that "communion as a liturgical event was only complete when a congregation made an experience of God's

---

[16] The Orthodox Creed XIX, in William L. Lumpkin, ed., *Baptist Confessions of Faith*, rev. ed. (Valley Forge, Pa.: Judson Press, 1969), 311–12.

[17] Thomas Grantham, *Christianismus Primitivus; or, The Ancient Christian Religion* II.7.IV (London: Francis Smith, 1678), 88.

[18] Thomas Grantham, *St. Paul's Catechism*, 2nd ed. (London: J. Darby, 1693), 47.

[19] *The Book of Common Prayer* (Whitechurch, 1552; repr., London: William Pickering, 1844), §12 (emphasis added).

[20] Diarmaid MacCulloch, *Thomas Cranmer: A Life* (New Haven, Conn.: Yale University Press, 1996), 616. Marion J. Hatchett suggests that the 1552 revision replaced the earlier Catholic sentence with Zwingli language, doubtless because of the insertion of the word "remembrance," in her *Commentary on the American Prayer Book* (San Francisco: Harper, 1995), 386. This puzzling assertion lacks any explanation. Surely not every instance of reciting the words of institution that contain the words "in remembrance of me" is Zwinglian. Both sentences have survived in the Book of Common Prayer in both Anglican-Episcopal eucharistic liturgies, thus blending Catholic and Reformed language and theology. The range of views in

grace effectual by its act of willing acceptance in faith."[20] This language of sacramental realism linked with personal faith appealed to Grantham and provided Baptists with a theological alternative to the external and objective sacramentalism exemplified among Anglo-Catholics and the internal and subjective spiritualism that they encountered among the Quakers.[21] General Baptists were careful to avoid any suggestion that the sacraments work instrumentally as means of grace. John Smyth thus described the sacraments as "a visible word" that "doe not confer, and convey grace and regeneration to the participants, or communicants: but as the word preached they serve only to support and stir up the repentance, and faith of the communicants till Christ come."[22]

The early Particular Baptists, being closer than the General Baptists to Calvin, drew more freely from the theology of the sacraments in the wider Reformed tradition as means of grace. Though they sometimes preferred language of "the ordinances," they too conceived of the elements, as did Augustine, as signs of the divine things that do more than

---

mid-seventeenth-century sacramental theology ran the gamut from "High-Church" Anglo-Catholics who held that the sacraments *confer* and *confirm* grace to "No-Church" Radicals who averred that the sacraments neither *confer* nor *confirm* grace, with "Low-Church" Puritans seeking a mediating position in which the sacraments *confirm* grace but do not *confer* it. Radical Puritans like the Quakers settled in the antisacramental position while Baptists modulated between the antisacramental and mediating views. See Peter Lake, *The Boxmaker's Revenge: "Orthodoxy," "Heterodoxy" and the Politics of the Parish in Early Stuart London* (Stanford, Calif.: Stanford University Press, 2001), 290–92, 358–59; and Geoffrey F. Nuttall, *The Holy Spirit in Puritan Faith and Experience* (Oxford: Basil Blackwell, 1946), 90–101. Ashley Null argues that for Cranmer "sacraments *did indeed confer grace*, but not as a separate, second channel in addition to Scripture." Null contends that for Cranmer the sacraments "were *means of grace* precisely because their use of elements made the promises of Scripture sink more easily into the depths of human hearts, since people's senses were more fully engaged by the presentation." Null also points out that Cranmer's revision dropped the *epiclesis* prayer over the elements, making their reception the response to the words of institution. "As a result," Null explains, "receiving the sacramental bread and wine, not their prior consecration, became the liturgy's climax. Now the sacramental miracle was not changing material elements but reuniting human wills with the divine." Null, "Conversion to Communion: Thomas Cranmer on a Favourite Puritan Theme," *Churchman* 116, no. 3 (2002): 251–52.

[21] Clint C. Bass argues that Grantham and the General Baptists held a memorialist view of the Lord's Supper with the central theme of "commemorating Jesus' death," in his *Thomas Grantham (1633–1692) and General Baptist Theology* (Oxford: Centre for Baptist History and Heritage, Regent's Park College, 2013), 100-101. Bass shows that a noninstrumental view in which the elements were not considered to be a means of grace was the consensus of the General Baptists at the time of Grantham. He notes, however, that the General Baptists signatories of the Orthodox Creed did hold to a theology of the table closer to the instrumentalism of Calvin in which the sacraments were thought of as a means of grace, though he rightly notes that the Orthodox Creed was not representative of wider General Baptist thought.

[22] Smyth, *A Confession of Faith* §73, in *The Works of John Smyth*, ed. W. T. Whitley (Cambridge: Cambridge University Press, 1915), 2:746.

[23] First London Confession XL, in Lumpkin, *Baptist Confessions of Faith*, 167.

simply point to a reality beyond themselves.[23] To emphasize their continuity with the wider Puritan community, the Second London Confession of Particular Baptists drew heavily from the Westminster Confession,
which was an amalgam of Reformed theology.[24] But the Baptists differed
slightly with the Presbyterians on the language about baptism and the
Lord's Supper. Whereas the Westminster Confession referred to the "sacraments" as actions in which there is a "sacramental union, between the
sign and the thing signified," the Particular Baptists substituted the word
"ordinances."[25] Yet the Particular Baptists borrowed language that had
recognition in the wider church, as did Grantham, affirming that those
who partake of the gifts at the Lord's table "do then also inwardly by faith,
really and indeed, yet not carnally, and corporally, but spiritually receive,
and feed upon Christ crucified & all the benefits of his death." With this
borrowed language of feeding by faith, the Particular Baptists declared
that participation in the Supper is a real sharing in Christ and not merely
a recollection or commemoration, as they are nourished by "the Body
and Blood of Christ, being then not corporally, or carnally, but spiritually present to the faith of Believers, in that Ordinance, as the Elements
themselves are to their outward senses."[26]

This sense of sacramentalism found its way into the language of early
Particular Baptist ministers. Citing John 6:54 as warrant, William Kiffin,
the London pastor and leading signatory of the two London confessions,
maintained that the Lord's Supper "is a Spiritual participation of the Body
and Blood of Christ by Faith" and so "is a means of Salvation."[27] And he

---

[24] Bryan Spinks, *Sacraments, Ceremonies, and the Stuart Divines: Sacramental Theology and Liturgy in England and Scotland 1603–1662* (Burlington, Vt.: Ashgate, 2002), 128–29; and B. A. Gerrish, "The Lord's Supper in the Reformed Confessions," in his *Major Themes in the Reformed Tradition*, ed. Donald K. McKim (Grand Rapids: Eerdmans, 1992), 252.

[25] The Westminster Confession XXVII.2, in Jaroslav Pelikan and Valerie Hotchkiss, eds., *Creeds and Confessions of Faith in the Christian Tradition* (New Haven, Conn.: Yale University Press, 2003), 2:640; The Second London Confession XXVIII.1, in Lumpkin, *Baptist Confessions of Faith*, 290.

[26] Second London Confession XXX.7, in Lumpkin, *Baptist Confessions of Faith*, 293. Michael A. G. Haykin points out that the Baptists omit a phrase from the Westminster Confession and Savoy Declaration that borrows language from Luther, describing Christ as present "in, with, or under the bread and wine," in Haykin's "'His Soul-Refreshing Presence': The Lord's Supper in Calvinistic Baptist Thought and Experience in the 'Long' Eighteenth Century," in *Baptist Sacramentalism*, ed. Anthony R. Cross and Philip E. Thompson (Carlisle, U.K.: Paternoster, 2003), 179–80.

[27] William Kiffin, *A Sober Discourse of Right to Church-Communion* (London: George Larkin, 1681), 25. Here Kiffin appropriates familiar language from Calvin and contemporary Presbyterians that speaks of the sacraments as "efficacious signs" or "means of grace," which as Gerrish points out is the focal point of Calvin's sacramental theology. Gerrish, *Grace and Gratitude*, 160–73; and "Lord's Supper in the Reformed Confessions," 231.

further warned about the danger of a reactionary antisacramental theology, saying that anyone who "cares not for Christ in the Word, Christ in the Promise, Christ in the Minister, Christ in the Water, Christ in the Bread and Wine, Christ Sacramental; cares as little for Christ God, Christ Flesh, Christ Emanuel," adding that "by these he comes near."[28] Benjamin Keach, another leading pastor and signatory of the Second London Confession, declaimed, "There is a mystical conveyance or communication of all Christ's blessed merits to our souls through faith."[29] And in his *Orthodox Catechism*, Hercules Collins, pastor of the Wapping Church in London, answered that, in the sacrament of the Lord's Supper, "we are as verily partakers of [Christ's] Body and Blood, through the working of the Holy Ghost."[30] In sum, both the early General and Particular Baptists shared in a broad theological consensus that combined practice and piety, objective and subjective, external and internal, because existential faith and sacramental practice were regarded as indispensable conditions for the reception of grace.[31]

Yet, ironically, in spite of the sacramental theology of early Baptists, sacramentalism has rarely been a live option among subsequent generations, in spite of the quite remarkable developments in eucharistic

[28] Kiffin, *Sober Discourse*, 42–43. Kiffin is here approvingly quoting Daniel Rogers.

[29] Benjamin Keach, *Tropologia: A Key to Open Scripture Metaphors* (London: William Hill Collingridge, 1858), 4:638–39.

[30] Hercules Collins, *An Orthodox Catechism* (London, 1680), 42. Collins describes baptism and the Lord's Supper as sacraments, though he shares the wider Reformed theology of the sacraments as sacred "signs" and "seals" of God's covenant of grace (25).

[31] Stanley K. Fowler has shown that, from the beginning of the Baptist movement in the seventeenth century, there have always been Baptist sacramentalists. Fowler, *More than a Symbol: The British Baptist Recovery of Baptismal Sacramentalism* (Carlisle, U.K.: Paternoster, 2002), 128–62; and Fowler, "Is Baptist Sacramentalism an Oxymoron? Reactions in Britain to *Christian Baptism* (1959)," in Cross and Thompson, *Baptist Sacramentalism*, 129–50.

[32] E.g., Henri de Lubac calls attention to the migration of terminology whereby language describing the Eucharist as the mystical body was gradually applied to the Church. The result is that by the twelfth century the Eucharist was understood as the true body (*corpus verum*) while the Church became known as the mystical body (*corpus mysticum*). See Lubac, *Corpus mysticum: L'eucharistie et l'église au moyen age* (Paris: Aubier, 1948), 162–88; and idem, *Corpus Mysticum: The Eucharist and the Church in the Middle Ages*, trans. C. J. Gemma Simmonds, with Richard Price and Christopher Stephens, ed. Laurence Paul Hemming and Susan Frank Parsons (Notre Dame, Ind.: University of Notre Dame Press, 2007), 143–67. See also Susan K. Wood, *Spiritual Exegesis and the Church in the Theology of Henri de Lubac* (Grand Rapids: Eerdmans, 1998), 63–70; and Hans Urs von Balthasar, *The Theology of Henri de Lubac* (San Francisco: Ignatius Press, 1991), 36–37. The displacement of the Eucharist from the social aspects of ecclesiology paved the way for individualistic eucharistic piety among Catholics in much the same way that the disjunction of the visible and invisible church in Protestantism made possible the movement to private experiential religion. De Lubac's attention to the "real" presence located in the church and the "spiritual" presence in the Eucharist suggests new possibilities and contours for sacramental discussions between Catholics and Baptists.

theology in the twentieth century.[32] Spiritualism, however, has remained an ever-present challenge, especially in North American Free Churches, which are haunted by the specter of Ralph Waldo Emerson, who resigned as minister when he was unsuccessful in getting his congregation to displace the observance of the Lord's Supper with a more pleasing mode of remembrance.[33] Emerson revered Jesus but refused to administer the Supper because it was unmeaningful and disagreeable to his feelings. Baptist spiritualists today are probably closer to their American forebear John Leland, who explained that he had "no complaint against communing with bread and wine." Leland's reasons for refusing to administer the Supper were more pragmatic: he had seen many brought to faith through preaching, praying, singing, and baptizing but had known "no instance that God evidently blessed the observance of [the Lord's Supper] for the conversion of sinners." Leland confessed that in "more than thirty years experiment I have had no evidence that the bread and wine ever assisted my faith to discern the Lord's body."[34] A minority of the congregation regarded his views as disorderly, coming perilously close to the Quakers, who nullified all external ordinances. After an unsuccessful attempt to remove him as pastor, the dissenting group appealed for disciplinary action to the local Baptist Association, who supported their complaint and resolved "to hold fellowship with no man or church, embracing or countenancing such sentiments."[35]

Although there was enough of a sacramental residue in early nineteenth-century New England among Unitarians and Baptists to steer through the swirling romantic and pragmatic currents, the same cannot be said for contemporary Free Churches. The problem, as with Leland, perhaps stems more from neglect than contempt. Yet, no matter the motive, the Lord's Supper has become an empty relic as the spirituality of unmediated and individualistic piety reigns supreme in American religion.[36] The Supper consequently suffers from an infrequent and enfeebled

---

Interestingly de Lubac's work was not mentioned in the bilateral Catholic-Baptist discussions on grace. See William E. Reiser, "Roman Catholic Understanding of the Eucharist," *Southwestern Journal of Theology* 28, no. 2 (1986): 85–89.

[33] Ralph Waldo Emerson, *The Lord's Supper*, in *The Complete Writings of Ralph Waldo Emerson* (New York: Wm. H. Wise, 1929), 2:1104–5.

[34] John Leland to the Shaftsbury Association, in *The Writings of the Late Elder John Leland*, ed. L. F. Greene (New York: G.W. Wood; repr., New York: Arno Press, 1969), 59–60.

[35] Stephen Wright, *History of the Shaftsbury Association, From 1800–1829* (New York: Macmillan, 1951), 151–52; and *Writings of the Late Elder John Leland* (ed. Greene), 62.

[36] Robert N. Bellah et al., eds., *Habits of the Heart: Individualism and Commitment in American Life*, updated ed. (Berkeley: University of California Press, 1996), 142–63.

practice. As a result, many Christians are spiritually starved. The question at hand, then, is whether Baptists and other Free Churches can reclaim a healthy sacramental faith and practice so that Christians receive spiritual nourishment from the Lord's table.

From Private Devotion to Common Prayer

For many Baptists, the Lord's Supper is a matter of individual piety. If individualism is the sickness of Baptist life, the antidote is healing grace that in part lies in recovering a sense of the Lord's Supper as an act of common prayer. Although it is something shared with other Christians, the ordinance is widely regarded as a private experience of remembrance and a personal matter of obedience.[37] Baptist observance of the Supper, which was rooted in the rich soil of an earlier, more communal life, gradually became democratized.[38] As personal autonomy became for many the preeminent value to be preserved and served, the American ideal of the confident individual displaced the Baptist sense of the gathered community.[39] It goes too far to suggest that Baptists are the source of this culture of autonomous individualism, although they have often embraced it as their own.[40] It is probably fair to say that if American Christianity became democratized in the nineteenth century by populist individualism, no denomination embodied this shift more than did the Baptists.[41] There is perhaps no better representative figure or harbinger of the Baptist

[37] John Wayland, "Lord's Supper, Administration of." In *Encyclopedia of Southern Baptists* (Nashville: Broadman, 1958), 2:794.

[38] For the story of the democratization of American Christianity and Baptists in particular, see Nathan O. Hatch, *The Democratization of American Christianity* (New Haven, Conn.: Yale University Press, 1989).

[39] Barry Alan Shain displays how the communal and republican vision of the American founders was gradually replaced by the expressivist voices of individualism through a fundamental misreading of history, but more importantly he shows how mistaken revisionists invented the myth of individualism as the original ethos of America, in his *The Myth of American Individualism: The Protestant Origins of American Political Thought* (Princeton, N.J.: Princeton University Press, 1994). Robert C. Walton argues that among English Baptists the decline of communal life and the rise of individualism was more a result of the disintegrating economic pressure of the Industrial Revolution, in his *The Gathered Community* (London: Carey Press, 1946), 110–17. Both American and English Baptists were deeply influenced by the cultural forces of individualism.

[40] Robert Bellah, "Is There a Common American Culture?" *Journal of the American Academy of Religion* 66, no. 3 (1998): 620. For my critique of Bellah, see "A New Perspective on Baptist Identity," *Perspectives in Religious Studies* 26, no. 1 (1999): 60–65.

[41] Winthrop Hudson notes that this highly individualistic and democratized account of Baptist identity "was derived from the general culture of the nineteenth century rather than from any serious study of the Bible," in his "Shifting Patterns of Church Order in the Twentieth Century," in *Baptist Concepts of the Church*, ed. Winthrop S. Hudson (Philadelphia: Judson Press, 1959), 215.

future in America than the great post-Revolutionary prophet of religious individualism, John Leland. Whether he was opposing state-supported churches, mission societies, slavery, hierarchical religion, or the Lord's Supper, the source of his protest was the conviction that nothing should come between God and the soul. Leland maintained the conviction of "the inalienable right that each individual has, of worshipping his God according to the dictates of his conscience, without being prohibited, directed, or controlled therein by human law."[42] Leland defended to the end "an unvarnished, undiluted, individualism."[43]

Insofar as it concerned individualism, Leland was no outlier to Baptists, who came to embrace "the gospel of individualism" in America through the influence of Puritan experientialism, Enlightenment individualism, Romantic expressivism, frontier independence, and liberal economics.[44] This anthropological turn virtually identified the gospel of Christ with the gospel of individualism and eroded the earlier Baptist concerns about the gathered community and associational connectionalism. Carlyle Marney seems to have in mind this sort of stripped-down version of liberty, which some Baptists have come to claim as the "competency of the individual to deal with God" but which has been transmogrified into "a stupid folk-lie" that "every tub should set on its own bottom." This profound "mis-reading of the universal priesthood," Marney continued, has "virtually destroyed the notion of Church and fellowship."[45]

This rugged individualism has been fostered by an anthropocentric account in which observing the Supper "in remembrance" of Christ has been thought of entirely as the mental exercise of memory. When an evangelical pastor was asked by a church member why their congregation did not observe the Lord's Supper more frequently, the pastor explained that when communion is done too often "it tends to mean less to the

---

[42] Leland, *A Blow at the Root*, in *Writings of the Late Elder John Leland* (ed. Greene), 239.

[43] J. Bradley Creed, "John Leland, American Prophet of Religious Individualism" (Ph.D. diss., Southwestern Baptist Theological Seminary, 1986), 203.

[44] Robert T. Handy, foreword to *Baptists in Transition: Individualism and Christian Responsibility*, by Winthrop S. Hudson (Valley Forge, Pa.: Judson Press, 1979), 9–13. See also my two essays on how individualism came to be identified as the Baptist orthodoxy: "Can Baptist Theology Be Revisioned?" *Perspectives in Religious Studies* 24, no. 3 (1997): 273–302; and "E. Y. Mullins and the Siren Songs of Modernity," *Review and Expositor* 96, no. 1 (1999): 23–42.

[45] Carlyle Marney, "Hail and Farewell!" the Dickson Lectures at Myers Park Baptist Church, Charlotte, North Carolina, published as *Beyond Our Time and Place* (Charlotte: Myers Park Baptist Church, 1974), 38. Marney's critique of individualism is an indictment of the tradition that runs from Leland to Mullins.

[46] Chuck Swindoll, In Case You've Wondered (column), in *Connection*, June 2002. *Connection* is the newsletter of Stonebriar Community Church in Frisco, Texas, where Swindoll is senior pastor (www.stonebriar.org).

participants."[46] For such evangelically minded believers, the regular observance of the Lord's Supper is not necessary because it is simply a means of
strengthening individual piety. Even though it is shared with fellow Christians, the observance is regarded as a personal experience of commemoration and a private communion with Christ. What makes it "meaningful"
is that it becomes affectively significant to each individual worshiper. Yet
the imagery of remembrance and memorial, which is central to the Lord's
Supper in two of the accounts (Luke 22:19; 1 Cor 11:24-25), has a much
richer and fuller meaning. The Greek word *anamnesis*, the Hebrew term
zakar, and their cognates in both Testaments do not suggest a mere subjective recollection. Rather, they indicate an objective act to memorial-
ize. These words are part of the rich liturgical language of Israel and the
church that recalls God's past redemption as historically paradigmatic,
God's present deliverance as sacramentally signified, and God's coming
salvation as eschatologically anticipated. The association of these liturgical words (i.e., *anamnesis*, *zakar*, etc.) in the biblical narrative displays that
the Passover, the feast of unleavened bread, acts of charity, the lives of
saints, and preeminently the Lord's Supper perform the enacted prayers of
God's people. As remembering signs, they place before God the covenant
promises and saving acts of the Exodus and the cross and resurrection.
As common prayers, they invoke God's coming to complete the work of
salvation already begun.[47]

Put simply, "for Christians 'to remember' or 'to make remembrance'
is the equivalent of 'to pray,' and, for God, it is the equivalent of 'to hear,
to grant, to show mercy.'"[48] The *anamnesis* in which the church remem-
bers Jesus in the Supper stands in continuity with Old Testament covenant
language that does not call merely for God to bring to mind what has
been promised but rather pleads for God to act decisively so as to complete
the work of salvation already begun by bringing in the kingdom through
the *parousia*. Each celebration thus affirms the eschatological horizon of
the Supper as a covenant meal that proclaims "the Lord's death until he
comes" (1 Cor 11:26).[49] So, gathered at the table, the church lifts up a prayer
shared through the ages with the earliest Christians: *marana'tha*—come

---

[47] Max Thurian, *The Eucharistic Memorial: The New Testament*, vol. 2 of *The Eucharistic Memorial*, trans. J. G. Davies, Ecumenical Studies in Worship 8 (Richmond, Va.: John Knox, 1961), 5–33.

[48] Thurian, *Eucharistic Memorial: The New Testament*, 33.

[49] Joachim Jeremias, *The Eucharistic Words of Jesus* (New York: Charles Scribner's Sons, 1966), 249–55. See also Geoffrey Wainwright, *Eucharist and Eschatology* (New York: Oxford University Press, 1981), 64–68.

[50] The Aramaic words *marana'tha* were used by earliest Christians as a closing prayer associated with the Eucharist invoking Christ to come. 1 Corinthians 16:22 and also the *Didache*

Lord!⁵⁰ The Lord's Supper, then, is not merely a matter of subjective recollection or private devotion. It is a performative act of common prayer
by a covenant community that recalls as a memorial before the Father the
unique sacrifice of the Son and invokes God's abiding and eschatological
presence through the Spirit. And as such it prefigures and indeed hastens
the very future it signifies.

What makes this act of common prayer sacramental is not the action
performed, the words invoked, or even the faith believed. It is thus sacramental because God promises to be present in and through the performance of the words, actions, and reception. It is a sacrament because it
is "a sign through and in which God freely accomplishes that which is
signified, not in a manner that can be presumed or manipulated, but in a
manner that is truly gracious."⁵¹ Those who enact this prayer trust that the
Father will act to make Christ present through the Spirit because God has
promised to do so. This prayer enacts Jesus' promise that "those who eat
my flesh and drink my blood have eternal life, and I will raise them up on
the last day" (John 6:54). So, in anticipation of the future fulfillment of
the eschatological kingdom of God, the community gathers around the
table to lift up a common prayer as a testimony to the belief that God will
act according to God's promise "until he comes" (1 Cor 11:26). Thus the
gifts of bread and wine are received as a grateful response to God's promise and in hopeful expectation of God's action.

From Obligatory Ordinance
to Life-Giving Practice

Though most Baptists today prefer to speak of the Lord's Supper (and baptism) as an "ordinance," in the seventeenth century Baptists used a variety
of terms interchangeably to describe these acts, frequently employing the
language of "sacraments."⁵² The use of sacramental language continued
in the eighteenth and early nineteenth centuries among Baptists in England and America. For example, the English Baptist pastor Daniel Turner
described the minister as one set apart "for the due administration of the

---

10.6, in *The Didache, The Epistle of Barnabas, The Epistles and The Martyrdom of St. Polycarp, The
Fragments of Papias, The Epistle to Diognetus*, trans. James A. Kleist, Ancient Christian Writers
6 (New York: Newman Press, 1948), 21.

⁵¹ John E. Colwell, *Promise and Presence: An Exploration of Sacramental Theology* (Milton
Keynes, U.K.: Paternoster, 2005), 11.

⁵² John Smyth, *Short Confession of Faith in XX Articles by John Smyth* (1609), 13, in
Lumpkin, *Baptist Confessions of Faith*, 100–102; and The Orthodox Creed XIX, XXVII, and
XXXIII, in Lumpkin, *Baptist Confessions of Faith*, 311–13, 317, and 321. See also Kiffin, *Sober
Discourse*, 59; Keach, *Tropologia* 4.632–41; Collins, *Orthodox Catechism*, 25–46; and Thomas
Lambe, *A Confutation of Infants Baptisme* ([London?], 1643), 27, 37, and 45.

word and sacraments," and, in an appeal to London Baptists for more ministers to come to America, Middletown, New Jersey, minister Abel Morgan stated that most of the churches in the Philadelphia Association "administer the sacrament once a month."[53] In the antebellum South, where Baptist churches were often biracial in membership, one slave narrative describes white preachers inviting black members to come down from the gallery to receive the "sacrament."[54] Adoniram and Ann Judson, who in 1812 became the first American Baptist foreign missionaries, referred to the Lord's Supper and baptism as "sacraments" throughout their ministry.[55] Though antisacramentalist forces dominated much of Baptist life in North America and Great Britain in the latter half of the nineteenth century, the mid-twentieth century began to see a resurgence of sacramental theology.[56] The Baptist Union of Great Britain affirmed the "two sacraments of Believers' Baptism and the Lord's Supper as being of the Lord's ordaining," and their *Orders and Prayers for Church Worship* described the observance of the Lord's Supper as "the ministry of the sacrament."[57]

[53] Daniel Turner, *A Compendium of Social Religion of the Nature and Constitution of Christian Churches*, 2nd ed. (Bristol, U.K.: W. Pine, 1778), 49–50 and 36; Abel Morgan, letter to London Baptists, in *Baptist Life and Thought, 1600–1980*, ed. William H. Brackney (Valley Forge, Pa.: Judson Press, 1983), 85.

[54] Anonymous slave narrative in Norman R. Yetman, *Life under the Peculiar Institution* (New York: Holt, Reinhart & Winston, 1970), 266–67; cited in Brackney, *Baptist Life and Thought*, 218.

[55] When asked by a Burman inquirer about the "rules" that must be observed when converting to Christianity, Adoniram Judson replied, "The disciples of Christ, after baptism, were associated together; that they assembled every Lord's day for worship; and that, from time to time, they received the sacrament of bread and wine." Quoted in Ann H. Judson, *An Account of the American Baptist Mission to the Burman Empire: In a Series of Letters, Addressed to a Gentleman in London* (London: J. Butterworth & Son, 1823), 250–51. Earlier in his missionary diary, Adoniram Judson refers to baptism as an ordinance: "We felt satisfied, that they were humble disciples of Jesus, and were desirous of receiving this ordinance purely out of regard to his command, and their own spiritual welfare" (202).

[56] Michael J. Walker attributes the diminishing of sacramental theology among English Baptists to the backlash against the Oxford movement, in his *Baptists at the Table: The Theology of the Lord's Supper amongst English Baptists in the Nineteenth Century* (Didcot, U.K.: Baptist Historical Society, 1992), 91–97. In America the decline of sacramentalism among Baptists was due to the influence of evangelical revivalism, which emphasized personal faith and devalued ritual. Baptists in the American South were significantly shaped by the theology of Landmarkism, which was framed in reaction to the sacramentalism of the Campbellites, who held to baptismal regeneration and observed communion weekly.

[57] The Baptist Doctrine of the Church, statement approved by the Council of the Baptist Union of Great Britain and Ireland, March 1948, in *Baptist Union Documents 1948–1977*, ed. Roger Hayden (London: Baptist Historical Society, 1980), 5–6; and Ernest A. Payne and Stephen F. Winward, eds. *Orders and Prayers for Church Worship* (London: Baptist Union, 1967), 14. This emphasis on the sacramental dimension of worship has been continued in subsequent iterations of *Patterns and Prayers for Christian Worship* (Oxford: Oxford University Press, 1991);

As Baptists in America experienced rapid growth due to evangelical revivalism, they also grew gradually less comfortable with sacramental language that attempted to say something about God's activity at the
table, and they began to speak of its observance more as an "act of obedience."[58] Descriptions of the Lord's Supper as an ordinance consequently
became more dominant. Typical of the new theology were the Separate
Baptists of North Carolina, who declared that "baptism and the Lord's
Supper are ordinances of the Lord . . . to be continued by his church until
his second coming."[59] It is important to note that there is nothing inherently wrong with the nomenclature of "ordinance" as commonly used by
Baptists and other Christians.[60] Jesus Christ did in fact institute the Supper
to be performed regularly as a memorial until his return. Understanding
the Supper as an ordinance underscores its connection with Christian
obedience and discipleship.

One obvious tactical advantage of describing the Lord's Supper as an
ordinance was that it gave Baptists the greatest rhetorical traction to oppose
what they considered to be the "erroneous views" of "transubstantiation"
and "consubstantiation."[61] When it came to the Lord's Supper, Baptists
knew they were not Catholics or Protestants. Yet following the well-worn
paths of the Reformation debates on the sacraments often provided some
heat but rarely shed any light. This language borrowed from the elements
inherited from the history of earlier debates offered little room for Baptists
to say anything about God's activity in the Supper, which for them seemed
to stop with the Lord's command. From that point on, the Supper was
viewed as a matter of personal and communal piety.

A deeper problem is that the term "ordinance" carries a certain sense
of arbitrariness—of something to be done simply because it has been
commanded—often leading to blind obedience and legalism. The with-
ering of an earlier and more vital sacramental theology in Baptist life

---

and *Gathering for Worship: Patterns and Prayers for the Community of Disciples*, ed. Christopher J.
Ellis and Myra Blyth (Norwich, U.K.: Canterbury Press, 2005).

[58] The Baptist Faith and Message (1963) VII, in Lumpkin, *Baptist Confessions of Faith*, 396.

[59] Principles of Faith of the Sandy Creek Association (1816) VII, in Lumpkin, *Baptist
Confessions of Faith*, 358.

[60] Although the two most widely regarded Baptist confessions of the seventeenth century do not exclude other, more sacramental terminology about the Supper, they employ
the language of ordinance. See Second London Confession XXVIII.1, in Lumpkin, *Baptist
Confessions of Faith*, 290; and The Orthodox Creed XXVII, in Lumpkin, *Baptist Confessions
of Faith*, 317.

[61] E.g., Augustus Hopkins Strong, *Systematic Theology*, 8th ed. (Philadelphia: Judson
Press, 1909), 3:965–69.

is explicable given that the word "ordinance" has all but fallen out of conventional discourse in the wider culture. The conspicuous exceptions are the specialized meanings in legal and military jargon: "In accordance with city ordinance 165B you are hereby summoned to appear in municipal court," or "The aircraft discharged its ord[i]nance on the enemy target." Neither of these connotations, however, commends the continued use of the language of ordinance in theology or liturgy.

Earlier generations of Christians in the Free Church tradition had another way of speaking about the Lord's Supper. In 1651 a group of English General Baptists issued a statement that they called The Faith and Practise of Thirty Congregations, in which they declared that the Lord's Supper as a "practise is left upon record as a memorial of [Christ's] suffering."[62] Free Church Christians found the language of practice congenial to their understanding of living according to the primitive and apostolic pattern. Early Baptists clearly saw themselves as a mean between the formalist ritualism of Anglo-Catholics and the formless pietism of Quakers and Familists, but it was the latter that was the greatest temptation. For example, Thomas Grantham rightly worried that, where the practice of godliness is neglected, "religion will in a little time either vanish, or become an unknown conceit, every man being at liberty to follow (what he supposes to be) the motions of the Spirit of God, in which there is so great a probability of being mistaken as in nothing more." He warned that human "ignorance being very great, and Satan very subtile, and the way of the Lord neglected, Men ly open to every fancy which pleaseth best."[63] Baptists like Grantham emphasized that the church is spiritually fed and renewed through observance of gospel practices. Focusing on the notion of practice attends more closely to Christ's command, which was not simply to "remember me" but rather "*do this* in remembrance of me."

Retrieving this language of practice from the storehouse of tradition is timely given the contemporary interest in practice for Christian theology.[64] Recent reflections have begun to describe practices as "shared activities that address fundamental human needs and that, woven together, form a way of life" or simply as "a life-giving way of life."[65] As shared activities, practices are by definition complex, socially established, and cooperative.

---

[62] The Faith and Practise of Thirty Congregations, 53, in Lumpkin, *Baptist Confessions of Faith*, 183.

[63] Thomas Grantham, *Christianismus Primitivus; or, The Ancient Christian Religion* II.1.I (London: Francis Smith, 1678).

[64] E.g., Miroslav Volf and Dorothy C. Bass, *Practicing Theology* (Grand Rapids: Eerdmans, 2002).

[65] Dorothy C. Bass, *Practicing Our Faith* (San Francisco: Jossey-Bass, 1997), xi and 2.

Moreover, they address fundamental human need in terms of goods that are internal to the practice. And, as a life-giving way of life, they promote the advance of shared conceptions of what is good.[66] In the case of the Lord's Supper, the practice is commended to gathered communities, not individual Christians, for performance. Moreover, the Supper is to be observed in service of a good that is internal to the practice (i.e., remembering Jesus), not for any pragmatic reasons (e.g., Leland's conversion of sinners). Finally, as a gospel practice the Lord's Supper advances the Christian life by offering a real way of knowing the abiding presence of Jesus Christ and nourishing the faith of believers. Whereas theological debates about the elements in search of ecclesial orthodoxy have long since fallen along predictable lines, theological conversations about eucharistic practice that aim toward ecumenical orthopraxy offer signs of hope about a way forward. These gestures toward a common understanding of Christian practice should not be taken as attempts to smother diversity of liturgical expression but rather are to be received as efforts to display for those who gather in his name what Jesus commended with his words "do this."

The practice by the Abingdon church led by Daniel Turner of admitting both believer- and infant-baptized Christians to commune at the Lord's table serves as a shining example of catholic practice. Quoting the apostolic principle that "all things are yours" (1 Cor 3:21), Turner defends the practice of "free communion" on the basis that all those who have received the grace of Jesus Christ, who "live by faith upon him as their *Saviour,* and conscientiously obey him as their *Lord,* must have *an equal right* to ALL the privileges of the Gospel."[67] Turner can thus find no scriptural warrant to withhold the means of grace from any of God's children regardless of their "sentiments" or "mistakes" about baptism.[68] The fact that Christ undeniably accepts infant-baptized Christians at his table when they remember him leads one to ask why fellow Christians should not also be admitted freely when Christ is remembered at the table by Baptist Christians.[69] Indeed, Scripture expressly commands the reception of "the weak in faith" and respect for the liberty of conscience of those who differ in judgment (Rom 14:1).[70] Turner further argues that the matter of baptism is "not *so* clearly stated in the Bible (however clear to us) but

---

[66] Alasdair MacIntyre, *After Virtue* (Notre Dame, Ind.: University of Notre Dame Press, 1981), 175.

[67] Daniel Turner, *A Modest Plea for Free Communion at the Lord's Table* (London: J. Johnson, 1772), I–II, 3–4 (emphasis in original).

[68] Turner, *Modest Plea*, III, 4–5.

[69] Turner, *Modest Plea*, IV, 5–6.

[70] Turner, *Modest Plea*, V, 6.

that even *sincere Christians* may mistake them." Consequently, he reasons, "a private opinion . . . can never be *justly* made an *indispensable term of communion at the Lord's Table*" because it is "an ordinance *equally* binding upon *all* true Christians, and *equally* the privilege of all."[71] He concludes with an appeal to "forbearance and charity," and commends his readers to the "*uniting spirit*" in the Gospel.[72]

A more recent example of coming to the table on the basis of shared practice comes from the constructive proposals by the joint liturgical group in Great Britain entitled *Initiation and Eucharist*. The study suggests that the practice of the Supper at minimum conform to the fourfold action set forth in the biblical pattern: That Christ "took . . . blessed (or gave thanks) . . . broke . . . gave."[73] Other Baptists might make their move toward a deeper participation in the mystery of Christ's presence and a richer communion with the saints by following a threefold action. The first is *paradosis* that proclaims the gospel story of God's salvation beginning with Israel and its covenant, continuing through Jesus and his way, and culminating in the cross and resurrection. Here the move is to construe the actions of breaking bread within the drama of redemption so as to understand them as a performative practice. The second is *anamnesis* that recalls the words of institution either from one of the Gospels or Paul. Because Free Church worship tends to be more at home with the words of the Pauline account and sometimes from one the Synoptic Gospels but rarely in the Gospel of John, care should be taken to embrace the language of all three sources in liturgical *anamnesis*. The final feature is *paraclesis* that invokes the presence of the Holy Spirit to unite in mystery this practice with the sacrifice of Christ so God's people may by faith receive nourishment from the table. Remembering Jesus in the Supper is more than an obligatory ordinance. It is a life-giving practice that is offered to all God's children.

From Real Absence to Real Presence

When it comes to the question of God's omnipresence, Free Church faith and practice affirms that God can be present anywhere—almost anywhere, that is, except on the communion table. This curious doctrine

---

[71] Turner, *Modest Plea*, VI, 6–7 (emphasis in original).

[72] Turner, *Modest Plea*, VII–VIII, 7–8 (emphasis in original).

[73] The Joint Liturgical Group, *Initiation and Eucharist*, ed. Neville Clark and Ronald C. D. Jasper (London: SPCK, 1972), 24.

[74] C. W. Dugmore attributes the doctrine of real absence to Zwingli, in his *The Mass and the English Reformers* (London: Macmillan, 1958), 160. I will show in the next section that this reading of Zwingli is mistaken. Of course, the doctrine of real absence is more common in

of real absence is informed by several heterodox factors.[74] One factor is a deep-rooted tradition of suspicious antimagicalism based on a medieval stereotype of the sacraments as automatic media of grace coupled with a rigid tropism inherited from the Radical Reformation that posits an absolute ontological barrier between the sign (e.g., bread and wine) and the signified (e.g., body and blood). A second factor is a latent Gnosticism that sharply distinguishes between spiritual and material and is thus skeptical of identifying the divine presence with anything in the physical (or biological) world, often accompanied by an incipient Marcionism that separates the spheres of creation and redemption. A third factor is a persistent Donatism that assumes effective grace depends entirely on the faithfulness of the administrative agent and an individualistic spiritualism that tends to reduce all things sacramental to merely outward signs of inward experience. It is not surprising, then, that the belief that the risen Christ is not really present through the Holy Spirit at the table but that the Lord's Supper is merely of symbolic significance has become a new kind of popular consensus among Baptists and other Free Churches. Other Baptists seek to reconsider the ways early Christians expressed their faith when coming to the table.

The Sayings of the Desert Fathers relate the story of an old hermit who said that "the bread which we receive is not really the body of Christ, but a symbol." Two other monks confronted him and exhorted him saying, "Do not hold this position, Father, but hold one in conformity with that which the catholic Church has given us," namely "that the bread itself is the body of Christ and that the cup itself is his blood, and this in all truth and not a symbol." The three returned to their cells, where they prayed that God would reveal the truth to them. The answer to their prayers came by way of a vision, in which an angel appeared to them in church on Sunday, pouring the blood of a child into the chalice and transforming the eucharistic bread into bloody flesh. Seeing the vision, the old monk cried out, "Lord, I believe that this bread is your flesh and this chalice is your blood."[75] While some might be troubled that this truth was revealed through a vision, what many contemporary Baptists and other Free Church Christians find more troubling is the assertion that sacramental

---

populist rhetoric than in careful theology. E.g., Baptist theologian W. T. Conner explains that the symbolic view of the Lord's Supper "does not deny the spiritual omnipresence of Christ, but it does deny that Christ is present in the bread and wine of the Supper any more than he is present in any other material substance." Conner, *Christian Doctrine* (Nashville: Broadman, 1937), 287.

[75] Benedicta Ward, trans., *The Sayings of the Desert Fathers: The Alphabetical Collection* (Kalamazoo, Mich.: Cistercian, 1975), 53–54.

realism in the eucharistic meal is catholic (i.e., universal) teaching and symbolic significance is at odds with the apostolic faith. They are conditioned to assume that the notion of real presence is a later corruption that departs from the New Testament teaching of personal remembrance, but in fact the monks were right.[76] In the early second century, Ignatius of Antioch described the Eucharist as "the medicine of immortality, and the antidote which prevents us from dying . . . that we should live in God through Jesus Christ,"[77] and he noted that, because those with heterodox opinions reject the catholic teaching that the Eucharist is "the flesh of our Saviour Jesus Christ," they absent themselves from the table and prayer unto their own destruction.[78] Other writings from the second century confirm that a sense of sacramental realism was indeed regarded to be a matter of apostolic teaching shared by the whole church as Justin Martyr, Irenaeus of Lyons, Clement of Alexandria, and others attest.[79]

The struggle that Baptists and other Free Church Christians have in seeing Christ as really present in the Eucharist is puzzling. They do not doubt Christ's promise to be present with his disciples in worship (Matt 18:20) or on mission (Matt 28:20), but yet they are suspicious about his promise to meet them in the bread and wine of the Lord's Supper (Matt 26:26–29). Perhaps more than anything this reticence about the real presence in communion has to do with the default theological categories in the received tradition that rejected the transubstantiation teaching of Catholicism and the consubstantiation doctrine of Lutheranism and tended toward a memorial view that became associated with Zwinglian understandings of the Supper that became the consensus view among Baptists in the nineteenth century.[80] Not all Free Churches, however, hold to a memorial understanding of the Supper. The early nineteenth-century English Baptist Robert Hall railed against the inadequate consideration of the Lord's table as "a mere commemoration" and contended that the Supper is "a spiritual participation of the blood . . . and body of the crucified

---

[76] Steven R. Harmon, "Qualitative Catholicity in the Ignatian Correspondence—and the New Testament: The Fallacies of a Restorationist Hermeneutic," *Perspectives in Religious Studies* 38, no. 1 (2011): 33–34. Harmon shows that the idea that sacramental realism is a later corruption of Catholicism rests on an antihistoricism that is grounded in restorationist biblicism. This point has been made in greater detail in ch. 3, pp. 121–28.

[77] Ignatius, *To the Ephesians* 20.2, in *The Ante-Nicene Fathers*, 1:57.

[78] Ignatius, *To the Smyrnaeans* 7.1, in *The Ante-Nicene Fathers*, 1:89.

[79] Justin Martyr, *First Apology* 66, in *The Ante-Nicene Fathers*, 1:185; Irenaeus, *Against Heresies* 5.2.2–3, in *The Ante-Nicene Fathers*, 1:528; and Clement, *Who Is the Rich Man That Shall Be Saved?* 223, in *The Ante-Nicene Fathers*, 2:598.

[80] Walker, *Baptists at the Table*, 3–8.

[81] Hall, *Terms of Communion* I.3, in *The Works of Robert Hall* (London: Henry G. Bohn, 1851), 3:45.

Saviour."[81] Hall continued that those who receive communion "are actual partakers by faith of the body and blood of the Redeemer offered upon the Cross."[82]

Nor was Hall alone in rejecting mere memorialism in quest of a more sacramental theology. None other than Charles Haddon Spurgeon joined his voice to the growing Free Church sacramental chorus:

> *"We firmly believe in the real presence of Christ which is spiritual, and yet certain."* By spiritual we do not mean unreal; in fact, the spiritual takes the lead in real-ness to spiritual men. *I believe in the true and real presence of Jesus with His people*: such presence has been real to my spirit. Lord Jesus, Thou Thyself hast visited me. As surely as the Lord Jesus came really as to His flesh to Bethlehem and Calvary, so surely does He come really by His Spirit to His people in the hours of their communion with Him. We are as conscious of that presence as of our own existence.[83]

While clearly rejecting a stereotypical corporeal understanding of Catholicism, Spurgeon nevertheless used language closer to Calvin than to Zwingli to affirm the real presence of Christ in communion. Spurgeon's sacramental theology shared Calvin's concern about two faulty extremes to be avoided. The first is, "by too little regard for the signs, [to] divorce them from their mysteries, to which they are so to speak attached." This Calvin believed was the error of the Zwinglians. The second is, "by extolling them immoderately, [to] seem to obscure somewhat the mysteries themselves." This Calvin argued was the mistake of Lutherans and Catholics.[84] By all accounts Spurgeon avoided any attempt to reduce Christ's presence to a mere commemoration. It is a real presence, albeit a spiritual one, that Spurgeon avowed.[85]

Thomas Grantham also attempted to strike a balance between formalism and spiritualism. Like other General Baptists of the seventeenth century, he was more concerned about the spiritualism that left no room for God's acts in history or in the continuing incarnation of sacramental

---

[82] Hall, *Terms of Communion* II.1, in *Works*, 3:62.

[83] C. H. Spurgeon, "Mysterious Visits," in *Till He Come* (London: Passmore & Alabaster, 1894), 17 (emphasis added).

[84] Calvin, *Institutes* IV.17.5 (ed. McNeill), 2:1364–65.

[85] Tim Grass and Ian Randall, "C. H. Spurgeon on the Sacraments," in Cross and Thompson, *Baptist Sacramentalism*, 74–75; Peter J. Morden, "The Lord's Supper and the Spirituality of C. H. Spurgeon," in *Baptist Sacramentalism 2*, ed. Anthony R. Cross and Philip E. Thompson (Milton Keynes, U.K.: Paternoster, 2008), 189–91; and Morden, "The Spirituality of C. H. Spurgeon: Maintaining Communion; The Lord's Supper," *Baptistic Theologies* 4, no. 1 (2012): 41–45. Morden argues that Spurgeon's views on the Supper "grew more 'sacramental' as [his] ministry progressed."

practice. Not only did the Quakers refuse to observe the Lord's Supper; they went so far as to deny that the blood of Christ was ever seen with human eyes. On the basis of Luke 24, Grantham argued that Christ was (and continues to be) known in the breaking of bread, yet his residual anti-Catholic prejudice and the fixed doctrinal categories of the seventeenth century left him with little sacramental latitude and few theological resources to account for God's presence.[86]

In the sixteenth century, before a sub-Zwinglian memorial view became entrenched in Free Church theology, there was greater freedom when it came to reflection on the sacraments. One of the most notable and creative sacramental theologians of the Radical Reformers was Pilgram Marpeck, a leader among south German Anabaptists. His was not a theology of individual inwardness but of a gathered community. He did not offer a theology of the elements but a theology of the practices (or ceremonies). The goal of Marpeck's theology of the sacraments "was to create an apology for ceremonies as external works which were of one being with the inward reality they represented."[87] For Marpeck, unless the spiritual impulse was paired to the sacramental conviction, "the gospel would be reduced to a biblical, ahistorical, nonchurchly, individualized piety."[88] Marpeck's sacramental reflection was deeply christological. He considered the ceremony of the Lord's Supper to be an extension of the incarnation "that must remain . . . until the end of the world."[89] Just as the inner spiritual reality of Christ is revealed in the outer material form of his humanity, so the same spiritual reality is revealed in the outward ceremony of bread and wine.[90] The result is an understanding of the Lord's Supper as a means of conveying the nourishing spiritual food of grace. Marpeck's sacramental theology was also richly trinitarian. In the Supper the Father works internally through the Spirit, and the Son acts externally through his humanity.[91] The efficacy of the ceremony thus depends on the simultaneous interaction of all three persons of the Trinity: Father, Son, and Spirit. Likewise, only a trinitarian theology can adequately account

---

[86] Grantham, *Christianismus Primitivus* II.7.III.3, 86–87.

[87] John D. Rempel, *The Lord's Supper in Anabaptism* (Scottdale, Pa.: Herald Press, 1993), 97.

[88] John D. Rempel, "Toward an Anabaptist Theology of the Lord's Supper," in *The Lord's Supper: Believers Church Perspectives*, ed. Dale R. Stoffer (Scottdale, Pa.: Herald Press, 1997), 244.

[89] Marpeck, *A Clear Refutation* II, in *The Writings of Pilgram Marpeck*, ed. and trans. William Klassen and Walter Klaassen (Scottdale, Pa.: Herald Press, 1978), 47.

[90] Marpeck, *A Clear and Useful Instruction*, in *Writings of Pilgram Marpeck* (ed. and trans. Klassen and Klaassen), 78–79.

[91] Marpeck, *The Admonition of 1542*, in *Writings of Pilgram Marpeck* (ed. and trans. Klassen and Klaassen), 195.

for Christ's presence in the Supper: as regards his physical presence, Christ is in heaven, but as regards his spiritual presence, he is on earth with the fellowship of the Holy Spirit who gather in Jesus' name and partake of the bread and wine in faith and love.[92]

Baptists have been careful to point out that the Lord's Supper does not magically *confer* grace. Rather, it *confirms* grace that is mystically present to the faithful gathered around the table when as promised the risen Christ becomes really and truly known through the Holy Spirit in the breaking of bread and in the sharing of the cup. Other Baptists affirm the Lord's Supper as a sacrament of the Lord's ordaining and a means of grace to those who receive the bread and wine in faith. To share in the bread and the cup is to participate in a real communion with the living Christ. And to drink of the cup and eat the bread in faith is to feed upon Christ. No theory can explain this presence, and yet the reality of this knowledge requires no explanation to make it so. But when the covenant community gathers in faith at the table where the Lord has promised to be present in the enacted thanksgiving of bread and wine, Christ is really and spiritually known by his grace.

From Mere Symbols to Powerful Signs

In characterizing Baptist views on the Lord's Supper, it is clear that "some consider the elements mere symbols."[93] One preacher is said to have regularly admonished his congregation upon observing the Supper: "Now, remember that this doesn't mean anything. These are just symbols." It is not an overstatement to say that a sub-Zwinglian theology of the Lord's Supper has become entrenched as a de facto orthodoxy among Free Churches. British Baptist Robert Walton sounded a high note for those who would resist the theology of mere symbolism, declaring that the Lord's Supper is *a means of grace* in which *the real presence* of Christ is manifested. He insisted that "to interpret the Supper as a memorial feast and no more is to reduce it to a method of auto-suggestion," for the "sacraments are *not only symbols*: they are *also instruments*." They both "*tell the truth* and *convey the grace*." They do not just speak. They "speak with power."[94] To be sure, Baptists affirm that the bread and wine of the Supper have symbolic significance, but, as W. T. Conner noted, many Baptists have tended to resist saying that these symbols "contain or convey [Christ's] spiritual

---

[92] Marpeck, *Admonition of 1542*, in *Writings of Pilgrim Marpeck* (ed. and trans. Klassen and Klaassen), 288–91.

[93] *Encyclopedia of Southern Baptists*, s.v. "Lord's Supper," 2:794.

[94] Walton, *Gathered Community*, 170 (emphasis added).

presence." Instead, he continued, they have been more comfortable saying that they only "picture it so that it may be real to the mind and thus
strengthen faith."[95] Conner's younger colleague Franklin Segler, however,
argued that such "mere symbolism" is inadequate to convey the depth of
meaning and significance of the Lord's Supper. Indeed, Segler asserted,
"None of the historic views—Roman Catholic, Lutheran, Calvinistic,
Zwinglian—adequately delineates the dynamic, revelational aspects of
baptism and the Lord's Supper as acts of worship."[96] One thing is clear: the
consensus fidelium among Baptists and other Free Churches pertains more to
what the Supper is *not* than to what it positively signifies. Therein lies the
problem. The question remains whether Free Churches can move from
a theology of mere symbols to a rich and robust sense of powerful signs.

A shift in this direction requires a reassessment of Zwingli in context.[97] Misinterpretations of Zwingli as the champion of "mere memorialism" have become standard. In Victorian-era England the eucharistic
theology of Baptists and other Free Churches as well as the majority of
evangelical Anglicans was loosely Zwinglian.[98] It offered a view of the
Lord's Supper that did not intrude into the direct and immediate relationship between God and the individual believer. For example, Alexander
Maclaren, the minister of Union Chapel in Manchester and one of the
most popular Baptist preachers of the day, described his sacramental theology as "a poor, bald Zwinglianism," asserting of the Lord's Supper that
"there is no magic, no mystery, no 'sacrament' about it."[99] Zwingli has
been widely regarded by Catholic, Reformed, and Free Church theologians as a defender of all who observe the Supper with the understanding
that the bread and wine are but reminders of salvation already achieved.
According to the conventional account of Zwingli, the Supper enshrines
no mystery, Christ is not really present, and the elements convey no grace.
Yet more than a few observers have noted that "there was a recognition
of a mystical union with Christ in Zwingli's teaching which did not find
full expression in his controversies."[100]

Zwingli's sacramental theology went through several stages.[101] In his

---

[95] Conner, *Christian Doctrine*, 287.

[96] Franklin M. Segler, *Christian Worship* (Nashville: Broadman, 1967), 138–39.

[97] I allude here to David C. Steinmetz' careful treatments of Luther and Calvin, in his
Luther in Context (Bloomington: Indiana University Press, 1986); and *Calvin in Context* (New
York: Oxford University Press, 1995).

[98] Walker, *Baptists at the Table*, 3.

[99] Maclaren, *Expositions of Holy Scripture: Corinthians*, 173.

[100] Ernest A. Payne, *The Fellowship of Believers: Baptist Thought and Practice Yesterday and
Today* (London: Carey Kingsgate Press, 1952), 60.

[101] I have not attempted to give a close reading of Zwingli's text but rather have

early writings (1523), he criticized the abuses of the mass, referring to the Eucharist as "a memorial of the sacrifice" but not a sacrifice. The "remembrance" that Zwingli mentioned is no mere intellectual exercise but a reception by faith of God's gift. Moreover, the posture of the "memorial" is not merely looking back but rather bringing the past into the present. Zwingli at no point in these years denied the presence of Christ in the Eucharist.[102] During the period of the institutionalization of the reform (1524–1525), Zwingli developed a symbolic understanding of the Supper in dialogue with radicals on one extreme, pressing for changes along the lines of Karlstadt, and Catholics on the other end, wanting to hold the line against any changes. For example, in Zwingli's November 1524 letter to Matthew Alber, he equated "eating" the body and blood of Christ at the table (John 6:53) with "faith" (John 6:47).[103] In April of 1525, Zwingli began to interpret the Eucharist as a Passover meal. It is, he reasoned, the divinity of Christ, not the bodily presence in the Lord's Supper, that saves. Faith then is required for the spiritual meal, which is not merely the physical eating of the elements but is not unrelated to the Supper either. Those who receive the Lord's Supper signify their membership in the church.[104]

In the polemical period (1526–1529), Zwingli was concerned that Luther was opening the door to a return to Catholicism. It is important to note that even in these writings Zwingli did not exclude the presence of Christ in the Supper but preferred to speak of God's omnipresence through the Spirit.[105] In his *Friendly Exegesis* on the Eucharist addressed to Luther in 1527, Zwingli carefully distinguished his view from "memorialists" who commemorated Christ's "body" rather than his "passion and death" and who asserted that "faith makes God present." Zwingli here described Christ's presence as "spiritual."[106] In the final two years of Zwingli's ministry (1530–1531), he emerged as a reformed catholic theologian for whom the bread and wine are transformed not in substance but in significance. Zwingli asserted, "I do not believe it is the Supper unless Christ is there." What is present is not the physical body of Christ, which is in heaven, but the spiritual body of Christ received by faith.[107] But, whereas in his earlier and controversial periods, Zwingli emphasized the

---

summarized H. Wayne Pipkin's research from his *Zwingli: The Positive Value of His Eucharistic Writings* (Leeds, U.K.: Yorkshire Baptist Association, 1986).

[102] Pipkin, *Zwingli*, 10–11.

[103] Zwingli, letter to Matthew Alber, in *Writings* (trans. Pipkin), 2:134.

[104] Pipkin, *Zwingli*, 11–16.

[105] Pipkin, *Zwingli*, 16–19.

[106] Huldrych Zwingli, *Friendly Exegesis, that is, Exposition of the Matter of the Eucharist to Martin Luther*, in *Writings* (trans. Pipkin), 2:251–56.

[107] Pipkin, *Zwingli*, 19–22.

role of faith in the reception of the Supper, in his final work, an *Exposition of the Faith*, Zwingli spoke more about Christ's spiritual presence in the sacrament and argued that believers come to the Supper "to feed spiritually upon Christ."[108] Other studies have found even more sacramental realism in Zwingli's theology, suggesting that in the celebration of the Eucharist there is a transubstantiation not of the bread and the wine but of the gathered community that literally (not merely symbolically) becomes the body of Christ. It is in this transformation of the ecclesial community, not of the sacramental elements, that there is a doctrine of real presence in Zwingli's sacramental theology.[109] Other Baptists seeking to retrieve theological resources for a more powerful understanding of symbolism in the Lord's Supper may be surprised by what they find in a closer reading of Zwingli.

The bread and wine are "remembering signs" that the church enacts as repeatable monuments of faith and through which God acts to make effectual as God originally acted in the great historic signs of salvation.[110] As a part of a sacramental practice, they are more than symbols. They are signs of salvation that look backward and forward, declaring "the present presence of Christ with his people."[111] As signs these practices are not merely symbolic but "have the power to awaken spiritual response, so that Christ becomes 'more real to us as our Redeemer' when we eat and drink."[112] The observance of the Lord's Supper enacts the deep conviction that the Lord is present and active both in the performance of these remembering signs and with the community that performs them. Mere symbolism cannot satisfy the soul's hunger. Powerful signs can. The real and personal presence known in bread and wine can never be fully understood or explained, because it is a mystery. Yet this promised presence is the incontestable fact that stands over against spiritualized and magical notions. The Lord's Supper is *evangelical* because it participates in

---

[108] Zwingli, *An Exposition of the Faith*, in *Zwingli and Bullinger*, Library of Christian Classics, ed. B. W. Bromiley (Philadelphia: Westminster, 1953), 258–59.

[109] Jaques Courvoisier, *Zwingli: A Reformed Theologian* (Richmond, Va.: John Knox, 1963), 76. B. A. Gerrish thinks that the ecclesial transubstantiation in Zwingli has been overstated, but he concludes that "there can be no doubt that the ecclesial body, quite apart from any notion of a collective transubstantiation, was a strong concern in Zwingli's reflections on the Eucharist." Gerrish, *Grace and Gratitude*, 184–85; and Gerrish, *Continuing the Reformation* (Chicago: University of Chicago Press, 1993), 66–69.

[110] James Wm. McClendon Jr., *Doctrine: Systematic Theology, Volume II* (Waco, Tex.: Baylor University Press, 2012), 382.

[111] McClendon, *Doctrine*, 386.

[112] Paul Fiddes, *Tracks and Traces: Baptist Identity in Church and Theology* (Carlisle, U.K.: Paternoster 2003), 167. Fiddes is quoting John Clifford.

the fellowship of the gospel, and it is *sacramental* because it is an ordained means whereby grace is effective.[113] This is evangelical sacramentalism. So the community gathers at the table with a promise and a prayer desiring communion with Christ and with one another in Christ. And when the Eucharist is performed by remembering Jesus and invoking the Spirit, Christ makes himself really and personally known in the breaking of bread. For the table is a doorway into participation in the life of the triune God.[114] And so the invitation is extended:

> Come to this table, not because you must but because you may,
> Come, not because you are strong, but because you are weak.
> Come, not because any goodness of your own gives you a right to
>   come, but because you need mercy and help.
> Come, because you love the Lord a little and would like to love him
>   more.
> Come, because he loved you and gave himself for you.
> Come and meet the risen Christ, for we are his Body.[115]

All God's people are invited to come and be nourished at the table where spread before them is a spiritual banquet of divine grace to feed upon by faith. Other Baptists take steps toward this generous hospitality by seeking ways to move from a theology of simple faith, private devotion, obligatory ordinance, real absence, and mere symbol to a theology of sacramental participation, common prayer, life-giving practice, real presence, and powerful signs. For all things are ours, and we are Christ's; and Christ is God's (1 Cor 3:21, 23). These are the gifts of God for the people of God.

---

[113] Anthony R. Cross, *Recovering the Evangelical Sacrament: Baptisma Semper Reformadum* (Eugene, Ore.: Pickwick, 2013), 35–37.

[114] Fiddes, *Participating in God: A Pastoral Doctrine of the Trinity* (Louisville, Ky.: Westminster, 2000), 281–82.

[115] Ellis and Blyth, *Gathering for Worship*, 14 and 22. An earlier version of this invitation to the table is included in Payne and Winward, *Orders and Prayers for Church Worship*, 14–15 (bracketed sentence added):

> Come to this sacred table, not because you must, but because you may; come not to testify that you are righteous, but because you sincerely love our Lord Jesus Christ, and desire to be his true disciples; come not because you are strong, but because you are weak; come not because you have any claim on heaven's reward, but because in your frailty and sin you stand in constant need of heaven's mercy and help; [come for Christ himself wishes to meet with you here.]

Both versions are reprinted in *Patterns and Prayers for Christian Worship*, 81.

9

One Lord, One Faith, One Baptism

On August 20, 1961, twenty-five members of the Ruth Bible Class sent a letter to the board of deacons of the Watts Street Baptist Church in Durham, North Carolina. The letter contained a resolution calling for the congregation to "accept into full membership *all confirmed Christians*, who present themselves for membership, *without requiring a second baptism.*"[1] The newly revised church covenant had already gestured toward ecumenical openness, declaring that "as we hold to our Baptist heritage, we shall seek with all Christians a unity of spirit and action."[2] The deacons wondered how they could properly recognize the faith of Christians from other denominational traditions as genuine and still remain faithful to their historic conviction of believer's baptism. For Warren Carr, the pastor at Watts Street, the answer was clear: *infant baptism plus confirmation equals believer's baptism.* The deacons were not convinced, but they agreed to study the matter further. This question about baptism and membership did not come out of the blue. Several North Carolina Baptist congregations had already adopted open-membership policies, including the Olin T. Binkley Memorial Baptist Church in neighboring Chapel Hill. After two years of being under the watchcare of the Yates Baptist Association, the Binkley Church was informed in October of 1960 that their application for full membership had been refused because they did not require the baptism of believers by immersion for all who sought membership in

---

[1] Watts Street Baptist Church, Deacon Board, Minute Book, September 18, 1961, 144A; and Watts Street Baptist Church, Minutes of Church Meeting, November 1, 1961, 6. The wording of the resolution referring to "confirmed Christians" was understood to denote those who had been baptized in a Christian church of another denomination and had been through the catechetical process of confirmation. A committee comprised of deacons was appointed to study the resolution.

[2] The Covenant of Watts Street Baptist Church, Durham, N.C., 1957.

the church. Warren Carr, who served on the committee considering Binkley's admission into the association, asked whether the unstated reason
for their exclusion might be their practice of open membership toward
those of a different race as much as the stated reason of open membership toward those baptized by a different mode. The Yates Association
did not answer his question directly but stated that any congregation that
shared the same faith and practice as the other churches was eligible for
membership.[3]

Motivated by the ecumenical dilemma, Carr began writing a book
on Christian baptism, which he completed in April 1963.[4] His openness
to receiving Christians from other denominations was not without reservations. Indeed he candidly expressed concern that the practice of infant
baptism was deficient, resulting in a loss of the missional character of the
church.[5] Yet he asserted with equal vigor that rebaptism is not the answer,
insisting that baptism in any form is an act of Christian initiation. No
matter what explanations are given, Carr declared that rebaptism "can
only indicate that the first baptism was not only invalid but that its subjects are not in the Church." He affirmed the credobaptist conviction
that paedobaptist churches improperly embark on mission by baptizing
candidates before they have become disciples, but, following Karl Barth,
Carr argued that believer-baptizing churches cannot correct a mistake
that "has occurred outside the scope of their ministry." The choices for
Baptists are clear: "paedobaptist institutions must either be labeled as false
churches because of infant baptism and its implications, or they must be
confronted with correcting improper faith and practice within their own
congregations and denominations."[6] Yet he added the caveat that the brokenness of infant baptism can only be corrected by the Spirit. And by
insisting on rebaptism, Carr noted the irony that Baptists cannot escape
the contradiction that though they assert the nonsacramental nature of
baptism, "it becomes a sacrament by presuming to be the only means by

[3] Minutes of the Yates Baptist Association, North Carolina, October 25, 1960, Yates
Baptist Association, Durham, N.C., 28; and Courtland Smith and John L. Humber, *Olin T.
Binkley Memorial Baptist Church: A Twenty Year View 1958–1978* (Chapel Hill, N.C.: Binkley
Baptist Church, 1978), 2.

[4] Warren Carr, *Baptism: Conscience and Clue for the Church* (New York: Holt, Reinhart
& Winston, 1964). Carr dated the preface April 1963, and though he stated that he could not
"say with assured specificity" why he wrote the book, it is clear that the deliberations in the
Watts Street Baptist Church, the Yates Baptist Association, and the Baptist State Convention
of North Carolina were instrumental in this theological project.

[5] Carr, *Baptism*, 195. Carr approvingly cited Lesslie Newbigin on the relation between
baptism and mission in *The Household of God* (New York: Friendship, 1954), 13.

[6] Carr, *Baptism*, 196. Here Carr appealed to Karl Barth, *The Teaching of the Church regarding
Baptism*, trans. Ernest Payne (London: SCM Press, 1945), 35–36.

which the Spirit can perform its remedial task."[7] Moreover, when a Baptist church baptizes "a recognized Christian from a recognized Christian church," it makes "a mockery of its own baptismal faith and practice," turning "an inclusive missionary event . . . into an exclusive, nonmissionary, 'country club' bath!"[8] Rebaptism, Carr concluded, deservedly stands in a bad light. If it is understood as Christian initiation, "it presupposes that its subjects have neither been baptized nor have become members of the Church," and if it is simply a ritual of joining a local church of a particular denomination, "it reduces baptism to a status far below that of Christian initiation."[9]

Carlyle Marney praised Carr's book for stating both sides of the ecclesial question so sharply while presenting an ecumenical solution so graciously. Yet even though he agreed with the message, Marney noted that it would be costly for anyone actually to practice what Carr was preaching, implying it would likely remain a theological conviction without a practice to sustain it.[10] Most Baptists in North Carolina and elsewhere were, in the words of Southern Baptist leader Herschel Hobbs, "closed baptismists."[11] But for Other Baptists, Carr's book became a manifesto for the church of the future.[12] In 1968, four years after Carr was called to serve another congregation and seven years after the women's Bible class had sent their letter and resolution to the deacon board, a committee on the church and its ministry submitted a report recommending a change in the Rules of Church Order to include the reception of members "by transfer of letter from another Christian Church giving evidence of baptism by immersion *or another mode.*" The report was approved by the deacons and subsequently by the congregation. Though they would continue to

[7] Carr, *Baptism*, 197.

[8] Carr, *Baptism*, 199.

[9] Carr, *Baptism*, 201.

[10] Carlyle Marney, review of *Baptism: Conscience and Clue for the Church*, by Warren Carr, *Religion in Life* 34, no. 1 (1964–1965): 157–58.

[11] Herschel H. Hobbs, *The Baptist Faith and Message* (Nashville: Convention Press, 1971), 91.

[12] In his study on Baptists and ecumenism, William R. Estep Jr. held to a traditional line, maintaining the necessity of rebaptism, although he noted that some Baptist churches accept members without requiring rebaptism in his *Baptists and Christian Unity* (Nashville: Broadman, 1966), 173. Estep cited as evidence of open-membership churches an article by Robert G. Torbet, "Baptists and Protestantism in America," *Southwestern Journal of Theology* 6, no. 2 (1964): 108. Estep does not seem to be aware of Carr's work or the open membership churches in North Carolina. At the time Carr began his study, British Baptists had already begun ecumenical explorations, as is evident in the collection of essays in Alec Gilmore, ed., *Christian Baptism: A Fresh Attempt to Understand the Rite in Terms of Scripture, History, and Theology* (Philadelphia: Judson Press, 1959).

practice believer's baptism by immersion, rebaptism would no longer be required for membership.[13]

The change in membership policy by the Watts Street Baptist Church continued to be a matter of concern for the wider Baptist community. In 1971 the Yates Baptist Association considered proposed changes in its bylaws that would seat as voting messengers at any meeting "only individuals who are baptized (immersed) believers," and the Baptist State Convention of North Carolina debated a change to its constitution that would define a cooperating church as one that practices "believer's baptism by immersion only."[14] Both efforts failed. In 1972 the state convention appointed a committee to investigate congregations with an open-membership policy. A committee was charged to "plead with the churches differing" and ask them to follow the practice of "insisting on believer's baptism by immersion in water as a prerequisite to church membership."[15] The committee discovered eleven churches that had open-membership policies.[16] In the decades since the "differing" churches in North Carolina reported on their policies of open church membership, many more have followed their example. Others are now in the process of discerning how they can open up their membership policy without watering down their theological

[13] Watts Street Baptist Church, Deacon Board, Minute Book, October 15, 1968, 80; and Watts Street Baptist Church, Minutes of Church Meeting, February 26, 1969, 2. The motion to amend the Rules of Church Order was approved by the deacons by a vote of 12 to 5 with 1 abstention. The recommendation was presented "for information only" at the church meeting on October 30, 1968. The final report of the committee on church and its ministry is included in the minutes from the November 18, 1969, meeting of the deacons. It was studied and discussed on two Sundays in January during church school and was presented for consideration at the church meeting on February 26, 1969, where it was approved by ballot vote of 125 for and 31 against.

[14] "Proposals for Special Yates Association Meeting," February 23, 1971, in Watts Street Baptist Church, Deacon Board, Minute Book, 126F; and *Annual of the Baptist State Convention of North Carolina* (North Carolina: the Convention, 1971). The Yates Association subsequently wrote a letter to the Watts Street Church stating that it was not in compliance with the association's constitution requiring the reporting of "immersed members only" in its annual letter. The deacon chair, moderator, and pastor replied on behalf of the deacons that the church would not comply with the request to report only immersed members. Letters dated November 2, 1972, and November 11, 1972, in Watts Street Baptist Church, Deacon Board, Minute Book, 156A–C.

[15] G. McLeod Bryan, cited in the forward of *Documents concerning Baptism and Church Membership: A Controversy among North Carolina Baptists*, Perspectives in Religious Studies, Special Studies Series no. 1 (Macon, Ga.: Association of Baptist Professors of Religion, 1977), v.

[16] The appeal to the "differing" churches to identify themselves was published in the *Biblical Recorder* (March 24, 1973). The churches were Nashville First, Pullen Memorial Raleigh, Binkley Memorial Chapel Hill, Wake Forest Winston Salem, St. Johns Charlotte, Myers Park Charlotte, Lakeside Rocky Mount, Wedgewood Charlotte, Watts Street Durham, North Wilkesboro First, and Park Road Charlotte. They are listed in order of the adoption of open membership from 1936–1972. The church documents are included in Bryan's edited collection.

commitments. It is a hopeful sign that Baptists are beginning to understand themselves not as a sect but as the church united with all Christians by "one Lord, one faith, one baptism" (Eph 4:5). It is not a new idea. It is the oldest truth. Yet for some it appears that it is more important to be true to the Baptist heritage, or at least their interpretation of it (which may or may not be accurate), than to the apostolic faith. A careful examination of historic Baptist faith and practice seems warranted to determine whether the choices are really between sectarianism *or* apostolicity, or whether a return to the sources may provide a way to be both Baptist *and* catholic.

Crossing the Baptismal Bar to Communion

The earliest Baptists protested against an indiscriminate and undisciplined baptismal practice that created a nominal Christianity and identified the established church with the nation-state. Although the Baptist movement began with the baptism of John Smyth in 1609, those looking for an orderly pattern of baptismal practice must look beyond Smyth, whose self-baptism by affusion, not immersion, presents as many questions as answers. The earliest account of a Baptist arguing for believer's baptism by immersion is Edward Barber's *A Small Treatise of Baptisme or Dipping*, written in 1641. Barber began his tract with this declaration:

> Thus it is cleare, that the Lord Christ commanded his Apostles; and servants of the Gospel, first of all to teach, and thereby to gather Disciples: And afterward to dip those that were taught and instructed in the mysteries of the Gospell, upon the manifestation of their faith: which practice ought to continue to the end of the world, Matth. 28.20. Eph. 4.5. Heb. 13.8.[17]

From this mandate Barber concluded that "they onely are to be dipped that are made Disciples by teaching, Matth. 28.19. Infants cannot be made Disciples by teaching, therefore Infants are not to be dipt."[18] Although there is much more to say about Barber, his small treatise, and its influence on the retrieval of believer's baptism by immersion, it is clear that for the early English Baptists instituting believer's baptism as an ecclesial practice was deemed to be a necessary and essential reform, which they believed

---

[17] Edward Barber, *A Small Treatise of Baptisme or Dipping Wherein Is Cleerly shewed that the Lord Christ Ordained Dipping for those only that professe Repetance and Faith* ([London?], 1641), 2. For more about Barber and his role in the recovery of believer's baptism by immersion, see Stephen Wright, "Edward Barber (c. 1595–1663) and His Friends (Part 1)," *Baptist Quarterly* 41, no. 6 (2006): 354–70; and Wright, *The Early English Baptists, 1603–1649* (Woodbridge, U.K.: Boydell Press, 2006), 95–99.

[18] Barber, *Small Treatise of Baptisme*, 4.

would ensure that the church consisted only of disciples who were committed to following the precepts of the gospel.

Barber's treatise was followed by a rash of at least thirty-four baptismal tracts between 1640 and 1645, including those by Baptist ministers Andrew Ritor, John Spilsbury, Christopher Blackwood, William Kiffin, John Thombes, Henry Denne, Hanserd Knollys, Paul Hobson, and Robert Garner.[19] Like Barber, they contended for credobaptism and against paedobaptism, arguing that the gospel mandates a baptismal practice that results in disciple making. These baptismal treatises stirred the transatlantic controversy in Old and New England. But perhaps the most significant of all was a fifty-one-page tract published in 1643 entitled *A Confutation of Infants Baptisme*, written by Thomas Lambe, the popular London pastor.[20] Lambe published his book in answer to the views of George Philips, a Congregationalist minister in Watertown, Massachusetts. Lambe became aware of Philips' views through a mutual friend named Nathaniel Briscoe, who had been engaged in a theological conversation with Philips about the validity of infant baptism. Shortly after he arrived in New England, Philips wrote but never published a manuscript defending the sacraments against Baptist views. Philips sketched out a summary of his argument on infant baptism, and Briscoe apparently passed these notes on to Lambe back in London, which he then used as a basis for his book confuting infant baptism. Lambe's book was apparently so effective in spreading the antipaedobaptist message on both continents that it prompted Philips to revise his text for publication to refute Lambe.[21]

---

[19] Andrew Ritor, *A Treatise of The Vanity of Childish-Baptisme* (London, 1642); John Spilsbury, *A Treatise Concerning The Lawfull Subject of Baptisme* (London, 1643); Christopher Blackwood, *The Storming of Antichrist* (London, 1644); William Kiffin, *To Sions Virgins* (London, 1644); John Thombes, *Two Treatises And An Appendix To Them Concerning Infant-Baptisme* (London: George Whittington, 1645); Henry Denne, *Antichrist Unmasked* (n.p., 1645); Hanserd Knollys, *The Shining of a Flaming-fire in Zion* (London: Jane Cob, 1645); Paul Hobson, *The Fallacy of Infants Baptisme Discovered* (London, 1645); Robert Garner, *A Treatise of Baptisme* (n.p., 1645).

[20] Thomas Lambe, *A Confutation of Infants Baptisme* ([London?], 1643). Lambe published a second treatise on baptism, *Truth Prevailing Against Fiercest Opposition; or, An Answer to Mr. John Goodwins Water-Dipping No Firm Footing for Church Communion* (London: G. Dawson, 1655). Neither of Lambe's works on baptism are available on the Early English Books Online database. Both books are in the Angus Library of Regent's Park College, Oxford University. On the circulation of the Baptist baptismal writings in New England, see William G. McLoughlin, *New England Dissent, 1630–1833: The Baptists and the Separation of Church and State*, 2 vols. (Cambridge, Mass.: Harvard University Press, 1971), 1:27–28.

[21] George Philips, *A Reply to a Confutation of Some Grounds for Infant Baptisme: As Also, Concerning the Form of a Church Put Forth Against Mee By One Thomas Lamb* (London: Matthew Simmons, 1645). Timothy L. Wood, "'A Church Still by Her First Covenant': George Philips and a Puritan View of Roman Catholicism," *New England Quarterly* 72, no. 1 (1999): 32–33; Wood, *Agents of Wrath, Sowers of Discord: Authority and Dissent in Puritan Massachusetts,*

The first five propositions of Lambe's book were concerned with contending against the various arguments offered by Philips and other Congregationalists. Philips and the paedobaptists asserted that the Old Testament practice of circumcision provided both the pattern and the justification for infant baptism. Lambe for the credobaptists declared "that whensoever Baptisme is administred upon such a subject as maketh no externall manifestation of Faith [i.e., an unbelieving infant], this Baptisme hath no being from God, but is a humane device."[22] The visible church, Lambe continued, was not constituted by the natural descendants of Abraham but rather "by spirituall regeneration of Abrahams spiritual seed, by the means of the preaching of the Gospel."[23] Lambe and the Baptists distinguished between the time of the Old Testament Law, when acceptable standing before God was dependent on being circumcised "and observing the Rites and Ceremonies of the Law," and the church of Jesus Christ, in which acceptable standing "is by faith, and being baptised into the same faith."[24] No one, Lambe argued, was a true member of "the visible Church according to the Gospell, unlesse they did manifest faith, and bee in Covenant with Abraham according to the Spirit and baptised into the same faith."[25] Toward the end of the book, Lambe asserted that the church is "constituted by participation, and visibly by visible participation, and that is onely Baptisme, . . . therefore," he concluded, "Baptisme of believers," not the covenant, "is the constitution of the visible Church of Christ."[26] By denying the efficacy of infant baptism, Lambe and the Baptists set forth a controversial account of the *ordo salutis*, requiring repentance and faith followed by baptism. But more troublesome for the Church of England and Independent Churches, the Baptists denied the ecclesiality of all churches that practiced infant baptism.[27]

Before the publication of Lambe's book, Baptists had already emerged onto the public stage when on October 17, 1642, a little-known glover and later a leader of the Particular Baptists named William Kiffin disputed

---

1630–1655 (New York: Routledge, 2006), 41–42; and Philip F. Gura, *A Glimpse of Sion's Glory: Puritan Radicalism in New England, 1620–1660* (Middletown, Conn.: Wesleyan University Press, 1984), 110–11. Though Philips died before the completion of the project, his book *A Reply to a Confutation of Some Grounds for Infants Baptisme* appeared posthumously and was welcomed by Independents in Old and New England.

[22] Lambe, *Confutation of Infants Baptisme*, 7.

[23] Lambe, *Confutation of Infants Baptisme*, 8.

[24] Lambe, *Confutation of Infants Baptisme*, 12–13.

[25] Lambe, *Confutation of Infants Baptisme*, 13.

[26] Lambe, *Confutation of Infants Baptisme*, 49.

[27] The rejection of the ecclesiality of infant-baptizing communities was made in 1609 by the first Baptist, John Smyth, *The Character of the Beast*, in *The Works of John Smyth*, ed. W. T. Whitley (Cambridge: Cambridge University Press, 1915), 2:565.

in favor of believer's baptism against Daniel Featley, the well-known Anglican clergyman and controversialist. Featley later published his account of the argument under the provocative title *The Dippers Dipt., or, The Anabaptists Duck'd and Plung'd over Head and Eares, at a Disputation in Southwark*.[28] The debate, however, was not limited to the question of baptism but pertained more generally to the matter of the constitution of the church. Kiffin asserted that, because in the Church of England the Word is not "sincerely preached, or the Sacraments rightly administered," its churchly validity must be denied.[29] If he was not yet a convinced Baptist, he was surely leaning toward the view that a visible church is constituted on the basis of the baptism of believers only by immersion only.[30] Featley warned that the Baptists were doubly dangerous. As heretics they "pervert the Catholique doctrine," and as schismatics they "subvert the Aposto-like discipline of the Church." He recommended that they be "severely punished, if not utterly exterminated and banished out of the Church and Kingdome."[31] Though Featley argued that the Baptists simply "cover a little rats-bane in a great quantity of sugar," their theological orthodoxy on the weightier matters of doctrine was largely cleared up with the publication of A Confession of Faith in 1644 by Kiffin and the ministers of seven "Churches of Christ in London."[32] But, as to the charge of breaking the unity of the church, it proved a more difficult case to make.[33] John Spilsbury, one of the signatories of the confession, argued that for the Baptists baptism constituted the *esse*, not merely the *bene esse*, of the church. As he explained, "The ordinance of baptism instituted by Christ is so essential to the constitution of the church under the new Testament that none can be true in her constitution without it." He went on to assert that "where there is not a true constituted Church, there is no true constituted Church ordinance: and where there is a true Church ordinance in its constitution, there is at least presupposed a true Church also."[34] The Baptists seemed to leave little room for communion with those differing from them.

[28] Daniel Featley, *The Dippers Dipt., or The Anabaptists Duck'd and Plung'd over Head and Ears, at a Disputation in Southwark* (London: N.B. and Richard Royston, 1647), 1–19. Featley refers to Kiffin as "Cufin" throughout the manuscript.

[29] Featley, *Dippers Dipt.*, 4.

[30] Featley, *Dippers Dipt.*, 181–82. Featley objected to the Baptist claims that Scripture teaches baptism "onely" for "persons professing faith" and that Scripture defines baptism as "dipping or plunging" (i.e., immersion) on the basis that neither point is clearly stated in Scripture.

[31] Featley, epistle dedicatory, *Dippers Dipt.*, A4.

[32] Featley, *Dippers Dipt.*, 178.

[33] Featley, *Dippers Dipt.*, 180–86. The Baptists, revisions of Articles 38–41 and 45 in light of Featley's critiques suggest their concerns to clarify their theology of baptism and the church.

[34] Spilsbury, *Treatise Concerning The Lawfull Subject of Baptism*, 32.

At the time of the disputation at Southwark, Kiffin was leading a congregation in London that was moving toward but not yet exclusively believer baptized.[35] The Kiffin community had earlier branched out of another Independent church led by the prominent London minister Henry Jessey, which contained a mixed communion of both believer- and infant-baptized members. But a crisis of fellowship was on the horizon for the Jessey church. When Hanserd Knollys refused to have his child baptized in January 1644, the relation of baptism and the constitution of the church could no longer be avoided.[36] Jessey and the other elders deliberated for several months in search of a resolution to the conflict, but in March of 1644 sixteen members departed to join Kiffin's gathered community. Yet the elders of the Jessey church refused to censure or admonish them, resolving instead to remain in communion with them insofar as was possible. It came as no surprise, then, that, when the seven Particular Baptist congregations issued their confession of faith later in the year, they defined the church as a "company of visible saints, called and separated from the world" and gathered by believer's baptism by immersion.[37] The conversations about baptism continued after the separation, eventually convincing Jessey to submit to rebaptism in June 1645 at the hands of Knollys, whose conviction had started the controversy. But even though the congregation subsequently began receiving members through believer's baptism by immersion, it remained an *open-membership* church, not requiring rebaptism to share in all the benefits of membership. The Particular Baptists soon defined themselves as *closed-membership* churches, as Benjamin Cox made clear in his appendix to the 1646 edition of their confession of faith, stating that their churches "do not admit any to the use of the Supper, nor communicate with any in the use of this ordinance, but disciples baptized."[38] Thomas Patient, a signatory of the first Particular

[35] B. R. White, "How Did William Kiffin Join the Baptists?" *Baptist Quarterly* 23, no. 5 (1970): 201–7; Larry J. Kreitzer, *William Kiffen and His World*, part 1 (Oxford: Regent's Park College, 2010), 24–26; Wright, *The Early English Baptists*, 77–84.

[36] The same issue was publically debated between Baptists and Presbyterians on December 3, 1645, in London at the church of St. Mary's Aldermanbury, near St. Paul's Cathedral. Benjamin Coxe, Hanserd Knollys, and William Kiffen, *A Declaration Concerning the Publike Dispute . . . Concerning Infants-Baptisme* (London, 1645). William L. Pitts, "Debating the True Church on the Grounds of Believer's Baptism: The Ecclesiology of Hanserd Knollys," *Baptist History and Heritage* 47, no. 2 (2012): 55–67.

[37] The First London Confession XXXIII, XXXIX–XL, in William L. Lumpkin, ed., *Baptist Confessions of Faith*, rev. ed. (Valley Forge, Pa.: Judson Press, 1969), 165 and 167.

[38] Benjamin Cox, An Appendix to A Confession of Faith or A More Full Declaration of the Faith and Judgement of Baptized Beleevers XX (London, 1648), in *Confessions of Faith*, ed. Edward Bean Underhill (London: Haddon, Brothers, 1854), 59. A distinction should be made between open and closed membership that pertains to the reception of members into

Baptist confession and a former associate of William Kiffin, was even more pointed in his call for strict separation of membership. Writing to a group of Baptists who joined an Independent church gathered in Dublin, his Baptist congregation in Waterford, Ireland, admonished them for holding communion with unbaptized Christians:

> But the very end of Church-fellowship is the observation of all Christ's commands, as the Commission holds forth, but this your practice crosseth in that you agree to walk with such as have not, nor practice, the Ordinance of dipping Believers, and by your communion with them in Church-administrations, you are made guilty of their sins of disobedience. . . . That you admit one that walks in disobedience to the Ordinance of baptisme, whether through ignorance or error, you may admit all manner of disobedience into your Society upon the same ground, which is a total destroying the end of Church-fellowship, which is to bring up every member to a visible subjection to all the Lawes of Christ their King, or else cast them out of that Society as old leaven.[39]

Though the vast majority of English Baptist congregations in the seventeenth century aligned themselves with the closed-membership ecclesiology, not all Baptists held to such strict separationism.[40] It has long been recognized that some congregations among the early Baptists like Jessey's were open membership, practicing believer's baptism but also accepting infant-baptized members.[41] And as has recently been shown, during the same time the majority of Independent (Congregational) churches also held open-membership policies in which professing believers were received by subscription to the church covenant regardless of their views on baptism.[42] As a result, many Baptists remained in mixed congregations while identifying themselves as "Baptist."[43] It is not surprising, then,

---

the church and open and closed communion that concerns the admission of Christians to the Lord's table. Some churches that maintained closed membership were open communion.

[39] John Rogers, *Ohel or Beth-Shamesh, A Tabernacle for the Sun* (London: Printed for R. Ibbitson, 1653), 304–5. The letter was dated January 14, 1651.

[40] B. R. White, *The English Baptists of the Seventeenth Century* (Didcot, U.K.: Baptist Historical Society, 1996), 10–11.

[41] White, "Open and Closed Membership among English and Welsh Baptists," *Baptist Quarterly* 24, no. 7. (1972): 330–34.

[42] Joel Halcomb, "A Social History of Congregational Religious Practice during the Puritan Revolution" (Ph.D. diss., University of Cambridge, 2009), 144–67.

[43] A similar arrangement of baptists and paedobaptists coexisting in mixed-communion churches occurred in the 1740s among New England Congregationalists who were influenced by the New Light revival. The mixed-congregational experiment, however, was short lived, as the Baptists began to form their own Separate congregations in the 1750s. See Clarence C.

that Thomas Edwards observed that "the best Independent churches and congregations are mixed assemblies and medlies, consisting of persons whereof some are Anabaptists."[44] The historical record provides evidence of an extensive network of churches stretching from Hexham and Northumbria in the north to East Anglia in the east to Gloucestershire, Herefordshire, and Wales in the west to Bedfordshire in the midlands and London at the center. At the heart of these open-membership churches were influential ministers including Henry Jessey, John Tombes, Thomas Tillam, John Bunyan, Walter Cradock, and Vavasor Powell, who gathered around themselves others of kindred mind in circles of fellowship where baptism was no bar to ecclesial communion.

The earliest Baptists in Wales were in mixed-communion churches, gathered by the ministry of Walter Cradock and Vavasor Powell. Cradock once stated that, when he had communion with a saint, he did not think about "whether he be of such and opinion, or whether he have taken the covenant, or have been baptized once or twice or ten times, but see if he have fellowship with the Father and with Jesus Christ."[45] The Particular Baptist Association of Wales encouraged the gathering of congregations that were "professedly Baptist" and discouraged the practice of mixed-communion congregations. When a new church was gathered at Abergavenny in 1652, about fifty Baptist members came out of the mixed congregation, greatly disturbing the paedobaptists. They agreed to debate the issue of baptism, naming John Tombes, the vicar of Leominster in nearby Herefordshire, as the disputant for the believer's baptism side. The influence of the open-membership ecclesiology was evident at the meeting of the Welsh Baptist Association in 1654, where the association admonished the Abergavenny congregation to "take heed of mixed communion with unbaptized persons, or any others walking disorderly."[46] The churches in the Welsh Association, like the London Particular Baptists, held to closed membership and thought that the churches within the Cradock and Powell circles opened the door too wide.

In 1653 a circle of nine open-membership churches near Herefordshire and associated with Tombes corresponded with the church in Hexham

---

Goen, *Revivalism and Separatism in New England, 1740–1800* (New Haven, Conn.: Yale University Press, 1962), 258–67.

[44] Thomas Edwards, *Gangraena: The First and Second Part*, 3rd ed. (London: Ralph Smith, 1646), 2:13.

[45] Geoffrey F. Nuttall, *The Puritan Spirit: Essays and Addresses* (London: Epworth Press, 1967), 120.

[46] Joshua Thomas, *A History of the Baptist Association in Wales, From the Year 1650, To the Year 1790* (London, 1795), 10 and 86; and Thomas, *History of the Welsh Association, 1639–1780*, handwritten manuscript in the Angus Library, Regent's Park College, Oxford University, 10.

gathered by Tillam, reaching out for fellowship. Among the signatories were the leaders of the church in Abergavenny, where Tombes disputed on baptism. The letter is baptistic in theology, seeking communion with "the baptized churches that hold the faith purely," but irenic in tone, reminding them that they share "one Lord, one faith, one baptism" and urging them "to keep the unity of the spirit in the bond of peace."[47] It was followed by another letter to the Hexham church from Jessey's Swan Alley church in London that acknowledged their communion with the Tombes circle in Herefordshire. It also reported on Jessey's preaching tour in the summer of 1653 in which he was received by thirty-six congregations in Essex, Suffolk, Norfolk, and Middlesex. The letter reported that the churches were all "sound in the faith, and holy in life, though differing from some about the subject and manner of the ordinance of baptism." Yet it emphasized the importance of respecting those who differ, not excluding them "from the visible kingdom of God, merely for weakness' sake."[48] The entrance of the Broadmead Church in Bristol to the circle of open churches began in 1654 when the minister, Thomas Ewins, went to London to receive baptism from Jessey. From that time forward, Broadmead was Baptist, but like Swan Alley it remained an open-membership congregation.[49] Ewins stated that he administered the Lord's Supper to all believers, though he added, "some of them misbaptised." Nevertheless, he declared that, until such time "as farther light comes in, they are willing to walk up to it, in the mean time we can bear with them in love, as we desire them and others to bear with us in other things."[50]

Jessey's most complete thoughts on the subject of church communion are contained in a collection of letters and reflections entitled *A Storehouse of Provision*.[51] There he left no doubt of his Baptist convictions. Following "the Grand Commission" of Christ in Matthew 28:19, he named three essential elements of baptism. First, the baptizer must be a "professed Disciple." Second, the baptized is to be one who is "made a Disciple." And, third, the baptized is "dipped in water" in the name of the Father, the Son, and the Holy Spirit, or (in deference to those who follow the alternative

---

[47] Edward Bean Underhill, ed., *Records of the Churches of Christ, Gathered at Fenstanton, Warboys, and Hexham, 1640–1720* (London: Haddon, Brothers, 1854), 341–46.

[48] Underhill, *Records of the Churches of Christ*, 346–48.

[49] Roger Hayden, ed., *The Records of a Church of Christ in Bristol, 1640–1687* (Bristol, U.K.: Bristol Record Society, 1974), 111.

[50] Thomas Ewins, *The Church of Christ in Bristol Recovering Her Vail* (London, 1657), 59; cited in Hayden, *Records of a Church of Christ in Bristol*, 29–30.

[51] Henry Jessey, *A Storehouse of Provision, to Further Resolution in Severall Cases of Conscience, and Questions Now in Dispute* (London: Charles Sumptner, 1650).

biblical warrant of Acts) in the name of Jesus Christ.[52] Because infant baptism falls short on at least two counts, it is deficient. Yet, given that faith is an essential element of baptismal practice, believer's baptism must not be understood simply as the *negation* of infant baptism but rather as the ecumenical *restoration* of the gospel ordinance.[53] He thus cautioned against setting limits that would deprive the spiritual privilege of union with Christ and with one another in Christ, because, as he says, if "the Lord puts no difference between" Christians, "neither should wee."[54] Key to this stance of ecclesiological forbearance is the conviction to respect the conscience of each believer who walks according to the light received.[55] Those who have been infant baptized may be deficient in light, but because light is a gift from God, believers who are satisfied with their baptism must not be excluded from the other ordinances of the church.[56] Indeed, Jessey argued that for fellow Christians to go where they have no light would be asking them to transgress their conscience. Because he found no explicit biblical warrant to exclude believers from the church on baptismal grounds, he maintained that the door of membership and communion must remain open. Moreover, he urged believer-baptized Christians to recognize the differently baptized as fellow Christians and their gathered communities as true churches, making every effort to hold communion with them.[57]

In 1672 John Bunyan published his personal *Confession of Faith*, in which he argued that faith, not baptism, makes one a visible saint, and thus water baptism should not be a condition of church membership or communion.[58] Though Bunyan practiced only the baptism of believers, like Jessey he admitted into the visible church any who showed themselves to be believers, and though he did not go so far as to suggest that water baptism was unnecessary, he argued that it was inferior to the baptism of the Holy Spirit by which believers are brought into the communion of saints.[59] Bunyan's call for unity among the visible saints was met by

---

[52] Jessey, *Storehouse of Provision*, 59–60.

[53] Jessey, *Storehouse of Provision*, 80.

[54] Jessey, *Storehouse of Provision*, 95–96.

[55] Jessey, *Storehouse of Provision*, 49, 80, 84, 96, 148, and 190–91. See ch. 7 above, "More Light from the Word."

[56] Jessey, *Storehouse of Provision*, 119, 123, 127, 119 [misnumbered but after 128], and 127 [the second 127].

[57] Jessey, *Storehouse of Provision*, 200.

[58] Bunyan, *A Confession of My Faith, and a Reason of my Practice*, in *The Works of John Bunyan*, ed. George Offor (Glasgow: W. G. Blackie & Son, 1854), 2:606.

[59] E.g., William Dell, rector of the parish church in Yeldon, Befordshire, argued that water baptism was unnecessary in his *The Doctrine of Baptismes, Reduced from Its Ancient and Moderne Corruptions* (London: Giles Calvert, 1648), 17–24. Peter Lake discusses John

strong criticism from more strict Baptists. Thomas Paul accused Bunyan
of using Machiavellian arguments to "throw dirt" on the Baptists, hoping that "some of it will be sure to stick."[60] But, worst of all, Paul began
with a condescending reference to Bunyan's social rank and occupation,
suggesting that if he were open about his beliefs and practices, he might
gain more work than he could handle.[61] Kiffin was more measured in
his critique, asserting in the preface to Paul's book that Scripture plainly
teaches believer's baptism as a requirement for church membership and
communion and that Christ's rules cannot be surrendered even in the
name of love.[62]

Bunyan's response in *Differences in Judgment About Water-Baptism* articulated the evangelical position shared by his fellow Baptists, urging that "they
only that have before received the doctrine of the gospel, and so shew it us
by their confession of faith, they only ought to be baptized."[63] Yet he reiterated an ecumenical understanding of the church that defended the open
view of membership and communion proposed in his *Confession*, declaring
that "the church of Christ hath not warrant to keep out of the communion
the Christian that is discovered to be a visible saint of the word, the Christian that walketh according to his own light with God."[64] Bunyan replied
again to his strict discipline critics who accused him of disloyalty to the
Baptist name, saying that he hoped to be known simply as a Christian.[65]
Kiffin did not immediately enter the fray, waiting eight years to publish
his *Sober Discourse of Right to Church-Communion*, which upheld the strict

---

Etherington's account of two baptisms, the outward of which was simply "elementish" and
merely an external form that conveyed no saving grace; the inward of which was true participation in spiritual regeneration, or baptism "into Christ." Lake, *The Boxmaker's Revenge:
"Orthodoxy," "Heterodoxy" and the Politics of the Parish in Early Stuart London* (Stanford, Calif.:
Stanford University Press, 2001), 104–6.

[60] Thomas Paul, *Some Serious Reflections on That Part of Mr. Bunion's Confession of Faith:
Touching Church Communion with Unbaptized Persons* (London: Francis Smith, 1673), 42.

[61] Paul, *Some Serious Reflections*, 1. Paul's snobbery about social rank was a common rhetorical ploy of Presbyterian and Anglican critics of nonconformists, but was unusual among
Baptists.

[62] William Kiffin, "To the Reader," preface to Paul, *Some Serious Reflections*. A second
critique of Bunyan's *Confession* was subsequently published by John Denne, *Truth Outweighing
Error; or, An Answer to a Treatise Lately Published by J. B. Entitled, A Confession of his Faith and a
Reason of his Practice; or, With Who He Can, and With Who He Cannot Hold Church-Fellowship*
(London: F. Smith, 1673). For a discussion of the baptism controversy, see Richard L. Greaves,
Glimpses of Glory: John Bunyan and English Dissent (Stanford, Calif.: Stanford University Press,
2002), 291–301.

[63] Bunyan, *Differences in Judgment About Water-Baptism No Bar to Communion*, in *Works of
John Bunyan* (ed. Offor), 2:640.

[64] Bunyan, *Differences in Judgement About Water-Baptism*, in *Works of John Bunyan* (ed.
Offor), 2:617.

[65] Bunyan, *Peaceable Principles and True*, in *Works of John Bunyan* (ed. Offor), 2:648–49.

view of admitting "none into Church-Fellowship or Communion, that are Unbaptized."[66] It defined the closed-membership and closed-communion ecclesiology that became dominant in Baptist life for centuries, looking upon infant baptism as "absolutely invalid and so *no Baptism*."[67]

Open communion gradually gained greater acceptance among Baptists in England and around the world. Open membership has found less receptivity.[68] The Jessey-Bunyan tradition provides a source of retrieval for those seeking to identify a pathway for an evangelical ecumenism in Baptist life. For, though they did not regard infant baptism as satisfying the apostolic pattern, neither did they regard it as absolutely invalid. Yet this approach was not without problems. The sharp distinction between water and Spirit baptism, which seems unwarranted in Scripture, surely diminishes the importance of water baptism if it does not render it altogether unnecessary.[69] The antisacramentalism in contemporary evangelicalism strongly suggests this tendency to elevate faith as an essential but baptism as a nonessential. Moreover, the practice among Baptists of open communion and closed membership, though widely held up as a sign of church unity, actually does so by making the antiecclesial move of severing access to the Lord's table from church membership. It may be that on this matter Kiffin was right in arguing that Scripture and the church fathers insist that baptism is necessary for church membership but wrong in equating infant baptism with no baptism.[70]

A century after the publication of Bunyan's *Differences in Judgment*, a group of differing churches led by Daniel Turner, a Baptist minister in Abingdon, England (near Oxford), sought to combine the ecclesiological understanding of baptism expressed in the Kiffin position with the ecumenical generosity of the Bunyan view. Turner offered *A Modest Plea For Free Communion*, in which he suggested that, by excluding any of God's children from the means of grace, "we are guilty of invading the prerogative of Christ." Turner warned against offending and injuring fellow Christians "by denying them, as far as in us lies, the means of their spiritual comfort, and edification; forcing them to live in the neglect of a known and important duty, and exposing them to many temptations,

---

[66] William Kiffin, *A Sober Discourse of Right to Church-Communion* (London: George Larkin, 1681), 2.

[67] Kiffin, *Sober Discourse*, 9 (emphasis added).

[68] Peter Naylor, *Calvinism, Communion and the Baptists: A Study of English Calvinistic Baptists from the Late 1600s to the Early 1800s* (Milton Keynes, U.K.: Paternoster, 2004).

[69] George Beasley-Murray approvingly quotes H. Wheeler Robinson that "baptism, in its New Testament context, is always a baptism of the Spirit," in his *Baptism in the New Testament* (Grand Rapids: Eerdmans, 1962), 277.

[70] Paul S. Fiddes, foreword to Kreitzer, *William Kiffen and His World*, xii.

in violation of the express commands of the Gospel, and contrary to that spirit of divine benevolence that ever where breathes in it."[71] Not surprisingly, Turner was the guiding influence behind the covenant for a gathered church in nearby Oxford, which admitted into its membership both credobaptists and paedobaptists. After noting the difference of sentiment on the baptismal views of the two groups, the covenant pledged "to receive one another into the same affection and love," offering among its reasons "because the Lord Jesus receiving and owning them on both sides of the question, we think we ought to do so too."[72]

For Turner's congregation in Abingdon and for the other differing churches, the questions of communion and membership remained integrally related, as all Christians were invited to come to the table not because they showed themselves to be visible saints but as a sign of the visible communion of the whole church.[73] The Lord's Supper so conceived, Turner believed, is a "visible, external pledge and means, of that divine union and fellowship, all true Christians have with Christ, and one another in one body."[74] Thus open communion is not merely the expression of the individualistic principle of private faith but rather a manifestation of the visible catholicity of the church.[75]

Other Baptists will surely find promise in the ecumenical outlook of these differing voices, yet it remains unclear how the majority of the Baptists, particularly in the southern United States, came to close the door of membership even more tightly in their baptismal practice.[76] So, before continuing in the direction toward the open door to which Turner pointed, it seems important to tell the story of how believer's baptism

---

[71] Daniel Turner, *A Modest Plea for Free Communion at the Lord's Table* (London: J. Johnson, 1772), 5. Because of the controversial nature of his subject, Turner wrote under the pseudonym Candidus.

[72] New Road Baptist Church, Oxford, England, The Church Covenant of 1780, accessed March 26, 2012, http://www.newroadbaptistchurchoxford.co.uk/content/pages/documents/1312454439.pdf.

[73] Daniel Turner, *A Compendium of Social Religion* (London: John Ward, 1758), 119–20.

[74] Turner, *Compendium of Social Religion*, 120.

[75] Paul S. Fiddes, *Tracks and Traces: Baptist Identity in Church and Theology* (Carlisle, U.K.: Paternoster, 2003), 177.

[76] There was a move toward open membership among English Baptists in the nineteenth and twentieth centuries. John Clifford claimed that, in the late nineteenth century, two out of every three of the leading Particular Baptists churches in England were open membership, in his "Conference on the Conditions of Church Membership," *General Baptist Magazine* 85 (1883): 53–54; cited in Fiddes, *Tracks and Traces*, 177n79. B. R. White indicated that the trend in the twentieth century among English Baptists was more toward open membership, in his "Open and Closed Membership among English and Welsh Baptists," 334. Baptists in the United States and especially in the South until recently have been predominantly closed communion and closed membership.

ceased to be a sign of the one, holy, catholic, and apostolic church and became a denominational distinctive of the Baptists.

Does Our Baptismal Theology Hold Water?

In 1791 a controversy erupted among the churches in the Ketocton Association of Virginia about the validity of baptism. A Baptist preacher named James Hutchinson was visiting relatives in Loudoun County, where he was invited to preach. His sermon resulted in several converts who presented themselves for baptism, which Hutchinson immediately observed. When it became more widely known that Hutchinson had been converted and baptized under the ministry of a Methodist preacher and that he was subsequently received on the basis of that baptism into membership by the Baptists in Georgia, the validity of the baptism of Hutchinson and his converts was called into question. The Ketocton Association took the opposite view from the Georgia Baptists, deciding not to receive Hutchinson or his disciples without rebaptism. After extensive conversation and deliberation, Hutchinson and his disciples submitted to rebaptism.[77] The action of the Ketocton Association, however, stood in contrast to an earlier decision by the Dover Association in Virginia, which in May of 1790 approved baptisms performed by an "unordained person" (i.e., a minister from another denomination) as valid. The Dover Baptists resolved that "persons so baptized might be admitted as members of the church upon hearing and approving their experience."[78] The Ketocton Association was more strict than the other Virginia Baptists who "either deemed it unnecessary to rebaptize or left it to the conscience of the party to be rebaptized or not."[79] Summarizing the dominant view, Robert Semple observed that "the most important prerequisite to baptism was faith in the subject; that, although it was expedient to have a fixed rule for qualifying persons for the administration of the ordinances, yet the want of such qualifications in the administrator ought not to be viewed as having sufficient weight to invalidate the baptism."[80]

But with spread of the evangelical awakening through the South a controversial spirit emerged between denominations.[81] Doctrinal disputations intensified as credobaptists and paedobaptists began competing for

---

[77] Robert B. Semple, *A History of the Rise and Progress of the Baptists in Virginia*, rev. G. W. Beale (Richmond, Va.: Pitt & Dickerson, 1894), 391.

[78] Semple, *History of the Baptists in Virginia*, 122–23

[79] Semple, *History of the Baptists in Virginia*, 391.

[80] Semple, *History of the Baptists in Virginia*, 391.

[81] Philip N. Mulder, *A Controversial Spirit: Evangelical Awakenings in the South* (Oxford: Oxford University Press, 2002), 3–10 and 168–71.

the same converts. Anglican itinerate Charles Woodmason, who prior to the American Revolution encountered Separate Baptists in the Carolina backcountry, dismissed adult baptism as a lascivious public bath, writing, "I know not whether it would not be less offensive to modesty for them to strip wholly into the buff at once, than to be dipp'd with those very thin linen drawers they are equipp'd in—which when wet, so closely adheres to the limbs, as exposes the nudities equally as if none at all. If this be not offensive and a greivous insult on all modesty and decency among civiliz'd people I know not what can be term'd so."[82] Anglican clergyman Devereux Jarratt, who embraced New Light religion and labored along-side Methodist preachers in fanning the flames of revival throughout south central Virginia, reported that the harmony and accord among Christians was disrupted in 1769–1770, when the Baptists introduced "contentious disputes and discord" on the subject of baptism, demanding that their converts leave the Anglican Church.[83]

Members of the established church saw Baptists as "disturbers of the peace" who "cannot meet a man upon the road, but they must ram a text of Scripture down his throat."[84] They were regarded as "false prophets" who have "intoxicated the brains of poor people until they are horribly deluded."[85] Jarratt documented this controversial spirit in his book *An Argument Between an Anabaptist and a Paedo-baptist*, which portrays the Baptist as "a man of strife and contention."[86] The paedobaptist by contrast is shown to be a man of truth and peace, making a case for the validity of infant baptism by sprinkling on the basis of Scripture only. His parting words to the credobaptist are telling:

[82] Richard J. Hooker, ed., *The Carolina Backcountry on the Eve of the Revolution* (Chapel Hill: University of North Carolina Press, 1953), 103.

[83] Devereux Jarratt, *The Life of the Reverend Devereux Jarratt* (Baltimore: Warner & Hanna, 1806), 105–6; and Wesley M. Gewehr, *The Great Awakening in Virginia, 1740–1790* (Durham, N.C.: Duke University Press, 1930), 142–66. The Baptists to whom Jarratt alluded is likely a reference to William Mullen, who began preaching in Amelia in 1769, and especially John Waller and John Burrus, whose preaching in Middlesex in November 1770 brought out great crowds and evoked enormous controversy. See Semple, *History of the Baptists in Virginia*, 27. Jarratt actually mentions John Waller as well as Samuel Harris, the leading Baptist minister among the Virginia Baptists, in his *An Argument Between an Anabaptist and a Paedo-baptist* (n.p., 1803), 60. Jarratt eventually concluded that the Methodists were just as full of "party zeal, party interest and party spirit" as the Baptists. Quoted in Francis Asbury, *Journal and Letters*, ed. Elmer T. Clark, J. Manning Potts, and Jacob S. Payton (Nashville: Abingdon, 1958), 3:138–39n.

[84] Semple, *History of the Baptists in Virginia*, 30.

[85] William Bradley, a magistrate, to Nathaniel Saunders, a Baptist preacher, October 6, 1770, in Gewehr, *Great Awakening in Virginia*, 130.

[86] Jarratt, *Argument Between an Anabaptist and a Paedo-baptist*, 4.

I beseech you for the future to pray more and dispute less, and be more anxious to grow in grace than to make proselytes to an opinion which has no more scripture on the side of it—and you will lead a quiet and peaceable life, in all godliness and christian love—you will find more happiness in your own breast, by a submission to this good advice, than ever was found by a submission to a second baptism, or rather a submission to be dipped into the waters of strife.[87]

Methodist bishop Francis Asbury expressed exasperation with the Baptists who preyed on the weak and endeavored "to persuade the people that they have never been baptized."[88] He disappointingly admitted that, for many Baptists, immersion is "the *ne plus ultra* of Christian experience."[89] Methodist itinerant John Early was even more pointed in his criticism of the Baptist fixation on believer's baptism by immersion, complaining that "they are always ready to steal our lambs or turn our chickens into ducks by putting them into water."[90] But, comparing the Baptist religion to an old horseshoe, he continued, "Heat it and push it into the water and it will hiss for a while but soon get cold again."[91]

The early Baptists in North Carolina initially seemed to have a more open approach toward those who went through the baptismal waters outside their denominational supervision. When in May of 1783 the Kehukee Association in eastern North Carolina addressed a query as to whether the baptism of a believer is "a legal baptism if performed by an unauthorised minister" (viz., "alien immersion"), they answered that "as it was done in faith, we esteem it legal."[92] Yet this surprising openness to believer's baptism performed by non–Baptists apparently did not extend to communion with those sprinkled as infants, whom the Baptists did not consider to be "legally baptized." When a query was raised at the 1778 meeting of the Kehukee Association by the church in the Isle of Wight about what to "do with a minister who labors to make them believe, that difference in judgment about water baptism, ought to be no bar to communion," alluding to John Bunyan's famous line, the answer given was that "such a practice is disorderly, and [the minister] ought to be dealt with as an

---

[87] Jarratt, *Argument Between an Anabaptist and a Paedo-baptist*, 68.

[88] Asbury, *Journal and Letters*, 1:166.

[89] Asbury, *Journal and Letters*, 2:651.

[90] John Early, "Diary of John Early, Bishop of the Methodist Episcopal Church, South," *Virginia Magazine of History and Biography* 39, no. 1 (1931): 44.

[91] John Early, "Diary of John Early, Bishop of the Methodist Episcopal Church, South," *Virginia Magazine of History and Biography* 34, no. 4 (1926): 306.

[92] Joseph Biggs, *A Concise History of the Kehukee Baptist Association* (Tarborough, N.C.: George Howard, 1834), 58.

offender."[93] This early openness to the possibility of God's work beyond their own baptismal waters gradually closed as Baptists contended for converts with Presbyterians, Anglicans, and Methodists. The Sandy Creek Baptist Association affirmed "that true believers are the only fit subjects of baptism, and that immersion is the only mode," and they continued "that the church has no right to admit any but regular baptized church members to communion at the Lord's table."[94] Yet it was still unclear whether those who underwent so-called alien immersion were to be considered "regularly baptized."

At the meeting of the association in 1839, the question was raised whether it was "consistent with the spirit of the gospel, and according to the Scriptures, for any regular Baptist church to receive into her fellowship any member or members of another denomination, who have been baptized by immersion without baptizing them again." The answer of no was unanimous. The delegates went on to declare, "We cannot admit the validity of their baptisms without admitting that they are true and scriptural gospel churches, if we do this we *unchurch ourselves*."[95] In his commentary on the action, Elder George Washington Purefoy asserted that Baptists were the only denomination to come into being without schism, not having their origin in Roman Catholicism or any other paedobaptist denomination. And therefore, he argued, "we cannot admit the validity of their baptisms without admitting that they are true and scriptural gospel churches."[96] Baptists, he continued, were the only denomination with a legitimate claim to apostolicity because they alone maintained the primitive practice of believer's baptism. Purefoy was a staunch denominational loyalist and arch-controversialist, but he was by no means alone in the growing belief that the one true church established by God was Baptist and that paedobaptist gatherings were merely "human societies." This was the subject of his sensational 1857 sermon at the dedication service for a new meeting house of the Gum Springs Baptist Church in Chatham County, North Carolina, and later that year at the annual meetings of the Sandy Creek and Raleigh Baptist Associations.

In his sermon Elder Purefoy set out to show that God had established only one true church, which was Baptist in its membership, ordinances, polity, and discipline. He went on to argue that all the paedobaptist Protestant denominations were offspring of the Whore of Babylon—the

---

[93] Biggs, *History of the Kehukee Baptist Association*, 46.

[94] Principles of Faith, in George W. Purefoy, *A History of the Sandy Creek Baptist Association* (New York: Sheldon, 1859), 105.

[95] Purefoy, *History of the Sandy Creek Baptist Association*, 179 (emphasis in original).

[96] Purefoy, *History of the Sandy Creek Baptist Association*, 179.

apostate Roman Catholic Church, contending that "they were of and came out of Rome, hence they are called 'Protestants,' and 'the Reformed Churches.'" Baptist churches, Purefoy maintained, were neither Catholic nor Protestant but descended in uninterrupted succession from the days of the first Baptist—John. Thus, he asserted, "Baptists are not of the Reformation, but before it."[97] Purefoy was not alone in this belief of successionism, which had popular appeal among Baptists, as suggested by the hymn that intoned:

> John was a Baptist preacher,
> When he baptiz'd the Lamb;
> Then Jesus was a Baptist,
> And thus the Baptists came.

The final verse concluded with a point shaped on the anvil of interdenominational controversy:

> If you would follow Jesus,
> As Christians ought to do,
> You'd come and be immersed,
> And be a Baptist too.[98]

Purefoy wound down his stem-winding sermon, warning that, "if Baptists ever retrograde from their present high position as the advocates of the true principles of the Gospel" by countenancing "Paedobaptist convictions," they "render themselves unworthy of their predecessors, the ancient witnesses." He left no doubt as to what he thought of those who disagreed, suggesting that the Baptist minister who does not have "the moral courage to defend, on all proper and necessary occasions, the doctrines and practices of his Church, has mistaken his calling."[99]

The contentious tone of Elder Purefoy's sermon was widely shared by a growing movement of Baptists who called themselves Landmarkers, encouraged by the recent printing of G. H. Orchard's *History of the Baptists* and J. R. Graves' *The Great Iron Wheel* by the Baptist Publication Society of North Carolina. So it is not surprising to discover that Graves, the Landmark Baptist editor and author from Tennessee who attacked

---

[97] Purefoy, *A Sermon* (Nashville: Southwestern Publishing House, 1858), 64. See also Purefoy, *Pedobaptist Immersions: A Desultory Treatise* (Forestville, N.C.: North Carolina Baptist Bible & Publication Society, 1854).

[98] Starke Dupuy, *Hymns and Spiritual Songs*, ed. John M. Peck (Louisville, Ky.: John P. Morton, 1843).

[99] Purefoy, *Sermon*, 92.

Methodism as "clerical despotism," was invited to preach a sermon on June 23, 1855, at the Baptist Church in Chapel Hill Purefoy had recently helped establish.[100] The five converts who made a profession of faith were baptized that same afternoon. The meeting drew a large crowd, and the sharp attacks on infant baptism irritated the local Methodist minister, who accused Graves of preaching "false and slanderous" doctrine and being "destitute of character." Graves' supporters posted a challenge for several weeks in the *Biblical Recorder*, offering to debate the Methodists, who refused, saying they did not wish to "pollute their mouths."[101] A Baptist reporting on the events replied that "they no doubt dread the exposure of their polluted system, more than having their mouths polluted by entering into a discussion with the author of *The Wheel*."[102] Purefoy, whose father-in-law, William Merritt, was a friend and supporter of Francis Asbury before converting over to the Baptists, subsequently published his own scathing critique under the provocative title *The Tekel of Methodism*. In it he denounced the evils of Methodism and dismissed it as a schism of human origin, for he argued, "that God is the author of but one Church or Christian denomination, is evident from his word."[103] And, he claimed, that one true denomination that alone is the Church of Christ is the Baptists.

If Landmarkism represented the right flank of Baptists in the South, barring communion not only with the nonimmersed but even with immersed believers who were not members of the same congregation, when it came to the matter of baptism, the main body of Southern Baptists

---

[100] J. R. Graves, *The Great Iron Wheel or Republicanism Backwards and Christianity Reversed* (New York: Sheldon, 1855).

[101] The ad dated June 18, 1855, reported that *The Great Iron Wheel* was being denounced widely by Methodist clergy as a "false, foul, and slanderous book." Rev. Dr. Leroy M. Lee, the editor of the *Christian Advocate* in Richmond, had editorialized against Graves' book and the Baptist Publication Society of North Carolina. Lee declined to debate Graves, and the offer was extended to other Methodist clergy. James McDaniel, A. McDowell, G. W. Johnson, "A Challenge," *Biblical Recorder*, July 12, 1855, 2, accessed July 14, 2013, http://recorder.zsr.wfu.edu/Repository/ml.asp?Ref=QkNSLzE4NTUvMDcvMTIjQXIwMDIwMA%3D%3D&Mode=Gif&Locale=english-skin-custom. Graves eventually debated the renowned Methodist minister Jacob Ditzler on the subjects of baptism, the Lord's Supper, the church, and the perseverance of the saints. The debate was published in an 1184-page book by Graves under the title *The Great Carrolton Debate* (Memphis, Tenn.: Southern Baptist Publication Society, 1876).

[102] "Rev. J. R. Graves at Chapel Hill," *Biblical Recorder*, June 28, 1855, 1, accessed July 14, 2013, http://recorder.zsr.wfu.edu/Default/skins/WakeforestA/client.asp?skin=WakeforestA.

[103] Purefoy, *The Tekel of Methodism: History of Episcopal Methodism in Which Its Claims to Being a Church of Christ Are Investigated* (Chapel Hill, N.C.: The Gazette, 1858), 5. Purefoy acknowledged that Roger Williams founded a church 1639, but he denied that this is the origin of Baptists in America, claiming that Baptists have earlier origins in the English Baptists, which may be traced in unbroken succession to the days of the apostles (40–43).

was not that far away. Perhaps the most definitive and surely the most contentious statement on the subject by a Southern Baptist was produced by Robert Boyte C. Howell, pastor of the Second Baptist Church of Richmond, Virginia, whose book *The Evils of Infant Baptism* claimed to speak "for the million" Baptists of the South.[104] Howell argued that infant baptism was evil—not that it had bad consequences or was based on mistaken theological assumptions. It was, he asserted, an inherent and monstrous evil. His first and principle reason for the evil of infant baptism was that, "since it is not enjoined, nor taught, nor authorized in any way," it "is unsupported by the word of God."[105] And if it is not "*directly* enjoined in the word of God . . . then it is plainly *prohibited.*"[106] Infant baptism, Howell argued, "is no baptism at all" and is therefore "a sin against God" no less evil than witchcraft or idolatry.[107] He charged infant baptism with creating a barrier to Christian unity that "must forever remain impassible."[108] And he concluded with an appeal to paedobaptists to reexamine their opinions, condescendingly adding that they "have probably never at any time, closely investigated the subject."[109]

The reaction was swift and sharp, especially from the Methodists. Elder Leonidas Rosser dismissed Howell's book as erroneous, illogical, contradictory, dogmatic, arrogant, ignorant, uncharitable, and insidious.[110] He observed that the problem was not so much that Howell disagreed with paedobaptist writers but that he so shamefully misrepresented them that it scarcely seemed possible that he had even taken the time to read their books at all.[111] Elder Thomas Summers explained how paedobaptists understood the church as a fulfillment of the Abrahamic covenant and infant baptism as "the sign and seal of the covenant now, as

---

[104] Robert Boyte C. Howell, *The Evils of Infant Baptism* (Charleston, S.C.: Southern Baptist Publication Society, 1851), viii.

[105] Howell, *Evils of Infant Baptism*, 7.

[106] Howell, *Evils of Infant Baptism*, 12 (emphasis added). Howell's argument that what is not directly commanded is prohibited is a familiar line that appears in earlier baptismal controversies. E.g., in 1525 Balthasar Hubmaier contended with Oecolampadius against infant baptism that "what is not commanded in Scripture is already forbidden." Hubmaier, "On Infant Baptism," in *Baptist Roots: A Reader in the Theology of a Christian People*, ed. Curtis W. Freeman, James Wm. McClendon Jr., and C. Rosalee Velloso Ewell (Valley Forge, Pa.: Judson Press, 1999), 35.

[107] Howell, *Evils of Infant Baptism*, 14–17.

[108] Howell, *Evils of Infant Baptism*, 229.

[109] Howell, *Evils of Infant Baptism*, 244.

[110] Leonidas Rosser, *Reply to Evils of Infant Baptism* (Richmond, Va.: by the author, 1855), 6. Two years earlier Rosser had published a book on the subject, *Baptism: Its Nature, Obligation, Mode, Subjects, and Benefits* (Richmond, Va.: by the author, 1855).

[111] Rosser, *Reply to Evils of Infant Baptism*, 17–19.

circumcision was formerly."[112] And he took Howell to task for seeming to be unaware that his own Baptist ecclesiology is also based on a theology of being grafted into God's covenant with Israel when he charged paedo-baptists for the same reason with "engrafting Judaism upon the gospel of Christ."[113] The Methodists readily admitted that infant baptism has led to abuses in the history of Christianity, yet they complained that Howell's self-congratulatory account refused to acknowledge any fallout to adult baptism, such as "antinomian licentiousness."[114] The Methodists conveyed their hope for the Wesleyan revival as a source of renewal for the whole church, but they expressed concern that the Baptists had turned immersion into a shibboleth among the people of God.[115] In the end few if any were convinced by either side, yet for Baptists in the South these controversies succeeded in transforming believer's baptism by immersion from a practice of renewal for the church catholic into a denominational distinctive upheld by the Baptists over against all other denominations.

As a result, Southern Baptists in principle have held a strict line on closed membership and closed communion, and more importantly they have refused to recognize any shade or variation of difference, thus asserting this sectarian outlook to be the only legitimate position ever held by the Baptists from their origins to the present day. So, for example, when the respected Southern Baptist historian Albert Henry Newman summarized the historic view of Baptists about infant baptism, he channeled the voice of R. B. C. Howell, albeit in a more congenial tone, saying:

> Baptists have always regarded infant baptism not simply as an unauthorized and useless innovation, but as involving a radical departure from the purpose of Christ in instituting the ordinance: supplanting believers' baptism, making the symbol antedate the thing symbolized, striking at the root of regenerate church-membership, tending to bring the entire population of Christianized community into church fellowship, and making possible and fostering State-churchism. And so the consequences of any other radical departures from New Testament precept and example may be shown to be far-reaching and destructive.[116]

---

[112] Thomas O. Summers, *Baptism: A Treatise on the Nature, Perpetuity, Subjects, Administrator, Mode, and Use of the Initiating Ordinance of the Christian Church* (Richmond, Va.: John Early, 1853), 27.

[113] Summers, *Baptism*, 178.

[114] Summers, *Baptism*, 180.

[115] George W. Langhorne, review of *Baptism: Its Nature, Obligation, Subjects, and Benefits*, by Leonidas Rosser, *Quarterly Review of the Methodist Episcopal Church, South* 9, no. 2 (1855): 282.

[116] Albert Henry Newman, *A History of Anti-Pedobaptism* (Philadelphia: American Baptist Publication Society, 1897), 28–29.

It is not surprising, then, that a recent policy statement by the Southern Baptist International Mission Board made the claim that "Baptists have emphatically and categorically denied infant baptism and have insisted on baptizing anyone who truly comes to a saving faith in Christ at some point subsequent to a prior baptism." The statement continued that "as a true follower of Christ, one must receive baptism in its proper order—after salvation."[117] While there is strong support for the position of these guidelines as a majority view, it overstates the case by not recognizing the voices of Other Baptists who have differed. Such an extreme sectarian view is difficult and painful to maintain in light of contemporary ecumenical conversations.

Yet the impact of this interdenominational controversy for Baptists in the South extended beyond infant baptism to the rejection of so-called alien immersion—namely, a baptism performed in the name of the Trinity, on confession of faith in Jesus Christ, by an administrator of a different ecclesial fellowship or church order.[118] The large majority of Southern Baptist churches still does not accept without rebaptism those whose baptism they regard as alien. The example of Henry Noble Sherwood, who once served as president of Georgetown College, illustrates the problem. In the fall of 1934, the annual meeting of the General Association of Baptists in Kentucky passed a resolution calling for Sherwood's resignation on the grounds that he was improperly baptized and therefore unfit to serve as president of the state's (and the South's) oldest Baptist college. Although Sherwood had been baptized by immersion and upon confession of his faith, his baptism was administered by the Disciples of Christ, with whom the Baptists of Kentucky had been involved in a bitter and protracted controversy for more than a century. The Disciples, or Campbellites as the Baptists derisively called them, held to the doctrine of baptismal regeneration—the teaching that salvation is mediated by the act of baptism. It mattered not that a Northern Baptist church in Franklin, Indiana, had accepted his baptism as valid, receiving him into membership and even calling him as pastor. Kentucky Baptists considered Sherwood's baptism to be "alien immersion." Though the General Association commended Sherwood for following his conscience, which he continued to do, never submitting to rebaptism, they withheld their annual contribution to the

---

[117] International Mission Board of the Southern Baptist Convention, "Guideline on Baptism," March 6, 2006.

[118] W. W. Barnes, *Encyclopedia of Southern Baptists*, s.v. "Alien Immersion" (Nashville: Broadman, 1958), 1:32.

college until the trustees finally voted in December 1941 "that President Sherwood's services would no longer be required."[119]

Though few Baptists today would openly describe infant baptism as an evil or a sin against God, most all Baptist congregations in the South still regard infant baptism to be of no value, requiring infant-baptized Christians to be rebaptized before they can become members, even those who are confirmed Christians who show themselves to be faithful disciples of Jesus Christ. Yet many of these same churches ironically have an open communion practice that says "whosoever will may come" regardless of baptismal status or church membership. On the question of alien immersion, little has changed since the days of Sherwood, as most Southern Baptists still receive members by transfer of letter only if their baptism was administered by a church of "like faith and order." This policy in effect refuses to recognize as valid any baptism unless the candidate was dipped in a Baptist baptistery. Baptism so practiced has ceased to be a biblical mandate and a sign of union with Jesus Christ and his universal body. Instead it has devolved into a denuded ritual of club membership. Only a lingering Landmarkism that clings to the parochial assertion that Baptists have the only true churches, and thus the only true baptism, can justify the refusal to admit into membership those who have been baptized by immersion upon their profession of faith in Jesus Christ no matter who the administrator was. It is time to recognize that the strictly denominational view of membership and communion does not hold water.

When the Baptists began arguing for believer's baptism by immersion, they were alone. The twenty-first-century ecclesial landscape looks quite different. *Baptism, Eucharist and Ministry*, the most widely distributed and studied ecumenical document, states, "While the possibility that infant baptism was also practiced in the apostolic age cannot be excluded, baptism upon personal profession of faith is the most clearly attested pattern in the New Testament documents."[120] Non-Baptist churches commonly practice believer's baptism by immersion. Even the Catholic rite of Christian initiation of adults recognizes adult believer's baptism as the normal way for unbaptized persons to become Catholic Christians, and as the norm adult conversion baptism makes the exception of infant baptism make sense.[121] As churches continue to adopt the practice of believer's

---

[119] James Duane Bolin, *Kentucky Baptists, 1925–2000: A Story of Cooperation* (Brentwood, Tenn.: Baptist History and Heritage Society, 2000), 128–29; and Frank M. Masters, *A History of Baptists in Kentucky* (Louisville, Ky.: Baptist Historical Society, 1953), 523–24.

[120] *Baptism, Eucharist and Ministry* IV.A.11, Faith and Order Paper no. 111 (Geneva: World Council of Churches, 1982), 4.

[121] *Rite of Christian Initiation of Adults*, study ed. (Washington, D.C.: United States Catholic Conference, 1988).

baptism by immersion, it is time to recognize the fruit of the Baptist witness. A modest proposal, then, is for Baptists to look for marks of true Christian baptism, which may not always be indicated by a sign out front with the word "Baptist" on it. Faithfulness to the Baptist heritage means that, whenever Christian baptism is practiced according to the apostolic pattern, it must be recognized and received.

Opening Up without Watering Down

The Baptist churches of the Old South had a lovely image for describing entrance into church membership. They would announce that a door of the church was open. Anyone who came forward was asked to give a verbal confession of their "experience of grace." When everyone was satisfied, "the right hand of fellowship" was extended to the new members. In those days the door of church membership was open to those baptized as believers by immersion only and into churches of like faith and order only. For all others, the church door remained closed. But if the local congregation is to be understood as a manifestation of the church catholic, such a restrictive requirement for membership cannot be unrelated to the reality of the church as church. Most Baptists undoubtedly believe that anyone genuinely committed to Christ is part of the church, but their ecclesiology belies their intuition. Baptist theologian Malcolm Tolbert put it simply when he said that "a church that is limited only to people baptized by immersion is smaller than God's church."[122] Unlike their forebears, Other Baptists seek to acknowledge their fellow Christians as colaborers in God's mission to the world and to recognize the ecclesiality of their churches. As the Pauline formula "one Lord, one faith, one baptism" suggests, the three are linked. It is impossible to reject one and maintain the integrity of the gospel, for to deny that all Christians are united in baptism implies that all do not share a common faith or serve the same Lord. Other Baptists have reached the conclusion that they can no longer live with this contradiction. Yet they also have come to believe that the baptismal theology they have received no longer is coherent. The question that remains is whether there is a way forward that accepts the validity of divergent baptismal practices and opens the door to church membership without watering down their theology of baptism.

For the differing churches of North Carolina, Carr's equation that infant baptism plus confirmation equals believer's baptism suggested a pathway toward a more ecumenical future. This formulation of the

---

[122] Malcolm O. Tolbert, *Shaping the Church: Adapting New Testament Models for Today* (Macon, Ga.: Smyth & Helwys, 2003), 60.

problem, which presupposed the conditional validity of infant baptism, drew less on the historic negation of paedobaptism by many credobaptists and more from an internal critique among Protestant theologians. Emil Brunner hinted of a neopaganism during World War II that resulted from a deficient baptismal practice when he asked, "What does the fact of having been baptized mean for a large number of contemporary people who do not know and do not even care to know whether they have been baptized?"[123] Brunner, along with his Swiss colleague Karl Barth, wondered how much longer Protestantism could survive baptism as an undisciplined induction into nominal Christianity. Yet, as Barth argued, neither the faulty practice of the church nor the lack of religious experience on the part of the candidate is capable of rendering baptism "ineffective and therefore invalid."[124] Baptism, he explained, remains effective as a sacrament through which God speaks and acts. And though not grace in itself, it is "from first to last a means of grace."[125] Following this line of thought, Carr urged Baptists not to be impatient and take matters into their own hands but to entrust the remediation of the practice of infant baptism to the power of the Spirit.

There is a long tradition of internal criticism, beginning with Tertullian, the first critic of infant baptism, who recommended postponing baptism until a candidate has "become competent to know Christ."[126] Baptism, he argued, is a missional practice that makes sense only in the context of making disciples, and Baptists have been quick to appeal to this critique.[127] Methodist theologian and ecumenist Geoffrey Wainwright has affirmed that "Baptists are right to call for the abandonment of the practice of baptizing infants," not only because the baptism of believers is the clearest New Testament pattern, but also because "repentance, faith and righteous living form the proper human response to God's grace."[128] But the most trenchant critique from within has been offered by patristic scholar and reformed theologian David F. Wright, who asked, "What has infant baptism done to baptism?" His penetrating historical analysis has shown, much more persuasively than Brunner or Barth imagined, "the damaging ascendancy of infant baptism in practice and theology since the

[123] Emil Brunner, *The Divine Human Encounter* (Philadelphia: Westminster, 1943), 181.

[124] Karl Barth, *The Teaching of the Church regarding Baptism*, trans. Ernest Payne (London: SCM Press, 1945), 35.

[125] Karl Barth, *The Epistle to the Romans*, trans. Edwyn C. Hoskyns (London: Oxford University Press, 1977), 192.

[126] Tertullian, *Baptism* 18.5, in *Tertullian's Homily on Baptism*, trans. Ernest Evans (London: SPCK, 1964), 39.

[127] Smyth, *The Character of the Beast*, in *Works of John Smyth*, 2:568–69.

[128] Geoffrey Wainwright, *Christian Initiation* (London: Lutterworth, 1969), 49–50.

late patristic and early medieval centuries."[129] "One of the sad legacies of the long reign of infant baptism," Wright argued, is that "it has shrunk baptism even as an action or drama."[130] This unified practice came to rest on a theological account that reduced the validity and efficacy of baptism to the criteria of *water* and the *name* (i.e. the Trinity) but said nothing about the faith of the *candidate*.[131] Yet despite the suggestion that the credobaptist pattern might offer the best possibility for an ecumenical future, the internal paedobaptist critique carried no sweeping endorsement of Baptist practice.[132] As Baptist theologian Neville Clark reminded them, "Here also, confusion reigns."[133] So while it may be tempting to write off the problem of defective baptism as a unique trouble for paedobaptist churches, credobaptists must stop and ask whether their churches have done an effective job of making disciples of those whom they baptize. To be sure, Baptists maintain that believer's baptism is not merely the practice most clearly warranted by Scripture or simply a useful means of identifying the visible saints or even the most dramatic way of enacting the burial and resurrection of Christ. Baptists contend that, if consistently observed, the baptism of believers ensures the church will consist of true disciples. But too often they do not practice what they preach. Paedobaptists are not alone responsible for the breakdown of baptismal practice, for neither are credobaptists "immune from indiscriminate baptism."[134] Indeed, the suggestion that Baptists might be the source of ecumenical renewal may be little more than a theological idea without a practice to sustain it.[135] It seems fitting and fair then to ask *what believer's baptism has done to baptism.*

Considerable attention has been given to the fact that the annual number of baptisms in the Southern Baptist Convention, the largest Protestant denomination in America, has been in a slow but steady decline for the past fifty years.[136] The recognized crisis has resulted in challenges to

---

[129] David F. Wright, *What Has Infant Baptism Done to Baptism?* (Milton Keynes, U.K.: Paternoster, 2005), 9. What Wright's small book lacks in detail is more than compensated by his massive collection of essays, *Infant Baptism in Historical Perspective* (Milton Keynes, U.K.: Paternoster, 2007). For an excellent forum on Wright's argument, see *Evangelical Quarterly* 78, no. 2 (2006): 101–69.

[130] Wright, *What Has Infant Baptism Done to Baptism?* 77.

[131] Wright, *What Has Infant Baptism Done to Baptism?* 26.

[132] Wainwright, *Christian Initiation*, 82.

[133] Neville Clark, "The Theology of Baptism," in Gilmore, *Christian Baptism*, 325.

[134] James F. White, *Sacraments as God's Self-Giving* (Nashville: Abingdon, 1983), 46.

[135] G. R. Beasley-Murray, "Baptism in the New Testament," *Foundations* 3, no. 1 (1960): 15–31.

[136] Ed Stetzer, "Analysis of SBC Statistics," *Christianity Today*, June 10, 2011, accessed August 3, 2013, http://www.christianitytoday.com/edstetzer/2011/june/analysis-of-sbc -statistics.html; and Stetzer, "SBC 2011 Statistical Realities—Facts Are Our Friends but

"reach more people and plant more churches" to reverse the trend. There are indications, however, that suggest the trouble goes deeper than a mere downward statistical trajectory. One is the phenomenon of rebaptism. Of the total baptisms reported every year by the SBC, 60 percent are rebaptisms. Most are rebaptisms of people who have already been baptized as infants, but amazingly more than a third are rebaptisms of believers who have been previously baptized in Southern Baptist churches. In many cases these rebaptisms were deemed justified because the candidates stated that they did not think that they were really regenerate believers when they were previously baptized.[137] The prevalence of such repeat believer's baptisms, however, is a startling indication that the doctrinal integrity of believer's baptism itself may be collapsing under the pressures of evangelical decisionism, atomistic individualism, and theological minimalism.[138] When the faith decision of the candidate is elevated as the sole criterion of validity, it is but a short turn down the road of neo-Donatism, leaving open the possibility of an infinite regress of rebaptism.[139] Baptists from most other communities around the world would likely refuse to rebaptize Christians already baptized as believers, encouraging them instead to

These Are Not Very Friendly Facts," June 13, 2012, accessed August 3, 2013, http://www .christianitytoday.com/edstetzer/2012/june/sbc-2011-statistical-realities—facts-are-our -friends-but.html.

[137] "Adults Baptized in Southern Baptist Churches," *Research Report*, January 1995, 1–4, a publication of the Home Mission Board, SBC; and Phillip B. Jones et al., *A Study of Adults Baptized in Southern Baptist Churches, 1993* (Atlanta: Home Mission Board of the Southern Baptist Convention, 1995), 5. Though these data are twenty years old, there is no indication that the occurrence of rebaptism has decreased. One of the implications of the 1995 report was the identification of "rededication" as the motivation for 40 percent of all people being baptized. The report stated, "This raises questions about why they feel a need to be rebaptized."

[138] Timothy George, "The Reformed Doctrine of Believers' Baptism," *Interpretation* 47, no. 3 (1993): 251. The 1995 SBC report concluded that the lack of clarity about the meaning of baptism was troubling, stating as a particular concern pastoral pressure to be rebaptized rather than counseling inquirers on the assurance of salvation. It asked, "Is the true meaning of baptism being taught in our churches?" "Adults Baptized in Southern Baptist Churches," 3.

[139] The SBC's most notorious serial rebaptizer is surely Bailey Smith, who during his ministry as pastor of the Del City Baptist Church in Oklahoma consistently led the SBC in baptisms. As Timothy Bonney has related in his journal observations from the 1980 Oklahoma Youth Evangelism Conference, rebaptism was standard practice. In a sermon, Bailey Smith declaimed that the vast majority of church members were "lost" and going to hell. Afterward Smith asked for all the adults who previously thought they were saved but who had accepted Christ as a result of his sermon to raise their hands. This was followed by an appeal to Sunday school teachers and deacons. The point, as Bonney so vividly describes, was not to lead people to Christ but to use scare tactics to sow seeds of doubt among Christians, leading them to be born again, and again, and again, and to be baptized over, and over, and over. Timothy Bonney, journal entry, December 30, 1980, accessed July 30, 2013, http://www.baptistlife .com/flick/images/Tares.htm.

see their growing experience as a renewal of their baptismal vows and as a fulfillment of God's promised outpouring of the Spirit.

But repeat believer's baptism is not the only indication that the theology and practice of believer's baptism is in crisis. For several decades, the immersion of children has accounted for a growing number of the baptisms reported by the Southern Baptists, and the baptism of children even four and five years old, which might better be described as toddler baptism, is not uncommon, pushing the distinction between believer and infant baptism to the limits of credibility. The data from the 2011 Annual Church Profile indicate that children under age eleven comprised approximately one-third of the total baptism reported by SBC churches. At a time when the overall number of baptisms among the Southern Baptists is in decline, the baptism of children continues to increase.[140] When rebaptisms (60 percent) and children (33 percent) make up such a large number of all baptisms, it would seem to be time to ask not about the downward numerical trend of baptisms but about whether the underlying baptismal theology is sufficiently missional.[141]

A more subtle sign of confusion in baptismal theology among Baptists is the disconnect in a growing number of churches between admission to the Lord's table and church membership. In earlier generations, baptism and the Lord's Supper were tightly linked, as the table was "hedged" from those who were not regularly baptized. It was unusual for congregations, especially in the southern United States, to practice open communion. Today it is hard to find a Baptist church that still practices closed communion, though the Baptist Faith and Message through all its revisions has never wavered from the declaration that believer's baptism by immersion "is prerequisite to the privileges of church membership and to the Lord's Supper."[142] To the extent that churches that practice open

---

[140] "2011 Southern Baptist Statistics—Number of Baptisms," *Lifeway Insights*, August 14, 2012. Thorwald Lorenzen observed that in 1976 Baptist congregations connected with the SBC baptized 35,562 children under eight years of age. Lorenzen, "Baptists and Ecumenicity with Special Reference to Baptism," *Review and Expositor* 72 (1980): 42n2. In 1989, out of a total of 351,107 recorded baptisms, SBC congregations baptized 45,224 children eight years of age or younger; see *Quarterly Review* 50 (1990): 21.

[141] The 1995 SBC report suggested that, given the fact that only 40 percent of all baptisms were identified as "first-time commitments to Jesus," the missional impact of Southern Baptists is far less than the raw baptism statistics might indicate. "Adults Baptized in Southern Baptist Churches," 1.

[142] Baptist Faith and Message (1963/2000) VII; see Lumpkin, *Baptist Confessions of Faith*, 396. The earlier confession similarly states that believer's baptism by immersion is "prerequisite to the privileges of a church relation and to the Lord's Supper." Baptist Faith and Message (1925) XIII; see Robert A. Baker, *A Baptist Source Book* (Nashville: Broadman, 1966), 202. In a recent poll conducted by Lifeway Research, more than half (52 percent) of SBC pastors

communion and closed membership have any theological rationale, it is the evangelical conviction that *faith, not baptism, makes the church*, thus turning baptism into a recommended but still optional step, rather than a gospel ordinance essential for the church to be the church.[143] In any case, there is too little reflection on the tension between baptismal theology and communion practice. It would be a mistake, however, to construe these examples as a suggestion that the contemporary baptismal crisis is limited to Southern Baptists.[144] The fact that significant numbers of Baptist congregations in Great Britain and Australia have decoupled baptism from church membership indicates that the issue is not confined to the United States. Indeed, it suggests that all of these examples are symptomatic of a deeper problem extending to the wider fellowship of Baptists, in which baptism is conceived as just a symbol of human response, signifying nothing of God's activity.

Although Baptists claim to follow the light of the plain and clear teaching of Scripture, it is ironic that they often struggle to see any indication of divine activity in the biblical descriptions of baptism. Baptists, however, are not alone in this difficulty of discerning God's action in the baptismal waters, as even late in life Karl Bath reversed his earlier, more sacramental understanding in favor of the view that water baptism is only a "human work" that responds to the prior divine work of the baptism of the Holy Spirit.[145] Speaking directly to this conclusion, George

---

stated that any professing believer can participate in communion. Only a third of those polled (35 percent) stated that believer's baptism is prerequisite to the Lord's Supper. Carol Pipes, "Lord's Supper: LifeWay Surveys Churches' Practices, Frequency," *Baptist Press*, September 17, 2012, accessed July 14, 2013, http://www.bpnews.net/bpnews.asp?id=38730.

[143] Evangelical theologian Miroslav Volf has argued that faith linked with baptism is essential for the church to be the church in his *After Our Likeness: The Church as the Image of the Trinity* (Grand Rapids: Eerdmans, 1998), 152–53.

[144] A group of Southern Baptist theologians has made a significant contribution toward the ecumenical engagement of credobaptism and paedobaptism in the collection of essays in Thomas R. Schreiner and Shawn D. Wright, eds., *Believer's Baptism: Sign of the New Covenant in Christ* (Nashville: B&H Academic, 2006). A statement on the official SBC website continues to describe infant baptism as an ecumenical impasse: "When a Southern Baptist church requires baptism by immersion for membership, it is not inferring that a person who has been baptized by sprinkling is in any way inferior, or second class, or unsaved. It is not attempting to insult anyone or elevate itself as superior; it is merely striving to be faithful to the Lord and His command, and asking those who wish to be members to do the same. For the church to do otherwise would be compromise. Even worse, it would be disobedience." Accessed August 1, 2013, http://www.sbc.net/aboutus/faqs.asp#2.

[145] Barth, *Church Dogmatics* IV/4, trans. G. W. Bromiley (Edinburgh: T&T Clark, 1969), 101. Barth retreated from his earlier view that baptism is a "sacrament of truth and holiness" and a "means of grace" in his *Epistle to the Romans*, 192. He argued that the notion of "sacrament" was derived from the Hellenistic mystery religions rather than the New Testament in his *Church Dogmatics* IV/4, 108–9. Barth states in his preface that he was led to reverse

Beasley-Murray voiced a word of caution, warning that "the idea that baptism is a purely symbolic rite is out of harmony with the New Testament itself."[146] So the Apostle Paul can write that "when you were buried with him in baptism, you were also raised with him through faith in the power of God, who raised him from the dead" (Col 3:1). It is hard to miss the sense of divine activity in baptism as a participation in the death and resurrection of Christ. Baptism is surely an occasion for the candidate to offer a confession of faith (Rom 10:9-10), but it is also a witness to (and perhaps even a means of) the activity of God that brings the baptized into union with Christ (Rom 6:3) and his Body (1 Cor 12:13). Still it is fair to say that Baptists are not of one mind about whether the transformational grace of God is mediated by as well as depicted in baptism. Yet the claim that baptism is a "mere symbol" or an "empty sign" simply does not bear up to the plain and clear teaching of the Scripture. It is a "dynamic symbol" or an "effectual sign," and its effectiveness is precisely in the mysterious interplay between divine grace and human faith.[147]

The theological term historically used to describe such an action is "sacrament." Though many Baptists have resisted sacramental language, Other Baptists have used it with qualification, seeking to affirm the deep connection of grace and faith while wanting to avoid connotations of mechanical efficacy or *ex opere operato*.[148] Neville Clark was one who recommended sacramental terminology for baptism because, he attested, "it brings the disciple into a union with Christ too deep and realistic for words adequately to describe it," adding, "it has objective significance."[149] Following Augustine, baptism may be described as a sacrament because there is more going on here than meets the eye. But if baptism is a sacrament, it is so not because it is in itself grace. Rather it is a sacrament because God has ordained it as a means of grace.[150] It is an "evangelical

---

his thinking through the work of his Baptist son (Markus Barth, *Die Taufe—Ein Sakrament?* [Zollikon-Zürich: Evangelischer Verlag, 1951]).

[146] Beasley-Murray, *Baptism in the New Testament*, 263.

[147] Beasley-Murray, *Baptism in the New Testament*, 263–75. This same argument is made by Fiddes, *Tracks and Traces*, 145–48; and Paul S. Fiddes et al., *Pushing at the Boundaries of Unity: Anglicans and Baptists in Conversation* (London: Church House, 2005), 46–49.

[148] E.g., Thomas J. Nettles condemns Baptist sacramentalism as having "a corrupting influence on Baptist ecclesiology and soteriology," in his *The Baptists: Key People Involved in Forming a Baptist Identity* (Fearn, Scotland: Mentor, 2005–2007), 3:309. George Beasley-Murray, R. E. O. White, Neville Clark, and most of the other contributors to the collection *Christian Baptism* (ed. Gilmore), freely employed the term sacrament in relation to baptism.

[149] Neville Clark, *An Approach to the Theology of the Sacraments* (Chicago: Allenson, 1956), 32.

[150] John E. Colwell, *Promise and Presence: An Exploration of Sacramental Theology* (Milton Keynes, U.K.: Paternoster, 2005), 133.

sacrament" because it is both the visible word of God in water as well as a human response to God's word.[151] Suspicious evangelicals still hesitant about employing sacramental language may find James McClendon's use of speech-act theory to be a helpful way of retrieving a sense of baptism as an act in which God speaks. Baptism so construed actually *does* something rather than merely *describe* something already done.[152] It is performative. Yet if baptism is understood as a speech act, it is a complex semantic event that involves four distinct syntactical moves that do different but related things. First, there is the candidate's confession to God, which says, "I claim the power of the risen Lord for myself." Next is the church's reception of candidate, which affirms, "We receive you as our brother/sister in Christ." Then there is the candidate's confession to the church, which declaims, "Brothers and sisters, I take my place in your midst. Receive me!" And finally, there is God's word to the candidate, which declares, "You are my son/daughter; this day have I begotten you."[153] One striking feature of this scheme is that it not only retrieves a sense of God's action in baptism; it also reconnects Christian baptism with Christ's baptism in the Jordan (Matt 3:17; Mark 1:11; and Luke 3:22), as God speaks the same word to the candidate that was spoken to Jesus, thus identifying Christian baptism as the imitation of Christ. Such an approach would go a long way toward correcting the credobaptist reductionism of baptism as merely an individual human response limited to the first dimension named above.

Honest evaluation of believer's baptism reveals a theology and practice in serious crisis, no less than infant baptism. If paedobaptism hangs by a slender thread, it would seem that the frayed cord of credobaptism is near the breaking point as well. For, although believer's baptism by immersion may be the most clearly attested pattern in the New Testament, the earliest extrabiblical evidence from the *Apostolic Tradition* indicates that infants were routinely baptized from at least the mid-second century and perhaps earlier.[154] Indeed, from the descriptions in the Acts of the Apostles and the

---

[151] Anthony R. Cross, *Recovering the Evangelical Sacrament: "Baptisma Semper Reformadum"* (Eugene, Ore.: Pickwick, 2013), 35–37. Cross argues against the "myth" of Baptist antisacramentalism in Philip E. Thompson and Anthony R. Cross, eds., *Recycling the Past or Researching History? Studies in Baptist Historiography and Myths* (Milton Keynes, U.K.: Paternoster, 2005), 128–62. See also Stanley K. Fowler, *More than a Symbol: The British Baptist Recovery of Baptismal Sacramentalism* (Carlisle, U.K.: Paternoster, 2002); and Fowler, "Is Baptist Sacramentalism an Oxymoron?" in *Baptist Sacramentalism*, ed. Thompson and Cross (Carlisle, U.K.: Paternoster, 2003), 129–50.

[152] James Wm. McClendon Jr., "Baptism as a Performative Sign," *Theology Today* 23, no. 3 (1966): 407–8.

[153] McClendon, "Baptism as a Performative Sign," 410; and James Wm. McClendon Jr., *Doctrine: Systematic Theology, Volume II* (Waco, Tex.: Baylor University Press, 2012), 386–97.

[154] Hippolytus, *Apostolic Tradition* 21.4, in *The Apostolic Constitution: A Commentary*, ed.

Didache, it seems clear that baptism in water and in the name of the Trinity, though universally observed, was not uniformly practiced by the end of the apostolic era.[155] It is not inconceivable that Christian baptism at this early date may also have included infants.[156] And although most Baptists still would not regard infant baptism as conforming to the normative pattern of Scripture, Other Baptists are prepared to see infant baptism as a form of baptism derived from the norm of believer's baptism, while only practicing the normative form in their own communities. This is an important step. The pressing question is whether Baptists can exemplify a rich and robust practice of believer's baptism that might become a source of renewal for the whole church. As one Baptist theologian has argued, "Baptism is not only the solemn profession of a redeemed sinner . . . it is also a sacred and serious act of incorporation into the visible community of faith."[157] Such an understanding calls for the reform of baptismal

---

Paul F. Bradshaw, Maxwell E. Johnson, and L. Edward Phillips (Minneapolis: Fortress, 2002), 113. Bradshaw and colleagues date the *Apostolic Tradition* to be "an aggregation of material from different sources . . . from perhaps as early as the mid-second century to as late as the mid-fourth" (14). It is important to note that the "infants," literally those who cannot answer for themselves, may have included children from infancy to the age of seven (130). Everett Ferguson suggests that the earliest uncontested reference to infant baptism may be Irenaeus, *Against Heresies* 2.22.4, written in the late second century, which describes the baptism of "infants, children, boys, youths, and the old"; see Ferguson, *Baptism in the Early Church* (Grand Rapids: Eerdmans, 2009), 308.

[155] The Acts of the Apostles presents variations in baptismal practice that include the Spirit coming before and after baptism, with and without the laying on of hands, with and without manifestations in the gifts of the Spirit, baptism in the name of Jesus and baptism in the Holy Spirit. Beasley-Murray cautions that the evidence is complicated and ambiguous, defying formulas, in his *Baptism in the New Testament*, 302. The diversity of baptismal practice is reflected in the recommendation to baptize in the name of the Trinity in water that is running or still, cold or warm, by dipping or pouring. *Didache* 7.1–4, in *The Didache, The Epistle of Barnabas, The Epistles and The Martyrdom of St. Polycarp, The Fragments of Papias, The Epistle to Diognetus*, Ancient Christian Writers 6, trans. James A. Kleist (New York: Newman Press, 1948), 19.

[156] Geoffrey Wainwright, who has been a sympathetic critic of Baptist theology, concluded that "the *exclusive* insistence on believers' baptism has not done justice . . . to the distinct possibility (this is how I would rate the historical evidence) that infant baptism was practiced in the apostolic age," in his *Christian Initiation*, 81. Everett Ferguson has shown that Christian burial inscriptions from the late second and early third centuries provide conclusive evidence that young children and even newborns were in fact baptized. However, he suggests that there was (1) no common age for baptism, (2) no evidence of the routine baptism of newborn infants, and (3) strong motive for Christian parents to baptize gravely ill children. Ferguson points to the influence of John 3:5 on the second-century church, which was taken to mean that baptism was necessary for entrance in heaven. He contends that this "emergency practice eventually became the normal practice." It seems odd, however, that the Johannine baptismal theology would have left no similar impression on primitive Christians. Ferguson, *Baptism in the Early Church*, 372–79.

[157] George, "The Reformed Doctrine of Believers' Baptism," 251.

practice among all the churches, but meeting this challenge will require a new approach that moves beyond the intractable impasse of the past.

The book *Baptism, Eucharist and Ministry (BEM)* proposed the most significant ecumenical move in this direction. It explored the one baptism that unites all Christians to Christ. The basic conviction of the document is that the "one baptism" (Eph 4:5), which is the source of Christian unity, is a "common baptism." Though it acknowledged believer's baptism as "the most clearly attested pattern in the New Testament," it also commended infant baptism as an alternative practice. The troubling feature for most Baptists, however, was the declaration that baptism is "an unrepeatable act" and therefore "any practice which might be interpreted as 're-baptism' must be avoided."[158] This anabaptist prohibition is surely a nonstarter for those in closed-membership churches, but even Baptists who, following the Jessey-Bunyan approach, have been prepared to open the door to church membership out of respect for the conscience of paedobaptists still balk at the notion of infant-baptist and believer-baptist traditions as "equivalent alternatives."[159] To be sure, something like equivalency was at the core for Other Baptists who accepted Carr's equation that infant baptism plus confirmation equals believer's baptism. Closer examination, however, reveals that the equivalency implied in the notion of "common baptism" does not go quite deep enough. As a recent ecumenical document noted, "Baptist resistance to the phrase 'common baptism' rests on the implication that the present baptismal practices of the Christian Church are simply equivalent to each other." More specifically, "it implies that the baptism of a believer is exactly the same event as the baptism of a very young infant."[160] Rather than a "common baptism," the report recommends greater exploration into the biblical language of "one baptism" (Eph 4:5).

At the center of the link between "one Lord, one faith, one baptism" is the paschal mystery into which Jesus was immersed through the suffering and death of the cross (Mark 10:38-39).[161] His immersion into the deep waters of death is the reality that Christian baptism signifies and that all Christians are called to share in union with Christ (Rom 6:3, 5). As the early Baptist Leonard Busher wrote, to be baptized is to be "dipped

---

[158] *Baptism, Eucharist and Ministry* IV.A.11/13, 4.

[159] *Baptism, Eucharist and Ministry,* Commentary IV.A.12, 5.

[160] Fiddes et al., *Pushing at the Boundaries,* 31.

[161] *Believing and Being Baptized: Baptism, So-Called Re-baptism, and Children in the Church,* a discussion document by the Doctrine and Worship Committee of the Baptist Union of Great Britain (Didcot, U.K.: Baptist Union, 1996), 36.

for dead in water."[162] It is important to note that the word "baptism" (βάπτισμα) in the New Testament may be used in a metaphorical way as a collective term that can denote a constellation of ideas. In his book *Baptism in the Holy Spirit*, James D. G. Dunn suggests that "baptism" is a "shorthand description" for the entire process of becoming a Christian. Dunn explains that "it may be used simply for the actual act of immersion in water, or its meaning may be expanded to take in more and more of the rites and constituent parts of conversion-initiation until it embraces the whole."[163] There is reason to think that the "one baptism" in Ephesians 4:5 is just such a trope that refers to the whole conversion-initiation process through which believers become members of the body of Christ.[164]

In his book *The Customs of Primitive Churches*, the eighteenth-century Baptist historian Morgan Edwards offered a description of the process of Christian initiation and reception into membership among eighteenth-century Baptists. It began with the confession of faith and baptism, after which the minister addressed and prayed for the candidate, including the imposition of hands. Following the laying on of hands, the minister gave the baptized the right hand of fellowship and kiss of charity and wrote out a certificate of baptism. The baptismal service concluded with a benediction following the singing of a Watts hymn:

> Do we now know that solemn word,
> That we are bury'd with the Lord;
> Baptiz'd into his death, and then,
> Put off the body of our sin.[165]

The recent edition of *Patterns and Prayers* used among British Baptists includes a range of rites and practices under the rubric the "Welcoming of Disciples," which calls attention to the process of Christian initiation through the prayer for and the declaration of faith by candidates, baptism and the laying on of hands, making covenant promises and reception into membership, and the celebration of the Lord's Supper in which

---

[162] Leonard Busher, *Religion's Peace; or, a Plea for Liberty of Conscience*, in Edward Bean Underhill, *Tracts on Liberty of Conscience and Persecution* (London: Hanserd Knollys Society, 1846), 59. Busher's tract was first published in 1614, almost three decades before "dipping" or immersion was first practiced by Baptists.

[163] James D. G. Dunn, *Baptism in the Holy Spirit: A Re-examination of the New Testament Teaching on the Gift of the Sprit in Relation to Pentecostalism Today*, 2nd ed. (London: SCM Press, 2010), 5.

[164] Cross, *Recovering the Evangelical Sacrament*, 107. Cross specifically describes βάπτισμα as an example of synecdoche, in which the part refers to the whole.

[165] Morgan Edwards, *The Customs of Primitive Churches* (Philadelphia, 1774), 82–83.

new members are served first as a sign of hospitality and welcome.[166] It is important to note that baptism and initiation from the time of the ancient churches have been understood as a process with a number of rites and practices, from catechetical instruction and preparation, prayers of renunciation and thanksgiving, exorcism and confession of faith, anointing with oil and the laying on of hands, and the kiss of peace and eucharistic celebration.[167]

The "one baptism" that Christians are called to manifest, then, is not merely a punctual act but an extended process that includes everything implied in the gospel. Following this important insight of baptism as part of a process of Christian conversion and initiation, it seems reasonable to suggest that paedobaptists and credobaptists, though not sharing a "common baptism" in a strict sense, may work toward sharing a "common initiation." This approach was pursued in the international conversations between the Anglican Communion and the Baptist World Alliance, which explained in their 2005 report that "comparison should be made not simply between the ways in which baptism is practiced as a single event, but between varying shapes of the *whole journey* of initiation."[168] This journey includes baptism but also preparatory (or prevenient) grace, Christian nurture, responsible faith, first communion, and commissioning for service.[169] A similar approach was taken in the most recent international dialogue between the Baptist World Alliance and the Catholic Church, which stated that "initiation into Christ and his church is a process wider than the act of baptism itself" and continued that "we can work towards a mutual recognition of the different forms that *initiation* takes among us, as an entire 'journey' of faith and grace."[170]

---

[166] Christopher J. Ellis and Myra Blyth, eds., *Gathering for Worship: Patterns and Prayers for the Community of Disciples* (Norwich, U.K.: Canterbury Press, 2005), 64–93. It also includes liturgical resources for nurturing new faith and reaffirming baptismal vows.

[167] Edward Charles Whitaker, *Documents of the Baptismal Liturgy* (London: SPCK, 1960/1970/1997) is the most complete collection of documents of baptismal liturgy. See esp. *The Apostolic Tradition* §§16–21, pp. 2–7; and *The Apostolic Constitution* §§3.16–18 and §§7.22, 29–45, pp. 30–35. See also Aidan Kavanagh, *The Shape of Baptism: The Rite of Christian Initiation* (New York: Pueblo, 1978), 35–78; and William H. Willimon, *Remember Who You Are: Baptism, a Model for Christian Life* (Nashville: Upper Room, 1980), 15–21.

[168] Paul S. Fiddes and Bruce Matthews, eds., *Conversations around the World 2000–2005: The Report of the International Conversations between the Anglican Communion and the Baptist World Alliance* (London: Anglican Communion Office, 2005), 3.42, 46 (emphasis in original). This same approach was followed by the English Anglican and Baptist conversations. Fiddes et al., *Pushing at the Boundaries of Unity*, 41–46.

[169] Fiddes and Matthews, *Conversations around the World*, 3.42, 45.

[170] "The Word of God in the Life of the Church: A Report of International Conversations between the Catholic Church and the Baptist World Alliance 2006–2010" §101, *American Baptist Quarterly* 31, no. 1 (2012): 69 (emphasis in original).

Such an approach might set out alternate patterns of initiation. *Plan A* begins with (a) infant dedication, followed by (b) Christian nurture and catechetical instruction, leading to (c) baptism upon the confession of faith including the laying on of hands, and (d) reception into membership and participation in the Lord's Supper/Eucharist. *Plan B* starts with (a) infant baptism, followed by (b) Christian nurture and catechetical instruction, leading to (c) the confession and confirmation of faith including the laying on of hands, and (d) participation in the Lord's Supper/Eucharist. Each plan names a complex constellation of convictions and practices that move toward an understanding of *divergent patterns as equivalent alternatives.* Both patterns include a rich and robust account in which Christian baptism is not reduced to a singular act but rather traces a journey through which participants are made disciples.[171] *BEM* began with the declaration that the "one baptism into Christ constitutes a call to the churches to overcome their divisions and visibly manifest their fellowship."[172] That call has become more insistent in the three decades since its publication, so that a new World Council of Churches study document, simply entitled *One Baptism*, puts the issue more sharply, asking, "What does the 'mutual recognition of baptism' actually mean, theologically, ecclesiologically and pastorally?"[173] It asks churches to recognize one another as churches—that is, as genuine expressions of the one church of Jesus Christ—as well as to accept the validity of the baptism of those seeking membership from other churches and to acknowledge one another as fellow Christians.[174] Baptismal reform lies at the heart of the Baptist vision of reform and renewal for the church, and yet, as long as baptism continues to be a stumbling block to fuller relations with the wider church, it will remain an unfinished work.[175]

If Baptists desire to heed this call of overcoming divisions, it will require rethinking church membership. The continued insistence on *closed membership* that accepts only those baptized as believers by immersion not only rejects infant baptism as nothing but denies the working of the Holy Spirit though the process of infant baptism to confirmation, and consequently it does not regard communities that observe this practice to be Christian churches. Many closed-membership Christians will surely

---

[171] Wainwright, *Christian Initiation*, 66.

[172] *Baptism, Eucharist and Ministry* II.D.6, 3.

[173] *One Baptism: Towards Mutual Recognition* I.B.9, Faith and Order Paper no. 210 (Geneva: World Council of Churches, 2011), 3.

[174] *One Baptism* I.B.12, 4.

[175] Dale Moody, *Baptism: Foundation for Christian Unity* (Philadelphia: Westminster, 1967), 304.

protest, saying that by denying the baptismal initiation of other communities they are not questioning their churchly or Christian status. But as David Wright cautions, the refusal of one body of Christians to recognize the baptisms of another body "is tantamount to questioning the very character as 'church' of that other body."[176] A variation of this alternative seeks to recognize other churches as churches by regarding believer's baptism as a completion or renewal of infant baptism.[177] Though attempting to be ecumenically sensitive, the language of baptismal "repair" is still received by infant-baptizing communities in the same way as are more strict forms of closed membership: infant baptism is not really a churchly act, and those assemblies that practice it are not really Christian churches. Several other alternatives seek to modify closed membership by accepting infant-baptized believers as associate members or by receiving those who have been baptized as believers (and by immersion) in churches of different faith and order. Yet these variations leave unresolved the deeper questions of the validity of infant baptism and the ecclesial status of those who perform it.

The only viable option for Christians discerning the way forward toward the "mutual recognition of baptism" is *open membership*, in which a Baptist congregation practices baptism of believers by immersion only but allows baptized believers into full membership regardless of the mode or age of their baptism as long as the Christian initiation process has been completed. It is important to note that open membership considers infant baptism to be tacitly incomplete until a candidate has given evidence of a personal confession of faith, as in *Plan B* above. Yet open-membership churches have reached the conclusion that they can no longer countenance the unqualified denial of infant baptism unless they are prepared to "to 'unchurch' all Paedo-Baptist communities and to uphold separation at this point in the name of the One True Church."[178] Open-membership churches may wish to observe a rite of remembrance of baptism during the service for receiving Christians from non-Baptist churches. A variation of open membership is practiced by contemporary churches following a tradition from Bunyan to Spurgeon that considers someone initiated

---

[176] Wright, *Infant Baptism in Historical Perspective*, 381.

[177] McClendon, *Doctrine*, 393–96. Though McClendon proposes this as "an ecumenical solution," his unfortunate description of believer's baptism as a "repair" of infant baptism proves to be less than satisfactory. See Willie James Jennings, "Grace without Remainder: Why Baptists Should Baptize Their Babies," in *Grace Upon Grace: Essays in Honor of Thomas A. Langford*, ed. Robert K. Johnson, L. Gregory Jones, and Jonathan Wilson (Nashville: Abingdon, 1999), 202–5. While I disagree with the suggestion that Baptists should baptize infants, I nevertheless share suspicion about language of baptismal repair.

[178] Clark, "The Theology of Baptism," in Gilmore, *Christian Baptism*, 326.

into Christ and the church by a confession of faith (or conversion experience) regardless of baptism. Such churches can receive infant-baptized Christians into membership not by approving infant baptism but because they believe that faith rather than baptism is necessary for membership. But, as this chapter has shown, there have been Other Baptists "who have combined the belief in an indissoluble link between baptism and church membership with an 'open membership' approach."[179] And Other Baptists hope that, if they can display how divergent baptismal practices may be construed as part of the journey of discipleship, they might embody more fully the conviction of "one Lord, one faith, one baptism."[180] Such an approach avoids the blocking strategy of closed membership that "just says no" to ecumenical conversation partners who have a divergent baptismal practice as well as the unqualified acceptance that leaves the validity of baptism up to each person's own individual experience and judgment. Instead, the model of open membership proposed here suggests a way to continue together in the drama of salvation by overaccepting the offer of infant baptism based on the gospel story.[181]

One of the strengths of this strategy is that it ensures an intentional connection between personal-faith and divine-grace baptism. Early Baptist forebears were rightly concerned that personal faith and baptism be tightly linked. This was their major conviction and the basis of their apprehension about infant baptism. They argued that the proper order, indeed the only order explicitly warranted by Scripture, is profession of faith followed by baptism. What is proposed here is that the conviction of regenerate membership can be realized without insisting on that order as long as the link between faith and baptism is strong and intentional. Infant baptism aimed toward conversion of the baptized and believer's baptism observing baptism of the converted can both share the common goal of

---

[179] "Word of God in the Life of the Church" §110, 73.

[180] While open membership may be rare among Southern Baptists (around 1 percent), it is not uncommon among National Baptists, and almost one-third of American Baptists (30 percent) have open membership. Most participating churches in the Baptist Union of Great Britain are open membership, as only 17 percent require believer's baptism for membership and 51 percent admit to full membership people who have not been baptized as believers. Open membership is rare among European Baptists, though associate membership is quite common, except in Italy, and Denmark, where 90 and 40 percent of the churches are open, respectively. Open membership is universal among churches in Burma (Myanmar) and common among Baptists in the West Indies. Open-membership churches are not uncommon in Australasia, particularly in New South Wales, Victoria, South Australia, and New Zealand, where 50 percent of the churches are open membership. Fiddes and Matthews, *Conversations around the World*, 4.49–50.

[181] On the improvisational strategies of blocking, accepting, and overaccepting, see Samuel Wells, *Improvisation: The Drama of Christian Ethics* (Grand Rapids: Brazos, 2004), 103–42.

regenerate church membership. The Baptist scruple about baptism, then, must be understood not only as a matter of faith that must be brought to obedient discipleship. It is also a matter of grace, in that baptism seen as including endowment with *charismata* for service. Baptism in whatever mode must be connected to and accompanied by discipleship in which grace and faith are mingled.

Another value of this approach to open membership is that it forces Baptists to explore more deeply the connection between Spirit and water baptism. A downside to both closed membership and some expressions that regard baptism as no bar to communion is that both presuppose a radical distinction between Spirit and water baptism. Both strategies regard Spirit baptism as normative and so do not consider water baptism to be an initiatory rite. This tendency toward spiritualism was inherited from an earlier Puritanism as the Baptists split the difference on the sacraments between the Congregationalists and the Quakers.[182] Yet, both of these rejecting and accepting strategies water down the theology of baptism because there is no sense that anything might be stirring in the water other than their own feet. Baptists have rightly resisted ascribing any magical or regenerative power to the water that works *ex opere operato*. Yet in the New Testament, baptism in water and Spirit cannot be radically separated. The open-membership approach proposed here seeks to maintain a close connection between Spirit and water baptism without reducing one to the other. Baptists have been careful to maintain that forgiveness of sin described in Acts 2:38 is a condition, not a consequence, of baptism, but what has seemed to entirely escape their notice is that the injunction to "repent and be baptized" is followed by the clear promise that baptism is followed by "the gift of the Holy Spirit."[183] Such renderings miss that baptism is a sacrament because God has promised it as a means of grace. The journey to rediscovering the work of the Holy Spirit in baptism may be further strengthened by recovering the forgotten Baptist practice of the laying on of hands at baptism, which when integrated into the baptismal rite emphasizes the reality of the gift of the Spirit in baptism.[184]

---

[182] Geoffrey F. Nuttall, *The Holy Spirit in Puritan Faith and Experience* (Oxford: Basil Blackwell, 1946), 13.

[183] Beasley-Murray, *Baptism in the New Testament*, 106–8.

[184] Benjamin Keach, *The Laying on of Hands of Baptized Believers* (London: Benj. Harris, 1678; rev. 1698); and Thomas Grantham, *The Fourth Principle of Christs Doctrine Vindicated* (London, 1674). Both Keach and Grantham argue against Henry Danvers, *A Treatise of Laying on of Hands* (London, 1674). See J. K. Parratt, "An Early Baptist on the Laying On of Hands," *Baptist Quarterly* 21, no. 7 (1996): 325–27.

One of the most important questions Other Baptists will have to face is how to fulfill the commission to make disciples, "baptizing them in the name of the Father and of the Son and of the Holy Spirit, and teaching them to obey everything" he commanded them (Matt 28:19). The great commission is not just to evangelize. It is also to baptize and catechize. Perhaps they can pull a page from the ancient church, requiring candidates for baptism to undergo a period of catechetical instruction in the faith. By the third century, the office of the catechumenate was a well-developed institution. The church in Rome, for example, required three years of catechetical instruction before baptism for moral and doctrinal formation, though they were careful to note that "it is not the time that is judged, but the conduct."[185] The forty days before Easter were an especially intense time of preparation given to prayer, fasting, confession, and instruction, culminating with baptism on Easter dawn. To renew this missional commitment, churches might seriously consider retrieving the ancient Christian practice of the catechumenate.[186]

Other Baptists may not quite be prepared to call for the abolition of Sunday school, but they should have deep suspicions about the underlying assumptions of Christian education as it is currently practiced in the churches. The guiding philosophy of Christian education often has more to do with Erikson, Kóhlberg, and Piaget than it does with Jesus or the gospel. If the Sunday school is to be of use for evangelizing and catechizing Christians in the twenty-first century, it is in dire need of theological reimagination. Churches committed to renewing the practice of evangelism in a post-Christendom culture would do well to consider how they might implement the ancient-future practice of catechetical instruction, which has as its aim Christian formation, not age-appropriate information. Such an approach is not entirely new, as Baptists from John Bunyan to John Broadus utilized catechetical instruction.[187]

For missional churches to have a vital baptismal practice for the future, they would do well to reconsider the minimalist criteria of administering baptism immediately to anyone who will admit that he or she is a sinner and that Jesus is the savior. Conversion, as a preacher once observed, is the

---

[185] Hippolytus, *The Apostolic Tradition of St. Hippolytus*, 2nd ed., ed. Gregory Dix and Henry Chadwick (London: Alban, 1992), 28.

[186] A great resource for the contemporary retrieval of the catechumenate is Maxwell E. Johnson, *The Rites of Christian Initiation: Their Evolution and Interpretation*, rev. ed. (Collegeville, Minn.: Liturgical, 2007).

[187] For an excellent collection of articles on catechetical practice among Baptists see the issue entitled "Catechism" in the quarterly journal *Christian Reflection: A Series in Faith and Ethics*, published by the Center for Christian Ethics at Baylor University (2007), accessed February 14, 2014, http://www.baylor.edu/christianethics/index.php?id=46273.

end of the Christian life—the front end. It is an important first step, but as Tertullian intoned, "Let them be made Christians"—that is, baptized— "when they have become competent to know Christ." Baptists have been critical of the practice of infant baptism because, as they have argued, it does not make disciples. Perhaps it is time for Baptists themselves to be honest about the brokenness of their own baptismal practice, which more often than they would care to admit does not do an effective job of making disciples either. If the church is to have a vital evangelical mission in the future, baptism can no longer be viewed simply as a rite of membership. Retrieving the rich catechetical and baptismal practice of the Christian tradition would help the church better understand what it means to participate through baptism in the life of the triune God and so to be formed into a community that is sent out to extend God's mission to the world. Living into such a future will require a recommitment to the Great Commission to "make disciples of all nations, baptizing them in the name of the Father and of the Son and of the Holy Spirit" (Matt 28:19). Yet as Pope Benedict XVI rightly said, the church cannot simply continue in the pattern of the past. The new reality requires a "new evangelization," the challenge of which calls into question the universal church and demands a renewed commitment to the search for Christian unity.[188]

In his book *The Glad River*, Will Campbell tells the story of a young man from Mississippi named Doops Momber. He had never been baptized. In fact, he refused to be baptized because he came to the conclusion that there were not any Baptists around. Not the sort of Landmarkers, who claimed to be the *real* Baptists by tracing their genealogy back to John the Baptist, but the ones like the stories he read in *The Martyrs Mirror*.[189] Folks did not appreciate Doops' stickling on this matter. He was constantly pressured by his family, humiliated by the church, criticized by the community, and, at one point, even condemned by a court because he had not been baptized. But he held firm. He eventually decided to write a book about his search. When asked what his book was about, he said, "This story is about some people who lived a long time ago and aren't around anymore . . . an extinct species, I think."[190] Doops eventually got baptized but not by a Baptist. He was baptized by one of his Catholic friends, and not by immersion in the traditional Baptist style but by water

---

[188] Benedict XVI, "Homily of First Vespers on the Solemnity of the Holy Apostles Peter and Paul," accessed September 1, 2013, http://www.vatican.va/holy_father/benedict_xvi/homilies/2010/documents/hf_ben-xvi_hom_20100628_vespri-pietro-paolo_en.html.

[189] Thieleman J. van Braght, *The Bloody Theater; or, Martyrs Mirror*, 2nd ed. 1886 (Scottdale, Pa.: Herald Press, 1951).

[190] Will D. Campbell, *The Glad River* (Macon, Ga.: Smyth & Helwys, 2005), 163.

poured from cupped hands. It was time to be baptized because his friend's life was clearly shaped by the radical claim that all those who want to become followers of Jesus must deny themselves and take up their cross and follow him.

Methodist ecumenist Geoffrey Wainwright once remarked that he had always respected the emphasis that Baptists have historically placed on the link between discipleship and baptism, but he continued that he would respect them even more if they actually practiced what they preached. It would be well, then, to attend to the original conviction of the Baptists—not that everyone must be immersed and become a Baptist but that believer's baptism by immersion is the most clearly warranted pattern of Christian initiation in the New Testament and that it is a disciple-making practice waiting to be embraced by the whole church. Believer's baptism deserves, and indeed demands, to be practiced by Baptists. This is a gift to the church catholic. But any baptism in which the "signs of the common faith which Christians through the ages share"[191] can be discerned, especially when it leads to genuine Christian discipleship, also deserves—and indeed demands—to be recognized and received. Other Baptists seek a way forward that enables their churches to "accept into full membership *all confirmed Christians*, who present themselves for membership, *without requiring a second baptism*." This is the constraint of catholicity, and it is a constraint Other Baptists freely embrace.

---

[191] *One Baptism* 1.C.14.a, 5.

Conclusion

Recovering Baptists and the Coveted Future

In May of 1934, Edwin McNeill Poteat Jr., then the pastor of the Pullen Memorial Baptist Church in Raleigh, North Carolina, addressed the delegates of the Northern Baptist Convention. He reminded them that their common religious heritage was shaped by fierce antagonism to religious formalism, which over time led the Baptists to become innately liberal. This inchoate liberalism, Poteat argued, had motivated their Baptist forebears to oppose *creed* as the illiberalism of ideas, *liturgy* as the illiberalism of affections, and *sacrament* as illiberalism of the will. But he suggested that the question they needed to ask was not, "Who have Baptists been?" but rather, "Where are Baptists for such a time as this?"[1] The new liberalism that Poteat imagined, however, could not long endure. Something had changed. The Christendom culture that Baptists had both depended on and protested against was on the wane and was being replaced by an increasingly secular society in which the church was disestablished. In the past, Baptists had maintained what Paul Tillich called "the Protestant principle," but, with the disappearance of Christian civilization, they could no longer take for granted what Tillich called "the Catholic substance," in which "religion is the substance of culture" and "culture is the expression of religion."[2]

With the words of Poteat's question still ringing in their ears, a small group of Dixieland liberals that included Carlyle Marney, Warren Carr, Blake Smith, and James McClendon recognized the signs of

---

[1] Edwin McNeill Poteat Jr., *Jesus and the Liberal Mind* (Philadelphia: Judson Press, 1934), 225–27.

[2] Paul Tillich, *The Protestant Era* (Chicago: University of Chicago Press, 1957), v–xxvi and 55–65; and Tillich, *Systematic Theology* (Chicago: University of Chicago Press, 1967), 3:245.

passing modernity. They began to move toward an emerging theology that looked something like the generous liberal orthodoxy described by the Yale school of Robert Calhoun, Hans Frei, and George Lindbeck. In the final volume of his *Systematic Theology*, simply entitled *Witness*, McClendon reframed this issue of the relationship of church and culture. He suggested that whereas before modernity the unity of the church was assumed, in the twilight of modernity the church is being increasingly seen as fragmented, not always holy, diverse, and disconnected from its own past. The question to be asked, McClendon proposed, is not whether society is being transformed by Christ but rather "whether the church at some given times and places . . . is or is not itself fitly in step with the gospel of the kingdom."[3] Here McClendon followed John Howard Yoder, who, though firmly rooted in baptist soil, "increasingly understood himself to be 'radically catholic' in outlook."[4] It is to such an account of catholicity that Other Baptists look for help.

This study, then, represents the story not only of a recovering liberal but of a theology for recovering Baptists, seeking to retrieve some sense of continuity with the one, holy, catholic, and apostolic church. Other Baptists want to think of their connection in the church catholic with the hope that it might provide a theological basis for them to draw from the spiritual tradition of the whole church without defaulting to an eclecticism of personal preference.[5] They are inspired by Walter Rauschenbusch's affirmation that all are ours, "whether Francis of Assisi, or Luther, or Knox, or Wesley," echoing the words of the Apostle Paul that "all things are yours, and you are Christ's; and Christ is God's" (1 Cor 3:21, 23). But this gospel truth has not always been well received by Baptists, many of whom have suffered from an isolated sense of denominational identity. As Rauschenbusch put it, "The old Adam is a strict denominationalist; the new Adam is just a Christian."[6]

This book has attempted to understand more about what it might mean for Baptist Christians to leave their old Adamic denominationalism behind and claim their inheritance in Christ. Yet the strict denominationalists

---

[3] James Wm. McClendon Jr., *Witness: Systematic Theology, Volume III* (Waco, Tex.: Baylor University Press, 2012), 36.

[4] McClendon, *Witness*, 44–45. On his free-church ecumenism and radical catholicity, see John Howard Yoder, *The Royal Priesthood: Essays Ecclesiological and Ecumenical*, ed. Michael G. Cartwright (Grand Rapids: Eerdmans, 1994), 221–373.

[5] Gary A. Furr and Curtis W. Freeman, eds., *Ties That Bind: Life Together in the Baptist Vision* (Macon, Ga.: Smyth & Helwys, 1994), 83–97.

[6] Walter Rauschenbusch, "Why I Am a Baptist," *Rochester Baptist Monthly* (November 1905), reprinted in *Colgate Rochester Divinity School Bulletin* (1938): 24.

recoil from this vision of the new creation. Instead they protest with shrill invectives against those who call for a sharing in the wholeness of the church of Jesus Christ, suggesting that "Bapto-Catholics wish to dissolve Baptists into a cauldron of ancient Church creeds, repealing the Protestant Reformation on a pilgrimage to Rome."[7] Such language is little more than a thinly veiled disguise for the "ugly little secret" of anti-Catholicism, which is "as American as blueberry pie."[8] Yet the problem is not simply a matter of American nativism. It is a habit that comes naturally to Baptists, who as descendants of Anglo-Puritanism inherited a long tradition of anti-Catholicism.[9] And sectarianism is merely a manifestation of these latent Romophobic tendencies.

"There ought to be but three Christian denominations in the world," a mainline Protestant church official once opined: "the Catholics standing on one side for the authority of the church, and the Baptists standing on the other side for the authority of the Bible. The other denominations should be united, for the difference between them is that between Tweedledum and Tweedledee."[10] The old stereotype of Baptists and Catholics as the two big ecclesial bookends separated by a broad Protestant middle was a caricature, even in the 1950s, but the picture was true enough for everyone to get the point. Then came Vatican II. Just as the council was getting underway, Lutheran theologian Carl Braaten lamented that while Catholics did not understand the necessity of the Reformation, Protestants did not understand its tragedy.[11] It might be added that some Baptists understand neither. Having lost any memory of ecclesiality, they have

---

[7] Bruce Gourley, "Editorial: Baptists and Theology—Broad, Deep, and Diverse," *Baptist History & Heritage* 47, no. 2 (2012): 3.

[8] Andrew M. Greeley, *An Ugly Little Secret* (Kansas City, Mo.: Sheed Andrews & McMeel, 1977), 17.

[9] Peter Lake explains that the theology and politics of English Protestantism in the sixteenth and seventeenth centuries were preoccupied with the irrational fears of a nonexistent popish plot, in his chapter "Anti-popery: The Structure of a Prejudice," in *Conflict in Early Stuart England: Studies in Religion and Politics, 1603–1642*, ed. Richard Cust and Ann Hughes (London: Longman, 1989), 72–106. John Coffey demonstrates that when Protestants were in charge this "antipapist" ideology drove the policies that led the state-sponsored execution of Catholics. He provides tables and data on Catholic martyrs in sixteenth- and seventeenth-century England. E.g., 189 Catholics were executed in Elizabethan England. Coffey, *Persecution and Toleration in Protestant England, 1558–1689* (Essex: Pearson Education, 2000), 90 and 134–60. Modern anti-Catholicism, secular and religious, simply reveals its radical Protestant roots.

[10] "Religion: The Southern Baptists," *Time*, October 17, 1960, 90.

[11] Carl E. Braaten, "Rome, Reformation, and Reunion," *Una Sancta* 23, no. 2 (1966): 3–8. Braaten borrowed the point from Jaroslav Pelikan, *The Riddle of Roman Catholicism* (New York: Abingdon, 1959). Ch. 4 of Pelikan's book is entitled "The Tragic Necessity of the Reformation," 45–57.

become content to live a sectarian existence that rejects the reform of the church and leads to a religious autism without a connection to historic Christianity. The Protestant Reformers did not see their efforts through such a narrow sectarian lens. As Braaten attests, they "aimed to reform a church that lived in continuity with the church the Creed calls 'one, holy, catholic, and apostolic.'"[12] It makes perfect sense, then, to speak about the Reformation not as an effort to oppose the catholicity of the church but instead as an attempt to recover it.

American Baptists moved toward a more ecumenical stance in July of 1967, by establishing a Committee on Christian Unity to engage in a wider and deeper understanding of ecclesial relations. Noting that it was the 450th anniversary of the Protestant Reformation, the convention adopted a "Statement on Christian Unity," which declared that "the Holy Spirit calls us to continuing reformation, leading us from this separationist trend to a quest for new expressions of the unity for which Christ prayed."[13] The statement grew out of a study paper written by historian Robert G. Torbet that had been enthusiastically received by the General Council of the American Baptist Convention (ABC). Their intent, as Torbet characterized it, must be to move beyond the fragmentation and sectarianism that has unfortunately characterized much of Baptist life in the name of the Reformation.

On November 21, 1964, the Second Vatican Council approved its decree on ecumenism, *Unitatis Redintegratio*, which opened with a stirring call for "the restoration of unity among all Christians." The statement declared that the lack of accord among the followers of Jesus "openly contradicts the will of Christ, scandalizes the world, and damages the holy cause of preaching the Gospel to every creature."[14] The ABC quickly recognized the opportunity and entered into ecumenical conversations with the Catholics. From 1967 to 1973, representatives from the ABC that included Robert Handy and Robert Torbet met annually with a delegation from the United States Catholic Bishops' Committee for Ecumenical and Interreligious Affairs. Rather than being polar opposites, it became clear that Baptists and Catholics have much in common. Together they articulated a differentiated consensus grounded in a shared affirmation of faith in the triune God as the source of authority and in God's unique

---

[12] Carl E. Braaten and Robert W. Jenson, eds., *The Catholicity of the Reformation* (Grand Rapids: Eerdmans, 1996), vii.

[13] "Statement on Christian Unity," in *Year Book of the American Baptist Churches 1967–1968* (Valley Forge, Pa.: American Baptist Board of Education and Publication, 1967), 81–83.

[14] *Unitatis Redintegratio* §1, *Vatican Council II*, vol. 1, *The Conciliar and Postconciliar Documents*, rev. ed. (New York: Costello, 2004), 452.

self-revelation in the Scriptures. They recognized to their surprise that they shared common ground in the belief in salvation by grace through faith and a sense of urgency to take the good news to the whole world. And they also discovered that Catholics as well as Baptists respect freedom of conscience and religious liberty.[15] It was a step toward the catholicity Braaten described.

The basic intent of Braaten's 1965 ecumenical proposal was to address the question of how to affirm Lutheran identity with confessional integrity in an ecumenical age. He asked, "Who are Lutherans?" To which he answered: "Lutherans are Catholics in exile."[16] The aim of these reflections has been to speak to the question of Baptist identity with an eye to the new ecumenical future. Are some Baptists sectarians? Indeed they are. But what about Other Baptists? This book is offered as a vision of what it might look like for Other Baptists to see themselves as a radically reforming community of contested convictions within the church catholic. In short it answers, "Other Baptists are contesting Catholics." This approach follows the insight of G. K. Chesterton, who observed that the greatest part of the story of Daniel Defoe's novel *Robinson Crusoe* may be Crusoe's simple inventory of things saved from the wreckage of his ship. For it suggests that the future for Christians living in the wilderness of the modern world depends not on inventing the faith anew but in retrieving the faith from the church and its ancient traditions.[17] And in doing so perhaps it points a way for other castaways whose ecclesial ships have sunk as they seek to make a life on the desert island of modernity.

The suggestion that Other Baptist communities might exist as islands of catholicity separated from Rome will surely strike Catholics as deeply

---

[15] John A. Hardon, S.J., "Towards an American Baptist-Roman Catholic Dialogue"; and Robert T. Handy, "Areas of Theological Agreement from a Baptist Point of View," both in *Foundations* 10, no. 2 (1967): 150–72; George Peck and Robert Trisco, "Christian Freedom and Ecclesiastical Authority," *Foundations* 11, no. 3 (1968): 197–226; Robert G. Torbet and John S. Cummins, "Baptist-Roman Catholic Conversations: Two Papers on the Nature and Communication of Grace," *Foundations* 12, no. 3 (1969): 213–31; Lloyd M. Short, "The Role of the Church: A Baptist Layman's View"; and Emmet A. Blaes, "The Role of the Church: The Catholic Laity's View," both in *Foundations* 13, no. 4 (1970): 335–53; Robert T. Handy, "Toward a Theology of the Local Church"; and Robert Trisco, "The Catholic Theology of the Local Church," both in *Foundations* 15, no. 1 (1972): 42–71; John S. Cummins, "Clergy-Lay Issues and Relations: The Roman Catholic Perspective"; and L. Doward McBain, "Clergy-Lay Issues and Relations: The Baptist Perspective," both in *Foundations* 15, no. 2 (1972): 146–62; Lloyd M. Short, "Church-State Relations, Viewed by the Baptist Joint Committee on Public Affairs"; and Emmet A. Blaes, "The Relationship of Church and State: A Catholic View," both in *Foundations* 16, no. 3 (1973): 261–78.

[16] Carl E. Braaten, "Confessional Lutheranism in an Ecumenical World," *Concordia Theological Quarterly* 71, nos. 3 and 4 (2007): 221–23.

[17] G. K. Chesterton, *Orthodoxy: The Romance of Faith* (New York: Image Books, 1959), 64.

incoherent and Protestants as little more than a prescription for denomi-national suicide.[18] To their brothers and sisters in the wider church, Other Baptists can only attest that catholicity is not an option. It is the only reality. For either Baptist churches are expressions of the church catholic or they are not the church at all. And the catholicity to which Baptists must remain committed in order to manifest any semblance of ecclesial identity is not exclusively identified with the Roman Catholic Church. But neither is it the opposite. Rather, it consists in a whole way of life that includes basic convictions and practices that the gospel commends as normative for all Christians.[19] This is contesting catholicity. To put the matter sharply, the categorical rejection of all things catholic risks a loss not simply of the *catholic* substance of the faith but of its *Christian* substance as well. For catholicity in its most basic sense, as McClendon observed, is simply another way of describing the way that is authentically Christian because it includes within its scope "those apostolic qualities that make Christianity Christ-like."[20]

In 1941 a young Congregationalist theologian named Daniel Jenkins offered a remarkable account of ecclesiological renewal for contesting catholics. His book *The Nature of Catholicity* argued that catholicity is a quality that denotes the essence of the church's nature as the church.[21] The catholicity of the church, Jenkins argued, is particularly endangered among Free Churches, which tend to accept ecclesial divisions as "nor-mal, if not desirable."[22] This mind-set, he warned, is content to perpetu-ate one's own traditions and distinctives and to maintain separation from other churches simply out of preference for a particular denominational way of doing things. But regarding such denominationalism as ecclesio-logically normative, Jenkins declared, is a denial of the true nature of the church.[23] As C. C. Goen once observed, denominationalism in America is "ecclesiocracy without ecclesiology," which at its worst "degenerates into a gaggle of private societies competing with each other on the basis of their own self-interests."[24] Catholicity calls for the church to live out

---

[18] James Nuechterlein, "In Defense of Sectarian Catholicity," *First Things* 69 (1997): 12–13.

[19] E. S. Abbott et al., *Catholicity: A Study in the Conflict of Christian Traditions in the West* (Westminster: Dacre Press, 1947), 11.

[20] McClendon, *Witness*, 336.

[21] Daniel T. Jenkins, *The Nature of Catholicity* (London: Faber and Faber, 1941), 18. On Jenkins, see D. Densil Morgan, *Barth Reception in Britain* (London: T&T Clark, 2010), 174–83.

[22] Jenkins, *Nature of Catholicity*, 127.

[23] Jenkins, *Nature of Catholicity*, 128–29.

[24] Clarence C. Goen, "Ecclesiocracy without Ecclesiology: Denominational Life in America," *American Baptist Quarterly* 10, no. 4 (1991): 272.

of the apostolic memory to which the gospel points, but it also invites the church to live into a future hope toward which the Spirit leads. And, through the ministry of word and sacrament, the church seeks to discern what it might mean to be faithful to the apostolic witness and to be open to the Spirit's direction.

One thing is certain: This vision of catholicity is not the coveted future of Christendom. That time is past. Yet what lies ahead is anything but clear. The best indications are little more than gestures. In his novel *From a Christian Ghetto*, Geddes MacGregor offered a forecast of the future through the perspective of a twenty-fifth-century church historian exchanging a series of letters to a young man studying for ministry. The student is majoring in late medieval Christianity—that is, the church in twentieth-century America and Great Britain. In one letter the medievalist writes his young understudy:

> We twenty-fifth-century Christians are so completely disreputable in the eyes of the world that there is never any question of keeping up the "good name" of Christendom among those outside it. Our name is so vile that we can attend to our proper business of realizing the ideal Christian community free from fear of what the world may think or say.[25]

Who can know whether the vision MacGregor imagines is the one that lies ahead. But the post-Christendom future toward which the church is surely moving offers the opportunity to take leave of the grand delusion of majority consciousness and focus on the proper business of asking what it means for the church to be the church without worrying about what the world may think or say. Whatever that future is, it is in God's hands, not ours.[26]

In his poem "The Wheel," Wendell Berry offers an alternative vision. It is a description of the perichoretic dance of time and eternity.[27] The first stanza describes a room full of people. The music calls, they rise from their seats, and the dance begins. Couples join other couples, and soon they are moving as one. But the image of the dance is not a bourgeois ballroom in which everyone holds onto his or her own partner or a postmodern mosh pit of chaotic gyrations. The picture is that of a square

---

[25] Geddes MacGregor, *From a Christian Ghetto: Letters of Ghostly Wit, Written A.D. 2453* (London: Longmans, Green, 1954), 23.

[26] Daniel T. Jenkins, *The Strangeness of the Church* (Garden City, N.Y.: Doubleday, 1955), 165.

[27] Wendell Berry, *The Wheel* (San Francisco: North Point, 1982), 48.

dance in which couples move round from partner to partner, always to return home. This is the life of community. Alterity remains, yet no one stands alone, and each depends on all. Still, there is a love to which each returns, "and time is the wheel that brings it round." Suddenly the poet is caught up in ecstatic imagination of community that spirals upward. In this vision the dead join the living in an eternal dance. Sorrows cease. Darkness flees. All is light. Caught up in the transcendent participation, the dancers rise from the wheel of chronic time to the circle of kairotic timelessness. From every tribe and nation, they gather—one yet many. In this communion, humanity joins the perichoretic dance: the Father with the Son through the Spirit, three in oneness, "and timeless is the wheel that brings it round."

The contesting catholicity envisioned in these pages gestures toward that future. It is a vision in which Baptists are connected with all Christians in a quantitative sense of ecumenical relations and in a qualitative sense of a common faith enacted in Word and sacrament. These signs point to the eschatological future of the whole church as God's community of embodied truth. Yet these reflections are only the thoughts of one Other Baptist seeking recovery from the habits of life and mind that have shaped (and continue to shape) his life. They are an attempt to help other Other Baptists seeking a way to resist the alien powers that would otherwise determine their lives so that they may not be conformed to the world but transformed by the renewing of the mind (Rom 12:2). Let Other Baptists then, as McClendon urged, "congregation by congregation, local church by local church, Christian group by Christian group, seek to embody the completeness that is found in Christ Jesus and in his true saints ancient and modern," because when they embody that catholicity that is authentically Christian, they "shall of necessity come closer to one another."[28] In that spirit these pages are offered for pilgrims as they venture through this strange, new city of exile, toward that other city whose builder and maker is God (Heb 11:10).

---

[28] McClendon, *Witness*, 336.

Bibliography

"2008 Southern Baptist Convention Statistical Summary." *2008 Southern Baptist Convention's Annual Church Profile*. Nashville: Lifeway Christian Resources, April 20, 2009. Accessed July 21, 2009. http://www.lifeway.com/lwc/files/lwcF_corp_news_ACP2008_pdf.pdf.

"2011 Southern Baptist Statistics—Number of Baptisms." *Lifeway Insights*, August 14, 2012.

Abbott, E. S., et al. *Catholicity: A Study in the Conflict of Christian Traditions in the West*. Westminster: Dacre Press, 1947.

Acta apostolicae sedis 77. Vatican: Typis Polyglottis Vaticanis, 1985.

"Adults Baptized in Southern Baptist Churches." *Research Report*, January 1995. A publication of the Home Mission Board, SBC.

Aers, David. *Sanctifying Signs: Making Christian Tradition in Late Medieval England*. Notre Dame, Ind.: University of Notre Dame Press, 2004.

Ahlstrom, Sydney E. *A Religious History of the American People*. 2nd ed. New Haven, Conn.: Yale University Press, 2004.

———. "The Scottish Philosophy and American Theology." *Church History* 24, no. 3 (1955): 257–72.

Ainsworth, Henry. *A Reply to a Pretended Christian Plea for the AntiChristian Church of Rome*. 1620.

Allen, Bob. "Proposal Sparks Debate over Baptists and Creeds." *Ethics Daily*, July 16, 2004.

Allen, Daniel. *Moderate Trinitarian*. London: Mary Fabian at Mercers Chappel in Cheapside, 1699.

Allen, Jimmy R. "The Takeover Resurgence Is Creedalism." *Texas Baptists Committed*, August 2004.

Althaus, Paul. *The Theology of Martin Luther*. Translated by Robert C. Schultz. Philadelphia: Fortress, 1966.

Anonymous. *An Humble Advise To The Right Honorable The Lord Mayor, The Recorder, and the Rest of the Justices of the Honorable Bench. To the good men of the*

Jury, aud [sic] at the Sessions House in the Old–Bayley, London, in behalf of Mr. John Bidle, prisoner in Newgate (London, [1655?]).

———. *The Spirit of Persecution Again broken loose, By An Attempt to put in Execution against Mr. John Biddle Master of Arts, an abrogated Ordinance of the Lords and Commons for punishing Blasphemies and Heresies. Together with, A full Narrative of The whole Proceedings upon that Ordinance against the said Mr. John Biddle and Mr. William Kiffen Pastor of a baptised Congregation in the City of London.* London: Richard Moone, 1655.

———.*A True State of the Case of Liberty of Conscience in the Common-wealth of England.* London: Richard Moone, 1655.

Annual of the Northern Baptist Convention. Philadelphia: American Baptist Publication Society, 1922.

Annual of the Southern Baptist Convention. Nashville: Marshall & Bruce, 1914, 1925.

Annual of the Southern Baptist Convention. Nashville: Southern Baptist Convention, 1926, 1938, 1940, 1965, 1971, 1974, 1984.

Ambrose. "Where Peter is, there is the Church" (*Ubi ergo Petrus, ibi Ecclesia*). In *Enarratio in Psalmum* 40.30. Patrologia Latina 14. Paris: J. P. Migne, 1882.

Asbury, Francis. *Journal and Letters.* Edited by Elmer T. Clark, J. Manning Potts, and Jacob S. Payton. Nashville: Abingdon, 1958.

Asplund, John. *Universal Register of the Baptist Denomination in North America.* New York: Arno Press, 1980. First published 1794 by John W. Folsom, Boston.

Athanasius. *Four Discourses against the Arians.* In vol. 4 of *The Nicene and Post-Nicene Fathers.* 2nd series. Grand Rapids: Eerdmans, 1978.

———. *On the Incarnation of the Word.* Crestwood, N.Y.: St. Vladimir's Seminary Press, 1944.

Atherton, Ian, and David Como. "The Burning of Edward Wightman: Puritanism, Prelacy, and the Politics of Heresy in Early Modern England." *English Historical Review* 120, no. 489 (2005): 1215–50.

Augustine. *The City of God, Books XVII–XXII.* Fathers of the Church 24. Translated by Gerald G. Walsh. Washington, D.C.: Catholic University of America Press, 1954.

———. *City of God.* Patrologia Latina 41. Paris: J. P. Migne, 1900.

———. *Confessions.* Translated by John K. Ryan. New York: Image Books, 1960.

———. *Lectures or Tractates on the Gospel According to St. John.* Translated by John Gibb and James Innes. In vol. 7 of *The Nicene and Post-Nicene Fathers.* 1st series. Grand Rapids: Eerdmans, 1971.

———. *On Christian Doctrine.* In vol. 2 of *The Nicene and Post Nicene Fathers.* 1st series. Translated by Marcus Dods. Grand Rapids: Eerdmans, 1977.

———. *On Christian Doctrine.* Patrologia Latina 34. Paris: J. P. Migne, 1887.

———. *On the Epistle of John.* In vol. 7 of *The Nicene and Post-Nicene Fathers.* 1st series. Grand Rapids: Eerdmans, 1971.

———. *On the Spirit and the Letter.* In vol. 5 of *The Nicene and Post-Nicene Fathers.* 1st series. Grand Rapids: Eerdmans, 1971.

————. *On the Trinity*. Translated by Arthur West Haddan and Rev. William G. T. Shedd. In vol. 3 of *The Nicene and Post-Nicene Fathers*. 1st series. Grand Rapids: Eerdmans, 1971.

————. *Sermon 272, Ad Infantes, de Sacramento*. Patrologia Cursus Completus, Series Latina 38. Edited by J. P. Migne. Paris: J. P. Migne, 1844–1865.

Austin, John L. *How to Do Things with Words*. 2nd ed. Oxford: Oxford University Press, 1975.

Austin Study Group. *Report on the Table of the Lord*. North American Conference of Faith and Order, September 3–10, 1957. Box 111, the Carlyle Marney Papers, David M. Rubenstein Rare Book & Manuscript Library, Duke University, Durham, N.C.

Ayres, Lewis. "On Not Three People: The Fundamental Themes of Gregory of Nyssa's Theology as Seen in *To Ablabius: On Not Three Gods*." *Modern Theology* 18, no. 4 (2002): 445–74.

Backus, Issac. *An Appeal to the Public for Religious Liberty*. Boston: John Boyle, 1773. Reprinted in *Isaac Backus on Church, State, and Calvinism*. Edited by William G. McLoughlin. Cambridge, Mass.: Belknap Press, 1968.

Baillie, D. M. *God Was in Christ*. New York: Scribner, 1948.

Baillie, Robert. *Anabaptisme, the True Fountaine of Independency, Brownisme, Antinomy, Familisme, and Most of the Other Errours Which for the Time Doe Trouble the Church of England*. London: M. F. for Samuel Gallibrand, 1647.

Bainton, Roland H. *Yale and the Ministry: A History of Education for the Christian Ministry at Yale from the Founding in 1701*. San Francisco: Harper & Row, 1957 and 1985.

Baker, Robert A. *A Baptist Source Book*. Nashville: Broadman, 1966.

Baker, Robert A., and Paul J. Craven Jr. *Adventure in Faith: The First 300 Years of First Baptist Church Charleston, South Carolina*. Nashville: Broadman, 1982.

Balthasar, Hans Urs von. *The Theology of Henri de Lubac*. San Francisco: Ignatius Press, 1991.

Bantum, Brian. *Redeeming Mulatto: Theology of Race and Christian Hybridity*. Waco, Tex.: Baylor University Press, 2010.

Baptism, Eucharist and Ministry. Faith and Order Paper no. 111. Geneva: World Council of Churches, 1982.

"Baptist Dismissals." *Time*, April 12, 1954.

The Baptist Doctrine of the Church. Statement approved by the Council of the Baptist Union of Great Britain and Ireland, March 1948. In *Baptist Union Documents 1948–1977*, edited by Roger Hayden, 5–6. London: Baptist Historical Society, 1980.

Baptist Faith and Message. *SBCNet*. 2000. Accessed February 21, 2013. http://www.sbc.net/bfm/bfm2000.asp.

The Baptist Hymnal. Nashville: Convention Press, 1975, 1991.

Baptist State Convention of North Carolina: Annual of the Baptist State Convention of North Carolina. North Carolina: The Convention, 1971.

The Baptist World Congress. London, July 11–19, 1905. London: Baptist Union, 1905.

Barber, Edward. *A Small Treatise of Baptisme or Dipping Wherein Is Cleerly shewed that the Lord Christ Ordained Dipping for those only that professe Repetance and Faith*. [London?], 1641.

Barnes, Elizabeth B. *An Affront to the Gospel? The Radical Barth and the Southern Baptist Convention*. Atlanta: Scholars Press, 1987.

Barnes, Michel René. "Divine Unity and the Divided Self: Gregory of Nyssa's Trinitarian Theology in Its Psychological Context," *Modern Theology* 18, no. 4 (2002): 475–96.

Barnett, Das Kelly. "The New Theological Frontier for Southern Baptists." *Review & Expositor* 38, no. 3 (1941): 264–76. Reprinted in *Western Recorder*, September 18, 1941.

Barrington, John Shute. *An Account of the Late Proceedings of the Dissenting Ministers at Salters Hall*. London: J. Roberts, 1719.

Barron, Robert. *The Priority of Christ: Toward a Postliberal Catholicism*. Grand Rapids: Brazos, 2007.

Barrow, Henry. *A True Description Out of the Worde of God, Of the Visible Church* (1589). In *The Writings of Henry Barrow*, edited by Leland H. Carlson. Vol. 3 of *Elizabethan Non-conformist Texts*. New York: Routledge, 2003.

Barth, Karl. *The Church and the Churches*. Grand Rapids: Eerdmans, 1936/2005.

———. *Church Dogmatics*. Translated by G. T. Thomson, Harold Knight, G. W. Bromiley, and T. F. Torrance. Edinburgh: T&T Clark, 1956–1969.

———. *The Epistle to the Romans*. Translated by Edwyn C. Hoskyns. London: Oxford University Press, 1977.

———. *The Humanity of God*. Atlanta: John Knox, 1960.

———. *The Teaching of the Church regarding Baptism*. Translated by Ernest Payne. London: SCM Press, 1945.

Barth, Markus. *Die Taufe—Ein Sakrament?* Zollikon-Zürich: Evangelischer Verlag, 1951.

Bass, Clint. *Thomas Grantham (1633–1692) and General Baptist Theology*. Oxford: Regent's Park College, 2013.

Bass, Dorothy C. *Practicing Our Faith*. San Francisco: Jossey-Bass, 1997.

Bateman, Charles T. *John Clifford: Free Church Leader and Preacher*. London: National Council of the Evangelical Free Churches, 1904.

Baxter, Richard. *Richard Baxter's Confession of His Faith*. London: R. W. for Tho. Underhil, and Fra. Tyton, 1655.

Baylor, Michael G., ed. *The Radical Reformation*. Cambridge: Cambridge University Press, 1991.

A Beacon Set on Fire. London, 1652.

Beal, Rose M. "Priest, Prophet and King: Jesus Christ." In *John Calvin's Ecclesiology: Ecumenical Perspectives*, edited by Gerard Mannion and Eduardus Van der Borght, 90–106. London: T&T Clark, 2011.

Beasley-Murray, G. R. [George]. "Baptism in the New Testament." *Foundations* 3, no. 1 (1960): 15–31.

———. *Baptism in the New Testament*. Grand Rapids: Eerdmans, 1962/1990.

Beatus of Liebana. *Sancti beati a liebana commentarius in Apocalypsin*. Rome: Typis Officinae Polygraphicae, 1985.

Bebbington, David W. "Baptist Thought." In *The Blackwell Encyclopedeia of Modern Christian Thought*, ed. Alister E. McGrath, 28–30. Cambridge: Blackwell, 1993.

———. *Baptists through the Centuries: A History of a Global People*. Waco, Tex.: Baylor University Press, 2010.

Becker, Karl J. *L'Osservatore Romano*, December 14, 2005. Subsequently published in *Origins* 35, no. 31 (2006): 514–22.

Beeley, Christopher A. *Gregory of Nazianzus on the Trinity and the Knowledge of God: In Your Light We See Light*. New York: Oxford University Press, 2008.

Believing and Being Baptized: Baptism, So-Called Re-baptism, and Children in the Church. A discussion document by the Doctrine and Worship Committee of the Baptist Union of Great Britain. Didcot, U.K.: Baptist Union, 1996.

Bellah, Robert N. "Is There a Common American Culture?" *Journal of the American Academy of Religion* 66, no. 3 (1998): 613–25.

Bellah, Robert N., Richard Madsen, William M. Sullivan, Ann Swidler, and Steven M. Tipton, eds. *Habits of the Heart: Individualism and Commitment in American Life*. Updated ed. Berkeley: University of California Press, 1996.

Bender, Harold S. *The Anabaptist Vision*. Scottdale, Pa.: Herald Press, 1944.

Benedict, David. *Fifty Years among the Baptists*. New York: Sheldon, 1860.

———. *A General History of the Baptist Denomination in America and Other Parts of the World*. New York: Lewis Colby, 1848.

Benedict XVI. "Homily of First Vespers on the Solemnity of the Holy Apostles Peter and Paul." Accessed September 1, 2013. http://www.vatican .va/holy_father/benedict_xvi/homilies/2010/documents/hf_ben-xvi_hom _20100628_vespri-pietro-paolo_en.html.

Bentley, Richard. *Bentleii Critica Sacra*. Edited by Arthur Ayers Ellis. Cambridge: Deighton, Bell, 1862.

———. *The Correspondence of Richard Bentley, D. D.* Edited by Christopher Wordsworth. London: John Murray, 1842.

———. *Dr. Bentley's Proposals for Printing a New Edition of the Greek Testament, and St. Hierom's Latin Version*. London: Printed for J. Knapton, 1721.

Bercovitch, Sacvan. *The American Jeremiad*. Madison: University of Wisconsin Press, 1978.

Bernard, Richard. *Christian Advertisements And Counsels Of Peace Also Disswasions From The Separatists Schisme*. London: Felix Kyngston, 1608.

———. *Plain Evidences: The Church England is Apostolicall, the Separation Schismaticall*. London: T. Snodham for Weaver & Welby, 1610.

Berry, Wendell. *Jayber Crow*. Washington, D.C.: Counterpoint, 2000.

————. *Sex, Economy, Freedom, and Community.* New York: Pantheon Books, 1992.

————. *The Wheel.* San Francisco: North Point, 1982.

Biddle, John. *A Confession of Faith Touching the Holy Trinity According to the Scripture.* London, 1648.

Biggs, Joseph. *A Concise History of the Kehukee Baptist Association.* Tarborough, N.C.: George Howard, 1834.

Blackwood, Christopher. *The Storming of Antichrist.* London, 1644.

Blaes, Emmet A. "The Relationship of Church and State: A Catholic View." *Foundations* 16, no. 3 (1973): 274–78.

————. "The Role of the Church: The Catholic Laity's View." *Foundations* 13, no. 4 (1970): 343–53.

Bloom, Harold. *The American Religion: The Emergence of the Post-Christian Nation.* New York: Simon & Schuster, 1992.

Blundau, August. "The Comma Johanneum in the Writings of English Critics of the Eighteenth Century." *Irish Theological Quarterly* 17, no. 1 (1922): 66–67.

Blyth, Myra. *Celebrating the Trinity: Faith, Worship and Mission.* Cambridge: Grove Books, 2003.

Boer, Martinus C. de. *Johannine Perspectives on the Death of Jesus.* Kampen, Netherlands: Kok Pharos, 1996.

Boff, Leonardo. *Church, Charism and Power: Liberation Theology and the Institutional Church.* Translated by John Diercksmeier. New York: Crossroad, 1985.

Bolin, James Duane. *Kentucky Baptists, 1925–2000: A Story of Cooperation.* Brentwood, Tenn.: Baptist History & Heritage Society, 2000.

Bonhoeffer, Dietrich. *Ethics.* Edited by Eberhard Bethge. Translated by Neville Horton Smith. New York: Macmillan, 1955.

Bonney, Timothy. Journal entry. Accessed July 30, 2013. http://www.baptistlife .com/flick/images/Tares.htm.

The Book of Common Prayer. New York: Church Publishing, 1979.

The Book of Common Prayer. Whitechurch, 1552. Repr., London: William Pickering, 1844.

Boyce, James Petigru. *Abstract of Systematic Theology.* Philadelphia: American Baptist Publication Society, 1887.

Boyd, Lois A., and R. Douglas Brackenridge. *Presbyterian Women in America: Two Centuries of a Quest for Status.* 2nd ed. Westport, Conn.: Greenwood Press, 1996.

Bozeman, Theodore Dwight. *To Live Ancient Lives: The Primitivist Dimension in Puritanism.* Chapel Hill: University of North Carolina Press, 1988.

Braaten, Carl E. "Confessional Lutheranism in an Ecumenical World." *Concordia Theological Quarterly* 71, nos. 3 and 4 (2007): 219–31.

————. "A Harvest of Evangelical Theology." *First Things* 61 (1996): 45–48.

———— . "Rome, Reformation, and Reunion." *Una Sancta* 23, no. 2 (1966): 3–8.

Braaten, Carl E., and Robert W. Jenson, eds. *The Catholicity of the Reformation.* Grand Rapids: Eerdmans, 1996.

Brachlow, Stephen. *The Communion of Saints: Radical Puritan and Separatist Ecclesiology 1570–1625.* Oxford: Oxford University Press, 1988.

Brackney, William H., ed. *Baptist Life and Thought, 1600–1980.* Valley Forge, Pa.: Judson Press, 1983.

———. *The Baptists.* Westport, Conn.: Praeger, 1994.

———. *A Genetic History of Baptist Thought.* Macon, Ga.: Mercer University Press, 2004.

Bradford, William. *Bradford's History "Of Plimoth Plantation" from the Original Manuscript with a Report of the Proceedings Incident to the Return of the Manuscript to Massachusetts.* Boston: Wright & Potter, 1899.

———. *History of Plymouth Plantation, 1620–1647.* Edited by William Chauncey Ford. Boston: Houghton Mifflin, 1912.

Bradley, William. Letter to Nathaniel Saunders, October 6, 1770. In *The Great Awakening in Virginia, 1740–1790,* by Wesley M. Gewehr, 130. Durham, N.C.: Duke University Press, 1930.

Braght, Thieleman J. van. *The Bloody Theater; or, Martyrs Mirror.* 3rd ed. 1886. Repr., Scottdale, Pa.: Mennonite, 1951; Scottdale, Pa.: Herald Press, 1990.

Brantly, William T. "Trinitarians Rational." Augusta: Chronicle and Advertiser, 1824.

Briggs, John H. Y. *The English Baptists of the Nineteenth Century.* Didcot, U.K.: Baptist Historical Society, 1994.

———. *Pulpit and People: Studies in Eighteenth-Century Baptist Life and Thought.* Milton Keynes, U.K.: Paternoster, 2009.

———. "She-Preachers, Widows and Other Women: The Feminine Dimension in Baptist Life since 1600." *Baptist Quarterly* 31, no. 7 (1986): 337–52.

Broadway, Mikael. Introduction to "Festschrift for James Wm. McClendon Jr." Special issue, *Perspectives in Religious Studies* 27, no. 1 (2000): 5–9.

———. "The Roots of Baptists in Community, and Therefore Voluntary Membership Not Individualism; or, The High Flying Modernist, Stripped of His Ontological Assumptions, Appears to Hold the Ecclesiology of a Yaho." In *Recycling the Past or Researching History? Studies in Baptist Historiography and Myths,* edited by Philip E. Thompson and Anthony R. Cross, 67–83. Milton Keynes, U.K.: Paternoster, 2005.

———. "The Ways of Zion Mourned: A Historicist Critique of the Discourses of Church-State Relations." Ph.D. diss., Duke University, 1993.

Broadway, Mikael, Curtis W. Freeman, Barry Harvey, James Wm. McClendon Jr., Elizabeth Newman, and Philip Thompson. "Re-envisioning Baptist Identity: A Manifesto for Baptist Communities in North America." *Baptists Today,* June 26, 1997. Also published in *Perspectives in Religious Studies* 24, no. 3 (1997): 303–10

Broadway, Mikael, Curtis W. Freeman, Steven Harmon, Barry Harvey, Elizabeth Newman, Mark Medley, and Philip Thompson. "'Dangerous and Un-baptistic'? A Response from Supporters of the 'Baptist Manifesto.'" *Associated Baptist Press*, February 1, 2006. Accessed March 30, 2012. http://www.abpnews.com/archives/item/919-%E2%80%9Cdangerous-and-un-baptistic%E2%80%9D?-a-response-from-supporters-of-the-%E2%80%9Cbaptist-manifesto%E2%80%9D.

Brown, Charles Reynolds. *The Social Message of the Modern Pulpit*. New York: Scribner, 1906.

Brown, J. Newton. *The Baptist Church Manual*. Philadelphia: American Baptist Publication Society, 1853.

Brown, John. *John Bunyan: His Life Times and Work*. 3rd ed. London: Wm. Isbister, 1887.

Brown, Raymond E. *The Churches the Apostles Left Behind*. New York: Paulist, 1984.

———. *The Epistles of John*. New York: Doubleday, 1982.

———. *The Gospel according to John*. Garden City, N.Y.: Doubleday, 1966.

———. *New Testament Essays*. Garden City, N.Y.: Doubleday, 1968.

Browne, Robert. *A True and Short Declaration*. In *The Writings of Robert Harrison and Robert Browne*, edited by Albert Peel and Leland H. Carlson. Vol. 2 of *Elizabethan Nonconformist Texts*. London: George Allen & Unwin, 1953.

Brunner, Emil. *The Divine Human Encounter*. Philadelphia: Westminster, 1943.

———. *The Misunderstanding of the Church*. Translated by Harold Knight. Philadelphia: Westminster, 1953.

Bryant, Scott E. "An Early English Baptist Response to the Baptist Manifesto." *Perspectives in Religious Studies* 37, no. 3 (2010): 237–48.

Bullinger, Heinrich. *Der Wiedertäufferen Ursprung, etc*. Zurich, 1560.

Bultmann, Rudolf. *The Gospel of John: A Commentary*. Philadelphia: Westminster, 1971.

Bunker, Nick. *Making Haste from Babylon: The* Mayflower *Pilgrims and Their World*. New York: Vintage Books, 2011.

Bunyan, John. *A Confession of My Faith, and a Reason of my Practice*. In vol. 2 of *The Works of John Bunyan*. Edited by George Offor. Glasgow: W. G. Blackie and Son, 1854.

———. *Grace Abounding to the Chief of Sinners*. Edited by W. R. Owens. London: Penguin Books, 1987.

———. *The Pilgrim's Progress*. Edited by N. H. Keeble. Oxford: Oxford University Press, 1984.

———. *Sighs from Hell*. In *The Complete Works of John Bunyan*, edited by John P. Gulliver. Philadelphia: Bradley, Garretson, 1872.

Burgess, Walter Herbert. *John Robinson, Pastor of the Pilgrim Fathers: A Study of His Life and Times*. London: Williams and Norgate; New York: Harcourt, Brace & Howe, 1920.

Burrage, Champlin, *The Church Covenant Idea: Its Origin and Its Development*. Philadelphia: American Baptist Publication Society, 1904.

———. *The Early English Dissenters in Light of Recent Research*. 2 vols. Cambridge: Cambridge University Press, 1912.

Burtchaell, James Tunstead. *The Dying of the Light: The Disengagement of Colleges and Universities from Their Christian Churches*. Grand Rapids: Eerdmans, 1998.

Bush, L. Russ, and Tom J. Nettles. *Baptists and the Bible: The Baptist Doctrine of Biblical Inspiration and Religious Authority in Historical Perspective*. Chicago: Moody Press, 1980.

Byassee, Jason. *Praise Seeking Understanding: Reading the Psalms with Augustine*. Grand Rapids: Eerdmans, 2007.

Byrd, James P., Jr. *The Challenges of Roger Williams: Religious Liberty, Violent Persecution, and the Bible*. Macon, Ga.: Mercer University Press, 2002.

Caffyn, Matthew. *Envy's Bitterness Corrected*. London, 1674.

———. *Faith in Gods Promises The Saints best Weapon*. London: S. Dover, 1660.

———. *A Raging Wave Foming out his own Shame*. London: Francis Smith, 1675.

Calamandrei, Mauro. "Neglected Aspects of Roger Williams' Thought." *Church History* 21, no. 3 (1952): 239–58.

Calhoun, Robert L. "A Liberal Bandaged but Unbowed." In the series "How My Mind Has Changed in This Decade." *Christian Century*, May 31, 1939.

———. *Lectures on the History of Christian Doctrine*. New Haven, Conn.: Yale Divinity School, 1948.

Callahan, James Patrick. "*Claritas Scripturae*: The Role of Perspecuity in Protestant Hermeneutics." *Journal of the Evangelical Theological Society* 39, no. 3 (1996): 353–72.

Calvin, John. *Calvin's Commentaries: The Acts of the Apostles 1–13*. Edited by David W. Torrance and Thomas F. Torrance. Grand Rapids: Eerdmans, 1965.

———. *Calvin's Commentaries: The Epistles of Paul the Apostle to the Hebrews and the First and Second Epistles of St. Peter*. Edited by David W. Torrance and Thomas F. Torrance. Translated by William B. Johnston. Grand Rapids: Eerdmans, 1963.

———. *Calvin's Commentary on the Epistles of Paul the Apostle to the Corinthians*. Grand Rapids: Eerdmans, 1948.

———. *Institutes of the Christian Religion*. Edited by John T. McNeill. Translated by Ford Lewis Battles. Philadelphia: Westminster, 1960.

Campbell, Alexander. *The Christian System*. Bethany, Va.: Pittsburg, Forrester & Campbell, 1839. Repr., Salem, N.H.: Ayer, 1988.

Campbell, Douglas A. *The Deliverance of God: An Apocalyptic Rereading of Justification in Paul*. Grand Rapids: Eerdmans, 2009.

———. *The Quest for Paul's Gospel*. London: T&T Clark, 2005.

Campbell, Will D.. *Brother to a Dragonfly*. New York: Seabury, 1977.

———. *The Glad River*. Macon, Ga.: Smyth & Helwys, 2005.

Campbell-Reed, Eileen. "Anatomy of a Schism: How Clergywomen's Narratives Reinterpret the Fracturing of the Southern Baptist Convention." Ph.D. diss., Vanderbilt University, 2008. Accessed February 10, 2014. http://etd.library .vanderbilt.edu/ETD-db/available/etd-07232008-000207/unrestricted/ Campbell-Reed+Dissertation7-24-08.pdf.

Canons of the Second Council of Orange, A.D. 529. Translated by F. H. Woods. Oxford: James Thornton, 1882.

Carey, John J. *Carlyle Marney: A Pilgrim's Progress.* Macon, Ga.: Mercer University Press, 1980.

Carey, William. *An Enquiry into the Obligations of Christians to Use Means for the Conversion of the Heathens.* Leicester, 1792. Repr., London: Carey Kingsgate Press, 1961.

Carnell, Edward John. *The Case for Orthodox Theology.* Philadelphia: Westminster, 1959.

———. "Orthodoxy: Cultic vs. Classical." *Christian Century,* March 30, 1960.

Carr, Warren. *At the Risk of Idolatry.* Valley Forge, Pa.: Judson Press, 1972.

———. *Baptism: Conscience and Clue for the Church.* New York: Holt, Rinehart & Winston, 1964.

———. "The Community Which Waits." Sermon preached at Watts Street Baptist Church, Durham, N.C., March 4, 1973.

———. *Oral Memoirs of Warren Tyree Carr: April 18, 1985.* Baylor University Religion and Culture Project. Waco, Tex.: Baylor University Institute for Oral History, 1988.

———. "A Prayer for Durham, N.C." Sermon preached at Watts Street Baptist Church, Durham, N.C., December 12, 1993.

———. *Reflections on the August 9, 1964 Ordination of Addie Davis.* Watts Street Baptist Church, Durham, N.C., August 8, 2004.

Carrell, William. "The Inner Testimony of the Spirit: Locating the Coherent Center of E. Y. Mullins's Theology." *Baptist History and Heritage* 43, no. 1 (2008): 35–48.

Carroll, Benajah Harvey. *The Book of Revelation.* New York: Fleming H. Revell, 1913.

Carroll, J. M. *The Trail of Blood Following Christians Down through the Centuries; or, The History of Baptist Churches from the Time of Christ, Their Founder, to the Present Day.* Lexington, Ky.: Ashland Avenue Baptist Church, 1931.

Carson, D. A., and John D. Woodbridge. *Scripture and Truth.* Grand Rapids: Zondervan, 1983.

Carter, J. Kameron. *Race: A Theological Account.* New York: Oxford University Press, 2008.

Cary, Jeffrey W. *Free Churches and the Body of Christ.* Eugene, Ore.: Cascade Books, 2012.

Catechesis Ecclesiarium Quae in Regno Polonia. London: William Dugard, 1651.

Cathcart, William. *The Baptist Encyclopaedia*. Philadelphia: Louis H. Everts, 1881.

Cauthen, Kenneth. *The Impact of American Religious Liberalism*. 2nd ed. Washington, D.C.: University Press of America, 1983.

Chadwick, Rosie, ed. *A Protestant Catholic Church of Christ: Essays on the History and Life of New Road Baptist Church, Oxford*. Oxford: Alden, 2003.

Chafe, William H. *Civilities and Civil Rights*. New York: Oxford University Press, 1980.

The Chalice Hymnal. St. Louis, Mo.: Chalice Press, 1996.

Chalke, Steve, and Alan Mann, *The Lost Message of Jesus*. Grand Rapids: Zondervan, 2003.

Channing, William Ellery. "Unitarian Christianity." In *A Sermon Delivered at the Ordination of Rev. Jared Sparks to the Pastoral Care of the First Independent Church in Baltimore, May 5, 1819*. Reprint, Boston: Hew & Goss, 1819.

————. *Unitarian Christianity: Five Points of Positive Belief from a Discourse Delivered at Baltimore, U.S., 1819*. London: C. Green & Son, n.d.

Chaves, Mark. *Ordaining Women: Culture and Conflict in Religious Organizations*. Cambridge, Mass.: Harvard University Press, 1997.

Chaves, Mark, and Shawna Anderson. "Continuity and Change in American Religion, 1972–2006." In *Social Trends in American Life: Findings from the General Social Survey since 1972*, edited by Peter V. Marsden, 212–39. Princeton, N.J.: Princeton University Press, 2012.

Chesterton, G. K. *Orthodoxy: The Romance of Faith*. New York: Image Books, 1959.

Childs, Brevard S. *Isaiah*. Louisville, Ky.: Westminster John Knox, 2001.

"City Baptists Admit Two Negro Units: Issue Decided on 99–25 Vote." *Austin Statesman*, October 12, 1955.

Clapham, Henoch. *Antidoton; or, A Soveraigne Remedie Against Schisme and Heresie*. London: John Wolfe, 1600.

————. *The Syn, Against the Holy Ghoste*. Amsterdam, 1598.

Clark, Andrew, ed. *The Life and Times of Anthony Wood: Antiquary of Oxford, 1632–1695*. Oxford: Clarendon, 1891.

Clark, Neville. *An Approach to the Theology of the Sacraments*. Chicago: Allenson, 1956.

————. "The Theology of Baptism." In *Christian Baptism*, edited by Alec Gilmore, 306–26. Philadelphia: Judson Press, 1959.

Clarke, Samuel. *The Scripture Doctrine of the Trinity*. 1st ed. London: James Knapton, 1712.

Clarke, William Newton. *The Christian Doctrine of God*. New York: Charles Scribner's Sons, 1909.

————. *An Outline of Christian Theology*. New York: Charles Scribner's Sons, 1899. Repr., New York: Scribner, 1912.

Clement. *Who Is the Rich Man That Shall Be Saved?* In vol. 2 of *The Ante-Nicene Fathers*. Grand Rapids: Eerdmans, 1979.

Clifford, Catherine E., ed. *A Century of Prayer for Christian Unity*. Grand Rapids: Eerdmans, 2009.

Clifford, John. "Conference on the Conditions of Church Membership." *General Baptist Magazine* 85 (1883).

———. "The Great Forty Years." In *A Baptist Treasury*, edited by Sydnor L. Stealey, 98–113. New York: Thomas Y. Crowell, 1958.

Coakley, Sarah. *God, Sexuality and the Self: An Essay "On the Trinity."* Cambridge: Cambridge University Press, 2013.

———. *Powers and Submissions: Spirituality, Philosophy, and Gender*. Oxford: Blackwell, 2002.

Cobb, John. *Christ in a Pluralistic Age*. Philadelphia: Westminster, 1975.

Coffey, John. *Persecution and Toleration in Protestant England, 1558–1689*. Essex: Pearson Education, 2000.

Coffman, Elesha J. *"The Christian Century" and the Rise of the Protestant Mainline*. New York: Oxford University Press, 2013.

Coggins, James. *John Smyth's Congregation: English Separatism, Mennonite Influence, and the Elect Nation*. Scottdale, Pa.: Herald Press, 1991.

Cohen, Arthur A., and Marvin Halverson, eds. *A Handbook of Christian Theology*. 2nd ed. Nashville: Abingdon, 1984. First ed., Marvin Halverson and Arthur A. Cohen, eds. New York: Meridian Books, 1958.

Coles, Romand. *Beyond Gated Politics: Reflections for the Possibility of Democracy*. Minneapolis: University of Minnesota Press, 2005.

———. "The Wild Patience of Radical Democracy." In *Radical Democracy: Politics between Abundance and Lack*, edited by Lars Tønder and Lasse Thomassen, 68–85. New York: Manchester University Press, 2005.

Collins, Hercules. *An Orthodox Catechism*. London, 1680.

Collinson, Patrick. *The Elizabethan Puritan Movement*. Oxford: Clarendon, 1967.

———. *From Cranmer to Sancroft*. New York: Hambledon Continuum, 2006.

Colwell, John E. *Promise and Presence: An Exploration of Sacramental Theology*. Milton Keynes, U.K.: Paternoster, 2005.

Confessing the One Faith: An Ecumenical Explication of the Apostolic Faith as It Is Confessed in the Nicene-Constantinopolitan Creed (381). Faith and Order Paper no. 153. Geneva: World Council of Churches, 1991.

"Confirmatory Deed of Roger Williams and his wife, of the lands transferred by him to his associates in the year 1638." In *Records of Rhode Island*, also known as *Records of the Colony of Rhode Island and Providence Plantations*, vol. 1, 22-25. Providence: A. Crawford Greene & Brother, 1856–1865.

Congar, Yves. *Divided Christendom*. London: G. Bles, 1939.

———. *Lay People in the Church*. Translated by Donald Attwater. Westminster, Md.: Newman Press, 1957.

Congregation for the Doctrine of the Faith. "Responses to Some Questions regarding Certain Aspects of the Doctrine of the Church." Accessed January 29, 2013.

http://www.vatican.va/roman_curia/congregations/cfaith/documents/rc_con_cfaith_doc_20070629_responsa-quaestiones_en.html.

Conner, W. T. *Christian Doctrine*. Nashville: Broadman, 1937.

———. *The Gospel of Redemption*. Nashville: Broadman, 1945.

———. *Revelation and God*. Nashville: Broadman, 1936.

Conyers, A. J. "The Changing Face of Baptist Theology." *Review & Expositor* 95, no. 1 (1998): 21–38.

Cook, Henry. *What Baptists Stand For*. London: Carey Kingsgate Press, 1961.

Cotton, Priscilla, and Mary Cole. *To the Priests and People of England We Discharge Our Consciences, and Give Them Warning*. London: Giles Calvert, 1655.

Courvoisier, Jaques. *Zwingli: A Reformed Theologian*. Richmond, Va.: John Knox, 1963.

The Covenant of Watts Street Baptist Church, Durham, N.C., 1957.

Cox, Benjamin. An Appendix to A Confession of Faith or A More Full Declaration of the Faith and Judgement of Baptized Beleevers XX. London, 1648. In *Confessions of Faith*, edited by Edward Bean Underhill, 50–60. London: Haddon, Brothers, 1854.

Cox, Harvey. *Religion in the Secular City: Toward a Postmodern Theology*. New York: Simon & Schuster, 1984.

———. *The Secular City*. New York: Macmillan, 1965.

Coxe, Benjamin, Hanserd Knollys, and William Kiffen. *A Declaration Concerning the Publike Dispute . . . Concerning Infants-Baptisme*. London, 1645.

Crane, Richard, Nicholas M. Healy, Elizabeth Newman, and Maureen H. O'Connell. "A Book Symposium on Steven R. Harmon, *Towards Baptist Catholicity*." *Pro Ecclesia* 18, no. 4 (2009): 367–92.

Cranmer, Thomas. *The Collects of Thomas Cranmer*. Compiled by C. Frederick Barbee and Paul F. M. Zahl. Grand Rapids: Eerdmans, 1999.

Creed, J. Bradley. "John Leland, American Prophet of Religious Individualism." Ph.D. diss., Southwestern Baptist Theological Seminary, 1986.

Criswell, W. A. "The Curse of Liberalism." Speech to the Southern Baptist Convention, June 13, 1988. *The Criswell Sermon Library*. Accessed March 30, 2012. http://www.wacriswell.org/Search/videotrans.cfm/sermon/1222.cfm.

———. "The Curse of Modernism." Sermon preached at First Baptist Church of Dallas, Texas, June 12, 1949.

Cross, Anthony R. *Recovering the Evangelical Sacrament: Baptisma Semper Reformadum*. Eugene, Ore.: Pickwick, 2013.

Cross, Anthony R., and Ruth Gouldbourne, eds. *Questions of Identity: Essays in Honour of Brian Haymes*. Centre for Baptist History and Heritage Studies 6. Oxford: Regent's Park, 2011.

Cross, Anthony R., and Philip E. Thompson, eds. *Baptist Sacramentalism*. Carlisle, U.K.: Paternoster, 2003.

Cross, Anthony R., and Philip E. Thompson, eds. *Baptist Sacramentalism 2*. Milton Keynes, U.K.: Paternoster, 2008.

Cross, Claire. "The Church in England 1646–1660." In *The Interregnum: The Quest for Settlement, 1646–1660*, edited by G. E. Aylmer, 99–120. Hamden, Conn.: Archon Books, 1972.

Croxton, Derek, and Anuschka Tischer. *The Peace of Westphalia: A Historical Dictionary*. Westport, Conn.: Greenwood Press, 2002.

Cummins, John S. "Clergy-Lay Issues and Relations: The Roman Catholic Perspective." *Foundations* 15, no. 2 (1972): 146–55.

Cyprian. *The Unity of the Catholic Church*. In vol. 5 of *The Ante-Nicene Fathers*. Grand Rapids: Eerdmans, 1979.

Dagg, J. L. *Manual of Theology*. Charleston, S.C.: Southern Baptist Publication Society, 1857–1858.

D'Ambrosio, Marcellino. "*Ressourcement* Theology, *Aggiornamento* and the Hermeneutics of Tradition." *Communio* 18, no. 4 (1991): 530–55.

Danforth, Samuel. "Brief Recognition of New England's Errand into the Wilderness." Sermon delivered in May of 1670. In *The Wall and the Garden: Selected Massachusetts Election Sermons*, edited by A. William Plumstead, 53–80. Minneapolis: University of Minnesota Press, 1968.

Danvers, Henry. *A Treatise of Laying on of Hands*. London, 1674.

Darby, J. N. *The Origins of Sectarian Protestantism*. New York: Macmillan, 1964.

———. "What the Christian Has amid the Ruin of the Church." In *The Collected Writings of J. N. Darby*, edited by William Kelly, 14:272–300. Winschoten, Netherlands: H. L. Heijkoop, 1971–1972.

Dare, Helen, and Simon Woodman, eds. *The "Plainly Revealed" Word of God? Baptist Hermeneutics in Theory and Practice*. Macon, Ga.: Mercer University Press, 2011.

Davis, Addie E. Letters. Watts Street Baptist Church Heritage Room, Durham, N.C.

Davis, Ellen F., and Richard B. Hays, eds. *The Art of Reading Scripture*. Grand Rapids: Eerdmans, 2003.

Davis, James Calvin. *The Moral Theology of Roger Williams*. Louisville, Ky.: Westminster John Knox, 2004.

Dawson, Joseph Martin. *Baptists and the American Republic*. Nashville: Broadman, 1956.

DeHart, Paul J. *The Trial of the Witnesses: The Rise and Decline of Postliberal Theology*. Oxford: Blackwell, 2006.

Dehoney, Wayne. "Issues and Imperatives." In *Annual of the Southern Baptist Convention*, 95–100. Nashville: Southern Baptist Convention, 1965.

———. "Southern Baptists and Ecumenical Concerns." *Christianity Today*, January 29, 1965.

Dell, William. *The Doctrine of Baptismes, Reduced from Its Ancient and Moderne Corruptions*. London: Giles Calvert, 1648.

Demerath, N. Jay, III. "Cultural Victory and Organizational Defeat in the

Paradoxical Decline of Liberal Protestantism." *Journal for the Scientific Study of Religion* 34 (1995): 458–69.

Denne, Henry. *Antichrist Unmasked.* N.p., 1645.

Denne, John. *Truth Outweighing Error; or, An Answer to a Treatise Lately Published by J. B. Entitled, A Confession of his Faith and a Reason of his Practice; or, With Who He Can, and With Who He Cannot Hold Church-Fellowship.* London: F. Smith, 1673.

Derrida, Jacques. *Writing and Difference.* Translated by Alan Bass. Chicago: University of Chicago Press, 1978.

Descartes, René. *Meditations on First Philosophy.* Translated by Michael Moriarty. Oxford: Oxford University Press, 2008.

DeVane, Steve. "Educators Support BWA Recitation of Creed." *Biblical Recorder,* July 17, 2004.

Devin, Robert I. *A History of Grassy Creek Baptist Church, from Its Foundation to 1880, with Biographical Sketches of Its Pastors and Ministers.* Raleigh, N.C.: Edwards, Broughton, 1880.

Deweese, Charles W. *Baptist Church Covenants.* Nashville: Broadman, 1990.

DeWolf, L. Harold. *The Case for Liberal Theology.* Philadelphia: Westminster, 1959.

Didache. In *The Didache, The Epistle of Barnabas, The Epistles and The Martyrdom of St. Polycarp, The Fragments of Papias, The Epistle to Diognetus,* translated by James A. Kleist, 15–25. Ancient Christian Writers 6. New York: Newman Press, 1948.

Dilday, Russell H. "Mullins the Theologian: Between the Extremes." *Review and Expositor* 96, no. 1 (1999): 75–86.

———. "On Higher Ground." Reprinted in *Texas Baptists Committed,* April 1997.

———. "The Significance of E. Y. Mullins's *The Axioms of Religion.*" *Baptist History and Heritage* 43, no. 1 (2008): 83–93.

Dixon, Philip. *"Nice and Hot Disputes": The Doctrine of the Trinity in the Seventeenth Century.* London: T&T Clark, 2003.

Documents concerning Baptism and Church Membership: A Controversy among North Carolina Baptists. Perspectives in Religious Studies. Special Studies Series no. 1. Macon, Ga.: Association of Baptist Professors of Religion, 1977.

"Dogmatic Constitution on Divine Revelation" [*Dei Verbum*] §9. November 18, 1965. Translated by Robert Murray. In *Decrees of the Ecumenical Councils,* edited by Norman P. Tanner. Vol. 2, *Trent to Vatican II.* Northport, N.Y.: Costello, 2005.

Dorrien, Gary. *The Making of American Liberal Theology.* Vol. 1, *Imagining Progressive Religion, 1805–1900.* Vol. 2, *Idealism, Realism, and Modernity, 1900–1950.* Louisville, Ky.: Westminster John Knox, 2001–2003.

Doyle, Dennis M. *Communion Ecclesiology.* New York: Orbis Books, 2000.

Draper, James T. *Authority: The Critical Issue for Southern Baptists.* Old Tappan, N.J.: Revell, 1984.

Dugmore, C. W. *The Mass and the English Reformers*. London: Macmillan, 1958.

Dula, Peter, and Alex Sider. "Radical Democracy, Radical Ecclesiology." *Cross Currents* 55, no. 4 (2006): 482–504.

Dulles, Avery Cardinal. "Ratzinger and Kasper on the Universal Church." *Inside the Vatican*, June 9, 2001.

Dunn, James D. G. *Baptism in the Holy Spirit: A Re-examination of the New Testament Teaching on the Gift of the Sprit in Relation to Pentecostalism Today*. 2nd ed. London: SCM Press, 2010.

————. *Christology in the Making*. Philadelphia: Westminster, 1980.

Dunn, James M. "Church, State, and Soul Competency." *Review and Expositor* 96, no. 1 (1999): 61–73.

————. "No Freedom for the Soul with a Creed." In *Soul Freedom: Baptist Battle Cry*, edited by James M. Dunn and Grady C. Cothen, 83–88. Macon, Ga.: Smyth & Helwys, 2000.

Dupuy, Starke. *Hymns and Spiritual Songs*. Edited by John M. Peck. Louisville, Ky.: John P. Morton, 1843.

Durden, Robert F. *The Launching of Duke University, 1924–1949*. Durham, N.C.: Duke University Press, 1993.

Durso, Pamela R., and Keith E. Durso, eds. *Courage and Hope*. Macon, Ga.: Mercer University Press, 2005.

Early, John. "Diary of John Early, Bishop of the Methodist Episcopal Church, South." *Virginia Magazine of History and Biography* 34, no. 4 (1926): 299–312.

————. "Diary of John Early, Bishop of the Methodist Episcopal Church, South." *Virginia Magazine of History and Biography* 39, no. 1 (1931): 41–45.

Eco, Umberto. *The Limits of Interpretation*. Bloomington: Indiana University Press, 1990.

Edwards, Morgan. *The Customs of Primitive Churches*. Philadelphia, 1768/1774.

————. *Materials Toward a History of the Baptists in Pennsylvania*. Philadelphia: Joseph Crukshank & Isaac Collins, 1770.

————. *Materials Towards a History of the Baptists*. Edited by Eve B. Weeks and Mary B. Warren. Danielsville, Ga.: Heritage Papers, 1984.

————. *Materials Towards a History of the Baptists in New Jersey*. Philadelphia: Thomas Dobson, 1792.

Edwards, Paul, ed. *The Encyclopedia of Philosophy*. New York: Macmillan, 1967.

Edwards, Thomas. *Gangraena: The First and Second Part*. 3rd ed. London: Ralph Smith, 1646.

Eighmy, John Lee. *Churches in Cultural Captivity: A History of the Social Attitudes of Southern Baptists*. Knoxville: University of Tennessee Press, 1987.

Eliot, T. S. *T.S. Eliot: Collected Poems 1909–1962*. New York: Harcourt Brace, 1963.

Ellis, Christopher J. *Gathering: A Theology and Spirituality of Worship in Free Church Tradition*. London: SCM Press, 2004.

Ellis, Christopher J., and Myra Blyth, eds. *Gathering for Worship: Patterns and Prayers for the Community of Disciples.* Norwich, U.K.: Canterbury Press, 2005.

Ellis, Marion Arthur. *By a Dream Possessed: Myers Park Baptist Church.* Charlotte, N.C.: Myers Park Baptist Church, 1997.

Ellis, William E. *A Man of Books and a Man of the People: E. Y. Mullins and the Crisis of Moderate Southern Baptist Leadership.* Macon, Ga.: Mercer University Press, 1985.

Emerson, Ralph Waldo. *The Lord's Supper.* In *The Complete Writings of Ralph Waldo Emerson,* 2:1104–5. New York: Wm. H. Wise, 1929.

———. "Self-Reliance." In *The Complete Writings of Ralph Waldo Emerson,* 1:138–52. New York: Wm. H. Wise, 1929.

Encyclopedia of Southern Baptists. 4 vols. Nashville: Broadman, 1958.

Epistle of Diognetus. In *The Apostolic Fathers,* edited by Bart D. Ehrman, 2:121–60. Loeb Classical Library. Cambridge, Mass.: Harvard University Press, 2003.

Erickson, Millard J. *The Evangelical Left: Encountering Postconservative Evangelical Theology.* Grand Rapids: Baker Books, 1997.

———. *God in Three Persons: A Contemporary Interpretation of the Trinity.* Grand Rapids: Baker Books, 1995.

———. *Who's Tampering with the Trinity? An Assessment of the Subordination Debate.* Grand Rapids: Kregel, 2009.

Estep, William R., Jr. *Baptists and Christian Unity.* Nashville: Broadman, 1966.

———. "On the Origins of English Baptists." *Baptist History and Heritage* 22, no. 2 (1987): 19–26.

———. "Thomas Helwys: Bold Architect of Baptist Policy on Church-State Relations." *Baptist History and Heritage* 20, no. 3 (1985): 24–34.

Evangelical Quarterly 78, no. 2 (2006): 101–69. Full-issue discussion of the views of David F. Wright.

Evans, Benjamin. *The Early English Baptists.* London: J. Heaton & Son, 1862.

Evans, Christopher H. *Liberalism without Illusions: Renewing an American Christian Tradition.* Waco, Tex.: Baylor University Press, 2010.

Evans, James H. *We Shall All Be Changed: Social Problems and Theological Renewal.* Minneapolis: Fortress, 1997.

Ewins, Thomas. *The Church of Christ in Bristol Recovering Her Vail.* London, 1657.

"E. Y. Mullins in Retrospect." Special issue, *Southern Baptist Journal of Theology* 3, no. 4. (1999): 2–88.

Fact Book on Theological Education for the Academic Year 1997–1998. Edited by Matthew Zyniewicz and Daniel Aleshire. Dayton, Ohio: Association of Theological Schools, 1997–1998. Accessed January 31, 2013. http://www.ats.edu/uploads/resources/institutional-data/fact-books/1997-1998-fact-book.pdf.

Fact Book on Theological Education for the Academic Year 1999–2000. Edited by Louis Charles Willard. Dayton, Ohio: Association of Theological Schools, 1999–2000. Accessed January 31, 2013. http://www.ats.edu/uploads/resources/institutional-data/fact-books/1999-2000-fact-book.pdf.

Farley, Edward. *Ecclesial Reflection: An Anatomy of Theological Method.* Philadelphia: Fortress, 1982.

Faulkner, William. Press Conference at 202 Rouss Hall, University of Virginia, May 20, 1957. Tape T-134. Accessed September 10, 2012. http://faulkner.lib .virginia.edu/display/wfaudio17.

Featley, Daniel. *The Dippers Dipt., or The Anabaptists Duck'd and Plung'd over Head and Ears, at a Disputation in Southwark.* London: N.B. & Richard Royston, 1647.

Ferguson, Everett. *Baptism in the Early Church.* Grand Rapids: Eerdmans, 2009.

Ferré, Nels. *The Christian Understanding of God.* New York: Harper, 1951.

Fiddes, Paul S. "Church and Sect: Cross-Currents in Early Baptist Life." In *Exploring Baptist Origins*, edited by Anthony R. Cross and Nicholas J. Woo, 33–57. Oxford: Regent's Park College, 2010.

———. "Dual Citizenship in Athens and Jerusalem: The Place of the Christian Scholar in the Life of the Church." Founders Day address for a conference on Christian Life and Witness, "From the Academy to the Church," George-town College, Georgetown, Ky., January 24, 2012. See Fiddes' chapter by the same title in *Questions of Identity: Essays in Honour of Brian Haymes*, edited by Anthony R. Cross and Ruth Gouldbourne, 119–40. Centre for Baptist History and Heritage Studies 6. Oxford: Regent's Park College, 2011.

———. *Participating in God: A Pastoral Doctrine of the Trinity.* Louisville, Ky.: Westminster John Knox, 2000.

———. *Tracks and Traces: Baptist Identity in Church and Theology.* Carlisle, U.K.: Paternoster, 2003.

———, ed. *Under the Rule of Christ: Dimensions of Baptist Spirituality.* Macon, Ga.: Smyth & Helwys, 2008.

Fiddes, Paul S., and Bruce Matthews, eds. *Conversations around the World 2000–2005: The Report of the International Conversations between the Anglican Communion and the Baptist World Alliance.* London: Anglican Communion Office, 2005.

Fiddes, Paul S., et al. *Pushing at the Boundaries of Unity: Anglicans and Baptists in Conversation.* London: Church House, 2005.

Finger, Thomas N. *A Contemporary Anabaptist Theology.* Downers Grove, Ill.: InterVarsity, 2004.

———. "James McClendon's Theology Reaches Completion: A Review Essay." *Mennonite Quarterly Review* 76, no. 1 (2002): 125–26.

———. "The Way to Nicea: Some Reflections from a Mennonite Perspective." *Journal of Ecumenical Studies* 24, no. 2 (1987): 212–31.

Finke, Roger, and Rodney Stark. *The Churching of America, 1776–2005: Winners and Losers in Our Religious Economy.* New Brunswick, N.J.: Rutgers University Press, 2005.

First London Confession. Rev. 1646 ed. Rochester, N.Y.: Backus Book Publishers, 1981.

Fish, Stanley. *Is There a Text in This Class? The Authority of Interpretive Communities.* Cambridge, Mass.: Harvard University Press, 1980.

Fisher, Claude S., and Michael Hout. "How Americans Prayed: Religious Diversity and Change." In *Century of Difference: How America Changed in the Last One Hundred Years,* 186–211. New York: Russell Sage Foundation, 2006.

Fitzgerald, Allan D., ed. *Augustine through the Ages: An Encyclopedia.* Grand Rapids: Eerdmans, 1999.

Flew, Robert Newton, and Rubert Eric Davies. *The Catholicity of Protestantism.* London: Lutterworth Press, 1951.

Flowers, Elizabeth H. *Into the Pulpit: Southern Baptist Women & Power since World War II.* Chapel Hill: University of North Carolina Press, 2012.

Flynt, J. Wayne. *Dixie's Forgotten People: The South's Poor Whites.* Bloomington: Indiana University Press, 1979.

Ford, David F., ed. *The Modern Theologians.* 2nd ed. Cambridge, Mass.: Blackwell, 1996.

Forsyth, P. T. *The Church and the Sacraments.* 3rd ed. London: Independent Press, 1949.

Fosdick, Harry Emerson. *Christianity and Progress.* New York: Fleming H. Revell, 1922.

———. *The Living of These Days: An Autobiography.* New York: Harper & Brothers, 1956.

———. *The Modern Use of the Bible.* New York: Macmillan, 1924.

———. "Shall the Fundamentalists Win?" *Christian Work* 102 (June 10, 1922): 716–22.

Foster, George Burman. *The Finality of the Christian Religion.* Chicago: University of Chicago Press, 1906.

———. *The Function of Religion in Man's Struggle for Existence.* Chicago: University of Chicago Press, 1909.

Foster, James. *An Essay on Fundamentals: With Particular Regard to the Ever-Blessed Trinity.* 2nd ed. London: J. Noon, 1754. First edition published in 1720.

Fowler, Stanley K. *More than a Symbol: The British Baptist Recovery of Baptismal Sacramentalism.* Carlisle, U.K.: Paternoster, 2002.

Freeman, Curtis W., ed. "*All the Sons of Earth*: Carlyle Marney and the Fight against Prejudice." *Baptist History and Heritage* 44, no. 2 (2009): 71–84.

———. "Can Baptist Theology Be Revisioned?" *Perspectives in Religious Studies* 24, no. 3 (1997): 273–310.

———. "Can the Secular Be Sanctified?" In *The Future of Baptist Higher Education,* edited by Donald D. Schmeltekopf and Dianna M. Vitanza, 219–232. Waco, Tex.: Baylor University Press, 2006.

———. "Carlyle Marney on Pilgrim Priesthood." *Baptists Today,* June 2002.

———. "The 'Coming of Age' of Baptist Theology in Generation Twenty-Something." "Festschrift for James Wm. McClendon Jr." Special issue, *Perspectives in Religious Studies* 27, no. 1 (2000): 21–38.

————, ed. *A Company of Women Preachers: Baptist Prophetesses in Seventeenth-Century England*. Waco, Tex.: Baylor University Press, 2011.

————. "A Confession for Catholic Baptists." In *Ties That Bind: Life Together in the Baptist Vision*, edited by Gary A. Furr and Curtis W. Freeman, 83–97. Macon, Ga.: Smyth & Helwys, 1994.

————. "The 'Eclipse' of Spiritual Exegesis: Biblical Interpretation from the Reformation to Modernity." *Southwestern Journal of Theology* 35, no. 3 (1993): 21–28.

————. "E. Y. Mullins and the Siren Songs of Modernity." *Review and Expositor* 96, no. 1 (1999): 23–42.

————. Letter to the editor. *Baptist Standard*, May 15, 2000, 4, available online at http://assets.baptiststandard.com/archived/2000/5_15/pages/letters.html.

————. "'Never Had I Been So Blind': W. A. Criswell's 'Change' on Racial Segregation." *Journal of Southern Religion* 10 (2007). http://jsr.fsu.edu/Volume 10/Freeman.pdf.

————. "A New Perspective on Baptist Identity." *Perspectives in Religious Studies* 26, no. 1 (1999): 59–65.

————. "'Other Baptists,' Too, Are Keeping the Faith." *News and Observer*, August 6, 2003. Reprinted in *Baptists Today*, September 2003.

————. "Patterson Galvanized the Other Baptists." *Herald Sun*, July 24, 2003. Reprinted as "Other Baptists and Bossy Preachers," in *Biblical Recorder*, August 22, 2003, and *Baptist Standard*, August 5, 2003.

————. "Reading St. Augustine's *City of God* as a Narrative Theology." Ph.D. diss., Baylor University, 1990.

————. "Roger Williams, American Democracy, and the Baptists." *Perspectives in Religious Studies* 34, no. 3 (2007): 267–86.

————. "Toward a *Sensus Fidelium* for an Evangelical Church." In *The Nature of Confession: Evangelicals and Postliberals in Conversation*, edited by Timothy R. Phillips and Dennis L. Okholm, 162–80. Downers Grove, Ill.: InterVarsity, 1996.

————. "What Kind of Baptist Are You?" *Religious Herald*, September 25, 2003.

————. "Where Two or Three Are Gathered: Communion Ecclesiology in the Free Church." *Perspectives in Religious Studies* 31, no. 3 (2004): 259–72.

Freeman, Curtis W., Steven Harmon, Elizabeth Newman, and Philip Thompson. "Confessing the Faith." *Biblical Recorder*, July 8, 2004.

Freeman, Curtis W., James Wm. McClendon Jr., and C. Rosalee Velloso Ewell, eds. *Baptist Roots: A Reader in the Theology of a Christian People*. Valley Forge, Pa.: Judson Press, 1999.

Frei, Hans W. *The Eclipse of Biblical Narrative: A Study in Eighteenth and Nineteenth Century Hermeneutics*. New Haven, Conn.: Yale University Press, 1974.

————. *The Identity of Jesus Christ: The Hermeneutical Bases of Dogmatic Theology*. Eugene, Ore.: Wipf & Stock, 1997. First published 1975 by Fortress, Philadelphia.

————. "The 'Literal Reading' of Biblical Narrative in the Christian Tradition." In *Theology and Narrative: Selected Essays,* edited by George Hunsinger and William Placher, 117–52. New York: Oxford University Press, 1993.

————. "In Memory of Robert L. Calhoun 1896–1983." *Reflection* 82 (1984): 8–9.

————. *Types of Christian Theology.* New Haven, Conn.: Yale University Press, 1992.

Frend, W. H. C. *The Donatist Church: A Movement of Protest in Roman North Africa.* Oxford: Clarendon, 1952.

Friesen, Duane. "Normative Factors in Troeltsch's Typology of Religious Association." *Journal of Religious Ethics* 3, no. 2 (1975): 271–83.

Fristoe, William. *A Concise History of the Ketocton Baptist Association.* Harrisonburg, Va.: Sprinkle Publications, 2002. First published 1808 by William Gilman Lyford, Stauton, Va.

Fuller, Andrew. *The Complete Works of the Rev. Andrew Fuller.* Philadelphia: American Baptist Publication Society, 1845. Repr., Harrisonburg, Va.: Sprinkle, 1988, from the 3rd London edition with additions by Joseph Belcher.

Furman, Richard, John M. Roberts, and Joseph B. Cook. "Call for a State Convention in South Carolina. . . ." November 8, 1820. In *A Sourcebook for Baptist Heritage,* edited by H. Leon McBeth, 246–51. Nashville: Broadman, 1990.

Furr, Gary A., and Curtis Freeman, eds. *Ties That Bind: Life Together in the Baptist Vision.* Macon, Ga.: Smyth & Helwys, 1994.

Gallie, W. B. "Essentially Contested Concept." In *The Importance of Language,* edited by Max Black, 121–46. Englewood Cliffs, N.J.: Prentice-Hall, 1962.

Gambrell, J. B. "Obligations of Baptists to Teach Their Principles." In *Baptist Principles Reset,* edited by Jeremiah B. Jeter, 250–51. Richmond, Va.: Religious Herald Press, 1901.

Gardiner, Samuel Rawson, ed. *The Constitutional Documents of the Puritan Revolution 1625–1660.* Oxford: Clarendon, 1936.

Garner, Robert. *A Treatise of Baptisme.* N.p., 1645.

Garrett, James Leo, Jr. *Baptist Church Discipline.* Nashville: Broadman, 1962.

————, ed. *Baptist Relations with Other Christians.* Valley Forge, Pa.: Judson Press, 1974.

————. *Baptists and Roman Catholicism.* Nashville: Broadman, 1965.

————. *Baptist Theology: A Four Century Study.* Macon, Ga.: Mercer University Press, 2009.

Gaustad, Edwin S. "The Backus-Leland Tradition." In *Baptist Concepts of the Church,* edited by Winthrop Still Hudson, 106–34. Chicago: Judson Press, 1959.

————. *Liberty of Conscience: Roger Williams in America.* Grand Rapids: Eerdmans, 1991.

Gelasius. Letter of Pope Gelasius to Emperor Anastasius (494). In *Readings in*

European History, edited by James Harvey Robinson, 72–73. Boston: Ginn, 1906.

George, Timothy. *John Robinson and the English Separatist Tradition*. Macon, Ga.: Mercer University Press, 1982.

———. *Reading Scripture with the Reformers*. Downers Grove, Ill.: InterVarsity, 2011.

———. "The Reformed Doctrine of Believers' Baptism." *Interpretation* 47, no. 3 (1993): 242–54.

———. *Theology of the Reformers*. Nashville: Broadman, 1988.

George, Timothy, and David S. Dockery, eds. *Baptist Theologians*. Nashville: Broadman, 1990.

Gerrish, B. A. *Continuing the Reformation*. Chicago: University of Chicago Press, 1993.

———. *Grace and Gratitude: The Eucharistic Theology of John Calvin*. Minneapolis: Fortress, 1993.

———. "The Lord's Supper in the Reformed Confessions." In *Major Themes in the Reformed Tradition*, edited by Donald K. McKim, 245–58. Grand Rapids: Eerdmans, 1992.

Gewehr, Wesley M. *The Great Awakening in Virginia, 1740–1790*. Durham, N.C.: Duke University Press, 1930.

Giles, Kevin. *Jesus and the Father: Modern Evangelicals Reinvent the Doctrine of the Trinity*. Grand Rapids: Zondervan, 2006.

———. *The Trinity & Subordinationism: The Doctrine of God & the Contemporary Gender Debate*. Downers Grove, Ill.: InterVarsity, 2002.

Gill, Jill K. *Embattled Ecumenism: The National Council of Churches, the Vietnam War, and the Trials of the Protestant Left*. DeKalb: Northern Illinois University Press, 2011.

Gill, John. *The Body of Doctrinal Divinity*. Atlanta: Turner Lassetter, 1950. First published in 1769 by George Keith, London.

———. *The Doctrine of the Trinity Stated and Vindicated*. London: Aaron Ward, 1731.

———. *An Exposition of the New Testament*. London: George Keith, 1774–1776.

Gilmore, Alec, ed. *Christian Baptism: A Fresh Attempt to Understand the Rite in Terms of Scripture, History, and Theology*. Philadelphia: Judson Press, 1959.

Gilpin, Clark. *The Millenarian Piety of Roger Williams*. Chicago: University of Chicago Press, 1979.

Goen, Clarence C. "Ecclesiocracy without Ecclesiology: Denominational Life in America." *American Baptist Quarterly* 10, no. 4 (1991): 266–79.

———. *Revivalism and Separatism in New England, 1740–1800*. New Haven, Conn.: Yale University Press, 1962.

Goodwin, Everett C., ed. *Baptists in the Balance*. Valley Forge, Pa.: Judson Press, 1999.

Gordis, Lisa M. *Opening Scripture: Bible Reading and Interpretive Authority in Puritan New England.* Chicago: University of Chicago Press, 2003.

Gordon, Alexander. *Addresses Biographical and Historical.* London: Lindsey Press, 1922.

———. *Heads of English Unitarian History.* London: Philip Green, 1895.

Gordon, James. "Spirituality and Scripture: The Rule of the Word." In *Under the Rule of Christ: Dimensions of Baptist Spirituality,* edited by Paul S. Fiddes, 103–34. Macon, Ga.: Smyth & Helwys, 2008.

Gourley, Bruce. "Editorial: Baptists and Theology—Broad, Deep, and Diverse." *Baptist History & Heritage* 47, no. 2 (2012): 2–3.

Grantham, Thomas. *Christianismus Primitivus; or, The Ancient Christian Religion.* London: Francis Smith, 1678.

———. *The Fourth Principle of Christs Doctrine Vindicated.* London, 1674.

———. *St. Paul's Catechism.* 2nd ed. London: J. Darby, 1693.

Grass, Tim, and Ian Randall, "C. H. Spurgeon on the Sacraments." In Cross and Thompson, *Baptist Sacramentalism,* 74–75.

Graves, J. R. "Baptist Corollaries." *Baptist,* July 20, 1867.

———. *The Great Carrolton Debate.* Memphis, Tenn.: Southern Baptist Publication Society, 1876.

———. *The Great Iron Wheel or Republicanism Backwards and Christianity Reversed.* New York: Sheldon, 1855.

Greaves, Richard L. *Glimpses of Glory: John Bunyan and English Dissent.* Stanford, Calif.: Stanford University Press, 2002.

Greef, Wulfert de. "Calvin's Understanding and Interpretation of the Bible." In *John Calvin's Impact on Church and Society, 1509–2009,* edited by Martin Ernst Hirzel and Martin Sallmann, 67–89. Grand Rapids: Eerdmans, 2009.

Greeley, Andrew M. *An Ugly Little Secret.* Kansas City, Mo.: Sheed Andrews & McMeel, 1977.

Greene-McCreight, Kathryn. *"Ad Litteram": How Augustine, Calvin, and Barth Read the "Plain Sense" of Genesis 1–3.* New York: Peter Lang, 1999.

Gregory of Nazianzus. *The Fifth Theological Oration: On the Holy Spirit.* In vol. 7 of *The Nicene and Post-Nicene Fathers,* Second Series. Grand Rapids: Eerdmans, 1976.

———. *The Third Theological Oration: On the Son.* In vol. 7 of *The Nicene and Post-Nicene Fathers.* 2nd Series. Grand Rapids: Eerdmans, 1976.

Gregory of Nyssa. *On 'Not Three Gods.' Letter to Ablabius.* In vol. 5 of *The Nicene and Post-Nicene Fathers.* 2nd Series. Grand Rapids: Eerdmans, 1976.

Grenz, Stanley J. *The Named God and the Question of Being: A Trinitarian Theoontology.* Louisville, Ky.: Westminster John Knox, 2005.

———. *Rediscovering the Triune God: The Trinity in Contemporary Theology.* Minneapolis: Fortress, 2004.

———. *Revisioning Evangelical Theology.* Downers Grove, Ill.: InterVarsity, 1993.

————. *The Social God and the Relational Self: A Trinitarian Theology of the* Imago Dei. Louisville, Ky.: Westminster John Knox, 2001.

————. *Theology for the Community of God.* Grand Rapids: Eerdmans, 2000.

Griffith, Benjamin. *A Short Treatise of Church Discipline.* Philadelphia: Philadelphia Baptist Association, 1743.

Griffith, John. *Gods Oracle and Christs Doctrine; or, The Six Principles of Christian Religion as They Were Taught and Delivered by Christ and His Apostles.* London: Richard Moon, 1655.

Griffiths, Olive M. *Religion and Learning.* Cambridge: Cambridge University Press, 1935.

Grudem, Wayne. *Systematic Theology: An Introduction to Biblical Doctrine.* Grand Rapids: Zondervan, 1995.

Guild, Reuben Aldridge. *Early History of Brown University.* Providence, R.I.: Snow & Farnham, 1897.

Gunton, Colin. *The One, the Three and the Many.* Cambridge: Cambridge University Press, 1993.

Gura, Philip F. *A Glimpse of Sion's Glory: Puritan Radicalism in New England, 1620–1660.* Middletown, Conn.: Wesleyan University Press, 1984.

Gustafson, James. *Can Ethics Be Christian?* Chicago: University of Chicago Press, 1975.

————. "The Sectarian Temptation: Reflections on Theology, the Church and the University." *Proceedings of the Catholic Theological Society* 40 (1985): 83–94.

Gutiérrez, Gustavo. *Las Casas: In Search of the Poor of Jesus Christ.* Translated by Robert R. Barr. Maryknoll, N.Y.: Orbis Books, 1993.

Haines, Richard. *His Appeal to The General Assembly of Dependent Baptists Convened in London, from most Parts of the Nation, the Third day of June; 1680.* [London?], 1680.

————. *New Lords, New Laws.* London, 1674.

Halcomb, Joel. "A Social History of Congregational Religious Practice during the Puritan Revolution." Ph.D. diss., University of Cambridge, 2009.

Hall, David D., ed. *The Antinomian Controversy, 1636–1638: A Documentary History.* 2nd ed. Durham, N.C.: Duke University Press, 1990.

Hall, Douglas John. *The End of Christendom and the Future of Christianity.* Valley Forge, Pa.: Trinity International, 1997.

Hall, Robert. *The Doctrine of the Trinity Stated.* Coventry: J. W. Piercy, 1776.

————. *The Works of Robert Hall.* London: Henry G. Bohn, 1851.

Hancock-Stefan, George. "Would the ABC-USA Ecclesiology Be Able (Willing) to Declare Arius a Heretic?" *American Baptist Quarterly* 30, nos. 3–4 (2011): 217–23.

Handy, Robert T. "Areas of Theological Agreement from a Baptist Point of View." *Foundations* 10, no. 2 (1967): 159–72.

————. "Toward a Theology of the Local Church." *Foundations* 15, no. 1 (1972): 42–52.

Hankins, Barry. "Southern Baptists and Northern Evangelicals: Cultural Factors and the Nature of Religious Alliances." *Religion and American Culture* 7, no. 2 (1997): 271–98.

———. *Uneasy in Babylon: Southern Baptist Conservatives and American Culture.* Tuscaloosa: University of Alabama Press, 2002.

Hanson, R. P. C. *The Search for the Christian Doctrine of God.* Edinburgh: T&T Clark, 1988.

Harder, Leland. *Doors to Lock and Doors to Open: The Discerning People of God.* Scottdale, Pa.: Herald Press, 1993.

Hardon, John A. "Towards an American Baptist-Roman Catholic Dialogue." *Foundations* 10, no. 2 (1967): 150–58.

Harink, Douglas Karel. *Paul among the Postliberals: Pauline Theology beyond Christendom and Modernity.* Grand Rapids: Brazos, 2006.

Harmon, Steven R. "Baptists and Ecumenism." In *The Oxford Handbook of Ecumenical Studies*, edited by Geoffrey Wainwright and Paul McPartian. New York: Oxford University Press, forthcoming.

———. "*Dei Verbum* §9 in Baptist Perspective." *Ecclesiology* 5, no. 3 (2009): 299–321.

———. "Do Real Baptists Recite Creeds?" *Baptists Today*, September 2004.

———. *Ecumenism Means You, Too: Ordinary Christians and the Quest for Christian Unity.* Eugene, Ore.: Cascade Books, 2010.

———. "Qualitative Catholicity in the Ignatian Correspondence—and the New Testament: The Fallacies of a Restorationist Hermeneutic." *Perspectives in Religious Studies* 38, no. 1 (2011): 33–45.

———. "A Time for Exchanging Ecclesial Gifts." *Baptists Today*, January 2010.

———. *Towards Baptist Catholicity: Essays on Tradition and the Baptist Vision.* Milton Keynes, U.K.: Paternoster, 2006.

———. "Why Baptist Catholicity, and by What Authority?" *Pro Ecclesia* 18, no. 4 (2009): 386–92.

Harnack, Adolf von. *The Constitution and Law of the Church of the First Two Centuries.* Translated by F. L. Pogson. New York: G. P. Putnam, 1910.

———. *History of Dogma.* Translated by Neil Buchanan. New York: Dover, 1961.

———. *What Is Christianity?* Translated by Thomas Bailey Saunders. New York: Putnam, 1901. Repr., New York: Harper & Row, 1957.

Harper, Keith. *The Quality of Mercy: Southern Baptists and Social Christianity, 1890–1920.* Tuscaloosa: University of Alabama Press, 1996.

Harrington, Michael. *The Other America.* New York: Macmillan, 1962.

Harvey, Barry. *Another City: An Ecclesiological Primer for a Post-Christian World.* Harrisburg, Pa.: Trinity Press, 1999.

———. *Can These Bones Live? A Catholic Baptist Engagement with Ecclesiology, Hermeneutics, and Social Theory.* Grand Rapids: Brazos, 2008.

Harvey, Hezekiah. *The Church: Its Polity and Ordinances.* Philadelphia: American Baptist Publication Society, 1879.

Hatch, Nathan. *The Democratization of American Christianity.* New Haven, Conn.: Yale University Press, 1989.

Hatchett, Marion J. *Commentary on the American Prayer Book.* San Francisco: Harper, 1995.

Hauerwas, Stanley. *After Christendom? How the Church Is to Behave if Freedom, Justice, and a Christian Nation Are Bad Ideas.* Nashville: Abingdon, 1991.

———. *Against the Nations.* New York: Harper & Row, 1985.

———. *Character and the Christian Life.* San Antonio, Tex.: Trinity University Press, 1975.

———. *Christian Existence Today: Essays on Church, World, and Living in Between.* Durham, N.C.: Labyrinth Press, 1988.

———. *A Community of Character.* Notre Dame, Ind.: University of Notre Dame Press, 1981.

———. *Dispatches from the Front.* Durham, N.C.: Duke University Press, 1994.

———. "How Christian Ethics Became Medical Ethics." *Christian Bioethics* 1 (1995): 11–28.

———. *The Peaceable Kingdom.* Notre Dame, Ind.: University of Notre Dame Press, 1983.

———. *Revisions: Changing Perspectives in Moral Philosophy.* Edited by Stanley Hauerwas and Alasdair MacIntyre. Notre Dame, Ind.: University of Notre Dame Press, 1983.

———. *Unleashing the Scripture: Freeing the Bible from Captivity to America.* Nashville: Abingdon, 1993.

———. *Vision and Virtue.* Notre Dame, Ind.: University of Notre Dame Press, 1981.

———. *With the Grain of the Universe: The Church's Witness and Natural Theology.* Grand Rapids: Brazos, 2001.

Hauerwas, Stanley, and William H. Willimon. *Resident Aliens.* Nashville: Abingdon, 1989.

Hayden, Roger, ed. *The Records of a Church of Christ in Bristol, 1640–1687.* Bristol, U.K.: Bristol Record Society, 1974.

Haymes, Brian. "On Religious Liberty: Re-reading *A Short Declaration of the Mystery of Iniquity* in London in 2005." *Baptist Quarterly* 42, vol. 3 (2007): 197–217.

Hays, Richard B. *The Moral Vision of the New Testament: A Contemporary Introduction to New Testament Ethics.* San Francisco: HarperCollins, 1996.

Hedstrom, Matthew. *The Rise of Liberal Religion: Book Culture and American Spirituality in the Twentieth Century.* New York: Oxford University Press, 2013.

Heim, S. Mark. *Saved from Sacrifice: A Theology of the Cross.* Grand Rapids: Eerdmans, 2006.

Helwys, Thomas. *A Short Declaration of the Mistery of Iniquity.* Repr., London: Kingsgate, 1935.

———. *A Short Declaration of the Mystery of Iniquity* (1611/1612). Edited by Richard Groves. Macon, Ga.: Mercer University Press, 1998.

Henry, Carl F. H. *The Uneasy Conscience of Modern Fundamentalism*. Grand Rapids: Eerdmans, 1947.

Heyerman, Christine Leigh. *Southern Cross: The Beginnings of the Bible Belt*. Chapel Hill: University of North Carolina Press, 1997.

Hick, John. *The Myth of God Incarnate*. Philadelphia: Westminster, 1977.

Higton, Mike. "Frei's Christology and Lindbeck's Cultural-Linguistic Theory." *Scottish Journal of Theology* 50, no. 1 (1997): 83–95.

Hill, Christopher. *The Collected Essays of Christopher Hill*. Vol. 2, *Religion and Politics in 17th Century England*. Amherst: University of Massachusetts Press, 1986.

———. *A Turbulent, Seditious, and Factious People: John Bunyan and His Church*. Oxford: Clarendon, 1988.

———. *The World Turned Upside Down*. New York: Penguin, 1991.

Hill, Samuel S. *Religion and the Solid South*. Nashville: Abingdon, 1972.

———. *Southern Churches in Crisis*. New York: Holt, Rinehart & Winston, 1967.

———. *Southern Churches in Crisis Revisited*. Tuscaloosa: University of Alabama Press, 1999.

Hinson, E. Glenn. "Creeds and Christian Unity." *Journal of Ecumenical Studies* 23, no. 1 (1986): 25–36.

———. "E. Y. Mullins as Interpreter of the Baptist Tradition." *Review and Expositor* 96, no. 1 (1999): 109–22.

———. "The Nicene Creed Viewed from the Standpoint of the Evangelization of the Roman Empire." In *Faith to Creed: Ecumenical Perspectives on the Affirmation of the Apostolic Faith in the Fourth Century*, edited by S. Mark Heim, 117–28. Grand Rapids: Eerdmans, 1991.

Hippolytus. *Apostolic Tradition*. In *The Apostolic Constitution: A Commentary*, edited by Paul F. Bradshaw, Maxwell E. Johnson, and L. Edward Phillips. Minneapolis: Fortress, 2002.

———. *The Apostolic Tradition of St. Hippolytus*. 2nd ed. Edited by Gregory Dix and Henry Chadwick. London: Alban, 1992.

Hobbs, Herschel H. *The Baptist Faith and Message*. Nashville: Convention Press, 1971.

Hobson, Paul. *The Fallacy of Infants Baptisme Discovered*. London, 1645.

Hodge, Charles. *Systematic Theology*. New York: Scribner, Armstrong, 1872–1873.

Hodgson, Peter C. *Liberal Theology: A Radical Vision*. Minneapolis: Fortress, 2007.

Holifield, E. Brooks. *The Gentlemen Theologians*. Durham, N.C.: Duke University Press, 1978.

Hollinger, David A. *After Cloven Tongues of Fire: Protestant Liberalism in Modern American History*. Princeton, N.J.: Princeton University Press, 2013.

Holmes, Stephen R. *Baptist Theology*. London: T&T Clark, 2012.

———. "Cur Deus Po-mo? What St. Anselm Can Teach Us about Preaching the Atonement Today." *Epworth Review* 36, no. 1 (2009): 6–17.

————. "Death in the Afternoon: Hebrews, Sacrifice and Soteriology." In *Hebrews and Christian Theology*, edited by Richard Bauckham, Daniel R. Driver, Trevor A. Hart, and Nathan MacDonald, 229–52. Grand Rapids: Eerdmans, 2009.

————. *The Holy Trinity: Understanding God's Life*. Milton Keynes, U.K.: Paternoster, 2011.

————. "Of Babies and Bathwater? Recent Evangelical Critiques of Penal Substitution in the Light of Early Modern Debates concerning Justification." *European Journal of Theology* 16, no. 2 (2007): 93–105.

————. *The Wondrous Cross: Atonement and Penal Substitution in the Bible and History*. London: Paternoster, 2007.

Hooker, Richard J., ed. *The Carolina Backcountry on the Eve of the Revolution*. Chapel Hill: University of North Carolina Press, 1953.

Hordern, William. *The Case for a New Reformation Theology*. Philadelphia: Westminster, 1959.

————. "Young Theologians Rebel." *Christian Century* 69, no. 11, March 12, 1952.

Horn, Patrick Hodges. Letter to the editor. *Baptists Today*, August 2002, 8.

Hovey, Alvah. *Manual of Christian Theology*. 2nd ed. New York: Silver, Burdett, 1900.

————. *Manual of Systematic Theology and Christian Ethics*. Philadelphia: American Baptist Publication Society, 1877.

Howell, Robert Boyte C. *The Evils of Infant Baptism*. Charleston, S.C.: Southern Baptist Publication Society, 1851.

Hubmaier, Balthasar. *Balthasar Hubmaier: Theologian of Anabaptism*. Edited and translated by H. Wayne Pipkin and John Howard Yoder. Scottdale, Pa.: Herald Press, 1989.

Hudson, Winthrop S., ed. *Baptist Concepts of the Church*. Philadelphia: Judson Press, 1959.

————. *Baptists in Transition: Individualism and Christian Responsibility*. Valley Forge, Pa.: Judson Press, 1979.

————. "Baptists Were Not Anabaptists." *Chronicle* 16, no. 4 (1953): 171–79.

————. "Who Were the Baptists?" *Baptist Quarterly* 16, no. 7 (1956): 303–12.

————. "Who Were the Baptists?" *Baptist Quarterly* 17, no. 2 (1957): 53–55.

Humphreys, Fisher. *Baptist Theology: A Really Short Version*. Brentwood, Tenn.: Baptist History and Heritage Society, 2007.

————. *The Death of Christ*. Nashville: Broadman, 1978.

————. "Father, Son and Holy Spirit." *Theological Educator* 12, no. 1 (1982): 78–96.

————. Review of *The Catholicity of the Reformation*, ed. Carl E. Braaten and Robert W. Jenson; *The Catholicity of the Church*, by Avery Dulles; and *Soul of the World*, by George Weigel. *Perspectives in Religious Studies* 26, no. 1 (1999): 91–95.

———. *The Way We Were: How Southern Baptist Theology Has Changed and What It Means to Us All*. Rev. ed. Macon, Ga.: Smyth & Helwys, 1984.

Hunsinger, George. "Postliberalism." In *The Cambridge Companion to Postmodern Theology*, edited by Kevin J. Vanhoozer, 42–57. Cambridge: Cambridge University Press, 2003.

Hunsinger, George, and William Placher, eds. *Theology and Narrative: Selected Essays*. New York: Oxford University Press, 1993.

Huntington, William. *Forty Stripes Save None For Satan*. London: G. Terry, 1792.

Hurt, John J. "Should Southern Baptists Have a Creed/Confession?—No!" *Review and Expositor* 76, no. 1 (1979): 85–88.

Hutchison, William R. *The Modernist Impulse in American Protestantism*. Cambridge, Mass.: Harvard University Press, 1976.

Ignatius. *To the Ephesians*. In vol. 1 of *The Ante–Nicene Fathers*. Grand Rapids: Eerdmans, 1979.

———. *To the Smyrnaeans*. In vol. 1 of *The Ante–Nicene Fathers*. Grand Rapids: Eerdmans, 1979.

International Mission Board of the Southern Baptist Convention. "Guideline on Baptism." March 6, 2006.

Irenaeus. *Against Heresies*. In vol. 1 of *The Ante-Nicene Fathers*. Grand Rapids: Eerdmans, 1979.

Isserman, Maurice. *The Other American: The Life of Michael Harrington*. New York: Public Affairs, 2000.

James I. "A Narration of the Burning of Edward Wightman." In *A True Relation of the Commissions and Warrants for the Condemnation and Burning of Bartholomew Legatt and Thomas Withman* [*sic*], 7–13. London: Michael Spark, 1651.

James, Robison B., ed. *The Unfettered Word: Southern Baptists Confront the Authority-Inerrancy Question*. Waco, Tex.: Word Books, 1987.

James, William. *Varieties of Religious Experience*. New York: Collins, 1960.

Jarratt, Devereux. *An Argument Between an Anabaptist and a Paedo-baptist*. N.p., 1803.

———. *The Life of the Reverend Devereux Jarratt*. Baltimore, Md.: Warner & Hanna, 1806.

Jefferson, Thomas. A Bill for Establishing Religious Freedom. In *The Papers of Thomas Jefferson*. Vol. 2, *1777 to June 18, 1779*, edited by Julian P. Boyd, 545–47. Princeton, N.J.: Princeton University Press, 1950.

Jeffery, Steve, Michael Ovey, and Andrew Sach. *Pierced for Our Transgressions*. Wheaton, Ill.: Crossway Books, 2007.

Jenkens, Charles A., ed. *Baptist Doctrines*. St. Louis, Mo.: Chancy R. Barns, 1880.

Jenkins, Daniel T. *The Nature of Catholicity*. London: Faber & Faber, 1941.

———. *The Strangeness of the Church*. Garden City, N.Y.: Doubleday, 1955.

Jennings, Willie James. *The Christian Imagination: Theology and the Origins of Race*. New Haven, Conn.: Yale University Press, 2010.

————. "Grace without Remainder: Why Baptists Should Baptize Their Babies." In *Grace upon Grace: Essays in Honor of Thomas A. Langford,* edited by Robert K. Johnson, L. Gregory Jones, and Jonathan Wilson, 201–16. Nashville: Abingdon, 1999.

Jenson, Robert W. *Canon and Creed.* Louisville, Ky.: Westminster John Knox, 2010.

————. "Catholic and Evangelical?" *First Things* 86 (1998): 42–43.

Jeremias, Joachim. *The Eucharistic Words of Jesus.* New York: Charles Scribner's Sons, 1966.

Jeschke, Marlin. *Discipling in the Church.* Scottdale, Pa.: Herald Press, 1988.

Jessey, Henry. *A Storehouse of Provision, to Further Resolution in Severall Cases of Conscience, and Questions Now in Dispute.* London: Charles Sumptner, 1650.

John of Damascus. *The Orthodox Faith.* In vol. 9 of *The Nicene and Post-Nicene Fathers of the Christian Church.* 2nd series. Grand Rapids: Eerdmans, 1976.

John Paul II. *Ut Unum Sint.* May 25, 1995. Accessed January 29, 2013. http://www.vatican.va/holy_father/john_paul_ii/encyclicals/documents/hf_jp-ii_enc_25051995_ut-unum-sint_en.html.

Johnson, Elias H. *An Outline of Systematic Theology.* Philadelphia: American Baptist Publication Society, 1895.

————. *Outline of Systematic Theology.* Philadelphia: American Baptist Publication Society, 1891.

Johnson, Francis. *A Christian Plea Conteyning three Treatises.* Leiden: William Brewster, 1617.

Johnson, Keith E. "Trinitarian Agency and the Eternal Subordination of the Son: An Augustinian Perspective." *Themelios* 36, no. 1 (2011): 7–25.

Johnson, Maxwell E. *The Rites of Christian Initiation: Their Evolution and Interpretation.* Rev. ed. Collegeville, Minn.: Liturgical, 2007.

Johnson, Robert E. *A Global Introduction to Baptist Churches.* Cambridge: Cambridge University Press, 2010.

Johnson, W. B. *The Gospel Developed through the Government and Order of the Churches of Jesus Christ.* Richmond, Va.: H. K. Ellyson, 1846.

The Joint Liturgical Group. *Initiation and Eucharist.* Edited by Neville Clark and Ronald C. D. Jasper. London: SPCK, 1972.

Jones, Keith G. "Rethinking Baptist Ecclesiology." *Journal of European Baptist Studies* 1, no. 1 (2000): 4–18.

Jones, Phillip B., et al. *A Study of Adults Baptized in Southern Baptist Churches, 1993.* Atlanta: Home Mission Board of the Southern Baptist Convention, 1995.

Jones, Robert P. "Re-envisioning Baptist Identity from a Theocentric Perspective." *Perspectives in Religious Studies* 26, no. 1 (1999): 35–57.

Jones, Robert P., and Melissa C. Stewart. "The Unintended Consequences of Dixieland Postliberalism." *Cross Currents* 55, no. 4 (2006): 506–21.

Jones, Rufus. *Mysticism and Democracy in the English Commonwealth.* Cambridge, Mass.: Harvard University Press, 1932.

Jones, William. *The History of the Christian Church, from the Birth of Christ to the XVIII Century: Including the Very Interesting Account of the Waldenses and Albigenses.* 4th ed. Wetumpka, Ala.: Charles Yancey, 1845.

Judson, Ann H. *An Account of the American Baptist Mission to the Burman Empire: In a Series of Letters, Addressed to a Gentleman in London.* London: J. Butterworth & Son, 1823.

Justin Martyr. *First Apology.* In vol. 1 of *The Ante-Nicene Fathers.* Grand Rapids: Eerdmans, 1979.

Kadane, Matthew. "Anti-trinitarianism and the Republican Tradition in Enlightenment Britain." *Republics of Letters* 2, no. 1 (2010). Accessed October 11, 2011. http://arcade.stanford.edu/sites/default/files/article_pdfs/roflv02i01_Kadane_121510_1.pdf.

Kasper, Walter. "A Friendly Reply to Cardinal Ratzinger on the Church." *America*, April 23, 2001.

Katongole, Emmanuel M. *Beyond Universal Reason: The Relation between Religion and Ethics in the Work of Stanley Hauerwas.* Notre Dame, Ind.: University of Notre Dame Press, 2000.

———. *A Future for Africa: Critical Essays in Christian Social Imagination.* Scranton, Pa.: University of Scranton Press, 2005.

———. *The Relation between Religion and Ethics in the Work of Stanley Hauerwas.* Notre Dame, Ind.: University of Notre Dame Press, 2000.

———. *The Sacrifice of Africa: A Political Theology for Africa.* Grand Rapids: Eerdmans, 2011.

Kaufman, Gordon. *In the Face of Mystery.* Cambridge, Mass.: Harvard University Press, 1993.

Kavanagh, Aidan. *The Shape of Baptism: The Rite of Christian Initiation.* New York: Pueblo, 1978.

Keach, Benjamin. *The Laying on of Hands of Baptized Believers.* London: Benj. Harris, 1678; rev. 1698.

———. *Tropologia: A Key to Open Scripture Metaphors.* London: William Hill Collingridge, 1858.

Kell, Carl L., ed. *Exiled: Voices of the Southern Baptist Convention Holy War.* Knoxville: University of Tennessee Press, 2006.

Kell, Carl L., and Raymond Camp, eds. *In the Name of the Father: The Rhetoric of the New Southern Baptist Convention.* Carbondale: Southern Illinois University Press, 1999.

Kelly, J. N. D. *Early Christian Creeds.* 3rd ed. New York: Longman, 1972.

Kelsey, David H. *Proving Doctrine: The Uses of Scripture in Modern Theology.* Harrisburg, Pa.: Trinity International, 1999.

Kidd, Richard, ed. *On the Way of Trust.* Oxford: Whitley, 1997.

Kiffin, William. Preface to "A Glimpse of Syons Glory," by Thomas Goodwin. In *The Works of Thomas Goodwin*, vol. 12. Edinburgh: James Nichol, 1866.

————. *A Sober Discourse of Right to Church-Communion*. London: George Larkin, 1681.

————. *To Sions Virgins*. London, 1644.

————. "To the Reader." Preface to *Some Serious Reflections on That Part of Mr. Bunion's Confession of Faith: Touching Church Communion with Unbaptized Persons*, by Thomas Paul. London: Francis Smith, 1673.

Killinger, John. "The Changing Shape of Our Salvation." Breakout session at the General Assembly of the Cooperative Baptist Fellowship, Memphis, Tennessee, June 19, 2008.

————. *The Changing Shape of Our Salvation*. New York: Crossroad, 2007.

King, Henry Melville. *The Baptism of Roger Williams: A Review of Rev. Dr. W. H. Whitsitt's Inference*. Providence, R.I.: Preston & Rounds, 1897.

Knollys, Hanserd. *A Moderate Answer Unto Dr. Bastwicks Book: Called, Independency not Gods Ordinance*. London: Jane Coe, 1645.

————. *The Shining of a Flaming-fire in Zion*. London: Jane Cob, 1645.

Kostenberger, Andreas J., and Thomas R. Schreiner, eds. *Women in the Church: An Analysis and Application of 1 Timothy 2:9-15*. 2nd ed. Grand Rapids: Baker Academic, 2005.

Kovach, Stephen D., and Peter R. Schemm Jr. "A Defense of the Doctrine of the Eternal Subordination of the Son." *Journal of the Evangelical Theological Society* 42, no. 3 (1999): 461–76.

Kratt, Mary. *Marney*. Charlotte, N.C.: Myers Park Baptist Church, 1979.

Kreitzer, Larry J. *William Kiffen and His World*. Part 1. Oxford: Regent's Park College, 2010.

Kuhn, Thomas. *The Structures of Scientific Revolution*. 2nd ed. Chicago: University of Chicago Press, 1970.

Küng, Hans. *The Church*. Garden City, N.Y.: Image Books, 1976.

Lacan, Jacques. *The Seminar of Jacques Lacan*. Edited by Jacques-Alain Miller. New York: W. W. Norton, 1988.

LaCugna, Catherine Mowry. "The Baptismal Formula, Feminist Objections, and Trinitarian Theology." *Journal of Ecumenical Studies* 26, no. 2 (1989): 235–50.

Lake, Peter. "Anti-popery: The Structure of a Prejudice." In *Conflict in Early Stuart England: Studies in Religion and Politics, 1603–1642*, edited by Richard Cust and Ann Hughes, 72–106. London: Longman, 1989.

————. *The Boxmaker's Revenge: "Orthodoxy," "Heterodoxy" and the Politics of the Parish in Early Stuart London*. Stanford, Calif.: Stanford University Press, 2001.

————. *Moderate Puritans and the Elizabethan Church*. London: Cambridge University Press, 1982.

Lamb, Matthew, and Matthew Levering, eds. *Vatican II: Renewal within Tradition*. New York: Oxford University Press, 2008.

Lambe, Thomas. *A Confutation of Infants Baptisme*.[London?], 1643.

————. *Truth Prevailing Against Fiercest Opposition; or, An Answer to Mr. John*

Goodwins Water-Dipping No Firm Footing for Church Communion. London: G. Dawson, 1655.

Langford, Michael J. *A Liberal Theology for the Twenty-First Century.* Aldershot, U.K.: Ashgate, 2001.

Langhorne, George W. Review of *Baptism: Its Nature, Obligation, Subjects, and Benefits,* by Leonidas Rosser. *Quarterly Review of the Methodist Episcopal Church, South* 9, no. 2 (1855): 267–87.

Larson, Edward J. *Summer for the Gods: The Scopes Trial and America's Continuing Debate over Science and Religion.* New York: Basic Books, 1997.

Las Casas, Bartolomé de. *The Devastation of the Indies.* Translated by Herma Briffault. Baltimore: Johns Hopkins University Press, 1992.

Laud, William, and John Fisher. *A Relation of the Conference between William Laud, Late Lord Arch-Bishop of Canterbury, and Mr. Fisher the Jesuit.* Edited by C. H. Simpkinson. London: Macmillan, 1901.

Laws, Curtis Lee. "Convention Side Lights." *Watchman Examiner,* July 1, 1920.

Layman, David Wayne. "The Inner Ground of Christian Theology: Church, Faith, and Sectarianism." *Journal of Ecumenical Studies* 27, no. 3 (1990): 480–503.

Lee, Philip J. *Against the Protestant Gnostics.* New York: Oxford University Press, 1987.

Leith, John H., ed. *Creeds of the Churches.* Garden City, N.Y.: Doubleday, 1963.

Leithart, Peter. *Defending Constantine: The Twilight of an Empire and the Dawn of Christendom.* Downers Grove, Ill.: InterVarsity, 2010.

Leland, John. *The Writings of the Late Elder John Leland.* Edited by L. F. Greene. New York: G. W. Wood, 1845. Repr., New York: Arno Press, 1969.

Leonard, Bill J. *Baptist Ways: A History.* Valley Forge, Pa.: Judson Press, 2003.

———. *God's Last and Only Hope: The Fragmentation of the Southern Baptist Convention.* Grand Rapids: Eerdmans, 1990.

Letter to Keith Jones and BWA Resolutions Committee. June 23, 2004.

Levinas, Emmanuel. *Alterity and Transcendence.* Translated by Michael B. Smith. New York: Columbia University Press, 2000.

Levine, Joseph M. *The Autonomy of History.* Chicago: University of Chicago Press, 1999.

Lewis, C. S. Introduction to *On the Incarnation of the Word,* by Athanasius, 3–10. Crestwood, N.Y.: St. Vladimir's Theological Seminary Press, 1953.

———. *The Lion, the Witch and the Wardrobe.* New York: Macmillan, 1950.

Lewis, John. *A Brief History of the Rise and Progress of Anabaptism in England.* London, 1738.

Lienesch, Michael. *In the Beginning.* Chapel Hill: University of North Carolina Press, 2007.

Lienhard, J. T., E. C. Muller, and R. J. Teske, eds. *Collectanea Augustiniana. Augustine: Presbyter factus sum.* New York: Peter Lang, 1993.

Lim, Paul C. H. *Mystery Unveiled: The Crisis of the Trinity in Early Modern England.* New York: Oxford University Press, 2012.

Lindbeck, George A. "The Bible as Realistic Narrative." *Journal of Ecumenical Studies* 17, no. 1 (1980): 81–85.

———. *The Church in a Postliberal Age.* Edited by James J. Buckley. Grand Rapids: Eerdmans, 2002.

———. *The Nature of Doctrine.* Philadelphia: Westminster, 1984.

———. *Robert Lowry Calhoun as Historian of Doctrine.* Yale Divinity School Library Occasional Publication no. 12. New Haven, Conn.: Yale Divinity School Library, 1998.

———. "Scripture, Consensus and Community." In *Biblical Interpretation in Crisis: The Ratzinger Conference on Bible and Church*, edited by Richard John Neuhaus, 74–101. Grand Rapids: Eerdmans, 1989.

Lindsay, D. Michael. *Faith in the Halls of Power.* New York: Oxford University Press, 2007.

Lindsell, Harold. *The Battle for the Bible.* Grand Rapids: Zondervan, 1976.

Littell, Franklin H. *The Anabaptist View of the Church.* Boston: Starr King, 1958.

———. "The Historical Free Church Defined." *Brethren Life and Thought* 9, no. 4 (1964): 78–79. Reprinted in *Brethren Life and Thought* 50, nos. 3–4 (2005): 51–52.

Livingstone, E. A., ed. *The Oxford Dictionary of the Christian Church.* 3rd ed. Oxford: Oxford University Press, 1997.

Locke, John. *An Essay Concerning Human Understanding.* In *Great Books of the Western World*, vol. 35, edited by Robert Maynard Hutchins. Chicago: Encyclopaedia Britannica, 1952.

———. *A Letter Concerning Toleration.* New York: Liberal Arts, 1950.

Lorenzen, Thorwald. "Baptists and Ecumenicity with Special Reference to Baptism." *Review and Expositor* 72 (1980): 21–45.

Lubac, Henri de. *Corpus mysticum: L'eucharistie et l'église au moyen age.* Paris: Aubier, 1948.

———. *Corpus Mysticum: The Eucharist and the Church in the Middle Ages.* Translated by C. J. Gemma Simmonds, with Richard Price and Christopher Stephens. Edited by Laurence Paul Hemming and Susan Frank Parsons. Notre Dame, Ind.: University of Notre Dame Press, 2007.

———. *Medieval Exegesis: The Four Senses of Scripture.* 3 vols. Grand Rapids: Eerdmans, 1998–2009.

———. *The Mystery of the Supernatural.* London: G. Chapman, 1967.

———. *Paradoxes.* Paris: Livre français, 1946.

Lumpkin, William L., ed. *Baptist Confessions of Faith.* Rev. ed. Valley Forge, Pa.: Judson Press, 1969.

Luther, Martin. *Luther's Works.* American edition. 55 vols. St. Louis, Mo.: Concordia; Philadelphia: Fortress, 1955–1986.

————. "On the Bondage of the Will." In *Luther and Erasmus: Free Will and Salvation*, Library of Christian Classics, translated and edited by Gordon Rupp and Philip Watson, 101–334. Philadelphia: Westminster, 1969.

The Lutheran World Federation and the Catholic Church. Joint Declaration on the Doctrine of Justification. Accessed February 8, 2010. http://www.vatican.va/roman_curia/pontifical_councils/chrstuni/documents/rc_pc_chrstuni_doc_31101999_cath-luth-joint-declaration_en.html.

MacCulloch, Diarmaid. *Thomas Cranmer: A Life*. New Haven, Conn.: Yale University Press, 1996.

MacGregor, Geddes. *From a Christian Ghetto: Letters of Ghostly Wit, Written A.D. 2453*. London: Longmans, Green, 1954.

Macintosh, D. C. *Theology as Empirical Science*. New York: Macmillan, 1919.

MacIntyre, Alasdair. *After Virtue*. Notre Dame, Ind.: University of Notre Dame Press, 1981.

————. *Three Rival Versions of Moral Enquiry: Encyclopaedia, Genealogy, and Tradition*. Notre Dame, Ind.: University of Notre Dame Press, 1990.

Maclaren, Alexander. *Expositions of Holy Scripture: Corinthians*. Repr., Grand Rapids: Baker, 1974.

Maddox, Timothy D. "E. Y. Mullins: Mr. Baptist for the 20th and 21st Century." *Review and Expositor* 96, no. 1 (1999): 87–108.

Madison, James. "Memorial and Remonstrance against Religious Assessment." In *The Papers of James Madison*. Vol. 8, *March 10, 1784 to March 28, 1786*, edited by Robert E. Rutland and William M. E. Rachal, 295–306. Chicago: University of Chicago Press, 1984.

Malloy, Christopher J. "*Subsistit In*: Nonexclusive Identity or Full Identity?" *Thomist* 72 (2008): 1–44.

Manly, Basil, and A. Brooks Everett, eds. *Baptist Chorals: Tune and Hymn Book*. Richmond, Va.: T. J. Starke, 1859.

Manly, Basil, and B. Manly Jr., eds. *The Baptist Psalmody: A Selection of Hymns for the Worship of God*. Charleston, S.C.: Southern Baptist Publication Society, 1851.

Manly, Basil, Jr.. *A Sunday School in Every Church*. Charleston, S.C.: Southern Baptist Publication Society, 1858.

Manley, Kenneth R. "Origins of the Baptists: The Case for Development from Puritanism-Separatism." *Baptist History and Heritage* 22, no. 4 (1987): 34–46.

Mansell, Samuel. *An Appeal to the Christian Professing World; or the Doctrine of Three Co-Equal Divine Persons in the Godhead*. London: J. Parsons, 1796.

————. *A Second Address to Mr. Huntington*. London: J. Parsons, 1797.

Manz, Felix. "Protest and Defense." In *The Racial Reformation*, edited by Michael G. Baylor, 95–100. New York: Cambridge University Press, 1991.

Markus, Robert. *The End of Ancient Christianity*. Cambridge: Cambridge University Press, 1990.

Marlow, Isaac. *A Treatise of the Holy Trinunity*. London: Richard Baldwin, 1690.

Marney, Carlyle. "All the Sons of Earth." July 27, 1947. Box 52, Carlyle Marney papers. David M. Rubenstein Rare Book & Manuscript Library, Duke University.

———. *Beyond Our Time and Place*. Charlotte, N.C.: Endowment Fund of the Myers Park Baptist Church, 1975.

———. *The Carpenter's Son*. Nashville: Abingdon, 1967.

———. "Church and Race: A Never-Ending Winter?" Sermon preached at Riverside Church, New York City, October 18, 1964. Published in the *Pulpit*, February 1967, 4–6.

———. Column in the Myers Park Baptist *Church News*, Feb 27, 1962. Box 69, Carlyle Marney papers. David M. Rubenstein Rare Book & Manuscript Library, Duke University, Durham, N.C.

———. *The Coming Faith*. Nashville: Abingdon, 1970.

———. "Dayton's Long Hot Summer." In *D-Days at Dayton: Reflections on the Scopes Trial*, edited by Jerry R. Tompkins, 125–41. Baton Rouge: Louisiana State University Press, 1965.

———. "The Emancipation of a White." *Christian Century*, November 17, 1954.

———. "Escape from Provincialism." Handwritten notes, 1963. Box 69, Carlyle Marney papers. M. Rubenstein Rare Book & Manuscript Library, Duke University, Durham, N.C.

———. "The Eternal Security of the Believer." Sermon preached to the Baptist General Convention of Texas in San Antonio, Texas, 1953. Box 55, Carlyle Marney papers. David M. Rubenstein Rare Book & Manuscript Library, Duke University, Durham, N.C.

———. "For This Cause" (part II). Sermonpreached at First Baptist Church, Austin, Texas, October 16, 1955. Box 61, Carlyle Marney papers. David M. Rubenstein Rare Book & Manuscript Library, Duke University, Durham, N.C.

———. "From These Stones." In *The Pulpit Speaks on Race*, edited by Alfred T. Davis, 87–95. New York: Abingdon, 1965.

———. "Fundaments of Competent Ministry." *Duke Divinity School Review* 41, no. 1 (1976): 5–15.

———. "Hail and Farewell!" The Dickson Lectures at Myers Park Baptist Church, Charlotte, North Carolina. Published as *Beyond Our Time and Place*. Charlotte, N.C.: Myers Park Baptist Church, 1974.

———. *He Became Like Us*. Nashville: Abingdon, 1964.

———. Introduction to "Tragic Man—Tragic House." Unpublished manuscript, 1958. Box 63, Carlyle Marney papers. David M. Rubenstein Rare Book & Manuscript Library, Duke University, Durham, N.C.

———. "Learn to Live Together." From *These Things Remain*, televised message, September 30, 1955. Box 61, Carlyle Marney papers. David M. Rubenstein Rare Book & Manuscript Library, Duke University, Durham, N.C.

————. Letter from Carlyle Marney to J. G. Hughes, September 11, 1953. Box 24, Carlyle Marney papers. David M. Rubenstein Rare Book & Manuscript Library, Duke University, Durham, N.C.

————. "Liberalism: A Continuation—DeWolf on Continuity." *Religion and Life* 32, no. 3 (1963): 351–60.

————. "Peace but Not Yet." Sermon Preached at Myers Park Baptist Church, Charlotte, North Carolina, December 24, 1965. Box 70, Carlyle Marney papers. David M. Rubenstein Rare Book & Manuscript Library, Duke University, Durham, N.C.

————. "Preaching the Gospel, South of God: An Interview with Carlyle Marney," by Bill Finger. *Christian Century*, October 4, 1978.

————. "The Priest at Every Elbow." Sermon preached at Myers Park Baptist Church, Charlotte, North Carolina, June 14, 1964. Box 70, Carlyle Marney papers. David M. Rubenstein Rare Book & Manuscript Library, Duke University, Durham, N.C.

————. *Priests to Each Other.* Valley Forge, Pa.: Judson Press, 1974.

————. "The Prospect of Baptist Unity." Address in Atlantic City, New Jersey, May 22, 1964. Box 69, Carlyle Marney papers. David M. Rubenstein Rare Book & Manuscript Library, Duke University, Durham, N.C.

————. "The Recovery of Center." In Recovery of the Church Series—Pamphlet 1. Published for Members and Friends of Myers Park Baptist Church, Charlotte, North Carolina, 1958.

————. "The Recovery of Center." Message to the American Baptist Convention in Rochester, New York, 1960. Box 65, Carlyle Marney papers. David M. Rubenstein Rare Book & Manuscript Library, Duke University, Durham, N.C.

————. *The Recovery of the Person.* Nashville: Abingdon, 1963.

————. "Report on Graduate Work: Year, 1941–42" and "Report on Graduate Work: Year, 1943–44." Box 121, Carlyle Marney papers. David M. Rubenstein Rare Book & Manuscript Library, Duke University., Durham, N.C.

————. Review of *Baptism: Conscience and Clue for the Church*, by Warren Carr. *Religion in Life* 34, no. 1 (1964–1965): 157–58.

————. "The Rise of Ecclesiological Externalism to 337 A.D." Th.D. diss., Southern Baptist Theological Seminary, 1946.

————. *Structures of Prejudice.* Nashville: Abingdon, 1961.

————. "The Tent of Meeting." September 22, 1963. Box 69, Carlyle Marney papers. David M. Rubenstein Rare Book & Manuscript Library, Duke University, Durham, N.C.

————. "The Unity of the Faith." Pastors' Conference, Southern Baptist Convention, May 22, 1961. In *The Recovery of the Church.* Unpublished manuscript, ch. 1. Carlyle Marney papers. David M. Rubenstein Rare Book & Manuscript Library, Duke University, Durham, N.C.

————. "We Have This Treasure." Lecture 4 at the Summer School on "The Church and Evangelism," July 9, 1959. Sponsored by the Council of Southwestern Theological Schools.

————. "World Council of Churches: Christ, Our Hope." Sermon delivered at First Baptist Church, Austin, Tex., August 22, 1954. Box 57, the Carlyle Marney Papers. David M. Rubenstein Rare Book & Manuscript Library, Duke University, Durham, N.C.

"Marney's Sermon to Nation: Peace Requires a New Man." *Charlotte News*, December 25, 1965.

Marpeck, Pilgram. *The Writings of Pilgram Marpeck*. Edited and translated by William Klassen and Walter Klaasen. Scottdale, Pa.: Herald Press, 1978.

Marsden, George M. *Fundamentalism and American Culture*. New York: Oxford University Press, 1980.

Marsden, George M., and Bradley J. Longfield. *The Secularization of the Academy*. New York: Oxford University Press, 1992.

Marsh, Charles. *God's Long Summer: Stories of Faith and Civil Rights*. Princeton, N.J.: Princeton University Press, 1997.

Marshall, Molly T. "Reading Scripture with the Spirit." *Baptistic Theologies* 3, no. 2 (2011): 8–12.

Marty, Martin E. "Baptistification Takes Over." *Christianity Today*, September 2, 1983.

Masters, Frank M. *A History of Baptists in Kentucky*. Louisville, Ky.: Baptist Historical Society, 1953.

Mathews, Donald G. *Religion in the Old South*. Chicago: University of Chicago Press, 1977.

Mathews, Shailer. *The Faith of Modernism*. New York: Macmillan, 1924.

Mays, Benjamin E. "Democratizing and Christianizing America in This Generation." *Journal of Negro Education* 14, no. 4 (1945): 527–34.

————. "The Moral Aspects of Segregation." In *The Segregation Decisions: Papers Read at a Session of the Twenty-First Annual Meeting of the Southern Historical Association, Memphis, Tennessee, November 10, 1955*, edited by William Faulkner, 13–18. Atlanta: Southern Regional Council, 1956.

————. *The Negro's God as Reflected in His Literature*. Boston: Chapman & Grimes, 1938. Repr., New York: Negro Universities Press, 1969.

————. *Seeking to Be a Christian in Race Relations*. New York: Friendship Press, 1957.

McBain, L. Doward. "Clergy-Lay Issues and Relations: The Baptist Perspective." *Foundations* 15, no. 2 (1972): 156–62.

McBeth, H. Leon. *The Baptist Heritage*. Nashville: Broadman, 1987.

————. *A Sourcebook for Baptist Heritage*. Nashville: Broadman, 1990.

McCabe, Herbert. *God Matters*. London: Geoffrey Chapman, 1987.

McClendon, James Wm., Jr. "Baptism as a Performative Sign." *Theology Today* 23, no. 3 (1966): 403–16.

―――. *Doctrine: Systematic Theology, Volume II.* Nashville: Abingdon, 1994. Reprinted with a new introduction by Curtis W. Freeman. Waco, Tex.: Baylor University Press, 2012.

―――. *Ethics: Systematic Theology, Volume I.* Nashville: Abingdon, 1986. 2nd ed., rev. and enlarged. Nashville: Abingdon, 2002. Repr. with a new introduction by Curtis W. Freeman. Waco, Tex.: Baylor University Press, 2012. The Baylor University Press edition is a reprint of the Abingdon 2nd ed., rev. and enlarged (2002) and follows the pagination of that edition.

―――. "A New Way to Read the Bible." The A. O. Collins Lectures, Houston Baptist University, Houston, Tex., April 1995.

―――. "Philippians 2:5-11." *Review and Expositor* 88, no. 4 (1991): 439–44.

―――. "The Radical Road One Baptist Took." *Mennonite Quarterly Review* 74, no. 4 (2000): 503–10.

―――. "Some Reflections on the Future of Trinitarianism." *Review and Expositor* 63, no. 2 (1966): 149–56.

―――. "What Is a Southern Baptist Ecumenism?" *Southwestern Journal of Theology* 10, no. 2 (1968): 73–78.

―――. *Witness: Systematic Theology, Volume III.* Nashville: Abingdon, 2000. Repr. with a new introduction by Curtis W. Freeman. Waco, Tex.: Baylor University Press, 2012.

McClendon, James Wm., Jr., and James M. Smith. *Convictions: Defusing Religious Relativism.* Rev. ed. Valley Forge, Pa.: Trinity International, 1994.

McClendon, James Wm., Jr., and John Howard Yoder. "Christian Identity in Ecumenical Perspective: A Response to David Wayne Layman." *Journal of Ecumenical Studies* 27, no. 3 (1990): 561–80.

McDaniel, James, A. McDowell, and G. W. Johnson. "A Challenge." *Biblical Recorder,* July 12, 1855. Accessed July 14, 2013. http://recorder.zsr.wfu.edu/Repository/ml.asp?Ref=QkNSLzE4NTUvMDcvMTIjQXIwMDIwMA%3D%3D&Mode=Gif&Locale=english-skin-custom.

McDonnell, Kilian. "The Ratzinger/Kasper Debate: The Universal Church and Local Churches." *Theologial Studies* 63, no. 2 (2002): 227–50.

McGrath, Alister E., ed. *The Blackwell Encyclopedia of Modern Christian Thought.* Cambridge: Blackwell, 1993.

McKim, Donald K., ed. *Major Themes in the Reformed Tradition.* Grand Rapids: Eerdmans, 1992.

McKnight, Edgar V. "How to Read and How Not to Read the Bible: Lessons from Münster." *Perspectives in Religious Studies* 24, no. 1 (1997): 77–99.

McLachlan, H. John. *Socinianism in Seventeenth-Century England.* Oxford: Oxford University Press, 1951.

McLaren, Brian D. *A Generous Orthodoxy.* Grand Rapids: Zondervan, 2004.

McLoughlin, William G. *New England Dissent, 1630–1833: The Baptists and the Separation of Church and State.* 2 vols. Cambridge, Mass.: Harvard University Press, 1971.

————. *Soul Liberty: The Baptists' Struggle in New England, 1630–1833.* Providence: Brown University Press, 1991.

Mencken, H. L. "The Monkey Trial: A Reporter's Account." In *D-Days at Dayton: Reflections on the Scopes Trial,* edited by Jerry R. Tompkins, 35–51. Baton Rouge: Louisiana State University Press, 1965.

Metzger, Bruce Manning. *The Text of the New Testament.* 2nd ed. New York: Oxford University Press, 1968.

Miller, Donald E. *The Case for Liberal Christianity.* San Francisco: Harper, 1981.

Miller, Perry. *The New England Mind: From Colony to Province.* Cambridge, Mass.: Belknap Press, 1953.

————. "Roger Williams: An Essay in Interpretation." In *The Complete Writings of Roger Williams,* 7:5–25. New York: Russell & Russell, 1963. Repr., Paris, Ark.: Baptist Standard Bearer, 2005.

————. *Roger Williams: His Contribution to the American Tradition.* Indianapolis, Ind.: Bobbs-Merrill, 1953.

Miller, Robert Moats. *Harry Emerson Fosdick: Preacher, Pastor, Prophet.* New York: Oxford University Press, 1985.

Milton, Anthony. *Catholic and Reformed: The Roman and Protestant Churches in English Protestant Thought, 1600–1640.* Cambridge: Cambridge University Press, 1995.

Milton, John. *John Milton Complete Poems and Major Prose,* edited by Merritt Y. Hughes. New York: Macmillan, 1957.

Minus, Paul M. *Walter Rauschenbusch: American Reformer.* New York: Macmillan, 1988.

Minute Book of the Deacon Board, Watts Street Baptist Church, Durham, North Carolina, Watts Street Baptist Church, Heritage Collection.

Minutes of the Austin Baptist Association, October 10–11, 1955. Texas Baptist Historical Collection, Dallas, Tex.

Minutes of the Philadelphia Baptist Association (1707–1807). Edited by A. D. Gillette. Philadelphia: American Baptist Publication Society, 1851.

Minutes of the Watts Street Baptist Church, Durham, North Carolina. Watts Street Baptist Church, Heritage Collection.

Minutes of the Yates Baptist Association, North Carolina. October 25, 1960. Yates Baptist Association, Durham, N.C.

Mohler, R. Albert, Jr. Introduction to *The Axioms of Religion,* by E. Y. Mullins, 1–32. Nashville: Broadman & Holman, 1997.

Monck, Thomas. *A Cure for the Cankering Error of the New Eutychians.* London, 1673.

Moody, Dale. *Baptism: Foundation for Christian Unity.* Philadelphia: Westminster, 1967.

————. *The Word of Truth.* Grand Rapids: Eerdmans, 1981.

Moore, LeRoy. "Roger Williams and the Historians." *Church History* 32, no. 4 (1963): 432–51.

————. "Roger Williams as an Enduring Symbol for Baptists." *Journal of Church and State* 7, no. 2 (1965): 181–89.

Moore, Russell. "The Moderates Were Right." *Baptist Press News,* July 7, 2004.

Morden, Peter J. "The Lord's Supper and the Spirituality of C. H. Spurgeon." In *Baptist Sacramentalism 2,* ed. Anthony R. Cross and Philip E. Thompson (Milton Keynes, U.K.: Paternoster, 2008).

————. "The Spirituality of C. H. Spurgeon: Maintaining Communion. The Lord's Supper," *Baptistic Theologies* 4, no. 1 (2012): 41–45.

Morgan, Abel. Letter to London Baptists. In *Baptist Life and Thought, 1600–1980,* edited by William H. Brackney, 85. Valley Forge, Pa.: Judson Press, 1983.

Morgan, D. Densil. *Barth Reception in Britain.* London: T&T Clark, 2010.

Morgan, David T. *The New Crusades, the New Holy Land: Conflict in the Southern Baptist Convention, 1969–1991.* Tuscaloosa: University of Alabama Press, 1996.

Morgan, Edmund Sears. *Roger Williams: The Church and the State.* New York: Harcourt, Brace & World, 1967.

————. *Visible Saints: The History of a Puritan Idea.* New York: New York University Press, 1963.

Mortimer, Sarah. *Reason and Religion in the English Revolution: The Challenge of Socinianism.* Cambridge: Cambridge University Press, 2010.

Mueller, William A. *A History of Southern Baptist Theological Seminary.* Nashville: Broadman, 1959.

Mulder, Philip N. *A Controversial Spirit: Evangelical Awakenings in the South.* Oxford: Oxford University Press, 2002.

Mullins, E. Y. [Edgar Young]. *The Axioms of Religion.* Philadelphia: Judson Press, 1908.

————. *Baptist Beliefs.* Philadelphia: Judson Press, 1925.

————. *The Christian Religion in Its Doctrinal Expression.* Nashville: Sunday School Board of the Southern Baptist Convention, 1917.

————. "The Contribution of Baptists to the Interpretation of Christianity." *Review & Expositor* 20, no. 4 (1923): 383–95.

————. "Is Jesus Christ the Author of Religious Experience?" *Baptist Review and Expositor* 1, no. 2 (1904): 55–70.

————. *Talks on Soul Winning.* Nashville: Sunday School Board of the Southern Baptist Convention, 1920.

————. "The Testimony of Christian Experience." In *The Fundamentals: A Testimony to the Truth,* edited by R. A. Torrey and A. C. Dixon, 4:314–23. 1917. Repr., Grand Rapids: Baker Books, 1980.

Murphy, Nancey. *Beyond Liberalism and Fundamentalism.* Valley Forge, Pa.: Trinity Press, 1996.

Murray, Paul D., ed. *Receptive Ecumenism and the Call to Catholic Learning: Exploring a Way for Contemporary Ecumenism.* New York: Oxford University Press, 2008.

Nation, Mark Thiessen. "Jim McClendon, Jr.: A Particular Baptist Theologian." *Journal of European Baptist Studies* 1, no. 2 (2001): 51–55.

The Nature and Mission of the Church: A Stage on the Way to a Common Statement. Faith and Order Paper no. 198. Geneva: World Council of Churches, 2005.

Naylor, Peter. *Calvinism, Communion and the Baptists: A Study of English Calvinistic Baptists from the Late 1600s to the Early 1800s.* Milton Keynes, U.K.: Paternoster, 2004.

Neal, Daniel. *The History of the Puritans.* London: Thomas Tegg & Son, 1837.

Nettles, Thomas J. *The Baptists: Key People Involved in Forming a Baptist Identity.* Fearn, Scotland: Mentor, 2005–2007.

————. *By His Grace and for His Glory.* Grand Rapids: Baker, 1986.

————. "The Rise and Demise of Calvinism among Southern Baptists." *Founders Journal* 19, no. 20 (1995): 6–21.

Neuhaus, Richard John. *Freedom for Ministry.* Rev. ed. Grand Rapids: Eerdmans, 1992.

————. "The Unhappy Fate of Optional Orthodoxy." *First Things* 69 (1997): 57–60.

Nevin, John Williamson. *Catholic and Reformed: Selected Theological Writings of John Williamson Nevin.* Edited by Charles Yrigoyen Jr. and George H. Bricker. Pittsburgh, Pa.: Pickwick, 1978.

————. "The Sect System." *Mercersburg Review* 1, no. 5 (1849): 482–507; and *Mercersburg Review* 1, no. 6 (1849): 521–39. Republished in *Catholic and Reformed: Selected Theological Writings of John Williamson Nevin,* edited by Charles Yrigoyen Jr. and George H. Bricker. Pittsburgh, Pa.: Pickwick, 1978.

————. "The Theology of the New Liturgy." *Mercersburg Review* 14, no. 1 (1867): 23–45.

Newbigin, Lesslie. *The Household of God.* London: SCM Press, 1953. Repr., New York: Friendship Press, 1954.

Newman, Albert Henry. *A History of Anti-Pedobaptism.* Philadelphia: American Baptist Publication Society, 1897.

————. *A History of the Baptist Churches in the United States.* New York: Christian Literature, 1894.

Newman, John Henry. *An Essay on the Development of Christian Doctrine.* 6th ed. Notre Dame, Ind.: University of Notre Dame Press, 1989.

————. *On Consulting the Faithful in Matters of Doctrine.* New York: Sheed & Ward, 1961.

Newman, Stewart A. *W. T. Conner: Theologian of the Southwest.* Nashville: Broadman, 1964.

New Road Baptist Church, Oxford, England. The Church Covenant of 1780. Accessed March 26, 2012. http://www.newroadbaptistchurchoxford.co.uk/content/pages/documents/1312454439.pdf.

Ney, Julius. *Geschichte des Reichstages zu Speyer im Jahre 1529: Mit einem Anhange ungedruckter Akten und Briefe.* Hamburg: Angentur des Rauhen Hauses, 1880.

Niebuhr, H. Richard. "The Doctrine of the Trinity and the Unity of the Church." *Theology Today* 3, no. 3 (1946): 371–84.

―――. *The Social Sources of Denominationalism*. New York: H. Holt, 1929.

Nixon, Pat Ireland. *A History of the Texas Medical Association 1853–1953*. Austin: University of Texas Press, 1953.

Noll, Mark A. "Common Sense Traditions and American Evangelical Thought." *American Quarterly* 37, no. 2 (1985): 216–38.

―――. *The Scandal of the Evangelical Mind*. Grand Rapids: Eerdmans, 1994.

"'Nones' on the Rise: One-in-Five Adults Have No Religious Affiliation." *Pew Forum on Religion & Public Life*, October 9, 2012. Accessed January 12, 2013. http://www.pewforum.org/uploadedFiles/Topics/Religious_Affiliation/ Unaffiliated/NonesOnTheRise-full.pdf.

Norris, R. A. *The Christological Controversy*. Philadelphia: Fortress, 1980.

North Creek Baptist Church. Minute book, North Creek Primitive Baptist Church, 1790–1890. Box 1, folder 1. David M. Rubenstein Rare Book & Manuscript Library, Duke University, Durham, N.C.

Nuechterlein, James. "In Defense of Sectarian Catholicity." *First Things* 69 (1997): 12–13.

Null, Ashley. "Conversion to Communion: Thomas Cranmer on a Favourite Puritan Theme." *Churchman* 116, no. 3 (2002): 239–57.

Nutt, Thomas, and Edward Barber. *The Humble Request of Certain Christians Reproachfully Called Anabaptists*. London, 1643.

Nuttall, Geoffrey F. *The Holy Spirit in Puritan Faith and Experience*. Oxford: Basil Blackwell, 1946.

―――. *The Puritan Spirit: Essays and Addresses*. London: Epworth Press, 1967.

Nye, Stephen. *A Brief History of the Unitarians, Called also Socinians in Four Letters, Written to a Friend*. London, 1687.

―――. *The Faith of One God, who is only the Father*. London, 1691.

Oden, Thomas C. *The Rebirth of Orthodoxy: Signs of New Life in Christianity*. San Francisco: HarperSanFrancisco, 2003.

―――. *Systematic Theology*. 3 vols. San Francisco: Harper & Row, 1987–1992.

Odle, Joe T. "Should Southern Baptists Have a Creed/Confession?—Yes!" *Review and Expositor* 76, no. 1 (1979): 89–94.

"Official Documents of the Joint Ecumenical Commission with Regard to the Assignment 'The Condemnations in the Protestant Confessions and in the Doctrinal Decisions of the Council of Trent Which No Longer Apply to Our Partner Today,'" May 6–7, 1981. In *The Condemnations of the Reformation Era: Do They Still Divide?* edited by Karl Lehmann and Wolfhart Pannenberg, 168–69. Minneapolis: Fortress, 1990.

Ogden, Schubert. *The Reality of God*. New York: Harper, 1966.

Olson, Roger. "Post-conservative Evangelicals Greet the Postmodern Age." *Christian Century*, May 3, 1995.

————. *Reformed and Always Reforming: The Postconservative Approach to Evangelical Theology*. Grand Rapids: Baker Academic, 2007.

————. *The Story of Christian Theology: Twenty Centuries of Tradition & Reform*. Downers Grove, Ill.: InterVarsity, 1999.

O'Malley, John W. *What Happened at Vatican II?* Cambridge, Mass.: Belknap/Harvard University Press, 2008.

One Baptism: Towards Mutual Recognition. Faith and Order Paper no. 210. Geneva: World Council of Churches, 2011.

Orchard, G. H. *A Concise History of the Baptists*. Nashville: Graves, Marks & Rutland, agents of Tenn. Publication Society; New York: Sheldon, Lamport, 1855.

Owen, John. *Vindiciae Evangelicae; or, The Mystery of the Gospell Vindicated, and Socinianisme Examined*. Oxford: Leon Lichfield, 1655.

Owen, John, et al. *The Humble Proposals*. London: Robert Ibbitson, 1652.

Parratt, J. K. "An Early Baptist on the Laying On of Hands." *Baptist Quarterly* 21, no. 7 (1996): 325–27.

Parrington, Vernon Louis. *Main Currents in American Thought*. New York: Harcourt, Brace, 1927.

Parry, Robin. *Worshipping Trinity: Coming Back to the Heart of Worship*. Milton Keynes, U.K.: Paternoster, 2005.

Patterns and Prayers for Christian Worship. Oxford: Oxford University Press, 1991.

Patterson, James A. *James Robinson Graves: Staking the Boundaries of Baptist Identity*. Nashville: Broadman & Holman, 2012.

Patterson, W. Morgan. *Baptist Successionism: A Critical View*. Valley Forge, Pa.: Judson Press, 1969.

————. "The Southern Baptist Theologian as Controversialist." *Baptist History and Heritage* 15 (1980): 7–14, 57.

Paul, Thomas. *Some Serious Reflections on That Part of Mr. Bunion's Confession of Faith: Touching Church Communion with Unbaptized Persons*. London: Francis Smith, 1673.

Payne, Ernest A. *The Baptist Union: A Short History*. London: Carey Kingsgate Press, 1959.

————. "Contacts between Mennonites and Baptists." *Foundations* 4, no. 4 (1961): 39–55.

————. *The Fellowship of Believers: Baptist Thought and Practice Yesterday and Today*. Enlarged ed. London: Carey Kingsgate Press, 1952.

————. *Free Churchmen, Unrepentant and Repentant*. London: Carey Kingsgate Press, 1965.

————. Preface to *The Teaching of the Church Regarding Baptism*, by Karl Barth, 5–7. London: SCM Press, 1948.

————. *Thomas Helwys and the First Baptist Church in England*. 2nd ed. London: Baptist Union, 1966.

————. "Who Were the Baptists?" *Baptist Quarterly* 16, no. 8 (1956): 339–42.

Payne, Ernest A., and Stephen F. Winward, eds. *Orders and Prayers for Church Worship*. London: Baptist Union, 1967.

Peck, George, and Robert Trisco. "Christian Freedom and Ecclesiastical Authority." *Foundations* 11, no. 3 (1968): 197–206.

Peirce, James. *Plain Christianity Defended*. London: J. Noon, 1719.

Pelikan, Jaroslav. *Credo: Historical and Theological Guide to Creeds and Confessions of Faith in the Christian Tradition*. New Haven, Conn.: Yale University Press, 2003.

————. *The Riddle of Roman Catholicism*. New York: Abingdon, 1959.

Pelikan, Jaroslav, and Valerie Hotchkiss, eds. *Creeds and Confessions of Faith in the Christian Tradition*. 4 vols. New Haven, Conn.: Yale University Press, 2003.

Pelt, Michael R. *A History of Original Free Will Baptists*. Mt. Olive, N.C.: Mt. Olive College Press, 1996.

Perkins, William. *A Reformed Catholike; or, A Declaration Shewing How Neere We May Come to the Present Church of Rome in Sundrie Points of Religion*. Cambridge: John Legat, 1598.

————. *The Work of William Perkins*. Edited by Ian Breward. Abingdon, U.K.: Sutton Courtenay Press, 1970. Originally published 1607 by Felix Kyngston, London.

The Petition of Divers Gathered Churches, and others wel affected, in and about the city of London, for declaring the ordinance of the Lords and Commons, for punishing blasphemies and heresies, null and void. London, 1655.

Pharr, Clyde, ed. and trans. *The Theodosian Code*. Princeton, N.J.: Princeton University Press, 1952.

Philips, Dietrich. "The Church of God." In *Enchiridion*, translated by A. B. Kolb, 386–88. Elkhart, Ind.: Mennonite, 1910.

Philips, Dirk. *The Writings of Dirk Philips, 1504–1568*. Translated and edited by Cornelius J. Dyck, William E. Keeney, Alvin J. Beachy. Scottdale, Pa.: Herald Press, 1992.

Philips, George. *A Reply to a Confutation of Some Grounds for Infant Baptisme: As Also, Concerning the Form of a Church Put Forth Against Mee By One Thomas Lamb*. London: Matthew Simmons, 1645.

Phillips, Timothy R., and Dennis L. Okholm, eds. *The Nature of Confession: Evangelicals and Postliberals in Conversation*. Downers Grove, Ill.: InterVarsity, 1996.

Pinnock, Clark H. *The Scripture Principle*. San Francisco: Harper & Row, 1984.

Pipes, Carol. "Lord's Supper: LifeWay Surveys Churches' Practices, Frequency." *Baptist Press*, September 17, 2012. Accessed July 14, 2013. http://www.bpnews.net/bpnews.asp?id=38730.

Pipkin, H. Wayne. *Zwingli: The Positive Value of His Eucharistic Writings*. Leeds, U.K.: Yorkshire Baptist Association, 1986.

Pitts, William L. "Debating the True Church on the Grounds of Believer's

Baptism: The Ecclesiology of Hanserd Knollys." *Baptist History and Heritage* 47, no. 2 (2012): 55–67.

Placher, William C. "Christ Takes Our Place: Rethinking Atonement." *Interpretation* 53, no. 1 (1999): 5–20.

———. "How Does Jesus Save?" *Christian Century*, June 2, 2009.

Pleasants, Phyllis Rodgerson. "E. Y. Mullins: Diplomatic Theological Leader." *Review and Expositor* 96, no. 1 (1999): 43–60.

Pope, Liston. *The Kingdom beyond Caste*. New York: Friendship, 1957.

———. *Millhands and Preachers: A Study of Gastonia*. New Haven, Conn.: Yale University Press, 1942.

Poteat, Edwin McNeill, Jr. *Jesus and the Liberal Mind*. Philadelphia: Judson Press, 1934.

Powell, Vavasor. *Spirituall Experiences, of Sundry Beleevers*. London: Robert Ibbitson, 1653.

Proceedings of the Southern Baptist Convention. Richmond, Va.: H. K. Ellyson, 1845.

Purefoy, George W. *A History of the Sandy Creek Baptist Association*. New York: Sheldon, 1859.

———. *Pedobaptist Immersions: A Desultory Treatise*. Forestville, N.C.: North Carolina Baptist Bible & Publication Society, 1854.

———. *A Sermon*. Nashville: Southwestern Publishing House, 1858.

———. *The Tekel of Methodism: History of Episcopal Methodism in Which Its Claims to Being a Church of Christ Are Investigated*. Chapel Hill, N.C.: The Gazette, 1858.

Quinter, James. *A Debate on Trine Immersion, the Lord's Supper, and Feet-Washing*. Cincinnati: H. S. Bosworth, 1867.

———. *A Defence of Trine Immersion*. Columbiana, Ohio: Gospel Visitor, 1862.

———. *A Vindication of Trine Immersion as the Apostolic Form of Christian Baptism*. Huntingdon, Pa.: Brethren's Publishing, 1886.

Rahner, Karl, ed. *Encyclopedia of Theology: The Concise* Sacramentum Mundi. New York: Seabury, 1975.

———. *The Trinity*. Translated by Joseph Donceel. New York: Continuum, 1974.

Ramm, Bernard. *Protestant Biblical Interpretation*. Boston: Wilde, 1950.

Ranck, George W. *The Traveling Church: An Account of the Baptist Exodus from Virginia to Kentucky in 1781 under the Leadership of Rev. Lewis Craig and Capt. William Ellis*. Louisville, Ky.: n.p., 1910.

Randall, Ian M. *Communities of Conviction*. Schwarzenfeld: Neufeld Verlag, 2009.

———. "'Counsel and Help': European Baptists and Wider Baptist Fellowship." Paper presented at a symposium on the local church at the German Baptist Seminary in Elstal, March 21–24, 2007.

———. *The English Baptists of the Twentieth Century*. Didcot, U.K.: Baptist Historical Society, 2005.

———. "Every Apostolic Church a Mission Society." In *Ecumenism and History*, edited by Anthony R. Cross, 281–301. Carlisle, U.K.: Paternoster, 2002.

Ratzinger, Joseph. *Call to Communion.* San Francisco: Ignatius Press, 1991.

————. "The Local Church and the Universal Church." *America,* November 19, 2001.

Raughley, Ralph C., Jr., ed. *New Frontiers of Christianity.* New York: Association Press, 1962.

Rauschenbusch, Walter. *Christianity and the Social Crisis.* New York: Macmillan, 1907, 1912. Repr., Louisville, Ky.: Westminster John Knox, 1991.

————. *Christianizing the Social Order.* New York: Macmillan, 1912. Repr., Waco, Tex.: Baylor University Press, 2010.

————. "Why I Am a Baptist." *Rochester Baptist Monthly,* November 1905. Reprinted in *Colgate Rochester Divinity School Bulletin,* 1938.

Rawson, George. "We Limit Not the Truth of God." In *The Baptist Church Hymnal,* 211. London: Psalms and Hymns Trust, 1900.

Receptive Ecumenism and the Local Church. Newsletter of the project in Receptive Ecumenism. Accessed February 14, 2010. https://www.dur.ac.uk/theology .religion/ccs/projects/receptiveecumenism/phasetwo/.

Records of Rhode Island. Also known as *Records of the Colony of Rhode Island and Providence Plantations.* Providence: A. Crawford Greene & Brother, 1856–1865.

Reimer, A. James. "Theological Orthodoxy, Constantinianism, and Theology from a Radical Protestant Perspective." In *Faith to Creed: Ecumenical Perspectives on the Affirmation of the Apostolic Faith in the Fourth Century,* edited by S. Mark Heim, 129–61. Grand Rapids: Eerdmans, 1991.

Reiser, William E. "Roman Catholic Understanding of the Eucharist." *Southwestern Journal of Theology* 28, no. 2 (1986): 85–91.

"Religion: The Southern Baptists." *Time,* October 17, 1960.

Rempel, John D. *The Lord's Supper in Anabaptism.* Scottdale, Pa.: Herald Press, 1993.

————. "Toward an Anabaptist Theology of the Lord's Supper." In *The Lord's Supper: Believers Church Perspectives,* edited by Dale R. Stoffer, 243–49. Scottdale, Pa.: Herald Press, 1997.

"Rev. J. R. Graves at Chapel Hill." *The Biblical Recorder,* June 28, 1855. Accessed July 14, 2013. http://recorder.zsr.wfu.edu/Repository/ml.asp?Ref=QkNSL ze4NTUvMDYvMjgjQXIwMDIxMg%3D%3D&Mode=Gif&Locale=en glish-skin-custom.

Richey, Russell E., Kenneth E. Rowe, and Jean Miller Schmidt. *The Methodist Experience in America: A History.* Vol. 1 of *The Methodist Experience in America.* Nashville: Abingdon, 2010.

Ricœur, Paul. *The Symbolism of Evil.* Boston: Beacon, 1967.

Rite of Christian Initiation of Adults. Study ed. Washington, D.C.: United States Catholic Conference, 1988.

Ritor, Andrew. *A Treatise of The Vanity of Childish-Baptisme.* London, 1642.

Rivera, Luis N. *A Violent Evangelism: The Political and Religious Conquest of the Americas.* Louisville, Ky.: Westminster John Knox, 1992.

Roach, David. "CBF Presenter Questions Christ's Deity." *Baptist Press*, June 19, 2008. Accessed September 10, 2009. http://www.baptistpress.org/bpnews .asp?id=28326.

Robert, Henry M. *Pocket Manual of Rules and Order for Deliberative Assemblies*. Chicago: S. C. Griggs, 1876.

————. *Robert's Rules of Order*. Chicago: Scott, Foresman, 1915.

Roberts, Alexander, and James Donaldson, eds. *The Ante-Nicene Fathers: Translations of the Writings of the Fathers Down to A.D. 325*. American reprint of the Edinburgh ed., rev. and chronologically arranged with brief prefaces and occasional notes by A. Cleveland Coxe. Grand Rapids: Eerdmans, 1978-1981.

Roberts-Thomson, Edward. *With Hands Outstretched: Baptists and the Ecumenical Movement*. London: Marshall, Morgan & Scott, 1962.

Robinson, James Harvey. *Readings in European History*. Boston: Ginn, 1906.

Robinson, John. *Honest to God*. London: SCM Press, 1963.

————. *The Works of John Robinson: Pastor of the Pilgrim Fathers*. Edited by Robert Ashton. 3 vols. London: John Snow, 1851.

Rogers, Jack B., and Donald K. McKim. *The Authority and Interpretation of the Bible: A Historical Approach*. New York: Harper & Row, 1979.

Rogers, John. *Ohel or Beth-Shamesh, A Tabernacle for the Sun*. London: Printed for R. Ibbitson, 1653.

Rosser, Leonidas. *Baptism: Its Nature, Obligation, Mode, Subjects, and Benefits*. Richmond, Va.: by the author, 1855.

————. *Reply to Evils of Infant Baptism*. Richmond, Va.: by the author, 1855.

Ruberstone, Patricia. *Grave Undertakings: An Archaeology of Roger Williams and the Narragansett Indians*. Washington, D.C.: Smithsonian Institution, 2001.

Ruddy, Christopher. *The Local Church: Tillard and the Future of Catholic Ecclesiology*. New York: Herder & Herder, 2006.

Ruth, Lester. "How Great *Is* Our God: The Trinity in Contemporary Christian Worship Music." In *The Message in the Music: Studying Contemporary Praise and Worship*, edited by Robert Woods and Brian Walrath, 29–42. Nashville: Abingdon, 2007.

————. "*Lex Amandi, Lex Orandi*: The Trinity in the Most-Used Contemporary Christian Worship Songs." In *The Place of Christ in Liturgical Prayer*, edited by Bryan D. Spinks, 342–59. Collegeville, Minn.: Liturgical, 2008.

Said, Edward W. *Orientalism*. New York: Vintage Books, 1979.

————. "Representing the Colonized: Anthropology's Interlocutors." *Critical Inquiry* 15, no. 2 (1989): 205–25.

"Salters' Hall 1719 and the Baptists." *Transactions of the Baptist Historical Society* 5, no. 3 (1917): 172–89.

Sanders, Fred. *The Image of the Immanent Trinity: Rahner's Rule and the Theological Interpretation of Scripture*. New York: Peter Lang, 2005.

Sandy Creek Baptist Association. Principles of Faith. In *A History of the Sandy*

Creek Baptist Association, by George W. Purefoy, 105. New York: Sheldon, 1859.

Sayers, Dorothy. *Creed or Chaos*. New York: Harcourt, Brace, 1949.

Scalise, Charles. Review of *Towards Baptist Catholicity*, by Steven R. Harmon. *Perspectives in Religious Studies* 35, no. 4 (2008): 433–35.

Schaff, Philip. *The Creeds of Christendom*. New York: Harper, 1877.

———. *The Principle of Protestantism*. Translated by John Nevin. Chambersburg: Publication Office of the German Reformed Church, 1845.

———. *A Select Library of the Nicene and Post-Nicene Fathers of the Christian Church, First Series*. Grand Rapids: Eerdmans, 1978-1979.

Schaff, Philip, and Henry Wace. *A Select Library of Nicene and Post-Nicene Fathers of the Christian Church, Second Series*. Grand Rapids: Eerdmans, 1978-1979.

Schlabach, Gerald W. "The Correction of the Augustinians: A Case Study in the Critical Appropriation of a Suspect Tradition." In *The Free Church and the Early Church: Bridging the Historical and Theological Divide*, edited by D. H. Williams, 47–74. Grand Rapids: Eerdmans, 2002.

Schleiermacher, Friedrich. *The Christian Faith*. Edited and translated by H. R. Macintosh and J. S. Stewart. Edinburgh: T&T Clark, 1928. Repr., Philadelphia: Fortress, 1976.

———. *On Religion: Speeches to Its Cultured Despisers*. Translated by John Oman. Louisville, Ky.: Westminster John Knox, 1994.

Schmeltekopf, Donald D., and Dianna M. Vitanza, eds. *The Future of Baptist Higher Education*. Waco, Tex.: Baylor University Press, 2006.

Schmidt, Leigh, and Sally Promey, eds. *American Religious Liberalism*. Bloomington: Indiana University Press, 2012.

Schreiner, Thomas R., and Shawn D. Wright, eds. *Believer's Baptism: Sign of the New Covenant in Christ*. Nashville: B&H Academic, 2006.

Schuessler, Jennifer. "A Religious Legacy, with Its Leftward Tilt, Is Reconsidered." *New York Times*, July 23, 2013.

Schweiger, Beth Barton. "Max Weber in Mount Airy; or, Revivals and Social Theory in the Early South." In *Religion in the American South: Protestants and Others in History and Culture*, edited by Beth Barton Schweiger and Donald G. Mathews, 31–66. Chapel Hill: University of North Carolina Press, 2004.

Searle, John R. *Speech Acts*. London: Cambridge University Press, 1969.

A Second Beacon Fired. London, 1654.

Segler, Franklin M. *Christian Worship*. Nashville: Broadman, 1967.

Semple, Robert B. *A History of the Rise and Progress of the Baptists in Virginia*. Revised by G. W. Beale. Richmond, Va.: Pitt & Dickinson, 1894.

Several Queries. April 1652.

Shain, Barry Alan. *The Myth of American Individualism: The Protestant Origins of American Political Thought*. Princeton, N.J.: Princeton University Press, 1994.

Shakespeare, J. H. *Baptist and Congregational Pioneers*. London: Kingsgate, 1907.

Sharmon, Edward. *A Caution Against Trinitarianism*. Market-Harborough: W. Harrod, 1799.

———. *A Letter on the Doctrine of the Trinity; Addressed to the Baptist Society at Guilsborough, Northamptonshire*. London: J. Johnson, 1795.

———. *A Second Caution Against trinitarianism . . . In a Letter Addressed to The Rev. Mr. Fuller, Kettering*. Market-Harborough: W. Harrod, 1800.

———. *A Second Letter on the Doctrine of the Trinity: Addressed to the Baptist Society at Guilsborough, Northamptonshire*. Market-Harborough: W. Harrod, 1796.

Sherman, Robert. *King, Priest, and Prophet: A Trinitarian Theology of the Atonement*. New York: T&T Clark, 2004.

Short, Lloyd M. "Church-State Relations, Viewed by the Baptist Joint Committee on Public Affairs." *Foundations* 16, no. 3 (1973): 261–73.

———. "The Role of the Church: A Baptist Layman's View." *Foundations* 13, no. 4 (1970): 335–42.

Shurden, Walter B. *Associationalism among Baptists in America, 1707–1814*. New York: Arno Press, 1980.

———. "The Baptist Identity and the Baptist Manifesto." *Perspectives in Religious Studies* 25, no. 4 (1998): 321–40.

———. *The Baptist Identity: Four Fragile Freedoms*. Macon, Ga.: Smyth & Helwys, 1993.

———. "The Coalition for Baptist Principles." *Baptist Studies Bulletin* 6, no. 6 (2007). Accessed August 26, 2009. http://www.centerforbaptiststudies.org/bulletin/2007/june.htm.

———. *Not a Silent People: Controversies That Have Shaped Southern Baptists*. Nashville: Broadman, 1972.

———, ed. *Proclaiming the Baptist Vision: The Church*. Macon, Ga.: Smyth & Helwys, 1996.

———. "Southern Baptist Responses to Their Confessional Statements." *Review and Expositor* 76, no. 1 (1979): 69–84.

Shurtleff, Nathaniel E., ed. *Records of the Governor and Company of Massachusetts Bay in New England*. Boston: William White, 1853.

Sierra, Joel. "Latin American Perspectives on Baptist-Catholic Dialogue." Baptist World Alliance, Doctrine and Church Unity Commission, Santiago, Chile, July 5, 2012.

Simpson, Alan. "How Democratic Was Roger Williams?" *William and Mary Quarterly* 13, no. 1 (1956): 53–67.

Skoglund, John E. *A Manual of Worship*. Valley Forge, Pa.: Judson Press, 1968.

Slatton, James H. *W. H. Whitsitt: The Man and the Controversy*. Macon, Ga.: Mercer University Press, 2009.

Smith, Andrew Christopher. "Searching for the Hidden Church: William Jones and the Common Roots of Landmarkist and Restorationist Ecclesiology." *Perspectives in Religious Studies* 36, no. 4 (2009): 421–31.

Smith, Christian, with Patricia Snell. *Souls in Transition: The Religious and Spiritual Lives of Emerging Adults*. New York: Oxford University Press, 2009.

Smith, Courtland, and John L. Humber. *Olin T. Binkley Memorial Baptist Church: A Twenty Year View 1958–1978*. Chapel Hill, N.C.: Binkley Baptist Church, 1978.

Smith, James A. "Is CBF Baptist? Christian?" *Florida Baptist Witness*, June 23, 2008. Accessed September 10, 2009. http://www.gofbw.com/News.asp?id=9034.

Smith, Jonathan Z. "What a Difference a Difference Makes." In *"To See Ourselves as Others See Us": Christians, Jews, and "Others" in Late Antiquity*, edited by Jacob Neusner and Ernest S. Frerichs, 3–48. Chico, Calif.: Scholars Press, 1985.

Smith, Nigel. "And if God Was One of Us: Paul Best, John Biddle, and the Anti-trinitarian Heresy in Seventeenth-Century England." In *Heresy, Literature, and Politics in Early Modern English Culture*, edited by David Loewenstein and John Marshall, 160–84. New York: Cambridge University Press, 2006.

Smith, Oscar Blake. "Jesus, Liberal or Conservative?" Sermon, 1944. Box 1, Blake Smith papers, David M. Rubenstein Rare Book & Manuscript Library, Duke University, Durham, N.C.

———. *Oral Memoirs of Oscar Blake Smith*. Interviewed by Thomas L. Charlton. Waco, Tex.: Baylor University Institute for Oral History, 1974.

———. "Race Relations." Radio talk, December 12, 1950. Box 1, Blake Smith papers, David M. Rubenstein Rare Book & Manuscript Library, Duke University, Durham, N.C.

Smyth, John. *The Works of John Smyth*. Edited by W. T. Whitley. Cambridge: Cambridge University Press, 1915.

Sobel, Mechal. *Trabelin' On: The Slave Journey to an Afro-Baptist Faith*. Westport, Conn.: Greenwood Press, 1979.

Southern Baptist Convention Statement on Infant Baptism. Accessed August 1, 2013. http://www.sbc.net/aboutus/faqs.asp#2.

Spain, Rufus B. *At Ease in Zion*. Nashville: Vanderbilt University Press, 1967.

"Special Committee Recommendation on Reception of Members"; and "Open—and Responsible Membership." *Myers Park Baptist Church News*, February 15, 1966.

Spencer, Aída Besançon, Mimi Haddad, Royce Gruenler, Kevin Giles, I. Howard Marshall, Alan Myatt, Millard Erickson, Steven Tracy, Alvera Mickelsen, Stanley Gundry, and Catherine Clark Kroeger. "An Evangelical Statement on the Trinity." Accessed December 3, 2011. http://www.trinitystatement.com/wp-content/files/Trinity%20Statement%20Spencer.pdf.

Spilsbury, John. *A Treatise Concerning the Lawfull Subject of Baptisme*. London: John Spilsbury, 1643.

Spini, Maggie. "Hays Named New Divinity School Dean." *Chronicle*,

February 14, 2012. Accessed March 3, 2012. http://dukechronicle.com/article/hays-named-new-divinity-school-dean.

Spinks, Bryan. *Sacraments, Ceremonies, and the Stuart Divines: Sacramental Theology and Liturgy in England and Scotland 1603–1662.* Burlington, Vt.: Ashgate, 2002.

Spivak, Gayatri Chakravorty. "Can the Subaltern Speak?" In *The Post-Colonial Studies Reader,* edited by Bill Ashcroft, Gareth Griffiths, and Helen Tiffin, 24–28. New York: Routledge, 1995.

Spurgeon, C. H. "Another Word concerning the Down-Grade." *The Sword and Trowel,* August 1887.

———. *The Down Grade Controversy.* Edited by Bob Ross. Pasadena, Tex.: Pilgrim, 1978.

———. "A Fragment upon the Down Grade Controversy." *The Sword and Trowel,* November 1887.

———. *Till He Come.* London: Passmore & Alabaster, 1894.

Stackhouse, Max L. Rejoinder to McClendon. *Journal of the American Academy of Religion* 56, no. 3 (1988): 555–56.

———. Review of *Ethics: Systematic Theology: Volume I,* by James Wm. McClendon Jr. *Journal of the American Academy of Religion* 55, no. 3 (1987): 615–17.

Stanley, Brian. *The History of the Baptist Missionary Society 1792–1992.* Edinburgh: T&T Clark, 1992.

"Statement on Christian Unity." In *Year Book of the American Baptist Churches 1967–1968,* 81–83. Valley Forge, Pa.: American Baptist Board of Education & Publication, 1967.

Steinmetz, David C. *Calvin in Context.* New York: Oxford University Press, 1995.

———. *Luther in Context.* Bloomington: Indiana University Press, 1986.

———. *Memory and Mission: Theological Reflections on the Christian Past.* Nashville: Abingdon, 1988.

Stendahl, Krister. "Biblical Theology, Contemporary." In *The Interpreter's Dictionary of the Bible,* edited by George A. Buttrick, et al., 1:420. Nashville: Abingdon, 1962.

Stetzer, Ed. "Analysis of SBC Statistics." *Christianity Today,* June 10, 2011. Accessed August 3, 2013. http://www.christianitytoday.com/edstetzer/2011/june/analysis-of-sbc-statistics.html.

———. "SBC 2011 Statistical Realities—Facts Are Our Friends but These Are Not Very Friendly Facts." June 13, 2012. Accessed August 3, 2013. http://www.christianitytoday.com/edstetzer/2012/june/sbc-2011-statistical-realities--facts-are-our-friends-but.html.

Stone, Brad Elliott. "Making Religious Practices Intelligible in the Public Sphere: A Pragmatist Evaluation of Scriptural Reasoning." *Journal of Scriptural Reasoning* 10, no. 2 (2011). Accessed March 6, 2012. http://jsr.lib.virginia.edu/volume-10-no-2-december-2011-public-debate-and-scriptural-reasoning/making-religious-practices-intelligible-in-the-public-sphere/.

Stone, Bryan. *Evangelism after Christendom: The Theology and Practice of Christian Witness.* Grand Rapids: Brazos, 2007.

Stow, Baron, and Samuel F. Smith, eds. *The Psalmist: A New Collection of Hymns for the Use of Baptist Churches.* Boston: Gould & Lincoln, 1854.

Stracener, W. G. "The Ordination of a Woman Pastor." *Alabama Baptist,* December 10, 1964.

Straton, John Roach. *The Famous New York Fundamentalist-Modernist Debates: The Orthodox Side.* New York: George H. Doran, 1924/1925.

———. *Fighting the Devil in Modern Babylon.* Boston: Stratford, 1929.

———. *The Menace of Immorality in Church and State: Messages of Wrath and Judgment.* New York: George H. Doran, 1920.

———. "Shall the Funny Monkeyists Win?" Sermon delivered at Calvary Baptist Church, New York City, September 24, 1922. In *Religious Searchlight* (published occasionally by the Religious Literature Department of Calvary Baptist Church, New York, Alfred Stokes, manager) 1, no. 7 (October 1, 1922): 1–8.

Stricklin, David. *A Genealogy of Dissent: Southern Baptist Protest in the Twentieth Century.* Lexington: University Press of Kentucky, 1999.

Strong, Augustus Hopkins. *Annual Report.* New York Baptist Union for Ministerial Education, 1906.

———. *Christ in Creation and Ethical Monism.* Philadelphia: Roger Williams Press, 1899.

———. "Dr. Robinson as a Theologian." In *Ezekiel Gilman Robinson: An Autobiography, with Supplement by H. L. Wayland and Critical Estimates,* edited by E. H. Johnson, 161–208. New York: Silver, Burdett, 1896.

———. *Systematic Theology.* 8th ed. 3 vols. Philadelphia: Judson Press, 1907–1909.

———. *A Tour of the Missions: Observations and Conclusions.* Philadelphia: Griffith & Rowland Press, 1918.

Sullivan, Clayton. *Called to Preach, Condemned to Survive: The Education of Clayton Sullivan.* Macon, Ga.: Mercer University Press, 1985.

Sullivan, Francis A. "The Meaning of *Subsistit in* as Explained by the Congregation for the Doctrine of the Faith." *Theological Studies* 69, no. 1 (2008): 116–24.

———. "A Response to Karl Becker, S.J., on the Meaning of *Subsistit in.*" *Theological Studies* 67, no. 2 (2006): 395–409.

Summary of Church-Discipline. Charleston, S.C.: Charleston Baptist Association, 1774.

Summers, Thomas O. *Baptism: A Treatise on the Nature, Perpetuity, Subjects, Administrator, Mode, and Use of the Initiating Ordinance of the Christian Church.* Richmond, Va.: John Early, 1853.

Swartley, Willard M. *Covenant of Peace: The Missing Peace in New Testament Theology and Ethics.* Grand Rapids: Eerdmans, 2006.

Swatos, William H., Jr. "Sects and Success: *Missverstehen* in Mt. Airy." *Social Analysis* 43, no. 4 (1982): 375–79.

Sweet, William Warren. *Religion on the American Frontier: The Baptists 1783–1830.* New York: H. Holt, 1931.

Swindoll, Chuck. In Case You've Wondered (column). *Connection,* June 2002.

Synodis, Hilarius de. *An Account Of all the Considerable Books and Pamphlets That have been wrote on either Side in the Controversy Concerning the Trinity Since the Year MDCCXII.* London: James Knapton, 1720.

———. *An Account of the Pamphlets Writ this Last Year each Side by the Dissenters.* London: James Knapton, 1720.

Taylor, Charles. *Sources of the Self.* Cambridge, Mass.: Harvard University Press, 1989.

Taylor, Dan. *Fundamentals of Religion in Faith and Practice.* Leeds, 1775.

Taylor, James B. *Lives of Virginia Baptist Ministers.* 2nd ed. Richmond, Va.: Yale & Wyatt, 1838.

Taylor, John. *A History of Ten Baptist Churches.* Frankfort, Ky.: J. H. Holeman, 1823.

Taylor, Mark C. *Altarity.* Chicago: University of Chicago Press, 1987.

Taylor, Michael J. *The Protestant Liturgical Renewal: A Catholic Viewpoint.* Westminster, Md.: Newman Press, 1963.

Tertullian. *Baptism.* In *Tertullian's Homily on Baptism,* translated by Ernest Evans. London: SPCK, 1964.

Thomas, Joshua. *A History of the Baptist Association in Wales, From the Year 1650, To the Year 1790.* London, 1795.

———. *History of the Welsh Association, 1639–1780.* Handwritten manuscript in the Angus Library, Regent's Park College, Oxford University.

Thomas, Roger. "The Non-subscription Controversy amongst Dissenters in 1719: The Salters' Hall Debate." *Journal of Ecclesiastical History* 4, no. 2 (1953): 162–86.

Thombes [Tombes], John. *Two Treatises And An Appendix To Them Concerning Infant-Baptisme.* London: George Whittington, 1645.

Thompson, Philip E. "A New Question in Baptist History: Seeking a Catholic Spirit among Early Baptists." *Pro Ecclesia* 8, no. 1 (1999): 51–72.

———. "Re-envisioning Baptist Identity: Historical, Theological, and Liturgical Analysis." *Perspectives in Religious Studies* 27, no. 3 (2000): 287–302.

———. "Toward Baptist Ecclesiology in Pneumatological Perspective." Ph.D. diss., Emory University, 1995.

Thompson, Philip E., and Anthony R. Cross, eds. *Recycling the Past or Researching History? Studies in Baptist Historiography and Myths.* Milton Keynes, U.K.: Paternoster, 2005.

Thurian, Max. *The Eucharistic Memorial: The New Testament.* Vol. 2 of *The Eucharistic Memorial.* Translated by J. G. Davies. Ecumenical Studies in Worship 8. Richmond, Va.: John Knox, 1961.

Thurman, Howard. *Jesus and the Disinherited*. Boston: Beacon Press, 1976.

Tilley, Terrence. "The Baptist Theology of J. W. McClendon, Jr., and Practical Faith in a Pluralistic Context." In *Postmodern Theologies: The Challenge of Religious Diversity*, edited by Terrence Tilley, 142–52. Maryknoll, N.Y.: Orbis Books, 1995.

―――. *The Disciples' Jesus: Christology as Reconciling Practice*. Maryknoll, N.Y.: Orbis Books, 2008.

―――. "Why American Catholic Theologians Should Read 'Baptist' Theology." *Horizons* 14, no. 1 (1987): 129–37.

Tillich, Paul. *The Protestant Era*. Chicago: University of Chicago Press, 1957.

―――. *Systematic Theology*. Chicago: University of Chicago Press, 1967.

Timmer, Kirsten T. "John Smyth's Request for Mennonite Recognition and Admission: Four Newly Translated Letters, 1610–1612." *Baptist History and Heritage* 44, no. 1 (2009): 8–19.

Tolbert, Malcolm O. *Shaping the Church: Adapting New Testament Models for Today*. Macon, Ga.: Smyth & Helwys, 2003.

Tolmie, Murray. *The Triumph of the Saints: The Separatist Churches in London, 1616–1649*. Cambridge: Cambridge University Press, 1977.

Tombes [Thombes], John. *Apology for the Two Treatises Concerning Infant-Baptisme*. N.p., 1645.

―――. *Emmanuel or God-Man*. London: F. Smith, 1669.

Toom, Tarmo. "Baptists on Justification: Can We Join the Joint Declaration on the Doctrine of Justification?" *Pro Ecclesia* 13, no. 3 (2003): 289–306.

Torbet, Robert G. "Baptists and Protestantism in America." *Southwestern Journal of Theology* 6, no. 2 (1964): 94–110.

―――. *A History of the Baptists*. 3rd ed. Valley Forge, Pa.: Judson Press, 1973.

―――. *Ventures of Faith: The Story of the American Baptist Foreign Mission Society*. Philadelphia: Judson Press, 1955.

Torbet, Robert G., and John S. Cummins. "Baptist-Roman Catholic Conversations: Two Papers on the Nature and Communication of Grace." *Foundations* 12, no. 3 (1969): 213–31.

Torrance, James B. *Worship, Community, and the Triune God of Grace*. Downers Grove, Ill.: InterVarsity, 1996.

Torrey, R. A., and A. C. Dixon, eds. *The Fundamentals: A Testimony to the Truth*. 4 vols. 1917. Repr., Grand Rapids: Baker Books, 1980.

To the Officers and Souldiers of the Army. London, 1656.

Toulmin, Joshua. *Memoirs of the Life, Character, Sentiments, and Writings, of Faustus Socinus*. London: J. Brown, Southwark, 1777.

――― to Joseph Fownes, Shrewsbury, July 7, 1778. In *Baptist Autographs in the John Rylands University Library of Manchester, 1741–1845*, translated and edited by Timothy D. Whelan, 36–37. Macon, Ga.: Mercer University Press, 2009.

Toulmin, Stephen. *Cosmopolis*. Chicago: University of Chicago Press, 1990.

Towns, James E. *The Social Conscience of W. A. Criswell.* Dallas, Tex.: Crescendo, 1977.

Tracy, David. *The Analogical Imagination.* New York: Crossroad, 1981.

Tran, Jonathan. "The New Black Theology: Retrieving Ancient Sources to Challenge Racism." *Christian Century,* February 8, 2012.

Trisco, Robert. "The Catholic Theology of the Local Church." *Foundations* 15, no. 1 (1972): 53–71.

Troeltsch, Ernst. *The Social Teaching of the Christian Churches.* Translated by Olive Wyon. New York: Harper Torchbooks, 1960.

Truett, George W. *Baptists and Religious Liberty.* Nashville: Baptist Sunday School Board, 1920. Reprinted in *Christian Ethics Today* 7, no. 1 (2001). Accessed November 25, 2011. http://christianethicstoday.com/cetart/index .cfm?fuseaction=Articles.main&ArtID=266.

————. "Baptists and Religious Liberty." In *Readings in Baptist History: Four Centuries of Selected Documents,* edited by Joseph Early Jr., 145–52. Nashville: B&H, 2008.

————. "Baptists and Religious Liberty." In *A Sourcebook for Baptist Heritage,* edited by H. Leon McBeth, 467–77. Nashville: Broadman, 1990.

Turberville, Arthur Stanley. *A History of Welbeck Abbey and Its Owners, 1559–1715.* London: Faber & Faber, 1938.

Turcescu, Lucian. "'Person' Versus 'Individual,' and Other Modern Misreadings of Gregory of Nyssa." *Modern Theology* 18, no. 4 (2002): 527–39.

Turner, Daniel. *Charity the Bond of Perfection. A Sermon, The Substance of which was Preached at Oxford, November 16, 1780. On Occasion of the Re-establishment of a Christian Church of Protestant Dissenters in that City; with a Brief Account of the State of the Society, and the Plan and Manner of their Settlement.* Oxford: J. Buckland, 1780.

————. *A Compendium of Social Religion.* London: John Ward, 1758.

————. *A Compendium of Social Religion of the Nature and Constitution of Christian Churches.* 2nd ed. Bristol, U.K.: W. Pine, 1778.

————. *A Modest Plea for Free Communion at the Lord's Table.* London: J. Johnson, 1772.

Turner, Victor. *The Ritual Process.* Ithaca, N.Y.: Cornell University Press, 1969.

Turner, William C. *Discipleship for African American Christians: A Journey through the Church Covenant.* Valley Forge, Pa.: Judson Press, 2002.

Tyconius. *The Turin Fragments of Tyconius' Commentary on Revelation.* Edited by Francesco Lo Bue. Cambridge: Cambridge University Press, 1963.

Underhill, Edward Bean, ed. *Records of the Churches of Christ, Gathered at Fenstanton, Warboys, and Hexham, 1640–1720.* London: Haddon, Brothers, 1854.

————. *Tracts on Liberty of Conscience and Persecution.* London: Hanserd Knollys Society, 1846.

Underwood, A. C. *A History of the English Baptists.* London: Baptist Union, 1847.

Underwood, Bill. "Address for Baptist Summit." *Associated Baptist Press*, February 1, 2006. Accessed March 30, 2012. http://www.abpnews.com/archives/item/920-address-for-baptist-summit#.UvAwLKW5Mts.

Vanhoozer, Kevin J. *The Drama of Doctrine: A Canonical Linguistic Approach to Christian Theology.* Louisville, Ky.: Westminster John Knox, 2005.

Vatican Council II. Vol. 1, *The Conciliar and Postconciliar Documents.* Rev. ed. New York: Costello, 2004.

Volf, Miroslav. *After Our Likeness: The Church as the Image of the Trinity.* Grand Rapids: Eerdmans, 1998.

———. "'The Trinity Is Our Social Program': The Doctrine of the Trinity and the Shape of Social Engagement." *Modern Theology* 14, no. 3 (1998): 403–23.

Volf, Mioslav, and Dorothy C. Bass. *Practicing Theology.* Grand Rapids: Eerdmans, 2002.

Votes of Parliament Touching the Book commonly called The Racovian Catechism. London: John Field, 1652.

Wacker, Grant. *Augustus H. Strong and the Dilemma of Historical Consciousness.* Macon, Ga.: Mercer University Press, 1985.

———. Review of *Autobiography of Augustus Hopkins Strong. Christian Century,* May 18, 1983.

Wainwright, Geoffrey. *Christian Initiation.* London: Lutterworth, 1969.

———. "The Doctrine of the Trinity: Where the Church Stands or Falls." *Interpretation* 45, no. 2 (1991): 117–32.

———. *Doxology: The Praise of God in Worship, Doctrine, and Life.* New York: Oxford University Press, 1980.

———. *Embracing Purpose: Essays on God, the World, and the Church.* Peterborough, U.K.: Epworth, 2007.

———. *Eucharist and Eschatology.* New York: Oxford University Press, 1981.

———. *Methodists in Dialogue.* Nashville: Kingswood Books, 1995.

Walker, Michael J. *Baptists at the Table: The Theology of the Lord's Supper amongst English Baptists in the Nineteenth Century.* Didcot, U.K.: Baptist Historical Society, 1992.

Walker, William, ed. *The Southern Harmony and Musical Companion.* New ed. Philadelphia: E. W. Miller, 1854.

Walton, Robert C. *The Gathered Community.* London: Carey Press, 1946.

Ward, Benedicta, trans. *The Sayings of the Desert Fathers: The Alphabetical Collection.* Kalamazoo, Mich.: Cistercian, 1975.

Ware, Bruce A. *Father, Son, and Holy Spirit: Relationships, Roles, and Relevance.* Wheaton, Ill.: Crossway Books, 2005.

———. "How Shall We Think about the Trinity?" In *God under Fire: Modern Theology Reinvents God,* edited by Douglas S. Huffman and Eric L. Johnson, 253–78. Grand Rapids: Zondervan, 2002.

Warfield, Benjamin Breckinridge. *Revelation and Inspiration.* New York: Oxford, 1927.

————. Review of *Der zekerheid des geloofs*, by Herman Bavinck. *Princeton Theological Review* 1 (1903): 138–43.

Washington, James Melvin. *Frustrated Fellowship: The Black Baptist Quest for Social Power*. Macon, Ga.: Mercer University Press, 1986.

Watts, Isaac. *The Works of the Late Reverend and Learned Isaac Watts*. London: T. and T. Longman, 1753.

Watts, Michael. *The Dissenters*. Vol. 1, *From the Reformation to the French Revolution*. Vol. 2, *The Expansion of Evangelical Nonconformity*. Oxford: Clarendon, 1978–1995.

Watts Street Baptist Church. Minutes of Church Meeting, February 26, 1964, 7; March 13, 1963; and July 29, 1964, 2.

Watts Street Baptist Church, Deacon Board. Minute Book, July 21, 1964, 203; and August 18, 1964, 205.

Watts Street Baptist Church Historical Collection. Watts Street Baptist Church, Durham, N.C.

Wayland, Francis. *Notes on the Principles and Practices of Baptist Churches*. New York: Sheldon, Blackmon, 1857.

Weaver, Alain Epp. "Missionary Christology: John Howard Yoder and the Creeds." *Mennonite Quarterly Review* 74, no. 3 (2000): 423–39.

Weaver, C. Douglas. "The Baptist Ecclesiology of E. Y. Mullins: Individualism and the New Testament Church." *Baptist History and Heritage* 43, no. 1 (2008): 18–34.

————. *In Search of the New Testament Church: The Baptist Story*. Macon, Ga.: Mercer University Press, 2008.

Weaver, J. Denny. "Nicea, Womanist Theology, and Anabaptist Particularity." In *Anabaptists & Postmodernity*, edited by Susan Biesecker-Mast and Gerald Biesecker-Mast, 251–59. Telford, Pa.: Pandora, 2000.

————. *The Nonviolent Atonement*. Grand Rapids: Eerdmans, 2001.

Webb, Stephen. Review of *Heaven: The Logic of Eternal Joy*, by Jerry L. Walls. *Christian Century*, December 4–17, 2002.

Webber, Robert E. *Ancient-Future Faith*. Grand Rapids: Baker, 1999.

Weber, Marianne. *Max Weber: A Biography*. Translated and edited by Harry Zohn. New York: John Wiley & Sons, 1975.

Weber, Max. *The Methodology of the Social Sciences*. Edited by Edward Shils and Henry Finch. New York: Free Press, 1949.

————. *The Protestant Ethic and the Spirit of Capitalism*. Translated by Talcott Parsons. New York: Charles Scribner's Sons, 1958.

————. "The Protestant Sects and the Spirit of Capitalism." In *From Max Weber: Essays in Sociology*, translated and edited by H. H. Gerth and C. Wright Mills, 302–22. New York: Oxford University Press, 1946.

Wells, Samuel. *Improvisation: The Drama of Christian Ethics*. Grand Rapids: Brazos, 2004.

West, Cornell. *Prophesy Deliverance! An Afro-American Revolutionary Christianity.* Philadelphia: Westminster, 1982.

Whitaker, Edward Charles. *Documents of the Baptismal Liturgy.* London: SPCK, 1960/1970/1997.

White, B. R. *The English Baptists of the Seventeenth Century.* Didcot, U.K.: Baptist Historical Society, 1996.

————. *The English Separatist Tradition: From the Marian Martyrs to the Pilgrim Fathers.* London: Oxford University Press, 1971.

————. "How Did William Kiffin Join the Baptists?" *Baptist Quarterly* 23, no. 5 (1970): 201–7.

————. "Open and Closed Membership among English and Welsh Baptists." *Baptist Quarterly* 24, no. 7 (1972): 330–34.

————. "The Practice of Association." In *A Perspective on Baptist Identity,* ed. David Slater. Kingsbridge, U.K.: Mainstream, 1987.

White, James F. *Sacraments as God's Self-Giving.* Nashville: Abingdon, 1983.

White, Jim. "Dan Vestal Corrects Claim that CBF Is 'Unchristian.'" *Religious Herald,* July 10, 2008. Accessed September 10, 2009. http://www.religious herald.org/index.php?option=com_content&task=view&id=2433&Itemid=113.

Whiting, C. E. *Studies in English Puritanism from the Restoration to the Revolution, 1660–1668.* New York: Macmillan, 1931.

Whitley, W. T. *The Baptists of London, 1612–1928.* London: Kingsgate, 1928.

————. *A History of the British Baptists.* London: C. Griffin, 1923.

————, ed. *Minutes of the General Assembly of the General Baptist Churches in England.* London: Kingsgate, 1909.

Whitsitt, William H. *A Question in Baptist History: Whether the Anabaptists in England Practiced Immersion before the Year 1641?* Louisville, Ky.: C. T. Dearing, 1896.

Wicks, Jared. "Not-So-Fully Church: The Pope's Message to Protestants—and Catholics." *Christian Century,* August 21, 2007.

————. "Questions and Answers on the New Responses of the Congregation for the Doctrine of the Faith." *Ecumenical Trends* 36, no. 7 (2007): 97–112.

Williams, D. H. *Evangelicals and Tradition: The Formative Influence of the Early Church.* Grand Rapids: Baker Academic, 2005.

————. *The Free Church and the Early Church: Bridging the Historical and Theological Divide.* Grand Rapids: Eerdmans, 2002.

————. *Retrieving the Tradition and Renewing Evangelicalism: A Primer for Suspicious Protestants.* Grand Rapids: Eerdmans, 1999.

Williams, E. Neville, ed. *The Eighteenth Century Constitution, 1688–1815.* Cambridge: Cambridge University Press, 1960.

Williams, Roger. *The Complete Writings of Roger Williams.* 7 vols. New York: Russell & Russell, 1963.

————. *A Testimony to the Said Fourth Paper [Presented by Maior Butler] By way of Explanation upon the four Proposals of it.* London: Giles Calvert, 1652.

Williams, Rowan, ed. *The Making of Orthodoxy.* Cambridge: Cambridge University Press, 1989.

Willimon, Will [William]. *Pastor: The Theology and Practice of Ordained Ministry.* Nashville: Abingdon, 2002.

————. "A Prophet Leaves Us: Carlyle Marney." *Christian Century,* July 19, 1978.

————. *Remember Who You Are: Baptism, a Model for Christian Life.* Nashville: Upper Room, 1980.

Willis-Watkins, David. *Calvin's Catholic Christology: The Function of the So-Called Extra Calvinisticum in Calvin's Theology.* Leiden: E. J. Brill, 1966.

Wills, Gregory A. *Democratic Religion: Freedom, Authority, and Church Discipline in the Baptist South 1785–1900.* New York: Oxford University Press, 1997.

————. *Southern Baptist Theological Seminary, 1859–2009.* New York: Oxford University Press, 2009.

Wilson, Charles Reagan. *Baptized in Blood.* Athens: University of Georgia, 1980.

Winchester, Elhanan. *The Universal Restoration: Exhibited in Four Dialogues Between a Minister and His Friend.* London: T. Gillet, 1792. Repr., Bellows Falls, Vt.: Bill Blake, 1819.

Winslow, Edward. *Hypocrisie Unmasked: A True Relation of the Proceedings of the Governor and Company of the Massachusetts Against Samuel Gorton of Rhode Island.* London: Rich. Cotes, 1646. Repr., New York: Burt Franklin, 1968.

Winstanley, Gerrard. *The Works of Gerrard Winstanley.* Edited by George H. Sabine. Ithaca, N.Y.: Cornell University Press, 1941.

Winter, Sean. *More Light and Truth? Biblical Interpretation in Covenantal Perspective.* The Whitley Lecture. Oxford: Whitley, 2007.

————. "Persuading Friends: Friendship and Testimony in Baptist Interpretative Communities." In *The "Plainly Revealed" Word of God?* edited by Helen Dare and Simon Woodman, 253–70. Macon, Ga.: Mercer University Press.

Winthrop, John. *The Journal of John Winthrop, 1630–1649.* Edited by Richard S. Dunn, James Savage, and Laetitia Yaendle. Cambridge, Mass.: Belknap Press, 1996.

————. *A Model of Christian Charity.* In *The Puritans,* edited by Perry Miller and Thomas H. Johnson, 1:198–99. New York: Harper & Row, 1963.

————. *Winthrop Papers, 1631–1637.* Edited by Allyn Bailey Forbes. Boston: Massachusetts Historical Society, 1943.

Wood, Susan K. *Spiritual Exegesis and the Church in the Theology of Henri de Lubac.* Grand Rapids: Eerdmans, 1998.

Wood, Timothy L. *Agents of Wrath, Sowers of Discord: Authority and Dissent in Puritan Massachusetts, 1630–1655.* New York: Routledge, 2006.

————. "'A Church Still by Her First Covenant': George Philips and a Puritan View of Roman Catholicism." *New England Quarterly* 72, no. 1 (1999): 28–41.

Woodward, Kenneth L. "Sex, Sin and Salvation." *Newsweek*, November 2, 1998.

"The Word of God in the Life of the Church: A Report of International Conversations between the Catholic Church and the Baptist World Alliance 2006–2010." *American Baptist Quarterly* 31, no. 1 (2012): 29–122.

Worden, Blair. "Toleration and the Cromwellian Protectorate." In *Persecution and Toleration*, edited by W. J. Sheils, 199–233. Oxford: Published for the Ecclesiastical Historical Society by B. Blackwell, 1984.

Wright, David F. *Infant Baptism in Historical Perspective*. Milton Keynes, U.K.: Paternoster, 2007.

———. *What Has Infant Baptism Done to Baptism?* Milton Keynes, U.K.: Paternoster, 2005.

Wright, G. Ernest. *The Old Testament and Theology*. New York: Harper & Row, 1969.

Wright, N. T. *The Climax of the Covenant: Christ and the Law in Pauline Theology*. Minneapolis: Fortress, 1992.

Wright, Nigel Goring. *Disavowing Constantine: Mission, Church and Social Order in the Theologies of John Howard Yoder and Jürgen Moltmann*. Carlisle, U.K.: Paternoster, 2000.

———. *Free Church, Free State: The Positive Baptist Vision*. Milton Keynes, U.K.: Paternoster, 2005.

Wright, Stephen. *The Early English Baptists, 1603–1649*. Woodbridge, U.K.: Boydell Press, 2006.

———. "Edward Barber (c. 1595–1663) and His Friends (Part 1)." *Baptist Quarterly* 41, no. 6 (2006): 355–70.

———. *History of the Shaftsbury Association, from 1800–1829*. New York: Macmillan, 1951.

Wuthnow, Robert, ed. *"I Come Away Stronger": How Small Groups Are Shaping American Religion*. Grand Rapids: Eerdmans, 1994.

———. *The Restructuring of American Religion*. Princeton, N.J.: Princeton University Press, 1988.

Wyclif, John. *Select English Works of John Wyclif*. Edited by Thomas Arnold. Oxford: Clarendon, 1869–1871.

Year Book of the American Baptist Convention: 1965–66. Valley Forge, Pa.: Judson Press, 1965.

Yetman, Norman R. *Life under the Peculiar Institution*. New York: Holt, Reinhart & Winston, 1970.

Yoder, John Howard. *Body Politics: Five Practices of the Christian Community before the Watching World*. Scottdale, Pa.: Herald Press, 1992.

———. *For the Nations*. Grand Rapids: Eerdmans, 1997.

———. "Karl Barth: How His Mind Kept Changing." In *How Karl Barth Changed My Mind*, edited by Donald McKim, 166–71. Grand Rapids: Eerdmans, 1986.

————. Preface to *Theology: Christology and Theological Method*. Grand Rapids: Brazos, 2002.

————. *The Priestly Kingdom: Social Ethics as Gospel*. Notre Dame, Ind.: University of Notre Dame Press, 1984.

————. *The Royal Priesthood: Essays Ecclesiological and Ecumenical*. Edited by Michael G. Cartwright. Grand Rapids: Eerdmans, 1994.

Zizioulas, John. *Being as Communion: Studies in Personhood and the Church*. Crestwood, N.Y.: St. Vladimir's Orthodox Seminary Press, 1985.

————. *Communion and Otherness*. London: T&T Clark, 2006.

Zwingli, Huldrych. *An Exposition of the Faith*. In *Zwingli and Bullinger*, Library of Christian Classics, edited by B. W. Bromiley. Philadelphia: Westminster, 1953.

————. *Huldrych Zwingli: Writings*. Translated by H. Wayne Pipkin. Allison Park, Pa.: Pickwick, 1984.

————. "Of the Clarity and Certainty of the Word of God." In *Zwingli and Bullinger*, Library of Christian Classics, edited by G. W. Bromiley, 49–95. Philadelphia: Westminster, 1953.

Author Index

Aers, David, 71n59
Ahlstrom, Sydney, 121
Ainsworth, Henry, 16
Alber, Matthew, 336
Allen, Jimmy, 102
Ambrose, 229n12, 296
Angus, Joseph, 97
Asbury, Francis, 357, 360
Asplund, John, 170
Athanasius, 113–14, 205n53
Augustine, 32–33, 35, 262–63, 296, 315, 371
Austin, John, 287

Backus, Isaac, 73–74
Bacon, Benjamin, 94
Bacon, Francis, 77
Baillie, Robert, 162
Barber, Edward, 291, 343–44
Barnett, Das Kelley, 54
Barrow, Henry, 222, 235
Barth, Karl, 43, 89, 91, 118, 135n158, 208, 220, 260n138, 262, 304, 366, 370
Baxter, Richard, 18–19
Beasley-Murray, George, 14n48, 370–71
Bebbington, David, 14
Benedict XVI, 253, 382
Benedict, David, 173
Bentley, Richard, 164–65, 181

Bernard, Richard, 227–28, 230, 236
Berry, Wendell, 391
Biddle, John, 147–48, 150–53, 172
Binkley, Olin T., 54
Blackwood, Christopher, 344
Bonhoeffer, Dietrich, 51n103
Bowne, Borden Parker, 86
Boyce, James Petigru, 77–78, 178, 181
Braaten, Carl, 10, 387–89
Brackney, William, 86n128
Brantly, William T., 176
Briggs, R. C., 304
Briscoe, Nathaniel, 344
Broadus, John, 381
Brown, Charles R., 93
Brown, Raymond E., 314n10
Browne, Robert, 15–16
Brunner, Emil, 366
Bryan, William Jennings, 53, 56, 58–59
Buckley, James J., 2n3
Bunyan, John, 9, 191, 216, 218, 295–96, 349, 351–53, 357, 374, 378, 381
Burroughs, Joseph, 162
Busher, Leonard, 374

Caffyn, Matthew, 110, 145–48, 150n26, 153–56, 158, 160
Calhoun, Robert, 5, 94, 386
Calvin, John, 116, 219n101, 220, 222, 229n12, 280–81, 288, 290, 313n9, 317, 332, 335

455

Subject Index